Industry Use Cases on Blockchain Technology Applications in IoT and the Financial Sector

Zaigham Mahmood
University of Northampton, UK & Shijiazhuang Tiedao University, China

A volume in the Advances in Data Mining and
Database Management (ADMDM) Book Series

Published in the United States of America by
IGI Global
Engineering Science Reference (an imprint of IGI Global)
701 E. Chocolate Avenue
Hershey PA, USA 17033
Tel: 717-533-8845
Fax: 717-533-8661
E-mail: cust@igi-global.com
Web site: http://www.igi-global.com

Library of Congress Cataloging-in-Publication Data

Names: Mahmood, Zaigham, editor.
Title: Industry use cases on blockchain technology applications in IoT and
 the financial sector / Zaigham Mahmood, editor.
Description: Hershey, PA : Engineering Science Reference, an imprint of IGI
 Global, [2021] | Includes bibliographical references and index. |
 Summary: "This book investigates the blockchain technology, its adoption
 and effectiveness in banking and other industry, and in general, for IoT
 based applications"-- Provided by publisher.
Identifiers: LCCN 2020043464 (print) | LCCN 2020043465 (ebook) | ISBN
 9781799866503 (hardcover) | ISBN 9781799866510 (paperback) | ISBN
 9781799866527 (ebook)
Subjects: LCSH: Blockchains (Databases)--Industrial applications.
Classification: LCC QA76.9.B56 I53 2021 (print) | LCC QA76.9.B56 (ebook)
 | DDC 005.75--dc23
LC record available at https://lccn.loc.gov/2020043464
LC ebook record available at https://lccn.loc.gov/2020043465

This book is published in the IGI Global book series Advances in Data Mining and Database Management (ADMDM)
(ISSN: 2327-1981; eISSN: 2327-199X)

British Cataloguing in Publication Data
A Cataloguing in Publication record for this book is available from the British Library.

All work contributed to this book is new, previously-unpublished material. The views expressed in this book are those of the authors, but not necessarily of the publisher.

For electronic access to this publication, please contact: eresources@igi-global.com.

Advances in Data Mining and Database Management (ADMDM) Book Series

David Taniar
Monash University, Australia

ISSN:2327-1981
EISSN:2327-199X

MISSION

With the large amounts of information available to organizations in today's digital world, there is a need for continual research surrounding emerging methods and tools for collecting, analyzing, and storing data.

The **Advances in Data Mining & Database Management (ADMDM)** series aims to bring together research in information retrieval, data analysis, data warehousing, and related areas in order to become an ideal resource for those working and studying in these fields. IT professionals, software engineers, academicians and upper-level students will find titles within the ADMDM book series particularly useful for staying up-to-date on emerging research, theories, and applications in the fields of data mining and database management.

COVERAGE

- Cluster Analysis
- Neural Networks
- Customer Analytics
- Educational Data Mining
- Database Testing
- Data Mining
- Quantitative Structure–Activity Relationship
- Data Warehousing
- Heterogeneous and Distributed Databases
- Data Quality

IGI Global is currently accepting manuscripts for publication within this series. To submit a proposal for a volume in this series, please contact our Acquisition Editors at Acquisitions@igi-global.com or visit: http://www.igi-global.com/publish/.

Titles in this Series

For a list of additional titles in this series, please visit: http://www.igi-global.com/book-series/advances-data-mining-database-management/37146

Applications of Big Data in Large- and Small-Scale Systems
Sam Goundar (The University of the South Pacific, Fiji) and Praveen Kumar Rayani (National Institute of Technology, Durgapur, India)
Engineering Science Reference • © 2021 • 330pp • H/C (ISBN: 9781799866732) • US $245.00

Developing a Keyword Extractor and Document Classifier Emerging Research and Opportunities
Dimple Valayil Paul (Department of Computer Science, Dnyanprassarak Mandal's College and Research Centre, Goa University, Goa, India)
Engineering Science Reference • © 2021 • 229pp • H/C (ISBN: 9781799837725) • US $195.00

Intelligent Analytics With Advanced Multi-Industry Applications
Zhaohao Sun (Papua New Guinea University of Technology, Papua New Guinea)
Engineering Science Reference • © 2021 • 392pp • H/C (ISBN: 9781799849636) • US $225.00

Handbook of Research on Automated Feature Engineering and Advanced Applications in Data Science
Mrutyunjaya Panda (Utkal University, India) and Harekrishna Misra (Institute of Rural Management, Anand, India)
Engineering Science Reference • © 2021 • 392pp • H/C (ISBN: 9781799866596) • US $285.00

Blockchain and AI Technology in the Industrial Internet of Things
Subhendu Kumar Pani (Orissa Engineering College,BPUT, India) Chittaranjan Hota (Birla Institute of Technology and Science, India) Guangzhi Qu (Oakland University, USA) Sian Lun Lau (Sunway University, Malaysia) and Xingcheng Liu (Sun Yat-sen University, China)
Engineering Science Reference • © 2021 • 330pp • H/C (ISBN: 9781799866947) • US $225.00

Challenges and Applications of Data Analytics in Social Perspectives
V. Sathiyamoorthi (Sona College of Technology, India) and Atilla Elci (Hasan Kalyoncu University, Turkey)
Engineering Science Reference • © 2021 • 324pp • H/C (ISBN: 9781799825661) • US $245.00

Multidisciplinary Functions of Blockchain Technology in AI and IoT Applications
Niaz Chowdhury (The Open University, Milton Keynes, UK) and Ganesh Chandra Deka (Ministry of Skill Development and Entrepreneurship, New Delhi, India)
Engineering Science Reference • © 2021 • 255pp • H/C (ISBN: 9781799858768) • US $245.00

701 East Chocolate Avenue, Hershey, PA 17033, USA
Tel: 717-533-8845 x100 • Fax: 717-533-8661
E-Mail: cust@igi-global.com • www.igi-global.com

This is my 32nd book. It is dedicated to:

My (late) parents: Ghulam Hussain Bhatti and Mukhtar Begum;
My siblings: Khalida baji, Masood, Tahir, Zahid and Irfana;
My immediate family: Rehana, Zoya, Imran, Hanya, Arif, Ozair, Eyaad and Zayb.

Table of Contents

Section 1
Blockchain Technology Applications

Detailed Table of Contents

Section 1
Blockchain Technology Applications

Chapter 1

    Zaigham Mahmood, University of Northampton, UK & Shijiazhuang Tiedao University,
       China

Blockchain technology is one of the latest innovations in computer science that has world-wide scale and reach. A blockchain is a mathematical structure for storing digital transactions in a distributed and decentralized digital ledger consisting of multiple blocks that are linked using cryptographic signatures and spread across multiple computers. Each block records digital transactions data securely and has a hash link pointing to the previous block in the network in an efficient manner. New blocks can be added and removed through an agreed consensus of all nodes that each share the distributed ledger without the need for a centralized controlling authority. This chapter aims to introduce the blockchain technology, also known as distributed ledger technology (DLT), and discuss its applications in various sectors of the society including banking, healthcare, transportation, manufacturing, supply chain, and education. Extension of the internet of things vision using the DLT is also briefly discussed.

Chapter 2

    Nhlanhla Andrew Sibanyoni, University of Johannesburg, South Africa

Blockchain technology and robotic process automation are increasingly the focus of attention in research, as these are both used successfully in business, marketing, manufacturing, and finance. However, their application in educational contexts is still emerging. This chapter uses an illustrative example of an online school registration system to explore how a blockchain-based robotic process automation mechanism can resolve the inherent challenges. The proposed system allows parents to register their Grade 1 and Grade 8 children for their school of choice. There is competition for places in certain schools and a history of unfair allocation of educational resources; hence, there is mistrust. To counter this threat, this study proposes a blockchain-based robotic automation process mechanism to fairly and transparently allocate educational resources. It recommends that further design science research be conducted in which the blockchain is supplemented by additional technological processes to enhance data-sharing in educational settings.

Chapter 3

Olefhile Mosweu, University of Johannesburg, South Africa
Forget Chaterera-Zambuko, Sorbonne University, Abu Dhabi, UAE & University of South
Africa, South Africa

The fourth industrial revolution (4IR) has ushered in several emerging and disruptive technologies. Southern Africa's records management practices have for a long time been reported to lag behind in embracing new technologies. Several studies have revealed lack of requisite skills to manage electronic records while others still lament the un-procedural management of paper records. The intention of this chapter is, therefore, to initiate a discourse that challenges information management practitioners to embrace disruptive technologies lest they themselves get disrupted. There are several emerging technologies, but this chapter focuses on blockchain technology and its possible benefits for records management. Guided by the technology acceptance model, the study established that archivists and records managers in Botswana and Zimbabwe would adopt blockchain if it is easy to use and useful for records management. The chapter ends by proposing a model for the adoption of blockchain technology for records management.

Chapter 4

Kosala Yapa Bandara, National University of Ireland Galway, Ireland
Subhasis Thakur, National University of Ireland Galway, Ireland
John G. Breslin, National University of Ireland Galway, Ireland

Modern supply chain applications are complex systems that play an important role in many different sectors. Supply chain management systems are implemented to handle increasing complexity and flows of goods. However, most of these systems are also increasing the complexity of providing trust and a global view of transactions in a distributed supply chain system. Blockchain technology introduces a new architectural style to support the traceability and trust of transactions performed by participants in a network. This chapter uses this emerging technology to realize a supply chain use case from JLP Meats in the UK with improved transparency, trust, and end-to-end querying while discussing potential challenges of realizing large-scale enterprise blockchain applications. The process of farm-to-fork is implemented and tested for traceability, item recall, block analysis, congestion enabling food safety, and sustainable agriculture. Potential challenges are highlighted in complex supply chains that need heterogeneous trade compliance and scalability.

Chapter 5

Güneş Çetin Gerger, Manisa Celal Bayar University, Turkey

Cryptocurrencies often also serve money laundering activities, terrorist financing, tax evasion, and other illegitimate activities with a market value of more than 7 billion euros across the globe, though the total amount is hardly measurable. Indeed, the blockchain technology involves many virtual currencies, including bitcoin, to conduct various financial transactions related practices throughout the world economies. Besides, other blockchain applications are making positive contributions to a wide array of other industries including healthcare, supply chain, manufacturing, etc. This technology which constitutes the backbone of digital assets transactions currencies is characterized by anonymity, privacy, security, and speed. In this sense, for tax administration authorities, detection of financial fraud and regulations with respect to taxation of virtual transactions pose newer emerging challenges. This chapter aims to examine the blockchain technology, cryptocurrencies, especially bitcoin, and look into regulations by world governments to combat tax evasion and illegal transactions.

Chapter 6

In recent years, blockchain has emerged as a popular data structure for use in software solutions. However, its meteoric rise has not been without criticism. Blockchain has been the subject of intense discussion in the field of cybersecurity because of its structural characteristics, mainly the permanency and decentralization. However, the blockchain technology in this field has also received intense scrutiny and caused to raise questions, such as, Is the application of blockchain in the field simply a localized trend or a bait for investors, both without a hope for permanent game-changing solutions? and Is blockchain an architecture that will lead to lasting disruptions in cybersecurity? This chapter aims to provide a neutral overview of why blockchain has risen as a popular pivot in cybersecurity, its current applications in this field, and an evaluation of what the future holds for this technology given both its limitations and advantages.

Chapter 7

In financial trading, cryptocurrencies like bitcoin use decentralization, traceability, and anonymity features to perform transactional activities. These digital currencies, using the emerging blockchain technologies, are forming the basis of the largest unregulated markets in the world. This creates various regulatory challenges, including the illicit purchase of drugs and weapons, money laundering, and funding terrorist activities. This chapter analyzes various legal and ethical implications, their effects, and various solutions to overcome the inherent issues that are currently faced by the policymakers and regulators. The authors present the result of an analysis of 30 recently published peer-reviewed scientific publications and suggest various mechanisms that can help in the detection and prevention of illegal activities that currently account for a substantial proportion of cryptocurrency trading. They suggest methods and applications that can also be used to identify the dark marketplaces in the future.

Post-trade securities settlements entered the electronic age between 1980 and 2000. The introduction of technologies such as secure electronic messaging, and improvements in database technology, enabled the inception of central securities depositories (CSDs) as trusted third parties or intermediaries within the securities settlements post-trade landscape. The study reported in this chapter has a focus on CSDs and the application of the blockchain technology to securities settlements. The objective is to develop a model for securities settlements using blockchain technology for a CSD, as currently, globally, no CSD has introduced a production-ready blockchain-based solution for securities settlements. A conceptual model was created from the reported literature that was evaluated by international post-trade securities professionals. The findings have resulted in the acceptance of the main components of the model, with a focus on the cost of the solution, and with the identification of prerequisites to such a solution (e.g., legal/regulatory enablement).

Section 2
Blockchain Technology Use Cases

Chapter 9
Zaigham Mahmood, University of Northampton, UK & Shijiazhuang Tiedao University, China

Blockchain technology is probably the most attractive innovation since the emergence of the internet. Blockchain refers to an open distributed ledger spread across multiple computers that hold digitally recorded transactions in a much more efficient, transparent, and secure manner. A blockchain consists of a number of blocks, each containing data relating to digital assets and a hash header that links it to the previous block in the chain. The blocks are linked together, and new blocks can be added and removed, following a process of consensus. Also, those involved in the transactions can share the distributed digital ledger without needing a centralized intermediary. This chapter aims to introduce blockchain technology and discuss the use cases and initiatives in various sectors of the society, in particular within the blockchain product vendors and service providers. Characteristics, benefits, types, underlying technologies, and platforms are also discussed for the sake of completeness.

Chapter 10
Somayya Madakam, FORE School of Management, New Delhi, India
Harshita, Institute of Management Technology, Ghaziabad, India

Currently, the financial transactions between individuals, organizations, and companies are taking place with the help of third-party approval of intermediaries such as banks, financial institutions, standardizing bodies, or credit card providers. These transactions involve multilevel approvals, costs, and inefficient processes in some cases, which also lead to waste of time and resources. To resolve these issues, blockchain technology has appeared as a new financial digital innovative solution. Here, financial transactions are online, open, and transparent. In this chapter, the authors present systematic literature of relevant research on blockchain technology. The objective is to understand the historical evolutions, current ongoing research, base technologies, and applications. The authors have extracted research articles from scientific databases including EBSCO, Scopus, Web of Science, and Google Scholar. The online blogs, wikis, media articles, YouTube videos, and companies' white papers on blockchain technology are also used for content analysis.

    Daniel Schönle, Furtwangen University of Applied Science, Germany
    Kevin Wallis, Furtwangen University of Applied Science, Germany
    Jan Stodt, Furtwangen University of Applied Science, Germany
    Christoph Reich, Furtwangen University, Germany
    Dominik Welte, Offenburg University of Applied Science, Germany
    Axel Sikora, Offenburg University of Applied Science, Germany

Digital transformation strengthens the interconnection of companies in order to develop optimized and better customized, cross-company business models. These models require secure, reliable, and traceable evidence and monitoring of contractually agreed information to gain trust between stakeholders. Blockchain technology using smart contracts allows the industry to establish trust and automate cross-company business processes without the risk of losing data control. A typical cross-company industry use case is equipment maintenance. Machine manufacturers and service providers offer maintenance for their machines and tools in order to achieve high availability at low costs. The aim of this chapter is to demonstrate how maintenance use cases are attempted by utilizing hyperledger fabric for building a chain of trust by hardened evidence logging of the maintenance process to achieve legal certainty. Contracts are digitized into smart contracts automating business that increase the security and mitigate the error-proneness of the business processes.

    Atakan Gerger, Ege University, Turkey

Even though the automotive industry was among the key players of the industrial revolution in the last century, striking transformations experienced in other sectors did not have significant repercussions on this industry until a few years ago. However, general advancements in technology and Industry 4.0 have presented new opportunities for the reconfiguration of the business environment. Developments in cryptocurrencies such as bitcoin, in particular, have attracted the attention to what is known as blockchain technology. Several successful examples of blockchain applications in different industries have tempted the automotive industry to be rapidly involved with efforts in this direction. As a consequence, the application of the blockchain technology to highly diverse areas in the automotive industry was set in motion. The purpose of this chapter is to explore the application of blockchain technology in the automotive industry, to analyse its advantages and disadvantages, and to demonstrate its successful in general.

    Vijayaraghavan Varadharajan, Infosys Ltd, India
    Divik Bansal, Infosys Ltd, India
    Sanal J. Nair, Infosys Ltd, India
    Rian Leevinson J, Infosys Ltd, India

The fragmented and disorganized nature of data in healthcare poses a variety of challenges to scientific research and medical applications. This mainly stems from the lack of traceability of transactions, complex disconnected networks, and lack of data interoperability. This complexity leads to difficulties in conducting research and clinical trials, and to the problem of counterfeit drugs in the market. This triggers lack of availability and accessibility of data for researchers and medical experts. Blockchain technology offers comprehensive solutions to these problems, and hence it has been of enormous interest in the healthcare sector. Blockchain technology with its innate transparency, traceability, data security, and distributed nature can help to overcome the data related problems in healthcare. This chapter provides an overview of the use of blockchain in the healthcare industry and explores various use-cases and applications. This chapter also discusses case-studies and various challenges faced while adapting blockchain in the healthcare industry.

Following the globalization initiated by containerization of logistics, supply chains might be due another revolution by the integration of the disruptive blockchain technology that addresses the current issues with the management of complex global supply chains. Blockchains are distributed digital ledgers that require no central authority to operate while offering a tamper-proof and transparent history of each transaction from the very beginning. Distributed nature of these ledgers ensure that every participant of the supply chain has access to trusted data. The industry has already begun experimenting with blockchain integration into their operations. For the majority of the organizations, however, these experiments stay in proof-of-concept stages or small pilot studies. In this chapter, the authors discuss the supply chain characteristics that make blockchain integration favorable, lay the groundwork for how blockchain can be used for supply chain operations and how it has been used so far.

Preface

OVERVIEW

Today's financial transactions are complex and costly. These are prone to human error and even fraud as each participant has their own separate ledgers. Intermediaries are also needed for validation that causes inefficiencies; and there are often delays and monitory losses. However, with the emergence of the Blockchain Technology, also known as Distributed Ledger Technology, it has been recognised that this new technology can provide highly efficient solutions to some of the issues with financial transactions that currently exist, especially when transactions involve cryptocurrencies.

Blockchain (BC) seems complicated, and it certainly can be, but its core concept is quite simple. A Blockchain is a particular type of database: a data structure that consists of a growing list of data records, called blocks, that are linked together using cryptography. It is an open and decentralised ledger that can record transactions between participants across a peer-to-peer network, without the need for a central certifying authority. Formally, as per the definition by McKinsey in Garson (2018), Blockchain is a decentralised, shared, and trusted distributed ledger (or database) that consists of encrypted 'blocks' of information added to a chain of existing blocks of linked records. The World Economic Forum estimate that by 2025, at least 10% of the world's GDP, currently at USD 100 trillion, will be managed via the Blockchain technology (Hance, 2020). According to Yahoo Finance (2020), the Blockchain market size is expected to grow from USD 3.0 billion in 2020 to USD 39.7 billion by 2025.

Blockchain technology is highly attractive due to the numerous advantages that it offers including increased transparency, reduced transaction costs, faster transaction settlement, automation of information, increased traceability, improved customer experience, improved digital identity, better cyber security, and user-controlled networks in real time. Potential applications and use cases include funds transfer, smart contracts, e-voting, efficient supply chain management, and financial transactions using cryptocurrencies such as Bitcoin; covering nearly every sector of the society including finance, healthcare, law, trade, real estate, and many more. As is always the case, challenges and limitations also exist due to the newness of this technology but mainly due to lack of adequate regulations and controls. The inherent issues include high energy consumption, limited scalability, complexity, security, network size, and lack of regulations; and also, unethical and illegal activities such as money laundering and avoidance of tax. Nevertheless, Blockchain is an attractive technology, and has much to offer to the modern-day industry.

It is in this context that the current book, *Industry Use Cases on Blockchain Technology Applications in IoT and the Financial Sector,* is developed. The aim is: 1) to investigate the Blockchain technology, and its adoption and effectiveness in banking and other industries; 2) to present use cases from industrial and financial sectors; and 3) to fill a gap and extend the existing body of knowledge in the suggested field. With this objective, this current volume presents relevant methodologies and applications of the Blockchain technology, case studies and major initiatives taken from various sectors of the society, and major development initiatives from the technology vendors.

This book is a collection of 14 chapters authored by well-known academics and industry practitioners from around the world. Hopefully, the book will serve as a reference text in the subject areas of Blockchain Technology, cryptocurrencies, financial transactions, and further extend the existing body of knowledge in these fields.

BOOK OBJECTIVE

This book, *Industry Use Cases on Blockchain Technology Applications in IoT and the Financial Sector*, aims to serve as a reference text that presents applications, case studies and relevant methodologies in the field of Blockchain technology. The objective is to discuss the following:

- Current research and practice in the field of Blockchain Technology and Cryptocurrencies
- Adoption of Blockchain Technology in banking, industry, and other sectors of the society
- Benefits and inherent limitations of Blockchain Technology, and suggested solutions
- Applications, initiatives and use cases from industry and financial services providers

TARGET AUDIENCE

This reference text is aimed at supporting a number of potential audiences, including the following:

- University students and lecturers interested in the emerging field of Blockchain Technology and adoption of virtual currencies for financial transactions
- Information systems specialists, technology professionals, security experts, business users, and managers working in commercial and financial sectors
- Research students and practitioners who wish to further advance the body of knowledge in the Distributed Ledger Technologies and trading in digital currencies

BOOK ORGANISATION

This book is organised in two sections with a total of 14 chapters, authored by 31 well known academics and practitioners from around the world. Brief descriptions of these chapters are as follows:

Section 1: Blockchain Technology Applications

There are eight contributions in this section. The first chapter discusses the Blockchain (BC) technology and presents BC applications in the industry, mainly to set the scene for further discussion that appears in other contributions in this section. The 2nd chapter presents a Blockchain based robotics automation mechanism suitable foe educational settings. The next contribution has a focus on the application of

Blockchain technology for records management and presents its adoption in Botswana and Zimbabwe. The 4th chapter discusses the tracing and congestion mechanism using BC and presents a supply chain use case using the Hyperledger Fabric. The following contribution aims to discuss the general issue of tax evasion through financial transaction using virtual currencies. The 6th contribution examines the use of BC to improve cyber security, and presents relevant applications. Chapter 7 presents an analysis of the legal and ethical issues relating to digital transactions made via the use of cryptocurrencies. The final contribution in this section proposes a securities settlement model using Blockchain.

Section 2: Blockchain Technology Use Cases

This section has six chapters. The first three chapters have a similar focus. The first of these discusses the Blockchain (BC) technology and presents industry initiatives and use cases, mainly to set the scene for further discussion in other contributions in this section of the book. The 2nd contribution presents the core concepts and main components of BC as well as some notable use cases. The 3rd chapter also has a similar focus on use cases from within the industry and various other sectors of the society. The next chapter in this section provides a Blockchain use case from the automotive industry and presents statistical evaluation of the case study. The fifth contribution provides an overview of the use and applications of Blockchain technology in the healthcare industry. The 6th chapter in this section and the final in the book considers the case of supply chain and provides an analysis of case studies in this subject area.

CHAPTER DESCRIPTIONS

Full abstracts of book chapters appear in the *Detailed Table of Contents* section in the book. Here, we present very brief outlines of each chapter.

Chapter 1 is titled "Blockchain Technology: Applications in the Industry." Authored by Zaigham Mahmood, it presents the essential terminology, concepts and processes relating to the Blockchain (BC) Technology, also known as Distributed Ledger Technology. This chapter presents some well-known applications of Blockchain in various sectors of the society including banking, healthcare, transportation, manufacturing, supply chain, and education. The aim is to introduce this latest technology and its uses to set the scene for further discussion on Blockchain-related topics, applications and case studies, that appear in later chapters in this book.

Chapter 2 is authored by Nhlanhla Sibanyoni. Titled as "A Blockchain-Based Robotic Process Automation Mechanism in Educational Setting," it suggests a robotics process automation (RPA) mechanism based on the Blockchain technology. Using example of an online school registration system, the chapter illustrates how Blockchain processes can help to overcome the inherent challenges often faced by the school administration, ICT technical staff, and parents, with respect to allocation of student places in a fair, transparent and trustworthy manner. The contribution presents an application and case study in educational setting.

Chapter 3 is jointly authored by Olefhile Moswen and Forget Chaterera-Zambuko. Titled as "Blockchain Technology for Records Management in Botswana and Zimbabwe," this contribution proposes the use of Blockchain technology for records management in Botswana and Zimbabwe. Methodology includes a survey to collect the required data. Based on the analysis, a model is proposed for the adoption of Blockchain, that also includes a proposal for a strategic roadmap for records and archives management professionals on how to embrace the Blockchain technology. TAM is used to investigate and review the uptake of Blockchain for records management.

Chapter 4, titled as "End-to-End Tracing and Congestion in a Blockchain: A Supply Chain Use Case in Hyperledger Fabric," is authored by Kosala Yapa Bandara, Subhasis Thakur, and John Breslin. This chapter uses the Blockchain technology to realise a supply chain (SC) use case for a UK based company, with the aim to achieve improved transparency, trust, and end-to-end querying while also discussing potential challenges of realising large-scale enterprise Blockchain applications. The SC process is detailed, implemented and tested for end-to-end traceability and items recall. The chapter suggests a clear need for heterogeneous trade compliance and scalability.

Chapter 5 is titled as "Blockchain Technology and General Issue of Tax Evasion via Bitcoin." Contributed by Gunes Cetin Gerger, this chapter examines the use of Blockchain technology for financial transaction of digital currencies. Discussing the advantages and limitations of trading in Bitcoin and other virtual currencies, this contribution has a focus on tax avoidance, tax evasion and money laundering scenarios. The contribution also examines the taxation regulations for cryptocurrencies, that international organizations are in the process of developing, in relation to combating tax evasion, money laundering, and related monitory fraud.

Chapter 6 is jointly developed by Muath Obaidat and Joseph Brown. Under the heading of "Perspectives of Blockchain in Cybersecurity: Applications and Future Developments," this chapter aims at presenting an historic perspective on Blockchain technology development, and provides an overview of why Blockchain has risen so much as a popular pivot in cybersecurity. The focus is on relevant applications of the said technology within the cybersecurity field. The contribution also includes an evaluation of the possible issues and implications of a Blockchain-centric future for this emerging technology given both its influence, attraction, limitations, and advantages.

Chapter 7 is jointly authored by Neha Mason, Malka N Halgamuge and Kamalani Aiyar. Titled as "Blockchain and Cryptocurrencies: Legal and Ethical Considerations," this chapter presents an analysis of the legal and ethical issues, and implications of transactions made via the use of cryptocurrencies using Blockchain technology. It looks into strategies to overcome the inherent issues with respect to such implications and considerations. To this end, thirty recently published scientific papers are analysed and necessary recommendations made to help with the detection and prevention of illegal activities relating to cryptocurrency trading.

Chapter 8 is titled as "A Securities Settlement Model Using Blockchain Technology: For Central Securities Depository" and developed by Andre Calitz, Jean Greyling and Steve Everett. This study has a focus on Central Securities Depositories (CSD) and discusses the application of the Blockchain technology to securities settlements. The authors have reviewed the published literature, evaluated their findings using a survey approach, and presented a suitable Blockchain-based production model for distributed securities depository. Critical success factors have been analysed; review and evaluation of the proposed model have also been presented.

Chapter 9 is developed by Zaigham Mahmood. Under the heading of "Blockchain Technology: Initiatives and Use Cases in the Industry," the author presents the basic terminology and essential concepts relating to the Blockchain technology, also known as Distributed Ledger Technology (DLT). The chapter introduces the relevant technologies and presents some well-known use cases and initiatives in various sectors of the society, mainly from the Blockchain product vendors and service providers. Relevant technology platforms are also discussed. The aim is to set the scene for further discussion on Blockchain case studies that appear later in 2nd part of the book.

Chapter 10 is jointly authored by Somayya Madakam and Harshita Susanto. Titled as "Blockchain Technology: Concepts, Components, and Cases," this contribution aims to present a systematic literature review of relevant research on Blockchain technology, with the objective to understand the historical evolution of the technology, current ongoing research, underlying technologies, applications, and use cases in sectors such as banking, insurance, real estate, smart cities, manufacturing, supply chain, energy, and telecommunication. In doing so, the authors also discuss the core concepts and Blockchain related mechanisms for the sake of completeness.

Chapter 11 is another collaborative effort authored by Danial Schonle, Kevin Wallis, Jan Stodt, Christoph Reich, Dominik Welte, and Axel Sikora. This contribution, under the heading of "Industry Use Cases on Blockchain Technology," demonstrates how equipment maintenance use cases can utilize the Hyperledger Fabric for building a chain of trust relating to the maintenance processes to achieve legal certainty. It is maintained that business contracts digitized into Blockchain smart contracts, can help to automate business operations that increase security of operations and trust in the processes, and thus mitigate the error-proneness of the business processes.

Chapter 12 is authored by Atakan Gerger and titled as "Blockchain Technology in Automotive Industry: Use Cases and Statistical Evaluation." This chapter discusses the Blockchain technology in some detail, presents relevant use cases and explores the current applications of the technology in the automotive industry. Discussing production processes, supply chain, financial transactions, vehicle safety, data security, and smart contracts, the contribution explores the inherent issues and presents strategies for more relevant process implementation. Best practices from the motor industry are highlighted and statistical evaluation is presented.

Chapter 13 is titled as "Blockchain: Reinventing the Healthcare Industry – Use Cases and Applications." It is jointly developed by Vijayaraghavan Varadharajan, Divik Bansal, Sanal J Nair, and Rian Leevinson. Focusing on the use of Blockchain in the healthcare industry, this contribution explores the relevant use-cases and applications in this domain. The emphasis is on regulatory compliance, operational efficiencies, electronic health records, reduction in costs, and improvement in productivity. The chapter also discusses case-studies and various industry initiatives to illustrate inherent challenges in adapting the Blockchain technology in the said industry.

Chapter 14, the final contribution in this book is titled as "Blockchain Integration Into Supply Chain Operations: An Analysis With Case Studies." Authored by Yigit Sever and Pelin Angin, it has focus on the use of the Blockchain technology on supply chain management (SCM). Discussing the potential issues in SCM, the contribution looks into the suitability of using the Blockchain technology to resolve the issues of traceability, transparency, immutability, efficiency, digitization, decentralisation, and security. Use of smart contracts and the Internet of Things paradigm are also discussed and practical suggestions provided. Various case studies are also explored.

OTHER BOOKS BY ZAIGHAM MAHMOOD

Web 2.0 and Cloud Technologies for Implementing Connected Government

This book is an essential reference source that presents various dimensions of the connected government visions, offering development methodologies, practical examples, best practices, case studies, and latest research, including in-depth examinations of mobile technologies, automation, business intelligence, as well as the ethical and security issues relating to citizens' data. ISBN: 978-1799-84570-6

Developing and Monitoring Smart Environments for Intelligent Cities

This reference text presents technological frameworks and device connectivity approaches, suitable for building and managing intelligent cities. The aim is to develop smart environments appropriate for Internet of Things applications such as Internet of Vehicles vision, Intelligent transportation, smart healthcare, and Industrial IoT, etc. ISBN: 978-1799-85062-5

Software Engineering in the Era of Cloud Computing

This book has a focus on developing scalable complex software for distributed computing applications. It presents and discusses state of the art of software engineering (SE) in terms of methodologies, trends and future direction for cloud SE. Domain modelling, SE testing in the cloud, SE analytics, and software process improvement as a service rare also discussed. ISBN: 978-3030-24891-8

The Internet of Things in the Industrial Sector: Security and Device Connectivity, Smart Environments, and Industry 4.0

This reference text has a focus on the development and deployment of the Industrial Internet of Things (IIoT) paradigm, discussing frameworks, methodologies, benefits and inherent limitations of connected smart environments, as well as providing case studies of employing the IoT vision in the industrial domain. ISBN: 978-3030-24891-8

Security, Privacy and Trust in the IoT Environment

This book has a focus on security and privacy in the Internet of Things environments. It also discusses the aspects of user trust with respect to device connectivity. Main topics covered include: principles, underlying technologies, security issues, mechanisms for trust and authentication as well as success indicators, performance metrics and future directions. ISBN: 978-3030-18074-4

Guide to Ambient Intelligence in the IoT Environment: Principles, Technologies and Applications

This text discusses the AmI element of the IoT paradigm and reviews the current developments, underlying technologies, and case scenarios relating to AmI-based IoT environments. The book presents cutting-edge research, frameworks, and methodologies on device connectivity, communication protocols, and other aspects relating to the AmI-IoT vision. ISBN: 978-3-030-04172-4

Fog Computing: Concepts, Frameworks and Technologies

This reference text describes the state of the art of Fog and Edge computing with a particular focus on development approaches, architectural mechanisms, related technologies, and measurement metrics for building smart adaptable environments. The coverage also includes topics such as device connectivity, security, interoperability, and communication methods. ISBN: 978-3319-94889-8

Smart Cities: Development and Governance Frameworks

This text/reference investigates the state of the art in approaches to building, monitoring, managing and governing smart city environments. A particular focus is placed on the distributed computing environments within the infrastructure of smart cities and smarter living, including issues of device connectivity, communication, security and interoperability. ISBN: 978-3-319-76668-3

Data Science and Big Data Computing: Frameworks and Methodologies

This book has a focus on data science, and provides practical guidance on big data analytics. Expert perspective is provided by an authoritative collection of 36 researchers and practitioners, discussing latest developments and emerging trends; presenting frameworks and innovative methodologies; and suggesting best practices for efficient data analytics. ISBN: 978-3-319-31859-2

Connected Environments for the IoT: Challenges and Solutions

This comprehensive reference presents a broad-ranging overview of device connectivity in distributed computing environments, supporting the vision of IoT. Expert perspectives are provided, covering issues of communication, security, interoperability, networking, access control and authentication. Corporate analysis is also offered via several case studies. ISBN: 978-3-319-70102-8

Connectivity Frameworks for Smart Devices: The Internet of Things from a Distributed Computing Perspective

This is an authoritative reference that focuses on the latest developments on the Internet of Things. It presents state of the art on the current advances in the connectivity of diverse devices; and focuses on the communication, security, privacy, access control and authentication aspects of the device connectivity in distributed environments. ISBN: 978-3-319-33122-5

Cloud Computing: Methods and Practical Approaches

The benefits associated with cloud computing are enormous; yet the dynamic, virtualized and multi-tenant nature of the cloud environment presents many challenges. To help tackle these, this volume provides illuminating viewpoints and case studies to present current research and best practices on approaches and technologies for the emerging cloud paradigm. ISBN: 978-1-4471-5106-7

Cloud Computing: Challenges, Limitations and R&D Solutions

This text reviews the challenging issues that present barriers to greater implementation of the Cloud Computing paradigm, together with the latest research into developing potential solutions. This book presents case studies, and analysis of the implications of the cloud paradigm, from a diverse selection of researchers and practitioners of international repute. ISBN: 978-3-319-10529-1

Continued Rise of the Cloud: Advances and Trends in Cloud Computing

This reference volume presents latest research and trends in cloud related technologies, infrastructure, and architecture. Contributed by expert researchers and practitioners in the field, this book presents discussions on current advances and practical approaches including guidance and case studies on the provision of cloud-based services and frameworks. ISBN: 978-1-4471-6451-7

Software Engineering Frameworks for the Cloud Computing Paradigm

This is an authoritative reference that presents the latest research on software development approaches suitable for distributed computing environments. Contributed by researchers and practitioners of international repute, the book offers practical guidance on enterprise-wide software deployment in the cloud environment. Case studies are also presented. ISBN: 978-1-4471-5030-5

Cloud Computing for Enterprise Architectures

This text, aimed at system architects and business managers, examines the cloud paradigm from the perspective of enterprise architectures. It introduces fundamental concepts, discusses principles, and explores frameworks for the adoption of cloud computing. The book explores the inherent challenges and presents future directions for further research. ISBN: 978-1-4471-2235-7

Cloud Computing: Concepts, Technology & Architecture

This is a text book (in English but also translated in Chinese and Korean) highly recommended for adoption for university level courses in distributed computing. It offers a detailed explanation of cloud computing concepts, architectures, frameworks, models, mechanisms, and technologies - highly suitable for both newcomers and experts. ISBN: 978-0133387520

Software Project Management for Distributed Computing: Life-Cycle Methods for Developing Scalable and Reliable Tools

This unique volume explores cutting-edge management approaches to developing complex software that is efficient, scalable, sustainable, and suitable for distributed environments. Emphasis is on the use of the latest software technologies and frameworks for life-cycle methods, including design, implementation and testing stages of software development. ISBN: 978-3319-543246

Requirements Engineering for Service and Cloud Computing

This text aims to present and discuss the state-of-the-art in terms of methodologies, trends and future directions for requirements engineering for the service and cloud computing paradigm. Majority of the contributions in the book focus on requirements elicitation; requirements specifications; requirements classification and requirements validation and evaluation. ISBN: 978-3319513096

User Centric E-Government: Challenges & Opportunities

This text presents a citizens-focused approach to the development and implementation of electronic government. The focus is twofold: discussion on challenges of service availability, e-service operability on diverse smart devices; as well as on opportunities for the provision of open, responsive and transparent functioning of world governments. ISBN: 978-3319594415.

Cloud Computing Technologies for Connected Government

This text reports the latest research on Electronic Government for enhancing the transparency of public institutions. It covers a broad scope of topics including citizen empowerment, collaborative public services, communication through social media, cost benefits of the Cloud paradigm, electronic voting systems, identity management, and legal issues. ISBN: 9781466686298

Human Factors in Software Development and Design

This reference text brings together high-quality research on the influence and impact of ordinary people on the software industry. With the goal of improving the quality and usability of computer technologies, topics include global software development, multi-agent systems, public administration Platforms, socio-economic factors, and user-centric design. ISBN: 9781466664852

IT in the Public Sphere: Applications in Administration, Government, Politics, and Planning

This nook evaluates current research and best practices in the adoption of e-government technologies in developed and developing countries, enabling governments to keep in touch with citizens and corporations in modern societies. Topics covered include citizen participation, digital technologies, globalisation, strategic management, and urban development. ISBN: 9781466647190

Emerging Mobile and Web 2.0 Technologies for Connected E-Government

This reference discusses the emerging mobile and communication technologies including social media, for use by governments and citizens. It presents a reference source for researchers, practitioners, students, and managers interested in the application of recent technological innovations to develop open, transparent and more effective e-government environment. ISBN: 9781466660823

E-Government Implementation and Practice in Developing Countries

This volume presents research on current undertakings by developing countries towards the design, development, and implementation of e-government policies. It proposes frameworks and strategies for the benefits of project managers, government officials, researchers, and practitioners involved in the development and implementation of e-government planning. ISBN: 9781466640900

Developing E-Government Projects: Frameworks and Methodologies

This text presents frameworks and methodologies for strategies for the design, implementation of e-government projects. It illustrates the best practices for successful adoption of e-government and thus becomes essential for policy makers, practitioners and researchers for the successful deployment of e-government planning and projects. ISBN: 9781466642454.

Zaigham Mahmood
University of Northampton, UK & Shijiazhuang Tiedao University, China
30 November 2020

REFERENCES

Garson, B. (2018, June). *Blockchain Beyond the Hype.* Available at: https://www.mckinsey.com/business-functions/mckinsey-digital/our-insights/Blockchain-beyond-the-hype-what-is-the-strategic-business-value?cid=other-eml-nsl-mip-mck-oth-1807&hlkid=5424a29008e445239371a81cc83b3dbb&hctky=10291646&hdpid=bb9f89f0-458b-4b4e-a1ee-ad99e602294e

Hance, M. (2020). *What is Blockchain and How Can it be Used in Education?* Available at: https://mdreducation.com/2018/08/20/Blockchain-education/

Yahoo Finance. (2020), *The Global Blockchain Market Size is Expected to Grow from USD 3.0 Billion in 2020 to USD 39.7 Billion by 2025, at a Compound Annual Growth Rate (CAGR) of 67.3%.* Available at: https://finance.yahoo.com/news/global-Blockchain-market-size-expected-140000250.html

Acknowledgment

The editor acknowledges the support and efforts of a number of colleagues. First and foremost, I would like to thank the contributors to this book, 31 authors and co-authors from academia as well as industry from around the world who collectively developed and submitted a total of 14 chapters. Without their efforts in developing quality chapters conforming to the required guidelines and meeting often the strict deadlines, this text would not have been possible. Their names and brief biographical notes are listed in a separate section in this book.

Secondly, my grateful thanks are due to the members of the advisory and editorial board of this book who willingly volunteered their time in reviewing the book chapters and providing further advisory and editorial support. Their names and affiliations also appear in a separate section in this book.

Finally, I would like to thank members of my immediate family - Rehana, Zoya, Imran, Hanya, Arif and Ozair - for their continued support, love, and encouragement. Every good wish, also, for the youngest and the most delightful in our family: Eyaad Imran Rashid Khan and Zayb-un-Nisa Khan.

Thank you all.

Zaigham Mahmood
University of Northampton, UK & Shijiazhuang Tiedao University, China
30 November 2020

Section 1
Blockchain Technology Applications

Chapter 1
Blockchain Technology:
Applications in the Industry

Zaigham Mahmood
ⓘ https://orcid.org/0000-0001-7411-7496
University of Northampton, UK & Shijiazhuang Tiedao University, China

ABSTRACT

Blockchain technology is one of the latest innovations in computer science that has world-wide scale and reach. A blockchain is a mathematical structure for storing digital transactions in a distributed and decentralized digital ledger consisting of multiple blocks that are linked using cryptographic signatures and spread across multiple computers. Each block records digital transactions data securely and has a hash link pointing to the previous block in the network in an efficient manner. New blocks can be added and removed through an agreed consensus of all nodes that each share the distributed ledger without the need for a centralized controlling authority. This chapter aims to introduce the blockchain technology, also known as distributed ledger technology (DLT), and discuss its applications in various sectors of the society including banking, healthcare, transportation, manufacturing, supply chain, and education. Extension of the internet of things vision using the DLT is also briefly discussed.

INTRODUCTION

Blockchain Technology is one of the newest innovations in the field of computer science, that has world-wide scale and reach. Blockchain has long been associated with cryptocurrency e.g. Bitcoin. However, this emerging technology is destined to disrupt the global economy in the foreseeable future. It has a huge potential to positively impact on the various industries including healthcare, transportation, manufacturing, finance, automotive, education, and government. The World Economic Forum estimates that by 2025, at least 10% of the world's GDP, currently at USD 100 trillion, will be managed via the Blockchain technology (Hance, 2020).

The idea of Blockchain, originally termed as 'block chain', was first put forward in 2008. This was essentially the realisation that the technology that underlined the operation of 'Bitcoin' could be separated from the currency and used for all kinds of other interorganisational cooperation. There was, then,

DOI: 10.4018/978-1-7998-6650-3.ch001

further exponential development over the period of about 10 years in terms of 'smart contracts', 'proofs of work', and Blockchain 'scaling'. Since its origin in 2008, The Blockchain technology has gone through a number of phases but most notably by the three as follows (Goyal, 2018):

- Transactional: around 2012-2014
- Contracts based: around 2014-2016
- Applications: from 2017 onwards

The timeline of the development of Blockchain technology can be presented as mentioned below.

2009-12: White paper on Bitcoin; emergence of Bitcoin cryptocurrency; Blockchain as backbone of digital currency; Bitcoin magazine

2012-14: Bitcoin marketplace and start-ups; Ethereum based projects; Blockchain attraction for financial services sector

2014-15: Over 40 Blockchain implementations; smart contracts; Hyperledger; Endorsement for Blockchain from technology companies

2016-17: Blockchain adoption beyond proofs of concept; EOS.IO protocol; Blockchain mainstream adoption across different industries

2018-20: Blockchain protocols and standards; accelerated investment from ISPs; Rise of IPOs and Blockchain start up ecosystem

2020-: New business models combining Analytics, IoT and Blockchain; Endorsement by World Economic Forum

Blockchain technology presents numerous highly attractive characteristics including decentralisation, transparency, immutability, security, consensus, and smart contracts (Rosic, 1016; Tasca, 2019). Witscad (2020) divides the main characteristics into two varieties: functional and emergent. Refer to Figure 1. These are explained in detailed in a later section of this chapter.

Because of the attraction of these features, Blockchain has been gaining enormous attention in areas beyond its cryptocurrency roots, since about 2014. This technology has gone beyond its first application in Bitcoin cryptocurrency; and is now being applied to nearly every sector of the society including banking, healthcare, manufacturing, transportation, logistics, supply chain management, and education, amongst others. Some of these applications are also discussed later in this contribution.

The organisation of this chapter is as follows. The next main section defines the Blockchain technology, describes the essential terminology, outlines the characteristics, describes the underlying concepts and varieties of Blockchain, and summarises the generic Blockchain transactional process. The next section is the main focus of the chapter, that lists various case studies and applications currently being pursued in various different industries, including banking, healthcare, transportation, manufacturing, supply chain, and education. Extension of the Internet of Things (IoT) vision using the Distributed Ledger Technology (DLT) is also briefly discussed. The final section presents the conclusion.

It is hope that this chapter sets the scene for further discussion on various Blockchain related topics, that appear in later chapters in this book.

Figure 1. Blockchain characteristics

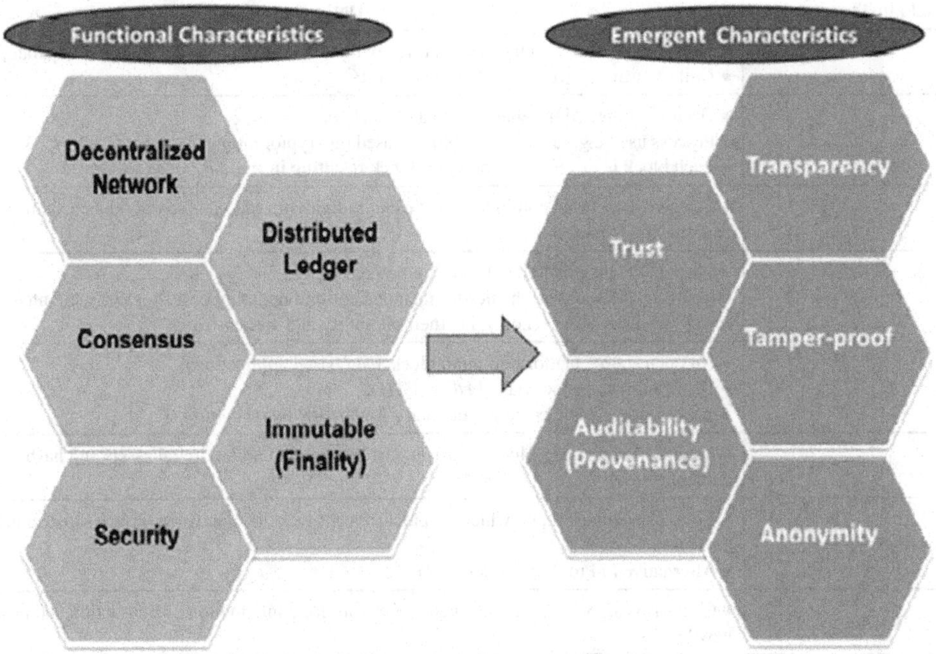

BLOCKCHAIN TECHNOLOGY

A Blockchain is a distributed database spread across many computers with no central control, that can transform governance, business models and the functioning of organisations. A Blockchain is a perfect place to store information on digital assets (representing values, identities, agreements, property rights, credentials, etc). It promises a more efficient, secure and transparent way of handling transactions, that can save a huge amount of administration, bureaucracy, effort and time.

According to McKinsey in Garson (2018), Blockchain can be described as *a decentralised, shared and trusted distributed ledger (or database) that consists of encrypted 'blocks' of information added to a chain of existing blocks of records*. The ledger relies on the *consensus* of a global peer network to operate. Modifying the data in one block is impossible without modifying the entire chain and without an agreed consensus of the entire peer network. Before a new block is added, it must first be validated by other participants (i.e. other blocks, also called nodes) to prevent fraud and to preserve security. Blocks are immutable so once data in a block is added to the chain, it cannot be edited; unless the Blockchain is initially created with ability to edit blocks, which is something that is subject to consensus (Robinson, 2018). Blockchain allows information to be verified and exchanged without relying on a third-party central or management authority. The Blockchain technology is based on a complex branch of mathematics called *cryptography*.

Blockchain applications include: *Bitcoin* (cryptocurrency), *Sia* (decentralised cloud storage), and *Ethereum* (virtual machine to run smart contracts). But, before proceeding any further, it is in order to define certain commonly used terms, for the sake of completeness. These are listed in Table 1.

Table 1. Blockchain terms and definitions

Blockchain Terms	Definitions
Bitcoin	• First and the most popular cryptocurrency that uses blockchain technology to operate; • Unit of currency where one bitcoin = 1 BTC
Block	• Group of transactions entered into a blockchain; • Process used e.g. to add a new block, based on cryptography; • Each block is linked to the previous block resulting in a chain
Cryptography	• Science of securing communication using individualized codes so only the participating parties can read the messages
Consensus	• Mechanism by which the blockchain process works; • Refers to rules and mechanics for maintenance and updating of ledger that guarantees trustworthiness of the records, i.e. their reliability and authenticity
Ethereum	• An open source platform to build blockchain based applications; • Distributes a currency called *ether* (ETH); • Allows storage and execution of code allowing for *smart contracts*
Hash	• Digital signature of a block (consisting of information about digital assets and hash pointer) for authentication
Proof of Stake (PoS)	• Consensus algorithm by which cryptocurrency blockchain network achieves distributed consensus; • Alternative to Proof of Work (PoW)
Proof of Work (PoW)	• Consensus algorithm for a blockchain network for confirmation of transaction and production of new blocks
Smart Contract	• Program code associated with a blockchain that allows to add a transaction based on a certain agreed trigger event; • Also known as Chaincode

Blockchain Characteristics

As mentioned before, some of the most important properties of Blockchain which have formed the reasons for its use in various applications include: decentralisation, transparency, immutability and smart contracts (Rosic, 1016; Tasca, 2019). These are briefly discussed below. Refer also to Figure 1 for a more detailed set of characteristics, divided into functional and emergent properties of the said technology.

- **Decentralisation**: The traditional client-server model is a centralised approach that has served the industry well but it has vulnerabilities. In a decentralised system, data is owned by all actors in the network. Also, interaction between two nodes in the network does not need to go through a third party. This is exactly the main idea behind Bitcoin and the Blockchain.
- **Transparency**: In a Blockchain, this is achieved by hiding a person's identity via cryptography so users' real identity is secure. However, transactions can be seen via their public addresses; but this is for the sake of accountability, which, in turn, translates into trust and honesty with respect to transactions between clients.
- **Immutability**: In the case of Blockchain, this refers to digital content of a block, which once entered remains unaltered; and any attempt to modify it gets stopped. This is achieved through using cryptographic hash functions. Since, a block comprises data and a hash (that points to data in the previous block), it makes the system more reliable.

- **Smart Contracts**: For a Blockchain, contracts are written in such a way that there is no need for human intervention, verification or arbitration. Also, there is a measure to ensure that conflicting or double transactions cannot be written in the Blockchain. Any conflict is automatically reconciled and each valid transaction is added only once (Tasca, 2019).

A simple approach to explain the way the Blockchain process works, is illustrated in Figure 2.

Figure 2. How Blockchain works

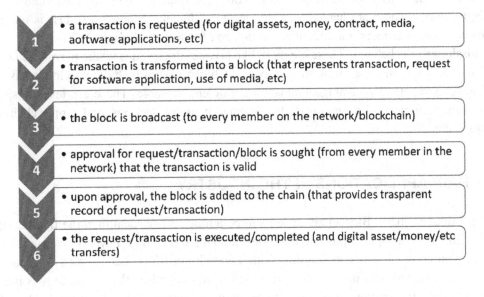

Blockchain Types

There are generally three main types of Blockchain: public, private and federated (Bhasin, 2019). Public and Private Blockchains can be permissioned or permissionless (Singh, 2020). Federated Blockchain are also known as consortium. Brief explanation of these now follows.

- **Public Blockchain**: Here, anyone is allowed to participate in the network to add and run a public node. These Blockchains are decentralised and slower in nature as compared to private blockchain, however, they offer better anonymity. All members of the network can see the blocks and participate in consensus for validation. This variety has true decentralised structure and offers the greatest transparency and immutability. Examples are: Bitcoin and Ethereum.
- **Private Blockchain**: In this case, the organisation that owns the Blockchain has the authority over who can join and access the network. It is, therefore, a centralised-decentralised network; where access permissions vary from node to node. Anonymity is not offered; however, these networks are less expensive to run than public Blockchains. This variety is more power efficient than Public networks, less volatile, and offers better privacy. Examples are: R3 and Corda.
- **Federated or Consortium Blockchain**: Here, multiple organisations form a federation that owns the network. It acts as a hub for multiple organisations to share and work concurrently. Networks

are highly scalable and energy efficient, and offer the fastest output and lowest costs. This variety offers lower transaction fees and more robustness as criminal activity is much reduced as compared to public or private Blockchains. Examples are: Multichain and Monax.

Another classification is as follows:

- **Permissionless** Blockchains: These require no permission to join the network (like public Blockchains) and therefore these are ideal for running and managing digital assets. Their characteristics include: anonymity, true decentralisation, transparency, trusting, immutability with enhanced security. These are harder to scale, and less efficient. Ethereum (ETH) is one example. Some use cases include: digital identity, voting, and fundraising (Singh, 2020).
- **Permissioned** Blockchains: These are more like private Blockchains where permission is required to join, from the owner organisations e.g. banks. Characteristics include: varying levels of decentralisation, governed by owning organisation, efficient, scalable. These are less transparent but more energy efficient. Use cases include: research, bank transactions, and supply chain management (Singh, 2020).

BLOCKCHAIN APPLICATIONS IN THE INDUSTRY

As stated in I-Scope (2020), Blockchain appears to be a much bigger deal than the Internet of Things (IoT) vision. Blockchain applications and use cases in the industry go far beyond the financial transactions using cryptocurrencies such as Bitcoin. With the ability of Blockchain to provide more transparency and robustness, and with its characteristics such as immutability, this technology is impacting a wide variety of industries including finance, manufacturing, supply chain, logistics, and healthcare, to name a few. Some of the Blockchain applications in the said industries, and more, are now elaborated in the following sub-sections.

Banking

The financial institutions and the banking sector connect various groups of people and allow them all kinds of opportunities relating to trade and commerce. In this context, Blockchain provides a tool that can accomplish the same but on a wider scale, more securely and transparently. Therefore, Blockchain technology has a potential for global commerce. It can make trade more efficient by removing the manual and paper-based processes, and introducing streamlined and automated processes instead. A public Blockchain can be a great collaborative tool because it is decentralized. Besides, there is no human intervention in its operation. The following bullet points briefly discuss a number of use cases of the Blockchain technology in the banking sector (Concise Software, 2020; Shumsky, 2019).

- Faster payments: The banking sector is moving towards decentralised channels for payments and money transactions. And so, Blockchain technology is already being used for this purpose. By adopting this technology, payments become faster and banks are able to cut down on processing fees as well as the need for verification from third parties or intermediaries. There is every indication that Blockchain would change the banking industry fundamentally by 2025 (Concise Software, 2020).

- Reduction in fraud: Possibility of cyber-attacks is probably the main challenge facing the banking industry today. Blockchain technology, which is decentralized and therefore less prone to this type of fraud, would not only execute payments in real time but also with complete transparency which, in turn, would also enable real-time fraud analysis and prevention. The Blockchain ledger can also keep and provide a historical record of all actions and documents shared (Shumsky, 2019).

- Buying and selling assets: In securities market, there is much reliance on financial assets brokers and custodian banks for buying and selling. This also involves a fee to be paid. Using Blockchain (and currencies such as Bitcoin and Ethereum) removes the middlemen, eliminates the exchange fees, makes the process more automatic, resilient and secure, and helps to create decentralised database of digital assets.

- Peer-to-peer transfers: This allows customers to transfer funds online, however, there are many limitations e.g. large commission fees and, at times, lack of security of customer data. Here, Blockchain technology can help to decentralize applications for peer-to-peer transfers as Blockchain has no geographical limitations. Transactions are immutable and can take place in real time, and thus recipients will not need to wait until they receive the digital assets (Concise Software, 2020).

- Accounting and auditing: Accounting and auditing has been relatively slow to digitize, mainly because of the regulatory requirements for integrity, accuracy and validity of data. Thus, accounting is another area that can be transformed with Blockchain technology that can simplify compliance and streamline the traditional bookkeeping systems. Here, businesses are able to add transactions directly into a joint register that is distributed. As a result, records are more transparent and secure. Blockchain smart contracts can be used to pay for invoices automatically, as well.

Healthcare

The healthcare industry is beginning to adopt the Blockchain technology to provide integrated care to the patients; as well as to address the challenges of synchronising patient data that exist in multiple disparate Hospital Information Systems (HIS) while ensuring data security and privacy. It can also provide opportunities to ensure interoperability, integrity, patient identity, privacy, traceability, reduced operational costs, and ubiquitous access to its services (CitiusTech, 2018). Some of these features are briefly elaborated below.

- Nationwide interoperability: Healthcare organisations, forming part of a nation's healthcare, follow different standards for exchange and sharing of data e.g. FHIR, CDA, or HL7 etc. This can result in reduced operability between different systems. The exchange of personal health records and Health Information Exchange (HIE) data via the Integrated Healthcare Enterprise (IHE) protocol is an important part of addressing the challenges of system interoperability and accessibility of medical records. Blockchain can help to resolve the issues by accessing and transferring data through the use of APIs. While Blockchain technology is not a panacea for data standardization or system integration challenges, it does offer a promising new distributed framework to amplify and support integration of health care information across a range of uses and stakeholders. It addresses several existing pain points and enables a system that is more efficient, disintermediated, and secure.

- Security: A growing concern that healthcare organisations have is to do with the possibility of tampering of sensitive data and various forms of security breaches from hackers. Since the data in a Blockchain is encrypted with private key of the sender and only the intended recipient can decrypt using the same key, it is very difficult for a hacker to tamper or modify such data. Also, the modification of data in a block requires validation from all other blocks in the chain, therefore, Blockchain also offers in-built security features.

- Integrity: Blockchain is a distributed ledger and its transactions are immutable (i.e. they remain unchanged). This is a feature that ensures integrity of transaction (i.e. data in the blocks) while encryption of data enhances security across the entire network. With the implementation of Blockchain technology, multiple instances of obsolete patient data with various healthcare organisations are replaced with single source of latest patient information.

- Ubiquitous access: Managing timely access to patient data across healthcare organisations spread around the nation is a challenge. It is here that Blockchain technology can also help. Blockchain architecture ensures that required data is present at every node (i.e. in each block) and is available for use to the authorized users based on the access rights provided through smart contracts or other mechanisms.

- Cost of maintenance: Information Systems need to be maintained for the rest of their operational life. This involves, amongst other activities, operations such as regular backups and having recovery mechanisms in place. Here, the Blockchain technology can come to rescue. In case of Blockchain, data is distributed across the network and there is no single point of failure that could lead to inherent backup mechanism; also, a single version of data is copied on every node of the Blockchain. This reduces transaction volume that occurs between each information system reducing the burden on the healthcare ecosystem.

For more applications of Blockchain in the healthcare sector, reader is referred to CitiusTech (2018).

Manufacturing

Manufacturing is a sector where Blockchain has probably the greatest potential to deliver business value. According to Forbes in Columbus (2019), cost savings, traceability, and transparency are the top three drivers behind the industry's investment in Blockchain. Mire (2018) lists ten use cases in manufacturing where Blockchain technology can be usefully employed including supply chain management, 3-D printing, reducing systematic failures, improving trust in products, authentication of IoT based devices, and better tracking and maintenance. Some of these are briefly discussed below.

- Improving supply chain management: With time, Supply Chains (SC) are becoming more complex as businesses continues to globalize. Lack of skills in the sector is also becoming more obvious, and supply chains are becoming increasingly more expensive. It is in this context that Blockchain solutions can result in simplification of SC management to help maintain production levels and improve efficiency. As an example, businesses can develop systems by which all participants on a supply chain can refer to and update a single record for all to see. These systems can then allow manufacturers to reduce product loss, provide a measure of provenance to those who they pass the finished products to, and also to play a major role in regulatory compliance. Forbes in Columbus (2019) predict that the most investment in Blockchain will be in its adoption for the following five areas: digital market places, tracking supply chain parameters, tracking product quality, preventing counterfeits, tracking asset maintenance. Blockchain application in SC is further elaborated later in this chapter.

- Reducing systematic errors: Manufacturing is not immune to data breaches. This sector which is so reliant upon supply chains may be particularly vulnerable, as <u>39% of executives</u> surveyed, reported being the victims of data breaches in the previous 12 months; and 38% of them reported losing up to $10 million because of such breeches (Mire, 2018). One characteristic of the Blockchain is that it requires the consensus of all nodes in the chain to approve data entry or changes to the ledger; this is part of Blockchain security mechanism. Because manufacturing requires near-constant communication between suppliers, and a single data breach can easily compromise the operations of each party, appropriate level of security in the Blockchain can prevent fraudulent attempts and the resultant system failure.

- Improving trust in products: Fraud in the manufacture and shipment, especially in case of ingestible products, is particularly dangerous, and can result in serious problems with health and even death. Manufacturers are also subjected to extensive certification and quality processes, and there is no reason that consumers should not be made party to such information. In this context, the Blockchain decentralized technology can allow this information to be shared, but not compromised or changed. Also, the information about supply chain provenance can be accessed fairly quickly. Through the employment of Blockchain technology, manufacturers can establish their credibility as reliable, and therefore, in turn, garnering stronger customer trust, loyalty and relationship.

- Authentication of networked devices: The Internet of Things (IoT) is impacting nearly all sectors of the society including manufacturing and logistics. According to one survey reported in Mire (2018), between 2016 and 2017, the IoT based device connections in manufacturing <u>grew by 84%</u>. Some issues relating to device connectivity via any network include: generation of huge amounts of diverse data, and safety and integrity of such data. Use of Blockchain technology provides a secure networking mechanism by which IoT based devices can be authenticated and monitored in a more robust manner. Here, information can also be securely passed along and immediately shared by the authorised users.

Supply Chain

Managing today's supply chains can be extraordinarily complex as successful supply chain operations rely on robust, transparent and end-to-end communication across geographically dispersed partners and other relevant organisations. Due to the complexity and lack of transparency in existing supply chains, the role of Blockchain for Supply Chain Management (SCM) is becoming an area of increasing interest. Some of the features of the Blockchain technology that SCM find attractive include consensus, provenance, immutability, trust, and finality (Morley, 2020). These features result in the following benefits for a more efficient SCM:

- Automation: Many supply chain processes are slow and paper based. Blockchain technology can replace these with an end-to-end digital process that delivers better visibility and transparency. However, this requires the creation of 100% digitally-enabled supply chain necessary for Blockchain to operate.

- Better traceability: Increasing regulatory demand for provenance information is already driving the change. Companies are already turning to Blockchain for increased supply chain transparency, with the track and trace style application of Blockchain. This, in turn, leads to better delivery times, improved quality and traceability, and reduced loss of revenue.
- Reduced transaction costs: The ability of Blockchain-based transfer of funds without the need of an intermediary can speed up payments while saving on transaction and administration costs. Also, because of smart contracts, many operations can be triggered automatically (e.g. what should happen if the delivery is delayed), which can significantly reduce costs.
- Accelerated speed of operations: Blockchain technology protects the integrity of information and the transactions so that there are fewer errors and disputes. The entire process becomes faster as there is less need for product recalls or re-filling a missed order. In addition, the use of smart contracts means that the need for intermediaries (e.g. clearing houses) is reduced.
- More ethical operations: Consumers demand ethical operations. Here, Blockchain can help in two ways: 1) supply chain professionals can use Blockchain provenance to establish where everything they use has come from, and pass this information to customers; and 2) because of inherent transparency, customers know how products are manufactured and shipped.

Transportation and Logistics

Opportunities that Blockchain offers to the industry are well recognised, and this is also true for the transportation sector. Blockchain in Transport Alliance (BiTA) is an example of the interest in Blockchain that was created (with members such as UPS and FedEx) as a forum for Blockchain education and standards development for the freight industry (Robinson, 2018). In transportation and logistics, Blockchain can usefully help in the following ways:

- To increase the efficiency and transparency of the entire shipping process including matching shippers with carriers - through the use of Blockchain smart contracts
- To streamline payments - through using a Blockchain platforms such as Ethereum, and without human intervention
- To reduce the number of intermediaries - as Blockchain technology does not require human intervention at any stage
- To show greater visibility of the entire supply chain - since each party in a Blockchain validates and records transactions throughout the process
- To increase transparency and tracking ability of transportation and shipping – which, in turn, would discourage attempts for cargo theft
- To enhance the level of trust in the transportation and shipping process – as, through the use of Blockchain, multiple parties would be able to validate the process.

Blockchain is changing the face of transportation and logistics in a number of other ways as well including the following (Winnesota, 2020):

- Better freight tracking: With the increase in on-demand deliveries, customer expectations are also increasing but scaling up the process has proved to be problematic, especially when it comes to authentication. By using Blockchain for data authentication, the entire network can contribute and validate data which then becomes less susceptible to tempering by malicious outsider agents; efficiency of tracking also improves.
- Reduction in costs: This is always one of the core objectives to achieve, for all businesses. In this respect, smart contracts can be the single most impactful Blockchain enabled feature to the freight industry. Smart Contracts are essentially self-executing tasks that are coded through the Blockchain and executed when certain conditions are met. Blockchain smart contracts would completely eliminate the need for various administrative steps, cutting costs and virtually also removing all possibilities of human error.
- Increased liquidity in the supply chain: There are many inefficiencies in the supply chain management mainly due to interaction between multiple partner organisations. Most of the inefficiencies can be removed by employing Blockchain based technologies stack e.g. *Sweetbridge* as mentioned in Winnesota (2020). Such technologies can help to improve the efficiency of settlements (in case of disputes) between parties within the supply chain, and hence increase liquidity.

Education

The possibilities of use of Blockchain Technology (BC) in the education sector are many. As education becomes more diversified, democratised, and decentralised, there is an urgent need to maintain reputation and trust in the certification process and the learning experience, and to ensure more transparency in the educational processes. Blockchain can provide just such a system. Clark (2016) suggests ten ways where Blockchain can be used in education including: keeping a national database, organising global assessments, better continuous professional development, delivering corporate learning, providing vocation education e.g. apprenticeships, etc. Byon (2020) also suggests a number of ways that can help curb the issues with educational technologies relating to digital classrooms, smart classroom boards, remote learning, etc; and looks at what is driving the interest of educational institutes to implement Blockchain technology. Some of the ways in which Blockchain can prove useful, are briefly articulated below (Hance, 2020; Clark, 2016; Alacrity, 2020; Maaghul, 2019):

- Safe keeping of student records: These records (consisting of attendance, programmes of study, payment of fees, grades achieved, and coursework materials etc.) can become part of students' personal Blockchain records. Since these records are immutable (i.e. cannot be deleted or modified without Blockchain consensus), it helps with the data security. Also, these records will now belong to students, rather than the institutions (Hance, 2020; Alacrity, 2020). Faculty records can also be kept safe and secure, using the same approach.
- Learning platform for all: It is important that there is a connect between students, teachers, course developers, and other academics. In this context, Blockchain and digital tokens (as part of Blockchain technology) can power an innovative learning platform to build an open-source internal learning education system where students can access materials and work on innovative projects. Digital tokens on the platform can be rewarded to students for their activities on the platform. Students can, then, use their tokens to access new study materials and keep the learning going on (Alacrity, 2020).

- Standardisation and authenticity: There is need for a unified approach to tracking and managing student certificates from educational bodies, professional societies, trade associations, and state examination boards. A single database that is digitally accessed from anywhere and anytime creates a standard for verified credentials. If data is stored on a public Blockchain, it is stored on every node on the network (of institutions and educational bodies). If one node is compromised, the ledger would remain unaffected. Additionally, if any data were tampered with, this would affect the cryptographic hashing of the block, thus breaking the chain between the blocks. In this case, the breach would be broadcast to the entire network, and the compromised block would be rejected. This provides security and authenticity of standardised data (Maaghul, 2019).

Internet of Things (IoT)

Currently, the convergence of Blockchain and the IoT is on the agenda for many organisations, not only in the financial services sector, but in nearly all sectors of the society, as already illustrated in the previous sections above. Core benefits that can be achieved from using Blockchain for the IoT can be summarised as follows:

- Building trust between users and IoT devices and reducing risk of collusion and tampering
- Reducing costs by removing overheads associated with the involvement of middlemen
- Accelerating speed of transactions by reducing settlement time between parties
- Increasing security of device connectivity and transmission of data.

In the following bullet point, some use cases of Blockchain in the IoT based applications are presented.

- Insurance: The main use case of Blockchain and IoT in insurance is with reference to smart contracts and the enhancement of processes such as claims management. Other applications include fraud management and reduction in security related threats, legally required applications and compliance, and even the use of technologies in an insurance context. The IoT data and Blockchain can lead to smart automated insurance policies (I-Scope, 2020).
- Enterprise Resource Planning (ERP): Blockchain technology and the IoT are already playing an important role in supply chain management and production within the ERP systems domain. Blockchain can create a single version of relevant information and data, and ensure that all related systems speak through a Blockchain, without intervention of intermediaries. Blockchain can work as a complementary supplement that simplifies the integration between the parties and reduces the applications vulnerabilities due to the system's inherent security (Active Business Systems, 2020).
- Autonomous vehicles: Currently, in terms of sharing machines like self-driving cars (e.g. through Uber or Google), data is centralised with service providers. Using a Blockchain-based service and the vehicles connected through the IoT, any number of individuals are able to form an agreement between themselves to purchase or share a self-driving vehicle and share its maintenance amongst themselves. Each cooperative group can then agree contracts with other groups and share usage of their vehicles amongst a wider group of peers (ConsenSys, 2016).

CONCLUSION

Blockchain technology appears to be a much bigger deal than the Internet of Things vision (I-Scope, 2020). Blockchain case studies and applications in the industry go far beyond the financial transactions and transfer of cryptocurrencies. This is due to its ability for transparency, openness and fairness and with its highly attractive properties (such as immutability) and features such as consensus between the nodes, this technology is impacting a wide variety of industries including finance, manufacturing, healthcare, logistics, supply chain, automotive, and transportation, to name but a few.

In this chapter, we have introduced the Blockchain technology and discussed its applications and case studies in various sectors of the society including banking, healthcare, transportation, manufacturing, supply chain, and education. Extension of the Internet of Things (IoT) vision using the Distributed Ledger Technology is also briefly discussed. We have described the essential terminology, outlined the essential characteristics and benefits, and described the underlying concepts and the Blockchain process.

REFERENCES

Active Business Systems. (2020). *Blockchain and the ERP*. Available at: https://www.activebs.com/en/news/2018/blockchain-and-erp

Bhasin, H. (2019, April). *3 Main Types of Blockchain: Classification of Blockchain*. Available at: https://www.marketing91.com/types-of-blockchain/

Byon/Alacrity. (2020, May). *Blockchain in Education: three Promising Reforms*. Available at: https://alacritys.net/2020/05/27/blockchain-in-education-three-promising-reforms/

CitiusTech. (2018, May). *Blockchain for Healthcare*. Available at: https://www.ehidc.org/sites/default/fi:les/resources/files/blockchain-for-healthcare-341.pdf

Clark, D. (2016). *10 Ways Blockchain could be used in education*. Available at: https://oeb.global/oeb-insights/10-ways-blockchain-could-be-used-in-education

Columbus, L. (2019). *How Blockchain Can Improve Manufacturing in 2019*. Available at: https://www.forbes.com/sites/louiscolumbus/2018/10/28/how-blockchain-can-improve-manufacturing-in-2019

Concise Software. (2020). *10 Use Cases of Blockchain in Banking*. Available at: https://concisesoftware.com/10-use-cases-of-blockchain-in-banking

ConsenSys. (2016). *5 Incredible Blockchain IoT Applications*. Available at: https://blockgeeks.com/5-incredible-blockchain-iot-applications/

Garson, B. (2018, June). *Blockchain Beyond the Hype*. Available at: https://www.mckinsey.com/business-functions/mckinsey-digital/our-insights/blockchain-beyond-the-hype-what-is-the-strategic-business-value?cid=other-eml-nsl-mip-mck-oth-1807&hlkid=5424a29008e445239371a81cc83b3dbb&hctky=10291646&hdpid=bb9f89f0-458b-4b4e-a1ee-ad99e602294e

Goyal, S. (2018, Nov). *The History of Blockchain Technology: Must Know Timeline*. Available at: https://101blockchains.com/history-of-blockchain-timeline/

Hance, M. (2020). *What is Blockchain and How Can it be Used in Education?* Available at: https://mdreducation.com/2018/08/20/blockchain-education/

I-Scope. (2020). *Blockchain and the Internet of Things: the IoT blockchain opportunity and challenge.* Available at: https://www.i-scoop.eu/internet-of-things-guide/blockchain-iot/

Maaghul, R. (2019, Oct). *Blockchain in Education: The Future of Records Management.* Available at: https://blogs.odem.io/blockchains-bright-future-in-the-education-industry

Mire, S. (2018, Nov). *Blockchain For Manufacturing: 10 Possible Use Cases.* Available at: https://www.disruptordaily.com/blockchain-use-cases-manufacturing

Morley, M. (2020, Feb). *Top 5 Use Cases of Blockchain in the Supply Chain in 2020.* Available at: https://blogs.opentext.com/blockchain-in-the-supply-chain/

Robinson, J. (2018, Aug). *The Future of Blockchain in Transportation.* Available at: https://www.fleetio.com/blog/future-of-blockchain-in-transportation

Rosic, A. (1916). *What is Blockchain Technology? A Step-by-Step Guide For Beginners.* Available at: https://blockgeeks.com/guides/what-is-blockchain-technology/

Shumsky, P. (2019, Sep). *Blockchain Use Cases For Banks In 2020.* Available at: https://www.finextra.com/blogposting/17857/blockchain-use-cases-for-banks-in-2020

Singh, N. (2020, May). *Permissioned vs. Permissionless Blockchain: A Comparison Guide.* Available at: https://101blockchains.com/permissioned-vs-permissionless-blockchains/

Tasca, P., & Tessone, C. J. (2019). *A Taxonomy of Blockchain Technologies: Principles of Identification and Classification, Ledger.* LedgerJournal.org.

Winnesota. (2020). *How Blockchain is Revolutionising the World of Transportation and Logistics.* Available at: https://www.winnesota.com/blockchain

Witscad. (2020). *Blockchain Characteristics.* Available at: https://witscad.com/course/blockchain-fundamentals/chapter/blockchain-characteristics

ADDITIONAL READING

R3. (2020), Corda Enterprise: A Next-Gen Blockchain Platform, Available at: https://www.r3.com/corda-platform/

Consensys, (2020), Smart Dubai: Blockchain Case Study for Government in the UAE, Available at: https://consensys.net/blockchain-use-cases/government-and-the-public-sector/smart-dubai/

Consensys, (2020a), Real World Blockchain Case Studies, Available at: https://consensys.net/blockchain-use-cases/case-studies/

Crypto Digest. (2020), EOS Platform: What you should know, Available at: https://cryptodigestnews.com/eos-platform-what-you-should-know-58da830d2aa8

Daley, S. (2020, March), 25 Blockchain Applications & Real World Use Cases Disrupting the Status Quo, Available at: https://builtin.com/blockchain/blockchain-applications

Economic Point. (2020), What is the Ethereum Platform, Available at: https://economicpoint.com/ethereum

Garson, B. (2018, June), Blockchain Beyond the Hype, Available at: https://www.mckinsey.com/business-functions/mckinsey-digital/our-insights/blockchain-beyond-the-hype-what-is-the-strategic-business-value?cid=other-eml-nsl-mip-mck-oth-1807&hlkid=5424a29008e445239371a81cc83b3dbb&hctky=10291646&hdpid=bb9f89f0-458b-4b4e-a1ee-ad99e602294e

Hyperledger Fabric. (2020), Hyperledger Fabric, Available at: https://hyperledger-fabric.readthedocs.io/en/release-2.0/whatis.html

IEEE Spectrum, (2020, April), Spanish Researchers Use Blockchain and AI to Flatten the Curve, Available at: https://spectrum.ieee.org/news-from-around-ieee/the-institute/ieee-member-news/researchers-spain-blockchain-ai-app-flatten-the-curve

Infura, (2020), Partnering with Horizon Games to Power a New Dimension of Gaming, Available at: https://infura.io/customers/skyweaver

ISO, (2016), Information technology, Patent No. ISO/IEC 10118–1:2016

Kashyap, P. (2018, Feb), What are Different Types of Blockchain and its Components? Available at: http://www.beingcrypto.com/what-are-different-types-of-blockchain-and-its-components/

Komgo, (2020), Streamlining Trade Finance, Available at: https://komgo.io/

Mahmood, Z. (2021). Blockchain Technology: Initiatives and Use Cases in the Industry. In Z. Mahmood (Ed.), *Industry Use Cases on Blockchain Technology: Initiatives and Use Cases in the Industry, IGI Global, 2021.*

Malhotra, M. (2020, March), A COMPREHENSIVE LIST OF BLOCKCHAIN PLATFORMS TO LOOK FOR IN 2020, Available at: https://www.valuecoders.com/blog/technology-and-apps/a-comprehensive-list-of-blockchain-platforms-to-look-for-in-2019/

MarketWatch. (2020, June), Blockchain Technology Market Share, Growth to record over US $25 billion by 2025 – Press Release, Available at: https://www.marketwatch.com/press-release/blockchain-technology-market-share-growth-to-record-over-us-25-billion-by-2025-2020-06-09

MultiChain. (2020), MultiChain for Developers, Available at: https://www.multichain.com/developers/

OpenChain. (2020), Overview of OpenChain, Available at: https://docs.openchain.org/en/latest/general/overview.html

OpenZeppelin. (2020), The standard for secure blockchain applications, Available at: https://openzeppelin.com/

Project Khokha: An Enterprise Ethereum Banking and Finance Case Study, (2020), Available at: https://pages.consensys.net/consensys-banking-and-finance-project-khokha-v2?utm_campaign=Enterprise%20Ethereum%20&utm_source=Website&utm_medium=Direct&utm_term=EntEth&utm_content=CaseStudyKhokha

Ripple, (2020), University Blockchain Research Initiative, Available at: https://ubri.ripple.com/faq/

Robinson, J. (2018, Aug), The Future of Blockchain in Transportation, Available at: https://www.fleetio.com/blog/future-of-blockchain-in-transportation

Tepper School of Business. (2020), Tepper Blockchain Initiative, Available at: https://www.cmu.edu/tepper/faculty-and-research/initiatives/blockchain-initiative/

Zaky, D. (2020, March), What is Blockchain Technology and How Does It Work? Available at: https://fxdailyreport.com/blockchain-technology/

KEY TERMS ANS DEFINITIONS

Bitcoin: Bitcoin is a digital currency created for use in peer-to-peer online transactions, Introduced in 2008. It is the most prominent of a group of virtual currencies.

Blockchain: A blockchain is a distributed database spread across many computers with no central control, that can transform governance, business models and the functioning of organisations. A Blockchain stores information on digital assets (representing values, identities, agreements, property rights, credentials, etc.).

Chaincode: It is another name for a self-executing smart contract, in the context of blockchain technology.

Consensus: It is a fault-tolerant mechanism used in blockchain systems to achieve the necessary agreement on a single data value or a single state of the network among distributed processes or multi-agent systems, such as with cryptocurrencies.

Cryptography: This is the science of securing communication using individualized codes (e.g. public and private keys) so only the participating parties can read the encrypted messages.

Ethereum: An open source platform to build Blockchain based applications. It permits distribution of a currency called ether (ETH); and allows storage and execution of code allowing for smart contracts.

Hash: This is a digital signature (comprising public and private keys) of a block (consisting of information about digital assets and hash pointer) for authentication and verification purposes. It is the process that blockchain uses to confirm its state; each transaction in a blockchain requires one or more digital signatures.

Hyperledger Fabric: It is a platform for distributed ledger solutions, developed by IBM, underpinning a modular architecture delivering high degrees of confidentiality, resiliency, flexibility, and scalability. It is designed to support pluggable implementations of different components of the blockchain technology.

Proof of Stake (PoS): It is a type of consensus algorithm by which a cryptocurrency blockchain network aims to achieve distributed consensus. In PoS-based cryptocurrencies, the addition of the next block is organised considering various combinations of random selection e.g. wealth or age (i.e., the stake).

Proof of Work (PoSW): It is a consensus mechanism that helps to stop or reduce denial of service attacks and other security abuses such as spam on a network by requiring some work from the service requester, usually meaning processing time by a computer.

Smart Contract: A smart contract is a computer protocol that facilities the transfer of digital assets between parties considering the already agreed-upon stipulations or terms. It is a self-executing code that comes into action when pre-agreed conditions are met.

Chapter 2
A Blockchain–Based Robotic Process Automation Mechanism in Educational Setting

Nhlanhla Andrew Sibanyoni

https://orcid.org/0000-0002-5393-905X

University of Johannesburg, South Africa

ABSTRACT

Blockchain technology and robotic process automation are increasingly the focus of attention in research, as these are both used successfully in business, marketing, manufacturing, and finance. However, their application in educational contexts is still emerging. This chapter uses an illustrative example of an online school registration system to explore how a blockchain-based robotic process automation mechanism can resolve the inherent challenges. The proposed system allows parents to register their Grade 1 and Grade 8 children for their school of choice. There is competition for places in certain schools and a history of unfair allocation of educational resources; hence, there is mistrust. To counter this threat, this study proposes a blockchain-based robotic automation process mechanism to fairly and transparently allocate educational resources. It recommends that further design science research be conducted in which the blockchain is supplemented by additional technological processes to enhance data-sharing in educational settings.

INTRODUCTION

This chapter explores the Online School Registration System for a regional group of South African schools as an illustrative example. This is an official online application system that is used by parents to register their Grade 1 and Grade 8 children in South African schools for the following academic year. This system is part of a citizen facing e-government system as it is operated by the state and meets the definition of e-government as given by Silcock (2001).

E-government is defined as the use of information and communication technology (ICT), which may include wide area networks, systems, the Internet, Internet of Things and mobile computing, to enhance

DOI: 10.4018/978-1-7998-6650-3.ch002

the access to and delivery of government services to benefit citizens, business partners, and employees (Silcock, 2001). This facilitates a new mode of public service where government agencies have an opportunity to deliver a technologically advanced, integrated and seamless service for their citizens (Bakon, Elias & Abusamhadana, 2020; Silcock, 2001). However, as Bélanger and Carter (2008) have established, mutual trust hinders citizen adoption of e-government services. Their study concludes that government agencies should directly address citizens' views concerning the credibility and trustworthiness of e-government systems, to increase citizens' perceptions of their value, accuracy and reliability. Through improved transparency and accountability, the trust needed by its citizens to adopt e-services can be further strengthened (Bélanger & Carter, 2008).

It is noted that gaining trust has proven to be a challenge for the Online School Registration System in South Africa. The competition for places in certain public schools is emotionally charged and has serious individual and social consequences. The distrust often arises from negative reports carried by newspapers and other media combined with the history of unfair allocation of educational resources in the context in which the system operates (Mokhaoli, 2020). This has compromised the issues of trust based on the perceived transparency and integrity of the Online School Registration System. These issues remain important even when, as is the case in the current chapter, the focus of the research reported is specifically on technology solutions. Future research will look at the Online School Registration System from other e-government perspectives.

In this chapter, a Blockchain-based, Robotic Process Automation mechanism is proposed, as a way to resolve some of the challenges faced by the community, schools' administration, ICT technical staff and the custodian government department of the system during the registration process. It is important to note that currently the Online School Registration System (OSRS) does not use Internet of Things or Robotic Process Automation (RPA) or Blockchain. These terms are defined in detail in later sections.

BACKGROUND

Parents are encouraged to register their children through the online system as depicted in Figure 1.

As part of the process, copies of certified documents, such as a birth certificate, identification document, school report cards from previous grades, and proof of residence, must be attached. The system also requires parents to 'take a picture of the registration process' as proof of registration and to submit hard copies of the documents submitted to the school on the same day (Gauteng Province, 2020). This additional process (that appears on left of Figure 1) may be intended to verify information provided and hence to lessen deliberate submission of misinformation and to check that online data has not been tampered with (Arslan, Jurdak, Jelitto & Krishnamachari, 2019). Parents can use a variety of devices to access the system (cellphones, laptops, desktop computer; as shown at the top part of Figure 1). The system has an intensive period of data input (with a fixed start and end times).

Despite the fact that parents have used the online system, they also need to submit hard copies of documents and present proof of registration to the chosen school (as shown at left of Figure 1). This 'backup system' helps the parents to prove any allegations that their online applications got lost, misplaced, were never received by schools or that their children have been unfairly placed in a school that is far from home. However, retaining the manual process causes duplication of effort and duplicate data that needs to be reconciled in the case of a dispute, and the dispute resolution process may still be prone to human failings including bias resulting once again in inappropriate or unfair placement of the learner.

Figure 1. Current Illustration of Online School Registration System Process

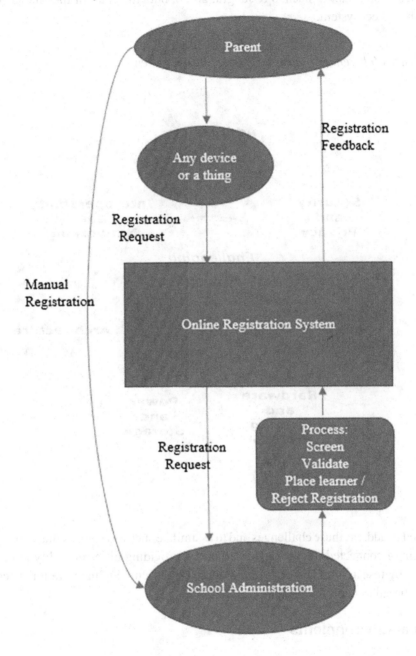

Therefore, trust issues remain valid when there is conflicting information and the double system results in an increase in the manual administration burden. In fact, many of the limitations of a manual system that the automated system seeks to address are simply magnified where two parallel systems are used.

Despite the obvious advantages, use of mobile devices by citizens to access e-government systems bring both opportunities and challenges. The security and privacy during transmission and storage of data is a major challenge. Figure 2 shows challenges arising from one specific Internet-based ecosystem,

Internet of Things (Lohachab, Lohachab & Jangra, 2020), but almost all of the challenges noted apply to any Internet-based ecosystem.

Figure 2. Challenges Inherent in Internet of Things Based Systems

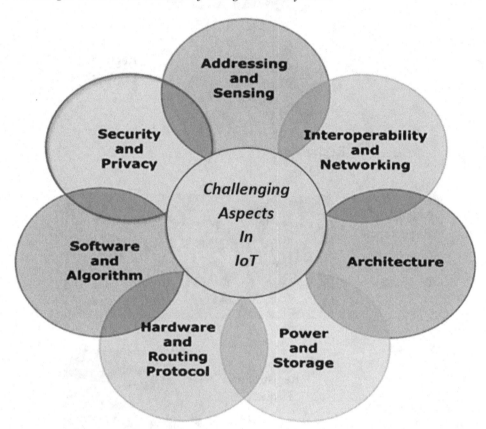

There is a need to address these challenges and to assimilate such a system as this allows to understand the new paradigm of connected mobile devices, thereby, providing ultra-reliability of communication. This can be done by researching and developing a universal secure architecture for successful deployment of Internet-based systems (Lohachab, et al., 2020).

Trust in Virtual Environments

The subject of trust is an important area for research as there is a general agreement that the broad success of virtual environments depends on the trust of the general public (Tan & Thoen, 2001). Trust consists of two elements: party providing the service (party trust), and control trust, which is the mechanism in which the service is provided (Bélanger & Carter, 2008). Tan and Thoen (2001) define control mechanism as dedicated procedures and protocols that ensure that the transaction is performed successfully through monitoring and control. Trust is defined as expectation that an individual or group can be relied upon their promise. According to the social learning theory, people develop different expectancies due to their experiences of promised negative or positive reinforcements. In the given scenario, some parents' applications go through as expected while others might experience difficulties as explained in the introduction. This chapter proposes that Blockchain technology, as suggested by Xing and Marwala (2018), can provide assistence in Robotic Process Automation (RPA) in ascertaining trust by changing the way online transactions are generally performed and ensure success (Makridakis Polemitis, Giaglis & Louca, 2018).

Potential of Blockchain-based RPA for Online School Registration System

The first part of the proposed solution put forward in this chapter is based on a claim that RPA can close the gap in terms of the security and privacy during transmission and storage of data to some extent, and that in addition, school administration efficiency and the fairness of the registration process can be improved. RPA is applied to human rule-based tasks that are repetitive and manual. For example, historically RPA has been used in industrial engineering processes to progressively automate tasks aimed at achieving economic efficiencies and improved product quality (Moffitt, Rozario & Vasarhelyi, 2018). RPA, also known as robots or bots, involves software agents that mimic user actions aimed at increasing operational efficiency to alleviate the workload of the human workforce (Syed et al., 2020). It is important to note that these are not the hardware robots that we are familiar with.

RPA has been used recently to automate organizational internal processes and applications that can bring immediate value to core business processes including employee payroll, employee status changes, new hire recruitment and on-boarding, accounts receivable and payable, invoice processing, inventory management, report creation, software installations, data migration, and vendor on-boarding (Madakam, Holmukhe & Jaiswal, 2019).

The second part of the proposed solution involves Blockchain technology, as the need to transmit confidential information accurately, reliably and securely between the parents, the Online School Registration System and the schools persists. As noted earlier, trust is a major factor that the system is grappling with as the parents do not trust that it is fair and transparent (that is, that it will place their children at the appropriate school based on language and location - proximity to school). A Blockchain creates an immutable record of interactions as all those interactions go through the Blockchain. This approach ensures that the quality of data is complete, correct, persist and retrievable (Reyna, Martín, Chen, Soler & Díaz, 2018).

Artificial intelligence (AI) embodied as robots or bots (terms used interchangeably with RPA) has the capability to perform complex, hard, dangerous, data-intensive tasks such as monitoring cybersecurity threats or boring tasks for humans. AI is everywhere and affects everyone in all aspects of our lives in the form of service, transportation, military robots and so on. AI robots can make decisions and act without human control (Dignum, 2017). In Blockchain-based RPA, the process of registration can be automated effectively and reliably using robots (bots). A Blockchain can ensure that records are not changed, history is retained, and transparency is maintained, thereby building trustworthy data-sharing (of personal data) (Shahaab, Hewage & Khan, 2020), as well as efficient and effective registration. Transparency, validation (including by home affairs departments if there are issues regarding birth certificates, etc.), traceability and immutability of the learners' registration records sent to the Online School Registration System and subsequently to the school concerned, are all improved. Traceability shows the status of a transaction including when it was received at a point in the process (workflow). This is particularly useful in a system which is distributed (the client does not visit an office and several different parties – in this case, the school and the centralized registration authority) are in different places. Blockchain supposed to safely store/transmit trustworthy data; AI on the other hand can ensure that this data is sent and received without human intervention making it even trustworthy to transact on the online systems. This combination makes Blockchain and AI a natural fit to handle complex tasks of safely storing/ transmitting data (Makridakis et. al., 2018).

A Blockchain consists of ordered and grouped transactions in blocks sharing the same timestamp. The blocks are managed by networks of miners or nodes (participants) that link the blocks. As this makes it difficult to change the records, a robust and auditable registry of all transactions is created even though the records are widely shared (Casino et al., 2019). In the Online School Registration System, there are issues at stake which may tempt parents, school administrators or independent dishonest people such as hackers to cheat the system, sometimes for financial reward. As registration systems cover all schools and learners throughout the country, manual systems are difficult to monitor and control. Rules relating to registration are complex; for example, if an older sibling is at the school subsequent siblings get entry automatically (as they are first in line). The Blockchain-based RPA mechanism can ensure that these rules are applied correctly. Blockchain has the ability to automate the validation of credentials using encryption technology and to provide access to a shared database, transactions, records, and logs in a decentralized, secure, transparent and trusted manner. While AI in the form of RPA (robots or bots) offers decision-making capabilities that mimic human intelligence, combination of these two technologies can provide massive benefits to the citizens (Salah, Rehman, Nizamudddin, & AI-Fuquaha, 2018).

This study contributes to Blockchain and RPA literature using an illustrative existing example in the education setting, the *Online School Registration System*. However, it is important that we acknowledge that no single solution can be expected to solve all the problems of the education system to register the Grade 1 and Grade 8 children; and therefore further empirical research should be conducted to find ways in which the Blockchain can be supplemented by additional solutions to enhance data-sharing in educational administration.

This chapter is organised as follows: The following section discusses related work in terms of how Internet of Things, robotic automation process and Blockchain technology of process data. The next section discusses the proposed solution about how the Online School Registration System should manage the issue of trust using a Blockchain based robotic process automation mechanism. In the final section, the chapter ends with the conclusion and prospective for future work in the field.

RELATED WORKS

There is enough literature discussing implementation techniques around Blockchain technology in education regarding trust, exchange, storing, validating and sharing of credentials and/or learning outcomes that the students have achieved but there is limited amount of literature discussing how to implement techniques to handle the challenges associated with unfair allocation of educational resources using a Blockchain-based robotic process automation.

Internet of Things (IoT)

The Internet of Things may create a massive network consisting of billions or trillions of smart devices of different kinds (or 'things') that are connected and communicate with each other without any interaction with a human (Arslan et al., 2019; Chen Xu, Liu, Hu & Wang, 2014). The term 'Internet of Things' has been defined as a combination of several objects which are physically connected to the Internet by associated sensors, e.g., RFID or Radio Frequency Identification (Albishi, Soh, Ullah & Algarni, 2017). The Internet of Things has also been defined as: 1) the growing number of connected digital devices used to process information by interacting over unreliable network links to reach a common objective (Arslan et al., 2019); 2) inter-connected smart devices that automatically collect data, relay information to each other and process the information collaboratively (Chen, 2012); 3) interconnected devices with virtual representations using standard communication protocols (Barnaghi, Wang, Henson & Taylor, 2012); and 4) an intelligent network (that is, an extension and expansion of an Internet-based network) which is used to expand the exchange and communication of information from human to human, from human to other things or from things to the Internet in accordance with agreed protocols, through information sensing devices (Chen et al., 2014). These definitions (and other definitions as listed in Table 1) are in broad agreement.

In this chapter, the IoT is viewed as involving several technologies such as RFID, short-range wireless communications, real-time localisation and sensor networks, that enable the Internet to reach out into the real world of physical objects or things with minimum or no human intervention (Feki, Kawsar, Boussard & Trappeniers, 2013). Many of these technologies were invented before the idea of the IoT; the innovation involves combining them and using them in new ways.

Table 1. Other Definitions of the Internet of Things Vision [adopted from Chen et al. (2014)]

Organisations	Definitions
California Charter Schools Association	A network infrastructure that supports communication between human and things or between things by collecting, transmitting, classifying and processing information from physical world objects. Hence the data is collected by non-human sensors and controlled through various deployed devices with the capability of perception, computation, execution and communication.
The Telecommunication Standardization Sector	A global network infrastructure that provides the information society with advanced services by leveraging existing and evolving interoperable information and communication technology, interconnecting both physical and virtual things.
Coordination and Support Action for Global RFID-related Activities and Standardisation	A global network infrastructure that leverages data captured and communication capabilities to link physical and virtual objects.
Internet Engineering Task Force	A world-wide network of interconnected objects or things uniquely controlled through standard communication protocols.

The Internet of Things model is seen as being the next generation of the Internet, whose development, implementation, impact and value depend on various actors (such as software developers and access technology providers) to enable the merger of different communication infrastructures. The new, combined structure can be deployed in a variety of sectors, such as, manufacturing, utility management, agriculture and healthcare. The application domain of the IoT is, therefore, broad and leads to the need to design smart gateways to interconnect the Internet of Things infrastructure and cloud computing as well as other ICT and communications technologies (Hameed, Khan & Hameed, 2018).

However, the design of any IoT architecture is complex as the system must be able to incorporate heterogeneous devices using a link layer of technology to open access to selected subsets of the data (Zanella et al., 2014). This needs to be done transparently, securely and seamlessly. The complexity and challenges faced by the Internet of Things (see Figure 2) require the following characteristics (Chen et al., 2014). Refer to Table 2.

Table 2. Characteristics of Internet of Things

Comprehensive Perception	Use identification and recognition technology to automatically obtain the object information at anytime and anywhere such as Radio Frequency Identification, sensors, and two-dimensional barcode. For example, a sensor network that enables citizens to interact with the real world remotely.
Reliable Transmission	Internet of Things should be able to create interaction between the physical world, the virtual world, the digital world, machine-to-machine (M2M), mobile-to-machine and human-to-machine by transmitting data and using a variety of existing and new infrastructure anytime and anywhere, wired or wireless and be able to switch between technologies, network technologies, and gateway technologies, such as, cloud computing, telecommunication networks, radio networks and the Internet.
Intelligent Processing	Supported by technology such as cloud computing, Internet of Things data should be collected efficiently, securely and processed instantly among the devices or things into a database without human intervention.

The existing online registration system is designed to be a component of the digital platform for the citizens of South Africa which provides access to relevant information by means of fast and easy service requests and incorporating tracking capabilities (Gauteng Provincial Government, 2020). The intention is to leverage advanced communication technologies to support added-value services for the parents. It is proposed that, using Blockchain-based RPA together with concepts from the Internet of Things architecture, the South African department of education must be able to provide access to selected subsets of the personal data without compromising security.

The parents are only given a certain period, for example, 20 May – 22 July (in year 2020), to register online. However, the volume of data collected into the Online School Registration System during that period is massive, making it a challenging task to integrate it, process it, and to base decisions on it quickly. Additionally, some parents show signs of frustration and complain that the system is inconvenient and unreliable, because even though they applied online and on time, their children were still not placed. As a result of these challenges, the associated education authority had to extend the registration period in 2020 (The Citizen, 2020). However, advancements in technology can change and improve lives. It has brought extremely small electronic devices with a large amount of computing power, storage, and battery capacities and with capabilities allowing identification, communication and interconnection. With this technology, it is possible to analyse and process massive amounts of information (Chen, 2012). Hence the three required characteristics as noted in Table 2 can be satisfied by new-generation technology. Rejeb, Keogh and Treiblmaier (2019) have demonstrated that the deployment of Blockchain technology as part of the Internet of Things infrastructure can streamline and benefit modern supply chains and enhance value chain networks.

Robotic Process Automation (RPA)

RPA software mimics human operations which are usually structured and repetitive in nature (Hofmann, Samp & Urbach, 2019). The processes use software such as, Microsoft tools, ERP systems using a rule-based structure (if, then, else and loop statements), by connecting to APIs on client servers or mainframes, or by using HTML code translated into an executable script controlled through a dashboard or other user interface which can be installed on a personal computer (van der Aalst, Bichler & Heinzl, 2018).

The term 'robot' or 'bot' indicates an electromechanical machine that is programmable and carries out a series of actions automaticlly, that can be at times complex and intelligent. For example, *Sophia* is a social humanoid robot developed by Hong Kong-based company Hanson Robotics using artificial intelligence software which can process virtual and emotional data. It can display more than 50 facial expression, and use this information to converse and create relationships with people. Swarm robotics, inspired by social insects, uses coordination techniques to control large numbers of relatively simple robots. In this context, the bots are assumed to possess the following important characteristics: (i) the bots are partially independent agents; (ii) the bots have limited representation, that is, they do not understand the whole system; and (iii) none of the bots manage the whole system, and so decentralisation is maintained (Zikratov, Lebedev, Gurtov & Kuzmich 2014). Swarm of bots can detect and trust their counterparts, where a public key cryptography technology allows any bot that wants to communicate and send information to a specific bot address, with the information that only the bot has a matching key to read the record. Even if the public key falls into the wrong hands, there is no risk since it is not used to decrypt the record (Ferrer, 2019). In addition, a permanent record that is auditable and can be used to coordinate an action, verify credentials stored in a synchronised copy of the Blockchain in a peer-to-peer version to ensure that they all share the same public database (Ferrer, 2019). Evolutionary robotics is an emerging technique, inspired by the Darwinian principle of selective reproduction of the fittest for the automatic creation of autonomous robots that develop their own skills in close interaction with the environment with little or no human intervention. Ambient robotics has the technical capability to reduce the complexity and the cost of service robotic system by focusing on the co-adaptation and the creation of compatibility in a physical and providing informational sense of assistive environments (Moore, 2016). RPA is a software-based solution and not a physical robot as already established above.

Managers structure, routinise and measure work to achieve organisational efficiency; and the development of RPA software today can supplement and augment human strengths (Lacity & Willcocks, 2016). However, the managers using such software or automation are facing resistance as there is a risk that certain human jobs will become redundant. The advantage of automation is that the burden of repetitive, monotonous, and simple humans tasks is reduced or even eliminated so that the human workforce can focus on unstructured, intellectual, creative and interesting tasks; the efficiency of day-to-day processing is also increased (Lacity & Willcocks, 2016; Uskenbayeva, Kalpeyeva, Satybaldiyeva, et al., 2019). Hence, companies are adopting fast-emerging business process automation technology such as RPA that uses software robots or bots to replicate or replace human tasks (Geyer-Klingeberg et al., 2018).

RPA is normally deployed and implemented within a period of 3-6 months at the human-computer interaction layer using rule-based and non-subjective processes in a manner that simulates human-machine interaction behaviour without changing the existing business processes or information communication and Technology (ICT) infrastructure. Vendors such as AutomationEdge, Automation Anywhere, Blue Prism, Cognizant, Conduent, Kofax, Kryon Systems, Pegasystems, Softomotive, and UiPath implement and offer RPA tools (van der Aalst, Bichler & Heinzl, 2018). In the study conducted by Lacity and Willcocks (2016), RPA was found to be mostly used in validating the sale of insurance premiums, generating utility bills, paying health care insurance claims, keeping employee records up-to-date, and generating news stories. This same review established that companies who implemented the RPA, were able to see immediate tangible benefits when they adopted three strategies. Firstly, have top management support for the implementation of automation; secondly, implement automated processes that deliver value to both customers and employees; and thirdly, build skills and capabilities that are enterprise wide. If implemented well, these authors say that the return on investment can be achieved within 9-12 months as the deployment is quick and cost effective with the quality of work guaranteed (Lacity and Willcocks, 2016). The return on investment can be achieved through this digital labour as it will reduce costs and free up human resources who would then focus more on important tasks and for robots to perform large number of human tasks frequently repeated, algorithmized, and labour-intensive tasks (Uskenbayeva et al., 2019; Maalla, 2019). Table 3 describes the criteria for the tasks to be automated by RPA for the robot to correctly perform its actions.

Table 3. Criteria for RPA [adapted from Asatiani and Penttinen (2016)]

Criteria	Description
High volume of transactions	A task or its sub-task is performed frequently in high volumes by one or more employees.
Need to access multiple systems	Repeated tasks execution steps that involve multiple systems, for instance, capturing data on the spreadsheet and uploading it into a system.
Stable environment	A task can be predefined and remain the same every time it is performed.
Low cognitive requirements	A task that does not involve creativity, subjective judgment or complex interpretation skills.
Easy to break down into unambiguous rules	A task without ambiguity or risk of misinterpretation which can be easily broken down into simple, straightforward and rule-based steps.
Proneness to human error	A task prone to human error, but not occurring to computers. Example - counting numbers across multiple columns.
Limited need for exception handling	A highly standardised task with little or few exceptions occurring during task execution.
Clear understanding of the current manual costs	Return on investment can be estimated and measured on RPA implementation using the current cost structure of a manual task.

The steps for effective implementation of RPA include the analysis of business processes, assessing business processes for robotization and calculation of the expected effect, development, implementation and scaling. Refer to Figure 3, and some brief explanation below:

Figure 3. Steps for effective implementation of RPA [adopted from Geyer-Klingeberg et al., (2018)]

- Assessing RPA Potential: The first decision for effective implementation of RPA (see Figure 3) depends on the assessed potential for process automation carried out using the criteria in Table 3. The processes should be scalable, repetitive and standardised for a successful RPA implementation. A process that is complex with many variants should not be replicated as it would require significant investment with cost of maintenance and servicing the robots outweighing the required savings.

- Developing RPA Application: The next step is to train and develop the RPA application within the existing workflow, as a pilot project. The generated process instances should be evaluated after a sound number of executions using the process mining applications. The most effective RPA implementations are identified, and the performance of different robots and the non-robotic supported processes should be benchmarked.
- Sustaining RPA Benefits: The last step is to continuously monitor the selected and implemented RPA applications using process mining to ensure that the impact of the RPA initiative and the return on investment is sustained. Through process mining, users can monitor process change and detect when a process evolves overtime and adapt the robots to align with an evolving or alternative business environment (Geyer-Klingeberg et al., 2018).

The current study explores how a Blockchain-based RPA mechanism resolves some of the challenges presented to the online registration system. As stated in the introduction, the current system is partly automated and partly manual, and it processes high volumes of transactions during the registration period. In this case, the RPA could be implemented to manage the processing, validation and to securely distribute of these transactions through a Blockchain mechanisms. The following section explores the Blockchain technology, as it is possible to use the robots to reach an agreement and record transactions without the involvement of a controlling authority through a Blockchain-based RPA mechanism (Ferrer, 2019).

Blockchain Technology

Blockchain is a peer-to-peer distributed database that provides immutable and transparent append-only register of all the transactions shared by participating members in the network. Each transaction contains details of who sent it, what was sent, at what time and to whom; transactions are then grouped into blocks in a chronological order (Reyna et al., 2018). The chain is formed by linking blocks together using a hash function, which forms a unique identifier, and this is used to create the link to the previous block. Each block uses a cryptographic technique to validate data linked to that block through proof of work, hash function, digital signature, and encryption mechanisms (Dubovitskaya, Novotny, Xu & Wang, 2019). The identity of the participants (also called nodes in the network) and their rights to participate are defined within a network. The consensus obtained from the members is represented digitally and allows each transaction to be recorded in the Blockchain. The distributed service of the database ensures that trustworthiness can be achieved by making the data available to all participants to verify that the data have not been tempered with since the first definition. This service also ensures that the data remains immutable (Reyna et al., 2018; Dubovitskaya et al., 2019). Once the transactions are recorded on the database they cannot be deleted or removed to keep the historical data. The basic characteristics of Blockchain are summarised in Table 4.

Table 4. Essential Characteristics of Blockchain [adapted from Cheng, Zeng & Huang (2017)]

Characteristic	Description
Identity	- Use scanner to establish identity of the participants
Data object	- Sequential data - Transactions stored in blocks of chains and in chronological order
Transaction structure	- No trusted central entity - No need for mutual trust between the transactional entities - Use of smart contracts to trade transactions in a Blockchain system
Information extension	- The information is always available and accessible - Each transaction is recorded and maintained by consensus of all the participants - All the transactions are kept from the beginning - Therefore, traceability and auditability are possible
Data security	- High security - The data are stored and publicly available in each node of the network - All nodes can maintain the data in other nodes.

The problem of trust in Internet-based e-government systems, including the Internet of Things, is complex, especially when sensitive information is transmitted and when no verification or audit mechanisms are available. The need to secure personal data collected from such systems has become more acute as the networks underlying these systems and access to them have become more widespread. This challenge has also prompted computer scientists involved in information security research and development to find new ways to protect the data (Reyna et al., 2018; Shahaab et al., 2020). Such building of trust has two components namely: trust in technology; and trust in institutions and people. These are not totally independent. The use of Blockchain is primarily addressing the trust in technology aspect and minimizing the need for trust in institutions and individuals.

As an example, Nakamoto (2008) conceptualised a peer-to-peer electronic transaction system that uses public-key cryptography technology in order to solve the double-spend problem where a private key is assigned to each participant and a public-key is known among the participants. This forms the backbone of cryptocurrency Bitcoin, where there is no need for third-party financial institutions to oversee and control the transactions. Here, cryptographic proof is the basis for trust in the network instead of a central financial institution or intermediary (Mougayar, 2016). However, it is important to note that the Blockchain is also prone to attacks when a single node controls more than half (51%) of processing power.

With the application of three generations of Blockchains, it is envisaged that sectors such as finance, accounting, management, and law could be revolutionised. Blockchain 1.0, which focused on digital currency, is the first Blockchain generation that uses an underlying technology platform such as mining, hashing, and the public ledger and transaction-enabling software for digital currency. Blockchain 2.0 broadened the focus to the digital economy and is the second generation of Blockchain. It involves smart contracts which are computer programs that can automatically execute the terms of a contract. Payments are automatically processed after a pre-configured condition in a smart contract is met by participants. Blockchain 3.0 extends the focus still further and its group of beneficiaries are digital society. Blockchain 3.0 refers to a variety of application areas such as art, health, science, identity, governance, education, public goods, and different aspects of culture and communication. It does not necessarily involve economic activity (money, currency, commerce or financial markets). The application of Blockchain 3.0 for digital society includes smart governance, smart mobility, smart living, the smart use of natural resources, smart citizens, and smart economy for smart cities. The use of peer-to-peer interaction on the Internet of Things platform to trade is based on the Blockchain technology and smart contracts. Similarly, machine-tomachine (M2M) interactions, concept of decentralisation that keeps transaction history to promote auditability, interoperability and accessibility, digital identity mechanism that enable the management of information on immutable Blockchain in the context of general data protection regulation are all related to Blockchain 3.0 for digital society (Zhao, Fan & Yan, 2016; Efanov & Roschin, 2018; Shahaab, Hewage & Khan, 2020; Sun, Yan & Zhang, 2016).

The combination of Blockchain and AI can enhance the shortcomings of both technological ecosystems. The Blockchain provides a platform that is credible, reliable, trusted and secure while AI algorithms can make informed decisions, learn and deduce faster with data or information collected from Blockchain platform. This technique can contribute significantly in securely transmitting data from various sectors including education, sources such as IoT devices, swarm robots, smart cities, buildings, vehicle and so on. Some of the features are summarised in table 5 (Marr, 2018; Strobel, Ferrer & Dorigo, 2018; Salah el al., 2018; Senthilkumar, 2020).

Table 5. Integration Benefits of Blockchain with AI [adopted from Salah el al. (2018)]

Artificial Intelligence	Blockchain	Integration Benefits
Centralised	Decentralised	Data Security Enhanced: Blockchain is famously known for storing sensitive, academic credentials and personal data in a distributed database. The data kept in the Blockchain database is digitally signed allowing AI algorithms to work on secure data protected through a private key, thus ensuring further trusted and credible decision outcomes.
Changing	Deterministic	Enhanced Trust on Robotic Decisions: Blockchain keeps logs in a decentralized, secure, transparent and trusted manner. Recording of decisions making process on the Blockchain ensures that users or consumers of AI can trust, understand and trace the AI decisions. In this way, transparency would increase and gain public trust to understand the robotic decisions. Hence a third-party auditor is not necessary in a swarm robotics ecosystem as there is absolute decentralised consensus.
Probabilistic	Immutable	Making Collective Decision: Agents in a robotic swarm ecosystem need to work in a coordinated effort to reach the swarm goal. Algorithms which are decentralised and distributed have been proven and adopted to make decisions without the need for a central authority in many applications of swarm robotics ecosystems. Swarm robots conclude through voting system where majority rules are determined the outcomes. If the Blockchain is public for all robots, each robot in the swarm network can submit its vote in the form of a transaction for verification by other robots, until the consensus is reached.
Volatile	Data Integrity	Decentralisation of Intelligence: Different individual cybersecurity AI agents can take intelligent decisions in a network where multiple agents are involved in main tasks and subtasks accessing the same training data should be combined to provide a more secure and coordinated effort to avoid the scheduling issues.
Data; Knowledge; and Decision Centric	Attack Resilient	Improving Efficiency: The integration of AI and Blockchain technologies can solve the inherently inefficiency in multiparty authorisation of business transactions which involve multiuser business processes and multiple stakeholders in government through automatic and fast validation of business transactions and transfer of data/value/ asset among different parties using the Intelligent Decentralised Autonomous Agents.

The following section is an overview of Blockchain technology application in educational setting.

Blockchain Technology in Educational Setting

The application of Blockchain in education is still emerging. It is mainly applied by a few educational institutions to validate and share credentials and/or learning outcomes that the students have achieved. However, researchers envisaged that Blockchain technology can offer much more than validating and sharing credentials. It could also delimit the central role of educational institutions and disrupt institutional norms to empower its citizens with the opportunity to transact with trust (Alammary, Alhazmi, Almasri & Gillani, 2019). It is important to first understand the concept of Blockchain before understanding its relevance in education (Sharples & Domingue, 2016). Blockchain, which is a distributed record of digital events, can be described as the linked data of items stored in blocks on every participants' computer to make a long block of chain, where a majority of those participating in a network can allow the addition of the next item/transaction to be added in a new block by consensus. There are two types of Blockchains: public and private. In a public Blockchains, anyone can access and possibly add to it; in the private Blockchain which is restricted to participants within the network who are the only ones allowed to access and add to the Blockchain (Nakamoto, 2008; Sharples & Domingue, 2016).

The wide usage of Blockchain in education is to store records of student's achievements and credits, for example, degree certificate and performance profiles. Blockchain in education provides a platform for persistent and secure public records where certificates and badges can be directly awarded to a student by trusted institutions, experts and teachers. The student can also access their credentials to share with potential employers, etc. The Blockchain technology does not verify the trustworthiness of the parties, it merely provides public evidence that the mentioned student has been awarded a certificate from a certain institution. The Blockchain solves the issue of recording occurrence of events and reliable checking of awarding of a degree, which may expose the awarding institution if, for example, the certificate is not valid (Bartolomé Castañeda, Torlà & Adell, 2017; Sharples & Domingue, 2016). In this way, Blockchain can introduce trust, transparency and efficiency, and create secure and connected networks of educational institutions, educational technology companies, and citizens to enable secure sharing and trusted exchange of data. To mitigate any issues and at the same time benefit from the Blockchain in terms of decentralise architecture, security offerings, anonymity, immutability, integrity and transparency are the attractive characteristics. Turkanović, Hölbl, M. and Košič (2018) proposed a system called EduCTX that can be globally trusted in higher education credit and grading systems. Their contribution was specifically related to the higher education credit system to provide a distributed and interoperable architecture model for higher education in order for students and institutions to have a unified viewpoint. Here, students can access a complete history of their course in a single and transparent view, and for universities to access student's educational records despite its origins. This benefit can also be extended to the potential employers which can use the system to validate students' credentials after their permission is received. For example, Grech and Camilleri (2017) predicted and described certain areas in educational sector that will be impacted by Blockchain technology, namely:

- In future, qualification and records of achievements, and other certificates will be reliably obtained from the Blockchain driven systems. Innovation in Blockchain could contribute towards lifelong learning where credentials are stored and verified, and automated awarding of certificates, recognition and transferring of credits, and accessed at any time. Ending the error of paper-based system.

- The Blockchain technology will remove the need for the users to contact the educational authority by providing the opportunity to access their certificates and validate their credentials directly against the Blockchain.
- The Blockchain technology could reduce the costs of organisations' data management and exposure to liability issues of data management by providing data management structures which give users the ability to have more ownership and control over their own data.
- Educational institutions are more likely to implement Blockchain-based cryptocurrencies to facilitate payments with other institutions, and the flexibility of providing custom cryptocurrencies could win countries to use the grant or voucher-based funder of education.

Another example of Blockchain in educational setting is the Massachusetts Institute of Technology (MIT) blockcerts project which was introduced as a reference point that has a platform and standards such as open-source libraries, tools, and mobile apps to provide a decentralized, standards-based, and recipient-centric ecosystem. These ultimately enable a trustless verification mechanism through blockchain technology to guide institutions when implementing a Blockchain technology in educational programs (Bartolomé, 2017; Gräther, Schütte, Kolvenbach, et al., 2018), with four basic components, namely: Issuer, Certificate, Verifier, and Wallet.

- The institution or issuer that issues or creates a digital certificate.
- The certificate that can provide detail of the Open badges as required, for example, by the Mozilla Foundation, which may contain skills, achievements and/or records in the blocks.
- Verifier is an independent person that confirms the origin of the certificate, by verifying that the certificate has not changed, the particulars of the issuing institution, and the particulars of the individual concern.
- Wallet, that each student has, enables them to store and share their certificates with others, for example, potential employer.

The current study explores the online system as an already automated process and with only disputes that involves the school, as shown in Figure 1, in terms of Blockchain 3.0 for digital society in the educational setting. As discussed earlier in this chapter, the parents do not trust the system and feel that there is not enough transparency. As illustrated in this section, we illustrate use of Blockchain in education. A Blockchain technology can provide the department of education with a technology to challenge the concentrated power of the school administration. This technology would be used to process the application and create a fair, transparent, sustainable, secure and decentralised registration process. The South African Department of Basic Education can solve some of these challenges at least in part with technology rather than by adding more rules and regulations as a decentralised technology has the potential to address many of the most pressing problems faced by the online registration system (Fenwick & Vermeulen, 2019). The next section provides a different perspective on how Blockchain-based robotic process automation mechanism can contribute to educational sector as discovered in the introduction of this chapter.

A BLOCKCHAIN-BASED ROBOTIC PROCESS AUTOMATION (RPA) MECHANISM

This section explores how South African Department of Basic Education can leverage the Blockchain-based RPA mechanism to streamline the process of registration of Grade 1 and Grade 8 learners in public schools. The problem of trust and distributed decision making can be resolved by a combination of Blockchain technology with swarm control techniques (Ferrer, 2019). When combined, these enabling technologies will help the Online School Registration System to overcome problems related to data acquisition from Internet of Things and to provide integrity, address security challenges, mitigate traceability and trust concerns, and reduce information irregularities. Documents such as birth certificate, identification, school report cards from previous Grades, and proof of residence contain crucial and delicate information of both the child and parent. Hence, a commissioner of oath needs to verify the hardcopies presented. Refer to Figure 4. In this context, in order to avoid human interference, the proposed new online registration system seeks to benefit from a Blockchain-based RPA mechanism. The Blockchain technology allows for the identification of participants and verification of participants' attributes by various authorities and a verification of the registration application to the Blockchain.

Figure 4. Proposed Online School Registration System Blockchain-based RPA Mechanism [adapted from Shahaab et al. (2020)]

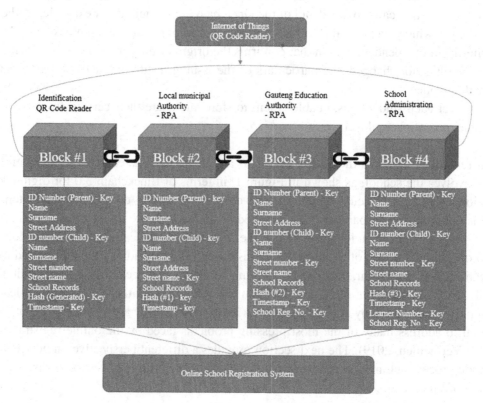

The proposed online registration system based on the Blockchain based robotic process automation (Figure 4) can solve some of the challenges faced by the South African Department of Basic Education at least in part with the technology rather than by adding more rules and regulations. This can be done by implementing the following measures and processes:

Identify

It is proposed that the online registration system must take the advantage of Internet of Things infrastructure technology such as a bar code reader or a QR code reader (available as an App on a smart phone or any other device with a camera) to identify the parents and their child(ren). In other words, the user cannot manually type in the ID number into the system, instead, they must use a QR or bar code reader. This sensor will read the code and automatically enter the ID number and associated name, surname and street address into the system. In this way, the first block, Block#01 in Figure 4, will be created. The encrypted private key identifier is the ID number of the parent and child(ren), hash (randomly generated numbers in each scan) and timestamp. The ID number of a parent can never change without authorization (possibly if a child has a new guardian), and that of a child can also never change while they are under 18 years of age. The Department of Home Affairs is the only authority to issue valid ID documents in South Africa. Other details, such as residential address will of course need to be updated and verified (see the next activity).

Data Objects

Following a successful identification, it is proposed that transactions are stored sequentially in blocks of chains and in chronological order. The next Block#02 in Figure 4 then matches the residential address to identify the nearest school. The bot 'owned by' the local municipality receives the file with the public key in the form of digital signature cryptography and decrypts it to access the record. The bot then logs into the local municipality system and retrieves the record utility bill record to confirm the street address using the ID number from Block#01 in Figure 4. If there is a match and the street address is confirmed, the bot creates a transaction with a private key consisting of the ID number of the parent and child(ren), hash from Block#01, street number and timestamp. Once the record is created, the bot sends the file with the public key to the Department of Basic Education to confirm the child's school records. If there is no match, an invalid message is sent to the parent. The bot at the node of the Department of Basic Education network receives the file in the form of digital signature cryptography and decrypts the public key to open the file. It will use the ID number from Block#02 (Figure 4) to access the child(ren)'s school records and to confirm if they have passed Grade 0 or Grade 7 to qualify for Grade 1 or Grade 8 respectively. The bot uses the address from Block#01 (Figure 4) to locate and check if there is space available at the nearest school using the street address of the applicant. If there is a space, the bot creates a record, say Block#03 as in Figure 4, with the private key containing ID number of the parent and child(ren), hash from Block#02 (Figure 4), street number, school registered number and timestamp, and sends the file to the school. If the child(ren) do not qualify or previous school records are not found, a message "invalid record" is sent immediately to the parent and department for checking and correction. Once the previous step has been successfully completed, the bot sends the file with digital signature cryptography to the next node, which is the school. The bot at the school node end of the series of steps uses its own private key to decrypt the file and the check number of learners to be placed compared with the space available at the school. Note that this node does not need to be physically located at the school but rather indicates that this is the logical location. At times there are learners who do not take up allocated places but do not inform the registration system of this decision. Hence, the bot at the school node needs to confirm placement of the applying learner in terms of space availability by sending a message to the onsite school administrators, particularly once classes have started. If a space is available, the bot creates a record, say in Block#04 as in Figure 4, with the private key combination consisting of ID number of the parent and child(ren), hash from Block#03 (Figure 4), street number, school registered number, learner number and timestamp. The bot creates and sends the message "Learner successfully placed at the school" to the parent, department of education and the school.

Information Extension

The information regarding school applications and school placements is always available and accessible. Each transaction is recorded and maintained by consensus of all the participants. All the transactions are kept from the beginning, and traceability and auditability are possible. The bots have access to the relevant data via the public key and each transaction recorded and maintained by consensus of all the participating bots.

Transaction Structure

No trusted central entity is required; there is no need for mutual trust between the transactional entities (institutions and individuals); and smart contracts are in place to validate transactions in a Blockchain system. The process is validated by different stakeholders including authorities to ensure that no privileged entity controls the registration application process and placement of a learner.

Data Security

High security is strengthened; the data are stored and publicly available in each node of the network, all the nodes can assist to maintain the data in other nodes. Placement of learners to a school takes place through an RPA after the steps in Blocks #01 to #03 (Figure 4) have been validated by all the nodes or participants in the intelligent network. The authorship is guaranteed by the fact that bots use their own private key to encrypt the file and other bots use the sender's public key to decrypt the digital signature cryptography. The receiving bot uses the sender's encrypted private key proves that it could not have been sent by just anyone else.

In the proposed solution as illustrated in Figure 4, only the first stage requires a human to initiate the registration process. Thereafter, the remaining steps are a combination of Blockchain and AI (bots) to complete the registration transaction. The proposed solution suggests the use of bots to detect and trust their counterparts, where public key cryptography technology provides any robot (that wants to communicate and send information to a specific robot addresses), with the information that only that bot has a matching key to read the record. Even if the public key falls into the wrong hands, there is no risk, since it is not used to decrypt the record. With this Blockchain technology, the bots can agree without the need for a controlling authority that the given record is credible. Once it is agreed, the block cannot be deleted or changed and is available to be certified by anyone on the network. After ensuring that all the new transactions that are supposed to be included in block#4 are valid, there is no need to invalidate previous credentials, for example, in block01# to block03#, as shown in Figure 4.

Hopefully, this section has demonstrated how to fairly and transparently allocate educational resources through a Blockchain-based RPA mechanism.

Proposals

This section explains the considerations when implementing a Blockchain-based RPA, on the basis of the illustrtive example as reviewed in this chapter. The proposals in table 6 serve as a guide and awareness for policy-makers who are pursing the creation of Online School Registration Systems that are trustworthy. These proposals also help to improve processes in allocating educational resources.

Table 6. Proposals i.e. Considerations when Implementing a Blockchain-based RPA

Proposals	
Decentralisation	Should the department of education in Gauteng consider the concept of a Blockchain-based RPA mechanism where educational credentials are decentralised for verification using robots, then this has to be defined in the policy in terms of the online registration system for Gauteng with standards and regulatory framework. The government should build expertise in order to understand and support the implementation of distributed database technology in the areas of storing sensitive, digital certificates, academic credentials and personal data using Blockchain-based RPA.
Enhanced Trust on Robotic Decisions	It is important being able to show who has received 'work' including when. Hence showing the status of an application (work flow) is very useful in a system which is distributed (the parents do not have to visit the schools and several different parties e.g. the home affairs, the centralised registration authority, etc) as they are in different places. Recording of decisions making process on the Blockchain ensures that parents, schools and government can trust, understand and trace the AI decisions.
Collective Decisions	It is proposed that the policy-makers in the department of education should further investigate and support a Blockchain-based RPA mechanism for the Online School Registration System using other use cases. Since the decisions of allocating educational resources will be shifted to the AI algorithms, there should be awareness and negotiations with the parents and schools regarding the introduction of a Blockchain-based RPA and its impact towards existing and planned activities.
Immutability	The proposed mechanism of a Blockchain-based RPA has a potential to accelerate the end of a paperbased system for issuing of academic credentials as they will be immutable and validated automatically through Blockchain, where parents do not have to provide hardcopies as proof of registration. Thereby, addressing citizens' views concerning the credibility and trustworthiness of the Online School Registration System, and to increase citizens' perceptions of its value, accuracy and reliability.
Strategic Partnerships	The proposed model to achieve the full potential of the Blockchain-based RPA is through a phased approach, for instance, starting with strategic public and private partnerships in order to align and creating awareness regarding the possible application and then deployment of a Blockchain-based RPA mechanism.
Further Research	Since the department of education has to prove that the Blockchain could offer considerable value to the parents, schools and themselves, the illustrative example of a Blockchain-based RPA serves as a way to make the department aware regarding the social advantage and potential it could have in increasing efficiency and effectiveness of allocating educational resources, using this mechanism; thereby creating a trusted Online School Registration System. Although a Blockchain-based RPA has been illustrated that is able to automatically store data in distributed database, verify educational credentials, and establish consesus between swarm robots without a central authority, the department of education is advised to conduct further research through a pilot study. It is proposed that this pilot study should collaborate with parents, schools, private sector, employee unions, and government agencies to get a buy-in and to create a policy framework for a Blockchain-RPA mechanism in educational setting. It is important to note that there is a possibility that bots can generate incorrect results due to changing business rules, partly because bots are unable to adapt their behavour to the new business rules. In order to lessen these disruptions, research in control and monitor mechanisms is needed to proactively adapt the bots in detecting changing business rules.

CONCLUSION

This chapter has presented some of the challenges faced by the Internet-based e-government systems which share characteristics with the Internet of Things. The chapter has suggested a Blockchain-based RPA mechanism as a possible solution for traceability, identification, validation and procession of registration without human intervention and a single central authority in control of placing learners at various school. Additionally, the chapter used an illustrative example from educational sector to demonstrate the Blockchain-based RPA mechanism in the registration process which includes cryptography, smart contracts, electronic school records, machine-to-machine communication (bots) and the implication of these within the Internet of Things scenario.

The combination of Blockchain and RPA has been shown to provide the possibility of storing the objects and all their changes, allowing complete, open and reliable traceability in an educational setting. Reliable identification is important, hence traditionally hardcopies of important documents are confirmed by a commissioner of oath and always accompanied by ID document. However, Blockchain identification verification has shown to be able to provide an open, trusted distributed ledger that can be used to verify identities, not only with respect to finance, but also in educational settings.

The chapter illustrated how different authorities, through machine-to-machine links, use consensus to significantly improve fairness and transparency using private and public keys in the process of placing a learner at a school through using Blockchain technology. This exploratory discussion was limited to a single example. Further research efforts should be made to ensure the security and privacy of educational records using more cases.

REFERENCES

Alammary, A., Alhazmi, S., Almasri, M., & Gillani, S. (2019). Blockchain-Based Applications in Education: A Systematic Review. *App. Sci.*, *9*(12), 2400. doi:10.3390/app9122400

Albishi, S., Soh, B., Ullah, A., & Algarni, F. (2017). Challenges and Solutions for Applications and Technologies in the Internet of Things. *Procedia Computer Science*, *124*, 608–614. doi:10.1016/j.procs.2017.12.196

Arslan, S. S., Jurdak, R., Jelitto, J., & Krishnamachari, B. (2019). Advancements in Distributed Ledger Technology for Internet of Things. *Internet of Things*, *9*, 100114. doi:10.1016/j.iot.2019.100114

Asatiani, A., & Penttinen, A. (2016). Turning Robotic Process Automation into Commercial Success – Case OpusCapita. *Journal of Information Technology Teaching Cases*, *6*(2), 67–74. doi:10.1057/jittc.2016.5

Bakon, K. A., Elias, N. F., & Abusamhadana, G. A. O. (2020). Culture and Digital Divide Influence on Government Success of Developing Countries: A Literature Review. *Journal of Theoretical and Applied Information Technology*, *98*(9).

Barnaghi, P., Wang, W., Henson, C., & Taylor, K. (2012). Semantics for the Internet of Things: Early progress and back to the future. *International Journal on Semantic Web and Information Systems*, *8*(1), 1–21. doi:10.4018/jswis.2012010101

Bartolomé, A., Castañeda, L., Torlà, C. B., & Adell, J. (2017), Blockchain in Education: Introduction and Critical Review of the state of the art. *EDUTEC, Revista Electrónica de Tecnología Educativa.*

Bélanger, F., & Carter, L. (2008). Trust and Risk in E-Government Adoption. *The Journal of Strategic Information Systems, 17*(2), 165–176. doi:10.1016/j.jsis.2007.12.002

Chen, S., Xu, H., Liu, D., Hu, B., & Wang, H. (2014). A Vision of IoT: Applications, Challenges, and Opportunities with China Perspective. *IEEE Internet of Things Journal, 1*(4).

Chen, Y. (2012), Challenges and Opportunities of Internet of Things, In *17th Asia and South Pacific Design Automation Conference* (pp. 383-388) IEEE. 10.1109/ASPDAC.2012.6164978

Cheng, S., Zeng, B., & Huang, Y. Z. (2017). Corrigendum: Research on Application Model of Blockchain Technology in Distributed Electricity Market. *IOP Conference Series. Earth and Environmental Science, 93*, 012065. doi:10.1088/1755-1315/93/1/012065

Coin Telegraph. (2015). *How Estonia Brought Blockchain Closer to Citizens: GovTech Case Studies.* https://cointelegraph.com/news/how-estonia-brought-Blockchaincloser-to-citizens-govtech-case-studies

Dignum, V. (2017). Responsible Artificial Intelligence: Designing AI for Human Values. *ITU Journal: ICT Discoveries, 1.*

Dubovitskaya, A., Novotny, P., Xu, Z., & Wang, F. (2019). *Applications of Blockchain Technology for Data-Sharing in Oncology: Results from a Systematic Literature Review. Oncology and Informatics - Review.* doi:10.1159/000504325

Efanov, D., & Roschin, P. (2018). The All-Pervasiveness of the Blockchain Technology. *Procedia Computer Science, 123*, 116–12. doi:10.1016/j.procs.2018.01.019

Feki, M. A., Kawsar, F., Boussard, M., & Trappeniers, L. (2013). The Internet of Things: The Next Technological Revolution. *Computer, 46*(2), 24–25. doi:10.1109/MC.2013.63

Fenwick, M., & Vermeulen, E. P. M. (2019). Decentralisation is Coming: The Future of Blockchain. *The JBBA, 2*(2), 2019. doi:10.31585/jbba-2-2-(8)2019

Ferrer, E. C. (2019), The Blockchain: A New Framework for Robotic Swarm Systems. *Proceedings of the Future Technologies Conference (FTC) 2018.*

Gauteng Province. (2020). *Online Admissions.* https://www.gdeadmissions.gov.za/Home/VideoTutorial

Gauteng Provincial Government. (2020). *Digital Platform.* https://www.gov.za/

Gräther, W., Schütte, J., Kolvenbach, S., Torres, C. F., Ruland, R., & Wendland, F. (2018). Blockchain for Education: Lifelong Learning Passport, In W. Prinz & P. Hoschka (Eds.), *Proceedings of the 1st ERCIM Blockchain Workshop 2018, Reports of the European Society for Socially Embedded Technologies.* Academic Press.

Grech, A., & Camilleri, A. F. (2017). *Blockchain in Education, JRC Science for Policy Report.* European Commission. doi:10.2760/60649

Hameed, S., Khan, F. I., & Hameed, B. (2018). Understanding Security Requirements and Challenges in Internet of Things (IoT): A Review. Journal of Computer Networks and Communications.

Hofmann, P., Samp, C., & Urbach, N. (2019). (2019), Robotic Process Automation. *Electronic Markets*. Advance online publication. doi:10.100712525-019-00365-8

Lacity, L. P., & Willcocks, M. C. (2016). A New Approach to Automating Service. *MIT Sloan Management Review*, *58*(1).

Lohachab, A., Lohachab, A., & Jangra, A. (2020). Comprehensive Survey of Prominent Cryptographic Aspects for Securing Communication in Post-Quantum IoT networks. *Internet of Things*, *9*, 100174. doi:10.1016/j.iot.2020.100174

Madakam, S., Holmukhe, R. M., & Jaiswal, D. K. (2019). The Future Digital Work Force: Robotic Process Automation (RPA). *Journal of Information Systems and Technology Management*, *16*, 1–17. doi:10.4301/S1807-1775201916001

Makridakis, S., Polemitis, A., Giaglis, G., & Louca, S. (2018). *Blockchain: The Next Breakthrough in the Rapid Progress of AI*. Artificial Intelligence-Emerging Trends and Applications. doi:10.5772/intechopen.75668

Marr, B. (2018). *Artificial Intelligence and Blockchain: 3 Major Benefits of Combining These Two Mega-Trends*. https://www.forbes.com/sites/bernardmarr/2018/03/02/artificial-intelligenceand-blockchain-3-major-benefits-of-combining-these-two-mega-trends/

Mokhaoli, V. (2020). *Parents Plead with Lesufi to Bring Back Manual School Registrations, Eyewitness News*. https://ewn.co.za/2020/01/15/parents-plead-with-lesufi-to-bring-back-manual-school-registrations

Moore, M. (Ed.). (2016). *Cybersecurity Breaches and Issues Surrounding Online Threat Protection*. IGI Global.

Mougayar, W. (2016). *The Business Blockchain: Promise, Practice, and Application of the Next Internet Technology*. John Wiley & Sons. http://ebookcentral.proquest.com

Nakamoto, S. (2008). *Bitcoin: A Peer-To-Peer Electronic Cash System*. https://bitcoin.org/bitcoin.pdf

Rejeb, A., Keogh, J. G., & Treiblmaier, H. (2019). Leveraging the Internet of Things and Blockchain Technology in Supply Chain Management. *Future Internet*, *11*(7), 161. doi:10.3390/fi11070161

Reyna, A., Martín, C., Chen, J., Soler, E., & Díaz, M. (2018). On Blockchain and its Integration with IoT. Challenges and Opportunities. *Future Generation Computer Systems*, *88*, 173–190. doi:10.1016/j.future.2018.05.046

Salah, K., Rehman, M. H., Nizamuddin, N., & Al-Fuqaha, A. (2019). Blockchain for AI: Review and Open Research Challenges. *IEEE Access: Practical Innovations, Open Solutions*, *7*, 10127–10149. doi:10.1109/ACCESS.2018.2890507

Senthilkumar, D. (2020). Cross-Industry Use of Blockchain Technology and Opportunities for the Future: Blockchain Technology and Aritificial Intelligence. In Cross-Industry Use of Blockchain Technology and Opportunities for the Future: Blockchain Technology and Aritificial Intelligence. IGI Global.

Shahaab, A., Hewage, R. M. C., & Khan, I. (2020). Managing Gender Change Information on Immutable Blockchain in Context of GDPR. The JBBA, 3(1).

Sharples, M., & Domingue, J. (2016). The Blockchain and Kudos: A Distributed System for Educational Record, Reputation and Reward. In K. Verbert, M. Sharples, & T. Klobučar (Eds.), Lecture Notes in Computer Science: Vol. 9891. *Adaptive and Adaptable Learning. EC-TEL 2016.* Springer. doi:10.1007/978-3-319-45153-4_48

Silcock, R. (2001). What is e-Government? *Parliamentary Affairs, 54*(1), 88–101. doi:10.1093/pa/54.1.88

Strobel, V., Ferrer, E. C., & Dorigo, M. (2018). Managing Byzantine Robots via Blockchain Technology in a Swarm Robotics Collective Decision-Making Scenario. *Proc. 17th Int. Conf. Auto. Agents MultiAgent Syst. International Foundation for Autonomous Agents and Multiagent Systems: Stockholm, Sweden,* 541–549.

Syed, R., Suriadi, S., Adams, M., Bandara, W., Leemans, S. J. J., Ouyanga, C., Hofstede, A. H. M., de Weerd, I., Wynn, M. T., & Reijers, H. A. (2020). Robotic Process Automation: Contemporary Themes and Challenges. *Computers in Industry, 115,* 103162. doi:10.1016/j.compind.2019.103162

Tan, Y. H., & Thoen, W. (2001). Toward a Generic Model of Trust for Electronic Commerce. *International Journal of Electronic Commerce, 5*(2), 61–67.

The Citizen. (2020). *Frustration and Anger over Dept's Online Registration System, The Citizen.* https://citizen.co.za/news/south-africa/education/2228424/frustration-and-anger-over--depts-online-registration-system/

Turkanović, M., Hölbl, M., Košič, K., Hericko, M., & Kamisalic, A. (2018). EduCTX: A Blockchain-Based Higher Education Credit Platform. *IEEE Access: Practical Innovations, Open Solutions, 6,* 5112–5127. doi:10.1109/ACCESS.2018.2789929

Uskenbayeva, R., Kalpeyeva, Z., Satybaldiyeva, R., Moldagulova, A., & Kassymova, A. (2019), Applying of RPA in Administrative Processes of Public Administration. In *2019 IEEE 21st Conference on Business Informatics (CBI)* (Vol. 2, pp. 9-12). IEEE.

van der Aalst, W. M. P., Bichler, M., & Heinzl, A. (2018). Robotic Process Automation. *Business & Information Systems Engineering, 60*(4), 269–272. doi:10.100712599-018-0542-4

Xing, B., & Marwala, T. (2018). *The Synergy of Blockchain and Artificial Intelligence.* https://arxiv.org/ftp/arxiv/papers/1802/1802.04451.pdf

Zhao, J. L., Fan, S., & Yan, J. (2016). Overview of Business Innovations and Research Opportunities in Blockchain and Introduction to the Special Issue. *Financial Innovation, 2*(1), 28. doi:10.118640854-016-0049-2

Zikratov, I. A., Lebedev, I. S., Gurtov, A. V., & Kuzmich, E. V. (2014). Securing Swarm Intellect Robots with a Police Office Model. *2014 IEEE 8th International Conference on Application of Information and Communication Technologies (AICT),* 1-5. 10.1109/ICAICT.2014.7035906

ADDITIONAL READING

Al-Turjman, F. (2019). *Intelligence in IoT-enabled smart cities.* Taylor and Francis, a CRC title, part of the Taylor and Francis imprint, a member of the Taylor and Francis Group, the academic division of T&F Informa, plc.

Amita, K. (2019). *Hands-On Artificial Intelligence for IoT: Expert Machine Learning and Deep Learning Techniques for Developing Smarter IoT Systems.* Packt Publishing, Limited.

Bwalya, K. (2018). *The e-Government development discourse: analysing contemporary and future growth prospects in developing and emerging economies.* AOSIS Publisher. doi:10.4102/aosis.2018.BK71

Kapoor, A. (2019). *Hands-On Artificial Intelligence for IoT: Expert Machine Learning and Deep Learning Techniques for Developing Smarter IoT System.* Packt Publishing Ltd.

Leben, D. (2019). *Ethics for robots: how to design a moral algorithm.* Routledge.

Mahmood, Z. (2009), E-Government: Stage Models for Successful Development, *Proceedings of 13th International IBIMA Conf,* Marrakech, Morocco, Nov 2009

Mahmood, Z. (2013). *E-Government Implementation and practice in Developing Countries.* IGI Global Publishers. doi:10.4018/978-1-4666-4090-0

Michael, E. A., Hanno, H., & Panarit, S. (2020), The Impact of the 4th Industrial Revolution on Engineering Education: *Proceedings of the 22nd International Conference on Interactive Collaborative Learning (ICL2019),* Volume 1, Bangkok, Thailand

Oppenheimer, A. (2019). *The robots are coming!: The future of jobs in the age of automation.* Vintage Books.

Oracle South Africa. (2020), Oracle South Africa / Database, https://www.oracle.com/za/database/what-is-database.html, Accessed July 2020

Paul, G. N., & Vassiliki, N. K. (2019). *E-government in Europe: re-booting the state.* Routledge Publisher.

Stanislav, I., & Craig, W. (2019). *Robots, artificial intelligence, and service automation in travel, tourism and hospitality.* Emerald Publishing Limited.

Tan, Y., & Zheng, Z. (2013, March). Research Advance in Swarm Robotics. *Defence Technology, 9*(1), 18–39. doi:10.1016/j.dt.2013.03.001

KEY TERMS AND DEFINITIONS

Algorithm: This refers to a procedure or finite list of instructions or rules, normally followed by a computer, to calculate and solve a mathematical problem. It refers to a finite sequence which is computer-implementable instructions to perform a computation.

Artificial Intelligence: This refers to machines that are programmed to simulate human intelligence, think like humans, and mimic their actions such as interpreting and detecting deviations in data, as well as problem-solving.

Blockchain Technology: It refers to a system that records information transparently and with consensus from other participants that make information immutable or difficult to change. It refers to a database that contains all the historical records that are publicly available and accessible to all the participants.

Cryptography: Also known as cryptology, it is the practice and study of techniques to ensure protect information and secure communications using codes such that only the intended recipient can read and process it.

Database: Refers to an organised collection of data or information stored in a structured form, usually in a computer, and accessed electronically from a computer system. It is controlled through a database management system and is modelled in rows and columns in a series of tables for efficient processing and querying of data.

E-Government: It is defined as the use of information communication and technology such as mobile devices, computers, and the internet to effectively and efficiently provide public or government services to citizens, businesses and other persons in a country.

Internet of Things: This refers to a system of interconnected and interrelated devices, network, software, electronics, mechanical and digital machines which are embedded with sensors to enable them to automatically collect and exchange data without requiring human-to-human or human-to-computer interaction.

Mechanism: It is a small part in a larger process or mechanical system to perform a specific function, in other words, a system of parts working together within a machine. Mechanism maybe an entire mechanical system.

Online School Registration System: An Internet system which provides for parents to electronically register their grade 1 and grade 8 children in a South African school. It is an e-service or e-government implemented by the Gauteng department of education to allocate scarce educational resources.

Public-Key Cryptography: Also known as asymmetric cryptography, it is a method of encrypting data with two pairs of keys, namely, public key which is available for anyone to use, and the private key known only to the owner.

Robotic Process Automation: Refers to a computer software or robot or bot that can be configured to mimic human actions with business systems to perform a business process. The steps used to train a software robot are illustrative.

Swarm Robotics: This refers to how swarm robotics algorithms can be designed to solve problems by learning from natural systems like swarms of birds, mammals, bees, or fish. It refers to the collective behaviour that is either natural or artificial of decentralised coordinated systems.

Chapter 3
Blockchain Technology for Records Management in Botswana and Zimbabwe

Olefhile Mosweu

https://orcid.org/0000-0003-4404-9458
University of Johannesburg, South Africa

Forget Chaterera-Zambuko

https://orcid.org/0000-0002-3379-0200
Sorbonne University, Abu Dhabi, UAE & University of South Africa, South Africa

ABSTRACT

The fourth industrial revolution (4IR) has ushered in several emerging and disruptive technologies. Southern Africa's records management practices have for a long time been reported to lag behind in embracing new technologies. Several studies have revealed lack of requisite skills to manage electronic records while others still lament the un-procedural management of paper records. The intention of this chapter is, therefore, to initiate a discourse that challenges information management practitioners to embrace disruptive technologies lest they themselves get disrupted. There are several emerging technologies, but this chapter focuses on blockchain technology and its possible benefits for records management. Guided by the technology acceptance model, the study established that archivists and records managers in Botswana and Zimbabwe would adopt blockchain if it is easy to use and useful for records management. The chapter ends by proposing a model for the adoption of blockchain technology for records management.

INTRODUCTION AND BACKGROUND TO THE STUDY

The adoption of new technologies is a fairly documented phenomenon. The use of Information and Communication Technologies (ICTs) in developed countries proliferated between the 1980s and 1990s. The same, however, cannot be said for countries in Sub Saharan Africa (SSA) as they were left trailing

DOI: 10.4018/978-1-7998-6650-3.ch003

behind, hence creating a global digital divide (Wamboye *et al.*, 2015). By 2011, more than half of the global population used a mobile phone with 13% having access to the Internet (ITU, 2018). Although this shows growth in the adoption of ICTs, the SSA region still falls behind other regions regarding the implementation of ICTs. This chapter focuses on two Sub Saharan countries namely Botswana and Zimbabwe. Both countries have a strong ICT framework supported by national policy (ITU, 2018). ICTs facilitate relatively easy information capture, processing, storage, and sharing (Burke, 1992). In turn, this leads to the generation of huge volumes of digital, electronic as well as paper records, hence the need to adopt emerging technologies so as to better manage the large volumes of records.

According to Mosweu *et al.* (2017, p. 97): *increasingly, public sector organizations are implementing records management* systems with a view of improving service delivery. However, adoption and use of these systems have been found wanting. This has also been observed by Mnjama and Wamukoya (2007) who indicated that managing records generated by ICTs have been a major challenge for archivists and records managers in the public sector in Africa. At national level, both Botswana and Zimbabwe have adopted electronic records management systems. Mosweu (2014) and Mosweu *et al.* (2017) have investigated factors that affected the adoption and use of an EDRMS at the Ministry of Trade and Industry, using the Unified Theory of Acceptance and Use of Technology (UTAUT) model as framework. Mosweu (2014) has reported the findings of a pilot study from an ongoing study whose findings revealed the adoption and use of an EDRMS was affected by computer attitudes, computer anxiety, social influences, facilitating conditions and performance expectancy. The eventual findings of the study as reported in Mosweu et al. (2017) showed that the four major UTAUT constructs accounted for 55% of the variance in explaining behavioral intention to adopt and use the EDRMS named the Document Workflow Management System. Empirical data indicated that key factors that affected to the low adoption and use of the system were technophobia, negative attitudes to system use, perceived system complexity and incompatibility with existing information systems as key factors contributing to low adoption and usage of the system.

Another study by Mosweu and Kenosi (2018) assessed whether the implementation of a Court Records Management System (CRMS) improved the delivery of justice in the Gaborone Magistrate District. The Motsaathebe and Mnjama (2007) studied the automation of records management processes in the High Courts of Botswana. The two preceding studies revealed that the implementation in both the High Courts and Gaborone Magistrate District improved case management and delivery as among others instances of missing files needed to argue cases were reduced significantly, file retrieval became easier and cases were successfully captured into the system. In yet another study, Moatlhodi and Kalusopa (2016) investigated the e-records readiness at the Ministry of Labour and Home Affairs and found that opportunities for increasing the depth of e-records readiness existed as system implementation funds were available and the ICT infrastructure was adequate, while management commitment was guaranteed. The studies by Kalusopa and Ngulube (2012), and Moloi and Mutula (2007) focused on e-records readiness among labour organisations and e-records readiness in an e-government setting respectively. The study by Kalusopa and Ngulube (2012) established that e-records readiness in labour organizations in Botswana was evident, low and evolving. The evidence for that was shown by the slow adoption of ICTs, inadequate records management standards and practices, and low integration in the national e-readiness framework. Shonhe and Grand (2019) investigated change management in EDRMS implementation at the Tlokweng Land Board (TLB). Communication came out as the most effective tool for managing change at TLB. However, due to lack of capacity in effecting change management, the desired change was yet to be reinforced. Rakemane and Serema (2018) investigated electronic records management practices at the Companies and the Intellectual Property Authority and found that ICTs are widely used in business processes, culminating in the massive production of electronic records. However, there is a lack of policies and procedures that govern their management.

Many other researchers studied email records management and success factors in EDRMS implementation (e.g. Keakopa, 2007; Mosweu, 2016). The study by Keakopa (2007) focused on the policies and procedures for the management of electronic records in Botswana, Namibia and South Africa. The findings established non-existence of the policies and procedures in Botswana and Namibia, while in South Africa, they were in place and operational. Mosweu (2016) assessed critical success factors for EDRMS implementation at the Ministry of Investment, Trade and Industry in Botswana and found that they included top management support, system user training, change management and project governance.

In Zimbabwe, several studies relating to electronic records management have been conducted. These include but not limited to research on managing email as electronic records, managing electronic records in financial services parastatals, e-records readiness, adoption and use of an EDRMS, digitization of historical records for preservation and enterprise digital records management (Sigauke & Nengomasha, 2012; Nkala *et al.*, 2012; Chaterera, 2013, Sigauke *et al.*, 2016; Chaterera, *et al.*, 2018; Chikomba, 2018; and Nengomasha & Chikomba, 2018). Despite their differences in approach and focus, these studies share the common ground that electronic records management in Zimbabwe is still in its infancy. A myriad of challenges, weaknesses and shortfalls in managing electronic records are yet to be addressed.

Awareness of technology promotes its uptake. For archivists and records managers in developing countries, electronic records management is still a distant practice as paper records management systems dominate. Over the years, archives and records management professionals in developing countries have embraced managing manual records and developed skills and competencies for the conventional paper records. The same cannot be said for electronic records management. As documented in extant literature, Southern Africa's records and archives management practitioners have struggled to embrace the advancements in technologies which have altered established existing archival theory, methodology and practice (Turnbaugh, 1997; Duranti, 2001). While other parts of the globe are now in the fourth Industrial Revolution (4IR), countries in the Sub Saharan Africa are still battling with the proper management of paper records.

Although researchers in Botswana and Zimbabwe have conducted studies in records management and issues of technology, there is dearth of literature that focuses on Blockchain as a records management technology, hence the need for this chapter. "Blockchain are an emerging recordkeeping technology producing new forms of records, and new modalities of recordkeeping with which records and information professionals will need to engage" (Lemieux, *et al.*, 2019), hence the need to establish the status quo in Botswana and Zimbabwe regarding the awareness and uptake of Blockchain technology for records management.

OBJECTIVES OF THE STUDY

Following the perceived problem that technology adoption seems to always come late in Africa, this study serves to enhance the understanding of, and promote the use of Blockchain technology for records management in Botswana and Zimbabwe. As such, the specific objectives of the study are, to:

- Establish if records managers and archivists in Botswana and Zimbabwe are aware and knowledgeable of Blockchain technology.
- Find out if archivists and records managers in Botswana and Zimbabwe use Blockchain for records management
- Ascertain the potential benefits of Blockchain technology in records management
- Determine if archivists and records managers in Botswana and Zimbabwe intend to use Blockchain if they perceive it to be useful for records management.
- Propose a strategic road map for records and archives management professionals on how to embrace Blockchain technology for records and archives management.

BLOCKCHAIN TECHNOLOGY

Blockchain technology is a collection of technologies that can be put together in different ways to create different results. The identifying factors of Blockchain are that the technology is politically decentralised; it does not have an infrastructural point of failure; it offers self-sovereignty; and it is attack resistant. These and other characteristics as discussed in Chaterera-Zambuko (2019) as depicted in Figure 1, influence the adoption of Blockchain technology across diverse disciplines.

Figure 1. Aspects of Blockchain technology

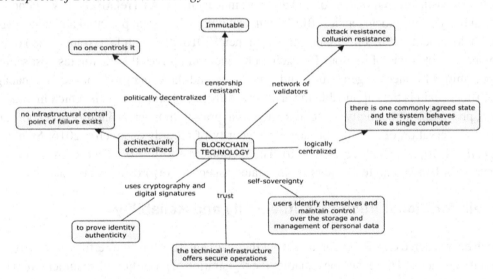

Blockchain technology enables the creation of a decentralized environment, where transactions and data are not under the control of any third-party organization. Any transaction completed is recorded in a public ledger in a verifiable, secure and transparent way, with a time stamp and other details (Holotescu, 2018). Understanding the Blockchain technology can be simplified by likening it to a book. A book has a series of pages and each page in a book contains text as well as information about that page (*not referring to the contents of the page but rather information about that page, technically known as metadata*). For example, at the top of the page there is usually the title of the book and sometimes the chapter number or title; at the bottom is usually the page number which tells you where you are in the book.

Similarly, in a Blockchain, each block has the contents of the block; and a header which contains the data about the block, and thus. it includes some technical information about the block e.g. a reference to the previous block, and a fingerprint (hash) of the data contained in this block, among other things. This hash is important for ordering. Blocks in a chain refer to previous blocks, like page numbers in a book. With books, predictable page numbers make it easy to know the order of the pages. If one ripped out all the pages and shuffled them, it would be easy to put them back into the correct order where the story makes sense. With Blockchains, each block references the previous block, not by 'block number', but by the block's fingerprint, which is wiser than a page number because the fingerprint itself is determined by the contents of the block (Lewis, 2015). Reference to previous blocks creates a chain of blocks, hence the term Blockchain.

BLOCKCHAIN TECHNOLOGY FOR RECORDS MANAGEMENT

Several studies show that Blockchain technology can be effectively used for records management (e.g. Begley, 2017; Stančić, 2018; Lemieux *et al.*, 2019). As such, governments and organisations have begun to seriously consider using the Blockchain technology to manage records. This is because records generated through Blockchain technology have been attested to be immutable and trustworthy (Lemieux, 2017), a characteristic revered in records and archives management. As a relatively new technology best known for underlying cryptocurrencies, Blockchain technology has great potential and may have a deep influence on document and records management (Stančić, 2018, p. 71). In fact, John (2019) opines that records management is one of the four Blockchain business initiatives that facilitates cost saving, provides opportunities for income generation and actually extend the capabilities of records management processes. Blockchain is thus applicable in various records management aspects which include records disposition, promoting authenticity of records, records appraisal, transfer, reliability of records and long term digital preservation of records, privacy and security of records (Lemieux, 2016; Stančić, 2018; Lemieux *et al.*, 2019; and Bhatia *et al.*, 2020). The sections that follow briefly present an overview of the application of Blockchain technology on the stated aspects of records management.

Blockchain for Digital Records Authenticity and Reliability

Records can be registered on a Blockchain to proof their authenticity. It is like certifying legal documents and financial statements. The technology enables the registration of an audit trail documentation for proof of process such as who did what, when and for how long (Jones, 2018). Authenticity is one of the four characteristics of a record, together with usability, integrity and reliability (ISO, 2016). It refers to the fact that the record has not been tampered with or corrupted, either accidentally or maliciously, and can thus be trusted as evidence of transactions completed (Duranti, 2009). Unlike centralised digital signature technologies, Blockchain does not use third parties but the authenticity of records can be demonstrated through signatures, finger prints and time stamps generated to authenticate them. These can be stored on the distributed ledger to provide proof of data integrity and authenticity. Storing signatures, along with a hash of the document, on a Blockchain removes the requirement for sequential signing and certificates. This could be particularly useful for long-term records, such as land deeds and wills (Bhatia *et al.,* 2020)

Lemieux (2017) asks whether Blockchain technology delivers on the promise of producing and keeping trustworthy records. Blockchain as a recordkeeping technology does indeed ensure that records of transactions are immutable and thus remain authentic after creation (Jones, 2018; Stančić, 2018; Bhatia *et al.,* 2020).

Blockchain and Issues of Reliability and Authenticity

A reliable record is one whose contents can be trusted as a full and accurate representation of the transactions or activities to which they attest and can be depended upon in the course of subsequent transactions or activities. Authenticity, on the other hand, is reliant upon establishing and preserving the identity and the integrity of a record from its point of creation and thereafter (Lemieux, 2019).

One of the fundamental issues for records management has been ensuring the authenticity and integrity of records. Blockchain presents records managers with a new way to ensure electronic systems offer integrity. Reliability of records starts from the point when they are created. Fundamental questions include who created the record and how it was exactly created. Digital signatures are one way of ensuring records reliability. They are a common form of transactional data. They can be stored on a Blockchain. Currently, when an electronic textual document such as a PDF is signed, the signature is stored in the document itself. To ensure the reliability of the record, it is crucial for signatures to be applied sequentially, and if the certificate expires, the validity of the document can be questioned. Storing signatures, along with a hash of the document, removes the requirement for sequential signing of certificates. This could be particularly useful for long-term records, such as land deeds and wills (NARA, 2019, p. 10).

A Blockchain could be used to provide authenticity for a record. When an organization provides a record to users, it usually provides provenance and certification that it is a true and accurate copy. If there is any question afterwards, the copy is compared to the original. If the certificate of authenticity is retained in a Blockchain, the record could be re-hashed to determine if any changes or alterations have been made. Photographs can be altered, cropped, or otherwise modified by a researcher and if the hash fails upon comparison, then they would be able to prove the image has been changed. To achieve this, Blockchain uses cryptographic signatures and public keys to form a chain linked record of transactions which cannot be forged (NARA, 2019, p.10).

There is a plethora of applications that can be used to manipulate video, audio, and photo files. This presents serious challenges to the 21st century records manager and archivist. There are video editing applications that can play around facial appearances and there are also highly accurate voice editing software, which allows users to easily create fake videos without detection. Bockchain technology can be used to solve this challenge through the use of hashes in the metadata of a file so that external entities are in a position to validate that the digital material has not been altered. Such characteristics of Blockchain are what makes the technology so attractive to records and archives management professionals.

Blockchain and Records Retention and Disposition

Records retention and disposition is at the centre of effective records management (Lemieux *et al..* 2019). With the appropriate records in place, an organisation fulfills its obligations and execute its mandate, protect and defend its interests. Despite the importance of records retention, organisations face problems emanating from lack of records retention schedules occasioned by disagreements over the business value of records (Lemieux *et al.*, 2019). Furthermore, Lemieux *et al.* (2019, p. 49) ask a number of questions related to records retention and these are:

- Can Blockchain reduce any of the investment required for records retention?
- Does it impose new challenges or risks?
- What could Blockchain records retention look like?

These questions need to be answered as archives and records management professionals grapple with Blockchain as a potential records management technology. From a records management perspective, "features that make data cryptographically inaccessible indicate records retention and disposition were not included as part of the original intention of Blockchain developers" (Bhatia *et al.*, 2020). The fact that records generated in Blockchain are immutable is both a good thing as it promotes records authenticity and also not so good for the retention of records. Blockchain technology is still nascent in terms of managing records, its capacity to integrate a solution with records retention schedules and classification systems remains undeveloped (Lemieux *et al.*, 2019). Records retention is an indispensable aspect of records management.

Blockchain and Long-Term Preservation of Digital Records

For records to remain accessible and useable in the long term, they need to be preserved properly. Amongst other records management functions, Blockchain can also be used in the long term preservation of digital records (Lemieux *et al.*, 2019). However, Blockchains are not custom designed for the preservation of records and archives. A related question is: what would then happen if traditional custodial approaches to long-term archival preservation fail to work in Blockchain recordkeeping contexts? This question arises in view of the fact that unlike archival systems which are designed to keep content accessible for long periods, Blockchain systems are limited in that regard. However, this does not dismiss Blockchain technology from being a potential records management tool. There are a couple of positive attributes of Blockchain technology which have to be given due consideration. The technology can be effectively used for ensuring the integrity and maintaining the provenance of digital records.

The InterPARES Trust *Truster* project led by researchers at the University of Zagreb in Croatia on the application of Blockchain in records management, addressed the challenge of archiving digitally signed documents whose tampering becomes possible if and when the certificate used in the signature expires, or possibly when the certificate authority stops functioning (Chaterera et al., 2018; Bralić, 2017). This challenge is resolved by the *Trust Chain*, a model for long-term preservation of digitally signed documents using Blockchain technology (Lemieux *et al.*, 2019). The core of the system is a Blockchain containing hashes of digital signatures (Bralić et al. 2017).

The proposed Trust Chain Model, that we proposed, is based on cooperation between multiple archival (or other interested) institutions. While there is no technical reason why a single institution could not run the needed software and hardware components, the trust in the envisioned system is in direct relation to the number of independent participating institutions. If a single institution runs the whole system, that institution is capable of manipulating records and would need to be trusted implicitly. This is the situation we have today. We are bypassing this need to trust a single institution by requiring multiple institutions to confirm the validity of a digitally signed document before writing it into an immutable Blockchain (Bralić et al., 2017, p. 91)

Blockchain Security and Confidentiality of Records

Breach of confidentiality of records comes with heavy penalties as it is outlawed by data protection legislation (Lemieux *et al.*, 2019). Four billion data breaches were reported in the first half of 2019. These were categorized as financial data breaches, entertainment data breaches, healthcare data breaches, education data breaches, government data breaches and other business data breaches (Norton Life Lock, 2020). Educational data breach reports from December 2018 to March 2019 indicated that an unknown entity breached 1.3 million records from a central database run by the Georgia Tech University. The database contained the names, addresses, social security numbers, and birth dates of current and former students, faculty members, and staffers at the school (Norton Life Lock, 2020). With Blockchain technology, organisational records are secured whilst simultaneously ensuring that only parties to a transaction can have access to records on a need to know basis. The removal of third parties improves the security of records.

Blockchain uses a distributed (peer-to-peer) network. The distributed network has no center(s) since all interconnected computers are treated equally. This type of network has no single point of control and therefore no single point of attack (Stančić 2018, p. 62). Comparatively, a centralised database is prone to costly security breaches as it exposes a single point of failure (John, 2019). Blockchain technology therefore leverages public key infrastructure and cryptography which can be powerful tools for protecting data privacy.

Overview of Blockchain Uptake for Records Management

This section briefly illustrates some of the use cases of Blockchain for records management. The illustrations are drawn from around the globe to give insights into the level of understanding and acceptance of Blockchain technology. The intention of this section is to instill confidence in records managers to the effect that the technology can be adopted as it has been successfully used elsewhere. It should however be acknowledged that Blockchain is not a silver bullet to digital records and archives management challenges as the technology is not immune from pitfalls.

Owing to its unique characteristics that are meant to ensure the integrity and authenticity of records, Blockchain technology has been applied in many areas of records management such as land title transfers, health records and financial records management. Several countries are contemplating to adopt Blockchain technology for recordkeeping. Table 1 illustrates some of the use cases of Blockchain technology (Lemieux *et al.,* 2019).

Table 1. Use cases of Blockchain technology

Country	Blockchain project
Georgia	-Piloted the registration of land titles using a private Blockchain in 2016. - has plans to expand Blockchain use to sales and purchases of land titles, mortgages, rentals & new land title registration
Brazil	- Blockchain technology was applied to land transfer registration in the municipality of Pelotas in 2017 -The application was done by the local real estate registration authority
Estonia	- Uses Blockchain to securely keep medical records and a host of other types of government records as well
UK (National Archives)	- Has been experimenting with the use of Blockchains in digital preservation

It is disappointing to note that a thorough online literature search on Blockchain and records management could not yield any result from the African continent. In this regard, the assumptions made from this observation are that:

1. Either records management practitioners in Africa are not aware of the Blockchain technology
2. Or Blockchain technology to manage records is being used but it has not been documented and published yet.

Considering the many reports that have been previously made by scholars in Africa, lamenting that professionals and practitioners lag behind in terms of adopting new technologies, the probability of assumption 1 above is likely to be true, hence the need for this chapter's initiative to bring the attention of archivists and records managers in Africa to the existence of Blockchain and the potential it holds for them. On the academic front, a few scholars are beginning to delve into the subject, notable amongst them, e.g. Marutha (2019) who in a conference presentation proposes a framework to interconnect healthcare facilities for universal patient records access using Blockchain technology.

Blockchain based solutions are increasing and there is added interest in using the technology to manage records (Lemieux, 2016). This calls for archives and records management professionals to gain an understanding of Blockchain as a viable technology for the management and preservation of authentic digital records. It is in this context that this study sought to take stock of Blockchain uptake for records management in Botswana and Zimbabwe.

UPTAKE OF BLOCKCHAIN TECHNOLOGY USING TAM

The adoption and use of ICTs is associated with success. The automation of work process brings efficiency in the form of limited errors, cost reduction and some consistency in the delivery of services. Hence, ICTs have been adopted in different sectors of the economy such as education, health, governance, manufacturing and the banking industry (Luka, 2012). In turn, researchers have focused their attention on getting to understand issues surrounding technology adoption. These include factors that promote and hinder adoption of technology, using different technology adoption models. Some of the commonly used models to anchor such studies include but are not limited to the Technology Adoption Model (TAM), Unified Theory of Acceptance and Use of Technology (UTAUT), Technology–Organization–Environment Framework (TOEF), and the Diffusion of Innovation (DOI) (Davis, 1989; Tornatzky and Fleischer, 1990; Rogers, 2003; and Venkatesh & Davis, 2003).

Jones et al. (2005) used TAM in a descriptive case study to establish significant system factors that contributed to the success of an Online Assignment Submission, Infocom System (OASIS) used by distance learners in an Australian academic institution. Those students who were technology savvy perceived the system to be easy to use unlike those who viewed technology as difficult. The system was said to be easy to use when there were support mechanisms in place. The conclusion reached by the study was that perceptions of the ease of use of the system promoted its adoption. A similar research approach was used by Radif et al. (2016) to gauge the intention to use a Learning Management System (LMS) at Al-Qadisiyah University in Iraq. Chaterera (2012) also used the same strategy to examine the factors that influence the adoption of e-government services by citizens in Zimbabwe.

Totolo (2007) utilised TAM to anchor a study which investigated Botswana secondary school principals' intention to adopt computer technology. The study found that there was substantial support for respondents to adopt and use computer technology for those who found it easy to use and also useful in their work. In addition, it emerged from the study that factors such as time constraints, phobia, lack of skills or training and the lack of practice with computers were barriers to adopt computer technology.

In a study that sought to develop a suitable model for the adoption of an online transaction platform for retailers in Zimbabwe, it emerged that perceived ease of use of the system was the main driver for the adoption of the technology, followed by perceived usefulness among retailers (Dube and Gumbo, 2017). The third factor was the reliability of the system. For bankers, the factors that drove the acceptance of the online transaction system were system reliability and management attitude.

The few studies explored using TAM to predict the adoption of technology show that the model is good to use for assessing technology adoption. This is true for both developed and developing countries. To this effect, the current study uses TAM to investigate the uptake of Blockchain as a records management technology among archivists and records managers in Botswana and Zimbabwe.

METHODOLOGY

A quantitative research approach through the use of a survey monkey tool was employed to conduct the study. The survey was distributed through electronic mail and the WhatsApp platform. Target population were archivists and records managers working in the public, private and parastatal organisations in Botswana and Zimbabwe. The respondents were selected through the snowball sampling strategy. Data collection started on 19 May 2020 and ended on 5 June 2020. A total of 95 questionnaire scripts were sent out and 54 were returned, giving a response rate of 56.8%. This was deemed adequate to make conclusions from the empirical data collected.

FINDINGS OF THE STUDY

This section presents the findings of the study obtained from empirical data collected from the participants. The results are presented and discussed thematically as derived in the study's objectives.

Blockchain Awareness

Archives and records management does not happen in a vacuum. It takes place within an organization where transactions are documented. As such, the initial question of our study requested respondents to state the type of organization they work for. Out of the 54 study participants, 28 (51.85%) said they work for parastatals, 22 (40.74%) indicated that they work for public organisations while the remaining 5 (9.26%) worked for private organizations. Amongst the driving force of this study was to establish if records and archives management practitioners in Botswana and Zimbabwe are aware of Blockchain technology. Accordingly, question two requested study participants to indicate if they are aware of Blockchain technology. The findings revealed that 38 (70.4%) respondents answered in the affirmative while 16 (29.6%) gave a negative response.

Blockchain technology has been touted to be technological innovation of the 21st century. However, since its inception in 2008, awareness about its application has not really come to the fore, except for Bitcoin, cryptocurrency that underpinned its coming into being (Nakamoto, 2008; Notheisen et al., 2017). Although Blockchain technology has been adopted in many areas including records management, its application has been largely embraced in the financial sector (Sadhya and Sadhya, 2018).

A follow up question on how they learnt about Blockchain technology was asked to the respondents who had indicated that they are aware of Blockchain technology. Their responses which could include more than one choice from a given list, are tabulated in Table 2.

Table 2. Source of knowledge about Blockchain (sample size n = 38)

Source of knowledge for Blockchain	Responses
Internet	32
Fellow professionals	15
University/College	2
Friends	3
Other	4

The results show that most of the respondents learnt about Blockchain technology from the Internet and from fellow professionals accounting for thirty-two and fifteen responses respectively. Four respondents indicated that they learnt about the technology through other means which they however did not specify. Three said that they learnt about Blockchain technology from friends while two indicated that they got to know about Blockchain via a university/college programme.

Another question posed to respondents was whether Blockchain could be used to manage records. Out of 54 respondents, 37 (80.43%) said it could be used to manage records, 3 (6.52%) said it cannot be used to manage records, 6 (13.04%) either gave answers such as "I don't know" or "I am not sure" while eight respondents skipped the question. As depicted in the study's findings, the majority of the respondents said Blockchain could be used to manage records.

From the study's findings, it is clear that the Internet is a major source of knowledge for archivists and records managers, at least for those in Botswana and Zimbabwe. Technological advances and the fast pace at which knowledge is acquired and gets outdated enables people to use additional forms of learning to update their knowledge in order to adapt to the ever-changing world and function in it. The Internet makes self-education easier due to the vast information resources online.

The Internet facilitates self-directed learning beyond the limitations of a classroom. This fact has become clearer in the face of Covid-19 pandemic of 2020, which has seen more people resorting to the internet for their various learning needs. Information has become ubiquitous and technology now plays a significant role in enabling the fast-paced acquisition of knowledge (Reader, 2018). The Internet facilitates self-conducted learning. An important factor which influences the effectiveness of Internet use in education is its ability to allow a user to work with information (UNESCO, 2003).

Blockchain Uptake for Records Management

The overarching aim of the study was to take stock of Blockchain uptake for records and archives management in Botswana and Zimbabwe. None of the study participants indicated actual use of Blockchain technology in their respective organisations. However, when asked on whether Blockchain can be used to manage records, the study informants supplied the responses as depicted in Figure 2.

Figure 2. Use of Blockchain for records management

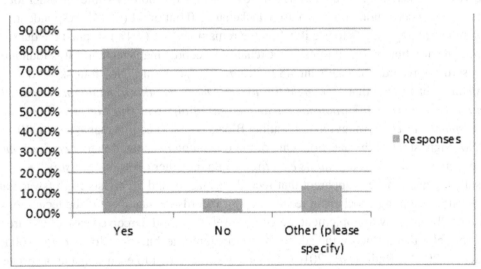

Figure 2 shows that the majority of the study participants believe that Blockchain can be used for records management. Nevertheless, there are a few who do not think that the technology is appropriate for records management. The large response to the effect that Blockchain can be used for records management is presumably because Blockchain has proven beneficial in application areas such as the financial sector, supply chain management, food industry and energy sector among others (Khatoon, 2020). This implies that records management can also benefit from Blockchain technology; hence the majority of the respondents indicated that Blockchain can be used for records management.

Uptake of Blockchain Based on Perceived Usefulness and Ease of Use

Amongst the objectives of the study was to establish if archivists and records managers in Botswana and Zimbabwe intend to use Blockchain if they perceived it to be useful for records management. As such, questions six up to nine (6 – 9) were structured in a related and interlinked manner that ultimately sought to establish the probable factors surrounding the potential uptake of Blockchain technology for records management. The questions were structured as follows:

- If Blockchain is introduced in your organisation for records management, would you use it if it is easy to use?
- If Blockchain is useful (improves records management), would you use it and encourage others to use?
- Do you intend to use Blockchain for records management if it is easy to use and useful for records management?
- Would you recommend Blockchain, toothers, as a records management technology?

48 out of 54 (88.9%) respondents revealed that they are willing to use Blockchain technology if it is easy to use, two indicated that they are not willing to try out the technology while the other four skipped the question. About encouraging others to use Blockchain, 50 out of 54 (92.6%) respondents indicated that they would encourage others to use it; while the remaining four (7.4%) skipped the question.

Regarding the question on intent to use Blockchain for records management if it is found to be easy to use and useful for records management, 48 indicated 'Yes', one said 'No', four skipped the question and the remaining one stated that "*I thought for now it is more popular in managing financial records only. Unless it encompasses the wholesome management of different types of records e.g. staff files, policy, correspondence etc.*" About recommending Blockchain for records management, 40 said 'Yes', four said 'No', eight skipped the question. One of the remaining two stated that "*I can recommend it if the security of information is good and its effective*" while the other one said "*not sure*".

The results obtained make it apparent that records managers and archivists in Botswana and Zimbabwe are keen on adopting Blockchain technology for records management if the technology is relatively user friendly and easy to implement. Perceived usefulness and perceived ease of use are amongst the critical variables that influence the adoption or rejection of technology (Jones *et al.*, 2005; Totolo, 2007; Chaterera, 2012 & Radif *et al.*, 2016). As such, it is important to ensure that appropriate support systems are put in place when a decision is made to adopt any form of technology. Additionally, the personnel targeted to use the technology must receive proper orientation and training on how to use the technology (Mosweu *et al.*, 2016). This is particularly important for records managers and archivists in Botswana and Zimbabwe as there have been numerous reports on poor records management owing to lack of training and expertise to manage electronic records.

The results obtained in this study also bear testimony to the need for adequate training if Blockchain technology is to be adopted as a records management tool. One of the respondents frankly stated that they thought Blockchain technology was only meant to manage financial records. Such findings are in line with Chaterera-Zambuko (2019) who established that there was confusion on what Blockchain is all about as the informants of her study confused it with mostly Bitcoin and sometimes databases.

Benefits of Blockchain for Records Management Technology

Being aware of Blockchain technology as a potential records management technology suggests that potential users would be aware of its benefits to an organisation. A question was posed to respondents to select the benefits of the use of Blockchain technology for records management from a number of choices. The findings as shown in Table 3 indicate that study respondents were indeed aware of the benefits of Blockchain for records management. The majority, 30 (73.17%) said that managing records in Blockchain ensures that they are immutable, authentic and have integrity. The least, 17 (41.46%) indicated that Blockchain established trust in the validity of records.

Table 3. Benefits of Blockchain as records management technology

Benefit	Responses	
Records are immutable, authentic and have integrity	30	73.17%
Flexibility	21	51.52%
Efficiency	23	56.10%
Cost savings (shorter processes without third parties)	22	53.66%
Improved security	27	65.85%
Establishes trust in the validity of a record	17	41.46%

The sections that follow now, discuss the benefits of Blockchain for records management as displayed in Table 3.

Records Immutability, Authenticity and Integrity

Records of transactions undertaken through Blockchain can never be erased once confirmed, thus they are immutable. Such records possess the value of integrity (Bhatia *et al.*, 2020), which is crucial in the management of records. The integrity of data is a topical issue in the technical world of computer security, and together with availability and confidentiality, they make up its central features. There is a general illusion that information on the Internet is fixed and accurate (Duranti and Rogers, 2019). The integrity and identity of a record makes it authentic. Authenticity, reliability, integrity and usability are key characteristics of a record as outlined in ISO 15489-1 (ISO, 2016).

The standard defines a record as one: a) that can be proven to be what it purports to be, b) that has been created or sent by the agent purported to have created or sent it; and c) that has been created or sent when purported (ISO, 2016, p. 4). The fact that records generated in Blockchain have integrity, are immutable and are authentic makes the technology attractive to records and archives management .

Flexibility, Efficiency and Cost Savings

Transactions using Blockchain technology are undertaken by two parties who do not know each other but go along with the transaction because of the issue of trust. By not involving third parties in the transactions, there is more efficiency. Blockchain technology is flexible. The technology is a peer to peer network that time stamps a transaction and eliminates the necessity for third party services to validate the transactions (Bhatia *et al.*, 2019). When using Blockchain technology, transactions that usually take days because of the involvement of many parties take incredibly lesser time to be concluded (Iron Mountain, 2020). Thus, Blockchain for records management promotes higher efficiency amongst other benefits (John, 2019).

Blockchain technology can lead to significant savings in costs. Its application can be affected in a number of functional areas such as across payments, capital markets, trade services, investment and wealth management, securities and commodities exchanges (Di Grigorio, 2017). For lodging claims, the technology can make sure that claims are paid only to deserving persons. As a whole, companies can expect to reduce financial services infrastructure cost between US$15 billion and $20 billion per annum by 2022, providing the possibility to decommission legacy systems and infrastructure and significantly reduce IT costs (Di Grigorio, 2017).

Improved Security and Trust in Records Validity

A trusted record is one that can serve as evidence of the performance of the transaction that led to its generation (Zhiliang *et al.*, 2019). Records generated in Blockchain systems are deemed trustworthy. Blockchain technology is increasingly discussed as a solution towards having trusted digital records (Lemieux 2016, p.11). Records generated in Blockchain are secure. The technology is designed to update all the ledgers that are kept by each member every time a new transaction occurs (Yoo, 2017). As a distributed database of records or public ledger of all transactions undertaken, parties to the transaction verify by consensus the transactions. The majority has to agree that the record generated is accurate and complete. Once entered, information can never be erased (Yoo, 2017). Although advancements in the health sector offered improved security and user experience through the implementation of Electronic Health Record (EHR) and Electronic Medical Record (EMR) systems, security issues still remained. Issues regarding security of medical records, user ownership of data and data integrity remain unresolved. Blockchain technology offers a more secure, temper-proof platform for storing medical records and other healthcare related information (Shahnaz, *et al.*, 2019).

PROPOSED MODEL FOR ADOPTING BLOCKCHAIN TECHNOLOGY IN RECORDS MANAGEMENT

Adopting a new technology can be a daunting task surrounded with scepticism and uncertainty. Various sectors are under pressure to embrace emerging technologies otherwise they risk becoming redundant, outdated and unattractive to their respective service communities. Much as it is critical to adopt disruptive technologies, it is imperative to do some pre-checks and thorough considerations. The proposed model illustrated in Figure 3 offers key variables to consider when adopting Blockchain for records management. The variables were determined from the findings of the current study.

Depicted in Figure 3 is the proposed model with critical elements that records managers and archivists should consider when adopting Blockchain technology in managing documentary heritage in their custody.

Figure 3. Proposed model for adoption of Blockchain technology in records and archives management

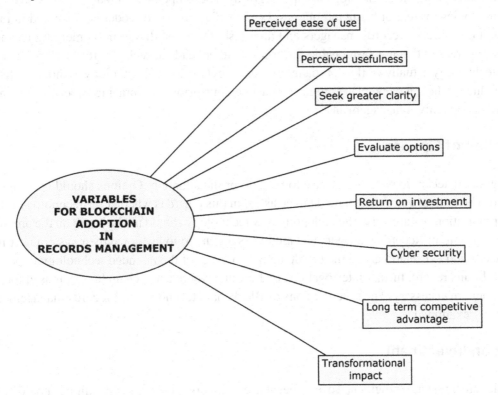

Perceived Ease of Use

Perceived ease of use is an essential element in technology adoption. As revealed in the results of this study, records managers and archivists are willing to adopt Blockchain technology if it is easy to use. This also implies that adequate training should be given to records managers and archivists on how to implement the technology. The visible error in many organisations is that training on adopting a new technology is usually reserved for Information Technology Departments. This has left many records managers and archivists as passive users of systems in which they have limited understanding on how technologies function. Consequently, several records managers and archivists have shunned technology on the basis of its complexity.

Perceived Usefulness

Perceived usefulness is equally important in inculcating the will to use newly implemented technology. The bulk of this study's respondents expressed interest in adopting Blockchain technology, if it is useful in records management. As such, adopting technology should not be driven by the need to keep pace with technological advancements. Rather, the technology should be vetted for its ability to get things done more effectively. The practical question that records managers and archivists should ask themselves is what they want the technology to do for them and whether the technology can do it. Use case should therefore drive the need to adopt technology.

The world is riding on a technological super highway. The temptation for many professionals to jump onto technologies for fear of being left out is very high. The proposed model is illustrated in Figure 3, however, it discourages records managers and archivists from just diving into emerging technologies for the simple reason that it is fashionable. Efforts should be made in seeking greater clarity in terms of how the technology actually works. It is dangerous to accept the use of technology without a satisfactory understanding on how it works. Due diligence must be done prior to embracing Blockchain technology for records and archives management.

Evaluation of Options

Adopting a new technology does not have to be a do or die situation. Options should be weighed and evaluated. The critical question that ought to be asked in this regard is whether the technology is the best for the organisation. As argued earlier, adopting new technology should not be based on the pressure that everyone is doing it. Records managers and archivists are urged to lay down their system user requirements, needs and expectations and then evaluate the capacity of the intended technology to perform as expected. In this regard, further interrogations on how and where Blockchain has been used for records management are necessary. The specifications of Blockchain technology for records management need to be closely examined.

Return on Investment

Economies are built and strengthened over time, hence every organisation's expenditure should be worthwhile. Decisions with financial implications must be carefully assessed. There has to be a meaningful return on investment. Records managers and archivists are advised to do a cost benefit analysis when contemplating the adoption of Blockchain for records management. There has to be a good understanding on the cost benefits offered by the technology. Ngulube (2011) posits that cost analysis is essential in planning for records management programmes. It leads to informed decision making about costs and benefits that may accrue to an organisation that desires to have a competitive edge having an effective and efficient system. However, available literature in Sub Saharan Africa indicates that undertaking cost benefit analysis is not a major area of concern for professionals in the sub-continent (Ngulube and Tafor, 2006; Kemoni *et al.*, 2007; Ngoepe, 2009). In reality, a detailed cost benefit analysis for the implementation of Blockchain in records management is a necessity as it will avail options for the implementing organisation to go ahead with implementation with full knowledge that doing so will justify the money spent.

Improved Cyber Security

Modern day organisations that seek to remain competitive, are compelled to embrace new technologies in order to survive (Qiang *et al.*, 2012). The adoption of new technologies may bring benefits to organisations but it comes with security risks in the form of breaches (Dohertya *et al.*, 2011). Caution must be exercised when implementing ICTs. Improved security had the second highest number of responses in terms of the perceived benefits of using Blockchain technology for records management accounting for 27 indications. This shows that the ability of a technology to offer security need not be overemphasised. As depicted in the proposed model, cyber security is a key factor to consider when adopting a new technology. Appropriate checks and verifications should be done on the strength of the technology from internal and external attacks such as illicit access and undetectable deletions and alterations that may threaten the authenticity of records. In cloud computing, for records management, the security of data is questionable (Mosweu *et al.,*2019). It is against this backdrop that McKemmish (2013) cautions that gains and benefits in technology implementation should be weighed against risks such as those pertaining to security and privacy. Although, McKemmish (2013)'s context was specifically for cloud-based records management, the same risks are also a concern in Blockchain based records management.

Transformational Impact

As reiterated in the preceding sections, adopting new technologies should not be driven by pressure of adoption on the basis that everyone else is also doing it. Records managers should assess the long-term competitive advantage of adopting the technology. They should visualise the transformational impact of the technology. For example, what radical changes, the profession or organisation are likely to experience by adopting the new technology? Or, what are the perceived long and short term benefits to be achieved, etc? Answers to these and other questions will help in making an informed decision on whether to adopt the technology or let it pass.

CONCLUSION

The Fourth Industrial Revolution (I4.0) has seen the emergence of disruptive technologies which many professionals and practitioners have found hard to ignore. Records managers and archivists have not been spared in this race to stay abreast of technological advancements. Overall, this study has established that records managers and archivists in Botswana and Zimbabwe are aware of the existence of Blockchain technology, although their respective organisations are not yet using the technology. Records managers and archivists in Botswana and Zimbabwe appreciate the potential benefits of Blockchain technology on records management and are willing to adopt the technology if the technology is indeed useful and easy to use. Apart from perceived usefulness and ease of use, other factors to be considered include seeking for greater clarity, evaluating options, looking at the return on investment and long term competitive advantage as well as cyber security.

The use of Blockchain technology should however not be considered a silver bullet. There are issues that must be considered such as how to deal with malicious users, how controls are applied, and the limitations of the implementations. It is imperative to note that Blockchain recordkeeping system does not fundamentally change the existing record keeping and archival systems but augments them by adding an integrity-checking layer. Blockchain recordkeeping, however, does not require the existence of certificate issuing authorities, since public-private key pairs are self-generated within the system. Thus, incoming archival records can be re-signed while their original certificates are still valid, and cryptographically secured in a Blockchain in time ordered sequential manner as a basis for establishing their continued authenticity. While the technology may not be immune from the potential risks associated with new technologies, records managers and archivists are encouraged to embrace the technology as it offers considerable benefits.

SUGGESTIONS FOR FURTHER RESEARCH

Blockchain technology is still new and should be investigated with the mindset of how it could potentially benefit records and information management professionals. The indisputable fact that nothing lasts forever raises the following three critical questions (Lemieux, 2019), which call for further research:

- How long will the Blockchain survive?
- Who and by what means will they ensure that a copy of the user's data will be preserved?
- Assuming a copy of the user's data is preserved, can it be verified using the data stored on the Blockchain?

The other drawbacks are the high costs of hardware, energy and time needed for the data mining process, also the fact that the technology is complex and maybe difficult to understand.

REFERENCES

Begley, R. (2017). *Information and Records Management and Blockchain Technology: Understanding its Potential* (Masters Dissertation). Northumbria University, New Castle.

Bhatia, S., Douglas, E. K., & Most, M. (2020). *Blockchain and records management: disruptive force or new approach?* Retrieved 17 May 2020, from https://www.emerald.com/insight/0956-5698.htm

Bralić, V., Kuleš, M., & Stančić, H. (2017). A Model for Long-Term Preservation of Digital Signature Validity: TrustChain. In *Future2017: Integrating ICT in Society, 2017*. Retrieved 30 March, 2020, https://www.researchgate.net/publication/321171227_A_Model_for_Long

Burke, F. G. (1992). Chaos through communications: archivists, records managers, and the communications phenomenon. In The Archival Imagination: Essays in Honour of Hugh A. Taylor (pp. 154-77). Academic Press.

Chaterera, F. (2012). Towards harnessing e-government adoption in Zimbabwe. 2012. *Mousaion: South African Journal of Information Studies*, 30(2), 78–93.

Chaterera, F. (2013). *Records surveys and the management of public records in Zimbabwe* (Masters Dissertation). University of South Africa, Pretoria.

Chaterera, F., Masuku, M., Bhebhe, S., Ngoepe, M. S., & Katuu, S. (2018). *Enterprise digital records management in Zimbabwe*. Retrieved 16 April, 2020, from https://interparestrust.org/assets/public/dissemination/AF03ZimbabweLitReviewJuly2018.pdf

Chaterera-Zambuko, F. (2019). *The integrity and authenticity of records: is Blockchain the silver bullet?* Paper presented at the 3rd Records Management Conference on Records management and sustainable development, Mombasa, Kenya.

Chikomba, A. (2018). *Management of digital records in selected financial services parastatals in Zimbabwe* (Masters Dissertation). University of South Africa, Pretoria.

Davis, F. D. (1989). *Perceived usefulness, perceived ease of use, and user acceptance of information technology.* Retrieved 12 May, 2020, from http://www.jstor.org/stable/249008

Di Grigorio, M. (2017). *Blockchain: a new tool to cut costs.* Retrieved 30 March, 2020 https://www.pwc.com/m1/en/media-centre/articles/Blockchain-new-tool-to-cut-costs.html

Dohertya, N. F., Anastakisa, L., & Fulfordb, H. (2011). Reinforcing the corporate security of information resources: A critical review of the role of the acceptable use policy. *International Journal of Information Management, 31*, 201–209.

Dube, C., & Gumbo, V. (2017). Technology Acceptance Model for Zimbabwe: The case of the retail industry in Zimbabwe. *Applied Economics and Finance, 4*(3), 56–76. doi:10.11114/aef.v4i3.2208

Duranti, L. (2001). The impact of digital technology on archival science. *Archival Science, 1*(1), 39–55. doi:10.1007/BF02435638

Duranti, L. (2009). From digital diplomatics to digital records forensics. *Archivaria: Journal of the Association of Canadian Archivists, 68*, 39–66.

Duranti, L., & Rogers, C. (2019). *Trusting in records and data online.* Retrieved 12 May, 2020, from https://www.researchgate.net/publication/337398175_Trusting_Records_and_Data_in_the_Cloud_The_Creation_Management_and_Preservation_of_Trustworthy_Digital_Content

Holotescu, C. (2018). *Understanding Blockchain technology and how to get involved.* Paper presented at the 14th International Scientific Conference eLearning and Software for Education, Bucharest, Romania.

International Organization for Standardization. (2016). *ISO 15489-1:2016 Information and Documentation–Records Management–Part1: Concepts and Principles.* ISO.

Iron Mountain. (2020). *What is Blockchain and why should records management professionals care?* Retrieved 6 May, 2020, from https://www.ironmountain.com/resources/general-articles

ITU. (2018). *Measuring the Information Society Report Volume 2.* Retrieved 30 March, 2020, from https://www.itu.int/en/ITU-D/Statistics/Documents/publications/misr2018/MISR-2018-Vol-2-E.pdf

John, C. (2019). *Blockchain for contract and records management.* Retrieved 26 March, 2020, from https://medium.com/vdcconsortium/Blockchain

Jones, A. (2018). *Blockchain brings proof of authenticity to records management.* Retrieved 20 March, 2020, https://www.alfresco.com/blogs/digital-transformation/Blockchain

Jones, D., Cranston, M., Behrens, S., & Jamieson, K. (2005). *What makes ICT implementation successful: A case study of online assignment submission.* Retrieved 29 March, 2020, from https://djon.es/blog/wp-content/uploads/2008/12/oasissubmit_v3.pdf

Kalusopa, T., & Ngulube, P. (2012). Developing an e-records readiness framework for labour organisations in Botswana. *Information Development, 28*(3), 199–215. doi:10.1177/0266666912446209

Keakopa, S. (2007). Policies and Procedures for the Management of Electronic Records in Botswana, Namibia and South Africa. *ESARBICA Journal, 26*(1), 54–64. doi:10.4314/esarjo.v26i1.31015

Kemoni, H., Ngulube, P., & Stilwell, C. (2007). Public records and archives as tools for good governance: Reflections within the recordkeeping scholarly and practitioner communities. *ESARBICA Journal: Journal of the Eastern and Southern Africa Regional Branch of the International Council on Archives, 26*(1), 3–18. doi:10.4314/esarjo.v26i1.31012

Khatoon, A. (2020). Blockchain-Based Smart Contract System for Healthcare Management. *Electronics (Basel), 9*(94), 1–23. doi:10.3390/electronics9010094

Lemieux, V. L. (2016). Trusting records: Is Blockchain technology the answer? *Records Management Journal, 26*(2), 110–139. doi:10.1108/RMJ-12-2015-0042

Lemieux, V. L. (2017). *A typology of Blockchain recordkeeping solutions and some reflections on their implications for the future of archival preservation.* Retrieved 26 April, 2020, from https://www.researchgate.net/publication/322511343

Lemieux, V. L. (2019). Blockchain and Public Record Keeping: Of Temples, Prisons, and the (Re) Configuration of Power. *Frontiers in Blockchain, 2*(5), 1–14. doi:10.3389/fbloc.2019.00005

Lemieux, V. L., Hofman, J. D., Batista, D., & Joo, A. (2019). *Blockchain technology and recordkeeping.* Retrieved 26 March, 2020, from http://armaedfoundation.org/wp-content/uploads/2019/06/AIEF-Research-Paper-Blockchain-Technology-Recordkeeping.pdf

Lewis, A. (2015). *A Gentle Introduction to Blockchain Technology.* Retrieved 17 July, 2020, from https://bitsonblocks.net/2015/09/09/gentle-introduction-Blockchain-technology/

Luka, M. (2012). The Impacts of ICTs on Banks: A Case study of the Nigerian Banking Industry. *International Journal of Advanced Computer Science and Applications, 3*(9), 145–149.

Marutha, N. S. (2019). *Using Blockchain technology to interconnect the entire healthcare universe for patients' records sharing.* Paper presented at the School of Arts Triennial Conference, Pretoria, South Africa.

McKemmish, S. (2013). *Record keeping and archiving in the cloud: is there a silver lining?* Retrieved 1 July, 2020, from https://infoz.ffzg.hr/INFuture/2013/papers/1-02%20McKemmish,%20Recordkeeping%20and%20Archiving%20in%20the%20Cloud.pdf

Mnjama, N., & Wamukoya, J. (2007). Egovernment and Records Management: An Assessment Tool for E-records Readiness in Government. *The Electronic Library, 25*(3), 274–284. doi:10.1108/02640470710754797

Moatlhodi, T., & Kalusopa, T. (2016). An Assessment of E-Records Readiness at the Ministry of Labour and Home Affairs, Gaborone, Botswana. Mousaion. *South African Journal of Information Studies, 34*(3), 1–22.

Moloi, J., & Mutula, S. (2007). E-records management records management. *Information Development, 23*(4), 290–306. doi:10.1177/0266666907084765

Mosweu, O. (2014). *Factors affecting the adoption and use of Document Workflow Management System (DWMS) by Action Officers and Records Officers at the Ministry of Trade and Industry in Botswana* (MA Dissertation). University of Botswana, Gaborone.

Mosweu, O. (2016). Critical success factors in electronic document and records management. *ESARBICA Journal, 35,* 1–13.

Mosweu, O., Bwalya, J., & Mutshewa, A. (2017). A probe into the factors for adoption and usage of electronic document and records management records management. *Information Development, 33*(1), 97–110. doi:10.1177/0266666916640593

Mosweu, T., Luthuli, L., & Mosweu, O. (2019). Implications of cloud - computing services in Africa: Achilles heels of the digital era? *South African Journal of Information Management, 21*(1), 1–12. doi:10.4102ajim.v21i1.1069

Mosweu, T. L., & Kenosi, L. (2018). Implementation of the Court Records Management System in the delivery of justice at the Gaborone Magisterial District, Botswana. *Records Management Journal, 28*(3), 234–251. doi:10.1108/RMJ-11-2017-0033

Motsaathebe, L., & Mnjama, N. (2007). The management of High Court records in Botswana. *Records Management Journal, 19*(3), 173–189. doi:10.1108/09565690910999175

Nakamoto, S. (2008). *Bitcoin: A peer-to-peer electronic cash system.* Retrieved 20 July, 2020, from https://bitcoin.org/bitcoin.pdf

National Archives and Records Administration (NARA). (2019). *Blockchain white paper.* Retrieved 2 May, 2020, from: http://www.archives.gov>policy

Nengomasha, C. T., & Chikomba, A. (2018). Status of EDRMS implementation in the public sector in Zimbabwe and Namibia. *Records Management Journal, 28*(3), 252–264. doi:10.1108/RMJ-08-2017-0023

Ngoepe, M. (2009). Organising public records to achieve service delivery: The role of the National Archives and Records Service of South Africa's Functional Subject File Plan in Government Departments. *ESARBICA Journal: Journal of the Eastern and Southern Africa Regional Branch of the International Council on Archives, 28*(1), 41–56. doi:10.4314/esarjo.v28i1.44397

Ngulube, P. (2011). Cost analysis and the effective management of records throughout their life cycle. *Journal of the South African Society of Archivists, 44,* 3–18.

Ngulube, P., & Tafor, V. F. (2006). An overview of the management of public records and archives in the member countries of the East and Southern Africa Regional Branch of the International Council on Archives (ESARBICA). *Journal of the Society of Archivists, 27,* 69–86.

Nkala, G., Ngulube, P., & Mangena, S. (2012). E-Records readiness at the National Archives of Zimbabwe. *Mousaion, 30*(2), 108–116.

Norton Life Lock. (2020). *2019 data breaches: 4 billion records breached so far.* Retrieved 2 May, 2020, from:https://us.norton.com/internetsecurity-emerging-threats-2019-data-breaches.html

Notheisen, B., Hawlitschek, F., & Weinhardt, C. (2017). *Breaking Down the Blockchain Hype - Towards a Blockchain Market Engineering Approach.* Retrieved 18 May 2020, https://www.researchgate.net/publication/317828531

Prasad, D. (2016). *A Study of ICT Use for Service Delivery in the Public Sector of Palau, Samoa, Kiribati and the Solomon Islands.* Retrieved 19 May 2020, from https://www.researchgate.net/publication/314281757

Qiang, Y., Fang, Y., & Gonzalez, J. J. (2012). Managing security risks during new technology adoption. *Computers & Security, 31*, 859–869.

Radif, M., Fan, I. S., & McLaughlin, P. (2016). *Employment Technology Acceptance Model (TAM) to adopt Learning Management System (LMS) in Iraqi Universities.* Paper presented at the 10th annual International Technology, Education and Development Conference, Valencia, Spain. Retrieved 2 May, 2020, from: https://www.researchgate.net/publication/298953343_EMPLOYMENT_TECHNOLOGY_ACCEPTANCE_MODEL_TAM

Rakemane, D., & Serema, B. C. (2018). Electronic records management practices at the Companies and Intellectual Property Authority in Gaborone, Botswana. *Journal of the South African Society of Archivists, 51*, 148–169.

Reader, S. (2018). *Self-learning: why it's essential for you in the 21st Century.* Retrieved 6 May, 2020, from: https://medium.com/wondr-blog/self-learning-why-its-essential-for-us-in-the-21st-century-9e9729abc4b8

Rogers, E. M. (2003). *Diffusion of innovations* (5th ed.). Free Press.

Sadhya, V., & Sadhya, H. (2018), Barriers to Adoption of Blockchain Technology. *Twenty-fourth Americas Conference on Information Systems*, New Orleans.

Shonhe, L., & Grand, B. (2019). Implementation of electronic records electronic records. *Records Management Journal, 30*(1), 43–62. doi:10.1108/RMJ-03-2019-0013

Sigauke, D. T., & Nengomasha, C. (2012), *Challenges and prospects facing the digitization of historical records for their preservation within the national archives of Zimbabwe.* Paper presented at the 2nd International Conference on African Digital libraries and Archives (ICADLA-2), University of Witwatersrand, Johannesburg, South Africa. Retrieved 16 April, 2020, from https://core.ac.uk/download/pdf/39670341.pdf

Sigauke, D. T., Nengomasha, C., & Chabikwa, S. (2016). Management of email as electronic records in state universities in Zimbabwe: Findings and implications for the National Archives of Zimbabwe. *ESARBICA Journal, 35*, 14–29.

Tornatzky, L. G., & Fleischer, M. (1990). *The processes of technological innovation.* Academic Press.

Totolo, A. (2007), *Information Technology Adoption by Principals in Botswana Secondary Schools.* Retrieved 30 April, 2020, from https://www.researchgate.net/publication/242407711_Information_Technology_Adoption_by_Principals_in_Botswana_Secondary_Schools

Turnbaugh, R. C. (1997). Information Technology, Records, and State Archives. *The American Archivist, 60*(2), 184–200. doi:10.17723/aarc.60.2.e6247tm502671537

UNESCO. (2003). *Internet in education.* Retrieved 3 May, 2020, from https://iite.unesco.org/pics/publications/en/files/3214612.pdf

Venkatesh, V., Morris, M. G., Davis, G. B., & Davis, F. D. (2003). *User Acceptance of Information Technology: Toward a Unified View.* Retrieved 16 April 2020, from https://www.researchgate.net/publication/220259897

Wamboye, E., Tochkov, K., & Sergi, B. S. (2015). Technology adoption and growth in sub-Saharan African countries. *Comparative Economic Studies, 57*(1), 136–167. doi:10.1057/ces.2014.38

Yoo, S. (2017). Blockchain based financial case analysis and its implications. *Asia Pacific Journal of Innovation and Entrepreneurship., 11*(3), 312–321. doi:10.1108/APJIE-12-2017-036

Zhiliang, D., Yongjun, R., Yepeng, L., Xiang, Y., Zixuan, S., & Hye-Jin, K. (2019). *Blockchain-Based Trusted Electronic Records Preservation in Cloud Storage.* Retrieved 16 July 2020, from https://vntechindia.com/wp-content/uploads/2020/04/004.pdf

ADDITIONAL READING

Bhatia, S., & de Hernandez, A. W. (2019). Blockchain is already here. What does that mean for records management and archives? *Journal of Archival Organization, 16*(1), 75–84. doi:10.1080/15332748.2019.1655614

Body, A. (2018), Blockchain: how to choose the right tech for your business. Retrieved 13 July, 2020, from https://medium.com/@abody/Blockchain-how-to-choose-the-right-tech-for-your-business-aa4597d7ee7c

Bwalya, K. (2019). *Relevance of archives in Fourth Industrial Revolution – redefining the terrain in the era of artificial intelligence and dynamic information governance.* Paper presented at the 2019 South African Society of Archivists, Johannesburg, South Africa.

Collomosse, J., Bui, T., Brown, A., Sheridan, J., Green, A., Bell, M., Fawcett, J and Higgins, J. (2018). *ARCHANGEL: Trusted archives of digital public documents.* Retrieved 30 March, 2020, fromhttps://arxiv.org/pdf/1804.08342.pdf

Connolly, A., & Kick, A. (2015). "What Differentiates Early Organization Adopters of Bitcoin From Non-Adopters?" In: AMCIS 2015 Proceedings. AIS Electronic Library: Association for Information Systems (AIS).

Consensys. (2018), *Blockchain Basics.* A Curated Collection. ConsenSys Academy

Day, M. S. (2019), "The shutdown problem: how does a Blockchain system end?", available at: arXiv: 1902.07254

Dhillon, V., Metcalf, D., & Hooper, M. (2017). *Blockchain Enabled Applications: Understand the Blockchain Ecosystem and How to make it Work for You.* Apress. doi:10.1007/978-1-4842-3081-7

Dollar, C. (1993). Archivists and Records Managers in the Information Age. *Archivaria, 36,* 37–52.

Fincham, J. E. (2008). Response Rates and Responsiveness for Surveys, Standards, and the Journal. *American Journal of Pharmaceutical Education, 72*(2), 1–3. doi:10.5688/aj720243 PMID:18483608

Hofman, D., Lemieux, V. L., Joo, A., & Batista, D. A. (2019). The margin between the edge of the world and infinite possibility': Blockchain, GDPR and information governance. *Records Management Journal, 29*(1/2), 240–257. doi:10.1108/RMJ-12-2018-0045

ICA. (2010), *Universal Declaration on Archives*. Retrieved 6 May, 2020, from https://www.ica.org/en/universal-declaration-archives

Mearian, L. (2018). The Blockchain market is hot; here's how to learn the skills for it. *Computerworld*.

Millar, L. (2009), *Understanding the context of electronic records management*. http://www.irmt.org/documents/educ_training/term%20modules/IRMT%20TERM%20Module%201.pdf

Morisse, M. (2015), "Cryptocurrencies and Bitcoin: Charting the Research Landscape." In: AMCIS 2015 Proceedings. AIS Electronic Library: Association for Information Systems (AIS).

Mosweu, O., Bwalya, K. J., & Mutshewa, A. (2016). Examining factors affecting the adoption and usage of document workflow management system (DWMS) using the UTAUT model. *Records Management Journal, 26*(1), 38–67. doi:10.1108/RMJ-03-2015-0012

Motlhasedi, N., & Mnjama, N. (2014). The management of electronic records at the Botswana Training Authority. *Journal of Theology. Religion and Philosophy, 4*(2), 361–382.

Motlhasedi, N. Y. (2012), E-records management at Botswana Training Authority. Masters Dissertation, University of Botswana, Gaborone.

Wattenhofer, R. (2016). *The science of the Blockchain*. Inverted Forest Publishing.

Yaga, D., Mell, P., Roby, N., & Scarfone, K. (2018), "Blockchain technology overview, NISTIR 8202", National Institute of Standards and Technology, available at: https://nvlpubs.nist.gov/nistpubs/ ir/2018/ NIST.IR.8202.pdf

Zyskind, G., Nathan, O., & Pentland, A. (2015). Decentralizing Privacy: Using Blockchain to Protect Personal Data. In *Security and Privacy Workshops (SPW)* (pp. 180–184). IEEE. doi:10.1109/SPW.2015.27

KEY TERMS AND DEFINITIONS

Adoption: Adoption refers to the use of a newly implemented technology. It also means the same as Uptake. Adoption in the context of this chapter refers to the acceptance by individuals or institutions to use Blockchain technology in the management of records and archives in their custody.

Authenticity: This is the concept of accepting a record as a true reflection of what exactly transpired. It refers to the fact that the record has not been tampered with or corrupted, either accidentally or maliciously, and can thus be trusted as evidence of transactions completed.

Blockchain Technology: This refers to the collection of technologies that can be put together to ensure that distributed ledger mechanisms work securely and more efficiently. The identifying factors of Blockchain are that the process is politically decentralised, it does not have an infrastructural point of failure, it offers self-sovereignty and trust, and it is attack resistant.

Cryptocurrencies: These are digital assets designed to work as a medium of exchange wherein individual coin ownership records are stored in a ledger existing in a form of computerized database using strong cryptography to secure transaction records.

Database: A database is an organized collection of data, generally stored and accessed electronically from a computer system. It can also be described as a data structure that stores organized information. Most databases contain multiple tables, which may each include several different fields.

Electronic Records: An electronic record is information recorded by a computer that is produced or received in the initiation, conduct or completion of an agency or individual activity. Examples of electronic records include e-mail messages, word- processed documents, electronic spreadsheets, digital images.

Emerging Technologies: These are technologies whose development, practical applications, or both are still largely unrealized, such that they are figuratively emerging into prominence from a background of nonexistence or obscurity.

Immutable: An immutable record object is one whose state cannot be modified after it is created, except through a 'consensus' mechanism involving all other participants. This implies that a records cannot be altered or deleted once it has been created, unless consensus is achieved.

Industrial Revolution: This refers to a period in which one or more technologies are replaced by other novel technologies in a relatively short period of time. It is an era of accelerated technological progress characterized by new innovations whose rapid application and diffusion typically cause an abrupt change in society.

Integrity: A document has integrity when nothing therein has been altered, added or deleted; it represents exactly what was created by its author. Integrity means that records are complete and authentic.

Records Management: This refers to the management function signifying the management of recorded information arising from the performance of business functions throughout their life cycle i.e. from creation and capture, use, maintenance, and disposal.

Security: It refers to the protection of records against various forms of damage or threats of attacks. These include physical damages, external data breaches, unauthorized alterations and deletions amongst others.

Chapter 4
End–to–End Tracing and Congestion in a Blockchain:
A Supply Chain Use Case in Hyperledger Fabric

Kosala Yapa Bandara

https://orcid.org/0000-0002-3616-7764

National University of Ireland Galway, Ireland

Subhasis Thakur

National University of Ireland Galway, Ireland

John G. Breslin

https://orcid.org/0000-0001-5790-050X

National University of Ireland Galway, Ireland

ABSTRACT

Modern supply chain applications are complex systems that play an important role in many different sectors. Supply chain management systems are implemented to handle increasing complexity and flows of goods. However, most of these systems are also increasing the complexity of providing trust and a global view of transactions in a distributed supply chain system. Blockchain technology introduces a new architectural style to support the traceability and trust of transactions performed by participants in a network. This chapter uses this emerging technology to realize a supply chain use case from JLP Meats in the UK with improved transparency, trust, and end-to-end querying while discussing potential challenges of realizing large-scale enterprise blockchain applications. The process of farm-to-fork is implemented and tested for traceability, item recall, block analysis, congestion enabling food safety, and sustainable agriculture. Potential challenges are highlighted in complex supply chains that need heterogeneous trade compliance and scalability.

DOI: 10.4018/978-1-7998-6650-3.ch004

INTRODUCTION

Supply Chain management is an integration of business processes that are implemented in distributed and heterogeneous systems from end-users to original suppliers (Cooper, Lambert, & Pagh, 1997). Current supply chain management systems have known limitations and the food supply chain is the most complex and fragmented of all supply chains (Martin, 2017). There are many participants involved in a supply chain and they are using distributed and heterogeneous systems increasing the complexity of integration, sharing information, end-to-end tracking, and compliance tracking. Moreover, various systems integrated with a supply chain can be exposed to cyber threats which will result in breaching the integrity of information in the supply chain (Gao, et al., 2018).

Blockchain Technology has emerged as a solution to the double-spending problem that promises traceability, immutability, and transparency of transactions (Nakamoto, 2008). As stated by Consensys (2020), the blockchain technology coupled with smart contracts can enable:

- Transparency of consumer goods from the source point to end consumption
- Accurate asset tracking
- Enhance the licensing of services, products, and software.

The shared IT infrastructure of blockchain can streamline workflows of all participants irrespective of the size of the business network. Moreover, this shared infrastructure enables the auditor greater visibility into the participant's activities along the supply chain.

In the context of supply chain for the food industry, the farm-to-fork food system is a complicated network of isolated systems. There is no widely adopted industry standard regarding how to record and track data for food traceability purposes. Since blockchain technology is emerging as a distributed, trusted, and immutable ledger, it can be used to record transactions in farm-to-fork food systems enabling traceability (Martin, 2017). The number of transactions in a supply chain network is always huge. As an example, Walmart is serving 260 million customers every week across 28 countries in nearly 12,000 stores (Yiannas, 2018). A few of such participants in one blockchain network create millions of transactions and blocks which are continuously growing, challenge the scalability of blockchain networks.

Moreover, product companies in a supply chain network are producing thousands of various types of products before distributing them to their clients. Some of the detail of these transactions is redundant information. For example, thousands of packets of meat are made from one commodity hence only the packet identifier is different. Moreover, most of this information is needed for a certain limited period. Therefore, creating blocks of transactions for these types and have them stored in distributed ledgers of all other participants is a costly process in terms of congestion in the blockchain network and storage. On the other hand, having the same copy of records in all the ledgers support item traceability and auditing. However, end-to-end tracing of items is necessarily required in the modern complex supply chain systems.

The globalisation of the business sector has increased the cross-border movement of commodities and goods, and hence increased the complexity of global supply chains (Martin, 2017). The regulator's role in a blockchain is extremely challenging in current complex supply chains with diverse established old laws, regulations, and institutions distributed in various countries (Kshetri, 2018). Playing a monitoring role as in Gao, et al (2018) is not sufficient since they need to approve or reject transactions providing reasons. Regulators are interested in only the relevant information required for compliance. It is not required for them to know heterogeneous transactions happening in various contexts of regulations.

Current blockchain architecture supports distributed ledgers of the equal state. A regulatory organization to become a participant of all the blockchain networks which need regulatory compliance and maintain ledgers of them is not a practical approach. Hence, the position of a regulatory organization in a blockchain network is still not clear.

The public blockchain frameworks are optimised for transparency hence they create challenges to share private and sensitive information and enable only authorised participants to participate in a supply chain; for example, Bitcoin (Bitcoin, 2020), Ethereum (Ethereum, 2020) and Litecoin (Litecoin, 2020). However, the permissioned blockchain platforms separate transactions into public transactions and private transactions and also enable authorisation, for example, Hyperledger Fabric (Hyperledger, 2020) and Quorum (Quorum, 2020). Hyperledger Fabric has a reliable technology stack to implement supply chain applications compared to other private and permissioned blockchains and that has been highly used for pilots in major organisations such as IBM and Walmart (Kshetri, 2018). Hyperledger Fabric is a modular blockchain framework that supports plug-and-play components that are aimed for use within private enterprises (Kenton, 2020). However, most of these pilots are focussing on end-to-end tracing and still need to elaborate on other challenges such as item recall, blockchain congestion, data redundancy, scalability, regulatory compliance, etc.

In this chapter, the authors discuss a supply chain use case implemented in Hyperledger Fabric (Hyperledger, 2020) for JLP Meats (JLP Meats, 2020) in the UK. Authors have selected Hyperledger Fabric framework because of its promise in developing supply chain applications, modular architecture which supports plug-and-play components required for private enterprises, and reliable technology stack for development and testing. Authors elaborate on the use case for end-to-end tracing, item recall, blockchain congestion, data redundancy, scalability, and position of a regulatory organization in a large scale blockchain network.

The organisation of this chapter is as follows: There are five main sections. Firstly, the authors discuss related work in the literature. Then, the authors discuss end-to-end tracing, blockchain congestion, and regulator's position in a blockchain. In the next section, this chapter describes a use case of JLP Meats, a wholesale meat distributer in London, UK. The fourth section of the chapter describes the design, implementation, and testing using Hyperledger Fabric to elaborate end-to-end tracing, item recall, and congestion analysis. Finally, the chapter summarises the contribution and highlights the future work and directions.

RELATED WORK

In this section, the authors review related work in blockchain technology and supply chain management systems for security, privacy, traceability, item recall, and transaction congestion.

Supply chain management is an integration of business processes that are implemented in distributed and heterogeneous systems from end-users to original suppliers (Cooper, Lambert, & Pagh, 1997). The participants in a large supply chain are generally operating in so many countries under various constraints and legislations. Besides, the food supply chains are trying to provide a more diverse, convenient, and economical source of food while facing enormous new challenges. Moreover, in today's food supply system, the output from one ingredient producer could end up in thousands of new products on a grocery store shelf (Yiannas, 2018). This distributed behaviour and the complexity of food supply chains becomes more complicated when also taking necessary actions for food contamination concerns such as the peanut butter Salmonella outbreak[1] in 2008, the E. coli. illness caused by contaminated flour[2] in 2016, Outbreak of E. coli. infections linked to clover sprouts[3] in 2020, etc. The food supply chain also suffers dynamic costs, prices, and regulatory compliance.

There is no widely adopted industry standard for how each segment of the food supply chain (farmer, processor, distributor, retailer, etc.) tracks and records data for food traceability purposes (Yiannas, 2018). Most of the participants are still recording their data on paper or their legacy systems which do not enable necessary mapping records and communications needed for detailed traceability and transparency. Moreover, current supply chain applications suffer from the integration of isolated systems and security breaches regarding the integrity of transactions. Radio-frequency identification (RFID), telematics, barcode and 2D codes, sensors-enabled technologies, Internet of Things(IoT), and numerous other technologies are used for tracking products through supply chains (Davor & Domagoj, 2018). However, the true potential of tracking data is not fully exploited as the underlying data is available only within companies or partially connected isolated systems. The communication between systems and the lack of trust between the segments of the systems are the main concerns in the current supply chain systems. The supply chain-related sustainability incidents suggest that firms with a global presence struggle to improve environmental, social, and economic outcomes in global supply chains (Esteban Koberg, 2018). The firms should be accountable for the environmental, social, and economic outcomes caused by their internal and supplier operations.

On the other hand, blockchain technology has emerged as a solution to the double-spending problem that promises traceability, immutability, and transparency of transactions (Nakamoto, 2008). The blockchain technology has evolved from cryptocurrency transactions and disrupts constantly enlarging areas of the economy (Davor & Domagoj, 2018). This technology can provide improved traceability, transparency, and tradability for supply chain systems (Consensys, 2020). Thus, blockchain and distributed ledger technologies are becoming increasingly popular in the supply chain applications domain (Martin, 2017). The blockchain technology promises overpowering trust issues and allows a secure and authenticated system for logistics and supply chains. This lead to revolutionise supply chain systems using blockchain technology. Pilot projects already exist within big organisations; for example, the farm-to-fork[4] process can adopt IoT and blockchain technologies to improve control and flexibility while increasing food trust and brand protection.

Siemens merges its Mindsphere platform, private track and trace repositories, and blockchain management applications to implement track and trace use cases as shown in Figure. 1 (Siemens, 2019). These solutions use the blockchain technology to implement trust throughout the process. This framework allows companies to limit information viewing privileges hence sensitive information can be kept behind closed doors while exposing only critical information to other members of the supply chain. This platform further enables leveraging IoT and blockchain for a "digital twin" (Meyvaert, 2020). A digital twin in IoT is a virtual representation of a physical product or process, used to understand and predict the physical counterpart's performance characteristics (Meyvaert, 2020). Digital twins are used throughout the product lifecycle and blockchain enables them to record all the information in immutable records.

Figure 1. Siemens Mindsphere for Supply Chains

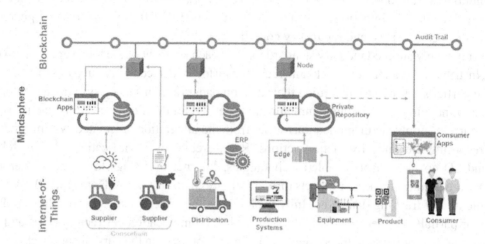

Blockchain technology can enable the creation of a decentralised, distributed, and trusted digital ledger that can be used to record transactions from multiple entities across a complex network (Yiannas, 2018). Data immutability and public accessibility of data streams can support compliance, reliability, and transparency of modern supply chain systems (Perboli, Musso, & Rosano, 2018). A supply chain as a blockchain, is a two-step block construction mechanism as suggested by Gao et al. (2018) classifies participants as ordinary users, third-party users, and supporting entities with different roles. In their approach, regulatory organizations are focusing on monitoring information. A monitoring agent to monitor and analyse blockchain transactions, nodes, blocks, and smart contracts to ensure blockchains operate legally, efficiently, and reliably are discussed in (Ko, Lee, Jeong, & Hong, 2018).

Authors in (Kshetri, 2018) summarize a set of successful use cases of blockchain implementations including: Danish shipping company Maersk (a blockchain application for international logistics), Provenance (a pilot project in Indonesia to enable the traceability in the fishing industry), Alibaba (a blockchain to fight for food fraud), Walmart (tracking produce from Latin America to the US, and Intel's solution to track seafood supply chain, etc.

Traceability in a supply chain is an important area to explore (Westerkamp, Victor, & Küpper, 2018). In the current blockchain architectures, distributed ledgers provide transaction information accessible to all the participants in the blockchain network providing greater transparency (Zheng, Xie, Dai, Chen, & Wang, 2017). However, organizations are reluctant to expose sensitive information in a public ledger, and hence private data collections are introduced by Benhamouda, Halevi & Halevi (2018) to manage sensitive information. Privacy, scalability, and lack of governance are still major concerns for large scale industrial adaptation of blockchain paradigms (Li, Sforzin, Fedorov, & Karame, 2017).

The public (permissionless) blockchain platforms are optimised for transparency, and transactions are public and transparent, for example, Bitcoin (Bitcoin, 2020), Ethereum (Ethereum, 2020), and Litecoin (Litecoin, 2020). However, the permissioned blockchain platforms separate transactions into public transactions and private transactions, for example, Hyperledger Fabric (Hyperledger, 2020) and Quorum (Quorum, 2020). The private transactions share private and sensitive data between participants in a network (Hyperledger2, 2020).

Ethereum is a secure decentralised ledger that is optimized for transparency, hence it is difficult to share secrets on the platform (Ethereum, 2020). The main components of Ethereum are Ethereum Virtual Machine (EVM), miner, block, transaction, consensus algorithm, account, smart contract, mining, Ether, and gas (Modi, 2018). These are illustrated in Figure. 2. The notion of private transactions and public transactions are introduced in Quorum (Quorum, 2020) which extends the transaction model of Ethereum to include an optional privateFor parameter and a new IsPrivate method to deal with such transactions.

Figure 2. Components of Ethereum

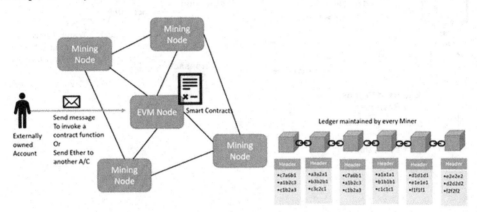

On the other hand, Hyperledger Fabric introduces private data collections, which allow a defined subset of organizations on a channel the ability to endorse, commit, or query the private data (Hyperledger2, 2020). The private data is sent peer-to-peer via gossip protocol to only the organisations authorised to see it. The ordering service is not involved here and the orderer does not see the private data. The hash of the private data is endorsed, ordered, and written to the ledgers of every peer on the channel as in Figure. 3 (Hyperledger2, 2020).

Figure 3. Private Data Store in Hyperledger Fabric

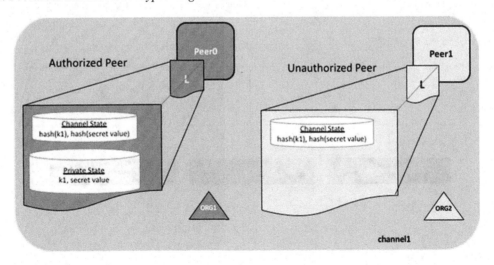

Figure 4. Transactions Invocation in Hyperledger Fabric

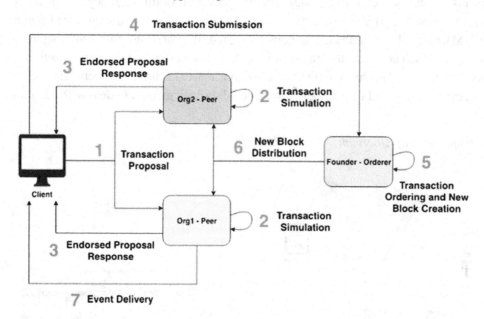

Figure 5. Hyperledger Fabric and Composer Technology Stack

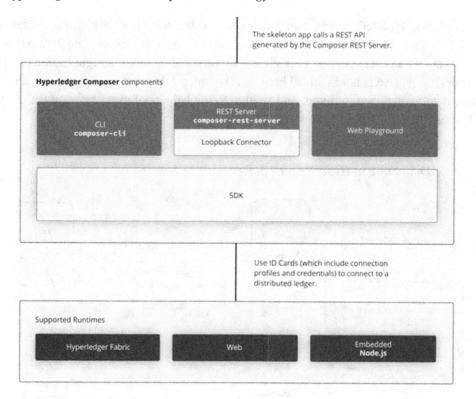

The hashes of private data go through the orderer to the public ledger and preserve privacy. The hash can be used for state validation and audit purposes. The flow of transactions invocation in Hyperledger Fabric is illustrated in Figure. 4 (Thummavet, 2020).

The Hyperledger fabric technology stack for blockchain applications is presented in Figure. 5 (Composer, 2020).

The technology stack in Figure. 5 enables architects and developers to quickly create "full-stack" blockchain solutions: for example, business logic that runs on the blockchain, REST APIs that expose the blockchain logic to the web or mobile applications, blockchain integration with existing systems, etc. (Composer, 2020). Hyperledger composer has been designed to support pluggable runtimes. The modular architecture of Hyperledger fabric separates the transaction processing workflow into three different processes: smart contracts called chaincode that comprises the distributed logic processing and agreement of the system, transaction ordering, and transaction validation and commitment (Kenton, 2020).

END-TO-END TRACING AND CONGESTION

Blockchain stores data chronologically in blocks that are chained together in a continuously growing series. Participants in the network are contributing to commit transactions and blocks into the blockchain. Adding blocks to a blockchain cannot be predicted and blocks are not sequenced based on transactions. However, all the distributed ledgers have the same state enabling reliable access and supporting end-to-end traceability of records from one ledger.

Figure 6. Transactions and Blocks in a Blockchain

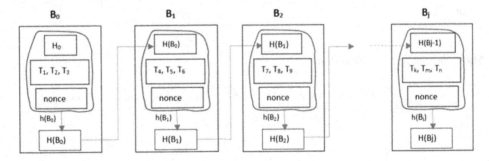

Figure. 6 illustrates a blockchain where B_0 to B_j are constituent blocks in the blockchain. $H(B_0)$ to $H(B_j)$ are hash keys of blocks. T_1 to T_k, T_m, T_n are transactions. k, m, n are Integers. h () is the hash function. Here, the authors assume a block is created including three transactions. Blockchain grows continuously based on the transactions created by the participants in the network. Participants will transact based on their own needs and blocks are added to the continuously growing blockchain. Transaction information retrieval is a challenge because there is no relationship between transactions. For example, item traceability needs all the transactions related to one item, auditing needs to audit a set of transactions, etc. However, different blockchain platforms provide various methods to retrieve transaction information. Hyperledger Fabric has the composer-rest-server which provides REST endpoints for each asset.

Figure. 7 shows participants P1...P6 and transactions T01 ...T04 and T11 ... T14. In a supply chain application, P1 to P6 can be considered as, commodity providers, logistic companies, importers, and retailers respectively.

Figure 7. Sequence of transactions in a blockchain

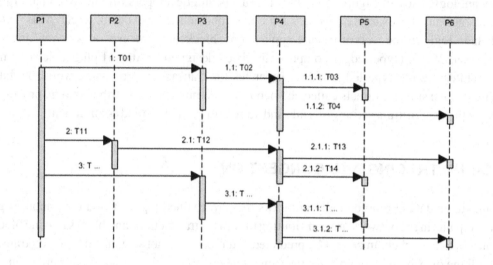

Commodity provider provides commodities continuously of various types through logistic companies to the importer company who will produce batches of products from the commodities and supply them to clients. Participants in the blockchain network contribute to add blocks to the blockchain network as shown in Figure. 8.

Figure 8. State change in the blockchain

The end-users finding end-to-end details about a product, that involves a set of transactions distributed in randomly distributed blocks in a blockchain, are not straightforward in the current blockchain architecture. Though blocks are connected using block hash mechanism, the chain concept and random blocks integration make it complicated to find the evolution of an item in a supply chain. However, the decentralized nature of records and having the same copy of up-to-date ledger allow participants to directly interact with end-to-end details of data.

The authors have created a REST-API which is creating REST endpoints to members on the blockchain, asserts, user-defined queries, and transactions in the blockchain. Queries are defined to extract necessary information from the ledger. Representational state of these resources can be extracted, filtered, and connected to find end-to-end details. The processes should be defined accordingly.

Blockchain Congestion

In supply chain applications, end-user products have gone through a list of transactions in the process of transforming resources to end-user products. There are intermediate participants in the blockchain network who develop the main resource into various products and distribute them to clients. These scenarios will add millions of records to the blockchain. This leads to several challenges regarding block congestion in the blockchain network and data redundancy at the participants. All the transactions happening in the product life cycle are not equally important to all the participants in the blockchain network, hence a compensation model for transaction verification is needed. As in Figure. 7, P4 makes different products from the main resource and distributes them to P5 and P6.

$$(T_{01}, T_{02}) \rightarrow (T_1 \ldots T_{n1}), (T_{n1} \ldots T_{n2}), (T_{n2} \ldots T_{n3}), \ldots\ldots \text{ where } n1, n2, n3 \in \mathbb{Z}$$
$$(T_{11}, T_{12}) \rightarrow (T_{11} \ldots T_{m1}), (T_{m1} \ldots T_{m2}), (T_{m2} \ldots T_{m3}), \ldots \text{ where } m1, m2, m3 \in \mathbb{Z}$$
$$(T_{\ldots}) \rightarrow (T_{21} \ldots T_{k1}), (T_{k1} \ldots T_{k2}), (T_{k2} \ldots T_{k3}), \ldots\ldots\ldots \text{ where } k1, k2, k3 \in \mathbb{Z}$$

At P4, transactions T_{01} and T_{02} result in creating sets of transactions based on product creation and requirements of clients. The same will apply to T_{11}, T_{12} and $T_{\ldots}$. If there are several intermediate participants of the type P4 who develop sub-products, this will add millions of records to the blockchain developing real-time congestion in the blockchain network. Moreover, this will add redundant data to the blockchain. This is a continuously growing real-time overhead which brings a negative impact to the scalability of blockchain networks. Managing temporal data to reduce transaction redundancy and transaction verification for supply chain applications still need major developments. IoT devices are integrated with supply chains and they generate millions of records throughout the supply chain. Ad hoc solutions can be adopted to manage these records, for example, Hyperledger Fabric support plug-and-play local data stores to record the IoT data, and only the hashes of sets of data are recorded in the blockchain. IoT integration to supply chains is a common scenario, hence new standards are necessary for blockchain integration with IoT.

Moreover, the supply chain applications need to comply with regulations set up in various territories. Regulatory organisations in various territories are interested in only a specific set of information regarding supply chain transactions for compliance checking. In the current blockchain architecture, participants will maintain the complete blockchain hence regulator's role as a participant in the blockchain network is not practical. So far, none of the blockchain architectures provide necessary standards to position regulators in blockchains.

As shown in Figure. 9, the authors propose a private channel for regulatory organizations to connect with only the required participants for compliance checking. Referring to Figure. 9, ORG 1 to 4 and ORG 1 to 3 are connected in two blockchain networks. REG ORG has a private channel connecting ORG3 and ORG 2 of two different blockchain networks. Regulatory organizations in various territories can become authorized members of this private channel and that eases quick validation of supply chain transactions without long delays as in the current system. This can further support transparent compliance checking for anyone who needs to send items through a supply chain. This topic area needs further elaboration because there are no proper standards or mature products so far, to fast track regulatory compliance and blockchain technology has shown a lot of promise in this area.

Figure 9. Regulatory organization in blockchains

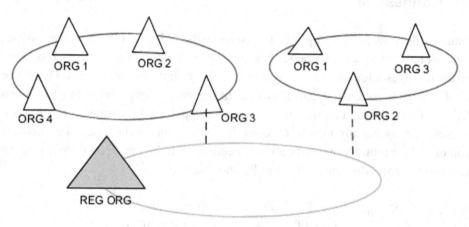

In our proposed architecture, transactions that need regulatory compliance will be directed to the regulatory organization, and distributed ledgers are updated with the blocks of approved or rejected transactions. A block of approved or rejected transactions are kept in the regulator data store as *{hash(block), block}*. The hash of the block is recorded on the blockchain. In this approach, regulators do not need to keep unnecessary records and they only keep records of their processed records (approved or rejected records). Future applications can use this recorded data. For example, since these blocks have necessary hash keys on the blockchain, audit trails can be done connecting to a ledger of a participant in the network.

USE CASE

JLP Meats Trading organization (JLP Meets, 2020) imports meat from Australia, South America, and Europe, and sells in the UK. Their customers are restaurants, retail shops, and butchers in the UK. JLP Meats produces hundreds of tailor-made meat products and distributes them to customers. An abstract view of the farm-to-fork process is illustrated in Figure. 10. The authors have implemented a blockchain solution using Hyperledger Fabric to illustrate end-to-end tracing, item recall, transaction congestion, etc.

Figure 10. Use Case of JLP Meats, London

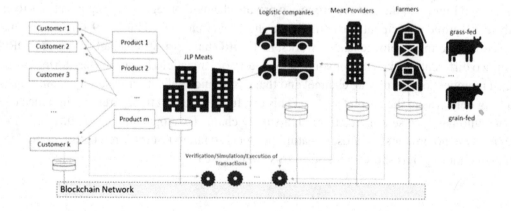

For the illustration purposes, authors considered a specific scenario as follows. Farmer Samex uses the logistic company Sandford group to export beef of the type grass-fed and grain-fed to JLP Meats in the UK. JLP Meats transforms beef into packets of 300 to 500 grams and supply them to their customers ASDA and TESCO stores. A buyer who buys a packet of beef from TESCO (or ASDA) wants to find end-to-end details about the product. Here, a typical set of ttransactions can be modelled as shown in Figure. 11.

Figure 11. Transactions in the Use Case scenario

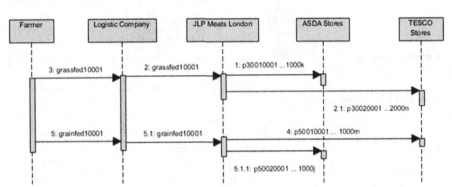

JLP Meats supplies various types of products that create thousands of transactions improving transaction congestion in the blockchain. Transactions verification is done by permitted verifiers in the network and this process should be compensated. However, this chapter does not cover the compensation process; and the quality control is governed by regulators. This chapter proposes a private channel network of regulators who can connect to blockchain networks to perform regulatory activities and necessary endorsements as illustrated in Figure. 9.

DESIGN, IMPLEMENTATION AND TESTING

The authors use a public and permissioned blockchain so that ledgers are decentralized, and a selected set of nodes participates in consensus procedure. The authors have implemented the above use case using Hyperledger Fabric[5], Composer Playground, Hyperledger Explorer, and Docker on Ubuntu 18.04.

The high-level architecture for the proposed solution using Hyperledger Fabric is illustrated in Figure. 12.

The peers are members of the blockchain network. The business network was developed and installed in the above peers and a REST-API[6] was created to perform end-to-end tracing of items. Hyperledger composer playground was used to implement and test scenarios and Hyperledger blockchain explorer was used to visualize blockchain statistics. Swagger[7] was used to visualise and test REST endpoints. The trading transaction for packets of meat was defined as in Figure. 13. The peers can be authorised miners or participants to mine supply chain transactions and a compensation model should be introduced for transaction verifications. However, there are no proper standards or miners available so far to mine supply chain transactions. These necessary developments can further revolutionise future supply chain systems.

Figure 12. The High-level Architecture Based on Hyperledger Fabric

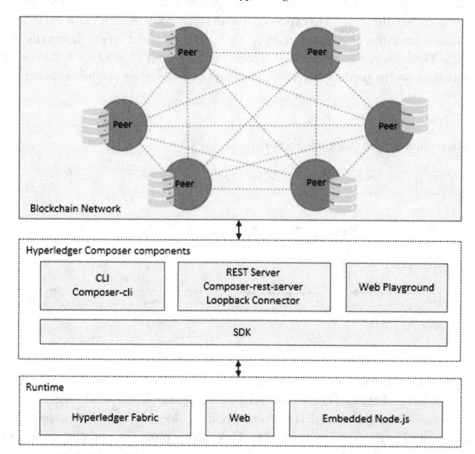

Figure 13. Trading Transaction for Packets

```
/**
 * Track the trade of a packet from one trader to another
 * @param (org.jlp.trading.TradePacket) trade - the trade to be processed
 * @transaction
 */
async function tradePacket(trade) { // eslint-disable-line no-unused-vars

    // set the new owner of the packet
    trade.packet.owner = trade.newOwner;
    const assetRegistry = await getAssetRegistry('org.jlp.trading.Packet');

    // emit a notification that a trade has occurred
    const tradePacketNotification = getFactory().newEvent('org.jlp.trading', 'TradePacketNotification');
    tradePacketNotification.packet = trade.packet;
    emit(tradePacketNotification);

    // persist the state of the packet
    await assetRegistry.update(trade.packet);
}
```

Referring to Figure. 13, the trading transaction has three main functionalities: setting the ownership for a packet of meat, emitting a notification that a trade has occurred, and persisting the state of the packet of meat. These are mostly common functionalities for trading transactions. The trading transaction for a commodity is defined in Figure. 14.

Figure 14. Trading Transaction for Commodities

```
/**
 * Track the trade of a commodity from one trader to another
 * @param {org.jlp.trading.Trade} trade - the trade to be processed
 * @transaction
 */
async function tradeCommodity(trade) { // eslint-disable-line no-unused-vars

    // set the new owner of the commodity
    trade.commodity.owner = trade.newOwner;
    const assetRegistry = await getAssetRegistry('org.jlp.trading.Commodity');

    // emit a notification that a trade has occurred
    const tradeNotification = getFactory().newEvent('org.jlp.trading', 'TradeNotification');
    tradeNotification.commodity = trade.commodity;
    emit(tradeNotification);

    // persist the state of the commodity
    await assetRegistry.update(trade.commodity);
}
```

End-to-End Tracing

Tracing end-to-end details were achieved using REST endpoints. These endpoints and their outcomes to achieve details of a packet, the commodity and its trader are detailed as follows:

```
http://localhost:3000/api/Packet/p3001001:
{
 "$class": "org.jlp.trading.Packet",
 "packetID": "p3001001",
 "mainExchange": "GBP",
 "quantity": 300,
 "unitprice": 2,
 "commodity": "resource:org.jlp.trading.Commodity#grassfedbeef",
 "owner": "resource:org.jlp.trading.Trade#tesco"
}
http://localhost:3000/api/Commodity/grassfedbeef:
{
 "$class":"org.jlp.trading.Commodity",
 "tradingSymbol": "grassfedbeef",
 "description": "Grassfed Beef",
 "mainExchange": "AUD",
 "slaughterDates": "20th December",
```

```
 "quantity": 500,
 "owner": "resource:org.jlp.trading.Trader#jlp"
}
http://localhost:3000/api/Trader/jlp:
{
 "$class":"org.jlp.trading.Trader",
 "tradeId": "jlp",
 "name":"JLP Meat",
 "address": "London"
}
```

The authors developed queries to retrieve information and deployed them as REST endpoints. The following REST endpoints output transaction details regarding trading commodities and farmer details. The endpoint to retrieve farmer details is a query-based REST endpoint.

```
http://localhost:3000/api/Trade:
{"$class": "org.hyperledger.composer.system.AddAsset",
"resource":[
        {
            "$class": "org.jlp.trading.Commodity",
            "tradingSymbol": "grassfedbeef",
            "description": "Grassfed Beef",
            "mainExchange": "AUD",
            "slaughterDates": "20th December",
            "quantity": 500,
            "owner": "resource:org.jlp.trading.Trader#samex"
}
]}
http://localhost:3000/api/queries/findAddAssertsTradeTransactions:
{
 "Packet id": "p3001001",
 "Type of Beef": "grass-fed beef",
 "Trader": "JLP Meats",
 "Logistic company used": "Sandford",
 "Farmer name": "Samex",
 "Slaughtered Date": "20th December"
}
```

The authors extracted the above details using REST endpoints and arranged them in a process to generate end-to-end details about a specific packet. That is, developers' intervention is needed to develop workflows connecting the endpoints to filter and provide requested information. This requested information can be a simple user request or a complex audit trail. However, this process enables users, participants and regulatory organisations to view end-to-end details, for example, farmers to get to know where their meat is being sold, some fair trade organisations to view records and ensure fair trade policies are properly applied, organisations to review statistics to ensure sustainable agriculture, etc.

Item Recall

In supply chain applications, it is necessary to quickly trace unsafe products back to their source and where they have been distributed.

In this implementation, the REST endpoint, *http://localhost:3000/api/Packet/p3001001* provides details of the packet p3001001.

```
{
"$class":" org.jlp.trading.Package",
"packetID": "p3001001",
"mainExchange": "GBP",
"quantity": 300,
"unitprice": 2,
"commodity": "resource.org.jlp.trading.Commodity#grassfed10001",
"owner": "resource.jlp.trading.Trade#tesco"
}
```

Finding all the packets made from the commodity "grassfed10001" can be extracted using the following REST endpoint and the filter *http://localhost:3000/api/Packet*

```
where ":{"commodity":"resource:org.jlp.trading.Commodity#grassfed10001"}}.
[
{
 "$class": "org.jlp.trading.Packet",
 "packetID": "p3001001",
 "mainExchange": "GBP",
 "quantity": 300,
 "unitprice": 2,
 "commodity": "resource:org.jlp.trading.Commodity#grassfed10001",
 "owner": "resource:org.jlp.trading.Trade#tesco"
},
{
"$class": "org.jlp.trading.Packet",
 "packetID": "p3001002",
 "mainExchange": "GBP",
 "quantity": 300,
 "unitprice": 2,
 "commodity": "resource:org.jlp.trading.Commodity#grassfed10001",
 "owner": "resource:org.jlp.trading.Trader#tesco"
},
{
 "$class": "org.jlp.trading.Packet",
 "packetID": "p3001003",
 "mainExchange": "GBP",
```

```
"quantity": 300,
"unitprice": 2,
"commodity": "resource:org.jlp.trading.Commodity#grassfed10001",
"owner": "resource:org.jlp.trading.Trade#jlp"
},
{
"$class": "org.jlp.trading.Packet",
"packetID": "p3001005",
"mainExchange": "GBP",
"quantity": 300,
"unitprice": 2,
"commodity": "resource:org.jlp.trading.Commodity#grassfed10001",
"owner": "resource:org.jlp.trading.Trader#asda"
}
]
```

Similarly, farmer and transport details of the commodity can also be found. The recall of items can be processed accordingly for the selected commodities. It is not necessary to recall all the packets provided by JLP or the farmer. This approach helps faster recall of all the items from clients and stores stopping further damage in terms of health and finance. The necessary workflows can be developed to expand as needed.

Blocks in Channels

Peer channel commands[8] implemented in Hyperledger Fabric were used to explore blocks and channels in the blockchain network. In this use case implementation, CLI command *"docker exec -it cli bash"* and *"peer channel getinfo -c mychannel"* were used to connect to a peer and extract blockchain information.

Blockchain info: {"height":37,"currentBlockHash":"avhlBTkndEjbj7GixWkvB9kC7RawTzhKmHh Cy7gXHuQ=","previousBlockHash":"+d+lYUBQzoWOXIn/wCRkI7uSAAcCd1Evloyzyau4jGM="}

Figure 15. Details of Block 16

The CLI command *"peer channel fetch 16 -c mychannel"* and *"configtxlator proto_decode --input mychannel_16.block --type common.Block"* enables fetching block 16, decoding, and extracting block information. All inside details of a block (data, payload, actions, creator, nonce, mspid, endorsements, signature, endorser, chain code details, channel details, data hash, previous hash, metadata, etc.) were extracted in this approach as in Figure. 15.

Congestion Analysis

Figure. 16 illustrates transactions in an 8-member blockchain network for 6 imports from the farmer. The authors computed a congestion analysis for a blockchain environment of 8 participants (p1 to p8 – p1: farmer, p2: logistic company, p3: logistic company, p4: JLP meats, p5 to p6 are clients) and 6 imports as illustrated in 6 series. Here, p4 is JLP Meats that creates thousands of products from commodities.

There are more than one P4 type participants in most of the supply chains and that leads to creating transaction congestion on blockchains and delays transaction verification. That is, future blockchain-based supply chain systems should have methods and standards to manage transaction congestion. For example, keeping redundant information locally while recording the hash of this information on the blockchain to assure trust. However, the private channels, local data stores, and plug-and-play modular architecture of Hyperledger Fabric can be improved to develop necessary solutions.

Figure 16. Congestion analysis for 6 imports in the 8-member blockchain network

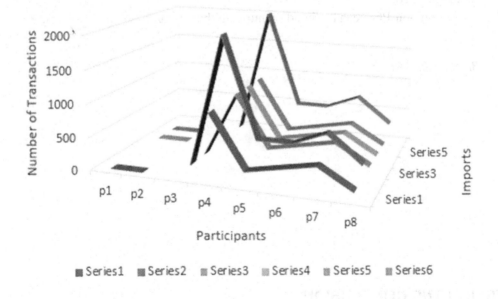

Figure. 17 illustrates a set of transactions for each import. The ordering service in Hyperledger Fabric is managing adding blocks to the blockchain network. P4 is an intermediate participant who creates thousands of products from imports. Having several such participants in a single blockchain network generates many records per import and increases the congestion in the blockchain.

Figure 17. Number of Transactions for Imports

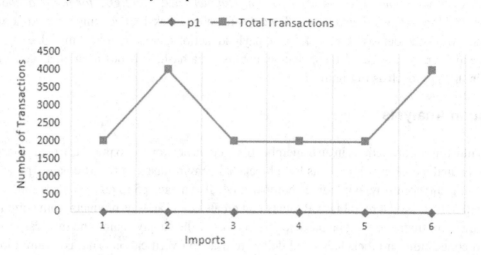

In supply chain applications, the regulator plays the role of checking regulations regarding various types of imports/exports, approving imports/exports, and keeping only the necessary records of them. The regulator cannot maintain ledgers of all the transactions and this proposed approach helps regulators to stay transparent to all other necessary blockchain networks. Moreover, the authors used blockchain explorer to visualize block statistics such as number, block hash, and previous hash as in Figure. 18, Figure. 19, and Figure. 20.

The source code of our POC can be found on https://github.com/kosalayb/JLPMeats.

Figure 18. Blockchain Details

Block Number	Channel Name	Number of Tx	Data Hash	Block Hash	Previous Hash	Transactions
19	mychannel	1	9c7b0f...	e5601c...	7c44b2...	e3866f...
18	mychannel	1	50fta2...	7c44b2...	5795c3...	82bcbc...
17	mychannel	1	c15e43...	5795c3...	8f9128...	18c32b...
16	mychannel	1	8bc5ef...	8f9128...	2aa8cc...	027234...
15	mychannel	1	c40a71...	2aa8cc...	d1637d...	67578f...

DISCUSSION AND CONCLUSION

Blockchain Technology is a potential technology to realize complex supply chain applications because of its nature of immutable and distributed ledgers which help to ease traceability and ensure the trust of heterogeneous transactions. Traceability and trust of transactions are extremely important in supply chain applications. Most of the pilot studies presented in the literature discuss traceability and they do not discuss in detail transaction verifications, congestion, regulatory compliance, and necessary standards.

Figure 19. Block Details

Block Details	
Channel name:	mychannel
Block Number	19
Created at	2019-02-15T14:31:50.559Z
Number of Transactions	1
Block Hash	c5601c309d2ad2fe5c6a3a396b05baed3f8e93712f68fe5124e8c3ed1bf39f0f
Data Hash	9c7b0faae5d33ab808ac1e6110e17b0365f880d07227a73b405cab688dd6d468
Prehash	7c44b2fc000ac8abe5795ed767ec17632ebb77a7629673b6f572bcafc6044597

Figure 20. Transaction Details

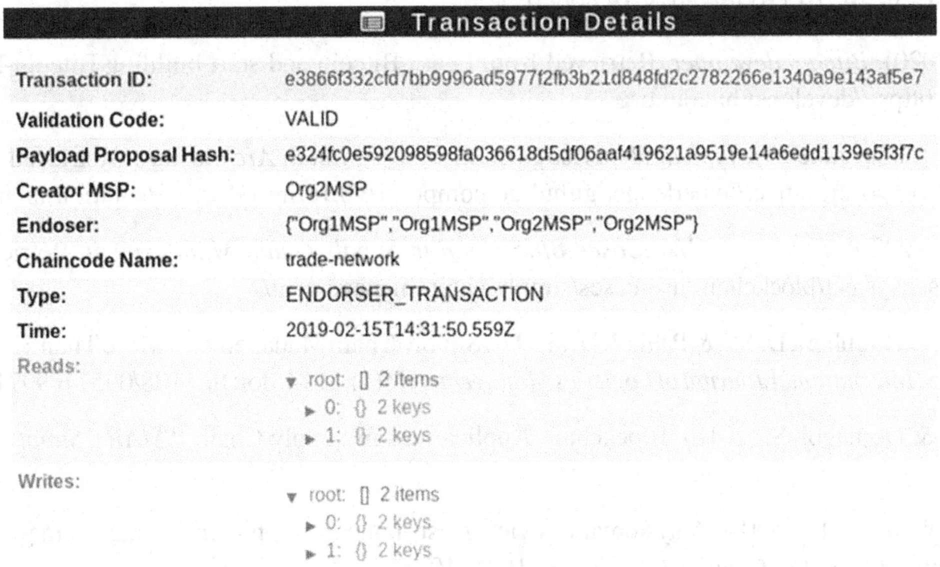

Transaction Details	
Transaction ID:	e3866f332cfd7bb9996ad5977f2fb3b21d848fd2c2782266e1340a9e143af5e7
Validation Code:	VALID
Payload Proposal Hash:	e324fc0e592098598fa036618d5df06aaf419621a9519e14a6edd1139e5f3f7c
Creator MSP:	Org2MSP
Endoser:	{"Org1MSP","Org1MSP","Org2MSP","Org2MSP"}
Chaincode Name:	trade-network
Type:	ENDORSER_TRANSACTION
Time:	2019-02-15T14:31:50.559Z
Reads:	▼ root: [] 2 items
	► 0: {} 2 keys
	► 1: {} 2 keys
Writes:	▼ root: [] 2 items
	► 0: {} 2 keys
	► 1: {} 2 keys

This chapter implements a supply chain use case using Hyperledger Fabric and illustrates the farm-to-fork process relating to the food supply industry, traceability, item recall, transaction congestion, regulatory compliance, necessary standards, etc. Moreover, authors are highlighting necessary improvements to realise complex supply chains with connecting regulators placed in various countries, integrating with IoT systems, managing redundant data, and managing a large volume of transactions.

It is noticeable that current blockchain architectures and key-value data stores do not directly support end-to-end traceability of assets, item recall, and lacking necessary standards. Developers should, therefore, involve and develop necessary workflows. The authors propose a private channel concept to position a regulator in a blockchain network, minimizing data redundancy and ensuring auditing. However, continuous improvements are needed to manage block congestion, transaction verification, and compensation management in real-time complex blockchain applications.

ACKNOWLEDGMENT

This publication has emanated from research supported in part by a research grant from Science Foundation Ireland (SFI) and the Department of Agriculture, Food and the Marine on behalf of the Government of Ireland under Grant Number SFI 16/RC/3835 (VistaMilk), and also by a research grant from SFI under Grant Number SFI 12/RC/2289_P2 (Insight), with both grants co-funded by the European Regional Development Fund.

REFERENCES

Benhamouda, F., Halevi, S., & Halevi, T. (2018). Supporting Private Data on Hyperledger Fabric with Secure Multiparty Computation. In *2018 IEEE International Conference on Cloud Engineering (IC2E)*. Orlando, FL: IEEE. 10.1109/IC2E.2018.00069

Bitcoin. (2020). *Bitcoin developer*. Retrieved from Learn Bitcoin and start building Bitcoin-based applications: https://developer.bitcoin.org/

Composer. (2020, June 23). *Typical Hyperledger Composer Solution Architecture*. Retrieved from Hyperledger Composer: https://hyperledger.github.io/composer/v0.19/introduction/solution-architecture

Consensys. (2020). *Blockchain Use Cases-Blockchain in Supply Chain Management*. Retrieved from https://consensys.net/blockchain-use-cases/supply-chain-management/

Cooper, M. C., Lambert, D. M., & Pagh, J. D. (1997). Supply Chain Management: More Than a New Name for Logistics. *International Journal of Logistics Management, 8*(1), 1–14. doi:10.1108/09574099710805556

Davor, D., & Domagoj, S. (2018). Blockchain Applications in Supply Chain. *SMART Supply Network*, 21-46.

Esteban Koberg, A. L. (2018). A systematic review of sustainable supply chain management in global supply chains. *Journal of Cleaner Production*, 1084–1098.

Ethereum. (2020, June 23). *Ethereum is a global, open-source platform for decentralized applications*. Retrieved from ethereum.org: https://ethereum.org/

Gao, Z., Xu, L., Chen, L., Zhao, X., Lu, Y., & Shi, W. (2018). CoC: A Unified Distributed Ledger Based Supply Chain Management System. *Journal of Computer Science and Technology*, 237–248.

Hyperledger. (2020a, June 23). *Hyperledger Fabric*. Retrieved from Hyperledger: https://www.hyperledger.org/use/fabric

Hyperledger. (2020b, June 23). *Private data*. Retrieved from Hyperledger Fabric: https://hyperledger-fabric.readthedocs.io/en/release-2.0/private-data/private-data.html

Kenton, W. (2020, June 24). *Hyperledger Fabric*. Retrieved from Investopedia: https://www.investopedia.com/terms/h/hyperledger-fabric.asp

Ko, K., Lee, C., Jeong, T., & Hong, J. W.-K. (2018). Design of RPC-based Blockchain Monitoring Agent. In *2018 International Conference on Information and Communication Technology Convergence (ICTC)*. Jeju, South Korea: IEEE. 10.1109/ICTC.2018.8539456

Kshetri, N. (2018). Blockchain's roles in meeting key supply chain management objectives. *International Journal of Information Management, 39*, 80–89. doi:10.1016/j.ijinfomgt.2017.12.005

Li, W., Sforzin, A., Fedorov, S., & Karame, G. (2017). Towards Scalable and Private Industrial Blockchains. In *BCC '17: Proceedings of the ACM Workshop on Blockchain, Cryptocurrencies and Contracts* (pp. 9-14). ACM. 10.1145/3055518.3055531

Litecoin. (2020, June 23). *The Cryptocurrency For Payments: Based on Blockchain Technology*. Retrieved from https://litecoin.org/

Martin, S. (2017). *Blockchain use cases for food traceability and control. Swedish county councils and regions: Kairos Future*. Retrieved from Kairos Future: https://tinyurl.com/y7hh6nup

Meyvaert, E. (2020, June 22). *Siemens Mindsphere and SettleMint's distributed middleware: the perfect match!* Retrieved from Medium: https://updates.settlemint.io/siemens-mindsphere-and-settlemints-distributed-middleware-the-perfect-match-b1ce77335c09

Modi, R. (2018). *Solidity Programming Essentials*. Packt Publishing.

Nakamoto, S. (2008). *Bitcoin: A Peer-to-Peer Electronic Cash System*. www.bitcoin.org

Perboli, G., Musso, S., & Rosano, M. (2018). Blockchain in Logistics and Supply Chain: A Lean Approach for Designing Real-World Use Cases. *IEEE Access: Practical Innovations, Open Solutions, 6*, 62018–62028. doi:10.1109/ACCESS.2018.2875782

Quorum. (2020, June 23). *The proven blockchain solution for business*. Retrieved from Evolve with Quorum: https://www.goquorum.com/

Siemens. (2019). *Trusted Traceability - Blockchain and the Internet of Things*. uremberg, Germany: Siemens AG 2019. Retrieved from https://assets.new.siemens.com/siemens/assets/api/uuid:de496ba4-0081-48f5-965b-4963879b2d43/version:1557493248/vrfb-b10033-00-7600sbblockchainfb-144.pdf

Thummavet, P. (2020, June 22). *Demystifying Hyperledger Fabric: Fabric Architecture*. Retrieved from Medium: https://tinyurl.com/y9yn33k5

Westerkamp, M., Victor, F., & Küpper, A. (2018). Blockchain-Based Supply Chain Traceability: Token Recipes Model Manufacturing Processes. In *IEEE/ACM Int'l Conference on Cyber, Physical and Social Computing (CPSCom)*. Halifax, NS, Canada: IEEE Xplore. 10.1109/Cybermatics_2018.2018.00267

Yiannas, F. (2018). A New Era of Food Transparency Powered by Blockchain. *Innovations: Technology, Governance, Globalization, 12*(1-2), 46–56. doi:10.1162/inov_a_00266

Zheng, Z., Xie, S., Dai, H., Chen, X., & Wang, H. (2017). An Overview of Blockchain Technology: Architecture, Consensus, and Future Trends. In *2017 IEEE International Congress on Big Data (BigData Congress)*. Honolulu, HI: IEEE. 10.1109/BigDataCongress.2017.85

ADDITIONAL READING

Ahamed, N. N. K. P, S. P. Anandaraj and V. R. Sea Food Supply Chain Management Using Blockchain, *6th International Conference on Advanced Computing and Communication Systems (ICACCS)*, 2020, pp. 473-476.

Du, M., Chen, Q., Xiao, J., Yang, H., & Ma, X. (2020). Supply Chain Finance Innovation Using Blockchain, in IEEE Transactions on Engineering Management, doi:10.1109/TEM.2020.2971858

Hastig, G. M., & Sodhi, M. S. (2019). Blockchain for Supply Chain Traceability: Business Requirements and Critical Success Factors. *Production and Operations Management*, 935–954.

Jabbar, A., & Dani, S. (2020). Investigating the link between transaction and computational costs in a blockchain environment. *International Journal of Production Research*, 58(11), 3423–3436. doi:10.10 80/00207543.2020.1754487

Li, Z., Guo, H., & Ali Vatankhah Barenji, W. M. (2020). A sustainable production capability evaluation mechanism based on blockchain, LSTM, analytic hierarchy process for supply chain network. *International Journal of Production Research*, 58(24), 1–21. doi:10.1080/00207543.2020.1740342

Subramanian, N, Chaudhuri, A, & Kayikci, Y. (2020). Blockchain Applications in Food Supply Chain. *Blockchain and Supply Chain Logistics*, 21-29. Springer.

Subramanian, N, Chaudhuri, A, & Kayikci, Y. (2020). Blockchain Applications in Health Care Supply Chain. *Blockchain and Supply Chain Logistics*, 31-38. Springer.

KEY TERMS AND DEFINITIONS

Digital Twin: Digital twin refers to a digital replica of potential and actual physical assets, processes, people, places, systems, and devices that can be used for various purposes.

Farm-to-Fork: The stage involves the growing, processing, and consumption of food – the entire food cycle, from supplier to the customer table.

IoT (Internet of Things): The Internet of things is a system of interrelated computing devices, mechanical and digital machines provided with unique identifiers and the ability to transfer data over a network without requiring human-to-human or human-to-computer interaction.

Miner: Miners validate new blockchain transactions and record them on the blockchain. Miners compete to solve a difficult mathematical problem based on a cryptographic hash algorithm.

Peer-to-Peer (P2P): P2P computing is a distributed application architecture that partitions tasks between peers. Peers are equally privileged in the application.

REST API: Representational state transfer (REST) is a software architectural style that defines a set of constraints to be used for creating Web services. The application programming interface (API) defines interface functions.

RFID: Radio-frequency identification (RFID) uses electromagnetic fields to automatically identify and track tags attached to objects.

Smart Contract: A smart contract is a vital component of a Blockchain; it is a self-enforcing agreement embedded in computer code managed by a blockchain. Agreement comes in force, automatically, when certain pre-agreed conditions are met.

ENDNOTES

1   https://www.cdc.gov/salmonella/2009/peanut-butter-2008-2009.html
2   https://www.cdc.gov/ecoli/2016/o121-06-16/index.html
3   https://www.cdc.gov/ecoli/2020/o103h2-02-20/index.html
4   https://www.arcweb.com/blog/supply-chain-transparency-farm-table
5   https://www.hyperledger.org/projects/fabric
6   https://github.com/hyperledger/composer/wiki/Composer-REST-Server
7   https://swagger.io/
8   https://hyperledger-fabric.readthedocs.io/en/release/commands/peerchannel.htm

Chapter 5
Blockchain Technology and General Issue of Tax Evasion via Bitcoin

Güneş Çetin Gerger
https://orcid.org/0000-0002-5823-7866
Manisa Celal Bayar University, Turkey

ABSTRACT

Cryptocurrencies often also serve money laundering activities, terrorist financing, tax evasion, and other illegitimate activities with a market value of more than 7 billion euros across the globe, though the total amount is hardly measurable. Indeed, the blockchain technology involves many virtual currencies, including bitcoin, to conduct various financial transactions related practices throughout the world economies. Besides, other blockchain applications are making positive contributions to a wide array of other industries including healthcare, supply chain, manufacturing, etc. This technology which constitutes the backbone of digital assets transactions currencies is characterized by anonymity, privacy, security, and speed. In this sense, for tax administration authorities, detection of financial fraud and regulations with respect to taxation of virtual transactions pose newer emerging challenges. This chapter aims to examine the blockchain technology, cryptocurrencies, especially bitcoin, and look into regulations by world governments to combat tax evasion and illegal transactions.

INTRODUCTION

The Blockchain is the software architectural structure of the new are. In fact, in the Blockchain as a database, data are recorded into blocks in an ordered manner. Each record has a time stamp. When a block is full, the next block is created, and the blocks are connected to each other in the form of a chain. Today, in information systems, databases are the most used constructs. This situation is also valid for the Blockchain. A Blockchain may be created for each project, each cryptocurrency and each recording system. In this sense, the Blockchain is a record book. We may call this a "general ledger" (Güven, Şahinöz, 2018).

DOI: 10.4018/978-1-7998-6650-3.ch005

The World Economic Forum defined the Blockchain technology as follows: "The Blockchain technology, or distributed ledger technology (DTL), is a technology protocol that makes it possible for the exchange of data between two parties without needing an intermediary." In terms of security, the Blockchain is superior, as all records in the chain are at the same level with same privileges, and cannot be changed, without an agreed consensus. It is not in question for the system to crash, be hacked or its data getting deleted. As an important discovery, the Blockchain may be used in terms of social, political and legal aspects. The most popular applications of the Blockchain technology are in the transaction of cryptocurrencies.

Creation of cryptocurrencies occurs without the control of any state or government, and does not show any physical aspect; these are virtual currencies. Cryptocurrencies are created by "miners" with the Blockchain technology and mathematical encryption methods. By adding a new link to the chain existing over the Internet, miners gain money in exchange. This amount of production is limited to 21 million units for Bitcoin, which is the most prevalently used virtual currency among the many cryptocurrencies. In the Blockchain, where Bitcoin operations are recorded, all past transactions can be seen and monitored. However, the account owners are not clearly known, therefore all operations take place anonymously. In this aspect, it is often also used for the purposes of money laundering and the underground economy. This in turn causes the prevalence of tax evasion. The main issue in tax evasion is the anonymity meaning that cryptocurrency users remain hidden, and their transactions cannot be taxed, which in turn creates an undetectable area. Accordingly, Bitcoin is sometimes described as a "tax haven".

States i.e. governments are also spending time and effort to find ways of bringing cryptocurrencies within the taxation systems. While these cryptocurrencies are now being taxed in some countries, they are still outside the taxing system in other countries. There is still no clear decision on how cryptocurrencies can be brought under the income tax systems. In general, Bitcoin income is being regarded as "commodity", rather than money. In the cryptocurrency scenario, money is created as much as the amount declared during establishment by following publicly available methods that are known by all concerned. On the other hand, in the conventional monetary system, the state may create as much money as it wants through the central bank, and the state is the guarantor in this process (Çarkacıoğlu, 2016). Bitcoin production requires a highly difficult process. However, looking at its usage, one may see that it is being used by many large organizations worldwide including Wikipedia, Virgin Galactic, Tesla, Microsoft, Overstock, Namecheap, etc. (White, 2018). The superior properties of cryptocurrency have made it prevalent. These properties are security, anonymity, portability, bidirectionality, offline capacity, unlimited term, broad acceptability and user-friendliness (Matonis, 1995). These superior properties may also lead to negative effects that may result in tax evasion.

It is a fact that digital technologies stand as a basis for complex tax fraud and tax scam schemes. Even though technology has been a significant facilitator of illegal economic activities, cyberspace consists of many tools that are used for money laundering and other illegal financial transactions. For example, banking products and services which are regulated mediators, electronic payment systems as non-bank mediators, cryptocurrencies which are mostly unregulated and may also be decentralized, online services and trading platforms, online gambling and e-commerce. Converting cryptocurrencies into cash or other means of traditional payments is used as a common way of illegal money transfer (Çetin Gerger and Bozdoğanoğlu, 2017).

Differences in the taxation systems and tax inspection forms of world governments, in addition to the technologies of information and communication they use, may lead to loss of tax revenue. Countries and international organizations have different mechanism, if any, regarding taxation on Bitcoin revenues.

While the Blockchain technology serves effective facilitation of taxation in some countries, some other countries are not yet utilizing this technology. Bitcoin operations depending on the Blockchain technology result in loss of taxes both due to shortcomings in legislation, lack of relevant regulations, and for reasons that this technology is not yet prevalent.

The organization of this chapter is as follows. It first examines the Blockchain technology, cryptocurrencies and Bitcoin in general terms, then discusses the advantages and disadvantages of Bitcoin currency in relation to taxation, and finally assesses the regulations that international organizations may already have in relation to tax evasion, money laundering and related monitory fraud.

BLOCKCHAIN TECHNOLOGY, CRYPTOCURRENCIES AND BITCOIN

The Blockchain may be defined as: *a system in which a record of transactions made in Bitcoin or another cryptocurrency are maintained across several computers that are linked in a peer-to-peer network* (https://www.lexico.com/en/definition/Blockchain). A "Blockchain" is a particular type of data construct that is utilized in some distributed ledgers which stores and transfers data in packages called "blocks" that are linked to each other in a digital "chain". Blockchains employ cryptographic and algorithmic techniques to record and synchronize data across a network in an immutable manner. The decentralized database managed by multiple participants is known as Distributed Ledger Technology (DLT). These are a specific application of the broader category of "shared ledgers", which are simply defined as a shared record of data across different parties (World Bank Group, 2017).

Blockchain applications are emerging under four main areas, viz: digital currencies, digital assets, smart contracts and identity. Figure 1 presents some more detail. The applications under "identity" includes healthcare developments, title records, ownership, voting, AML/KYC, passports and IP rights. The other main applications are on digital currency. A cryptocurrency is a specific Blockchain product (e.g. Bitcoin, Ethereum, Ripple, EOS, etc.) representing a new way of transferring digital assets which are like stock exchange, loyalty, provenance are other uses of Blockchain. The last area relates to smart contracts like mortgage and loans and transfer of ownership (Chandrasekaran et al., 2019). Focusing on Figure 1, we may also see the inherent Blockchain benefits. These being as follows:

- Identity: helps to remove increasing problems such as forged documents,
- Smart contracts: help to digitize and automate existing paper contracts,
- Digital assets: to make faster and cheaper settlement of trade by removing intermediaries
- Cryptocurrencies: can be transferred almost instantaneously to anyone and anywhere

Usually Blockchain technology is closer to virtual currency applications, payments and financial services. However, Blockchain may theoretically be applied in many different sectors, though this technology is specific to Bitcoin for problem solving of "double-spending". Prior to Bitcoin, an account holder was relieved of worries about their transactions and account balances by getting reconciled over a trustworthy independent platform. Now, however, an essential technology has been developed for digital currencies; this is known as Distributed Ledger Technology (DLT). With this, the institutional requirement for trust is eliminated since the security and safety system is of integrity in a localized ledger through a network of participants on the basis of anonymity (Natarajan et al., 2017).

Figure 1. Main Areas for Blockchain Applications

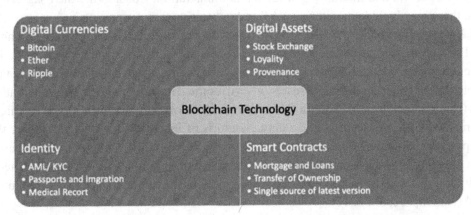

Decentralization needs a universal consensus provided by Bitcoin Blockchain depending on "proof of work", which was cautiously developed for anti-spamming action based on a specified set of leading zeros. The proof-of-work generation is referred as "mining". In the Bitcoin system, calibration is processed in a way where a proof-of-work is described as valid through evaluation performed in ten-minute periods, and a higher difficulty score makes the protocol valid, out of the two produced at one moment. "Miners" are individually remunerated with Bitcoins for every valid proof of work (Natarajan et al., 2017).

Figure 2. Bitcoin and Blockchain Technology

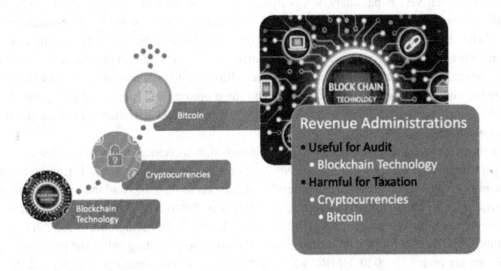

Bitcoin is the most frequently used among cryptocurrencies. Bitcoin uses the Blockchain technology infrastructure. Considering Figure 2, we may see that Bitcoin usage, one of the four main usage areas of the Blockchain technology, can be harmful for the tax administration as it may lead to tax evasion due to its anonymity characteristics, while the Blockchain is, generally, beneficial. The Blockchain is beneficial for inspection and monitoring at the tax administration. Considering the usage areas of the Blockchain, these may include monitoring VAT and preventing transfer pricing.

Blockchain, a special kind of the DLT system, offers data recording and data sharing among multiple databases. The stored datum is unique despite being collected by different sources, because a decentralized but integrated network of computer servers retains and checks all the data for avoiding double entry. Cryptography-based Blockchain either creates or verifies the data structure using certain mathematical algorithms (Natarajan et al., 2017). With this cryptographic solution, the institutional requirement for trust is eliminated since the security and safety system is of integrity in a localized ledger through a network of participants on the basis of anonymity. As a mechanism or data structure, Blockchain unalterably retains data through cryptographic and algorithmic techniques in a specific way. This technology has a potential in different contexts and is interchangeably used with another term, 'distributed ledger technology' (Natarajan et al., 2017).

In tax collection, the Blockchain technology will lead to reduction of especially the Missing Trader Intra Community (MTIC) fraud that is frequently encountered in the EU (Europol, 2020). It is one of the most commonly encountered forms of VAT fraud in Europe. The 2018-2021 EU Policy Cycle (https://www.europol.europa.eu/empact) showed MTIC fraud among the nine crimes representing the priority areas of crime. Additionally, Blockchain practices can also prevent double taxation and transfer pricing. Ainsworth, Alwohaibi, Cheetham and Tirand (2018) developed a model established on cryptocurrencies. Accordingly, in tax collection, they developed a system for Gulf countries as a "crypto tax currency" system. In these operations, VATcoin was be used, and all operations were dependent on the Blockchain. In Blockchain practices, it is sufficient for the customer to pay the bill to the business and businesses to pay these bills to their suppliers (Deloitte, 2017). In this way, VAT fraud can be prevented.

Where and when VAT is paid may be monitored with the Blockchain technology. It provides secure information flow to tax administrations, tax inspectors and other regulators. Microtransactions among individuals has also become more visible. In terms of tax inspection, the Blockchain technology allows provision for greater advantages. After all, inspection involves substantiation of recorded operations with relevant, secure, objective and confirmable evidence. Blockchain will provide positive effects such as achieving tax confidence between the employee and the employer and increasing the speed of tax collection (Johnston and Lewis, 2017). In the Value Added Tax, several operations in the tax chain may be no longer necessary with Blockchain practices.

Collecting taxes by using the Blockchain is a factor that increases efficiency in terms of the tax office operations. This is because close to zero errors are made with this method. Employment of the Blockchain system is highly useful for income administrations as well. In Thailand, the Bangkok Income Administration has been using this system since 2018 (Uti, 2018). Additionally, the United Kingdom is also among the pioneering countries (HMRC,2019). In the United Kingdom, HMRC has presented its "Making Tax Digital" project, an initiative with the purpose of getting rid of the paper-based, long-after-the-fact tax return by 2020. HMRC will gather and process information affecting tax in as close to real-time as possible, to prevent taxes due or repayments owed from further building up (Asquith, 2016). The World Economic Forum has discussed when countries will start to collect taxes with the means of the Blockchain, and most participants thought that such practices would start in the year 2013 (Ainsworth & Shact, 2016).

Cryptocurrencies and Total Market Capitalization

Considering the cryptocurrencies connected to the Blockchain technology, we see that they have started to be used highly prevalently today. Cryptocurrencies are electronically issued by private developers to substitute value for exchange as a denomination in a special unit of account (Dong He et al., 2016). Bitcoin became one of the first and most valuable currencies among cryptocurrencies. It is a digital asset which can be bought, sold and transferred between two parties securely over the Internet (Nooruddin, 2019). Like other cryptocurrencies, Bitcoin, a peer-to-peer electronic cash mechanism, can securely pay purchases in either real or digital world. Cryptocurrency developers build these protocols using advanced systems, so, they make it difficult to duplicate or alter the protected currencies and transactions (Martucci, 2018). Now, there are 2,247 different cryptocurrencies worldwide, all of varying value, utility and market capitalization (Coinmarketcap, 2019). Cryptocurrency exchanges are very important in creating liquid markets for popular cryptocurrencies. In 2019, BitPremier reviewed and named its top 13 cryptocurrency exchanges (BitPremier (2019). The list is presented in Table 1.

Table 1. Top 13 Cryptocurrencies

1.Coinbase
2. Coinmama
3. Bitpanda
4. CEX.IO
5. Kraken
6. LocalBitcoins
7. Bitstamp
8. Gemini
9. Crypto to Crypto Exchanges
10. Binance
11. Changelly
12. Bitfinex
13. Poloniex

Referring to Table 2, the total market capitalization of all cryptocurrencies is approximately $171 billion. In total, Bitcoin was the dominant currency with 54.66 percent of the market share, followed by Ethereum at only 9.7 percent and ripple at 7.3 percent (Prewett et al., 2019).

Table 2. Cryptocurrency Market Capitalization [Adopted from CoinMarketCap.com (2019)]

Date	Number of Cryptocurrencies	Market Capitalization
2013	7	$1,580,539,630
2014	237	$6,085,317,610
2015	564	$3,537,377,349
2016	577	$8,520,778,723
2017	777	$29,473,958,605
2018	1563	$388,027,865,010
2019	2140	$171,075,254,32

Characteristics of Bitcoin (BTC)

Bitcoin has typically no chance of being transformed to a physical form, so the ideal way of its representation is simply by a computer file. One can save Bitcoins virtually on a computing system or even on the Internet, in a digital wallet. In order that the combination of virtual characters can be printed out, the plain Bitcoin character should remain qualified (Kaplanov, 2012).

Bitcoins can be issued through "mining" processes using a PoW consensus mechanism. In a PoW system, the joiners of a network have to solve so-called "cryptographic puzzles" to be permitted to introduce new "blocks" on the Blockchain. If one wishes, they can open and share with the Bitcoin network the computer for trouble-shooting which involves sophisticated mathematics. The computer that manages to solve one problem like this is offered Bitcoin bonuses (Kaplanov, 2012). Nevertheless, mining is a poor way to create Bitcoins.

Bitcoin is operable on a free Blockchain with no requirement for authorization, meaning that an individual may login to or logout of the global network anytime without any notification by a central authority (Houben et al., 2018).

Bitcoin has convertibility from cryptocurrency into fiat currency. Bitcoins can be simply exchangeable or purchasable with fiat currency on a wide range of cryptocurrency types (Houben et al., 2018). Bitcoin is officially acceptable as a medium of exchange or an origin of funds by a great deal of traders such as financially big corporations (Houben et al., 2018). Bitcoin is a pseudo-anonymous coin.

A public ledger constitutes an institution like a notary for verification of the chain transactions although Bitcoin seems to have free direct contact with individuals. In other words, the property of anonymity is not indispensable for the Bitcoin technology, and any parties are detectable even if hidden in a Bitcoin transaction by merging the technical elements accompanying the transaction (Grinberg, 2012). Bitcoin has gained a significant place in the cryptocurrency market not only due to its market volume but also because of the superiority of its characteristic properties.

CRYPTOCURRENCIES: ADVANTAGES AND DISADVANTAGES

Cryptocurrencies have multiple advantages, mostly due to their technological properties including cybersecurity, cryptography, trust, decentralization and transparency. The double-spending problem disappears by means of the Blockchain technology which delegates the authority of verification from one center onto the global network. In this respect, the digital currency market is built on mistrust among users for conventional finance, and the third-party financial authority could be disqualified by the peer-to-peer consensus on its efficiency (Schipor, 2019; Gerger, 2020). As cryptocurrencies are not taxed in many countries, they are not subject to any tax cuts or tax revenues. Additionally, as they do not have a center, they do not require an administrator. Their costs and operational times are low in this matter. The operations are not monitored by anyone, and it is easy to transport, store and protect currency. As the cryptographic digital signatures method is used for the security of the system, this prevents the currency from being imitated. As the amount of created cryptocurrency is fixed, it does not have a risk of encountering inflation or disinflation (Kızıl 2019, Çarkacıoğlu 2016). Cryptocurrencies are tempting for illegal operations such as terrorist acts, drug dealing and money laundering because the account holder remains anonymous, and a financial intermediary is also unnecessary for digital transactions so that crime investigators can hardly get informed to catch criminals, and thereby, these stay out of their control area (Schipor, 2019).

It is suggested that the cryptocurrency exchange is a volatile and infective market influencing the overall financial system and global economy. Now that digital transactions are favorably less costly, it can be argued, without doubt, that it may establish a contemporary payment system across one nation or multiple nations (Schipor, 2019). Cryptocurrencies could become a main tool in financial systems, and there will be a risk on financial stability (Carstens, 2018). In the European Union, according to the chairman of BIS (Bank for International Settlements), the related policy intervention should be adopted, or otherwise, the financial administration will be late for averting the threat of financial instability that cryptocurrencies may pose due to their integration to the traditional financial system (Castens, 2018).

Bitcoin is not applicable to other decentralized virtual currencies as usual, so, there exist variations in taxation of this currency (Ram, 2017). Virtual currencies are taxed as commodities because these are different to normal currencies, and this characteristic may determine taxation for consumption taxes including the value added tax (VAT), income tax including capital gains, wealth tax including wealth transfers and other potential taxable items. The rising exchange rate provides income and capital gains, though there is no actual transaction, which in turn initiates taxing the value difference. This case may occur in different situations where the rate of multiple virtual currencies even in a basket changes or where these are directly non-exchangeable to a fiat currency. Furthermore, the decrease is also equally treated as being taxed like an increase (Ram, 2018).

Cryptocurrencies are risky as there is no state or country that will act as their guarantor. Cryptocurrency exists within a virtual environment, and thus, cyberattacks may affect it. As it is anonymous, it may be used in illegal activities. It is also difficult to monitor by income tax administrations. As cryptocurrencies are not on a legal basis, they do not have a regular exchange. This increases the volatility of the currency and makes it a target for speculators. Therefore, this results in an imbalanced pricing of the currency (Kizil, 2019).

If we assess the advantages and disadvantages of cryptocurrencies in general, while privacy, security, speed and easy usage make them advantageous, their openness to cyber-attacks, threat on financial stability and usage in illegal economic activities put them in a disadvantageous position.

TAXATION REGULATIONS FOR CRYPTOCURRENCIES AND BITCOIN

States perceive cryptocurrencies as a threat. One of the most important reasons for this is that monitoring of money laundering and terrorism financing becomes difficult, and tax evasion increases. Besides, other issues may include losing the monopoly of printing money, deprivation of seigniorage income, possibility of reducing the effectiveness of monetary policy, liquidity management becoming difficult, and concerns of deflation. For these reasons, states have rightfully approached cryptocurrencies from a certain distance (Güven and Şahinöz, 2018). To be able to eliminate such negative effects, governments have either preferred to take the usage of cryptocurrencies under control by issuing legal regulations about them or chosen to ban them by completely ignoring them.

In the 2018 Summit, G20 countries formed a mosaic of distinctive legislations for the concept of cryptocurrency on a global map and produced a list of countries displaying their status in terms of whether these currencies are designated neutral, restricted, legal or illegal (Global Cryptocurrency Report, 2018). Refer to Table 3.

Table 3. Worldwide Legality of Cryptocurrency [Adopted from Global Cryptocurrency Report (2018)]

Neutral	Restricted	Legal		Illegal
Argentina Senegal Rwanda India Indonesia Jamaica	Mexico Russia Saudi Arabia South Korea	Australia Netherlands Chile Brazil Canada France Singapore USA Malta	Germany South Africa Spain Italy Turkey UK Japan	China

EU members exchange information, as a matter of course, on tax issues mainly to fight against tax evasion; however, the current EU framework is limited since virtual currencies are excluded due to the anonymity of cryptocurrencies (Houben et al., 2018). The growth of virtual currencies needs appropriate regulations.

Cryptocurrencies have a lack of central authority. Japan became the first country to recognize Bitcoin and other cryptocurrencies as legal tender when it passed the Virtual Currency Act in early 2017 (Terazona, 2017). International agencies have the power to set regulations over cryptocurrency, but only a few agencies have declarations. International coordination among global regulators took risk management measures for virtual currencies at the G20 level, in 2017. The International Monetary Fund (IMF) stated that some regulation for Bitcoin is necessary (Alkhalsi, 2018). The US, Canada, Israel, the UK, Australia and Japan have issued guidance for taxpayers investing in virtual currencies (Bal, 2015). In the EU Parliament, the fourth anti money laundering (AML) directive passed on May 20th, 2015, and the fifth AML Directive passed on May 30th, 2018. These directives relate to virtual currencies having registration necessarily. EU member countries regulate their national laws complying with the EU's directives and implementations. The variation between national laws of different countries makes a difference between the virtual currency markets of EU countries. Finland accepted the fifth EU AML directive on March 13th, 2019 (EC, 2019).

AMLD5 defines virtual currencies and operations of virtual currency exchange, and prescribes due diligence obligations from custodian wallet providers for customer and reporting to financial intelligence units (FIUs) for suspicious transactions. This directive has made virtual currency exchange platforms and custodian wallet providers liable for cryptocurrencies and thereby introduced the phenomenon of "virtual currencies". When it is reported to FIU by a provider that cryptocurrency has been produced or by the platform that any transactions have been actualized, the institution informs the tax authority of potential tax evasion under the name of "suspicious transaction" (Houben et al., 2018); it then investigates such transactions (Article 32 AMLD4).

EU have also prepared a key project (called Titanium) regarding research, development and validation on innovative data-driven techniques and solutions to promote crime investigation agencies in charge of virtual currencies and/or undocumented markets on the darknet. The Titanium project was designed to digitally fight tax evasion, money laundering and terrorist financing that might occur in virtual transactions using cryptocurrencies (Keatinge et al., 2020).

According to the European Banking Authority, an EU framework concept should be adopted (Yeoh, 2017). In the description of the World Bank, cryptocurrencies are categorized under digital currencies and referred to as value representations in the electronic format via denominations in the special unit of account. Additionally, the Bank added into the definition that these are cryptography-based digital currencies for getting consensus (Natarajan et al., 2017).

The very common cryptocurrency, currently in use, is Bitcoin. Since criminals take advantage of the characteristic of anonymity, and limited regulatory framework and poor enforcement of regulations in virtual transactions, it urges them towards conducting illegal operations (Zola et al., 2019). Bitcoin processes do not collect any taxes from its users. Therefore, governments would like to regulate the organization of its citizens and businesses who wish to transact in Bitcoin. Governments should apply anti-money laundering regulations on its spread, seek to tax its use and prosecute those who use Bitcoin for illegitimate activities (IRS, 2014). It is crucial for tax administration to provide strong guidance on tax treatment of virtual currency transactions (Prewett et al., 2019). The IRS 2013 Annual Report to Congress addressed the lack of guidance. The IRS Notice 2014-21 provided the first, current and best guidance to the tax agency's perception of Bitcoin and other cryptocurrencies (IRS, 2014). Accordingly, personal income tax rate applies to Bitcoin received in exchange for goods or services.

When we look at taxation of Bitcoin incomes, we see that there is a different practice in each country. Bitcoin incomes are considered as securities, commodities or money based on the country, and taxation is made accordingly. In the USA, Bitcoin sales are considered as real estate sales, and when one wants to purchase goods as Bitcoin sale, Capital Gains Tax is collected over the sales operation (De, 2018). While the rate of taxation is between 15% and 23.8%, for a term longer than a year, the rate may increase up to 39% for those with a term less than a year (Köse, 2018). While there is 45% of taxation in France recently, where cryptocurrencies are considered as securities, it was decided to reduce this rate to 19% with a regulation that came in force in April 2018 (Zuckerman, 2018).

Cryptocurrencies are accepted as commodity in Canada and taxed over commercial gains or increased value gains, whereas they are considered as a barter agreement when used by commercial establishments when the net profit is taxed over the country's own currency. They are subject to corporate tax and value added tax. 50% of revenues obtained from individual purchases and sales is exempt from taxation. The tax base, on the other hand, is taxed over the normal tax regime. However, if there are short-term and continuous sales and purchases, the Canadian Tax Administration considers these activities as commercial (Uğurlu, 2018).

Australia considers and taxes purchases and sales via cryptocurrencies as barter operations. Firms are subject to corporate tax and transaction tax. For individual investors, good and service purchases made by under 10,000 Australian dollars in cryptocurrency are exempt from income and consumption taxes. Since 1 July 2017, the purchase and sale operations of cryptocurrencies have been exempted from good and service transaction taxes (Uçma Uysal and Aldemir, 2018).

In the United Kingdom, operations carried out with cryptocurrencies are exempt from value added tax. Those who take part in such operations are obligated to pay 20% corporate tax. Individual investors pay capital gains tax on the profit they make after a purchase or sale (Uğurlu, 2018). In South Korea, 22% corporate tax and 2.2% local income tax are applicable for Bitcoin revenues (Zuckerman, 2018).

Tax Evasion Via Bitcoin

Income administrations are disturbed by the prevalence of tax evasion due to the usage of cryptocurrencies. This is because preference of cryptocurrencies due to their superior properties in the unofficial economy such as anonymity and privacy has increased the illegal exchange of goods and services between people at distant locations. Additionally, if they do not wish to do so, taxpayers might not declare the value increases in their cryptocurrencies. Although it is possible to monitor large sums of investments, based on the idea that a person can open any desired number of accounts, it is possible for these individuals to divide illegal transactions into small volumes in a way that would not attract attention. Based on this, the FBI managed to crash the Silk Road market, and they arrested their leader (Fanusie and Robinson, 2018). It is not yet possible to calculate the loss of taxes arising from Bitcoin and other cryptocurrency usage. Cryptocurrencies may be employed to launder money or fund terrorism (Güven and Şahinöz, 2018).

The IMF prepared a report about the "virtual currencies and beyond" in 2016. In the report, it was stated that cryptocurrencies became a highly potential instrument to evade tax. The subjects of this criminal act tend to use cryptocurrencies mainly because they can stay anonymous while using the option to cover their identity and due to the peer-to-peer characteristic of the virtual transactions and the potentiality for international operations. Such digital currencies have tax implications depending on their connection to a currency function of a means of exchange or a store of worth in economics.

The taxable virtual currency (VC) transactions should be determined through a profound evaluation of sophisticated matters arising from the schematic structure and subtle operations (IMF, 2016). Blockchain practices will make Know Your Customer (KYC) and Anti Money Laundering (AML) actions both easy and highly practical. With Blockchain practices, it will be enough for an individual or firm to conduct a KYC operation only once (Güven and Şahinöz, 2018).

Usage of virtual currencies like Bitcoin for illegal activities by using the Blockchain technology will in time allow monitoring in an easier way than monitoring the flows within the central monetary system. This is why it is important to make it prevalent instead of banning it and allow it to develop within its own ecosystem. For example, there are cryptocurrency ATMs setup at the Prague metro (Konakçı, 2018). Again, in Switzerland, the largest railway company of the country has been selling Bitcoin from its own ticket sales ATMs spread around the country since November 2016. Such policies may help monitoring and inspection of cryptocurrencies easier by pulling it towards the public sphere (Güven and Şahinöz, 2018).

Reducing Tax Evasion by Blockchain Applications

Blockchain make faster digital reporting possible and provides multiple authorized parties with the capability to independently view the same unit of transaction information electronically. This may possibly make the act of VAT filing even more seamless and efficient in the future (Asquith, 2016). It helps businesses and tax authorities in terms of more control, simplifying compliance, and avoiding double taxation (Gerger&Firuzan, 2020). The implementation of such a scheme would allow obtaining various advantages that would contribute to almost complete elimination of tax evasion (Faccia and Roxana, 2019), as mentioned below:

- Simplification of tax obligations, lowering the costs of consulting for firms,
- Potential of conducting concrete and fast tax planning,
- Potential to pay corporate taxes monthly, but connecting the tax withholding of the invoices issued. The Government would also gain continuous cash flow and be able to get large advantages in terms of monitoring production and GDP,
- While calculating the markup, firms may easily consider the cost related to taxes. They may additionally prevent bearing unnecessary costs for the sole aim of lowering the tax burden, but exclusively emphasizing business efficiency,

- Lowering uncollectible tax credits by the Government, which could simultaneously validate the non-payment and prevent the activity of defaulting companies. Basically, the system of self-declaration (income tax return) trialed on a sample (source of temptation to escape) would be eliminated. Automated mechanisms, depending on electronic invoices issued in a centralized system, as well as the withholding tax implemented in payments, would instantly validate the payment of the taxes due in the next month.

Although Bitcoin leads to tax evasion, usage of Blockchain applications at the income administration and in the business world for taxation and accounting practices will lead to increased tax compliance by reducing tax loss. Additionally, by allowing the legitimate and efficient use of technology, Blockchain applications will also lower tax compliance risk, operational risk and reporting risks (Gerçek and Bakar Türegün, 2018).

CONCLUSION

Regulation of cryptocurrencies is a highly difficult issue. Thus, it could be suitable to broaden their usage but have strict right regulations and apply small amounts of taxes on operations conducted with these currencies. Banning or ignoring these currencies is not a realistic solution. This is because uncertainty brings costs. This is why the grey area needs to be clarified. The public authority needs to be not excessively limiting but balancing.

In general, the Blockchain technology has a great potential for all manner of industries. Therefore, in recent times, the Blockchain technology has surpassed Bitcoin, and it has advanced in the public and private sectors. The Blockchain technology is a field that is still continuing to develop. Many firms have started to develop their own prototype technologies for the purpose of understanding the Blockchain technology. The Blockchain allows real-time monitoring and recording of the transition of digital currency, financial assets and other digital documents between two or more parties. Especially in terms of the public sector, a Blockchain technology that is provided by the central government via allowed entries may make it easier for everyone to access the system and provide achievement of security and privacy principles.

Income administrations need to make clear and comprehensible regulations for cryptocurrencies in general and for Bitcoin that is prevalently used, in particular. Bitcoin is a new phenomenon on which there is inaccurate knowledge among taxpayers who believe that making transactions in digital currencies alleviates taxation and reporting liabilities. Bitcoin operations are legal and taxed in many countries. Additionally, income administrations have also started to adopt a taxation inspection system established on the Blockchain technology.

To be able to reduce loss of taxes and stop illegal financial activities, an Anti-Money Laundering program is being carried out in the European Union. It is well noted that usage of cryptocurrencies may be associated with illegal activities. Bitcoin is being used in issues such as terrorist activities, drug supply or money laundering. Taking this issue under control may be possible by also using the Blockchain technology at income administrations. Such administrations are already using and developing technologies such as Blockchain technologies, artificial intelligence, cloud computing and the Internet of Things (Gerger, 2020) for the said purpose.

REFERENCES

AinsworthR.AlwohaibiM.CheethamM.TirandC. (2018), A Vatcoin Solution To MTIC Fraud: Past Efforts, Present Technology, and the EU's 2017 Proposal. Boston University School of Law, Law & Economics Series Paper No. 18-08. SSRN: https://ssrn.com/abstract=3151394

Ainsworth, R., & Shact, A. (2016). Blockchain (Distributed Ledger Technology) Solves VAT Fraud. SSRN. doi:10.2139srn.2853428

Alkhalsi, Z. (2018). *IMF Chief: Cryptocurrency Regulation Is 'Inevitable'.* https://money.cnn.com/2018/02/11/investing/lagarde- bitcoin-regulation/index.html

Asquith, R. (2016). *How Blockchain could shape tax automation?* https://www.avalara.com/vatlive/en/vat-news/how-Blockchain-could-shape-tax-automation.html

Bal, A. (2015). *Bitcoin Transactions: Recent Tax Developments and Regulatory Responses.* https://www.ibfd.org/sites/ ibfd.org/files/content/pdf/dfi_2015_05_int_2.pdf

BitPremier. (2019). *Cryptocurrency Exchange Reviews.* https://www. bitpremier.com/best-exchanges

Çarkacıoğlu, A. (2016). *Kripto-Para Bitcoin.* Sermaye Piyasası Kurulu Araştırma Dairesi.

Carstens, A. (2018). *Money in the Digital Age: What Role for Central Banks?* Lecture at House of Finance, Goethe Univ. https://www.bis.org/ speeches/sp180206.pdf

Çetin Gerger, G., & Bozdoğanoğlu, B. (2017). *Evaluation of the problems regarding taxation of electronic commerce in the context of informal economy and tax evasion.* Issues in Public Sector Economics, Peter Lang.

Chandrasekaran, N., Somanah, R., Rughoo, D., Dreepaul, R. K., Cunden, T. S. M., & Demkah, M. (2019). Digital Transformation from Leveraging Blockchain Technology, Artificial Intelligence, Machine Learning and Deep Learning. In S. Satapathy, V. Bhateja, R. Somanah, X. S. Yang, & R. Senkerik (Eds.), *Information Systems Design and Intelligent Applications. Advances in Intelligent Systems and Computing* (Vol. 863). Springer. doi:10.1007/978-981-13-3338-5_25

CoinMarketCap. (2019). *All Cryptocurrencies.* https://coinmarketcap.com/all/views/all

De, N. (2018). *Germany Won't Tax you for Buying Coffee with Bitcoin.* https://www.coindesk.com/germany-considers-crypto-legal-equivalent-to-fiat-for-tax-purposes/

Deloitte. (2017). *Blockchain Technology and Its Potential in Taxes.* https://www2.deloitte.com/content/dam/Deloitte/pl/Documents/Reports/pl_Blockchain-technology-and-its-potential-in-taxes-2017-EN.PDF

EC. (2019). *Urgency for an EU blacklist of third countries in line with the Anti-Money Laundering Directive.* https://www.europarl.europa.eu/doceo/document/TA-8-2019-0216_EN.html

Europol. (2020). *Economic Crime.* https://www.europol.europa.eu/crime-areas-and-trends/crime-areas/economic-crime/mtic-missing-trader-intra-community-fraud

Faccia, N., & Mosteanu, R. (2019). Tax Evasion_Information System and Blockchain. Journal of Information Systems & Operations Management, 13(1), 65-74.

Fanusie, Y. J., & Robinson, T. (2018). *Bitcoin Laundering: An Analysis of Illicit Flows into Digital Currency Services*. https://www.fdd.org/analysis/2018/01/10/bitcoin-laundering-an-analysis-of-illicit-flows-into- digital-currency-services/

Gerçek, A., & Bakar Türegün, F. (2018). Şirketlerde Vergi Riski Algısı Ve Vergi Riski Yönetimi Üzerine Bir Araştırma. *Muhasebe ve Vergi Uygulamaları Dergisi, 11*(3), 307–332. doi:10.29067/muvu.368807

Gerger, A. (2020). Technologies for Connected Government Implementation: Success Factors and Best Practices. In Z. Mahmood (Ed.), Web 2.0 and Cloud Technologies for Implementing Connected Government. IGI Global.

Gerger, A., & Firuzan, A. (2020). Taguchi based Case study in the automotive industry: Nonconformity decreasing with use of Six Sigma methodology. *Journal of Applied Statistics*, 1–17. Advance online publication. doi:10.1080/02664763.2020.1837086

Grinberg, R. (2011). Bitcoin: An Innovative Alternative Digital Currency. *Hastings Science & Technology Law Journal, 4*, 164. https://papers.ssrn.com/sol3/papers.cfm?abstract_id=1817857

Güven, V., & Şahinöz, E. (2018). Blokzincir - Kripto Paralar - Bitcoin. Satoshi Dünyayı Değiştiriyor. Kronik Kitap.

He, D., Habermeier, K., Leckow, R., Haksar, V., Almeida, Y., Kashima, M., Kyriakos-Saad, N., Oura, H., Saadi Sedik, T., Stetsenko, N., & Verdugo Yepes, C. (2016). Virtual Currencies and Beyond: Initial Con-siderations. *IMF Staff Discussion Notes, 16*(3), 1. Advance online publication. doi:10.5089/9781498363273.006

HMRC. (2019). *Crypto Assets: Tax for Individuals*. https://www.gov.uk/government/publications/tax-on-cryptoassets/cryptoassets-for-individuals

Houben, R., & Snyers, A. (2018). *Cryptocurrencies and Blockchain*. https://www.europarl.europa.eu/cmsdata/150761/TAX3%20Study%20on%20cryptocurrencies%20and%20Blockchain.pdf

IBINEX. (2019). *Global Cryptocurrency Market Report*. https://www.financemagnates.com/wp-content/uploads/2018/10/Global-Cryptocurrency-Market-Report.pdf

IMF Monetary and Capital Markets, Legal and Strategy and Policy Review Departments. (2016). *Virtual Currencies and Beyond: Initial Considerations Prepared by an IMF Staff Team1*. https://www.imf.org/external/pubs/ft/sdn/2016/sdn1603.pdf

IRS. (2014). *Virtual Currency Guidance: Virtual Currency Is Treated as Property for U.S. Federal Tax Purposes; General Rules for Property Transactions Apply*. IRS. https://www.irs.gov/uac/newsroom/irs-virtual-currency-guidance

Johnston, S., & Lewis, A. (2017). New Frontiers: Tax Agencies Explore Blockchain. *Tax Notes International, 86*(9), 16-19. https://www.taxnotes.com/tax-notes-international/tax-system-administration/new-frontiers-tax-agencies-explore-Blockchain/2017/04/03/18884661

Kaplanov, N. M. (2012). Nerdy Money: Bitcoin, the private digital currency, and the case against its regulation. *Temple Law Review*. https://papers.ssrn.com/sol3/papers.cfm?abstract_id=2115203

Keatinge, T., Carlisle, D., & Keen, F. (n.d.). *Virtual currencies and terrorist financing: assessing the risks and evaluating responses.* Study commissioned by the Directorate General for Internal Policies, Policy Department for Citizens. https://www.titanium-project.eu

Kızıl, E. (2019). Türkiye'de Kripto Paranın Vergilendirilmesi ve Muhasebeleştirilmesi. *Mali Çözüm, 29*(155), 179–196.

Konakçı, A. E. (2018). *Prag Metro Sistemi Artık 10 Bitcoin ATM'sine Sahip!* https://koinbulteni.com/prag-metro-sistemi-artik-10-bitcoin-atmsine-sahip-19118

Martucci, B. (2018). *What Is Cryptocurrency: How it Works, History & Bitcoin Alternatives.* https://www.moneycrashers.com/cryptocurrency-history-bitcoin-alternatives/

Matonis, J. W. (1995). *Digital Cash and Monetary Freedom.* Economic Notes No. 63. http://libertarian.co.uk/lapubs/econn/econn063.pdf

Natarajan, H., Krause, S., & Gradstein, H. (2017). *Distributed Ledger Technology (DLT) and Blockchain.* FinTech note, no. 1. http://documents.worldbank.org/curated/en/177911513714062215/pdf/122140-WP-PUBLIC-Distributed- Ledger-Technology-and-Blockchain-Fintech-Notes.pdf

Nooruddin, S. (2019). *All about Blockchain.* Vieh Group.

Prewett, K., Dorsey, R. W., & Kumar, G. (2019). A Primer on Taxation of Investment in Cryptocurrencies. *Journal of Taxation of Investments, 36*(4), 3. Retrieved April 2020, from http://search.ebscohost.com/login.aspx?direct=true&db=edb&AN=138241160&site=eds-live

Ram, A. J. (2018). Taxation of the bitcoin: Initial insights through a correspondence analysis. *Meditari Accountancy Research, 26*(2), 214-240. http://www.emeraldinsight.com/doi/10.1108/MEDAR-10-2017-0229

Schipor, F. G.-L. (2019). Risks and Opportunities in the Cryptocurrency Market. *Ovidius University Annals, Series Economic Sciences, 19*(2), 879–883. http://search.ebscohost.com/login.aspx?direct=true&db=obo&AN=142315464&site=eds-live

Terazono, E. (2017). *Bitcoin Gets Official Blessing in Japan.* https://www.ft.com/content/b8360e86-aceb-11e7-aab9-abaa44b1e130

Uçma Uysal, T., & Aldemir, C. (2018). Dijital Kamu Mali Yönetim Sistemi ve Blok Zinciri Teknolojisi. *Muhasebe ve Vergi Uygulamaları Dergisi, 11*(3), 505–522. doi:10.29067/muvu.415066

Uğurlu, M. (2018). *Kripto Paraların Gelişimi ve Vergisel Konular.* https://coin-turk.com/kripto-paralarin-gelisimi-ve-vergisel-konular

Uti, T. (2018). *Bangkok's Revenue Department Will Use Blockchain Technology to Prevent Tax Evasion.* https://Blockchainreporter.net/bangkoks-revenue-department-will-use-Blockchain-technology-to-prevent-tax-evasion/

White, A. K. (2018). *Blockchain Discover the Technology Behind Smart Contracts, Wallets, Mining and Cryptocurrency.* CreateSpace Independent Publishing Platform.

World Bank Group. (2017). *FinTech Note No: 1, Distributed Ledger Technology (DLT) and Blockchain.* Author.

Yeoh, P. (2017). Regulatory issues in Blockchain technology. *Journal of Financial Regulation and Compliance, 25*(2), 196–208. doi:10.1108/JFRC-08-2016-0068

Zuckerman, M. J. (2018). S. *Korea to Tax Crypto Exchanges 24.2 Percent, in Line with Existing Tax Policy.* https:// cointelegraph.com/news/s-korea-to-tax-crypto-exchanges-242-percent-in-line-with-existing-tax-policy

ADDITIONAL READING

Bal, A. (2015), How to Tax Bitcoin? http://scitechconnect.elsevier.com/wp-content/uploads/2016/01/Chapter-14-%E2%80%93-How-to-Tax-Bitcoin.pdf, Accessed April 2020

Çetin, G. (2010). Bilişim Teknolojilerindeki Gelişmelerin Vergilemede Kayıt Düzeni ve Denetim Uygulamalarına Etkisi. Ekonomi Bilimleri Dergisi.2(1). ISSN: 1309-8020 (On- line). Retrieved September 3, 2012, from http://www.sobiad.org/eJOURNALS/dergi_EBD/arsiv/2010_1/09gunes_cetin.pdf

Çetin Gerger, G. (2019). Tax Services and Tax Service Providers' Changing Role in the IoT and AmI Environment. In Z. Mahmood (Ed.), *Guide to Ambient Intelligence in the IoT Environment. Computer Communications and Networks*. Springer. doi:10.1007/978-3-030-04173-1_9

ECB. (2012), Virtual Currency Schemes, https://www.ecb.europa.eu/pub/pdf/other/virtualcurrencyschemes201210en.pdf, Accessed April 2020

European Commission. (2016), The digital economy & society index (DESI), available at: www.ec.europa.eu/digital-single-market/en/desi, Accessed March 2020

Francesco, Z. et al. (2019), Bitcoin and cybersecurity: temporal dissection of Blockchain data to unveil changes in entity behavioral patterns. Applied Sciences 9.23, 5003.

Köse, B. (2018), Bitcoin'deki Düşüşün Gerekçesi Vergiler Olabilir, https://uzmancoin.com/bitcoin-vergi-2/, Accessed April 2020.

Nakamoto, S. (2009), Bitcoin: A Peer-to-Peer Electronic Cash System, https://bitcoin.org/bitcoin.pdf, Accessed May 2020 Gökbunar, R., & Utkuseven A. (2002). Elektronik Ticaretin Vergilendirilmesinde Yaşanan Gelişmeler: Yeni İpek Yolu Bir Vergi Cenneti Mi? İ.Ü. Siyasal Bilgiler Fakültesi Dergisi. 27.

KEY TERMS AND DEFINITIONS

Anti-Money Laundering: Anti-money laundering (AML) refers to a group of laws, regulations and processes aimed at preventing criminals from disguising illegally obtained funds as legitimate income.

Bitcoin: This refers to the decentralized and most popular virtual currency that can be sent from user to user on a peer-to-peer Bitcoin network without the need for intermediaries.

Blockchain: It refers to a form of distributed ledger spread over multi computers for sustaining a permanent and tamper-proof record of transactional information of digital assets.

Cryptocurrency: A digital currency for which encryption methods are used to regulate the generation of units of currency and verify the transfer of funds, operating independently of a central bank.

KYC (Know Your Customer): KYC related practices are especially relevant in user and client relationships with business. It is the first step in a customer's good relationship with a company.

Proof-of-Work: In a PoW system, network participants have to solve the so-called "cryptographic puzzles" to be permitted to introduce new "blocks" into a Blockchain.

Tax Compliance: Tax compliance means taxpayers' decision to comply with tax laws and regulations by paying taxes timely and accurately.

Tax Evasion: It refers to any criminal act or any offence of dishonesty punishable by civil penalties that is intended to lower or non-payment of taxation.

Chapter 6
Perspectives of Blockchain in Cybersecurity:
Applications and Future Developments

Muath A. Obaidat
Center for Cybercrime Studies, City University of New York, USA

Joseph Brown
City University of New York, USA

ABSTRACT

In recent years, blockchain has emerged as a popular data structure for use in software solutions. However, its meteoric rise has not been without criticism. Blockchain has been the subject of intense discussion in the field of cybersecurity because of its structural characteristics, mainly the permanency and decentralization. However, the blockchain technology in this field has also received intense scrutiny and caused to raise questions, such as, Is the application of blockchain in the field simply a localized trend or a bait for investors, both without a hope for permanent game-changing solutions? and Is blockchain an architecture that will lead to lasting disruptions in cybersecurity? This chapter aims to provide a neutral overview of why blockchain has risen as a popular pivot in cybersecurity, its current applications in this field, and an evaluation of what the future holds for this technology given both its limitations and advantages.

INTRODUCTION

As an emergent technology, blockchain has been a crux of discussion and experimentation in many fields. One among these is cybersecurity - a fast-moving, ever-changing industry which is constantly at the mercy of changing norms. The blockchain technology did not emerge with cybersecurity solely in mind, but rather as a means of decentralizing data while maintaining trust between users. However, as blockchain grew in notability, its purpose expanded to academia and commerce, where it quickly

DOI: 10.4018/978-1-7998-6650-3.ch006

developed in the cybersecurity area as well because of its intrinsic characteristics, commonly cited as immutability and decentralization.

Cybersecurity is a field which demands evolution at a more frequent rate than its constituent industries. As other technological norms evolve in tandem, cybersecurity must evolve at a relative rate in order to ensure the safety of - or alternatives to - such norms. To adhere to both the ever-changing norms of technology as well as the constant race for improved soundness and convenience for security, cybersecurity remains a field which is constantly evolving. As new architectures and protocols enter the public consciousness, such concepts always find their way into the sphere of cybersecurity discussion and research. Can these concepts be utilized to improve security? What implications do such concepts have for the field? One of these concepts is blockchain. The spur in discussion and research about blockchain has largely been fueled by both a desire for innovation as well as changing logistical cybersecurity structures which have already been considered as standard, such as the client-server or third-party authentication models. Blockchain stands as a contrast to historical architectures and security methodologies, and thus has brought some renewed hopes for researchers and businesses for the future, while others remain skeptical of its applicability.

The introduction of any elements considered ground-breaking or game-changing into a field, brings its own problems. These elements do exist in isolation, but alongside an omnipresent race for innovation, notability, or attracting the attention of investment without care for the integrity of proposed solutions. In the past few years, blockchain has shifted from a once curious concept into a pivotal discussion point in the fields of software, computer science, and cybersecurity. The exponential growth in popularity of blockchain has drawn rigorous debate; some voices purport blockchain to be a universal solution for filling prior gaps in historical fields, while others believe blockchain is simply a passing fad. As mentioned above, in cybersecurity especially, blockchain has remained a hot button yet also a controversial topic.

This chapter aims to present an investigation into the place of blockchain within the current field of cybersecurity, and evaluate its possible presence in the field in the future. The organization of this chapter is broken into three sections as follows. The first section outlines the characteristics of blockchain as they pertain to cybersecurity, discussing both the advantages of the blockchain architecture as well as the limitations and liabilities that its implementation could propose. The second section uses the first as a springboard to both discuss and evaluate the most popular currently discussed applications of blockchain within the cybersecurity field. The third section discusses the future implications of what impact blockchain will have on the cybersecurity field; it discusses both what opportunities blockchain has created which may continue to be influential in the future, as well as what issues a blockchain-centric future for cybersecurity may create.

CHARACTERISTICS OF BLOCKCHAIN

The usages of blockchain within cybersecurity and other perpendicular fields such as finance, typically lean on the core architectural traits of blockchain rather than more tangential extrapolations of its functionalities. Possible usages of blockchain within the field which have been promoted both by studies and private firms have included digital identity management, including digital signatures which is a direct derivative of the inherent functionality of the data structure. There are typically five core architectural characteristics of blockchain: *decentralized, immutable, anonymous, cryptographically encrypted,* and *trust-based.* Each of these elements has their own extrapolations within the field of cybersecurity (Yeasmin, 2019; Yassein, 2019). Brief explanation is as follows:

- **Decentralization** refers to the structure of inter-node communication within a blockchain network. This is dependent in part on the type of blockchain deployed, which is discussed within sections below. Decentralization, in general, typically means there is no centralized authority for assignment of permissions and storage.
- **Immutability** typically is a guarantee that data retains integrity and cannot be modified once stored; this is achieved in blockchain through the mutual agreement upon data between ledgers.
- **Anonymity** is facilitated in part through the decentralized nature of blockchain. Since there is no central authority, identities are distinct only through their communication, not their identity. Since blockchain is typically built on asymmetric encryption, identities are based around keys rather than being tied to personal identifiable information. It should be noted that the anonymity facilitated by blockchain is not a lack of identity, but rather a lack of publicly centralized identity. The identity which exists is tied to a key rather than to an individual. This distinction is what allows smart contracts to exist. Theoretically, blockchain applications can eliminate anonymity by assigning identities to keys, but this would done be through a middleware implementation, not through an inherent function of blockchain itself.
- **Cryptographic encryption** is a self-evident facet, as blockchain is built on asymmetric encryption between ledger storage and clients. Data within the ledger is encrypted while respective clients possess needed keys for decryption and management of their own data.
- **Trust**-based is a slightly more complicated characteristic. Trust refers to the overall integrity and legitimacy of actions between authorities manipulating data within a wider network. *Trust* is built differently, depending on blockchain structure; "proof" mechanisms are used for facilitating *access control*, which is the basis of trust.

While these traits may overlap with fundamental concepts within cybersecurity, one striking issue which researchers have struggled with is the imprecise nature of blockchain. As a result of its vast usage and asymmetric, decentralized deployments from a wide variety of sources and usages, it is hard to universally consider any non-theoretical traits as standard. This lack of standardized foundations has meant that, especially in a concrete field such as cybersecurity (where standardized information, outcome, and reliability are apropos to applicability), blockchain can be hard to coherently develop solutions with or to study consistently. This has led to a strong nuance in research, which has in turn led to a strong communal desire for general classification for the purpose of further judging accessibility and applicability (Yassein, 2019).

The architecture of blockchain itself is not singular; there are different categories for the structure of ledgers, such as the nature of visibility, or for what algorithm is used to guarantee trust. As such, some architectures are not suited for all applications in all given fields, and some are better suited than others. Intense research has been done for lending credence to the applicability of blockchain, both for the more generalized universal concept of blockchain itself, as well as the differentiations between variant architectures. This has been referred to as *blockchain applicability framework*. In this framework, the functionality of an application is contrasted with various variables to determine how its ecosystem fits (or fails to fit) not just into a blockchain itself, but also into individual categorizations of blockchain (such as public or private). It is divided into five domains; *data and participation, technical attributes, security, trust parameters,* and *performance/efficiency.* Each of these domains is constituted by several sub-domains, which themselves are structured around the aforementioned variables to determine the needs of a given system (Gourisetti, 2019).

Blockchain Architecture

Blockchain's extrapolation differs slightly depending on the architecture of the ledger. Although there are some elements which may overlap between categorizations, some categories of blockchain are best suited for certain applications over others, depending on the needs of the individual ecosystem.

Types of Blockchain

There are three main types of blockchain, each with its own distinct structures. These include *public, "consortium",* and *private.* Refer to Figure 1. In a public blockchain, every node within the ledger participates in verification, and thus creates a decentralized data structure. Public blockchains are permissionless, with every node carrying equal participation. This category of blockchain is typically deployed in ecosystems where every node is considered equal, most popularly, in cryptocurrencies. In a consortium blockchain, there are distributed permissions, unlike a public version. As a result, it is partially centralized; however, this creates a more secure environment, as the permissioned nodes allow relative security functionality. As such, the trust process is not universally mutual, but permissioned. Lastly, a private blockchain is one which is fully centralized. These blockchains are strictly permissioned and typically reserved for dictation by a central organization. Certain functionalities, such as read or write permissions, are controlled by centralized preference. As a result of centralization however, data is not guaranteed full integrity; thus, data tampering may occur in some environments, which may present an issue depending on the purpose the blockchain is meant to fulfill (Yeasmin, 2019; Gourisetti, 2019; Yassein, 2019).

Consensus Algorithms

As mentioned above, blockchain is built on the facilitation of trust between nodes. Within a given network, trust is one of the most important characteristics of any deployed system in cybersecurity. In order to build trust, blockchain architectures implement internal schemes called *consensus algorithms,* which are fundamental blueprints for how nodes communicate within a wider architecture. There are various different algorithms which can be used, and the choice of one over another typically relies on both the functionality as well as the category of blockchain in question. As such, choosing the correct algorithm, much like choosing the correct category of blockchain, is vital to an application's functionality. These algorithms are used for fostering both reliable data integrity as well as the distribution of access control among nodes. There are three popular versions of *consensus algorithms: proof of work, proof of stake,* and *proof of authority.* In a *proof of work* algorithm, iterative blocks are created through challenges which are exponentially hard to create, but easy to verify. Thus, nodes must work to create a proof, creating an environment in which blocks are probabilistically near impossible to modify, and also work in an iterative chain manner. In a *proof of stake* algorithm, the trust is distributed. Nodes compete by offering relative proportions of their stake in a system in order to be selected as valid. Selected nodes then verify transactions as valid. *Proof of authority* works as a modified version of *proof of stake;* in addition to competing for validation, the identity of the node itself is put at stake when competing for validation.

Figure 1. Visualization of blockchain architectures; from left to right: public, private, consortium.

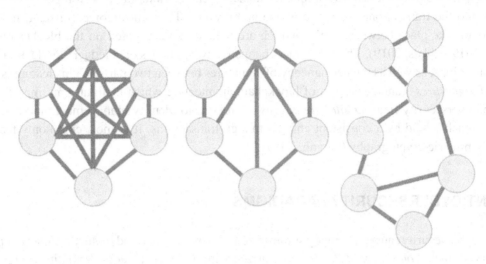

As such, limited nodes maintain authority for approval at any given time. It is important to note that these are not the only forms of consensus algorithms; there are at least a dozen popular other ones which have been employed by various blockchain applications. Other forms of consensus algorithms may include *proof of burn*, an algorithm where authority is proven by burning an amount of a stake in a system from a node. However, the three algorithms mentioned above are typically the most common in wider extrapolatable discussions (Yeasmin, 2019; Gourisetti, 2019).

Trust Factors

As seen above, trust is one of the most important factors which blockchain can be used to facilitate. This is, in part, why blockchain has been such a popular architecture within the field of information security. Trust can be most easily defined through the collective, foundational information security concepts of *confidentiality, integrity,* and *availability.* Research indicates that five primary factors support these operations: 1) the utilization of encryption algorithms to provide *privacy,* 2) identity-based algorithm through asymmetric or proof-of-identity techniques for *authentication,* 3) data immutability through storage and hash signatures for *integrity,* 4) the usage of digital operations such as signatures or certificates for guaranteeing *non-repudiation*, and 5) the *examinable degradation*, or presentable evidence regarding the norms of any given transactional operation. These five factors provide a continual foundation from which trust is built by the verifiability of transactions over time (Gorog, 2018).

There are also five categories of trust implementable through blockchain transactions: *suppression, validation, reliability, refutation,* and *deprivation.* Blockchain can be used to foster trust through the fulfillment of such categories; in doing so, blockchain can provide not just immutability, but also traceability, a caveat which would otherwise disallow blockchain's place in some fields (Gorog, 2018).

Smart Contracts

These are another important aspect of blockchain architecture. Similar to how anonymity and encryption are features which are derivative of intrinsic qualities of blockchain, smart contracts are derivative of both blockchain's inherent features of identity management and integral data storage. It is a protocol pre-baked into the transactional structure of the architecture. They allow for permanent, immutable agreements to take place between parties, which are then stored encrypted on the blockchain ledger (Yeasmin, 2019; Abbas, 2019). These contracts happen between nodes on a ledger, and facilitate guaranteed transactions, as well as the permanency of signatures between two parties. This feature is related to *"Digital Signatures",* another aspect of blockchain architecture which facilitates an important need within the cybersecurity field. *Digital signatures* are related to identity management, and allow for a node - presumably held by a consistent entity - to sign transactions. It is most commonly facilitated through asymmetric cryptography (Huynh, 2019).

CURRENT CYBERSECURITY PARADIGMS

The goal of cybersecurity can be succinctly summarized as managing risk and protecting assets. A popular subcategory, *information security*, can be summarized with three facets: confidentiality, integrity, and availability of data (Andriole, 2020). Researchers have noted that because of the exponential growth in reliance on technology, the demand for innovative cybersecurity tools and protocols has grown. Because of the timely presence and popularity of blockchain, it has become a popular staple within proposed cybersecurity whitepapers and studies. Some still ask, however, has blockchain proven itself as a pivotal concept to warrant such attention? Some academics, as well as business people, say it may be too early to tell, but the infant state of blockchain may foretell a future explosion of popularity, similar to the previous rise of cloud computing and cloud-based solutions (Andriole, 2020).

Blockchain's looming presence in cybersecurity has mimicked its place within the wider private business sector. Because of its trending and attractive nature to investors, blockchain has largely been proposed as a solution for bridging gaps and solving unresolved issues in the field, regardless of the actual viability of it within that sub-category. This has also been a result of unproven theory; many business pitches and studies which tout blockchain have not provided proof-of-concept or deployed solutions, and have simply existed as quantifiably vague theory. However, with that having been said, this does not mean that blockchain cannot separately be a useful tool within the cybersecurity field aside from the above also being true. Four particular usages of blockchain have been more popularly touted as extrapolatable features: data integrity and confidentiality aside from human oversight, previously discussed data immutability and mutuality between nodes, scalability of usership, and permanency of user identities (Sharma, 2019).

Application Determinacy

Due to the explosion of proposals, a need has emerged for determining if blockchain is truly needed for a given solution. Prior research has recommended a four-step process for assessing the applications of emerging technology, under which blockchain would fall. The steps include: 1) technology's background, 2) technology's potential impact, 3) pilot demonstration identification, and 4) planned demonstration development (Andriole, 2020). In the cybersecurity field, many applications of blockchain have stalled at step three; there is an abundance of discussion about the theorized impact of blockchain as well as the traits of it as an emerging technology, as well as theoretical applications within localized fields, but many theories have not manifested in active demonstrations. In the business sector, there have been more demonstrations of blockchain technology, but many have not managed to fully extrapolate the concept to where such demonstrations are more practical to use than current traditional methodologies.

Cryptocurrency & Tokens

It would also be impossible to discuss blockchain's current applicative presence without discussing cryptocurrency, and cryptocurrency's place in cybersecurity (Mohanta, 2019). While cryptocurrency is not a topic inherently related to cybersecurity, extrapolations of concepts introduced by cryptocurrency have found some level of integration - or at least discussion - within the field. This has been partially bolstered by the rise of features such as smart contracts popularized by the Ethereum platform (Polvora, 2020). Such extrapolations, besides smart contracts, have included ideas of permissioned policies and/ or access controls based on relative token holding (Polvora, 2020). Such discussion has been largely influenced by ICOs, or "Initial Coin Offerings", that are preliminary investment rounds of cryptocurrency ecosystems which mimic public company stock offerings. Ideas have included distributed token holdings, which in turn relate to relative access control or permissions in relation to an application's ecosystem. Since the tokens are possessed immutably by wallets tied to specific identities, the owner of such identity can be considered to have concrete relative control as such (Polvora, 2020). Despite being in early stages, there has still been some level of proof-of-concept of many of these techniques. While there has, to some degree, been proof of such working - at least on small levels, in whitepapers, or in nascent stages - worries have still stemmed from various issues, such as identities being more at risk if compromised through tangential means (such as phishing or otherwise), as well as other more typical worries such as the previously discussed limitations of blockchain networks, which still ring true here.

Blockchain vs. Cloud Computing

Blockchain has drawn significant comparisons to cloud computing. Refer to Figure 2 for virtualization for Cloud distributed computing. Cloud-based security solutions have grown significantly in popularity over the last decade and have targeted similar solutions in similar fields. Unlike blockchain, however, cloud computing solutions at times amplify narrow vulnerabilities, or can even create new surfaces of attack, like centralized data storage or shared access control. Blockchain has been proposed as a solution for replacing more centralized cloud-computing structures with decentralized architectures and eliminating vulnerabilities in turn. This is not to say that blockchain is fully impenetrable, but rather that the surfaces of attack are greatly distilled in comparison to simple cloud-computing solutions; this is partially because of the lack of singular points of entry on most implementations of blockchain architectures (Kshetri, 2017).

Figure 2. Visualization of Cloud Computing

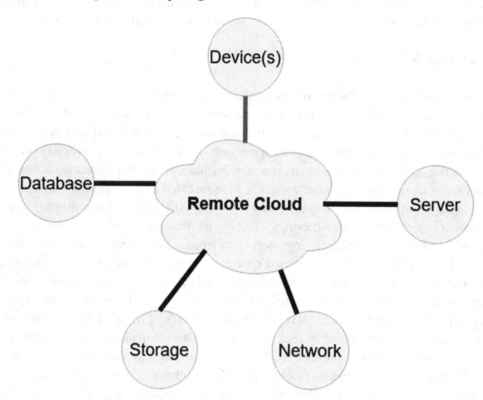

CYBERSECURITY SOLUTIONS AND DISCUSSION

Current applications of blockchain, whether in cybersecurity or in wider fields, are hard to evaluate in full, which in turn has led to segmented evaluations of their usage. This is because current designs vary greatly, and thus have made implementation as well as deployment and maintenance, difficult. Unlike many current systems, blockchain's relative infancy combined with its requirement of high levels of sophisticated technical knowledge and complex setup requirements make it harder to be adopted widely (Vance, 2019). This has raised questions, particularly in the field of cybersecurity where concrete knowledge of what one is working with is of utmost importance. Despite the constant desire for innovation within the field, precedent is also very important within the industry among professionals, and the lack of large-scale precedent for blockchain's usage has been a detriment to the spread of its adoption. This is not to say, however, that there have not been successful test cases or proof-of-concepts, simply that the wider application of blockchain within cybersecurity has been handicapped because of unfamiliarity and decency, as well as lack of historical usages proving its usefulness over more traditional implementations and architectures.

Blockchain and the Internet of Things

While there has been a general explosion in the popularity of blockchain, it has seen particular exponential interest in two cybersecurity fields: information security and Internet of Things (IoT) security.

Out of these two subcategories, blockchain has received serious innovative attention for the Internet of Things. This has been a result of two major factors - the relative infancy of the IoT, and thus its timely popularity intersecting with the popularity of blockchain, as well the lack of current standardization and security measures for the IoT (Obaidat, 2019; Obaidat, 2020). Information security has also remained a popular category; though this is because of an overlap in motives between the field and the features of blockchain, namely, data integrity and availability (Ahram, 2017). Blockchain's presence within the sphere of IoT cybersecurity discussion has been dual-faceted: the nature of the IoT can be said to simultaneously support and clash with blockchain architecture. On one hand, the need for standardized identity management, immutability of data, and peer-to-peer verification brought by blockchain perfectly suits the design structure of IoT devices and software. On the other hand, Blockchain's exponential resource usage, especially when juxtaposed with the limited resources of IoT devices (Obaidat, 2019; Hassebo, 2018; Khodjaeva, 2019), is a significant hurdle. While this has been an obstacle, it has not fully prevented possible solutions from manifesting; many theories have been proposed for circumventing this issue and maintaining the benefits of blockchain in turn, one such example being "LightChain" (Doku, 2019). The specifics of how blockchain may influence IoT spheres have been scattered and differ greatly between proposals and studies. Some ideas have included IoT devices as individual certified nodes, and all communications between such would be facilitated through smart contracts to guarantee validity, and track transactions (Kshetri, 2017).

IoT's intersection with blockchain has led to a fierce debate over leveled integration. The severity of IoT vulnerabilities alongside their popularity has led to such research being fast-tracked (Obaidat, 2019). Many startups have already started to roll out whitepapers and prototypes for the usage of blockchain in IoT systems. Large conglomerates such as IBM have taken interest in these and have begun to distribute blockchain services for supply chains to rely on. These inter-business facilitations have elevated blockchain to industrial level discussion. Blockchain-based protocols have been proposed for the deployment of such architectures as safeguards in industrial systems which rely on wireless communications. The use of blockchain to validate identities between sources has made it an important discussion point for devices that vitally rely on communication from a select source of valid entities (Kshetri, 2017). The intersection of IoT and blockchain proposals, however, have not been without issue; depending on the infrastructure of blockchain implementation, which would be determined by the type of blockchain, there are possible privacy issues, considering the vast amount of data collected and transferred between IoT devices. There are already large concerns about IoT device interactions in this regard which have not been solved by consensus yet, especially considering an industry-wide lack of standardization. Blockchain's integration with the IoT does not inherently solve these issues and may open up new issues because of its ledger-based distribution structure. Possible solutions to this have included tiered networks with individual private blockchains connected to wider public blockchains, distributed with fine-grained access controls. These architectures, however, have largely not been tested. Blockchain has been proposed also as a management platform for IoT devices, essentially functioning as a middleware for managing data, establishing permanent identities, and tokenizing privileges (Ali, 2019).

Facilitation of API Functionalities

Blockchain's cybersecurity functionality is by no means limited to IoT devices; blockchain as a non-IoT data management platform has also been tested separately as another popular means. Due to its node-based structure as well as its immutable nature, blockchain has been used as a platform for simplifying user management, particularly in relation to cloud-based applications. This assists in facilitating access control, as well as bolstering user authentication methods and implementing single sign-on capabilities. Blockchain has also been proposed methodically through other approaches, one being an "API Approach", where blockchain functions as an API to facilitate other functionalities rather than acting as a functional platform in and of itself. Some of these usages have included DevOps, cloud integration, and data analytics, particularly for apps, businesses, and ads (Ahram, 2017). As mentioned before, this may echo traits of cloud platforms. Much capacity has been given to comparing facets of cloud computing and blockchain platforms. Research has noted that some cloud platforms follow "zero trust" security models, and, similar to blockchain, fully employ encrypted transactional models. Blockchain, as a decentralized model for the most part (outside of modified architectures such as consortium), does lack the segmented control schemes which cloud computing allows, such as administrator oversight. However, blockchain arguably employs better identity management and data immutability, at the cost of compromising that client nodes bear more serious implications because of such. However, with current technology, hacking into a blockchain node would be significantly harder, as attacks would be limited to brute-forcing or client hijacking, both of which have a far lower rate of success than man-in-the-middle, masquerade, or replay style attacks. However, both models are still susceptible to attacks based on human error, such as phishing or social engineering (Kshetri, 2017).

Given the above evaluations of blockchain functionalities, it is not hard to see how most current applications of blockchain are comparable to current applications of cloud computing. However, there are nuances between the two which may affect which is more viable for an application (or user/enterprise, in turn) to utilize. Cloud computing relies on a third party with physical infrastructure, while blockchain is decentralized through a ledger, but may be facilitated through a third-party vendor. These options may fit different companies differently: some may want a third party for validatory oversight, while others may want to eliminate middlemen. Similarly, physical infrastructure may suit some, while ledger-based immutability may be better for other companies. Blockchain and cloud computing are very similar, however, not on all fronts. For example, while both carry nuances in how they are permissioned, blockchain can be selected to operate as permission-less, while this would be a risk under most cloud computing paradigms. Other nuances between the two, such as the level of encryption, would be left up to individual organizations to evaluate depending on target and vendor specifications. Both still face challenges, however; cloud computing is a less recent and more developed standard, while blockchain still faces early implementation issues such as lack of security mechanisms. In theory, both face resource management issues, albeit for different reasons - blockchain because of the exponential growth of needed resources for transactions and ledger-size, while cloud computing because of limited hardware resources for storage and speed (Kshetri, 2017).

Identity Management

Figure 3. Visualization of digital signing and signature verification process

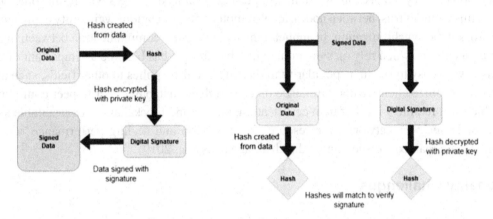

Another functional usage of blockchain is the facilitation of digital certificates and signatures, an inherent attractive feature of its architecture. Refer to Figure 3. As such, its implementation has been simplified, but has not largely been deployed en masse. Many private companies have started either developing or rolling out solutions in this light, but, because of a race for innovation, these competing brands have largely crowded each other out from reaching wider accessibility. Larger brands such as Facebook or Twitter, however, have announced their own initiatives for developing blockchain-based solutions, some of which have intersected desires for immutable identity management and signatures (Ahram, 2017). Popular applications of digital certification have promised a functionality for replacing notarization and have hinted at ideas for replacing infrastructure for intangible assets such as copyrights or licenses, as well as storage for public and private records, and taking advantage of smart contracts for implementation of arbitration and real-life contracts. Current implementations of many of these practices leave systems open to data tampering or theft; blockchain solutions promise to bolster cybersecurity standards for storage and transaction through increased confidentiality and integrity. Many private companies have undertaken these ideas already but have yet to break into the mainstream for further serious consideration (Alexander, 2019).

Other Applications

Further deployments of blockchain include email and endpoint security. The insecurity of current emailing services and protocols has remained an issue for multiple years; blockchain has been proposed as an alternative, and unlike many claims, has been backed by proof-of-concept tests. Blockchain has posed itself as a decentralized solution for email because of immutable transaction records and identity nonrepudiation. Current issues of message authenticity, from which phishing and fraud emails currently stem, could be eroded by the implementation of blockchain systems. Endpoint security, on the other hand, ties into the aforementioned intersection of Blockchain's popularity in relation to IoT security. Most IoT devices lack endpoint security measures, thus increasing the need for effective measures. Blockchain has been proposed as a solution primarily because attacks against blockchain-based architecture are weakened by the distributed architecture of blockchain, especially if data validation nodes are used. Much like email, use cases have been deployed for this as well, which have shown promising results (Vance, 2019).

Advantages of using blockchain for the above mentioned applications have a level of nuance between implementation but, beyond decentralization, also present certain advantages which suit some purposes over others; this includes trust between nodes, local-remote synchronization, availability of unchangeable data, and cross-node synchronization. In applications which require communication between individual nodes, or applications which rely on synchronization, blockchain has become an important discussion pivot. This is very easy to see in its popularity in the IoT, but also applies to other fields, such as fields looking to synchronize clients without reliance on a centralized database. Peer to peer communicative clients, which still require a level of trust certification, have found blockchain to be a suitable solution. However, for larger peer networks, the resource consumption and scaling performance issues with blockchain have remained a discouraging disadvantage (Yassein, 2019).

Functionality Challenges

Besides the inconsistencies between deployments of blockchain, other issues have been discussed widely in academic research of Blockchain's capabilities, especially in regards to security and privacy. Issues which the blockchain architecture possesses include balancing authority with integrity/data consistency, proportional control in a ledger's network by users, and exponential size of operations and size. Balancing confidentiality with the connective nature of blockchain has also remained an issue. Blockchain's immutability can be a double-edged sword as well, in the case of mistakes from users or organizations. The exponential cost and size of blockchain ledgers, as previously mentioned, has remained a massive issue, even for enterprise organizations (Yassein, 2019).

Various solutions have been proposed for solving many of these limitations, such as further deployment of encryption techniques, as well as the implementation of new data structures (Yassein, 2019). The infancy and lack of standardization of blockchain has been a catalyst in many of these limitations (Ahram, 2017). Blockchain is not only a complex system in and of itself, but also it does not suit a "plug and play" style of development. This is a potential drawback for two reasons. Firstly, as blockchain is a relatively nascent architecture, it discourages many from adopting such because of it being unproven. However, the lack of adoption, in turn, means a lack of widespread security mechanisms have been tested or developed on a wide scale basis, in comparison to traditional methods which are more easily tested. The complex and intended large, decentralized nature of blockchain makes proof-of-concepts hard to evaluate in low-density or testing environments (Kshetri, 2017). However, as blockchain matures as an architecture, many of these issues are expected to be solved, especially as it attracts more academic attention for research (Ahram, 2017; Kshetri, 2017).

Common Attacks and Threats

Figure 4. Example of a "majority" attack in a blockchain, where malicious blocks outweigh original blocks, and thus overwrite them.

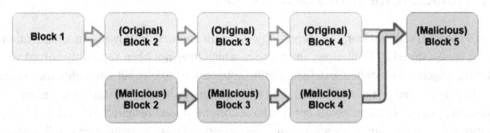

A variety of attacks also exist because of intrinsic features of blockchain networks. "Majority" attacks, as exemplified in Figure 4, remain an issue in many networks, which can occur when a node controls the majority of stakes in a given environment. Similarly, "selfish mining" has remained an issue, where miners participate in creating blocks on a private branch and then only broadcast them to the public network once the chain is longer than the public network, thus replacing them (Abbas, 2019; Huynh, 2019). Distributed Denial of Service (DDoS) attacks are also a threat to blockchain networks. This may occur when a dishonest node uses a large number of other nodes to attempt to overwhelm requests on the rest of the blockchain ledger (Huynh, 2019; Oksiiuk, 2020).

It is also important to note that, while blockchain bolsters authentication measures, because of its integrity of permanency and ability to foster digital signature and identity management, the immutable status of identities on a blockchain also brings its own worries. While authentication strength is partially dependent on the strength of cryptographic implementation, there are tangential vulnerabilities which may call for greater worry than their non-blockchain counterparts. Primarily, phishing and social engineering carry more grave risks for blockchain authentication than they do for other authentication procedures. This is because of the immutable, permanent nature of identities on a blockchain; if information regarding an identity is compromised, depending on the nature of the Blockchain's implementation, it may be permanently compromised (Oksiiuk, 2020).

Limitations

Blockchain is commonly brought up in information security discussions for "big data" applications but suffers from some limitations which are often ignored. Firstly, block capacity is a large limitation. Wider implementations of blockchain have low block capacities, and while larger blocks can store more data, they cause significant performance and scaling issues. Smaller blocks, on the other hand, are reliable, but obviously limit the actual space for records. Secondly, because blockchain is a distributed ledger, the storage mechanism for large blockchains often does not take into account that ledgers are copied to the side of all users. This is, of course, dependent on implementation: some may circumvent this by using vendors or applications which simply facilitate access to a blockchain rather than distributing client nodes. Nevertheless, this remains an issue for some implementations; while this data is encrypted, it still opens data to data mining and other attacks depending on how the ledgers are actually accessed. It also means that attackers can potentially store permanent malicious data in a ledger (Dai, 2017).

FUTURE TRAJECTORIES AND DISCUSSION

Blockchain's future is still unclear; the technology is bright and is still drawing much attention and investment but is also mired by limitations and worries which have not been verifiably solved yet, despite their continual subjection to academic debate. Future applications of blockchain within the cybersecurity sphere will largely depend on the scale under which blockchain protrudes into the wider technical sphere. Both private and public (governmental) entities have commissioned research for enterprise implementations, but many of such remain, as aforementioned, confined to theorization or small-scaling testing rather than large-scale deployment. Most cybersecurity implications of where blockchain may shine in the future lies in either information security derivative functionalities or the facilitation of trust between transacting entities (Gorog, 2018).

Studies largely fall into two camps when considering which path blockchain may take in the future. One position is an optimistic view of integration on the public, communal level, replacing the foundations of many inter-entity communications (Aggarwal, 2019). On the other hand, a more pessimistic view which either passes off blockchain as a fad or instead proposes that current limitations on blockchain application architecture are enough to prevent it from being further pervasive in the future. Much discussion derivative of the former point does not necessarily agree with the possibility of blockchain's ability to constitute such functionality. When it comes to the integration of blockchain with concepts such as contracts, financial transactions, or other communal activities, there is not much debate as to *if* such integration can be done, but rather if it *should* be done (Aggarwal, 2019). There is much technical consensus on how these concepts could be implemented, but there is less consensus from an organizational standpoint insofar as the realistic measures under which such applications could be deployed.

Propositions and Frameworks

Research has indicated that future public implementations of blockchain must be open, transparent, and auditable, in order to circumvent worries which may otherwise manifest from the nature of the architecture. Most research on the future of blockchain in cybersecurity, and in wider fields to an extent, has indicated that the strongest promises of the architecture come from its facilitation of decentralization, and the ability for mutual, decentralized validation without the need for arbitrary authority (Oksiiuk, 2020). Such future implementations of blockchain may not be restricted solely to using public architectures but will have to pay close attention to caveats in individual blockchain categorizations according to the need of their applications. For example, applications which seek better privacy protections and better performance are more likely to depend on consortium blockchain models (Cai, 2018). It is important to note, however, that moving forward, the usage of the prior mentioned "blockchain applicability framework(s)" will be vital for this reason. Incorrect blockchain application may result not just in decreased performance but also in heightened security risks.

Developing decentralized applications is a lucrative measure with a high demand but presents unique challenges. It requires extra scrutiny, which blockchain may not be fully self-sufficient to handle. When dealing with the trust and assets of enterprises at high levels in particular, decentralized applications must be evaluated as holistically secure. This means that individual parts of the architecture - the consensus algorithm, the category of blockchain, and even the separate structure of the application - must all be given strict security and performance guidelines (Cai, 2018). Future opportunities for blockchain in this light may not just present themselves as innovations utilizing blockchain but rather as innovations built off of blockchain perpendicularly aimed at making blockchain utilization more accessible and/or secure to either users or to commercial or governmental enterprises.

Blockchain-as-a-Service

Figure 5. Comparison of service infrastructures.

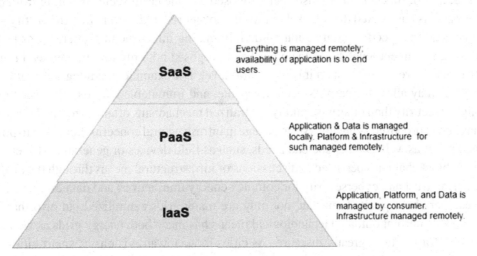

Future implementations of blockchain may replicate the current usage of cloud providers. Referring to Figure 5, just as cloud-based cybersecurity applications are provided as a *service*, alongside the rise of SaaS (Software-as-a-Service), PaaS (Platform-as-a-Service), and IaaS (Infrastructure-as-a-Service) models, research has indicated that the future of blockchain may popularize the model of *Blockchain-as-a-Service* (Andriole, 2020). This concept heavily ties into prior mentions of comparisons between blockchain and cloud computing; the similarity in service model and focused solutions also creates similarities on this front. Unlike cloud computing, however, a vendor would facilitate access rather than facilitate hosting. This is slightly different from the current cloud-computing model because a vendor is also liable for the actual maintenance of the core foundations of the platform. While the core functionality would be dependent on both the category of blockchain and consensus algorithm deployed, in this evolved model, a vendor would simply act as a front end for providing access to a ledger and, at best, moderate data on the application layer rather than the underlying data structure of blockchain. Some studies have noted that the rise of peer-to-peer ecosystems and contractor ("gig") platforms could be similarly bolstered by implementations of blockchain. This would be because of the identity management functionality of the architecture as well as the decentralized structure, the implementation of cryptocurrencies and tokens, and, most importantly, the smart contract functionality. Such implementations would likely mimic "as-a-service" infrastructures (Fraga-Lamas, 2019).

Blockchain as Infrastructure

As previously discussed, there is much discussion over Blockchain's possible place in replacing and/or aiding the foundational architectures of communal and legal activities, such as securing the integrity and availability of inter-entity contracts or providing a secure basis for voting (Aggarwal, 2019). While there has not been practical mass application of most of such proposals to date, surveyed and commissioned research has pinpointed that blockchain could be utilized as a cybersecurity tool for securing government level infrastructural needs; research into such has been commissioned by multiple governments, including the UK for energy infrastructure, the US for secured domestic messaging between officials and for identity certification, and Australia for securing communication between entities inside of wider "smart cities" (Vance, 2019). Blockchain has also been proposed as a means of securing voting from malicious influence; proposals have stated that blockchain would bolster risk reduction through identity validation as well as increase the speed of digitization while minimizing infrastructural interactions (Alexander, 2019). On this government level, blockchain has been proposed not only for civilian level transactions but also for trans-active systems on an infrastructural level. For example, the integration of blockchain into power grids may allow for permissioned, traceable, and immutable records of transactions which provide a higher security than otherwise purely centralized mechanisms often currently deployed. Smart contracts have been proposed as having a strong usage in infrastructural concerns, both akin to power grids as mentioned prior, as well as other societal needs, such as field devices or generators (Li, et al., 2019).

Elsewhere, blockchain has persisted in discussions of infrastructural means through the proposals for usage of ensuring trust and cybersecurity for complex energy transactions and data exchanges (Mylrea, 2017). Researchers have pointed out that, not only are many grids centralized but also that interconnectivity alongside current outdated technological means has made both energy grids as well as associated electrical infrastructure, greatly insecure. As cities move toward visions of smart cities, securing infrastructure becomes increasingly important as new vectors of attack become available. Blockchain's ability to create a decentralized "Energy Internet of Things" makes systematic attacks on infrastructural grids harder by decentralizing vulnerabilities. The usage of smart contracts may also increase resilience and more reliably track energy transactions within infrastructure. Researchers note that the integration of blockchain will also help both single out anomalous entities or transactions within a system and allow for a more streamlined intersection of infrastructural needs such as electricity and the reporting of data. These ideas have been tested on a small scale within testbeds but have not yet been extrapolated to apply to large cities. Much like other specialized, large-scale theories, these concepts are often found trapped in a limbo of not being able to be deployed because of a lack of proof but also not carrying proof because of their need for large-scale deployment in order to create such (Mylrea, 2017).

Specialized Usage

New opportunities regularly arise, such as those recently proposed within the automotive economy (Fraga-Lamas, 2019). The integration of blockchain within the sphere of automotive technology intersects with the recent rise of the intelligent automotive economy. The term "intelligent automotive" does not just apply to autonomous cars: it applies to any car with onboard technology for data processing. Many newer models of cars feature on-board computers, with some relying at least partially on cloud-based information. Given the absolute need for safety as a priority within an automobile, as computer systems are embedded in them, the need for cybersecurity arises. Cybersecurity for automotive may apply to different categorizations, not only the traditional categories of preventing cyber-attacks and ensuring reliability and validity of cloud information, but also new functionalities such as ensuring the validity of parts and protecting against counterfeits, and protecting the integrity of the production process. Studies say that blockchain may be utilized for the prevention of counterfeits through blockchain-based certificates; meanwhile, integrity during production processes may be facilitated through the usage of smart contracts. Other such benefits that blockchain may bring to smart-automobiles, essentially mimic the benefits blockchain brings to other integrations, namely information integrity and security through encryption, standardization, and decentralization (Narbayeva, 2020).

Whether or not blockchain can meet other more specialized purposes is still undecided. A significant amount of research has been dedicated to these more focused fields, as seen above, despite the otherwise scattered nature of scouting opportunities for blockchain to fulfill. Much like the considerations given to blockchain as a foundation for securing communal activities, much of the question of integration does not lay on *how* or *why*, but rather *if*. Surveyed research has found a significant number of benefits for blockchain, and, without a doubt, there will be continued discussion, especially for as long as a standard fails to exist otherwise for the IoT. Given the virtues and wide discussion of blockchain in relation to these narrow implementation ideas, there is much reason to think optimistically about their future. However, non-technical factors, such as business considerations, must also be taken into account in this regard (Ali, 2019).

Open Research and Current Challenges

As previously mentioned, if blockchain is to be deployed as massively accessible architecture, future implementations of blockchain will still have various hurdles to overcome which have not yet been solved. The most important of these includes the lack of scalability of blockchain - not of usership but instead with regards to processing transactions and consumption of resources. Furthermore, there are some privacy concerns within blockchain, e.g. those originating from the public nature of ledgers. Research has also indicated that bootstrapping could pose an issue for blockchain applications, as related to large commercial enterprise files and frameworks (Sharma, 2019). Accessibility is generally held back in a technical fashion; accessibility for blockchain must also be improved at a user-derivative level. As mentioned in the evaluation section, blockchain has been handicapped in its adoption because of the complexity surrounding its development, deployment, and maintenance. Experts in the cybersecurity field believe that, because of the importance of concrete understanding of employed metrics and concepts, the future of blockchain applications will be dependent on its ability to develop user friendly adaptations (Vance, 2019).

Performance

Many of the previously discussed limitations of blockchain, particularly in regards to performance and exponential resource usage, remain serious concerns for widespread adoption in the future. While individual implementations may not find these limitations as stifling due to their scope, many company products and academic studies which purport blockchain as a solution, intend for such to be deployed on a massive scale. Currently, these issues are generally incurred on wide scales and create worries in many of the organizations and clients who otherwise may be apt to adopt such innovative measures. The direct adoption, as well as the further discussion, of blockchain has not been fully blockaded by these issues. The reason being that there has been a significant interest in solving the issues, but progress has nonetheless been significantly slowed down. Many conclude that before blockchain can reach peak cybersecurity implementation in both the general public and within individual private sectors, these issues will have to be solved (or alternatively, at least addressed in part), due to them eclipsing the benefits blockchain otherwise brings (Alexander, 2019). These worries carry over to many of the more focused implementation ideas which outline blockchain as a solution, such as the previously discussed IoT, and thus may prove to be some of the biggest hurdles which blockchain will need to overcome before seeing wider implementation even within these narrow pigeonholes (Ali, 2019).

User Identification

While it has been previously discussed that decentralization, and thus strengthened anonymity measures, are possible future strengths for the Blockchain platform, this is a double-edged sword. Anonymity also implies a lack of traceability which may be a worry when considering the facilitation of illegal activity through blockchain. Since cybersecurity also involves offensive tactics rather than just defensive, blockchain architectures may hinder the ability of law enforcement to enforce laws regarding illegal transactions; alternatively, because of data permanency, the ability to hinder or delete the spread of illegal materials online (Oksiiuk, 2020).

Accessibility and Propagation

The future of blockchain's implementation in cybersecurity especially, parallel to its dependence on user accessibility, will also be heavily determined by the quality of research which discusses the concept. Academics have noted that claims about blockchain are tricky to make. For example, blockchain carries a reputation for immutability of data but is also vulnerable to majority or 51% of the attacks, which allows data to be modified. This creates concerns as to whether claims for the concept are fully understood and justified in how they are propagated between researchers, developers, governments, and business people. Current dissonances, for example, in claims of blockchain being fully immutable would be technically false because of the existence of these attacks. Nevertheless, such claims continue to be made (Vance, 2019).

As with the aforementioned topics, it is likely conclusive that, given the current status of blockchain as well as the consensus drawn around certain points, the future of blockchain will lie in specialized implementations rather than as a replacement for systems constituting historical methods and foundations. This is not to say that blockchain would not provide theoretical strengths in its implementation for these systems; rather, the viability of such will be likely limited to theory rather than practice. However, this is also not an ultimate conclusion but rather an evaluation of the current status of blockchain and its implementations which notes their highly volatile nature (Fraga-Lamas, 2019).

Applicability

The benefits of implementation within many of these new opportunities typically overlap with those proposed for other such systems. For example, we earlier discussed the possible usage of blockchain as a foundation for further technical standardization of communal activities (Fraga-Lamas, 2019). Many of these overlaps, even within these specialized systems, as seen with the above explanation of automotive integration, typically boil down to the same infrastructural benefits and limitations; these being standardization, identity management, and information security benefits, alongside limitations of scalability, complexity, and maintenance, amongst many others. Given that many of these benefits overlap concretely, it is hard to conclude whether blockchain is actually benefiting the individual fields or whether the field is simply absorbing the nature of blockchain. In other words, the discussion has often fallen on pivots of *"How would this function on blockchain?"* rather than *"How would this benefit from blockchain?"* Hence both the vague generality and the benefits being traits of blockchain rather than improved traits of the individual fields. It is important to note that this is not necessarily universal; fields such as the IoT have had far more conclusive discussion on the purpose and individualized benefits of blockchain implementation. However, from a wider generalized perspective, this harkens back to the early mentions of the *"blockchain applicability framework"*. The question is often not what traits of blockchain could be integrated with an application but rather if the application benefits enough from blockchain to render its integration as being worthwhile.

Summary of Open Research and Debate

To summarize, current research challenges in blockchain typically can be boiled down to six categories (Mohanta, 2019):

- Efficiency of distributed systems in regards to wider scalability
- Correct distribution of trust and/or permission between nodes without compromising usability and cybersecurity, depending on the architecture of the blockchain
- Exponential resource usage
- Universality of smart contract designs
- Task scheduling on blockchain networks
- Efficient validation of data between nodes as networks grow exponentially in size.

Several other discussed challenges also exist; however, such is the complexity of blockchain and its relative nascence (Fraga-Lamas, 2019) as well as the existence of prior mentioned cyber-attacks (Oksiiuk, 2020). Lastly, the actual applicability of blockchain itself for certain functionalities over others remains a debate, hence the discussed existence of applicability frameworks (Gourisetti, 2019).

CONCLUSION

Blockchain is an exciting, relatively new architecture which has spurred a significant interest in both public and private sectors, particularly regarding its possible place within the cybersecurity field. However, despite the significant proposed innovation and sheer amount of discussion taking place, there is still no consensus as to what the future may hold for wider implementation. There is certainly a significant amount of both research and theory for projecting that the future of blockchain is bright. However, these promising implementations are held back by current limitations for which there is yet to be a consensus on how to fix, such as scalability and exponential resource usage. Specialized niches, especially within narrow uses such as IoT security, show the most promise for blockchain as an application structure.

Researchers mostly agree that the future of blockchain will largely be dependent on the ability of the architecture to adapt to the needs of enterprises which wish to adopt it. While there is much consensus as to the security benefits the adoption of blockchain may bring, questions about its detractions or about the sheer complexity and maintenance of its implementation, particularly on a wide-scale, have acted as a barrier for it penetrating further within the sphere of cybersecurity. As discussed within this chapter, the universality of Blockchain's benefits have led to discussion about the actual benefits of blockchain, rather than if Blockchain's usage actually suits an application or if blockchain itself just carries certain traits which applications adopting it would adopt in turn. These have led to frameworks being developed for the purpose of determining whether or not blockchain is actually needed. Some may say the excitement surrounding blockchain has, in part, obscured its adoption, because through its wider proposals for almost all forms of cybersecurity gaps, specialized sectors, for which its implementation is better suited, have received less attention.

While blockchain continues to receive much attention, its place in cybersecurity is still uncertain. Although the benefits of the architecture may be inarguable, propositions of its integration beckon logistical and theoretical questions. Most importantly, the questions arise as to: should blockchain be integrated just because it can be? and do the benefits of blockchain outweigh the complexity and downsides? Unfortunately, there is no universal answer to such questions. Instead, the answers are largely determined by the individual factors of the application in question. Just as with the wider cybersecurity field, no matter what benefits may be innate to blockchain, the individual nuances and caveats of deployments are more determinate factors for integration than the supposed benefits of what is being integrated itself. As a result of this, it is no surprise that the proposed integrations of blockchain, which shine the most, are those which come from specialized systems, such as the Internet of Things. These systems do not benefit from blockchain solely because of the traits of blockchain but instead because the nature of such systems intersect with the structure and functionalities made available by blockchain architecture.

REFERENCES

Abbas, Q. E., & Sung-Bong, J. (2019). A Survey of Blockchain and Its Applications. *2019 International Conference on Artificial Intelligence in Information and Communication (ICAIIC)*, 1–3. 10.1109/ICAIIC.2019.8669067

Aggarwal, S., Chaudhary, R., Aujla, G. S., Kumar, N., Choo, K.-K. R., & Zomaya, A. Y. (2019). Blockchain. *Journal of Network and Computer Applications*, *144*, 13–48. doi:10.1016/j.jnca.2019.06.018

Ahram, T., Sargolzaei, A., Sargolzaei, S., Daniels, J., & Amaba, B. (2017), Blockchain technology innovations. *2017 IEEE Technology Engineering Management Conference (TEMSCON)*, 137–141. 10.1109/TEMSCON.2017.7998367

Alexander, C. A., & Wang, L. (2019), Cybersecurity, Information Assurance, and Big Data Based on Blockchain. 2019 SoutheastCon, 1–7. doi:10.1109/SoutheastCon42311.2019.9020582

Ali, M. S., Vecchio, M., Pincheira, M., Dolui, K., Antonelli, F., & Rehmani, M. H. (2019). Applications of Blockchains in the Internet of Things. *IEEE Communications Surveys and Tutorials*, *21*(2), 1676–1717. doi:10.1109/COMST.2018.2886932

Andriole, S. J. (2020). Blockchain cybersecurity. *IT Professional*, 22(1), 13–16. doi:10.1109/MITP.2019.2949165

Cai, C., Duan, H., & Wang, C. (2018). Tutorial: Building Secure and Trustworthy Blockchain Applications, 2018 IEEE Cybersecurity Development. SecDev. doi:10.1109/SecDev.2018.00023

Dai, F., Shi, Y., Meng, N., Wei, L., & Ye, Z. (2017), From Bitcoin to cybersecurity: A comparative study of blockchain application and security issues. *2017 4th International Conference on Systems and Informatics (ICSAI)*, 975–979. 10.1109/ICSAI.2017.8248427

Doku, R., Rawat, D. B., Garuba, M., & Njilla, L. (2019). LightChain: On the Lightweight Blockchain for the Internet-of-Things. *2019 IEEE International Conference on Smart Computing (SMARTCOMP)*, 444–448, 10.1109/SMARTCOMP.2019.00085

Fraga-Lamas, P., & Fernandez-Carames, T. M. (2019). A Review on Blockchain. *IEEE Access: Practical Innovations, Open Solutions, 7*, 17578–17598. doi:10.1109/ACCESS.2019.2895302

Gorog, C., & Boult, T. E. (2018). Solving Global Cybersecurity Problems by Connecting Trust Using Blockchain. *2018 IEEE International Conference on Internet of Things (IThings) and IEEE Green Computing and Communications (GreenCom) and IEEE Cyber, Physical and Social Computing (CPSCom) and IEEE Smart Data (SmartData)*, 1425–1432. 10.1109/Cybermatics_2018.2018.00243

Gourisetti, S. N. G., Mylrea, M., & Patangia, H. (2019). Evaluation and Demonstration of Blockchain. *IEEE Transactions on Engineering Management*, 1–15. doi:10.1109/TEM.2019.2928280

Hassebo, A., Obaidat, M. A., & Ali, M. (2018). *Commercial 4G LTE Cellular Networks for Supporting Emerging IoT Applications in Internet of Things*. Mechatronics and their Applications International Conference, as a part of the Advances in Science and Engineering Technology Multi-Conference (ASET), Dubai, UAE.

Huynh, T. T., Nguyen, T. D., & Tan, H. (2019). A Survey on Security and Privacy Issues of Blockchain Technology. *2019 International Conference on System Science and Engineering (ICSSE)*, 362–367. 10.1109/ICSSE.2019.8823094

Khodjaeva, M., Obaidat, M. A., & Salane, D. (2019). Mitigating Threats and Vulnerabilities of RFID in IoT through Outsourcing Computations Using Public Key Cryptography. In *Security, Privacy and Trust in the IoT Environment*. Springer-Cham.

Kshetri, N. (2017). Blockchain privacy. *Telecommunications Policy, 41*(10), 1027–1038. doi:10.1016/j.telpol.2017.09.003

Li, Z., Bahramirad, S., Paaso, A., Yan, M., & Shahidehpour, M. (2019). Blockchain. *The Electricity Journal, 32*(4), 58–72. doi:10.1016/j.tej.2019.03.008 PMID:32524086

Mohanta, B. K., Jena, D., Panda, S. S., & Sobhanayak, S. (2019). Blockchain privacy. *Internet of Things, 8*, 100107. doi:10.1016/j.iot.2019.100107

Mylrea, M., & Gourisetti, S. N. G. (2017). Blockchain for smart grid resilience: Exchanging distributed energy at speed, scale and security. Resilience Week. doi:10.1109/RWEEK.2017.8088642

Narbayeva, S., Bakibayev, T., Abeshev, K., Makarova, I., Shubenkova, K., & Pashkevich, A. (2020). Blockchain Technology. *Transportation Research Procedia, 44*, 168–175. doi:10.1016/j.trpro.2020.02.024

Obaidat, M. A., Khodjaeva, M., Obeidat, S., Salane, D., & Holst, J. (2019). Security Architecture Framework for Internet of Things. IEEE 10th Annual Ubiquitous Computing, Electronics & Mobile Communication Conference (UEMCON), 154-157. doi:10.1109/UEMCON47517.2019.8993096

Obaidat, M. A., Obeidat, S., Holst, J., Al Hayajneh, A., & Brown, J. (2020, May). A Comprehensive and Systematic Survey on the Internet of Things: Security and Privacy Challenges, Security Frameworks, Enabling Technologies, Threats, Vulnerabilities and Countermeasures, in Computers Journal. *MDPI, 9*, 44.

Oksiiuk, O., & Dmyrieva, I. (2020). Security and privacy issues of blockchain technology. *2020 IEEE 15th International Conference on Advanced Trends in Radioelectronics, Telecommunications and Computer Engineering (TCSET)*, 1–5. 10.1109/TCSET49122.2020.235489

Pólvora, A., Nascimento, S., Lourenço, J. S., & Scapolo, F. (2020). Blockchain. *Technological Forecasting and Social Change, 157*, 120091. doi:10.1016/j.techfore.2020.120091

Sharma, M. (2019), Blockchain for Cybersecurity: Working Mechanism, Application areas and Security Challenges. *2019 2nd International Conference on Intelligent Computing, Instrumentation and Control Technologies (ICICICT), 1*, 1182–1187. 10.1109/ICICICT46008.2019.8993204

Vance, T. R., & Vance, A. (2019). Cybersecurity in the Blockchain Era: A Survey on Examining Critical Infrastructure Protection with Blockchain-Based Technology. *2019 IEEE International Scientific-Practical Conference Problems of Infocommunications, Science and Technology (PIC S&T)*, 107–112. 10.1109/PICST47496.2019.9061242

Yassein, M. B., Shatnawi, F., Rawashdeh, S., & Mardin, W. (2019). Blockchain Technology: Characteristics, Security and Privacy; Issues and Solutions. *2019 IEEE/ACS 16th International Conference on Computer Systems and Applications (AICCSA)*, 1–8, 10.1109/AICCSA47632.2019.9035216

Yeasmin, S., & Baig, A. (2019). Unblocking the Potential of Blockchain. *2019 International Conference on Electrical and Computing Technologies and Applications (ICECTA)*, 1–5. 10.1109/ICECTA48151.2019.8959713

ADDITIONAL READING

Hasanova, H., Baek, U., Shin, M., Cho, K., & Kim, M. (2019). A survey on blockchain cybersecurity vulnerabilities and possible countermeasures. *International Journal of Network Management, 29*(2), e2060. doi:10.1002/nem.2060

Zhang, X., Li, R., & Cui, B. (2018). A security architecture of VANET based on blockchain and mobile edge computing. 2018 1st IEEE International Conference on Hot Information-Centric Networking (HotICN). 10.1109/HOTICN.2018.8605952

KEY TERMS AND DEFINITIONS

Access Control: A fundamental concept of cybersecurity facilitated through the regulation of who and/or what can view, maintain, and use individual resources within a system.

Availability: A principle of cybersecurity which states that authorized users should be able to not only access systems as needed, but also perform needed tasks and data transactions.

Cloud Computing: A method of distributed computing in which a network of remote servers are used to remotely provision, manage, store, and process rather than using local systems.

Confidentiality: A principle of cybersecurity which dictates that only those who should be able to have access to certain data, should be able to access it.

Cryptocurrency: A decentralized, blockchain-based system of digital currency assets where digital coins are stored in distributed ledgers, and units are generated through strongly protected cryptographic means.

End-Point Security: A method of protecting system networks which relies on the security of bridged devices participating in a network.

Immutability: The ability for data to exist within a source while maintaining definition and inarguable integrity, for connected systems to transmit such data without error.

Integrity: A principle of cybersecurity which dictates that data should be insured to be both accurate and untampered with, from any unauthorized entities.

Internet of Things (IoT): The interconnected web of devices spread between internet-connected computers and processors embedded within everyday systems, which receive and transmit data.

Peer to Peer (P2P): A method of networking in which a network is distributed across interconnected nodes for whom resources are shared, without a centralized source, thus coordinating outside of a traditional client-server model.

Transaction: An event between at least two systems or participants where a sequence of information is sent and received by participating entities.

Chapter 7
Blockchain and Cryptocurrencies:
Legal and Ethical Considerations

Neha Mason
Charles Sturt University, Australia

Malka N. Halgamuge
https://orcid.org/0000-0001-9994-3778
The University of Melbourne, Australia

Kamalani Aiyar
Charles Sturt University, Australia

ABSTRACT

In financial trading, cryptocurrencies like bitcoin use decentralization, traceability, and anonymity features to perform transactional activities. These digital currencies, using the emerging blockchain technologies, are forming the basis of the largest unregulated markets in the world. This creates various regulatory challenges, including the illicit purchase of drugs and weapons, money laundering, and funding terrorist activities. This chapter analyzes various legal and ethical implications, their effects, and various solutions to overcome the inherent issues that are currently faced by the policymakers and regulators. The authors present the result of an analysis of 30 recently published peer-reviewed scientific publications and suggest various mechanisms that can help in the detection and prevention of illegal activities that currently account for a substantial proportion of cryptocurrency trading. They suggest methods and applications that can also be used to identify the dark marketplaces in the future.

DOI: 10.4018/978-1-7998-6650-3.ch007

INTRODUCTION

Trading in cryptocurrencies has become a global phenomenon in recent years. These are decentralized anonymous virtual currencies, that do not require central control by any central authority (Nakamoto, 2019). Cryptocurrencies can adapt to the challenges in the emerging digital economies and for funding purposes while engaging communities through crowdfunding and the peer-to-peer technology platforms (Tschorsch & Scheuermann, 2016). Therefore, cryptocurrencies, with the use of Blockchain technologies, have hit the news headlines due to their rapid growth in terms of both market volume and value, since around 2012 (Tschorsch & Scheuermann, 2016).

The first initiative for cryptocurrencies was the white paper, that was released under Satoshi Nakamoto pseudonym in 2008. It combined the ideas of Blockchain technology, decentralization, finite supply, and perfect anonymity to pave the way for the first virtual currency known as Bitcoin (Nakamoto, 2019). Blockchain has been utilized in most of the business models, including supply chain (Alvarado & Halgamuge, 2019), multimedia (Shrestha et al., 2020), finance, and healthcare. In 2010, merchants like WordPress, Microsoft, and Expedia started accepting Bitcoin as their mode of payment, which led to the recognition of Bitcoin as a proper currency.

As Bitcoin gained popularity, the idea of encrypted and decentralized currencies emerged, and the first alternative cryptocurrency appeared. This currency, called Altcoin, focused on improving the original Bitcoin design by offering several advantages like higher speed and anonymity. Therefore, this period became attractive to new start-ups, with currencies such as Namecoin and Litecoin.

Unsurprisingly, as a currency designed with a lack of control and anonymity in mind, Bitcoin proved to be a lucrative and attractive target for criminals. For example, in June 2014, a Bitcoin exchange called Mt. Gox went offline making the owners losing almost 750,000 Bitcoins. This case is still under investigation as it led to a total estimated loss of 400 million dollars. Due to such reasons, many countries have disallowed the use of cryptocurrencies like Bitcoin, as they fear of them being used for illegal purposes such as trades involved in the black market (Fraser & Bouridane 2017; Kshetri & Voas 2017; Toyoda et al. 2017; Van Der Horst et al. 2017; Meiklejohn et al. 2013; Chadha & Kumar 2017).

Misuse of Bitcoin is easily possible through the exploitation of pseudo-anonymity and use of Blockchain transactions. Moreover, the evidence for Bitcoins used in terrorist funding and money laundering has already been found (Kshetri & Voas 2017; Toyoda et al. 2017; Van Der Horst et al. 2017; Chadha & Kumar 2017; Liu, Chen, et al. 2017). Therefore, there is a need for cooperation between the government agencies, with other agencies like banks and other financial regulators, to develop legal frameworks and to track the cryptocurrency transactions in order to put them in the tax domain.

Most digital currencies are unregulated. Some countries consider them as legal, whereas others have banned them outright. For instance, use of cryptocurrency is banned in China, and even applying for Initial Coin Offerings (ICO) in China is considered as an illegal activity. Countries that have adopted it into their financial system are facing problems related to taxation and the growth of illegal activities (Kshetri & Voas 2017; Toyoda et al. 2017; Van Der Horst et al. 2017; Meiklejohn et al. 2013; Chadha & Kumar 2017). Due to this reason, proper legislation needs to be framed (Shehhi et al., 2014).

With this background, this chapter attempts to analyze the legal and ethical implications of digital currencies to fill the gaps through the use of various relevant techniques.

Figure 1. Overview of Legal & Ethical Implications of Use of Cryptocurrencies

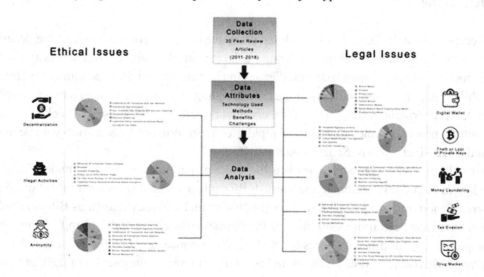

So far, however, there has been little discussion about the use of cryptocurrencies. Most of the cryptocurrency articles focus only on Bitcoin, and no major study describes legal and ethical issues in the use of cryptocurrencies through the use of Blockchain trading. This chapter attempts to provide a glimpse of various issues in the use of cryptocurrencies and also to suggest methods and techniques to mitigate them.

Being digital and virtual, cryptocurrencies have also led to the growth of darknet marketplaces. Therefore, the way the black markets operate has transformed into black-market e-commerce using these cryptocurrencies. The law enforcement agencies like the FBI are still investigating and tracking criminals who are using cryptocurrencies as their mode of money transfer in illegal activities. The solutions proposed in our chapter are through analyzing 30 scientific peer-reviewed articles, including techniques and solutions proposed by various authors, to discuss legal and ethical aspect of the topic. As per the analysis, most researchers have only observed one or a few issues in the use of cryptocurrencies; however, in our chapter, we analyze many more issues, together with providing practical workable suggestions. The applications that can be utilized to mitigate these issues and to track down the criminals behind these transactions are also investigated.

Another important research gap is with respect to the regulations in tracking those who are using cryptocurrencies as their mode of payment in money transactions. This happens due to the anonymity nature of cryptocurrencies. Therefore, many issues in tracing criminals involved in money laundering and tax evaders are still remaining to be resolved. Many researchers are developing applications to trace the defaulters and to take necessary actions against these criminals. The present contribution also attempts to provide mechanisms to help reduce the criminal activities and to assist the regulators in tracking down the criminals, through shedding light on the dark side of the use of cryptocurrencies.

The main purpose of this chapter is to get a deeper understanding of the negative aspects and the challenges of using cryptocurrencies to form a legal and ethical framework in controlling the use of cryptocurrencies. In this respect, the legal and ethical implications of cryptocurrencies as represented in Figure 1. Later in the chapter, we investigate the ethical and legal implications, and provide suggestions by analyzing the searched articles.

This chapter is divided into five parts. The introduction section deals with the necessary background information on the selected topic. The materials and methods section provides a detailed overview of the topic with the selection criterion of data acquisition for the data analysis, followed by data analysis Tables. The graphs illustrating recommendations and suggestions are presented in the Results section, followed by the discussion on relevant findings related to the literature and essential legal and ethical implications. Finally, this chapter concludes by suggesting important solutions for the future development of the related topic areas.

MATERIALS AND METHODS

Cryptocurrencies are decentralized structures that allow them to exist outside the control of the government bodies and other central authorities. So are the Blockchain structures that have characteristics of anonymity, security and no requirement of central authority to manage transactions. Since cryptocurrencies hold the promise of handling transactions easier without the need of third-party involvement, more money is flowing into the Bitcoin, Cryptocoin and other virtual currency ecosystems. In this section, we discuss the transactional areas where cryptocurrencies are being used and discuss the consequences of the manner in which these are transacted. Moreover, we attempt to analyze the legal and ethical implications of the use of cryptocurrencies, for a better understanding.

Collection of Raw Data for the Current Study

We collected data from 30 recently published peer-review research publications. These have mentioned and discussed different aspects related to cryptocurrencies. Most of the publications have focused on Bitcoin; however, our chapter examines various other cryptocurrencies as well. Here an attempt is made to bring out the legal and ethical effects of the use of cryptocurrencies taking into account attributes like the technologies used, methods of security, secret manners of sharing, benefits and challenges; and look to reducing the adverse effects of undesirable activities (such as money laundering).

Data Inclusion Criteria

For the literature analysis, we considered data from various studies from 30 research papers and examined algorithms used by authors of the papers to evaluate the security, and legal and ethical issues related to cryptocurrencies. Comparison Table 1-8 summarise our findings on legal and ethical implications as reported in the said research papers. As a result, the use of Hierarchical Cipher Text Policy Attribute Based Encryption (CP-HABE) scheme is recommended for the encryption of the user's identities, and a regulation node is suggested for the prevention of issues related to the currency. The different technologies that can be used to mitigate the adverse effects are also suggested. The scientific publications that are not peer-reviewed were excluded.

Analysis of Raw Data for the Current Study

Data relating to the legal and ethical issues was analyzed, as shown in Tables 1-8. The attributes used for comparison are: the wider effects of ethical and legal issues, countries affected, various measures undertaken, technologies used, benefits achieved, and the challenges noted of using cryptocurrencies. Legal issues referring to digital wallets, tax evasion, money laundering, drug markets, and theft of private keys were also analyzed and graphically presented in Figures 2-8. Ethical issues that involve decentralization, Illegal activities and anonymity were analyzed and are graphically rpresented in Figures 9 -11.

When presenting these results with tables, the use of CP-HABE scheme was adopted. CP-HABE method is recommended by Wang and Gao (2018). Using this method, that includes users' encrypted identities and Modified Signature (MS) algorithms for signatures, transactions are generated by users and sent to the blockchain first. The miners then verify the transactions, their signatures, and source of the used cryptocurrency. Finally, in the case where transactions are found suspicious, regulation nodes are used to decrypt the user's real identities. It can be used as a measurement in avoiding illegal transactions (Wang & Gao, 2018). This method, along with various other methods is used to fill the gaps in legal and ethical issues in cryptocurrencies as mentioned in Tables 1-8.

Studying these gaps, issues, and solutions with reference to relevant technologies enables regulators to develop a proper legal framework for cryptocurrencies. Hopefully, this also assists the regulators in tracking down the people behind the illegal activities and infringement of the relevant laws.

Legal Implications

Legal implications related to the use of cryptocurrencies in digital wallets, private keys, tax evasion, money laundering, and the drug market are now discussed here.

Digital Wallets

Digital wallets hold the private keys of users and allow them to access their public keys. Digital wallets are not insured by the Federal Deposit Insurance Corporation (FDIC) and are not protected. Most of the digital wallet companies are going out of business because of this reason. Since, cryptocurrency transactions are tied to the "digital wallet ID", rather than the user's actual name and their identity, these remain entirely anonymous. As a result of this, cryptocurrencies are being accepted as mode of transaction with respect to illegal products and services, for example, the "now-defunct Silk Road" (Kshetri & Voas 2017; Toyoda et al. 2017; Van Der Horst et al. 2017; Meiklejohn et al. 2013; Chadha & Kumar 2017).

Various threats and hacking incidents related to cryptocurrencies have been reported in recent years. Some of these are listed here. Bithumb, the top crypto exchange owned by North Korea and the world's fourth-largest stock exchange, was hacked in June 2017. The Digital Wallet of cryptocurrency named NiceHash was also hacked in December 2017. Ethereum, which is the Digital wallets of Parity Technologies containing Ether was one of the biggest hacks that happened in November 2017. The Wannacry ransom affected nearly 100 countries, demanding ransom in bitcoin. Petya cyber-attack targeted the Cadbury chocolate factory in Tasmania, demanding bitcoins as ransom money (Wang & Gao, 2018). There are no legal regulations regarding managing and regulating cryptocurrencies. Users want to keep their transactions confidential to ensure that their privacy is protected. According to this, gaining the confidence of these crowds would be difficult.

The key problem with digital wallets is with their security in preventing internal and external threats involving the private keys. There are two digital wallet types called Hot Wallets and Cold Wallets. Hot wallets require the private keys of the user to be stored on a machine that is connected to a network. On the other hand, Cold Wallets store private keys offline and not connected to a network. Based on this scenario, the threats that can take place using hot wallets and cold wallets work as follows.

1. Hot Wallets - where Private keys are stored online:
    a. Internal threats

These wallets are more prone to be attacked by insiders, and many incidents involve in theft or loss of private keys. For instance, the risk for theft of keys is exceptionally high in cases where the keys are printed and stored in a locker.

    b. External threats

External threats related to network security is high. In the past, there have been a few instances of stealing bitcoins via networks.

2. Cold Wallets - where Private keys stored offline:
    a. Internal threats

These wallets face threats related to the physical storage of private keys. The private keys are stored offline. These keys can be stolen by accessing the storage place only. Therefore, a firm's internal control policy is needed to mitigate such risks.

    b. External threats

The cold wallets are safe from external threats as they are not connected to a network. Hence, network-related threats are mitigated because private keys stored in cold wallets are not available online.

Table 1 presents the legal implications related to digital wallets, including their benefits and challenges.

Theft or Loss of Private Keys

Massive thefts like Mt. Gox have resulted in putting pressure on regulators to regulate and to bring bitcoin transactions under tax bracket. In case of deregulated nature of bitcoins, users can lose private keys, and then it becomes much harder to prove who still owns the coins. There have been many thefts related to the loss of private keys, using Denial of Service (DoS) attacks, also called the 51% attacks. Here, more than 51 present of computing power is needed to be capable of modifying, excluding, and self-reversing transactions. Such thefts have occurred in many countries in the past.

Techniques have been formulated to overcome issues with bitcoins that are based on transaction processing systems. The 51% attacks have been prevented through modifying the block header and by introducing extra bytes. During hash generation, the timestamp was effectively utilized to overcome issues related to this theft. However, proper formulation of strategies and implementation of security measures need to prevent this kind of theft. Detection of lost coins can be done by detecting the bitcoins having no movement on the blockchain. Table 2 shows the legal implications of the involvement of theft or loss of the private keys.

Evasion of Taxes

The evasion of taxes is caused mainly due to Pseudo anonymity of cryptocurrencies. Users generally tend to hide assets in order to avoid paying taxes. Taxes can be evaded through using online private keys, as there is no proper legal framework related to the taxation of cryptocurrencies. There have been cases where untaxed foreign currencies have been coming into the country through the use of cryptocurrencies. However, in some countries, cryptocurrencies are banned. In Australia, the Australian Taxation Office (ATO) considers cryptocurrency as a form of property, to bring it into tax brackets. The ATO is consulting tax experts and lawyers regarding the development of a proper regime to overcome the related issues. In order to do this, the government needs to track cryptocurrency transactions and make sure the payments of all its taxes are done on time. The ATO warns bitcoin as "neither money nor a foreign currency", and therefore, it should be taxed as an asset, and should not be a subject to the Goods and Services Tax (GST). Consequently, it should be treated as an asset as income to calculate it as the Capital Gains Tax (CGT).

Many countries are suffering from tax evasion problem. Formal meetings are often conducted to discuss the policies for taxation. Governments with their regulatory officials are also working to develop a proper method for the taxation of such currencies. Efforts are being made to devise systems to detect the indication of tax evasion and making authorities for controlling currencies and payment systems responsible for taxation on transactions. For taxation of cryptocurrencies, legal frameworks are being developed in many countries. It is advised to cryptocurrency owners to keep proper records of their intentions, transactions, and records of whoever are receiving payments; otherwise, huge penalties could be levied in case of detection. Table 3 depicts the legal implications involved in the evasion of taxes.

Money Laundering

Money laundering is a critical problem, as money can be moved between countries without anyone monitoring and tracking their movements, due to the nature of Blockchain operations. Bitcoins are not outlawed in some countries such as South Korea. However, there is strict prosecution, in case of illegal activities involving Bitcoin, in some other countries. Money laundering is always illegal, regardless of how it is done. However, many loopholes are still existing in legal frameworks, and therefore, government and other financial regulators are cooperating to develop proper legal frameworks to prevent the laundering of money. To track money laundering, a proper authority should be established, and the users indulging in such activities should be accordingly punished. Table 4 illustrates the legal implications involved in money laundering.

Drugs Market and Financing Terrorism

Cryptocurrencies are being used in online drugs marketplace and for financing terrorist groups. Dark marketplaces like Silk Road were reported to be closed. However, similar places are now actively transacting without being traced because of the use of anonymity nature of bitcoins. Bitcoins are used in black markets as a mode of payment of contracts undertaken by drug dealers and murders in their illegal businesses. Cryptocurrencies are offered for buying weapons. There is considerable trade related to buying drugs, weapons, and other illegal things in darknet market websites. In 2015, the founder of the Silk Road website was sent to prison for such transactions, and the Silk Road was shut down. Silk

Road, the Armory, and the General store have since been found active and transacting using cryptocurrencies. Every country is currently facing this problem. The governments and other financial regulators are cooperating to develop proper legal frameworks in this regard.

The dark web is the primary concern of the Federal Bureau of Investigation (FBI), the European Banking Authority, and others. It is essential to analyze how the network works, along with the associated mining processes. There should be a regulatory authority to track such activities. The extraction of illicit transactions can be done through Random Access Memory (RAM) analysis and hard disk analysis. Table 5 depicts the legal implications involved in the use of cryptocurrencies in the drug market.

Ethical Implications

The ethical implications related to the use of cryptocurrencies due to their decentralization and anonymity features, and how they are related to illegal activities, are now discussed here.

Decentralization

Decentralization is one of the key features of cryptocurrencies, which is making it beyond the control of any monetary controlling powers. Due to this and due to the way Blockchains work, all the transactions handled are irreversible. Proper maintenance of transaction ledgers at every node, and validation of transaction at the distributive node (not by the central authority), are necessary to make this process more secure. In the case of Bitcoin, users have transparency of the validating code used and can participate in software development. However, there is no government control in transactions handled in such a decentralized manner. Therefore, regulations may help in imposing taxes and preventing black money sustainably. Table 6 illustrates the ethical issues involved in decentralization.

Anonymity

There are untraceable electronic transfers due to the anonymity feature of cryptocurrencies. The Onion Routing (TOR) adds further to anonymity due to the layered encryption process. Due to the anonymity characteristic, users can transfer money without leaving a trace. Moreover, the Dark Net and ransomware are getting popular due to this. People behind these illegal activities go unnoticed due to this feature. Software like Tox allows us to make malware suitable, unfortunately, for malicious activities.

Various ethical issues are also caused due to anonymity. Around 100 countries were affected by the Wannacry ransom demanded in bitcoins. Similarly, the Petya cyberattack targeted the Cadbury chocolate factory in Tasmania. The criminals behind such attacks went unnoticed due to anonymity. Accounts cannot be frozen, and also nobody knows the real identity of the account holders. Therefore, regulation nodes are implemented to prevent this issue. These nodes are created to reveal the real identities of users. Suspicious and illicit transactions are automatically flagged and made to enable further investigation. True identities are revealed at regulation nodes. In this case, users are no longer allowed to mask their identity to surface the web. Even if ransomware is detected and deactivated, files are not restored, and therefore, framing appropriate laws in this regard is essential. Table 7 shows the legal issues related to anonymity feature of cryptocurrencies.

Illegal Activities

Cryptocurrencies are reportedly being used by drug cartels and for human trafficking, as already mentioned above. Users are combining cryptocurrencies with anonymity when dealing with illegal activities, such as trading drugs and weapons. Silk Road was closed with combined efforts of Interpol and FBI in 2013. However, due to the high demand in the use of cryptocurrencies, and due to decentralization and anonymity, other Dark web markets like Silk Road 2.0, Evolution, Hydra, and Agora have emerged. Thus, many countries are being affected by such illegal activities.

Therefore, there is a need to track down these activities and to administer necessary penalties to the criminals involved in such activities. Regulating transactions and using relevant techniques can help in tracking down doubtful transactions. The ethical and moral implications mentioned by various authors with their suggested applications, benefits, and challenges of such implications and applications are presented in Table 8.

RESULTS

The legal and ethical issues related to the technologies used, methods of security, methods of secret sharing, benefits, and the challenges of the use of cryptocurrencies are presented in Tables 1-8. An analysis of 30 peer review scientific publications was completed to determine the technologies used in each of the legal and ethical implications. Legal issues involving digital wallets, tax evasion, money laundering, drug markets, and theft of private keys were analyzed and now graphically presented in Figures 2-8. Ethical issues involving decentralization, illegal activities, and anonymity examined are graphically presented in Figures 9-11.

Evaluation of Legal Issues

Based on the analysis of the 30 peer-reviewed scientific publications, the legal issues, their impact and inherent challenges were evaluated. Our contribution now provides step by step suggestion regarding the problems related to legal issues. The COUNTIF formula was used to count the percentages of the applications used among the range of other applications.

The syntax of the COUNTIF function is COUNTIF (range, criteria). For instance, a Bitcoin Wallet application is mentioned by 23 authors among 30 different authors then, the range is equal to 31 applications (one author has compared two different wallets) and criteria is equal to Bitcoin Wallet. The syntax for counting Bitcoin Wallet within the specified range equals COUNTIF (C2: C33, Bitcoin Wallet), and therefore, the answer is 74%.

Table 1. Legal Implications Involving Digital Wallets

No	Authors	Technologies Used	Methods of Security	Benefits	Challenges
1	(Dikshit & Singh, 2017)	Bitcoin Wallet	Joint Control	Bitcoin Wallet is software or hardware storing digital credentials for Bitcoin holders. Wallet stores information related to transactions	It generates and stores private keys, and hence, the security is crucial
2	(Reid & Harrigan, 2013)	Bitcoin Wallet	Hot Wallets	Identify and track considerable portions of user activities	Entire history of Bitcoin transactions is available, which can have severe implications on user anonymity and security
3	(Gennaro et al., 2016)	Bitcoin Wallet	Hot & Cold Wallets	Bitcoin wallet is a software abstraction which seamlessly manages multiple addresses on behalf of a user	The wallet software chooses the input addresses, changes the address, and constructs the transaction
4	(Narayanan et al., 2016)	Bitcoin Wallet	Hot & Cold Wallets	Securing Bitcoin wallet through the use of threshold cryptography	It enables us to manage multiple addresses on behalf of the user seamlessly. Internal and external threats to Bitcoins are the most pressing problems
5	(Kshetri & Voas, 2017)	Bitcoin Wallet	Hot Wallets	Analysis of Illegal activities conducted using wallets	Ransomware can be detected and prevented
6	(Maurer et al., 2017)	CoinJoin	Hot Wallets	Multiple users merge their transactions into one substantial transaction. Pseudonymity is maintained	Maintaining the anonymity and securing the wallets
		Bitcoin Wallet	Hot Wallets	It is compatible with Bitcoin architecture and provides stronger anonymity	Using the methodology with the Bitcoin architecture to enhance anonymity
7	(Wang et al., 2018)	Bitcoin Wallet	Hot Wallets	Pattern analysis can be conducted for High Yield Investment program in Bitcoins	Maintaining the anonymity and securing the wallets
8	(Toyoda et al., 2017)	Bitcoin Core	Hot Wallets	Bitcoin, its applications, storage and trading of Bitcoins	Study between both the wallets to identify potential sources and relevant data related to Bitcoin keys, passphrases and transactions in both the wallets
9	(Van Der Horst et al., 2017)	Electrum	Hot Wallets	Electrum, its applications, storage and trading of Bitcoins	
		Testnet Bitcoin	Hot Wallets	Bitcoins payments and supervises transactions	Regulating Bitcoins can impact the anonymity and security
10	(Chen et al., 2017)	Bitcoin Wallet	Hot & Cold Wallets	Bitcoins related to various applications	Can be used in many industries, however; anonymity and security is an issue
11	(Tama et al., 2017)	Bitcoin Wallet	Hot Wallets	Buyer's protection will ensure much reliability in Bitcoins or any other cryptocurrency	Incorporating the concept to help in conflict resolution
12	(Yin et al., 2018)	Deterministic wallets	Hot Wallets	Blockchain is used to mitigate anti-quantum attacks	Regulating Bitcoins can impact the anonymity and security
13	(Liu, Liu, et al., 2017)	Bitcoin Wallet	Hot Wallets	Combines transaction hash and addresses balance to confirm the transaction completion. Attacks can be detected and mitigated through transaction malleability	It is compatible with Bitcoin network and easy to use and upgrade existing program; however, it can have an impact on anonymity
14	(He et al., 2018)	Social-network based cryptocurrency wallet	Hot & Cold Wallets	The scheme has the advantages of high security and security-enhanced storage, portable login on different devices, no-password authentication, flexible key delegation, blind wallet recovery, etc.	Deploying such a scheme is a difficult task
15	(Zhang & Li, 2016.)	Bitcoin Wallet	Hot & Cold Wallets	Instead of storing all the private key in cold wallets, the author suggested combining random seeds and passphrase for a user to generate private keys and thus, make more secure and less prone to theft	Generating random seeds and passphrase is much complicated task than storing the private key in a cold wallet
16	(Mehta et al., 2017)	Bitcoin Wallet	Hot & Cold Wallets	An attempt to study attacks to secure Bitcoins. It also suggests Bitcoin security algorithms	Thefts and attacks can be mitigated and cannot be effaced out totally
17	(Meiklejohn et al., 2013)	Bitcoin Wallet	Hot Wallets	Provide longitudinal changes in Bitcoin market, the stresses caused by them, and the users who use it for fraudulent purposes	Mitigating these risks can be done; however, the users using Bitcoins for criminal activities cannot be avoided
18	(Chadha & Kumar, 2017)	Bitcoin Wallet	Hot Wallets	An attempt to study various cryptocurrencies and taking the most popular among them, namely Bitcoins	Provides a more insight related to cryptocurrencies and their effects
19	(Shehhi et al., 2014)	Bitcoin Wallet	Hot Wallets	An attempt to study cybercrime and ransomware using Bitcoin wallet	Mitigating the threats involving cybercrime can be done; however, it cannot be eliminated
20	(Upadhyaya & Jain, 2016)	Bitcoin Wallet	Hot Wallets	An attempt to study dark web and ransomware using Bitcoin wallet	Threats can be mitigated and not completely avoided
21	(Baravalle et al., 2016)	Bitcoin Wallet	Hot & Cold Wallets	An attempt to study Bitcoins for the secure financial transactions	Mitigation of thefts and attacks can be done; however, it cannot be effaced out totally
22	(Quamara & Singh, 2016)	Bitcoin Core	Hot Wallets	Security risk related to Bitcoin wallets are discussed, and among them, the safest is Bitcoin core	Mitigating the threats involving Bitcoin wallets can be done; however, it cannot be eliminated
23	(Kaushal et al., 2017)	Bitcoin Wallet	Hot Wallets	Investigating security flaws in Bitcoins	Mitigating the threats involving Bitcoin wallets can be done; however, it cannot be eliminated
24	(Fraser & Bouridane, 2017)	Bitcoin Wallet	Hot Wallets	Review of Bitcoins used by cybercriminals	There are many security issues related to Bitcoins
25	(Shanmugam et al., 2017)	Bitcoin Wallet	Hot Wallets	Swot analysis is conducted to evaluate Bitcoins strengths and opportunities while mitigating its weaknesses and threats	Apart from developing strategies, implementing, and regulating Bitcoin trading, which is a significant issue
26	(Mirzayi & Mehrzad, 2017)	Cryptocurrency	Hot Wallets	It is used to detect ransomware and track the flow of the activities	It is difficult to trace out and catch the criminals behind ransomware
27	(Liu, Chen, et al., 2017)	Bitcoin Wallet	Hot Wallets	It provides insight to gain profit through Bitcoin mining pools	Implementing and gaining profit is difficult and volatile
28	(Barratt et al., 2016)	Bitcoin Wallet	Hot Wallets	An attempt to study the causes of money laundering and the actions can be taken against them	Regulations are being proposed to stop money laundering activities and track the criminals involved in those
29	(Tschorsch & Scheuermann, 2016)	Bitcoin Wallet	Hot Wallets	There is a regulation node which is responsible for the regulation of transactions and for encrypted identities. In the case of doubting transactions where illegal activities consist, the authorized regulation nodes can reveal the users' real identities and add the illegal identities to a public blacklist	Users favour anonymity and privacy rights. The regulation node might affect anonymity
30	(Wang & Gao, 2018)	Bitcoin Wallet	Hot Wallets	There is a regulation node which is responsible for the regulation of transactions and for encrypted identities. In the case of doubting transactions where illegal activities consist, the authorized regulation nodes can reveal the users' real identities and add the illegal identities to a public blacklist	Users favour anonymity and privacy rights. The regulation node might affect anonymity

Table 2. Legal Implications Involving Theft or Loss of Private Keys

No	Author	Technologies Used	Secret Sharing	Benefits	Challenges
1	(Dikshit & Singh, 2017)	Threshold Signature Scheme	Joint Random Zero Secret Sharing	Each player was given one or more shares of secret keys according to weightage/priority. Under New scheme, each player gets a single share while accomplishing the requirements of weightage	Handling or managing many keys by each player. This scheme will not work if players come together from two or more different groups to reconstruct the key
2	(Reid & Harrigan, 2013)	Combination of Transaction and User Networks	Combination of Transaction and User Networks	Analysis of theft of Bitcoins and forming a pattern through combining networks to trace the flow of Bitcoins, and to generate hypotheses	Theft and loss of private keys can be analyzed and traced out, without compromising anonymity
3	(Gennaro et al., 2016)	Threshold Signature Scheme	Multiplicative Secret Sharing	Threshold digital signature algorithm is used to prevent private keys from theft or loss. Without this, Bitcoins are subject to single point failure, and the risk of holding Bitcoins is high	It is for comparison only and does not provide full security of a proof
4	(Narayanan et al., 2016)	Threshold Signature Scheme	Multiplicative Secret Sharing	Keys can be stored at different locations to prevent threats to private keys	It makes compromise of keys and Bitcoins more difficult
5	(Wang et al., 2018)	Distributive Key Generation	Verifiable Secret Sharing	It strengthens the anonymity	Users' anonymity relies on the assumption that the mix does not log or reveal the relation between input and output addresses
6	(Toyoda et al., 2017)	Combination of Transaction and User Networks	Feature Extraction Scheme	Real-time fraud detection and classification of services can be done	Theft and loss of private keys can be analyzed and traced out, without compromising anonymity
7	(Van Der Horst et al., 2017)	Threshold Signature Scheme	Ethash	It is used to mitigate the risk of theft or loss of private keys	It makes compromise of keys and Bitcoins more difficult
8	(Chen et al., 2017)	Threshold Signature Scheme	SHA-256	It analyses how to mitigate the theft of keys by mentioning about regulating the Bitcoins for payments	It talks about Bitcoin 3.0 and about regulating the Bitcoins by the government
9	(Tama et al., 2017)	Threshold Signature Scheme	SHA-256	Private keys are stored in wallets and can be used in various applications.	It makes compromise of keys and Bitcoins more difficult.
10	(Yin et al., 2018)	Threshold Signature Scheme	SHA-256	Private keys are stored in wallets and can be used in various applications	It makes compromise of keys and Bitcoins more difficult
11	(Liu, Liu, et al., 2017)	Lattice-based bonsai tree signature	SHA-256 & RIPEMD 160 algorithm	It can resist quantum algorithm attacks	It resists a quantum attack and can be used to reduce the SIS hard problem on the lattice
12	(He et al., 2018)	Combination of Transaction and User Networks	SHA-256 & RIPEMD 160 algorithm	It combines transaction hash and addresses balance to confirm the transaction completion. Attacks can be detected and mitigated through transaction malleability	It removes an essential script from the transaction before the hash of the transaction is computed
13	(Zhang & Li, 2016)	HIKE Scheme	SHA-256 (Shamir)	It prevents loss and theft of keys and makes the wallet more secured	Difficulty in deploying the scheme
14	(Mehta et al., 2017)	Threshold Signature Scheme	SHA-256	Private keys can be stored offline using a cold wallet. Combine random seeds and passphrase for a user to generate private keys, therefore, the physical storage theft can be avoided completely	Deploying the scheme is a tedious task
15	(Chadha & Kumar, 2017)	Heuristic Clustering	SHA-256	Through this method, attempts are being made to analyze the potential threats to private keys and to mitigate it	Risk cannot be eliminated completely. New potential threats are emerging out, and illicit activities are still conducted using cryptocurrency

Table 3. Legal Implications Involving Tax Evasion

No	Author	Technologies Used	Benefits	Challenges
1	(Kshetri & Voas, 2017)	Behavior & Transaction pattern analysis, Data Retrieval, Know Your Client (KYC), Patching Software	It helps in monitoring the trading of Bitcoins to bring it into the tax bracket. Few countries like Malaysia and India, require proper registration of individuals to trade in Bitcoins by bringing them through exchanges and require them to submit KYC	Monitoring trading of Bitcoins in many countries for tax purposes is difficult
2	(Toyoda et al., 2017)	Behavior & Transaction pattern analysis	It helps in identifying undesirable and fraudulent activities such as HYIP (High Yield Investment Program)	It requires the study of a transaction and the frequency of each pattern to identify illicit activities
3	(Van Der Horst et al., 2017)	KYC, Customer Due diligence and Heuristic Clustering	Tax cannot be avoided. FBI has assessed with high confidence where the tax evaders will be detected and punished with huge penalties	Tax authorities are still finding difficulties in taxing the users indulged in trading of Bitcoins
4	(Chen et al., 2017)	Bitcoin Payment and Collection Scheme (BPCSS)	Regulatory mechanism to regulate the collection scheme and payment of taxes	Regulating may affect anonymity
5	(Tama et al., 2017)	Behavior & Transaction pattern analysis	Each block in the blockchain can be traced back to the genesis block. This can act as a regulation on the users and prevent them from tax evasion since they know about the regulators watching the transactions	Regulating may affect anonymity
6	(Yin et al., 2018)	Escrow Mechanism	It requires a third party to hold and regulate the transaction to protect the buyers. Regulators control the transactions	Regulating may affect anonymity
7	(Chadha & Kumar, 2017)	Heuristic Clustering	Many countries have started framing policies to take the cryptocurrency into tax brackets and to analyze its impact	Tax authorities are still finding difficulties in taxing the users indulged in trading of Bitcoins
8	(Tschorsch & Scheuermann, 2016)	Behavior & Transaction pattern analysis	Most of the countries have now a legal framework to tax the digital currency. Many tax laws framed to avoid tax evasion. Cryptocurrency classified as an asset to bring it in the tax domain. Pattern analysis will help in tracking transactions	There is always resistance for taxation. There is a lack of excellent and clear redemption mechanism for converting cryptocurrency to other currency like Dollars. Regulations for licensing Bitcoin exchange is vague. Compliance of customer data with Know your customer (KYC) policy should be implemented

Legal Issues Related to Digital Wallets

According to 30 peer-reviewed articles, the technologies used by various authors were analyzed and clustered together. The major categories being: Bitcoin Wallet, Bitcoin Core, Coin Join, Electrum, Testnet Bitcoin, Deterministic Wallets, Cryptocurrency Wallets, and the social-network based cryptocurrency wallets. The popularity of applications used in various studies is illustrated in Figure 2.

Table 4. Legal Implications Involving Money Laundering

No	Author	Technology Used	Benefits	Challenges
1	(Kshetri & Voas, 2017)	Behavior & Transaction pattern analysis, Data Retrieval, Know Your Client (KYC), Patching Software	Users can be traced through IP addresses and money flows. Artificial intelligence can be used to scan and analyze the Bitcoin network to identify suspicious behaviour patterns in Bitcoin transactions. It can trace transactions to individuals or groups	Framing a policy and monitoring it, and immediate detection in case of money laundering
2	(Toyoda et al., 2017)	Behavior & Transaction pattern analysis	It helps in identifying undesirable and fraudulent activities such as HYIP (High Yield Investment Program)	It requires the study of a transaction and the frequency of each pattern to identify illicit activities
3	(Van Der Horst et al., 2017)	KYC, Customer Due diligence and Heuristic Clustering	The author tested to reverse-engineer the behaviour of Transaction Anonymization services	Money Laundering activities should be prevented and tracked down
4	(Chadha & Kumar, 2017)	Heuristic Clustering	Combination of scalable, irrevocable and anonymous payments have proven Bitcoins to be more beneficial for money laundering purposes. Methods have been evaluated to analyze activities of money laundering through clustering	Law enforcement still face difficulty in identifying users, detecting suspicious activities and obtaining transaction records
5	(Liu, Chen, et al., 2017)	Machine learning algorithm	It is used to detect ransomware and track the flow of the activities	It is difficult to trace out and catch the criminals behind ransomware
6	(Tschorsch & Scheuermann, 2016)	Behavior & Transaction pattern analysis, Data Retrieval, Know Your Client (KYC), Patching Software	Tracking down the users through imposing regulatory mechanisms and attempts to study weaknesses in imposing regulations. This helps in strengthening the regulatory mechanism	Money Laundering activities should be prevented and tracked down; however, law enforcement is still facing difficulties
7	(Wang & Gao, 2018)	Hierarchical Ciphertext-Policy Attribute-Based Encryption (CP-HABE)	Lost cryptocurrency can be traced by a regulator. Identities can be verified for doubted and flagged transactions. The decryption of regulation nodes	Users feel the regulation node conflict with right to protect their privacy and free trade. Users insist on being unregulated and anonymous

Data analysis reveals that most of the authors preferred Bitcoin Wallet for their research because it provides the whole blockchain to the user. Electrum, on the other hand, is based on Simplified Payment Verification (SPV) wallets or lite wallets as they do not provide a full copy of the blockchain to verify the transactions. Electrum depends upon other computers on the network to provide the information; it is the most effective, robust, and secured desktop wallet.

According to the 30 peer-reviewed articles, the methods of storing keys referred by various authors (e.g. hot wallets or cold wallets) were analyzed and clustered together and now presented in Figure 3.

Legal Issues Related to Tax Evasion

The technologies mentioned by the various authors to prevent tax evasion include: Bitcoin Payment and Collection Scheme (BPCSS), Heuristic Clustering, behavior analysis, and pattern analysis. Various recommended methods like BPCSS, Escrow Mechanism, Heuristic Clustering, and combination of Transaction and User Networks were also evaluated in various studies. All this information is summarised in Figure 4.

Table 5. Legal Implications Involving Drugs Market

No	Author	Technologies Used	Benefits	Challenges
1	(Kshetri & Voas, 2017)	Behavior & Transaction pattern analysis, Data Retrieval, Know Your Client (KYC), Patching Software	Users can be traced through IP addresses and money flows. Artificial intelligence can be used to scan and analyze the Bitcoin network to identify suspicious behavior patterns in Bitcoin transactions. It can trace transactions to individuals or groups	Probability of detection using next-generation cryptocurrencies such as Monero, Dash, and Z-Cash. These have built-in anonymity features
2	(Toyoda et al., 2017)	Behavior & Transaction pattern analysis	It helps in identifying undesirable and fraudulent activities such as HYIP (High Yield Investment Program)	It requires the study of a transaction and the frequency of each pattern to identify illicit activities
3	(Van Der Horst et al., 2017)	Bit Iodine	It helps to investigate the Silk Road Wallets and addresses related to Crypto Locker ransomware	Analysis of the wallets used in illicit activities to prevent the illegal activities
4	(Meiklejohn et al., 2013)	Behavior & Transaction pattern analysis	It attempts to study various attacks, and mentions the causes of such attacks so the corrective steps can be taken to prevent such attacks	Bitcoins have anonymous nature and untraceable. The dark web users to buy drugs, weapons, and even hire hitmen still prevails
5	(Chadha & Kumar, 2017)	Heuristic Clustering	Combination of scalable, irrevocable, and anonymous payments have proven Bitcoins to be more beneficial for money laundering purposes. Methods have been evaluated to analyses activities of money laundering through clustering	Law enforcement still faces difficulty in identifying users, detecting suspicious activities and obtaining transaction records
6	(Shehhi et al., 2014)	Heuristic Clustering	The stolen Bitcoins can be traced out using the flow of transactions. Analysis over user graph can be made to track down the transactions related to Bitcoins in the drug market	Tracking and punishing the people involved in drug marketing using Bitcoins is still a difficult task
7	(Baravalle et al., 2016)	Tor (The Onion Routing) or I2P (Invisible Internet Project)	Dark web and other illicit websites like Agora can be studied, and the flow of transactions can be evaluated	Tracking and punishing the people involved in drug marketing using Bitcoins is still a difficult task
8	(Shanmugam et al., 2017)	Tor (The Onion Routing) or I2P (Invisible Internet Project)	Review of Bitcoins used by cybercriminals. It helps in tracking down of transactions. Criminal identities can be revealed. It helps in backing up the transactions offline and being easy to retrieve	There are many security issues related to Bitcoins. Distribution of exchanges and transactions have complex techniques. No tie-up with banks or any regulatory authority makes them popular in criminals
9	(Wang & Gao, 2018)	Ciphertext-Policy Hierarchical Attribute-Based Encryption (CP-HABE)	Lost cryptocurrency can be traced by the regulator. Identities can be verified for doubted and flagged transactions. The decryption of regulation nodes	Users feel the regulation node conflict with right to protect their privacy and free trade. Users insist on being unregulated and anonymous

Data analysis reveals that most authors preferred using behavior and transaction pattern analysis for tracking the flow of transactions in order to prevent tax evasion. A proper regime needs to be framed, which should include the Know Your Client (KYC) details, Data retrieval policies, and customer due diligence.

Table 6. Ethical Implications Involving Decentralization

No	Author	Technologies Used	Benefits	Challenges
1	(Reid & Harrigan, 2013)	Combination of Transaction and User Networks	Power to trace the flow of Bitcoins and generate hypotheses	Large centralized services can identify and track considerable portions of user activity
2	(Wang et al., 2018)	Distributive Key Generation	It is compatible with Bitcoin architecture and does not require modification in Bitcoin rules or scripts	Users' anonymity relies on the assumption where the mix does not log or reveal the relation between input and output addresses
3	(Toyoda et al., 2017)	Combination of Transaction and User Networks	Power to trace the flow of Bitcoins and generate hypotheses	Calculating the pattern for each transaction is a time-consuming method
4	(Van Der Horst et al., 2017)	KYC, Customer Due diligence and Heuristic Clustering	Regulations will be imposed to avoid illegal activities. FBI has assessed to deanonymized doubtful users when they exchange Bitcoins with Fiat money	Decentralization is still difficult, and a proper mechanism is still not available. Many countries have various policies and mechanisms in this regard
5	(Chen et al., 2017)	Threshold Signature Scheme	Author mentions about the payment and collection system using Bitcoins and how it is being regulated by the government	Users' anonymity relies on the assumption where the mix does not log or reveal the relation between input and output addresses
6	(Yin et al., 2018)	Threshold Signature Scheme	It is being regulated by another third node to protect the buyers	It can impact the anonymity of users since the third node controls the transactions
7	(He et al., 2018)	Combination of Transaction and User Networks	It combines transaction hash and addresses balance to confirm the transactions are completed. Attacks can be detected and mitigated through transaction malleability	Large centralized services can identify and track considerable portions of user activity
8	(Chadha & Kumar, 2017)	Heuristic Clustering	Thieves can be deanonymized using this technique and can be traced out. Thief steals thousands of Bitcoins, this theft is unavoidably visible within the Bitcoin network, and thus the initial address of the thief is known and he cannot simply transfer the Bitcoins directly from the theft to a known exchange. While he might attempt to use a mix service to hide the source of the money; however, these services do not currently have the volume to launder thousands of Bitcoins	Thieves have developed various strategies for hiding the source of the Bitcoins. Most of the strategies are studied, and causes are stated; however, many still prevail. It leaves behind high risk for theft
9	(Wang & Gao, 2018)	Ciphertext-Policy Hierarchical Attribute-Based Encryption (CP-HABE)	Relationship of identities and wallet addresses can reveal the real identities. It also prevents criminals from illegal acts	There are no legal regulations. Imposing regulation node can affect right to privacy. Gaining favor of the mass would be tough

Table 7. Ethical Implications Involving Anonymity

No	Author	Technologies Used	Benefits	Challenges
1	(Dikshit & Singh, 2017)	Elliptic curve digital signature algorithm using weighted threshold signature protocol.	Anonymity and privacy are maintained. No link between the transactions as Bitcoin wallet chooses input address, change address, and constructs a transaction	Maintaining anonymity and security while coming out with the solution in case of loss of keys
2	(Reid & Harrigan, 2013)	Combination of Transaction and User Networks	Entire history of transactions is publicly available, and there can be implications related to user anonymity	Tracing out the transactions, without revealing the identity to other users except the regulatory authorities
3	(Gennaro et al., 2016)	Elliptic curve digital signature algorithm using weighted threshold signature protocol.	It is not difficult to link various addresses belonging to a single user because the entire transaction log is public. Anonymity can be increased in change of an addresses provided by this method	Maintaining anonymity and security while coming out with the solution in case of loss of keys
4	(Narayanan et al., 2016)	Elliptic curve digital signature algorithm using threshold signature protocol.	It helps in enhancing internal financial controls. The method has the potential to dramatically improve Bitcoin security and moving it closer to widespread adoption as a currency	Maintaining anonymity and security while coming out with the solution in case of loss of keys
5	(Kshetri & Voas, 2017)	Behavior & Transaction pattern analysis	Transactions are recorded in a permanent public ledger, and financial movements can be traced	Only doubtful transactions should be reported to regulatory authorities
6	(Maurer et al., 2017)	Knapsack mixing	Through this methodology, enough ambiguity can be introduced to make linking highly unlikely for most of the coin pairs, regardless of available computation power. Thus, anonymity is most secured in this methodology	Mixing and analyzing can be costly
7	(Wang et al., 2018)	Elliptic curve digital signature algorithm	Everyone can only eavesdrop a list of output addresses; however, none of them can link the addresses to the related users, and even the real participants do not know the corresponding relationships	Users' anonymity relies on the assumption where the mix does not log or reveal the relation between input and output addresses
8	(Toyoda et al., 2017)	Behavior & Transaction pattern analysis	Recent studies, including FBI report, has shown the regulatory authorities keep track of transactions	The main challenge is to remove fraudulent activities using Bitcoins
9	(Van Der Horst et al., 2017)	Heuristic Clustering	Attempts to deanonymize the users to track doubtful by clustering techniques	Maintaining anonymity and security of genuine users while tracking doubtful users indulging in illicit activities
10	(Chen et al., 2017)	Bitcoin Payment and Collection Scheme (BPCSS)	Regulatory mechanism to regulate the collection scheme and payment of taxes of users who are under regulations	Regulating may affect anonymity
11	(Yin et al., 2018)	Escrow Mechanism	It requires a third party to hold and regulate the transaction to protect the buyers. Regulators control the transactions	Regulating may affect anonymity
12	(He et al., 2018)	Elliptic curve digital signature algorithm	It combines transaction hash and addresses balance to confirm the transactions are completed. Attacks can be detected and mitigated through transaction malleability	It removes an important script from the transaction before the hash of the transaction is computed
13	(Mehta et al., 2017)	Elliptic curve digital signature algorithm	Attacks can be detected and mitigated by combining random seeds and passphrase for the user to generate private keys	Difficulty in implementation; however, proper internal controls can be avoided
14	(Chadha & Kumar, 2017)	Heuristic Clustering	Attacks can be detected and mitigated through heuristic clustering. The clustering help in evaluating doubtful transactions	Thieves have developed various strategies for hiding the source of the Bitcoins. Most of the strategies are studied, and causes are stated; however, many still prevail. It leaves behind high risk for theft

Table 8. Ethical Implications Involving Illegal Activities

No	Author	Technologies Used	Benefits	Challenges
1	(Kshetri & Voas, 2017)	Behavior & Transaction pattern analysis	Users can be traced through IP addresses and money flows. Artificial intelligence can be used to scan and analyze the Bitcoin network to identify suspicious behavior patterns in Bitcoin transactions. It can trace transactions to individuals or groups	Probability of detection using next-generation cryptocurrencies such as Monero, Dash, and Z-Cash. These have built-in anonymity features
2	(Toyoda et al., 2017)	Behavior & Transaction pattern analysis	It helps in identifying undesirable and fraudulent activities such as HYIP (High Yield Investment Program)	It requires the study of a transaction and the frequency of each pattern to identify illicit activities
3	(Van Der Horst et al., 2017)	Bit Iodine	Various methods have been discussed by the authors to help in tracking down illegal activities	Analysis of the wallets used in illicit activities to prevent the illegal activities
4	(Meiklejohn et al., 2013)	Behavior & Transaction pattern analysis	It is necessary to study the transaction patterns and to avoid the untrusted transaction patterns, therefore the risk related to various attack can be mitigated	There is still high risk related to Bitcoins, and new risks and methods to steal Bitcoins are still coming out
5	(Chadha & Kumar, 2017)	Heuristic Clustering	Effort is made to study the flow of money in Silk Road Marketplace through clustering. Heuristic Clustering can be used to study the spread of Dirty money	Regulating the flow of money in illegal activities is difficult
6	(Upadhyaya & Jain, 2016)	Elliptic Curve Diffie Hellman (ECDH)	Various methods have been discussed by the authors to help in tracking down illegal activities	Imposing regulations can be difficult
7	(Shanmugam et al., 2017)	Tor (The Onion Routing) or I2P (Invisible Internet Project)	Review of Bitcoins used by cybercriminals. It helps in tracking down of transactions. Criminal identities can be revealed. It helps in backing up the transactions offline and is easy to retrieve	There are many security issues related to Bitcoins. Distribution of exchanges and transactions have complex techniques. No tie-up with banks or any other regulatory authority makes them popular in criminals
8	(Wang & Gao, 2018)	Ciphertext-Policy Hierarchical Attribute-Based Encryption (CP-HABE)	Lost cryptocurrency can be traced by the regulator. Identities can be verified for doubted and flagged transactions. The decryption of regulation nodes	Users feel the regulation node conflict with the right to protect their privacy and free trade. Users insist on being unregulated and anonymous

Legal Issues Related to Money Laundering

Cryptocurrency offers secure and private transactions. Therefore, it has been used to launder money by illicit means. Cryptocurrency offers the grounds for money laundering as it is unregulated, anonymous, and privacy prevailed. Many methods have been suggested by various authors, and much research is still undergoing. Methods suggested include: analyzing the behavior & Transaction pattern analysis, Data Retrieval, KYC, and Patching Software. These methods used in various studies are shown in Figure 5.

Data Analysis reveals that majority of authors favoured KYC details, Customer due diligence, Heuristic Clustering, and Hierarchical cipher text-policy attribute-based encryption (CP-HABE). CP-HABE is recommended as it involves a regulation node which monitors the transactions, and reports doubtful transactions to the regulatory authority. Therefore, money laundering can be prevented using the CP-HABE method.

Figure 2. Overview of Different Digital Wallets Discussed by Different Authors

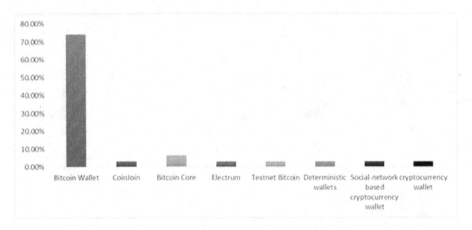

Figure 3. Overview of Methods Used for Digital Wallet Storage

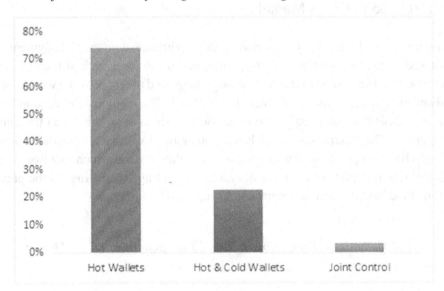

Figure 4. Overview of Methods for Prevention of Illegal Issues Related to Tax Evasion

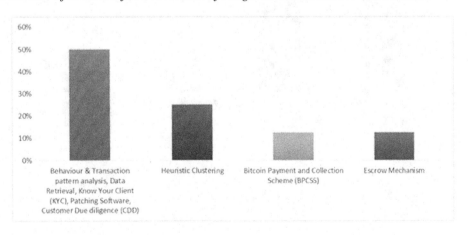

Figure 5. Overview of Methods for Prevention of Illegal Issues Related to Money Laundering

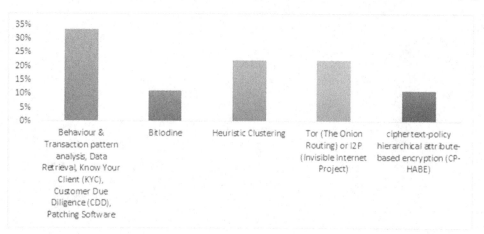

Legal Issues Related to Drugs Markets

Silk Road Drug dealers and WannaCry ransomware cybercriminals demand the payments in Bitcoins. Many methods have been suggested by various authors, and much research is still undergoing to detect illegal transactions. The data related to the methodology suggested in 30 peer-reviewed scientific articles was evaluated and analyzed, in order to evaluate the methods. The methods are listed in Figure 6.

Data Analysis reveals that behaviour and transaction pattern analysis can detect the transactions related to drugs markets. The patterns can be analyzed, and money flow that is considered doubtful can be traced out. CP-HABE is recommended as it involves a regulation node which monitors the transaction and reports doubtful transactions to the regulatory authority. Drugs marketing can be prevented using the CP-HABE method, and the doubtful transactions reported to authorities.

Figure 6. Overview of Methods for Prevention of Illegal Transactions in Drugs Market

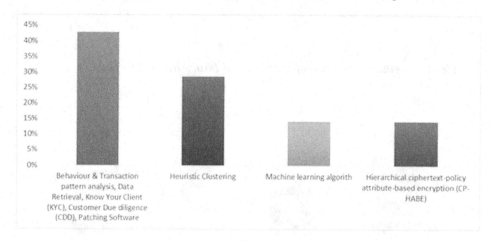

Legal Issues Related to Theft or Loss of Private Keys

Cryptocurrency offers secure and private transactions and has been used to launder money through illicit means. Users neither access nor do transactions in the case of theft or loss of private keys. Many methods have been suggested by various authors, and much research is still undergoing to make wallets strong enough to mitigate these risks. The data related to the methodologies as suggested in 30 peer-reviewed scientific articles are evaluated and clustered together to draw conclusions. The methods used to prevent theft or loss of private keys are presented in Figure 7.

Data Analysis reveals that threshold signature scheme is the one mostly used by many researchers. It is the most secure and helpful method in mitigating risks related to loss or theft of private keys. Secret sharing encryption techniques were also studied and presented in Table 2. These encryption techniques will surely enhance the security and help to mitigate the risk related to the loss or theft of private keys. According to the peer-reviewed articles, the methods of secret sharing used in wallets for encryption, as referred to by various authors, are analyzed and clustered together and presented in Figure 8.

Figure 7. Overview of Methods for Prevention of Theft or Loss of Private Keys

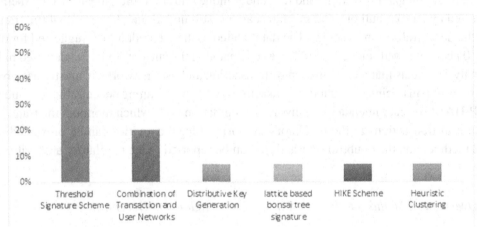

Figure 8. Overview of Methods Used in Secret Sharing for Prevention of Theft/Loss of Private Keys

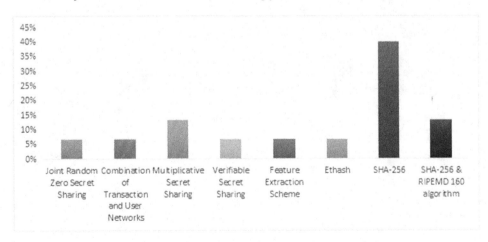

Data analysis reveals that Shamir method and Secure Hash Algorithm-256 (SHA-256) are reportedly the most used, for reasons such as strong encryption and compatibility with other methods, apart from the threshold signature scheme. Multiplicative Secret Sharing is also commonly used. However, it is not strong enough and is only compatible with a few other methods. A bitcoin wallet uses SHA-256 for stronger encryption.

Evaluation of Ethical Issues

Ethical issues on decentralization, illegal activities, and anonymity, noted from the 30 peer-reviewed scientific articles were analyzed and based on the analysis, the ethical issues, their impact, and inherent challenges were evaluated. Our contribution in this chapter makes suggestions with respect to the various problems under the ethical issues heading.

Ethical Issues Related to Decentralization

Cryptocurrencies offer secure and private transactions and is completely decentralized. Decentralization is used to facilitate illegal transactions and to launder money through illicit means. Many methods have been suggested by various authors, and much research is still undergoing to track doubtful transactions, following the decentralization structure. The data related to the methodologies suggested for decentralization in 30 peer-reviewed scientific articles, as evaluated in the current study, are depicted in Figure 9.

Data analysis reveals that a combination of transaction and user networks is mostly used by various authors as they help in tracing out doubtful transactions while maintaining decentralization and anonymity. The CP-HABE is recommended as it involves a regulation node which monitors the transaction and reports doubtful transactions to the regulatory authority. Illegal activities can be prevented using the CP-HABE method, and the doubtful transactions can be reported to the regulatory authority.

Figure 9. Overview of Methods to Prevent Ethical Issues Related to Decentralization

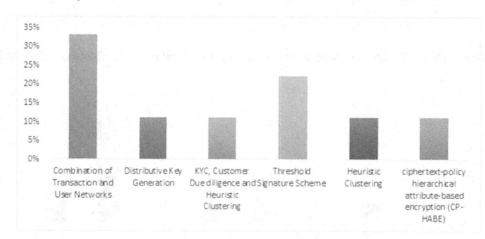

Ethical Issues Related to Illegal Activities

Unfortunately, cryptocurrency related transactions offer a secure and private transaction platform for criminals for the handling of illegal transactional activities. Many methods have been suggested by various researchers, and much research is still undergoing to track doubtful transactions. The data related to the methodologies, as suggested by 30 peer-reviewed scientific articles, for preventing illegal activities, are evaluated and depicted in Figure 10.

Figure 10. Overview of Methods to Prevent and Detect Ethical Issues Related to Illegal Activities

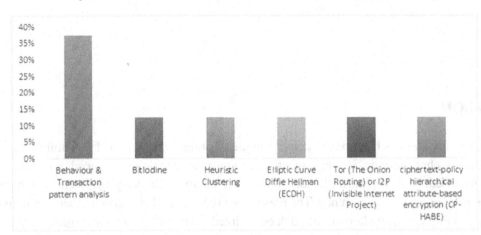

Data analysis reveals that illegal activities can be traced by user behaviour and transaction pattern analysis. Many authors have favored this method as it analyses the flow of transactions and reports doubtful transactions. The CP-HABE is recommended as it involves a regulation node which monitors the transaction and reports doubtful transactions to the regulatory authority. Illegal activities can be prevented using the CP-HABE method, and the doubtful transactions can be reported to the regulatory authority.

Ethical Issues Related to Anonymity

Cryptocurrency offers secure and private transactions due to its anonymity characteristic. Users' identity is not revealed and they remain completely anonymous, leading criminals to use cryptocurrencies for illegal transactions. Many methods have been suggested by various authors, and much research is still undergoing to track doubtful transactions. The methodologies suggested for preventing illegal activities related to anonymity, as suggested in 30 peer-reviewed scientific articles, are evaluated, clustered together, and presented in Figure 11.

Data analysis reveals that anonymity feature is used to deal with illegal activities and transactions. However, it can be traced by user behaviour and transaction pattern analysis. Many authors have favoured this method as it analyses the transactions flow and reports doubtful transactions. The Elliptic Curve Digital Signature Algorithm (ECDSA) is recommended as it is more secure and, for this reason, commonly used. Bitcoin wallet favors ECDSA because it enhances anonymity.

Figure 11. Overview of Methods Used to Prevent Ethical Issues Related to Anonymity

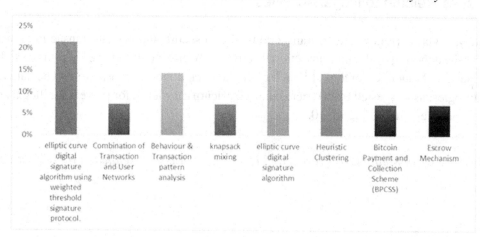

DISCUSSION

Bitcoin money transfer has become the favorite mode of online transactions for criminals as well, due to its anonymity characteristic. Because of this, criminals are unable to be traced, and their identities remain undisclosed. However, the initial idea of Satoshi Nakamoto was very different, when he paved the way for the Bitcoin, as virtual currency. The reason for creating the Bitcoin and other alternative digital currencies was to provide an alternative and decentralized payment system. Ever since these cryptocurrencies were introduced, they have been used for illegal transactions as well, such as buying and selling illegal goods, drugs, and weapons (Kshetri & Voas 2017; Toyoda et al. 2017; Van Der Horst et al. 2017; Meiklejohn et al. 2013; Chadha & Kumar 2017). Most people think that cryptocurrency is outside the view of regulators and authorities to track down, but this is not true (Reid & Harrigan 2013; Wang et al. 2018; Toyoda et al. 2017; Van Der Horst et al. 2017; Chen et al. 2017; Yin et al. 2018).

Our chapter has highlighted the methodologies used by various researchers to detect the illegal activities based on using cryptocurrencies (Dikshit & Singh 2017; Reid & Harrigan 2013; Gennaro et al. 2016; Narayanan et al. 2016; Kshetri & Voas 2017; Maurer et al. 2017; Wang et al. 2018). These solutions have helped and will support policymakers in making more informed decisions related to security and uncertainty of criminal activities through the use of cryptocurrencies.

The main contribution of this chapter is to focus on the areas of negative and illegitimate activities conducted online through using digital currencies like Bitcoin. The fact is that, at this point in time, there is a limited ability for policymakers to regulate cryptocurrencies, due to the reason that cryptocurrencies have allowed criminals to take advantage and to use them for unlawful activities. Therefore, our chapter is focused on helping the regulators and policymakers to make regulations and guidelines to control the unlawful activities being conducted online.

Another contribution of our chapter is presenting discussion on new applications that can be used to identify illicit activities and to regulate cryptocurrencies. The discussion on development of new approaches such as CP-HABE and Transaction and pattern analysis, and the way they can be utilized to detect illegal activities are the main aims of our chapter (Wang & Gao, 2018). Law enforcement authorities can use the applications mentioned in our chapter as surveillance mechanisms against the illicit activities such as selling drugs, weapons, and money laundering (Kshetri & Voas 2017; Toyoda et al. 2017;

Van Der Horst et al. 2017; Chadha & Kumar 2017; Liu, Chen, et al. 2017). Tracking illegal activities and monitoring them through the afore applications can deter the illegal activities being carried on. This will, hopefully, curb the illicit transactions and unlawful trading in cryptocurrencies.

This chapter has revealed the fact that dark web markets like Silk Road came into existence through Bitcoin and other digital currencies. People are buying illegal weapons, drugs from the dark web, and making their payments by using cryptocurrencies utilizing their anonymity feature (Kshetri & Voas 2017; Toyoda et al. 2017; Van Der Horst et al. 2017; Meiklejohn et al. 2013; Chadha & Kumar 2017). This is probably the reason why the street crime ratio has become smaller compared to the ratio of crimes handled online. There has been a migration of activities among people on trading drugs and illegal weapons online rather than on the streets. According to some authors, this has led to a reduction in violence occurring on streets (Christin, 2014). We have suggested in our present study that afore mentioned illegal activities can be prevented. The dark web can be prevented to a certain extent using applications mentioned in our chapter, and to "de-anonymize" the use of cryptocurrency to track the criminals.

Our chapter has revealed that the Elliptic curve, a digital signature using a weighted threshold signature protocol (Gennaro et al. 2016; Dikshit & Singh 2017), was used rather than a simple Elliptic curve digital signature using threshold signature protocol (Narayanan et al., 2016), as it gives one, share of secret keys to each player while accomplishing the requirements of weightage. This can be used as a solution to anonymity and for securing Bitcoin wallets. Our chapter can also help, in the future, for analyzing the scale of illegal activities and quantifying and comparing the illegal activities conducted online versus similar activities on the street. This contribution does not quantify the scale of operations done using the illegal websites, however; this can help to track down such websites by analyzing their activities, especially with respect to cryptocurrencies trade.

This chapter did not discuss the effects of price fluctuations that can occur in cryptocurrencies, although it highlighted the legal and ethical implications which can affect the prices drastically. For instance, genuine users of cryptocurrency are aware of the fact that it is being used in illegal activities, and this has some value in its trading prices online. In this scenario, a strict policy or a regulation by the government can affect prices adversely, to a large extent.

To the regulators, this chapter provides value in understanding the overall legal and ethical issues in the said context. It can help to curb the growth of dark web related marketplaces. There are other dark marketplaces apart from Silk Road 2.0, Armory, and Agora, which are operating in the dark web and are yet to be discovered. Our chapter can help in tracking down new dark market places through analyzing the behavior and transaction patterns of use of cryptocurrency.

Overall, the findings in our chapter summarize various illegal activities undertaken using cryptocurrencies and categorize them to give suggestions with recommended applications. Methods stated in our studies like behavior and transaction pattern analysis and network analysis can help in tracking these criminals. Our chapter can help the regulators and policymakers in developing a policy regime and regulating the use of cryptocurrencies. Additionally, our chapter provides some guidance to make the cryptocurrency wallets more secure by recommending the use of various applications. This can help to mitigate the risks, attacks, and theft related to the use of cryptocurrencies.

CONCLUSION

Many countries have banned certain virtual currencies e.g. Bitcoin, because the governments have no control over the transactions being carried out using these. Cryptocurrencies like Bitcoin should not be made illegal by nations just because these are used by criminals for illicit or undesirable activities. Digital currencies are considered as future currencies and have the potential to create a new revolution in the financial system of the economy. Therefore, restricting their use and banning them is not the solution. These currencies have their rightful place in further development of world economies.

This chapter has highlighted the various applications that can be used to regulate and to control the use of cryptocurrencies. We analyzed the data extracted from 30 peer-reviewed scientific publications (that appeared in years 2011- 2018) describing experimental observations covering the legal and ethical aspects of cryptocurrencies like Bitcoin. We have suggested various methods to prevent tax evasion and money laundering, so that criminals are unable to take the profit out of criminal activities, and the regulators can regulate people trading in cryptocurrencies by making those concerned pay taxes and to disclose their income. Behavior and Transaction pattern analysis, KYC, CDD, and patching software can serve as anti-money laundering and counter-terrorism financing. There are various methods suggested in our chapter to help to mitigate the risks of theft or loss of private keys and to secure digital wallets in cryptocurrencies. As an example, the threshold signature scheme is used as the most efficient and optimal among other schemes for securing digital wallets. The SHA-256 is considered to provide the best form of encryption.

Our research has revealed that Bitcoin wallets are the most used due to their popularity in recent years with respect to trading and price fluctuations. It is also revealed that this has become popular among criminals due to anonymity, which means that criminals are not traced, and their identities remain undisclosed. We have mentioned how decentralization and anonymity could be used to track the criminals. Criminals can be traced through the combination of transaction and user network. This chapter has also mentioned methods to help with the prevention of drug marketing and other illegal activities such as trading of weapons and terrorist funding using cryptocurrencies. We highlighted different applications to track down the illegal activities as a solution for this e.g. use of prior transactions to track down the use of cryptocurrency.

Many studies in the past have considered and discussed the legal issue related to cryptocurrencies, however, they have not satisfactorily studied the overall legal and ethical issues. Our chapter considered such concerns and provided informed suggestions along with existing applications to prevent illegal activities in relation to using cryptocurrencies. The anonymity feature of cryptocurrencies has made criminals think that they cannot be traced. Our chapter suggested various methods to de-anonymize cryptocurrencies and to track down the criminals. This can also prevent the growth of the dark web in the future.

Our current study can also assist the policymakers in making more informed decisions related to security enhancements that can remove the uncertainty that leads to the criminal activities being carried out through trading in cryptocurrencies.

AUTHOR CONTRIBUTION

N.M. and M.N.H. conceived the study idea and developed the analysis plan. N.M. analyzed the data and wrote the initial chapter. M.N.H. helped to prepare the figures and tables and finalized the manuscript. K.A. provided the final editing of the manuscript. All authors contributed to proofing of the manuscript.

REFERENCES

Alvarado, J., & Halgamuge, M. N. (2019). New Era in the Supply Chain Management With Blockchain: A Survey. In Industry 4.0 and Hyper-Customized Smart Manufacturing Supply Chains (pp. 1–37). IGI Global.

Baravalle, A., Lopez, M. S., & Lee, S. W. (2016). Mining the Dark Web: Drugs and Fake Ids. *2016 IEEE 16th International Conference on Data Mining Workshops (ICDMW)*, 350–356. 10.1109/ICDMW.2016.0056

Barratt, M. J., Ferris, J. A., & Winstock, A. R. (2016). Safer scoring? Cryptomarkets, social supply and drug market violence. *The International Journal on Drug Policy*, *35*, 24–31. doi:10.1016/j.drugpo.2016.04.019 PMID:27241015

Chadha, S., & Kumar, U. (2017). Ransomware: Let's fight back! *2017 International Conference on Computing, Communication and Automation (ICCCA)*, 925–930. 10.1109/CCAA.2017.8229926

Chen, P.-W., Jiang, B.-S., & Wang, C.-H. (2017). Blockchain-based payment collection supervision system using pervasive Bitcoin digital wallet. *2017 IEEE 13th International Conference on Wireless and Mobile Computing, Networking and Communications (WiMob)*, 139–146. 10.1109/WiMOB.2017.8115844

Christin, N. (2014). Commentary on Barratt *et al.* (2014): Steps towards characterizing online anonymous drug marketplace customers [Commentary]. *Addiction (Abingdon, England)*, *109*(5), 784–785. doi:10.1111/add.12519 PMID:24720826

Dikshit, P., & Singh, K. (2017). Efficient weighted threshold ECDSA for securing bitcoin wallet. *2017 ISEA Asia Security and Privacy (ISEASP)*, 1–9. doi:10.1109/ISEASP.2017.7976994

Fraser, J. G., & Bouridane, A. (2017). Have the security flaws surrounding BITCOIN effected the currency's value? *2017 Seventh International Conference on Emerging Security Technologies (EST)*, 50–55. 10.1109/EST.2017.8090398

Gennaro, R., Goldfeder, S., & Narayanan, A. (2016). Threshold-Optimal DSA/ECDSA Signatures and an Application to Bitcoin Wallet Security. In M. Manulis, A.-R. Sadeghi, & S. Schneider (Eds.), Applied Cryptography and Network Security (pp. 156–174). Springer International Publishing. doi:10.1007/978-3-319-39555-5_9

He, S., Wu, Q., Luo, X., Liang, Z., Li, D., Feng, H., Zheng, H., & Li, Y. (2018). A Social-Network-Based CryptocurrencyCryptocurrency. *IEEE Access: Practical Innovations, Open Solutions*, *6*, 7654–7663. doi:10.1109/ACCESS.2018.2799385

Kaushal, P. K., Bagga, A., & Sobti, R. (2017). Evolution of bitcoin and security risk in bitcoin wallets. *2017 International Conference on Computer, Communications and Electronics (Comptelix)*, 172–177. 10.1109/COMPTELIX.2017.8003959

Kshetri, N., & Voas, J. (2017). Do Crypto-Currencies Fuel Ransomware? *IT Professional*, *19*(5), 11–15. doi:10.1109/MITP.2017.3680961

Liu, Y., Chen, X., Zhang, L., Tang, C., & Kang, H. (2017). An Intelligent Strategy to Gain Profit for Bitcoin Mining Pools. *2017 10th International Symposium on Computational Intelligence and Design (ISCID)*, *2*, 427–430. 10.1109/ISCID.2017.184

Liu, Y., Liu, X., Zhang, L., Tang, C., & Kang, H. (2017). An efficient strategy to eliminate malleability of bitcoin transaction. *2017 4th International Conference on Systems and Informatics (ICSAI)*, 960–964. 10.1109/ICSAI.2017.8248424

Maurer, F. K., Neudecker, T., & Florian, M. (2017). Anonymous CoinJoin Transactions with Arbitrary Values. *2017 IEEE Trustcom/BigDataSE/ICESS*, 522–529. doi:10.1109/Trustcom/BigDataSE/IC-ESS.2017.280

Mehta, I. S., Chakraborty, A., Choudhury, T., & Sharma, M. (2017). Efficient approach towards bitcoin security algorithm. *2017 International Conference on Infocom Technologies and Unmanned Systems (Trends and Future Directions) (ICTUS)*, 807–810. 10.1109/ICTUS.2017.8286117

Meiklejohn, S., Pomarole, M., Jordan, G., Levchenko, K., McCoy, D., Voelker, G. M., & Savage, S. (2013). A fistful of bitcoins: Characterizing payments among men with no names. *Proceedings of the 2013 Conference on Internet Measurement Conference*, 127–140. 10.1145/2504730.2504747

Mirzayi, S., & Mehrzad, M. (2017). Bitcoin, an SWOT analysis. *2017 7th International Conference on Computer and Knowledge Engineering (ICCKE)*, 205–210. 10.1109/ICCKE.2017.8167876

Nakamoto, S. (2019). Bitcoin: A Peer-to-Peer Electronic Cash System. *Manubot*. https://git.dhimmel.com/bitcoin-whitepaper/

Narayanan, A., Bonneau, J., Felten, E., Miller, A., & Goldfeder, S. (2016). Bitcoin and Cryptocurrency Technologies: A Comprehensive Introduction. Princeton University Press.

Quamara, S., & Singh, A. K. (2016). Bitcoins and secure financial transaction processing, recent advances. *2016 2nd International Conference on Applied and Theoretical Computing and Communication Technology (ICATccT)*, 216–219. 10.1109/ICATCCT.2016.7911995

Reid, F., & Harrigan, M. (2013). An Analysis of Anonymity in the Bitcoin System. In Y. Altshuler, Y. Elovici, A. B. Cremers, N. Aharony, & A. Pentland (Eds.), Security and Privacy in Social Networks (pp. 197–223). Springer. doi:10.1007/978-1-4614-4139-7_10

Shanmugam, B., Azam, S., Yeo, K. C., Jose, J., & Kannoorpatti, K. (2017). A critical review of Bitcoins usage by cybercriminals. *2017 International Conference on Computer Communication and Informatics (ICCCI)*, 1–7. 10.1109/ICCCI.2017.8117693

Shehhi, A. A., Oudah, M., & Aung, Z. (2014). Investigating factors behind choosing a cryptocurrency. *2014 IEEE International Conference on Industrial Engineering and Engineering Management*, 1443–1447. 10.1109/IEEM.2014.7058877

Shrestha, B., Halgamuge, M. N., & Treiblmaier, H. (2020). Using Blockchain for Online Multimedia Management: Characteristics of Existing Platforms. In Blockchain and Distributed Ledger Technology Use Cases (pp. 289–303). Springer.

Tama, B. A., Kweka, B. J., Park, Y., & Rhee, K.-H. (2017). A critical review of blockchain and its current applications. *2017 International Conference on Electrical Engineering and Computer Science (ICECOS)*, 109–113. 10.1109/ICECOS.2017.8167115

Toyoda, K., Ohtsuki, T., & Mathiopoulos, P. T. (2017). Identification of High Yielding Investment Programs in Bitcoin via Transactions Pattern Analysis. *GLOBECOM 2017 - 2017 IEEE Global Communications Conference*, 1–6. 10.1109/GLOCOM.2017.8254420

Tschorsch, F., & Scheuermann, B. (2016). Bitcoin. *IEEE Communications Surveys and Tutorials*, *18*(3), 2084–2123. doi:10.1109/COMST.2016.2535718

Upadhyaya, R., & Jain, A. (2016). Cyber ethics and cybercrime: A deep dwelved study into legality, ransomware, underground web and bitcoin wallet. *2016 International Conference on Computing, Communication and Automation (ICCCA)*, 143–148. 10.1109/CCAA.2016.7813706

Van Der Horst, L., Choo, K.-K. R., & Le-Khac, N.-A. (2017). Process Memory Investigation of the Bitcoin. *IEEE Access: Practical Innovations, Open Solutions*, *5*, 22385–22398. doi:10.1109/ACCESS.2017.2759766

Wang, Q., Li, X., & Yu, Y. (2018). Anonymity. *IEEE Access: Practical Innovations, Open Solutions*, *6*, 12336–12341. doi:10.1109/ACCESS.2017.2787563

Wang, Y., & Gao, J. (2018). A Regulation Scheme Based on the Ciphertext-Policy Hierarchical Attribute-Based Encryption in Bitcoin. *IEEE Access: Practical Innovations, Open Solutions*, *6*, 16267–16278. doi:10.1109/ACCESS.2018.2814620

Yin, W., Wen, Q., Li, W., Zhang, H., & Jin, Z. (2018). An Anti-Quantum Transaction Authentication Approach in Blockchain. *IEEE Access: Practical Innovations, Open Solutions*, *6*, 5393–5401. doi:10.1109/ACCESS.2017.2788411

Zhang, Y., & Li, J. (2016, June 30). An Automatic Identification Authentic Work Anti-counterfeiting Algorithm Based on DWT-DCT. *International Journal of Security and Its Applications*, *10*(6), 135–144. doi:10.14257/ijsia.2016.10.6.14

Chapter 8
A Securities Settlement Model Using Blockchain Technology for Central Securities Depository

Andre P. Calitz
Nelson Mandela University, South Africa

Jean H. Greyling
https://orcid.org/0000-0002-6773-9200
Nelson Mandela University, South Africa

Steve Everett
Nelson Mandela University, South Africa

ABSTRACT

Post-trade securities settlements entered the electronic age between 1980 and 2000. The introduction of technologies such as secure electronic messaging, and improvements in database technology, enabled the inception of central securities depositories (CSDs) as trusted third parties or intermediaries within the securities settlements post-trade landscape. The study reported in this chapter has a focus on CSDs and the application of the blockchain technology to securities settlements. The objective is to develop a model for securities settlements using blockchain technology for a CSD, as currently, globally, no CSD has introduced a production-ready blockchain-based solution for securities settlements. A conceptual model was created from the reported literature that was evaluated by international post-trade securities professionals. The findings have resulted in the acceptance of the main components of the model, with a focus on the cost of the solution, and with the identification of prerequisites to such a solution (e.g., legal/regulatory enablement).

DOI: 10.4018/978-1-7998-6650-3.ch008

INTRODUCTION

The financial services industry has introduced new payment methods and services globally as new technologies have emerged. The use of mobile devices and banking applications (Apps) have made banking services more accessible that have improved the user experience. Electronic cash can now be sent on a peer-to-peer basis (transfer of value) without the need for a financial services intermediary (Nakamoto, 2008). Both the cash and stocks (e.g. securities traded on a financial exchange) have value and can be transferred typically between a buyer and a seller. A buyer of stock interacts directly with a seller of that stock or the issuer of stock (e.g. a company which issues either an equity or debt stock), having the ability in the network to view the transaction (Gibson and Kirk, 2016).

Cryptocurrencies, such as Bitcoin, Litecoin and Ethereum, have introduced a digital asset that can be exchanged between two parties. Peer-to-peer transactions are the core type of transaction which are undertaken in the Bitcoin Blockchain, that makes use of a cryptocurrency known as Bitcoin, which uses cryptography to secure peer-to-peer transactions in a verifiable database that cannot be changed or amended without detection (Swanson, 2015). Typically, these transactions can take place without geographical restriction and without the need to use the traditional banking services to do so.

Securities settlement is a business process whereby securities are delivered against a cash payment between two parties. The opportunity to achieve this type of peer-to-peer transaction in securities settlements (whereby an equity or debt instrument for example can be exchanged for cash) has resulted in much hype within the financial services sector, as the potential for disintermediation of financial services intermediaries exists within the securities settlements ecosystem (Gartner, 2020).

Gartner (2020) indicates that Blockchain technology is at the peak of inflated expectations. It is important to note that, although the technology in its current form is relatively new, many of the cryptographic techniques employed were developed as early as the 1970s (KPMG, 2018). Therefore, since the technology is underpinned by well-known cryptographic techniques and has been applied in the Bitcoin ecosystem, its application in securities settlements needs to be further explored.

Over the last two decades, the traditional trading floors at stock exchanges have been replaced by virtual trading floors, however, whether virtual or physical, each provided the ability to connect investors wishing to buy and sell stocks (O'Connor, 2004). The processes, thereafter, allow the exchange of cash and securities after the trade in what is commonly known as the 'post-trade' process. The process has not undergone a significant change in the last 10 to 15 years despite various technological advances in Financial Services over this period.

In the trade to the post-trade environments, there are multiple, trusted third parties, such as Exchanges, Brokers, Dealers and Central Securities Depositories (CSDs). Karp (2015) highlights the potential to disrupt this particular sector of Financial Services through the use of Blockchain. CSDs, for example, are typically a trusted third party in most markets, which may only have one, or a small number of CSDs responsible for securities settlements in a specific market.

Blockchain technology creates new opportunities and has great potential for securities settlements as a platform. The ability to exchange assets on a peer-to-peer basis, confirmed by an algorithm, is an appealing prospect to improve efficiency and reduce costs in any market. The technology, however, is not new and has been widely developed and documented for more than a decade.

This chapter aims to investigate why blockchain technology has not been successfully translated into a blockchain based production system for securities settlements. A model for securities settlements has been proposed using Blockchain technology. The model has been evaluated by a team of international role players.

PROBLEM STATEMENT AND RESEARCH OBJECTIVE

At the time of publication of this research study, no Central Securities Depository (CSD) exists that is settling securities using Blockchain technology globally, although many had issued press releases on planned research and implementations. In addition, the cryptocurrency market has continued to grow in parallel to the existing securities market. Therefore, the research problem investigated in this study is as follows:

No Central Securities Depository (CSD), nor any Capital Markets infrastructure presently utilise the Blockchain technology for securities settlements.

The current research was initiated by identifying what risks a CSD mitigates, given the actors, intermediaries and various settlement models employed; and how existing technology and processes assist in achieving a successful outcome. Once these were identified, the research explored what expectations of securities settlements exist amongst the primary role players in capital markets securities settlements (namely the regulators, issuers and investors). The research evaluated the most suitable approach to implement the new blockchain technology in an established securities settlement market. This provided a balanced evaluation, consisting of the inherent risks and the perceived benefits of available Blockchain technologies. A conceptual model was then presented and its acceptance evaluated, not only by CSDs, but also by the primary international role players in the industry.

The main research question for the study is:

What are the perceptions of the international role players in the industry, for a proposed model for securities settlements using Blockchain technology?

The main research objective of the study is:

To evaluate a proposed model for securities settlements using Blockchain technology for a Central Securities Depository by international role players.

This study is focused on CSDs and the application of the Blockchain technology to securities settlements. As most countries only have one or two CSDs, information had to be obtained from CSDs internationally as well as from the CSD in South Africa, namely Strate Ltd. The research was limited to evaluating a proposed model for securities settlements using blockchain technologies within a CSD of traditional CSD instruments, such as bonds, money markets and equities.

Due to the rapid developments and innovation in this area of technology specifically, this research was carried out within a two-year period without re-evaluating the latest available information and developments on Blockchain technology. No software application was developed in this study, as the primary aim of the study was focused on addressing broad-based principles to apply the use of Blockchain technologies for securities settlements.

This research is aimed at providing a pragmatic conceptual design of the application of Blockchain technology to securities settlement in a manner which balances the true benefits of the technology without introducing undue risk. The risk of failure of the technology of a CSD or a system which provides settlement services to a market can be catastrophic to the economies of countries. Thus, this research study aims to play a positive role in ensuring that robust models are considered, as the technology which underpins these markets is fast evolving.

LITERATURE REVIEW

The post-trade securities settlements ecosystem will be discussed in this section, followed by blockchain as a potential disrupter for CSDs and the use of distributed ledger technology for CSDs.

Post-Trade Securities Settlements Ecosystem

Before providing detail about the post-trade processes, it is important to understand the context of the total ecosystem of actors, intermediaries and regulators who are involved in this industry. Harris (2004) determines that stocks (equities or debt instruments for example) can take many forms, such as equities, commodities or debt instruments. Stocks can be bought and sold on exchanges through brokers who are members of an exchange. Harris (2004) further defines trading as a search problem whereby buyers need to find sellers and sellers need to find buyers. The primary actors involved in the trading of stocks are:

- Brokers: They assist clients to find traders who are willing to trade with them;
- Dealers: Thy trade with clients as and when they want to trade. Where dealers buy and sell, prices are 'bid' and 'offer' respectively; and
- Exchanges and Brokerages: they help to reduce search costs for buyers and sellers by placing both on the same electronic trading platform, thus engaging buyers with sellers and vice versa. These platforms also provide important information on the best bids and offers for a particular stock.

Once a buyer and seller have agreed on a price (between the bid and the offer) through their respective brokers at an exchange, the exchange sends a report to the brokers confirming the trade. A buyer must pay the broker who is purchasing stock (a term used interchangeably with security), then a number of days later (five days in South Africa), the seller receives payment for the stock while the buyer receives stock in the correct quantity, at the price already agreed (Harris, 2004).

The first electronic stock exchange, NASDAQ, was created in 1971 in the United States and became fully electronic in 1980 (Atack and Neal, 2009; Gorham and Singh, 2009). Electronic stock exchanges for the trading of securities require more efficient post-trade processing. Post-trade processing involves the processes of Clearing and Settlement. Loader (2002) describes clearing as the "the preparation through matching, recording and processing instructions of a transaction for settlement" and settlement as the "exchange of cash or assets in return for other assets" which includes the "exchange of legal ownership". Gorham and Singh (2009) describe the process of manually clearing and settling matched trades as both tedious and complex and requires many institutions in financial markets to co-operate and work together. Managing the complexity of clearing and settlement, is also a key component of post-trade risk management, in order to ensure that a seller receives payment and the buyer receives the contractually agreed asset, thus mitigating credit and default risk (Gorham and Singh, 2009).

Securities Settlement Systems (SSS), more specifically in the form of Central Securities Depositories (CSDs), were introduced over twenty years ago in order to provide a centralised, safekeeping function for local markets and to expedite the processing of clearing and settlement in a centralised and electronic way (Loader, 2002). Local market issuers would typically have their entire issue in safekeeping at the CSD (Dickinson, 2015). Dickinson (2015) further elaborates that CSDs dematerialised physical stocks, which were previously kept as physical certificates either at investors, issuers or custodians. These stocks were prone to loss, damage and theft in addition to being expensive to store.

Figure 1. Exchange Industry Value Chain [adapted from Floreani and Polato (2014)]

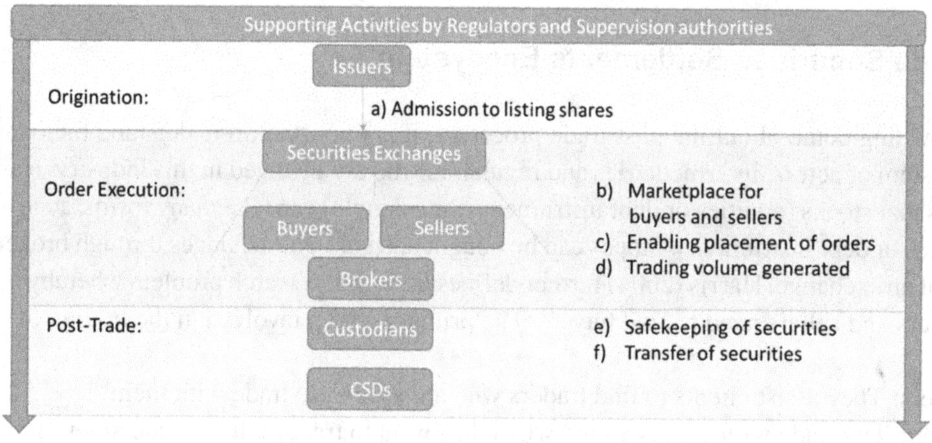

CSDs are found at the end of the post-trade settlements process, which forms a subset of the overall exchange-industry value chain, as illustrated in Figure 1, that suggests that there are three key phases in the value chain, namely Origination, Order Execution and Post-Trade; and that each of these activities is regulated and supervised in a given market or region (Floreani and Polato, 2014). CSDs are concerned with the post-trade activities of safekeeping and transfer of securities. Thus, a CSD could be considered as performing securities settlement per market or per region as part of the overall post-trade process. Caprio (2013) indicates that securities settlement is defined by four primary requirements, namely:

- Securities Ownership: Settlement must complete the legal requirements in respect of transfer of ownership, within the legal framework of the applicable jurisdiction;
- Cash settlement: Although cash payment is an important aspect of securities settlement, what is of primary importance is the delivery of the property (securities/stocks/shares). Therefore, buyers or sellers should maintain ownership in the event of insolvency of an intermediary while cash or securities are being processed;
- Settlements that are cost-effective and efficient: these should also be globally competitive and able to interoperate with other settlement systems globally; and

- Settlements that do not change the nature of a transferred security: If the security had a right (a voting right for example) attributed to it against an issuer, holders of such a security must be able to exercise the right attributed to the particular security.

CSDs however, are not the only trusted third party involved in the post-trade securities settlements between Issuers (i.e. institutions which issue debt or equities securities to raise capital) and Investors, as illustrated in Figure 2. Dickinson (2015) indicates the following differences inclusive of explanations for a) to h) as illustrated:

(a) A direct investor (who either buys or sells securities/stocks) can appoint a custodian and has the authority to select one or many brokers;

(b) A custodian, in turn, will have a nominee account at a CSD, made up of direct investors and institutional investors;

(c) Direct investors can also elect to have direct accounts at a CSD administered by a custodian;

(d) Direct investors who use brokers will have accounts with a broker who will in turn have an account at a CSD called a 'Brokers Participant Account';

(e) Institutional clients are able to open accounts with one or many custodians directly;

(f) Institutional clients would typically provide Investment Managers with access to their accounts as the custodian;

(g) Investment managers may also appoint their own custodians; and

(h) Institutional clients can appoint an Investment Manager who has his/her own custodian as an alternative.

Figure 2. Post-Trade Settlement Landscape [adapted from Dickinson (2015)]

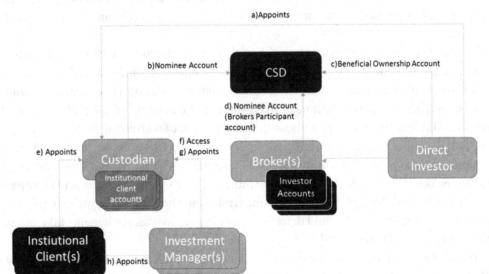

In Figure 2, the assumption is that Issuers have already issued securities (i.e. equities or debt). This provides an indication of the systemically important, interconnected, central role CSDs play in safekeeping and transferring securities. Any changes to the business model of how assets are transferred and kept in custody would impact all of the intermediaries depicted in Figure 2 and could even lead to an entirely new business model with disintermediation a distinct possibility for all intermediaries as represented by the World Economic Forum (2015).

Typically, each of these intermediaries interact with each other in some form as indicated in Figure 2. This implies that there are systems, processes and people involved within the interconnected nature of what is represented in Figure 2. Bitcoin, when it was first introduced, posed a question as to whether or not it was necessary to have these intermediaries at all and whether or not it was possible to merely have buyers and sellers transacting on a peer-to-peer basis (Swan, 2015).

Blockchain as a Potential Disrupter for CSD's

Zohar (2015) suggests that Blockchain Technology could be disruptive to existing business models, as no single entity is able to prevent transactions or charge fees. Blockchain technology effectively eliminates the need for a trusted third party to process transactions and provide record-keeping services, which poses threats to the core business functions of some intermediaries, such as CSDs.

Swan (2015) posits that Blockchain for securities settlement could need more development and customisation, describing the eventual outcome as 'Blockchain 2.0'. This is an interesting concept in itself, as the development of Blockchain technology up to 2015 had already undergone extensive improvement and changes since its inception in 2008. The application of Blockchain technology to the settlement of securities would need to enhance the four primary issues as defined by Caprio (2013), in order for there to be an appropriate business case as defined earlier by Evans (2003).

A decentralised Blockchain technology model for securities settlement is not clearly defined because of the interconnected nature of securities settlement. It would require market co-ordination and planning with regulators, intermediaries, issuers and investors in order to validate a business case to proceed with the technology as a replacement for currently used technologies (Committee on Capital Markets Regulation, 2019).

Blockchain technology continues to evolve, however the application of Blockchain technology for securities settlement is a complex exercise, given the interconnected landscape of the post-trade environment. A theoretical conceptual model for securities settlement using Blockchain technology could however be developed. This model will need to ensure that the benefits of Blockchain technology can be applied at CSDs for a given market without the introduction of additional risks.

Swan (2015) describes Blockchain as a disruptive technology. This is contextualised in the sense that Blockchain provides the potential for transactions to take place without trusted third parties. A Central Securities Depository (CSD) is the de facto trusted third party for securities settlement in a given market. Thus, a CSD, as a trusted third party could become irrelevant, should this technology introduce a fundamentally new set of rules, which could determine how capital market settlements take place, perhaps without the need for a CSD (Karp, 2015).

It is therefore important to understand why it has been more challenging to settle securities within the context of Blockchain technology, compared to peer-to-peer transactions using a cryptocurrency, such as Bitcoin. Almost, on a weekly basis, new prototypes or proof of concepts are announced by varying participants in capital markets, which aim to settle securities on a blockchain (Committee on Capital Markets Regulation, 2019). If this is technically feasible, there must be other conditions to consider beyond the technology itself.

A disruptive technology has the potential to elevate an unknown business in an established industry while discarding a proven, even dominant incumbent. Since CSDs are 'dominant' in given markets (there are normally one or two CSDs per market), they seem to be a prime use case for a disruptive technology such as Blockchain, as it is the 'trusted third party' in most markets. CSDs are typically found in the middle of the post-trade settlement processes in capital markets between multiple entities/intermediaries, although at the end of the post trade process. This disruptive technology therefore provides a differentiating opportunity to eliminate the need for a dominant intermediary, such as a CSD and enable peer-to-peer settled transactions between buyers and sellers of given stocks. The observation could also be that a CSD is the obvious starting point to enable the technology to, in essence, disrupt itself.

Blockchain technology has the potential to disintermediate any process in financial services (The Economist, 2014). This means that all financial service providers within the supply chain of a securities settlement transaction are potential points of disintermediation, including central banks, brokerages, custodian banks and CSDs. Disintermediation, however, would only take place if there are differentiating factors the technology could provide, which could lower cost, create efficiencies and increase information security (Committee on Capital Markets Regulation, 2019). At the time of writing, no disintermediation of any of the above-mentioned entities had taken place, even though the technology has been in use since 2008. There are many initiatives underway throughout the spectrum of participants globally in the capital markets, but none have successfully implemented the technology in post-trade securities settlement on an end to end basis (Committee on Capital Markets Regulation, 2019).

For Blockchain to realise its potential as a true disruptor, the technology needs to be a differentiator and not simply an enabler (Swan, 2015). Herein may be the key as to why there has been little disruption to date in post-trade securities settlement. It is important to note that there is much experimentation still taking place across the spectrum of intermediaries in capital markets, most of them accompanied by press releases about joint ventures with new fintech and established companies alike. This experimentation is necessary to understand the technology; however, the experimentation is not driven on a market-wide scale with a market-wide design to achieve common goals.

Securities Custody

This section introduces the concept of securities custody and how this is applied within the role of a CSD. Due to the physical nature of securities prior to dematerialisation, custodianship was sought by investors to keep their securities safe, effectively creating 'indirect asset holdings' (Eva, 2015). Advances in technology resulting in electronic securities holdings and in the use of CSDs, however, did not result in an elimination of indirect holdings, even though it significantly reduced risk and increased efficiencies. Eva (2015) mentions that the converse results in an increased number of indirect holdings at one or multiple custodians who administer and fulfil a safe-keeping function for the investor.

Although it is still possible to be a direct investor (buyers/sellers), the investor still has the option to appoint a custodian (typically a Bank) and has the ability to select one or many brokers (Swanson, 2015). A non-exhaustive list of intermediaries, who could operate in a series of 'custody chains' are:

- Brokers: have accounts at custodians either for their own positions or those of their clients;
- Custodians: have accounts with other custodians, typically sub-custodians or global custodians (European Central Bank, 2007);

- institutional clients: are able to open accounts with one or many custodians directly; they would typically provide investment managers with access to their accounts at the custodian; can appoint an Investment Manager who has his/her own custodian as an alternative; and
- investment managers: may also appoint their own custodians.

The custody chains listed above, represent a multi-layered account and an indirect holdings structure, which works together to support stable securities settlement (European Central Bank, 2016). Although these intermediaries co-operate to keep securities settlement stable, the custody chains have the ability to modify rights of investors, as there are multiple terms and conditions between custodians and their sub-custodians, which could be less beneficial for an investor (Eva, 2015).

The distance between the issuer and the investor in terms of custody relationship has been intermediated by between one and three custodians, before the record of ownership is realised at the CSD. Furthermore, rights of the investor have been altered within this procedure, thus leading to a case of 'indirect holding' for the ultimate investor (Eva, 2015). In addition, buyers and sellers each have their own custody arrangements. Custody services are typically offered as one service within a portfolio of services including tax, cash management, investment advice and brokerage; either only in a domestic market or in multiple geographic regions (European Central Bank, 2007). Settlement finality, which is supported by legal frameworks in each country, is a key component in the current settlement system within the custody chain and is typically affected by a transfer within a securities account at a custodian or at a CSD (Mori, 2016).

It is important to understand that buyers and sellers of stocks have, in effect, outsourced many of the administrative and operational functions required to settle securities to a series of intermediaries including custodians, sub-custodians, CSDs brokers and investment managers. According to the Financial Stability Board (2009), CSDs were introduced as a joint market initiative to electronically settle high volumes of dematerialised shares for a national market (country or region) and maintain a central register of ownership.

Eva (2015) asserts that CSDs are typically found between intermediaries of the custody chain with one or many custodians (sub-custodians) interacting in a coordinated and orchestrated manner with the CSD to safeguard assets of investors. CSDs typically serve a national market and play an important role for national regulators of a given country (European Central Bank, 2007) and differ subtly in their implementation in different countries (Euroclear and Oliver Wyman, 2016). Euroclear and Wyman (2016) further clarify that this implies that there is a sovereign (i.e. country specific) requirement with regard to CSDs, as regulators would require direct supervision, oversight and tailored reporting based on individual market requirements.

The Financial Stability Board (2009) concludes that CSDs are systemically important market infrastructures in the smooth functioning of capital markets, not only from a securities settlement perspective, but also for market conduct reasons (Euroclear and Wyman, 2016). Should a CSD experience distress or a failure because of the complexity and interconnectedness within capital markets, this would cause significant disruption to the wider financial system and to economic activity. According to Brennan and Lunn (2016), CSDs, a centralised ledger and by virtue of its current technology a record-keeping structure, are not immutable and are susceptible to censorship, forgery or transaction reversals. It is important to note that although the CSD record is not immutable, there are other logical and physical security controls in place which govern information security and data protection and have done so successfully. Given that CSDs also occupy a dominant position in a given market, the CSD system is required to interoperate with those of the various intermediaries and exchanges in local markets with pre-defined standards and protocols.

Distributed Ledger Technology

This section assesses the suitability of Distributor Ledger Technology (DLT) for the current expectations of securities settlement. The various approaches to adopt DLT are introduced, in order to assess whether DLT could enable the benefits for securities settlement or create a differentiator from existing practices and technology.

The adoption of a new platform for securities settlement in current markets globally, with incremental technology improvements or changes, is often implemented over a number of years. Typically, changes or improvements are considered by market committees and are implemented with synchronised timetables of each organisation matching those of other organisations in the ecosystem. One such example is Target 2 Securities (T2S), driven by the European Central Bank (2015), which has taken over seven years to implement in Europe to harmonise settlement across borders.

Although a disruptive change by the introduction of a new incumbent cannot be eliminated, the adoption of a relatively new technology would require a similar collaborative approach, given the interconnected nature of the entities affected. Morgan Stanley (2016), The European Securities and Market Authority (2016) as well as Euroclear and Oliver Wyman (2016) agree that the impact on connected legacy systems, processes and organisational changes are too complex to consider in a 'big-bang' manner and will in all probability be implemented in a coordinated approach using market forums or consortiums. There are a number of Blockchain consortiums comprising banks, market infrastructures and exchanges, focused on permissioned DLT solutions which have been formed as described by the World Federation of Exchanges (2016). These include R3 CEV, Hyperledger and the Post-Trade Distributed Ledger Group. This, however, does not mean that there are no other approaches to potential adoption, such as those identified by Euroclear and Oliver Wyman (2016).

Euroclear and Oliver Wyman (2016) state that collaboration could be another alternative. This is led by an existing market participant such as a CSD or an industry consortium, as described by DTCC (2016), which aims to develop the new technology in parallel with the existing technology. Typically, this is dependent on whether or not there is a business case to do so (Morgan Stanley, 2016). Finally, Mandated Policy is a further alternative, whereby a regulatory body mandates the use of the Blockchain technology to replace existing systems on a market-wide basis (Euroclear and Oliver Wyman, 2016).

Although there may not be a one-to-one match between functionality that DLT provides and what is required to facilitate securities settlements, it is important to acknowledge that DLT is still an emerging and evolving technology. Swan (2015) presents the concept of what the potential of 'Blockchain 2.0' could mean to the design of a DLT securities settlements system. There are indications of the technology evolving further, and this needs to be considered in the design of a new DLT based ecosystem.

Using Blockchain technology is challenging and it is important to understand the underpinning design and the consequences thereof for certain use cases as described by Natoli and Gramoli (2016). Although there are many more platforms available to evaluate, the pre-eminent consortia that have been involved in post-trade DLT development, as already stated above, are R3 CEV, ChinaLedger, Hyperledger and the Post-Trade Ledger Group (Swan, 2015). Since there is no widely used commercial DLT solution for capital markets and given the rapid development and emergence of new technology in this field, it is important to investigate new technology developments, which could support securities settlements, and assist in developing a technological framework or ecosystem to support such a service.

Figure 3. Sovereign Distributed Securities Ledger/Depository Platform DLT Ecosystem

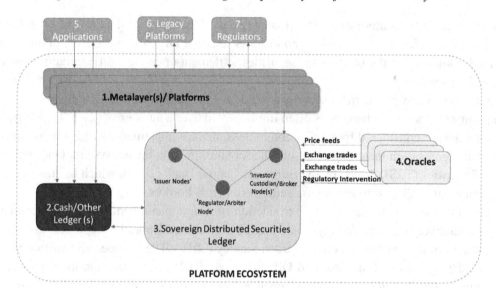

Multi-signature addresses are typically used in the Bitcoin Blockchain; however, the concept of multi-signature is a novel one when considering the custody chain. Payments or asset transfer can be affected by requiring more than one signature (i.e. the buyer, the seller and potentially a bank) and potentially the signature of an arbiter to complete the transaction (Natoli and Gramoli, 2016). This concept is further supported in the concept of a 'Threshold Signature Scheme', which reaches Byzantine agreement through the use of multi-signature (Pilkington, 2015).

A 'Control Layer' is further required for regulatory purposes. It is important to note the work that Ripple and Multichain have performed in order to have the concept of a 'metalayer', which operates independently and outside of the Blockchain 'layer'; and interacts with the ledger/Blockchain itself. Another option is Oracle, which is used extensively in the Ethereum protocol; it allows inputs from a third party into smart contracts (Wall and Malm, 2016).

The DLT ecosystem could probably be a multi-ledger environment that should enable cross-chain/ ledger delivery versus payment (DvP) (Wall and Malm, 2016). Thus, interoperability between ledgers is a key requirement of all DLT technologies for securities settlement in the future.

A CONCEPTUAL MODEL FOR DISTRIBUTED SECURITIES DEPOSITORY

In this section, a conceptual model for sovereign distributed securities depositories is presented. Figures 3 and 4 cover the design concept of the proposed sovereign distributed securities depository and the interoperability it requires, respectively. The conceptual model, depicted in Figure 3, is a 'sovereign' distributed securities depository, as opposed to a central securities depository, as it exists today. The significance of a 'sovereign' use case is that, typically, CSDs are operated on a country or regional basis. Thus, the proposed conceptual model should be built on this principle.

The identified design elements that have been graphically incorporated into a conceptual model represented in Figure 3, are summarised as follows:

- A permissioned Blockchain using Practical Byzantine Fault Tolerance (PBFT) is used as opposed to permissionless within the DLT network. This is used within the actual DLT network represented by *Sovereign Securities Distributed Ledger* (element 3 in Figure 3);
- As there are domestic laws, regulations and market disciplines, each domestic market requires its own 'sovereign' ledger. Most countries have their own CSD for these reasons (Euroclear and Oliver Wyman, 2016);
- Cash is kept and tracked in a separate cash ledger as described by Euroclear and Oliver Wyman (2016). The *'Cash/Other Ledger'* (element 2 in Figure 3), has the ability (through smart contracts) to interact bilaterally with the sovereign ledger to enable DvP transactions;
- All securities are within the 'sovereign' distributed securities ledger (depository) (SDSD) distributed across known nodes. These nodes are representative of the custody chain with known entities/intermediaries. This ensures no market fragmentation can take place whereby some securities are in one ledger and others in another;
- Known nodes within the ledger are given specific roles and access levels within a multi-signature discipline. For example, if an investor intends to purchase positions in stock from a particular seller, the investor mandates a broker to purchase the stock. The broker may have credit lines with a bank/custodian, who may also have bespoke applications built on top of the Metalayer (element 1 in Figure 3), in the ecosystem for their clients. The SDSD will use multi-signature technology to ensure that the investor purchases stock directly from a seller; however, the broker and bank/custodian signs/validates the transaction before it is concluded. This also means that since the DLT network provides the custodial functionality, the banks and brokers will focus on other customer service activities to retain customers;
- Regulatory intervention and oversight are catered for by the use of Oracles (Poelstra, 2014). Oracles (element 4 in Figure 3) are used to insert data into smart contracts or directly into the SDSD as well as regulatory read-access to information through the meta-layer platforms;
- The use of Oracles and multi-signature technology together adequately meet both the security and audit requirements of financial applications;
- Meta-layer platforms and Oracles act similarly to regular databases to read and write to the Blockchain, respectively. They should bear the computational and storage burdens, leaving the SDSD as scalable as possible. This also provides the opportunity for a 'full view' of transactions for regulators. In addition, the Oracles can provide necessary trade flow and price information as examples. It is clear that the Blockchain component of such a model is not the technical focus, but would affect the design of the entire ecosystem; and
- The combination of the above forms a platform whereby applications, legacy platforms and regulators as described by Caprio (2013) and Karp (2015) (elements 5, 6 and 7 in Figure 3) can interact with the DLT settlement ecosystem.

Given that the SDSD will only be applicable to one country/region, there is an important aspect that needs to be considered – the interoperability with other SDSDs, as markets require global asset mobility as the Bitcoin Blockchain provides. Figure 4 illustrates a conceptual model of how these sovereign ledgers could interface with each other.

Figure 4. Conceptual Model for SDSD

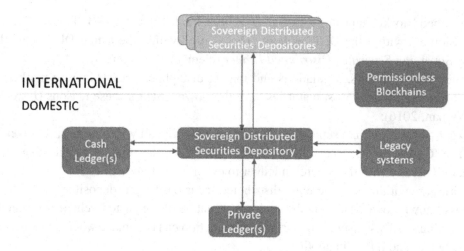

Figure 4 incorporates all elements of Figure 3 into the 'sovereign distributed securities depositories' block. This illustrates the importance of the SDSD to interoperate, as it will not operate in isolation and will need to have the ability to operate with on-chain and off-chain assets (such as legacy systems and cash ledgers), as well as other SDSDs in other markets, much like CSDs interoperate with each other today. Conceptually, SDSDs would need to be both trusted and known legal entities for each other, as the network between them would be yet another permissioned ledger to facilitate cross-border transactions.

Analysis of Success Factors for the Proposed Conceptual Model

The following are the critical success factors for implementing the proposed conceptual model (as shown Figure 4) against the requirements of a settlements system.

Securities Ownership

The immutability and consensus mechanism used e.g. Practical Byzantine Fault Tolerance (PBFT) provides settlement finality, especially in the case of Hyperledger. The model is designed to cater for the legal requirements in respect of transfer of ownership, within the legal framework of the applicable jurisdiction (Dickinson, 2015).

Cash Settlement

Dickinson (2015) indicates that ownership is maintained in the event of insolvency, through the use of smart contracts and a DvP process based on the escrow of the assets and cash on their respective ledgers. However, cash will need to be issued onto the Blockchain to ensure a clearly enhanced service compared to current DvP processing. The escrow method does not improve on the model currently in existence; however, it will need to at least maintain its effectiveness.

Cost-Effectiveness and Efficiency

The potential to reduce settlement timelines across asset types is both efficient that will assist in the reduction of capital costs, and reconciliations across multiple actors in the custody chain.

Interoperability with other Settlements Systems

The model (as shown in Figure 4) is conceptually designed to interoperate with other SDSDs globally, as well as with 'off-chain' and other ledgers (Dickinson, 2015). The collaborative approach to the development of this model in domestic markets also provides the ability for standardisation for 'off-chain' transactions and other ledgers. Interoperability without a global plan could eliminate any cost saving benefits of the technology.

The settlements must not change the nature of a transferred security. This requirement is an essential element in the current post-trade securities settlement environment and is included in the model. If the security had a right attributed to it (a voting right for example) against an issuer, holders of such a security must be able to exercise the right attributed to the particular security (Dickinson, 2015). Each security is tracked and signed by the ledger with the aid of smart contracts to assist in asset servicing.

Time to Market

The challenge that DLT solutions pose is due to the fact that no market-wide adoption exists, presently. The use of incumbents such as the CSD, custodians and brokers to work cooperatively with each other and the issuer, investor and regulators provide an evolutionary step towards implementing the technology in a domestic market without fragmenting markets. This also means that the majority of changes in initial stages should take place between custodians, brokers and the CSD, as a contained and manageable user-group.

RESEARCH DESIGN AND METHODOLOGY

The current study is based on the research paradigm where a proposed conceptual model for securities settlement, based on Blockchain technology, is presented as a theoretical contribution artefact and intended for use by Security Settlement Systems (SSS), such as CSDs, globally. Practitioners working for CSDs internationally, were requested to evaluate and validate the proposed model. The proposed model is part of a business case study, which was included in a paper published in an industry-recognised journal by Everett et al. (2017). Given the niche nature of this study (securities settlements and post trade infrastructure), the intention was that respondents, who are already knowledgeable in the field, would be best able to evaluate the model.

A positivistic research philosophy was used and data were collected through the use of a survey. Collis and Hussey (2013) assert that positivism is associated with quantitative analysis methodologies and requires quantitative research data. Yilmaz (2013) provides a generic set of characteristics of quantitative data inclusive of the following:

- A pre-constructed or standardised set of questions which are categorised;
- Conversion of data into numerical values for the purposes of analysis and generalisation (finding the 'norm'); and
- A randomly selected large representative sample. Note that this is a general requirement, however in the case of this study, there are only a limited amount of CSDs globally (normally 1 or 2 per developed country), thus the size of the representative sample was be constrained by the niche industry represented.

A deductive approach was used, whereby a proposed conceptual model was developed, published and evaluated. Given the limited potential size of the target audience (population) and that sample units needed to be uniquely screened by the researcher, a minimum of 30 respondents needed to be identified from both within South Africa and internationally. A sample of 47 appropriately judged sample units was selected from 7 countries, with 33 respondents ultimately participating from all 7 countries targeted.

Questionnaire and Evaluation Factors

The questionnaire, as presented in Appendix A, initially consisted of 6 factors (Figure 5) operationalised from literature and as discussed below. The six factors, after detailed statistical analysis and with the assistance of the university statistician, were mapped onto 10 factors (Figure 6).

Figure 5. The Factors used in the Sovereign Distributed Securities Depository Survey

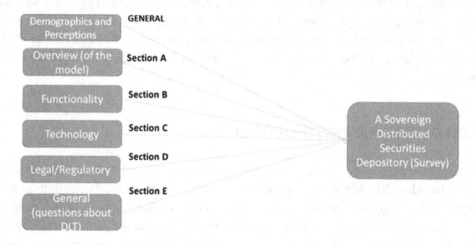

Demographics and Perception (General)

The purpose of this factor is to obtain basic information from respondents. However, given the context and the nature of this study, the perception and viewpoint of the respondent upfront is important to capture along with the age and designation of the respondent. The purpose of this factor is to provide general feedback on the conceptual model, which respondents were provided with. Primarily, respondents were asked to validate the foundational elements of the model, such as its sovereign nature versus public ledgers and general timelines around perceived implementations times.

Overview of the Model (Section A)

The purpose of this factor is to introduce and validate the conceptual model and to provide an overview and explanation of the conceptual model.

Functionality (Section B)

The purpose of this factor is to ascertain general functional requirements as considered in the conceptual model. Positively stated functional requirements to validate the model were included with questions which could validate the model.

Technology (Section C)

The purpose of this factor is to validate the principle technology components as discussed in the model.

Legal/Regulatory (Section D)

The purpose of this factor is to validate legal and regulatory assumptions about the model, including the validation of the custody chains that will remain in the model. Additionally, to investigate the legal and/or regulatory framework for securities settlements as applicable to the new technology.

General Questions about DLT (Section E)

The purpose of this factor is to consider generic questions around the implementation of DLT, specifically after answering questions about the proposed model. This is important as each of these questions has the potential to be linked to other factors and provide meaningful validation to the questions asked about the model earlier in the survey.

Survey Design and Sampling Methods

It is important to consider the nature of the questions in the survey which was later completed by respondents. Since a conceptual model was developed based on a technology, not yet fully proven in a production capacity, respondents are likely to provide their opinion rather than specific numeric or nominal answers. The design of the questionnaire therefore was of paramount importance and the sections discussed earlier, were used as a guideline to assist respondents. All questions were grounded in the literature review of the study. The questionnaire (in Appendix A) was sent to the target audience and was analysed using the Statistica software package to produce statistical results. In addition, Dr Danie Venter, a Nelson Mandela University statistical consultant was engaged to produce and analyse the statistical results.

Given the size of the sample and that each respondent is uniquely screened by the researcher, an appropriate non-probability sampling method was selected. Saunders et al. (2012) describe a sampling technique called *Judgement Sampling*, which permits an experienced individual to select units of the sample based on personal judgement on the most appropriate characteristics of the sample member. Given the information provided earlier, this option was the most logical choice for this research.

Data and Statistical Analysis

The study collected and analysed quantitative data using statistical analysis. The data were collected from respondents who read the case (Everett et al., 2017) for this study. The conceptual model (Figure 4) was tested by using both descriptive and inferential statistical methods.

The following descriptive statistics were conducted:

- Frequency distributions of understanding the respondent (age, understanding of the technology for example); and
- Central tendency and distribution per factor.

Statistical significance is an important objective and is represented by Alpha = 0.05 with a p-value of less than 0.05. Cohen's D is used for practical significance in a One-sample T-test. The ranges are illustrated in Table 1.

Table 1. Interpretation Intervals for Cohen's d (Gravetter and Wallnau, 2009: p 264)

Interpretation intervals for Cohen's d	
<0.20	Not significant
0.20 - 0.49	Small
0.50 - 0.79	Medium
0.80+	Large

Pearson's Product Moment Correlations analysis were also conducted with a correlation coefficient being statistically significant if the p-value is at 0.05 for n=33 (Gravetter and Wallnau, 2009). Pearson's Chi-Square tests, ANOVAs and t-tests were conducted in order to examine the relationships between various demographic variables. Furthermore, an inferential ranking was conducted.

Reliability and Validity

Research undertaken needs to be repeatable by other researchers, given that the same methods are applied to arrive at similar conclusions (Greener, 2008). Furthermore, Collis and Hussey (2014) are concerned with the robustness of a questionnaire and provide three possible reliability tests, which should be used in the design phase, namely:

- A re-test: This involved re-creating the conditions of the first survey and then requiring participants to re-test. This method is only recommended as a supplementary measure;
- Internal consistency: This method is statistically included to correlate the responses to questions in the questionnaire with other questions in the same questionnaire; and
- Alternative forms: This involves comparing responses to alternative/different forms of the same question.

For the purpose of this study, internal consistency and alternative forms were used to ascertain reliability. According to Greener (2008), it is important that research covers all three components of validity, namely: face validity, construct validity and internal validity. Greener (2008) furthermore explains the differences between the three components and how they are interlinked, viz:

- Face validity ensures that a non-researcher is able to easily determine that this method of research is appropriate to answer the questions presented. To explain this further, the measuring method should be able to be used in the measurement (Collis and Hussey, 2014);
- Construct validity focuses on measurability of what is being asked of respondents in a questionnaire. According to Greener (2008), this to ensure that the respondent understands the question correctly; and
- Internal validity, according to Greener (2008) is necessary to ensure that independent variables (or factors) are solely responsible for outcomes in dependent variables (or effects) and to ensure these are not merely assumptions.

The questionnaire items were operationalised from literature. In addition, academics in the Department of Computing Sciences and the NMU statistician were able to validate the questions to ensure the validity of the research instrument.

Ethical Requirements

Collis and Hussey (2014) indicate that research ethics are vital for the success of a research project. Furthermore, they elaborate on guidelines to facilitate ethical requirements as:

- Privacy, confidentiality and anonymity of all participants must be ensured;
- Participants need to have the ability to withdraw partially or in full;
- Any potential discomfort, anxiety or harm should be avoided;
- Participants have the right to informed consent in relation to the questionnaire; and
- Information should be collected transparently and honestly.

Full ethics approval was obtained from the Nelson Mandela University Ethics Committee, H18-SCI-CSS-006.

Table 2. Frequency Distribution per User Group

User Group	n	%
Legal/Regulatory	3	9%
Technologist/Consultant	6	18%
Senior Management	21	64%
Operations	3	9%
Total	33	100%

Table 3. Frequency Distribution - Age

Age	n	%
21-30	0	0%
31-40	11	33%
41-50	14	43%
50+	8	24%
Total	33	100%

RESEARCH RESULTS AND DISCUSSION

The results from the empirical study are presented and discussed in this section. The population of the study consisted of 47 international respondents, of which 33 completed the survey which is a 70% response rate.

Demographic Profile

The following Tables provide the basic demographic information about the 33 respondents. It is important to note that the target audience for this questionnaire all have a relatively extensive working knowledge of post-trade securities as a prerequisite.

Table 2 shows the frequency distribution of the user group of the respondents according to their current role or employment. The most frequent respondents were Senior Management, followed by Technologists/Consultants and finally with an equal share of Legal/Regulatory and Operations respondents.

Table 4. Frequency Distribution – DLT understanding

DLT understanding	n	%
Basic	9	27%
Intermediate	18	55%
Advanced	6	18%
Total	33	100%

Table 3 tabulates the frequency distribution of the age of the respondents. The respondents were generally middle-aged with only 8 being above 50 years of age.

DLT Perceptions

Table 4 provides an important qualitative aspect of this study. It shows the frequency distribution of the respondents' understanding of the DLT in the form of a self-assessment. Seventy three percent had an intermediate or advanced understanding of DLT.

In Table 5, the frequency distribution of respondents is presented, with regard to their opinion on how the technology can be viewed in light of possible implementation. It is important to note that 73% of respondents either claim to have an intermediate knowledge of the technology or better, while 27% maintain a basic understanding of the technology.

Table 5. Frequency Distribution – DLT view

DLT view	n	%
The change will be evolutionary	24	73%
The technology is immature and not suitable	2	6%
It is a 'fad' and will ultimately only be used for niche applications	3	9%
The change will be revolutionary	4	12%
Total	33	100%

The results reported in Tables 4 and 5 raise the following interesting points, namely:

- The number of respondents (n=24 respondents or 73%) who believe the change will be evolutionary, is similar to those who either claim to have an intermediate or better knowledge of the technology. Upon further investigation, 17 of the 24 respondents claimed to have an intermediate or better knowledge of the technology, while 21% (n=6) of these respondents claimed a basic understanding of the technology. Furthermore 17 (71%) of the 24 respondents are Senior Managers, while the remaining 7 (29%) of respondents are made up of Legal/Regulatory, Operations and Technologists/Consultants;
- Two respondents (6%) who believe the technology is immature and not suitable for securities settlement are designated as a Senior Manager with a basic understanding of the technology and an Operations respondent with an intermediate understanding of the technology;
- Three respondents (9%) who believe the technology is a 'fad' and will ultimately only be used for niche applications are designated as two Senior Managers with a basic and intermediate understanding of the technology respectively and one Technology/Consultant respondent with an intermediate understanding of the technology; and
- Four respondents (12%) who believe the technology will be revolutionary for securities settlements all have an intermediate or advanced understanding of the technology and are split between a single Senior Manager, Legal/Regulatory respondent and two Technologists/Consultant respondents.

Figure 6. Final 10 Factors for a Sovereign Distributed Securities Depository

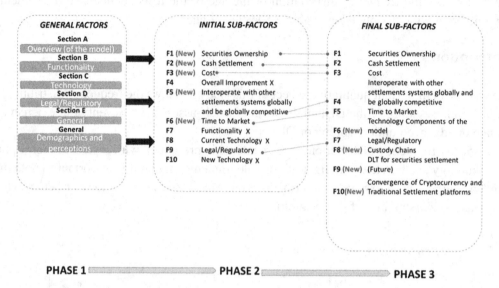

The results of the respondents' views can be further analysed in more detail as follows:

- None of the six Technologists/Consultants who responded (i.e. 18%) believe the technology is not suitable for Securities Settlement. It is important to note that Technologists/Consultants have the best overall understanding of the technology (with the most advanced understanding of any user group). This provides an implicit acknowledgement from the more technically oriented respondents, that the technology is suitable for securities settlement;
- Five respondents (15%), three Senior Managers one Operations and one Technologist/Consultant, are seemingly not in favour of using the technology and were the only user group to identify that the technology is immature and not suitable for securities settlement and that it is a 'fad' and will ultimately only be used for niche applications. It is also important to note that these respondents either have a basic or intermediate understanding of the technology. It is likely that these respondents are currently employed at intermediaries such as CSDs, Banks, etc.; and
- Most Senior Managers (n=19 or 58% of respondents) either believe the technology will be implemented in either an evolutionary or in a revolutionary way. It must be noted that the evolutionary option was considerably more of a popular option with approximately 90% of Senior Managers more in favour of an evolutionary implementation of the technology than a revolutionary one.

Figure 6 illustrates three phases relevant to the development of the final sub-factors to be used. The reason this exercise was undertaken was at the advice of the Nelson Mandela University statistician, Dr. Danie Venter, in order to improve the statistical relevance of the data gathered. This exercise was performed in three phases, whereby a set of statistical analysis was conducted on the factors in Phase 1 and then adjusted and re-performed in Phase 2. Finally, these factors were further adjusted for a third time to form the third and final Phase 3, which was used for statistical analysis.

Reliability of Summated Scores

In order to assess the internal reliability of the summated scores, Cronbach's alpha coefficients were used. The challenge with this particular study as mentioned was that the questionnaire refers to a potential future state and is not being applied to something current and tangible for the respondent. Therefore, the expectation for highly reliable scores from this measurement technique is not high. Hinton et al. (2004) provide an indication of the use of the Cronbach's alpha coefficients, which can be used after summating the scores and determining the consistency between factors. The Cronbach alpha values were interpreted as mentioned in Table 6.

Table 6. Cronbach's alpha value interpretation

Unacceptable	< 0.50
Acceptable	0.50 - 0.69
Good	0.70 - 0.79
Excellent	0.80 +

Table 7. Cronbach's alpha values

Factor	Cronbach's Alpha	Interpretation
F1- Securities Ownership	0.25	Unacceptable
F2- Cash Settlement	0.48	Unacceptable
F3- Cost	0.53	Acceptable
F4- Interoperate with other settlements systems globally and be globally competitive	0.16	Unacceptable
F5- Time to Market	0.79	Good
F6- Technology Components of the model	0.55	Acceptable
F7- Legal/Regulatory	0.60	Acceptable
F8- Custody Chains	0.37	Unacceptable
F9- DLT for securities settlement (Future)	0.57	Acceptable
F10- Convergence of Cryptocurrency and Traditional Settlement platforms	0.51	Acceptable

The Cronbach's alpha results, as reported in Table 7, showed five acceptable factors, namely F3 (Cost), F6 (Technology Components of the Model), F7 (Legal/Regulatory), F9 (DLT for Securities Settlement) and F10 (Convergence of Cryptocurrency and Traditional settlement platforms). One factor that showed 'good' reliability out of the possible ten factors was found, namely F5 (Time to Market).

Descriptive Statistics for the Factors

The following section discusses descriptive statistics for each of the finally agreed factors. Each question was designed as part of a 5-point Likert scale, however, for the purposes of describing these factors, *Very*

Negative and *Negative* were combined into *Negative* (1.00 to 2.59), while *Neutral* remains unchanged and *Positive* (3.41 to 5.00) includes the combination of *Positive* and *Very Positive*.

Table 8. Descriptive Statistics for the Factors (n = 33)

Factor	Negative 1.00 to 2.59		Neutral 2.60 to 3.40		Positive 3.41 to 5.00	
F1- Securities Ownership	6	18%	16	48%	11	33%
F2- Cash Settlement	5	15%	11	33%	17	51%
F3- Cost	3	9%	4	12%	26	79%
F4- Interoperate with other settlements systems globally and be globally competitive	2	6%	17	52%	14	42%
F5- Time to Market	14	42%	7	21%	12	36%
F6- Technology Components of the model	0	0%	10	30%	23	70%
F7- Legal/Regulatory	0	0%	5	15%	28	85%
F8- Custody Chains	2	6%	13	39%	18	55%
F9- DLT for securities settlement (Future)	8	24%	14	42%	11	33%
F10- Convergence of Cryptocurrency and Traditional Settlement platforms	9	27%	16	48%	8	24%

Table 9. Central Tendency and Dispersion of Factors (n = 33)

Variable	Mean	S.D.	H_1:m	t	p	Cohen's d
F1- Securities Ownership	3.22	0.69	≠3.40	-1.48	.148	n/a
F2- Cash Settlement	3.41	0.84	≠3.40	0.06	.951	n/a
F3- Cost	3.65	0.66	≠3.40	2.20	**.035**	**0.38**
F4- Interoperate with other settlements systems globally and be globally competitive	3.39	0.61	≠3.40	-0.06	.953	n/a
F5- Time to Market	2.88	1.11	≠2.60	1.44	.159	n/a
F6- Technology Components of the model	3.77	0.48	≠3.40	4.39	**<.0005**	**0.77**
F7- Legal/Regulatory	3.92	0.48	≠3.40	6.21	**<.0005**	**1.08**
F8- Custody Chains	3.44	0.47	≠3.40	0.44	.660	n/a
F9- DLT for securities settlement (Future)	3.20	0.78	≠3.40	-1.46	.154	n/a
F10- Convergence of cryptocurrency and Traditional Settlement platforms	2.96	0.56	≠2.60	3.72	**.001**	**0.64**

Table 10. Pearson's Product Movement Correlations for the factors (n=33)

Factor	F1	F2	F3	F4	F5	F6	F7	F8	F9	F10
F1- Securities Ownership	-	.205	*-.376*	.147	-.316	.295	.186	.211	.036	.265
F2- Cash Settlement	.205	-	-.342	-.019	-.121	.242	.174	.080	-.099	.216
F3- Cost	*-.376*	-.342	-	-.282	*.616*	-.027	-.020	-.302	*.366*	*-.463*
F4- Interoperate with other settlements systems globally and be globally competitive	.147	-.019	-.282	-	*-.514*	*-.455*	.059	.128	-.040	*.521*
F5- Time to Market	-.316	-.121	*.616*	*-.514*	-	.151	.157	*-.368*	*.509*	*-.473*
F6- Technology Components of the model	.295	.242	-.027	*-.455*	.151	-	.318	-.039	.168	-.335
F7- Legal/Regulatory	.186	.174	-.020	.059	.157	.318	-	.195	.193	.133
F8- Custody Chains	.211	.080	-.302	.128	*-.368*	-.039	.195	-	-.167	.273
F9- DLT for securities settlement (Future)	.036	-.099	*.366*	-.040	*.509*	.168	.193	-.167	-	-.327
F10- Convergence of cryptocurrency and Traditional Settlement platforms	.265	.216	*-.463*	*.521*	*-.473*	-.335	.133	.273	-.327	-

Table 8 highlights the highest descriptive statistic per factor, in red. This describes how, for each factor, the respondents answered that five of the factors had distinctly positive results and four factors were largely considered as neutral by respondents. Factor F5 (Time to Market) was the only factor, which had a material negative descriptive statistical factor.

Inferential Statistics on the Factors

The one-sample t-tests were used to determine if the respondents' mean scores for the various factors can be described as negative, neutral or positive. The results of these tests are reported in Table 9.

From Table 9, the highlighted population mean values are positive (M>3.40) for factors F3 (Cost with M =3.65) with a low practical and statistical significance. F6 (Technology Components of the model with M =3.77) generated a large statistical significance and medium practical significance. F7 (Legal/ Regulatory with M=3.92) garnered both a large statistical and practical significance.

The population mean value is neutral (2.60 <= M<= 3.40) for F10 (convergence of cryptocurrency and Traditional Settlement platforms) with M=2.9, although it has a medium practical significance. Inconclusive results were obtained for the other factors: population mean values for F1 (Securities Ownership), F2 (Cash Settlement) and F4 (Interoperate with other settlements systems globally and be globally competitive). F8 (Custody Chains) and F9 (DLT for securities settlement) could be either neutral or positive. The mean value for F5 (Time to Market) could be either negative (M<2.60) or neutral although it is of medium practical significance.

Table 11. Inferential Ranking of Mean per factor (n=33)

Factors	Ranking	Signif. Group	Mean	SD
F7- Legal/Regulatory	1	1	3.92	0.48
F6- Technology Components of the model	1	1	3.77	0.48
F3- Cost	1	1	3.65	0.66
F8- Custody Chains	4	2	3.44	0.47
F2- Cash Settlement	4	2	3.41	0.84
F4- Interoperate with other settlements systems globally and be globally competitive	4	2	3.39	0.61
F1- Securities Ownership	4	2	3.22	0.69
F9- DLT for securities settlement (Future)	4	2	3.20	0.78
F10- Convergence of cryptocurrency and Traditional Settlement platforms	9	3	2.96	0.56
F5- Time to Market	9	3	2.88	1.11

Pearson Product-Moment Correlation

Gravetter and Wallnau (2009) indicate practical significance in the correlations at 0.3, while a correlation coefficient above 0.5 is considered a strong correlation with statistical significance. Therefore, a factor of 3.44 (the intersection of the aforementioned) is both statistically and practically significant. Table 10, using Pearson Product-Moment correlation (n = 33), aims to conclude both statistically and practically significant correlations.

Table 10 presents mostly insignificant positive or negative correlations between the factors. However, it is important to highlight key positive and negative correlations and to understand how they can be interpreted. A strong positive correlation was found between F3 (Cost) and F5 (Time to Market) with M= .616; F4 (Interoperate with other settlement systems globally and be globally competitive) and F10 (Convergence of cryptocurrency and Traditional Settlement platforms) with M= .521; and F5 (Time to Market) with F9 (DLT for securities settlement) with M= .509. Significant positive correlation was found between F3 (Cost) and F9 (DLT for securities settlement) with M =. 366.

A strong negative correlation was found between F4 (Interoperate with other settlement systems globally and be globally competitive) and F5 (Time to Market) with M= -.514. Significant negative correlation was further found between F10 (Convergence of cryptocurrency and Traditional Settlement platforms) and F5 (Time to Market) with M=-473; F10 (Convergence of cryptocurrency and Traditional Settlement platforms) and F3 (Cost) with M=-.463; F4 (Interoperate with other settlement systems globally and be globally competitive) and F6 (Technology components of the model) with M= -.455. F1 (Securities Ownership) and F3 (Cost) with M= -.376; and F8 (Custody Chains) and F5 (Time to Market) completed the remainder of the significant negative correlations with M= -.368. In Table 11, the ten factors each of the three groupings ranked, are presented. The first group includes F7 (Legal/ Regulatory), F6 (Technology Components of the model) and specifically F3 (Cost).

Further analysis of Table 11 indicates that the 10 factors can be grouped and ranked into 3 statistical significance groupings:

- The first group includes F7 (Legal/Regulatory), F6 (Technology Components of the model) and F3 (Cost) and these have a positive mean. A key inference from the first group is the particular inclusion of the Cost factor (F3). Given that there are new technology components and more legal and regulatory prerequisites for the technology, there is a logical cost consequence to these. Thus, the inclusion of F3 (Cost) is of particular importance;
- The second group, with neutral means, include F8 (Custody Chains), F2 (Cash Settlement), F4 (Interoperate with other settlements systems globally and be globally competitive), F1 (Securities Ownership) and F9 (DLT for securities settlement), and as a group describe the functional requirements of the model; and
- The third group, which contains the fewest factors, namely, that of F10 (Convergence of cryptocurrency and Traditional Settlement platforms) and F5 (Time to Market), is consequently the lowest ranked.

This also seems to be a logical conclusion as given the additional technology requirements, costs and legal prerequisites from the first group and the functional requirements of the model from the second group. The primary reasoning from this inference is that cryptocurrency would potentially continue as it does currently, in parallel with traditional settlement and that given the potential complexity and cost of implementing DLT for Securities Settlement, Time to Market is less likely to be an important criterion.

Qualitative Analysis of Comments from Respondents

The questionnaire used in the study (Appendix A), provided the respondents with the opportunity to answer the open-ended questions. The general responses were that the model is well accepted. The respondents acknowledged the importance of large-scale industry support, collaboration and focus on the financial business case and related costs, would be key to implementing such a model.

The following noticeable themes emerged from the respondent's comments:

- The model is largely validated;
- Cost is a major factor to consider;
- The move to DLT for securities settlement will be an evolutionary one;
- The concept of disintermediation: In this instance, where it seems likely that although disintermediation of incumbents is possible, it is probable, however that they will remain, however they may fulfil different functions to what they perform at present; and
- Time to market is another key theme, which is prevalent, and it seems likely that to implement such a proposed model, could take longer than a decade and will require considerable co-ordination and support across multiple intermediaries and actors in the value chain.

A key criticism of the model is that the cash ledger should be included in the overall model and not as a separate ledger, which is interoperable. Furthermore, the most commented on subjects in order from highest to lowest number of comments were the following:

- Custody chains (existing intermediaries and/or interoperability between these);
- Time to Market: all agreed with the 10 to 15 years estimation;
- Cash settlement: needed to be solved for and included in the securities ledger; and

- Cost: of a potential solution would be a key factor to consider.

SUMMARY OF RESEARCH RESULTS

A summary of findings from the statistical analysis provides useful information for the development of the model. It also offers reasoning as to why DLT has not yet been implemented to the full post trade securities settlements industry. The major findings are summarised into various themes and discussed below.

Cost

The most consistent finding throughout the study relates to the Cost factor which, with an acceptable Cronbach Alpha score, seems to be more important due to the increased levels of understanding of the technology and is highly correlated to both Time to Market and the model used for a DLT solution in Securities Settlement. In addition, pre-requisites were identified such as additional technology components, legal and regulatory requirements, new interface requirements and integration to incumbents in inferential ranking. As each of these factors bears a cost, the inclusion of a cost consequence in the inferential ranking was important and relevant. This information provides both a model for future implementation of the technology in relation to cost considerations, as well as potential reasons why the technology has not yet been successfully implemented in a production environment.

Legal/Regulatory Requirements

The next consistent theme was that of legal/regulatory considerations, which also had an acceptable Cronbach Alpha score and ranked the highest in terms of inferential ranking on a group and individual question basis. Furthermore, this factor provided large statistical evidence and is likely to be of practical use. The primary finding here is that there needs to be a clear legal and regulatory framework, which precedes the building of a model such as this. This in essence means that this factor also becomes a key success factor in the building of these solutions for post-trade securities settlement.

Time to Market

Time to Market was strongly positively or negatively correlated with at least five other factors and has a strong association with interoperability and global competitiveness. This implies that a globally accepted solution, which solves interoperability needs for existing incumbents and technology, will be a key driver, which delivers the technology in a faster time to market. Furthermore, the indications from the open questions is that suitable global solutions are still at least a decade away.

Ancillary Narrative

In addition to the themes noted earlier, although the majority of respondents indicate that the change in this technology will be an evolutionary change, they support the notion that the Blockchain technology is, indeed suitable for securities settlements. Further to this, the narrative of collaborative evolutionary challengers is created from the findings of this study as an approach to manage the implementation of so-called disruptive technology (including DLT/Blockchain) in established markets. To explain this, the word 'disruptive' is associated with Blockchain. This association does the adoption of the technology in established markets no favours in terms of practical implementation of the technology, no matter what the purported benefits of the technology are. Incumbents are likely to develop technology isolation and thus not have industry support or alternatively focus on keeping current technology in place due to the threat of disruption.

In established markets, technology development is evidently evolutionary. Factors in this research, such as F4 (DLT for securities settlements) and F10 (the convergence of cryptocurrency and traditional settlements and technology components) point to a collaborative and inclusive approach to developing new technology models for the market. Although the aforementioned had acceptable Cronbach alpha values, essentially validating the conceptual model, the cash settlement (as a key component of the model) was not validated. Furthermore, cash settlement proved to be divisive in the open questions. This leads to the conclusion that cash settlement would need to be included as part of the settlements process; and ultimately would need to be solved for either in parallel to a securities settlement or prior to it.

The threat of short term and isolated disruption in the value-chain is unlikely. The need to interoperate and collaborate with both new technology, industry incumbents and regulators on an industry-scale will be necessary in order to see timely adoption of new technology. This narrative needs to be overlaid with the three key themes identified (Cost, Legal/Regulatory requirements and Time to Market) in a collaborative approach, will be the primary success factors responsible for implementing a model. In summary, an industry-wide business case would need to be concluded before a model such as this can be implemented successfully. Furthermore, the approach of introducing these new technologies should be guided with the concept developed here of collaborative evolutionary challengers instead of that of isolated disruptive fintech.

IMPLEMENTATION OF PROPOSED CONCEPTUAL MODEL

Blockchain technology has the potential to disintermediate any process in connection with the financial industry (The Economist, 2014). All financial service providers, within the supply chain of a securities settlement transaction, are potential points of disintermediation, including CSDs. Blockchain technology is a suitable platform for the securities settlements. The implementation of the proposed conceptual model using Blockchain technologies requires the collaboration of various role-players and stakeholders and also requires international collaboration. Presently, a prototype blockchain based application, using the Ethereum platform, is being developed for research purposes.

The prototype Blockchain project for securities settlement requires market co-ordination and planning with regulators, intermediaries, issuers and investors, in order to validate the proposed sovereign distributed securities depository conceptual model. The prototype uses an Ethereum blockchain to store the data. Here, a detailed analysis of the requirements from all stakeholders is required. Decisions on how to model the value chain and manage the requirements elicitation process with all stakeholders are managed by the NMU research team.

The proposed Blockchain application consists of three different components. The first component is the smart contract(s), which runs on an Ethereum Virtual Machine. The smart contract component is written in Solidity, the current language used on the Ethereum Virtual Machine. Decisions need to be made on how and what data need to be stored on the SDSD Blockchain, taking into consideration that some data may be better stored in a private database and other data on a Blockchain. The modelling of the proposed application is crucial and requires careful planning. Once the code is placed on a blockchain, it is there forever. The challenge in the smart contract component is not only planning what information is stored, but also how the data and information are stored. Special attention needs to be given to the storage of data and information as the developers are thinking of classes, as used in programming, which would likely come with an additional cost. The goal is to store enough data and information on the blockchain for the public to see what is happening in the process, but not to include additional data and information to leak or display any sensitive or confidential data.

The second component is the protocol for communicating between the blockchain and the user frontends or user interfaces. Once the model is designed and the smart contract is created, a protocol needs to be created. The protocol will dictate how, when and what needs to be written to the blockchain or retrieved from the blockchain. Creating the protocol involves ensuring that the backend programme can extract enough information from the blockchain to show relevant information to the user of the frontend system. Blockchain data structures are highly incompatible with other programming languages. It is thus important to create a simple way of exchanging the data.

The final component is the applications that provide user interfaces with the blockchain and presents the results. Programmes using any conventional programming language will be developed for all stakeholders that will make use of a blockchain to store and read data, as opposed to text files, databases, network requests, etc. The system needs to make use of the protocol to read relevant information, parse it and show the required information to the user. The programmes need to write to the blockchain and read from the blockchain to display updates in the value chain and write updates to the blockchain managing the SDSD process.

MANAGERIAL RECOMMENDATIONS

The main objective of this study was to create a model for securities settlement using Blockchain technology for a Central Securities Depository (CSD). Presently, globally, no CSD exists that has introduced a production-ready Blockchain-based solution for securities settlement. A conceptual model was created from the literature and was published in an international journal. This model formed the basis of the study which was sent to post-trade securities professionals globally to validate the conceptual model developed.

The managerial recommendations are generated in order to pragmatically bridge the gap between the literature results of the study and the empirical study. These recommendations are produced in order to improve the future implementation of Blockchain technology for securities settlement and to clearly articulate the potential benefits to markets.

The results from the study indicated that three primary components and design factors are included, namely: Cost, Legal/Regularly and Time to Market. In addition, to validate the inclusion of custody chains, technology components such as cryptocurrencies and traditional settlements systems will ultimately remain separated. Cash settlement, however, was found to be either a precursor or a parallel development required for the model's success. Furthermore, the research provided an over-arching approach to implement the technology, coining the phrase *collaborative evolutionary challengers* as an inclusive, consultative and collaborative market-wide approach to building business cases for new technologies. The focus in this approach is primarily on the three components and design factors which resulted, namely Cost, Legal/Regulatory and Time to Market.

Securities Ownership

Securities Ownership was originally included as a key requirement for securities settlement as highlighted in the literature. Given the Blockchain promise of immutability, Securities Ownership is ultimately a moot point as this is assumed in the use of the technology. The practicality of immutability was challenged in the model, however practical solutions were provided (Euroclear and Oliver Wyman, 2016).

Cash Settlement

Cash Settlement should be included within the same Ledger as Securities Settlements. This approach means that wider industry acceptance and engagement for cash settlement would need to be included before, or in parallel to securities settlements. Either way, there is negative impacts on Time to Market for potential solutions.

Cost

Given the additional technology components, legal requirements and co-ordination of multiple stakeholders involved, cost sensitivity to a model as presented is likely (Euroclear and Oliver Wyman, 2016). Cost ultimately ranks as the most significant factor over all in the study and the proposed approach of *collaborative evolutionary challengers'* approach to market-wide business case development is a major finding of this research.

Interoperability with other Settlements Systems

This factor is important to consider and is listed as an important requirement for any post-trade settlements system for securities. It is important to note that until the basic design elements (costs, time to market and a legal/regulatory framework) are concluded, this requirement will be secondary in nature to the other factors listed. This requirement would, ideally, be covered once the aforementioned are concluded.

Time to Market

Market consultation, legal/regulatory reform and implications of new technology are time consuming activities. It is not surprising that anecdotal feedback in the open questions show an expected 10-15 years implementation. This is in line with the time framing of large cross-geography projects such as T2S in Europe with similar incumbents.

Technology Components of the Model

The technology components were largely acceptable in this model and well received. Further development in the technology will need to be re-evaluated and a constant feedback mechanism to the wider market will need to take place. This is important, given the rate of change and changing market requirements. These will need to also be continually managed against the framework of pre-requisites already identified in this study.

Legal/Regulatory

Enabling legal/regulatory frameworks will need to be in place before projects of this nature can reasonably commence. The need for a clear and enabling legal and regulatory framework which precedes the building of a model such as this is a clearly observable requirement. Thus, this factor is a key success factor in building any of these solutions for post trade securities settlement in a pragmatic way.

Custody Chains

Existing incumbents are likely to remain over the time period established in this study of 10 to 15 years and these incumbents who form part of the custody chains will be critical to implementing new technology as long as the incumbents serve a purpose (Korman, 2017). The *collaborative evolutionary challengers'* approach will also be critically important in custody chains as this approach will need to prove beneficial to both incumbents and end users. This will be key to drive changes to realise the benefits of the Blockchain technology across the market.

DLT for Securities Settlement

Eighty five percent of respondents believe securities settlement will be concluded on DLT/Blockchain technology in future and most (73%) indicate this change will be evolutionary in nature. Given that the evolution will likely commence with existing incumbents, the *collaborative evolutionary challengers'* approach will again be an important aspect to employ in any given market.

Convergence of Cryptocurrency and Traditional Settlement Platforms

Although there is the practical implication of cryptocurrency destabilising securities settlement, either through criminal activity or fraud, it is unlikely that cryptocurrency will integrate with traditional settlements platforms. A reversal of potential disruption has been observed, namely *contrary disruption*. This is explained as instead of incumbent's business models being threatened, incumbents are offering cryptocurrency services (with similar safeguards and governance as are offered in traditional securities settlements) and directly competing with the fintech companies who are trying to disrupt them. This is an indirect result of the threat of disruption rather than seeking a collaborative approach to pragmatic solutions, which benefit an entire market.

LIMITATIONS AND FINAL CONCLUSIONS

The limitations of the study include items, which were reversed or removed due to insufficient factor loading. Four factors namely, Securities Ownership, Cash Settlement, Interoperability with other settlements systems globally, and Custody Chains, all had unacceptable Cronbach's Alpha scores. The recommendation is that pilot studies could have indicated any unsuitable questions to improve the Cronbach Alpha scores.

The study concludes that Securities Ownership and Cash Settlement, Interoperability with other settlements systems globally and global competitiveness, and Custody Chains, all had to be removed from the model. The remaining six factors (Cost, Time to Market, Technology Components of the Model, Legal/ Regulatory requirements, DLT for securities settlement (Future)) as well as Convergence of Cryptocurrency, and Traditional Settlement platforms, directly applied to validate the proposed conceptual model.

This study commenced with understanding of the so-called disruptive threat of Blockchain technology and cryptocurrencies, to post trade securities. On completion of the study, it seems likely that a CSD will transform into a Blockchain-based distributed depository for a given market, and that incumbents such as CSDs will participate in *contrary disruption* and offer both cryptocurrency and traditional settlements, as parallel service offerings. Presently, central bank digital coins (CBDC) represent the next step in having cash on chain and consequently the most important step as per this research to seeing the traditional Capital Markets moving to a Distributed Ledger platform. Future research need to focus on the implementation of CBDC and securities on the same or an interoperable chain which represent the most viable opportunity for realizing the benefits of the said technology in the industry.

REFERENCES

Atack, J., & Neal, L. (2009). *The origins and development of financial markets and institutions: From the seventeenth century to the present.* Cambridge University Press. doi:10.1017/CBO9780511757419

Brennan, C., & Lunn, W. (2016), The trust disrupter, https://www.finextra.com/finextra-downloads/newsdocs/document-1063851711.pdf, Accessed August 2016

Caprio, G. (2013). Securities settlement systems. In Handbook of Key Global Financial Markets, Institutions, and Infrastructure (pp. 547–563). Academic Press.

Collis, J., & Hussey, R. (2014). *Business Research* (4th ed.). Macmillan. doi:10.1007/978-1-137-03748-0

Committee on Capital Markets Regulation. (2019). *Blockchain and Securities Clearing and Settlement.* https://www.capmktsreg.org/wp-content/uploads/2019/04/CCMR_statement_ Blockchain_Securities_Settlement-Final.pdf

Dickinson, K. (2015). *Financial market operations management.* Wiley.

DTCC. (2016). *Embracing Disruption.* https://www.dtcc.com/~/media/Files/PDFs/DTCC-Embracing-Disruption.pdf

Euroclear and Oliver Wyman. (2016). *Blockchain in Capital Markets: The Prize and the Journey.* Brussels: Euroclear, Oliver Wyman. https://www.euroclear.com/en/campaigns/Blockchain-in-capital-markets.html

European Central Bank. (2007). *The securities custody industry.* https://www.ecb.europa.eu/pub/pdf/scpops/ecbocp68.pdf

European Central Bank. (2015). *TARGET2-Securities successfully launched today.* https://www.ecb.europa.eu/press/pr/date/2015/html/pr150622_2.en.html

European Central Bank. (2016). *Distributed ledger technologies in securities post-trading.* https://www.ecb.europa.eu/pub/pdf/scpops/ecbop172.en.pdf

European Securities and Market Authority. (2016). *The distributed ledger technology applied to securities markets.* https://www.esma.europa.eu/press-news/esma-news/esma-assesses-usefulness-distributed-ledger-technologies

Eva, M. (2015). Custody chains and asset values: Why crypto-securities are worth contemplating. *The Cambridge Law Journal, 73*(3), 505–533.

Evans, N. (2003). *Business innovation and disruptive technology harnessing the power of breakthrough technology for competitive advantage.* Upper Saddle River, NJ: Financial Times Prentice Hall.

Everett, S., Calitz, A. P., & Greyling, J. (2017). The case for a 'sovereign' distributed securities depository for securities settlement. *Journal of Securities Operations & Custody, 9*(3), 269-292. https://www.henrystewartpublications.com/jsoc/v9

Financial Stability Board. (2009). *Addressing SIFIs.* https://www.fsb.org/what-we-do/policy-development/systematically-important-financial-institutions-sifis/

Floreani, J., & Polato, M. (2014). *The economics of the global stock exchange industry.* Palgrave Macmillan. doi:10.1057/9781137321831

Gartner. (2020). *Gartner hype cycle for emerging technologies identifies three key trends that organizations must track to gain competitive advantage.* https://www.gartner.com/newsroom/id/3412017

Gibson, C., & Kirk, T. (2016). *Blockchain 101 for asset managers.* https://www.klgates.com/files/Publication/921292ec-0e76-4b4b-adf4-036b15c175fe/Presentation/PublicationAttachment/6489032d-7722-4dcc-a10c-09e7e9b4350e/Blockchain_101_for_Asset_Managers.pdf

Gorham, M., & Singh, N. (2009). *Electronic exchanges: The global transformation from pits to bits.* Elsevier.

Gravetter, F. J., & Wallnau, L. B. (2009). *Statistics for the Behavioral Sciences* (8th ed.). Wadsworth.

Greener, S. (2008). *Business research methods.* http://web.ftvs.cuni.cz/hendl/metodologie/introduction-to-research-methods.pdf

Harris, L. (2004). Trading and Exchanges: Market Microstructure for Practitioners. Oxford: Oxford UK

Hinton, P. R., McMurray, I., & Brownlow, C. (2004). *SPSS Explained.* Routledge. doi:10.4324/9780203642597

Karp, N. (2015). *Blockchain Technology: The Ultimate disruption in the Financial System.* https://www.bbvaresearch.com/wp-content/uploads/2015/07/150710_US_EW_Blockchain Technology.pdf

Korman, Z. (2017). *On Blockchain, Intermediaries and Hype.* https://www.zkorman.com/writing/blockchain/

KPMG. (2018). *The Changing Landscape of Disruptive Technologies.* https://home.kpmg/by/en/home/insights/2018/06/the-changing-landscape-of-disruptive-technologies.html

Loader, D. (2002). *Clearing, settlement, and custody.* Butterworth-Heinemann.

Morgan Stanley. (2016). *Global insight: Blockchain in banking: Disruptive threat or tool?* https://www.the-blockchain.com/docs/Morgan-Stanley-blockchain-report.pdf

Mori, T. (2016). Financial Technology: Blockchain and Securities Settlement. Deoitte and Touceh Tomatsu.

Natoli, C., & Gramoli, V. (2016). *The blockchain anomaly.* https://arxiv.org/pdf/1605.05438v1.pdf

Nakamoto, S. (2008). *Bitcoin: A Peer-to-Peer Electronic Cash System.* https://bitcoin.org/bitcoin.pdf

O'Connor, D. (2004). *The Basics of Economics.* Greenwood.

Pilkington, M. (2015). *Blockchain Technology: Principles and Applications.* http://ssrn.com/abstract=2662660

Poelstra, A. (2014). *Distributed consensus from proof of stake is impossible.* https://download.wpsoftware.net/bitcoin/old-pos.pdf

Saunders, M., Lewis, P., & Thornhill, A. (2012). *Research methods for business students.* Pearson Education Limited.

Swan, M. (2015), Financial Services. In Blockchain: Blueprint for a new economy. O'Reilly

Swanson, T. (2015). *Consensus-as-a-service: A brief report on the emergence of permissioned, distributed ledger systems.* https://www.weusecoins.com/assets/pdf/library/Consensus-as-a-service%20-%20 a%20brief%20report%20on%20the%20emergence%20of%20permissioned %20distributed%20ledger.pdf

The Economist. (2014). *Cryptocurrencies – the great hiccup.* https://www.economist.com/news/finance-and-economics/21596971-bitcoin-growing-too-fast-its-technology-keep-up-great-hiccup

Wall, E., & Malm, G. (2016). *Using blockchain technology and smart contracts to create a distributed securities depository.* http://lup.lub.lu.se/student-papers/record/8885750

World Economic Forum. (2015). *The Future of Financial Services.* http://www3.weforum.org/docs/ WEF_The_future__of_financial_services.pdf

World Federation of Exchanges. (2016). *Financial market infrastructures and distributed ledger technology.* https://www.world-exchanges.org/home/index.php/files/18/Studies%20-%20Reports/349/WFE%20 IOSCO%20AMCC%20DLT%20report.pdf

Yilmaz, K. (2013). European Journal of Education. *European Journal of Education,* 48, 311–325. doi:10.1111/ejed.12014

Zohar, A. (2015). *Bitcoin. Communications of the ACM.* doi:10.1145/2701411

ADDITIONAL READING

Accenture. (2020), The (R)evolution of Money II Blockchain Empowered CBDC, https://www.accenture. com/_acnmedia/PDF-105/Accenture-Revolution-of-Money-II-2019.pdf#zoom=50, Accessed May 2020

Ammous, S. (2016), Blockchain Technology: What Is It Good For? SSRN: https://SSRN.com/Abstract=2832751, Accessed September 2017

ECSDA. (2015), CSD Factbook, 1st ed. http://ecsda.eu/wp-content/uploads/2014_CSD_ Factbook.pdf, Accessed May 2020

European Commission. (2020), Central Securities Depositories (CSDs) - European Commission, http://ec.europa.eu/finance/financial-markets/central_securities_depositories/ index_en.htm, Accessed May 2020

Financial Conduct Authority. (2018), Central securities depositories, https://www.fca.org.uk/markets/central-securities-depositories, Accessed May 2020

Financial Conduct Authority. (2020), Securities Financing Transactions Regulation (SFTR), https://www.fca.org.uk/markets/sftr, Accessed May 2020

Inform, I. T. (2019), Blockchain technology. https://www.informit.com/articles/article.aspx?p=2955143, Accessed May 2020

Chase, J. P. M., & Wyman, O. (2020), Unlocking economic advantage with blockchain: A guide for asset managers, https://www.oliverwyman.com/content/dam/oliver-wyman/global/en/2016/july/joint-report-by-jp-morgan-and-oliver-wyman-unlocking-economic-advantage-with-blockchain-A-Guide-for-Asset-Managers.pdf, Accessed May 2020

KPMG. (2020), Seizing opportunity – Blockchain and beyond, https://assets.kpmg.com/content/dam/kpmg/pdf/2016/06/kpmg-blockchain-consensus-mechanism.pdf, Accessed May 2020

KPMG. (2016), Blockchain in hitting the big time, https://home.kpmg.com/content/dam/kpmg/us/pdf/blockchain-hitting-the-big.pdf, Accessed May 2020

Lafarre, A., & Van der Elst, C. (2018), Blockchain Technology for Corporate Governance and Shareholder Activism. European Corporate Governance Institute (ECGI) - Law Working Paper No. 390/2018, https://ssrn.com/abstract=3135209, Accessed May 2020

Mainelli, M., & Milne, A. (2016). The impact and potential of blockchain on the securities transaction lifecycle. *Computer*, *40*(9), 96–99.

SWIFT. (2020), SWIFT History, https://www.swift.com/about-us/history, Accessed May 2020

KEY TERMS AND DEFINITIONS

Blockchain Technology: Blockchain technology is not a new technology, as it has served as the backbone of the Bitcoin protocol since its inception in 2008. Blockchain technology eliminates the need for a trusted third party to process transactions and provide record-keeping services, which poses threats to the core business functions of some intermediaries, such as CSDs. Blockchain technology is still not a fully mature technology.

Central Securities Depository (CSD): Trusted third parties, such as Exchanges, Brokers, Dealers and Central Securities Depositories (CSDs) that operate in the trade to the post-trade environments. CSDs are a joint market initiative to electronically settle high volumes of dematerialised shares for a national market (country or region) and maintain a central register of ownership. **D**

istributed Ledger Technology (DLT): DLT can be considered as 'Blockchains' which provide the ability to distribute records across a network as opposed to keeping records with a centralised entity. In effect, the technology combines peer-to-peer networking, cryptography techniques and cryptographic hashing to affect transactions in chronological order.

Securities Settlement Model (SSM): This is a conceptual model to evaluate the use of blockchain related technologies for securities settlements.

Sovereign Distributed Securities (SDS): All securities are held within the 'sovereign' distributed securities ledger (depository) (SDSD) distributed across known nodes. The nodes are representative of the custody chain with known entities/intermediaries. In the SSM, the SDSD could use multi-signature technologies to ensure that the investor purchases stock directly from a seller; however, the broker and bank/custodian signs/validates the transaction before it is concluded.

APPENDIX A: QUESTIONNAIRE

A Sovereign Distributed Securities Depository - Pilot Evaluation Study

Participant Number:
User Group:
Senior management
Operations Technologist/consultant Legal/Regulatory
General:

How many years of experience do you have in the securities industry or post trade specifically?
- a. 1-3 Years
- b. 4-5 Years
- c. 6-10 Years
- d. 10 Years +

How would you rate your understanding of Distributed Ledger Technology (DLT)?
- e. Basic (Theoretical knowledge only)
- f. Intermediate (I understand the technology conceptually and have traded cryptocurrency at some point)
- g. Advanced (i.e. I have some experience in building these applications)

Select the option which best describes you with regards your view on the application of Distributed Ledger technology in securities settlements:
- h. The change will be revolutionary
- i. The change will be evolutionary
- j. The technology is immature and not suitable
- k. It is a 'fad' and will ultimately only be used for 'niche' applications

What age bracket do you fall in?
- l. 21-30
- m. 31-40
- n. 41-50
- o. 51+

	Questions	Strongly Disagree	Disagree	Neutral	Agree	Strongly Agree	N/A
	Section A – Overview						
5	After reviewing the attached paper, securities settlement will still be segregated by country in the next 5 to 10 years.	O	O	O	O	O	O
6	International securities settlements using DLT could be facilitated by connecting/ linking settlements systems of different countries.	O	O	O	O	O	O
7	Securities settlement platforms will service both traditional securities settlements as well as facilitate the buying and selling of crypto-assets, albeit in different platforms.	O	O	O	O	O	O
8	A model such the one described in the paper would be possible to implement within 5 to 10 years in your market.	O	O	O	O	O	O
9	A public ledger solution (agnostic to country/region) for all securities settlements will be possible to implement within 5 to10 years.	O	O	O	O	O	O
	Section B – Functionality						
10	DLT as implemented in this model will improve some aspect of securities settlement.	O	O	O	O	O	O
11	A cash ledger should be separate from a securities settlement system.	O	O	O	O	O	O
12	It is important that legacy systems integrate to the intended platform.	O	O	O	O	O	O
13	It is important for the model to support functionality for custody chains.	O	O	O	O	O	O
14	It is an important requirement to be able to amend securities records if required.	O	O	O	O	O	O
15	A platform such as described in the paper should provide functionality to other stakeholders of the securities settlement ecosystem such as Custodians, Asset managers, Exchanges, etc.	O	O	O	O	O	O
16	The platform should provide functionality to disintermediate incumbents in the securities settlement ecosystem, such as CSDs or Custodians.	O	O	O	O	O	O
17	Interoperation with other public ledgers will be an important (i.e. Ethereum) requirement.	O	O	O	O	O	O
	Section C – Technology						
18	A permissioned ledger is suitable for the model.	O	O	O	O	O	O
19	The use of oracles will be important to the success criteria of the model. Particularly as data feeds and for regulatory purposes.	O	O	O	O	O	O
20	The use of meta-layers will be important to the success of the model.	O	O	O	O	O	O
21	Technology development for DLT will be evolutionary and not disruptive for securities settlement.	O	O	O	O	O	O
22	Interfaces between ledgers (private or public) represent key risks which need to be mitigated in the model.	O	O	O	O	O	O
23	Given this is typically a high value, low volume environment. Proof of Work would be a suitable protocol to employ.	O	O	O	O	O	O
24	Given this is typically a high value, low volume environment. Proof of Stake would be a suitable protocol to employ.	O	O	O	O	O	O
	Section D- Legal/Regulatory						
25	Regulators would prefer native assets on the blockchain over tokenised assets.	O	O	O	O	O	O
26	Regulators are more likely to trial tryproduction- based settlements systems on this technology with incumbents rather than new-entrants.	O	O	O	O	O	O
27	Custody chains will remain in a DLT environment and so will the inherent legal risks.	O	O	O	O	O	O
28	Legal agreements will need to reflect risks associated with the technology (i.e. a total failure of the network in a public ledger).	O	O	O	O	O	O
29	Smart contracts could be implemented to automatically execute legal agreements and other legally binding settlement obligations.	O	O	O	O	O	O
30	Regulation will need to be expanded to detail use of DLT in securities Settlements, for native or tokenised assets.	O	O	O	O	O	O
	Section E- General						
31	The use of DLT will ultimately change the entire landscape and issuers and investors will be able to transact with no intermediaries.	O	O	O	O	O	O
32	Crypto currencies and securities (Crypto Assets) will ultimately trade the same way and traditional post trade infrastructure will be redundant.	O	O	O	O	O	O
33	DLT is not suitable for securities settlement.	O	O	O	O	O	O
34	DLT implementation for securities settlement will be more complex and costly than the current post trade infrastructure.	O	O	O	O	O	O
35	Banking led technology consortiums driving the technology will ultimately drive middle-of-the-road solutions which further entrench incumbents.	O	O	O	O	O	O
36	The technology is too immature and is not proven.	O	O	O	O	O	O
37	DLT implementation will ultimately lead to self-regulation of the network	O	O	O	O	O	O
38	The technology has not had a major failure as yet and the unknown implications are too great to risk entire economies.	O	O	O	O	O	O
39	An example such as the DAO (Ethereum) proves that even public ledgers ultimately need centralised decision making.	O	O	O	O	O	O
40	Immutability of records is not always a strength.	O	O	O	O	O	O

Please read the paper explaining the proposed model for a sovereign distributed securities depository. Answer the following questions after reading the paper please.

41. List the positive elements of the model:
42. List the negative elements of the model:
43. How can the model be improved?
44. If you believe incumbents will be disintermediated, please indicate who and why you think so.
45. Any other comments regarding the model?

Thank you for participating in the study.
End of survey

Section 2

Section 2
Blockchain Technology Use Cases

Chapter 9
Blockchain Technology:
Initiatives and Use Cases in the Industry

Zaigham Mahmood
ⓘD https://orcid.org/0000-0001-7411-7496
University of Northampton, UK & Shijiazhuang Tiedao University, China

ABSTRACT

Blockchain technology is probably the most attractive innovation since the emergence of the internet. Blockchain refers to an open distributed ledger spread across multiple computers that hold digitally recorded transactions in a much more efficient, transparent, and secure manner. A blockchain consists of a number of blocks, each containing data relating to digital assets and a hash header that links it to the previous block in the chain. The blocks are linked together, and new blocks can be added and removed, following a process of consensus. Also, those involved in the transactions can share the distributed digital ledger without needing a centralized intermediary. This chapter aims to introduce blockchain technology and discuss the use cases and initiatives in various sectors of the society, in particular within the block-chain product vendors and service providers. Characteristics, benefits, types, underlying technologies, and platforms are also discussed for the sake of completeness.

INTRODUCTION

The Blockchain technology is probably the most important innovation since the emergence of the Internet. It holds the same promise as the printing press or the Internet, to allow new forms of secure and anonymous communication to take place in many diverse sectors of the society and a multitude of industries. Areas that Blockchain is set to disrupt, include healthcare, transportation, supply chain, risk management, manufacturing, tourism, banking, education, and government, to name but a few. The Blockchain technology is still developing and yet it is already driving the digital revolution with the digitization of processes, automation, tokenization of physical resources, and codification of intricate contracts between stakeholders. Countries which have openly embraced this technology include China, USA, UK, UAE, Japan, Singapore and Australia. According to Market Watch (2020), Blockchain market share is expected to exceed USD 25 billion by the year 2025.

DOI: 10.4018/978-1-7998-6650-3.ch009

The idea of Blockchain technology, originally termed as *block chain*, was initially announced in a Bitcoin white paper published by Satoshi Nakamoto in 2008. The first implementation appeared in 2009 (Zaky, 2020). This was essentially the realisation that the technology that underlined the operation of 'bitcoin' (the cryptocurrency that can now be considered as the application of Blockchain) could be separated from the currency and used for all kinds of other inter-organisational cooperation. There was, then, further development over the period of about 10 years in terms of *smart contracts, proofs of work*, and Blockchain *scaling*. A brief timeline of the development of Blockchain technology is presented in Figure 1.

Figure 1. Timeline for evolution of Blockchain technology

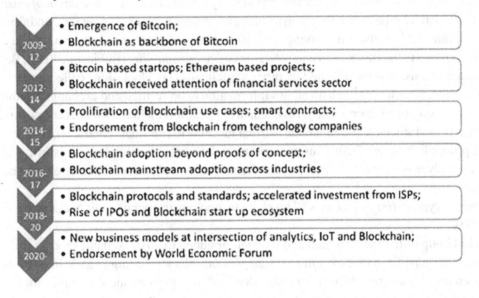

Characteristics of Blockchain technology include decentralisation, immutability, transparency, security, consensus, and smart contracts (Rosic, 2016; Tasca and Tessone, 2019). Witscad (2020) divides the characteristics into functional characteristics and emergent characteristics, as shown in Figure 2. These are explained in later sections of this chapter. Because of the attraction of these features, Blockchain has been gaining attention in areas beyond its cryptocurrency roots since about 2014. This technology has now gone beyond its initial application in cryptocurrencies (such as Bitcoin). It is now being applied to nearly every sector of the society including banking, healthcare, manufacturing, transportation, logistics, supply chain management, and risk management, to name but a few, as already mentioned.

The organisation of this chapter is as follows. The next main section defines the Blockchain technology, describes the essential terminology, outlines the main characteristics and benefits, describes the underlying concepts and varieties of Blockchain, and summarises the generic Blockchain process. Various well known Blockchain platforms are also summarised, for the sake of completeness. The next main section lists various use cases taken from different industries, vendors and service providers; and various initiatives that are currently in existence. The final section presents the conclusion.

It is hoped that this chapter sets the scene for further discussion on various Blockchain related investigations, that appears in other chapters in this book.

BLOCKCHAIN TECHNOLOGY

A Blockchain is a shared *distributed ledger* (database), spread across many computers with no central control or authority, in which digital assets (transactions representing values, identities, agreements, property rights, credentials, etc) are recorded and linked together so that they provide the entire history and the current state or the provenance of the assets. It promises a more efficient, secure and transparent way of handling transactions of digital assets, that can save a huge amount of administration, bureaucracy, effort and time. The Blockchain technology is based on a complex branch of mathematics called *cryptography*.

According to McKinsey in Garson (2018), Blockchain is *a decentralised, shared and trusted distributed ledger (or database) that consists of encrypted 'blocks' of information added to a chain of existing blocks of records*. The ledger relies on the *consensus* of a global peer network to operate. Modifying the data in a block is impossible without modifying the entire chain and receiving consensus of the entire peer network – this refers to the Blockchain characteristic called *immutability* (Robinson, 2018). Before a new block is added, it must first be validated by other participants (i.e. blocks also called nodes) to prevent fraud and increase security. Blockchain allows information to be verified and exchanged without relying on a central authority or an intermediary. Blockchain applications include: *Bitcoin* (cryptocurrency), *Sia* (decentralised cloud storage), and *Ethereum* (virtual machine to run smart contracts), to name but a few.

Before proceeding to any further discussion on the Blockchain technology, it is in order to define certain commonly used terms and concepts, for the sake of completeness. These are listed below.

- **Bitcoin**: Cryptocurrency that uses Blockchain technology to operate; unit of currency; one bitcoin = 1 BTC
- **Block**: Group of transactions gathered by a *minor* added to a Blockchain; Process used is known as *cryptography*; Each block is linked to the previous block resulting in a chain of blocks
- **Consensus**: Process by which Blockchain works; Refers to rules and mechanics for maintenance and updating of ledger that guarantees trustworthiness of the records, i.e. their reliability and authenticity
- **Ethereum**: An open source platform to build Blockchain based applications; Distributes a currency called *ether* (ETH); Allows storage and execution of code allowing for *smart contracts*
- **Hash**: Digital signature with public and private keys of a block for authentication
- **Proof of Stake (PoS)**: Consensus algorithm by which cryptocurrency Blockchain network achieves distributed consensus; Alternative to PoW
- **Proof of Work (PoW)**: Consensus algorithm for a Blockchain network for confirmation of transaction and production of new blocks
- **Smart Contract**: Code associated with a Blockchain that allows to add a transaction based on certain agreed requirements that trigger an event when agreed limitations are reached.

Blockchain Benefits

The Blockchain technology promises to revolutionize finance and business and many other sectors in the industry. One evidence is the numerous Blockchain project currently being researched and conducted in public domain, as discussed later in this chapter. Here are some of the generic advantages that Blockchain technology offers:

- **Reduced costs**: Since Blockchain establishes peer to peer network within one system, it cuts out the time and expense of intermediaries such as the middlemen.
- **Quick settlement and convenience**: The complexity of using Blockchain disparate ledgers and processes throughout the lifecycle of a transaction, for instance a stock purchase transacted in a Blockchain, get settles fairly quickly. There will be no need for another entity to process the transactions
- **Better security**: Each and every transaction is stored in a block that links to the ones before and after it helps increase in security. And, although nothing is hackproof, the Blockchain is considerably more secure than anything else today.
- **Transparency and Incorruptibility**: Blockchain data is not stored centrally, meaning that the transactions are truly transparent and easily verifiable. Also, the fact that it is decentralized makes it difficult for any hacker to corrupt the chain or transactions.

These benefits are further elaborated on, later in the chapter, when we discuss characteristics of Blockchain.

Although, there still are many challenges that are stopping the mass adoption of Blockchain technology, with further development, these are being addressed. Some of the issues relate to energy consumption which is normally very high, scalability which in some cases is relatively limited, skillset that is currently in short supply because of newness of the technology, and speed of operations that are often slow.

Blockchain Characteristics

As mentioned before, some of the most important properties of Blockchain which have formed the reasons for its use in various applications are decentralisation, transparency, immutability and smart contracts (Rosic, 2016; Tasca, 2019). These are briefly discussed below. Refer also to Figure 2 for a more detailed set of characteristics, divided into functional and emergent properties.

- **Decentralisation**: This refers to the occurrence of the fact that the Blockchain (i.e. the distributed ledger) exists on multiple computing systems, referred to as nodes. This is stark opposite to the traditional client-server model that is a centralised approach that has served the industry well but it has weaknesses. In a decentralised system, data is owned by all participants in the network. Also, interaction between nodes in the network does not need to go through an intermediary. This is exactly the main idea behind Bitcoins and the Blockchain.
- **Transparency**: In Blockchain, this is achieved by hiding a person's identity via cryptography so user' real identity is secure; also, every action on the Blockchain is driven by a digital signature that adds to further security. However, transactions can be seen via their public addresses; and this is for the sake of accountability, which, in turn, translates into trust, honesty and transparency with respect to transactions between clients.
- **Immutability**: This refers to the property of a system that prohibits alteration of data, once already entered into the system. This is an attractive characteristic of Blockchain, which stops any attempt to alter the digital content of a block. This is achieved through using cryptographic hash functions. Since, a block comprises data and a hash (of data in previous block) pointer to the previous block, it makes the system most reliable.

- **Smart Contracts**: These are lines of code that are stored on a Blockchain, that automatically execute when certain pre-defined conditions are met, without the need for human intervention, verification or arbitration. These contracts are used to enforce some type of agreement. Also, conflicting or double transactions cannot be written in the Blockchain. Any conflict is automatically reconciled and each valid transaction is added only once (Tasca and Tessone, 2019).

Figure 2. Blockchain characteristics

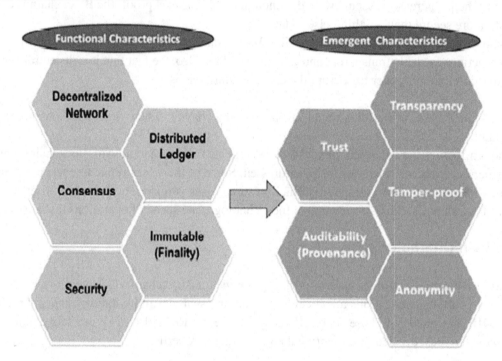

Blockchain Underlying Technologies

There are a number of existing technologies and concepts that, combined together, have given rise to the peer-validated decentralised cryptocurrency called Bitcoin, initially in 2018, and later to the Blockchain technology. These are: cryptography, distributed ledgers, hashing mechanisms, and consensus protocols. The following paragraphs briefly explain what these are.

- **Cryptography**: The general aim of cryptography is to create a secure identity for security purpose. Cryptography is of two varieties: *symmetric* and *asymmetric*. Asymmetric cryptography provides a much stronger algorithm that consists of public key (which is visible to all), and a private key (that is only available to the owner of the data that the key applies to). One of the applications of asymmetric cryptography is the *digital signatures*. Such signatures provide authenticity and integrity mechanisms for the data and documents; and provide strong control of owner of an asset (e.g. data or a document). In the case of a Blockchain: 1) a users' public key is their Blockchain *wallet* (e.g. Bitcoin or Ethereum address) that is visible to all participants with the chain; and 2) the private key is used to digitally sign a transaction for ensuring that particular transaction is indeed generated by the sender, is stored safely in a crypto wallet.

- **Distributed ledger**: A ledger is a file that contains a record of transaction (information and data). A distributed ledger uses independent computers (referred to as nodes) to record, share and synchronize transactions in their respective digital ledgers (instead of keeping data centralized as in a single traditional ledger). Blockchain is, in fact, a form of distributed ledger, which organizes digital assets and transactions into a database of blocks (residing of different nodes), which are chained together in an append only mode. The advantage of a distributed ledger is that, since it is decentralised and self-regulating, it eliminates the need for a central controlling authority or an intermediary to process, validate or authenticate transactions, or other forms of data exchange.

- **Hash function**: A Hash function is an important element of Blockchain architecture to ensure the immutability of transactions. It is a mathematical function/process that is used in Blockchain to represent its current state. The hash is used as part of the consensus mechanism to agree between all parties (nodes) that the Blockchain state is one and the same. Hashing involves taking an arbitrarily amount of input data, and then applying an algorithm to convert it to a fixed length data called the *hash* (ISO, 2016). Hashing and digital signatures are the two concepts that underpin cryptography.

- **Consensus protocol**: Such protocols are encoded rulesets of all access rights and obligations of all participants in a network. A consensus mechanism is a fault-tolerant process that is used to achieve the necessary agreement on a single data value or a single state of the network among a distributed process in multi-agent systems, such as with cryptocurrencies and Blockchain technology. It is useful for record-keeping and history of transaction events. Since, a Blockchain is dynamically changing, it is important that there is an efficient, fair, real-time, functional, reliable, and secure mechanism to ensure that all transactions occurring in the network are genuine. There is therefore a need for all participants to agree on a consensus on the status of the ledger. Two of the most commonly used consensus mechanisms are: *Proof of Work* (PoW), and *Proof of Stake* (PoS).

Blockchain Process

A simple approach to explain the way the Blockchain process works is illustrated in Figure 3.

Blockchain Types

There are generally three main types of Blockchain: *public*, *private* and *consortium* (Bhasin, 2019). Public and Private Blockchains can be further classed into permissioned or permissionless Blockchains (Singh, 2020). Consortium Blockchain are also known as Federated Blockchain.

- **Public**: Here, anyone is allowed to join and participate in the network i.e. download the code, read, write, audit, add and run a public node. These Blockchains are open, decentralised, and transparent but rather slower in nature. All who have joined can see the ledger and participate in consensus for validating new blocks. Decision making is through various consensus mechanism e.g. by PoW or PoS. Examples are Bitcoin, Litecoin, and Ethereum.

Figure 3. How Blockchain works

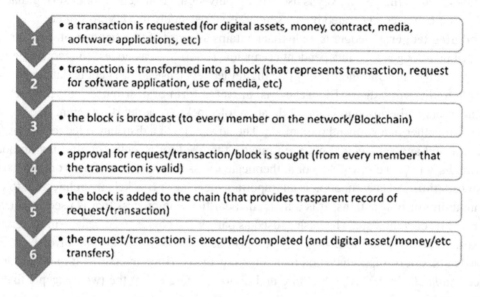

- a transaction is requested (for digital assets, money, contract, media, aoftware applications, etc)
- transaction is transformed into a block (that represents transaction, request for software application, use of media, etc)
- the block is broadcast (to every member on the network/Blockchain)
- approval for request/transaction/block is sought (from every member that the transaction is valid)
- the block is added to the chain (that provides trasparent record of request/transaction)
- the request/transaction is executed/completed (and digital asset/money/etc transfers)

- **Private**: Here, an individual or an organisation is the owner of the Blockchain and has the authority over who can join and have the access rights. It is, therefore, a centralised-decentralised network. Read and write access varies from node to node; and anonymity is not offered. These networks are less expensive than public Blockchains, but are more power efficient than Public networks and less volatile. Examples are: R3, Bankchain and Corda.
- **Consortium** or **Federated**: Here, multiple organisations form a federation who own the network. It is like a hub for multiple organisations to share and work concurrently. It is only the selected members who can run a node or make transactions. Networks are scalable and energy efficient. This variety offers lower transaction fees and more robustness as criminal activity is reduced. Examples are: Multichain, R3, and Monax.
- **Permissionless** Blockchains: In this variety, anyone can join, run and manage digital assets. These are public Blockchains, that are truly decentralised, transparent, trusting, immutable, and with enhanced security. However, these are harder to scale and less efficient. Here, PoW mechanism is used for reaching consensus. Ethereum and Bitcoin are examples of such Blockchains. Some use cases include: digital identity, voting and fundraising (Singh, 2020).
- **Permissioned** Blockchain: These are more like private Blockchains where permission to join is required from the owner organisation. Characteristics include: varying levels of decentralisation, governed and managed by the owning organisation, efficient, scalable, less transparent, and energy efficient. Use cases include: research, bank transactions, and supply chain management (Singh, 2020).

Within these varieties of Blockchain, we can identify the following components, as stated by Kashyap (2018), that a Blockchain generally consists of:

- Ledger: This consists of the elements of digital assets transactions
- Smart Contract: This refers to agreed terms that come into play when certain events occur

- Consensus Network: These are nodes of the Blockchain, linked in a certain order
- Events: These refer to Blockchain activities e.g. addition of a new block
- Wallet: This element keeps and mages a consumer's security credentials
- Management: This component manages ability to create, change, and monitor events
- Integration: This helps to manage links between a Blockchain and an external system.

BLOCKCHAIN PLATFORMS

The Blockchain ecosystem has grown rapidly in the last few years. As a result, many implementation platforms have appeared in the market. They fall in many multiple categories e.g. Blockchain enterprise platforms, Blockchain cloud platforms, and so on. Malhotra (2020) provides a review of fifteen most used Blockchain platforms. The following sections provide an overview of some of these (and also some other) platforms that support the development and implementation of Blockchain based applications.

Ethereum

Initially proposed in 2014, this is the second most attractive open-source decentralised public platform, after Bitcoin, for running smart contracts on the custom-built Blockchain network. It can be used to design and run applications on a Blockchain. It provides a cryptocurrency, called Ether (ETH). Programs based on Ethereum (using Ethereum embedded programming language) can run safely without human intervention, and payments made in ETH are automatic. Anyone can design and upload apps. to the Ethereum network (that is based on thousands of computers, distributed around the world) and anyone can participate as another node in the network that executes the apps. and verifies transactions. Benefits include security, reliability, and no need for intermediaries (Economic Point, 2020).

Hyperledger Fabric

This is another enterprise grade open-source permissioned distributed ledger technology platform, developed by IBM, that offers modularity, configurable architecture, and versatility for a broad set of industry use cases including banking, finance, insurance, healthcare, human resources, supply chain and even digital music delivery. It supports smart contracts authored in general-purpose programming languages such as Java, Python and Go (Hyperledger Fabric, 2020). It has support for pluggable consensus protocols that enable the platform to be more effectively customized to fit particular use cases and trust models. Fabric can leverage consensus protocols that do not require a native cryptocurrency; and provides security, privacy, confidentiality, scalability and pluggable consensus (CitiusTech, 2018).

OpenChain

This is also one of the most preferred Blockchain platforms based on secured open-source distributed ledger technology developed by Coinprism. It is a well-suited private network for organizations to manage and preserve their digital assets in a robust, secure and scalable manner. Although, OpenChain does not use the concept of blocks (its transactions are directly chained with one another, and they are no longer grouped in blocks), this distributed ledge is of real time; supports JavaScript; and its transactions are scalable and secure with customised permissions at different levels. Other features include: instant confirmation of transactions, immutability, assignment of aliases to users, transactions secured through digital signatures, and has multiple levels of controls with hierarchical account system (OpenChain, 2020).

MultiChain

This is an open-source platform for building Blockchains. A key design principle is maximal compatibility with <u>Bitcoin Core</u>, which includes Bitcoin's <u>network protocol</u>, <u>transaction format</u>, <u>block format</u> and <u>output scripts</u>. Almost all of the information in the <u>Bitcoin Developer Documentation</u> is applicable to MultiChain. It provides features such as customisation of Blockchain parameters, working with smart filters, API commends for controlling the MultiChain, and customisation of runtime parameters, fine-grain permissions, rapid deployment and unlimited assets. Some tools to help with MultiChain development includes MultiChain Explorer, Docker Multichain, and MultiChain Web Demo. C#, GO, Java, PHP, Python and Ruby can be used for programming (MultiChain, 2020).

R3 Corda

The Corda platform by R3 is an enterprise Blockchain platform that delivers security, scalability, enterprise integration, and interoperability. Distributed applications can be built on top of open-source Corda for usage across industries such as financial services, insurance, healthcare, trade finance, and digital assets (R3, 2020). Businesses can transact directly, privately (noting that most platforms lack privacy), securely and seamlessly, reducing transaction and record-keeping costs and streamlining business operations. The use of smart contracts makes it possible for the platform to execute tasks as soon as set conditions are met. Features include: reduced operational costs, increased revenues by monetizing networks, and delivering high levels of trust between parties. Corda does not have a native currency.

EOS

This is also an open-source Blockchain platform launched by a company called Block.One, only in early 2018. It allows buying and trading digital assets on smart contracts securely and relatively easily. Based on decentralised technology, unlike many other platforms that use Proof-of-Stake (PoS) algorithm, EOS performs consensus by using delegated PoS. Features include: commercial scalability, broad distribution, and flexibility. Currently, EOS is one of the top 20 cryptocurrencies worldwide as its token has market value of 500 million US dollars (Crypto Digest, 2020). Unlike Ethereum that operates on just a single chain (that usually results in micro transactions that can easily clog the network), EOS uses multiple chains and there is no or minimal risk of the network getting clogged and therefore, it does not affect other applications.

Other Platforms

There are numerous other Blockchain platforms including Ripple, Stellar, Quorum, Monero, IBM Blockchain platform, Hyperledger Sawtooth, Neo Blockchain Platform, Hedera Hashgraph, Hyperledger Iroha. These are well summarised in Malhotra (2020). And, there are many more platform available in the market e.g. Ardor, Cardanao, Konmodo, etc.

BLOCKCHAIN USE CASES AND INITIATIVES

As stated in I-Scope (2020), Blockchain technology appears to be a bigger deal than the Internet of Things (IoT) vision. Blockchain use cases and project initiatives in the industry go far beyond the financial transactions and transfer of cryptocurrencies. With its ability to create more transparency, openness and fairness and with its characteristics such as immutability, this technology is impacting a wide variety of industries including finance, manufacturing, healthcare, and transportation, to name a few. Some of the Blockchain use cases and initiatives within the industry, in particular within the Blockchain product vendors and Blockchain service providers, are elaborated in the following sub-sections.

Blockchain Use Cases

Here is a list of a number of vendors and business organisations that are using Decentralised Leger Technology for their services.

- **BURSTIQ**: This is a company in healthcare industry located in Denver in Colorado (Daley, 2020). They are using Blockchain contracts to help patients and medical staff to safely transfer sensitive and private patient data. The Blockchain contracts determine the parameters of what data can be stored and what information can to be displayed for each patient.
- **PROPY**: This is a real estate agency located in Palo Alto, California. It is a marketplace and transactional platform with a decentralised title registry system, that uses Blockchain technology to allow title issuance as and when required, in real time. The agency uses cryptocurrency for the purchase of properties (Daley, 2020).
- **CIRCLE**: This is a Boston based peer-to-peer payments technology company in the financial technology (FinTech) sector. They oversea approximately $2 billion a month in cryptocurrency investments and exchanges (Daley, 2020). Their portfolio features more than seven digital currencies including Bitcoin, Zcash and Monero.
- **HYPR**: This is a company, based in New York, operating in the cybersecurity sector. They use decentralised credential solutions to detect and resolve security risks in IoT based connected devices. They use biometric and password-free solutions; and develop IoT devices that are virtually unhackable (Daley, 2020).
- **KOMGO**: This company was established in late 2018, currently based in Switzerland, with the backing of institutions such as ABN-AMRO, BNP, and ING, with the purpose of automating global commodity trades by developing a decentralised, open-source and secure commodity trade network (Komgo, 2020).
- **HORIZON GAMES**: This is a Blockchain infrastructure company pioneering a new dimension of gaming that belongs to its players and creators (Infura, 2020). For their flagship game, called SkyWeaver, which consists of 500 collectable cards that players assemble into a deck, the cards are Ethereum ERC tokens which are digital cards with real world ownership and trade.
- **OPEN ZEPPELIN**: This company builds SDK (software development kit) platforms and other tools to help developers create faster and more interesting applications on top of Ethereum platform (OpenZeppelin, 2020). The company were able to reduce their technical overheads and seamlessly onboard their users to the Ethereum network, to securely build and deploy faster apps. improving their developer experience.

There are numerous use cases available and reported in the Blockchain literature. Refer to, for example, Consensys (2020a).

Blockchain Initiatives

Here is a list of a number of Blockchain related initiatives from around the world.

Smart Dubai

This is an initiative by UAE to make Dubai the 'happiest city on earth'. The aim is to make Dubai the *first city fully powered by Blockchain by 2021* (Consensys, 2020). This project is using Blockchain as a Service, developing a Blockchain powered Smart City University, developing Blockchain ecosystem for 100% of the government services, and ensuring paper-less processes. The sandbox environment is based on Ethereum.

Project Khokha

This project aims to assess the application and use cases of Distributed Ledger Technology to create a Blockchain-based interbank system, through the collaborated effort of South African Reserve Bank and the national banking community. The project has already exceeded the transaction performance target at achieving more than 70,000 transactions (interbank clearing and settlement) in less than two hours (Project Khokha, 2020a).

Tepper Blockchain Initiative

The Tepper School of Business at the Carnegie Mellon University have established an initiative to foster innovations in the design, use, ethics, and regulations of decentralised Blockchain based technologies (Tepper School of Business. 2020). The project serves as a hub for pursuing research topics, developing educational content and furthering industrial partnerships. Initiative also seeks to promote Blockchain and cryptocurrency activities for the faculty members and students.

IEEE Evolution of COVID-19 Project

This project uses Blockchain and AI technologies to design and develop an app. that predicts the evolution of the Corona Virus 2019 pandemic (IEEE Spectrum, 2020). Led by two IEEE members in Salamanca, Spain, the team are attempting to determine the factors affecting the COVID-19 corona virus spread, to support healthcare professionals by providing relevant information for decision making; and to predict future epidemics and pandemics.

Ripple UBRI Project

The University Blockchain Research Initiative (UBRI) is a partnership between Ripple and leading universities around the world, to support research, technical development and innovation in Blockchain, cryptocurrency and digital payments (Ripple, 2020). Ripple (also a Blockchain platform) is using this initiative to inspire students to pursue careers in Blockchain, distributed computing, FinTech and related fields.

CONCLUSION

The Blockchain Technology, also referred to as Distribute Ledger Technology (DLT), is probably the most important innovation since the emergence of the Internet. It holds the same promise but provides a new form of secure and anonymous communication to take place in many diverse sectors of the society and industries including healthcare, transportation, supply chain, risk management, manufacturing, tourism, banking, education, etc. It is a newer innovation in computer science; however, it is developing very fast, and all manner of industries and academia are embracing this emerging disruptive technology.

In this chapter, we have introduced the Blockchain technology and discussed the use cases and new initiatives in various sectors of the society, especially within the product vendor companies and Blockchain service providers. We have described the essential terminology, outlined the core characteristics, listed the benefits that Blockchain technology promises, and described the underlying concepts and the Blockchain process. Various well known Blockchain platforms are also summarised, for the sake of completeness.

REFERENCES

R3. (2020). *Corda Enterprise: A Next-Gen Blockchain Platform*. Available at: https://www.r3.com/corda-platform/

Bhasin, H. (2019, April). *3 Main Types of Blockchain: Classification of Blockchain*. Available at: https://www.marketing91.com/types-of-Blockchain/

CitiusTech. (2018, May). *Blockchain for Healthcare*. Available at: https://www.ehidc.org/sites/default/fi:les/resources/files/Blockchain-for-healthcare-341.pdf

Consensys. (2020). *Smart Dubai: Blockchain Case Study for Government in the UAE*. Available at: https://consensys.net/Blockchain-use-cases/government-and-the-public-sector/smart-dubai/

Consensys. (2020a). *Real World Blockchain Case Studies*. Available at: https://consensys.net/Blockchain-use-cases/case-studies/

Crypto Digest. (2020). *EOS Platform: What you should know*. Available at: https://cryptodigestnews.com/eos-platform-what-you-should-know-58da830d2aa8

Daley, S. (2020, March). *25 Blockchain Applications & Real World Use Cases Disrupting the Status Quo*. Available at: https://builtin.com/Blockchain/Blockchain-applications

Economic Point. (2020). *What is the Ethereum Platform.* Available at: https://economicpoint.com/ethereum

Garson, B. (2018, June). *Blockchain Beyond the Hype.* Available at: https://www.mckinsey.com/business-functions/mckinsey-digital/our-insights/Blockchain-beyond-the-hype-what-is-the-strategic-business-value?cid=other-eml-nsl-mip-mck-oth-1807&hlkid=5424a29008e445239371a81cc83b3dbb&hctky=10291646&hdpid=bb9f89f0-458b-4b4e-a1ee-ad99e602294e

Hyperledger Fabric. (2020). *Hyperledger Fabric.* Available at: https://hyperledger-fabric.readthedocs.io/en/release-2.0/whatis.html

I-Scope. (2020). *Blockchain and the Internet of Things: the IoT Blockchain opportunity and challenge.* Available at: https://www.i-scoop.eu/internet-of-things-guide/Blockchain-iot/

IEEE Spectrum. (2020, April). *Spanish Researchers Use Blockchain and AI to Flatten the Curve.* Available at: https://spectrum.ieee.org/news-from-around-ieee/the-institute/ieee-member-news/researchers-spain-Blockchain-ai-app-flatten-the-curve

Infura. (2020). *Partnering with Horizon Games to Power a New Dimension of Gaming.* Available at: https://infura.io/customers/skyweaver

ISO. (2016). *Information technology.* Patent No. ISO/IEC 10118–1:2016.

Kashyap, P. (2018, Feb). *What are Different Types of Blockchain and its Components?* Available at: http://www.beingcrypto.com/what-are-different-types-of-Blockchain-and-its-components/

Komgo. (2020). *Streamlining Trade Finance.* Available at: https://komgo.io/

Malhotra, M. (2020, March). *A comprehensive list of blockchain platforms to look for in 2020.* Available at: https://www.valuecoders.com/blog/technology-and-apps/a-comprehensive-list-of-Blockchain-platforms-to-look-for-in-2019/

MarketWatch. (2020, June). *Blockchain Technology Market Share, Growth to record over US $25 billion by 2025 – Press Release.* Available at: https://www.marketwatch.com/press-release/Blockchain-technology-market-share-growth-to-record-over-us-25-billion-by-2025-2020-06-09

MultiChain. (2020). *MultiChain for Developers.* Available at: https://www.multichain.com/developers/

OpenChain. (2020). *Overview of OpenChain.* Available at: https://docs.openchain.org/en/latest/general/overview.html

OpenZeppelin. (2020). *The standard for secure Blockchain applications.* Available at: https://openzeppelin.com/

Project Khokha: An Enterprise Ethereum Banking and Finance Case Study. (2020). Available at: https://pages.consensys.net/consensys-banking-and-finance-project-khokha-v2?utm_campaign=Enterprise%20Ethereum%20&utm_source=Website&utm_medium=Direct&utm_term=EntEth&utm_content=CaseStudyKhokha

Ripple. (2020). *University Blockchain Research Initiative.* Available at: https://ubri.ripple.com/faq/

Robinson, J. (2018, Aug). *The Future of Blockchain in Transportation*. Available at: https://www.fleetio.com/blog/future-of-Blockchain-in-transportation

Rosic, A. (1916). *What is Blockchain Technology? A Step-by-Step Guide For Beginners*. Available at: https://blockgeeks.com/guides/what-is-Blockchain-technology/

Singh, N. (2020, May). *Permissioned vs. Permissionless Blockchain: A Comparison Guide*. Available at: https://101Blockchains.com/permissioned-vs-permissionless-Blockchains/

Tasca, P., & Tessone, C. J. (2019). *A Taxonomy of Blockchain Technologies: Principles of Identification and Classification, Ledger*. LedgerJournal.org.

Tepper School of Business. (2020). *Tepper Blockchain Initiative*. Available at: https://www.cmu.edu/tepper/faculty-and-research/initiatives/Blockchain-initiative/

Witscad. (2020). *Blockchain Characteristics*. Available at: https://witscad.com/course/Blockchain-fundamentals/chapter/Blockchain-characteristics

Zaky, D. (2020, March). *What is Blockchain Technology and How Does It Work?* Available at: https://fxdailyreport.com/Blockchain-technology/

ADDITIONAL READING

Active Business Systems. (2020), Blockchain and the ERP, Available at: https://www.activebs.com/en/news/2018/Blockchain-and-erp

Byon/Alacrity. (2020, May), Blockchain in Education: three Promising Reforms, Available at: https://alacritys.net/2020/05/27/Blockchain-in-education-three-promising-reforms/

Clark, D. (2016), 10 Ways Blockchain could be used in education, Available at: https://oeb.global/oeb-insights/10-ways-Blockchain-could-be-used-in-education

Columbus, L. (2019), How Blockchain Can Improve Manufacturing in 2019, Available at: https://www.forbes.com/sites/louiscolumbus/2018/10/28/how-Blockchain-can-improve-manufacturing-in-2019/

Concise Software. (2020), 10 Use Cases of Blockchain in Banking, Available at: https://concisesoftware.com/10-use-cases-of-Blockchain-in-banking/

Consensys, (2016), 5 Incredible Blockchain IoT Applications, Available at: https://blockgeeks.com/5-incredible-Blockchain-iot-applications/

Goyal, S. (2018, Nov), The History of Blockchain Technology: Must Know Timeline, Available at: https://101Blockchains.com/history-of-Blockchain-timeline/

Hance, M. (2020), What is Blockchain and How Can it be Used in Education? Available at: https://mdreducation.com/2018/08/20/Blockchain-education/

Maaghul, R. (2019, Oct), Blockchain in Education: The Future of Records Management, Available at: https://blogs.odem.io/Blockchains-bright-future-in-the-education-industry

Mahmood, Z. (2021). Blockchain Technology: Applications in the Industry. In Z. Mahmood (Ed.), *Industry Use Cases on Blockchain Technology: Initiatives and Use Cases in the Industry, IGI Global, 2021.*

Morley, M. (2020, Feb), Top 5 Use Cases of Blockchain in the Supply Chain in 2020, Available at: https://blogs.opentext.com/Blockchain-in-the-supply-chain/

Shumsky, P. (2019, Sep), Blockchain Use Cases For Banks In 2020, Available at: https://www.finextra.com/blogposting/17857/Blockchain-use-cases-for-banks-in-2020

Winnesota, (2020), How Blockchain is Revolutionising the World of Transportation and Logistics, Available at: https://www.winnesota.com/Blockchain

KEY TERMS AND DEFINITIONS

Bitcoin: This is the first and the most popular cryptocurrency that uses blockchain technology to conduct digital transactions.

Blockchain: A blockchain is a mathematical structure for storing digital transactions in a distributed and decentralized digital ledger. It consists of multiple blocks, spread across multiple computing nodes, that are linked using cryptographic signatures.

Consensus Mechanism: This is the process that refers to rules and mechanics for maintenance and updating of ledger in a Blockchain that guarantees trustworthiness of the records, i.e. their reliability and authenticity.

Cryptography: This is the science of securing communication using individualized codes (e.g. public and private keys) so only the participating parties can read the encrypted messages.

Ethereum: An open source platform to build Blockchain based applications. It permits distribution of a currency called ether (ETH); and allows storage and execution of code allowing for smart contracts.

Hashing Mechanism: This is a digital signature (comprising public and private keys) of a block (consisting of information about digital assets and hash pointer) for authentication and verification purposes.

Hyperledger Fabric: This is enterprise grade open-source permissioned distributed ledger technology platform, developed by IBM. It offers modularity, configurable architecture, and versatility for a broad set of industries.

Proof of Stake (PoS): It is a type of consensus algorithm by which a cryptocurrency blockchain network aims to achieve distributed consensus. In PoS-based digital currencies, the addition of the next block is organised considering various combinations of random selection e.g. wealth or age (i.e., the stake)

Proof of Work (PoSW): It is a consensus mechanism that helps to stop or reduce denial of service attacks and other security abuses such as spam on a network by requiring some work from the service requester, usually meaning processing time by a computer.

Smart Contract: A smart contract is a computer protocol that facilities the transfer of digital assets between parties considering the already agreed-upon stipulations or terms.

Chapter 10
Blockchain Technology:
Concepts, Components, and Cases

Somayya Madakam
iD https://orcid.org/0000-0001-6708-2061
FORE School of Management, New Delhi, India

Harshita
Institute of Management Technology, Ghaziabad, India

ABSTRACT

Currently, the financial transactions between individuals, organizations, and companies are taking place with the help of third-party approval of intermediaries such as banks, financial institutions, standardizing bodies, or credit card providers. These transactions involve multilevel approvals, costs, and inefficient processes in some cases, which also lead to waste of time and resources. To resolve these issues, blockchain technology has appeared as a new financial digital innovative solution. Here, financial transactions are online, open, and transparent. In this chapter, the authors present systematic literature of relevant research on blockchain technology. The objective is to understand the historical evolutions, current ongoing research, base technologies, and applications. The authors have extracted research articles from scientific databases including EBSCO, Scopus, Web of Science, and Google Scholar. The online blogs, wikis, media articles, YouTube videos, and companies' white papers on blockchain technology are also used for content analysis.

INTRODUCTION

Experts deem blockchain as the most disruptive technology since the development of the Internet. Blockchain Technology, also known as Distributed Ledger Technology (DLT) will provide opportunity to build use cases based on industry and commerce, in the years to come. Hence, the software developing companies around the globe, but especially across India, are desperately looking to fill the following job positions in the blockchain technology domain: Blockchain Developer, Blockchain Lead Developer, Blockchain Architect, Application Architect, Blockchain Engineer, Blockchain Specialist,

DOI: 10.4018/978-1-7998-6650-3.ch010

Blockchain Expert, Blockchain Consultant, etc. This shows that the Indian software hubs of Hyderabad, Chennai, Kolkata, Pune, Kochi, NOIDA, Ahmedabad, Mumbai, and so on are in an urgent need of the development of Blockchain technologies and their allied applications in order to smoothen the financial services. This is the need of the hour, not only for the Indian based financial institutions, banks, and IT/ITes companies, but also for the other sectors located across the globe. Here are a few examples of the job calls, on LinkedIn on 07/05/2020, for roles such as: Blockchain Analyst for Smith + Crown Financial Services @ Portland, USA; Blockchain researcher in Onchain Company @ Shanghai, China; Director, Global PR & Branding, Blockchain Space Executive Company @ Bangkok Metropolitan Area; Head of Sales, Blockchain/Fintech in PERSOL @ Singapore and Senior Blockchain Engineer in Swisscom Blockchain @ Zurich, Switzerland.

The design, development, implementation and application of blockchain technologies involve distributed systems and storage, blockchains, cryptocurrencies, hash functions, cybersecurity, applied cryptography using different formal methods, tools and programming languages such as C, C#, Java, Ruby, Solidity, Java Script, Python, R, Go, Scala, Grafana, DataDog, Bash, Perl, MongoDB, MySQL, JSON, kotlin, and RESTful APIs, and so on, that are commonly used across various businesses. The blockchain development includes front/back-end, storage, networking, and security mechanisms. There are many applications of this disruptive financial technology including in distributed ledger technology (DLT)-based applications leveraging decentralization, digital scarcity and radical transparency delivering supply chain and stakeholder trust in the waste chain. The application domains, among others, include financial institutions, manufacturing, real estate, healthcare, judicial, education, governance, energy, telecom, and transportation.

In this book chapter, the authors discuss in detail the applications of blockchain technologies in banking, insurance, real estate, smart cities, manufacturing, supply chain, energy, and telecommunication sectors by used test cases along with blockchain concepts and underlying technologies. There are four main sections here. The first two sections explore the blockchain technologies in detail including definitions, genesis, components, and different cryptocurrencies. The subsequent section explains the blockchain concepts, background mechanisms, and case studies in diverse industries across the globe. The final short section presents conclusions.

BLOCKCHAIN CONCEPTS

The "Blockchain" technology is becoming one of the most demandable disruptive technologies along with Artificial Intelligence (AI), Machine Learning (ML), Deep Learning, Data Analytics, Internet of Things (IoT), and Cloud Computing. There is much in the literature on this emerging technology in the form of news scripts, journal articles, book chapters, analysis reports, and books. There are also vocal discussions on blockchain technologies in public speaking events, seminars, conferences, lectures, doctoral colloquium, webinars, and even special programs like conference-cum-exhibitions. This shows that there is a huge demand for this phenomenon. The past studies are giving evidence that there is increasing demand for this technology, as this is becoming highly attractive especially for financial transactions and banking services. Research by Blidholm & Johnson (2018); Coeckelbergh & Reijers (2016); Grigoriadou (2019); Hütten (2017); Khatal et al. (2020); Lundström & Öhman (2019); Manrique (2018); Mihigo (2019); Mushtaq & Haq (2019); Nehaï & Guerard (2017); Shi (2019); Songara & Chouhan (2017) amply sheds light on the need for blockchain technology, online distributed ledger, blockchain and InterPlanetary File System (IPFS) framework, and their value creation. Moreover, the seminal paper by Madakam & Kollu (2020) explains clearly about the fundamentals of blockchain technologies - perceptions, principles, procedures and practices.

The following are some of the vital studies on different aspects of blockchain and related technologies. Casey (2015) has voiced about blockchains without coins, which stirred tensions in the bitcoin community in The Wall Street Journal. Manuscript by Dash et al. (2017) has focused on a revolutionary bitcoin in the International Journal of Information Science and Computing. Felin & Lakhani (2018) has talked about how problems would solve with the blockchain technologies in MIT Sloan Management Review. Gatteschi et al. (2018) explained smart contracts for insurance in the Future Internet; Haber et al. (1991) described, in Journal of Cryptology, how to time-stamp a digital document. The study by Janssen et al. (2020) reported in International Journal of Information Management talks about blockchain technology adoption.

Köhler & Pizzol (2019) have explored the life cycle assessment of bitcoin mining in the Environmental Science & Technology Journal. Nian & Chuen (2015) in their Handbook of Digital Currency have discussed in detail about regulation for virtual currencies. Narayanan et al. (2016), in Princeton press edition, have discussed about bitcoin and cryptocurrency technologies in a comprehensive manner. The publisher of Nature News also talked about the future of cryptocurrencies i.e. Bitcoin and beyond (Extance, 2015). Katie Martin (2016) conveyed about the financial service company CLS Group ready to approve blockchain-based transactions in the Financial Times. Salsman (2013) have suggested, in Forbes magazine, that the financial crisis was due to a failure of government, not of free markets.

The subject of blockchain is interdisciplinary and technical in nature. One can find its literature through many predominated publishers and forums including IGI Global, IEEE, ACM, Springer conference proceedings and journals; apart from finance and accounting related journals. Additionally, John Wiley & Sons, Reuters, Elsevier, Inderscience, Emerald, Princeton University Press, and Academic Press are also active in blockchain technology knowledge dissemination. Studies with these publishers in the past have explored about blockchain and cryptocurrencies as a proof of trust, a decentralized technique for securing the IoT Things, implications for Industry 4.0, smart grid applications, and as a key driver of sustainable development.

In October 2019, Garter's Hype Cycle empirically suggested that by 2023, blockchain platforms will progress to be scalable, interoperable, and that they will support smart contract portability and cross-chain functionality. As per the Gartner prediction, some of the blockchain child technologies that will be flourishing in the coming next 5-10 years, are expected to be Blockchain UX/UI technologies, decentralize identity, ledger DBMS, smart contract oracle, Blockchain PaaS, cryptocurrency related soft/hardware wallets, Blockchain meta coin platforms, zero-knowledge proofs, and so on. Besides, much research is going on in the fields of blockchain business models, developments, blockchain distributed ledgers, hash functions, cryptocurrencies, stablecoin, smart contracts, smart assets, rewards and loyalty, ICOs, ACH payments, lead generation, decentralized autonomous organizations, strategic tokenization, security, digital signatures, policy, and regulations.

The latest blockchain technologies or applications can address human needs and make a huge difference in people's lives by providing even better Quality of Life (QoL) (Madakam & Kollu, 2020). In an exaggeration, no field seems to have excaped without Blockchain Technology applications. Because of its applications in every domain, this technology is penetrating in all the disciplines of human life. Even though it was initially meant for banking applications, it is now marrying with insurance, governance, telecom, education, research & development, healthcare, oil & gas, transportation, retail, media

& entrainment, advertising, supply chain & logistics, utilities, customer service, watering, energy, smart cities, gaming, 3-Dimensional (3D) printing, and IoT, to name but a few.

Blockchain technology refers to a data structure consisting of a growing list of online data records, so-called blocks, that are inter-linked using cryptography technique. Blockchain technology is an open, decentralised ledger that can record transactions between/among parties across a peer-to-peer computer network, without the need for a central financial certifying authority. According to The Economist of 31 Oct, 2015: *to understand the power of blockchain systems, and the things they can do, it is important to distinguish between three things that are commonly muddled up, namely the bitcoin currency, the specific blockchain that underpins it and the idea of Blockchains in general.*

Even though there is a huge amount of literature on this topic, there is no standard/operational definition, though many working definitions exist. Experts from different accounting regulating bodies, financial institutions, investment companies, and banks have their own way to define what Blockchain technology is. The academicians, researchers, and students have their own ways of explaining this. Moreover, the technology developers, policymakers and end-users have their own perspectives. For better understanding, we can consider the definition by Crosby et al. (2016): *Blockchain is a distributed database comprising records of transactions or digital events that have been executed and shared among participating parties. Each of these transactions is verified by the consensus of a majority of the participants in the system.*

Blockchain technology is an open, decentralised ledger technology in which online-distributed ledger records are stored in the form of blocks at node level at the time of peer-to-peer transaction over the fully connected computational networks. These technologies are transparent, peers are involved and miners are evident of the transactions without central authority like other traditional financial monitoring system. Blockchain technology is integrated, complex process of mining, peer-to-peer transaction, Proof-of-Work security mechanisms, to name but a few.

Blockchain History

Blockchain technology is data management technology that permits the financial online transactions to be gathered into blocks and finally recorded. It allows the resulting ledger to be accessed by different servers in a fully connected computer network. Individuals or entities with no basis to trust each other can also use it without a central controlling authority. According to Brito & Castillo (2013), originally, blockchain is a growing list of records, called blocks that are linked using cryptography. Although Blockchain Technology is becoming the base for entire financial service business using cryptocurrency, at first people knew about Bitcoin and only later, it developed into a technology. This suggests that initially, blockchain technology was used to record historical transactions of encrypted digital money such as Bitcoin (Nakamoto, 2008). So, before the introduction of Bitcoin, we had the online-distributed ledgers transactions, and there were distributed system records, which stored official information transactions at different nodes across the computer networks. Some background literature gives testimony that Stuart Haber and Scott Stornetta described the first work on a cryptographically secured chain of blocks in 1991 (Scott, 1991). They wanted to implement a system where document timestamps could not be tampered with. In 1992, Haber, Stornetta, and Bayer incorporated Merkle trees to the design, which improved its efficiency by allowing several document certificates to be collected into each block (Haber et al., 1991; Bayer et al., 1992; Narayanan et al., 2016). These were the stepping-stones for the development of Blockchain technology. From 2008 onwards, many global technology developing companies and new startups started new Blockchain related products and services as this technology promises many advantages for businesses. In 2009, the first Bitcoin was mined and became available, in digital form, online. In the subsequent year, i.e. in 2010, through cryptocurrency stock exchange, Bitcoin was launched and trading went live. In 2014, Microsoft started accepting Bitcoin for its business payments. Now Bitcoin created a decentralized environment for cryptocurrency, where the participants could buy and exchange goods with digital money (Yli-Huumo et al., 2016).

In this context, LeewayHertz, a company that specialize in building digital solutions, are providing smart contracts, dApps, Security Token Offering (STO)/Initial Exchange Offering (IEO), stablecoin, and public and private blockchain solutions to the clients. Whereas, Consensys are developing and deploying many enterprise Ethereum solutions, the team at Consensys also offer in-person and online blockchain education. Similarly, the ChromaWay is providing a blockchain platform, which delivers smart contracts solutions for real estate and finance industries. Besides, Blockchain Intelligence Group (BIG) aim at providing an optimum solution for reducing the risks associated with the cryptocurrency transactions. 4IRE LABS is developing robust solutions using blockchain, machine learning and Internet of Things. Globally, more than 1,000 companies are working on generation, planning, designing, funding, educating, consulting, developing and deploying blockchain products and services. These products could be used in different sectors in the form of blockchains, cryptocurrencies, mining processes, securing of transactions, smart contracts, Proof-of-Work, and many more.

Blockchain Cryptocurrencies

It was in 2012, that one of the authors heard about Onecoin through someone who invested in Onecoin and frequently attending related business meetings in Mumbai, India. Numerous digital currencies have appeared since 2012. These include Bitcoin, Lite coin, Blackcoin, Ethereum, Ripple, Monero, and many more. Table 1 presents the genesis of some of the cryptocurrencies.

Table 1. Cryptocurrencies - Genesis

S.No.	Cryptocurrency	Creator/Coined	Year	Langauge	Developers	Web Portal
1	Bitcoin (BTC)	Satoshi Nakamoto	2008/2009	C++, Java, JavaScript	BitCoin Foundation, Seattle, WA (USA)	https://bitcoin.org/en/
2	Litecoin (LTC)	Charlie Lee	2011	C++	Under the MIT/X11 license	https://litecoin.org/
3	Ripple (XRP)	Ryan Fugger	2012	C/C++, Java, JavaScript, Python, Go	Ripple Labs Inc. San Francisco, California (USA)	https://ripple.com/xrp/
4	DigiByte (DGB)	Jared Tate	2013/2014	Open Source Protocol	The DigiByte Foundation (DF),DigiByte Awareness Team	https://digibyte.io/
5	Ethereum (ETH)	Vitalik Buterin, Gavin Wood	2013/2015	C++, C#, Java, Python, Go, Rust	Ethereum	https://ethereum.org/
6	Tether	Reeve Collins	2014	Open Source Software	Tether Limited	https://tether.to/
7	LibrexCoin (LXC)	Anonymous	2014	C Innovative Libraries	Zerocoin library for native zerocash protocol support	http://www.librexcoin.com/
8	Monero (XMR)	Nicolas van Saberhagen	2014	Korvi, Monero Spelunker, XMR Stak, Wolfs Miner	Multiple people within a community working on the product	https://web.getmonero.org/
9	Dash (DASH)	Evan Duffield	2014	C++	Decentralized Autonomous Organization (DAO)	https://www.dash.org/
10	Zcash (ZEC)	Zooko Wilcox-O'Hearn	2016	C++, Python, Rust, Kotlin, Swift, Go	Electric Coin Company (zcashd), Zcash Foundation (zebra)	https://z.cash/

Blockchain Types

The Blockchain has received significant attention, mostly in the area of financial technology (FinTech). These blockchains are public distributed ledger records in the form of blocks online and inter-linked through computer networks. The Blockchain business has now leapfrogged, since 2017, around the world. Based on the source code, development process, access permissions and maintenance, blockchains are broadly categorized into three groups: Public; Private; and Federated. Refer to Figure 1.

Figure 1. Blockchain Types

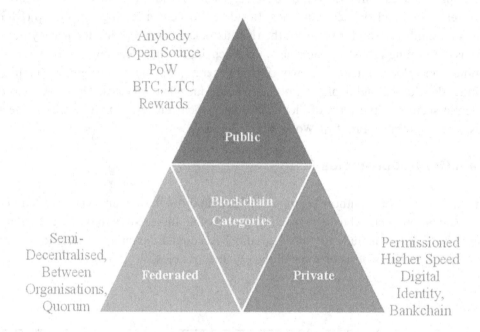

Public Blockchains

One category of blockchain is Public Blockchains. These are completely based on open source technologies. Anybody across the globe can participate anytime from anywhere with any device; the public node is accessible through his or her individual machines or devices. In a Public Blockchain, anyone can participate as user, miner, developer, and community member. All these transactions are anonymous and transparent. In a simple way, it is a platform in which every participant in the network would be able to read on and write to. Anyone can use the source code without any other's permission and run the code on their local systems as per the predefined rules in the Public Blockchain. The Proof of Work (PoW) algorithm is the backbone of the Public Blockchain. However, the auditing can be done by anybody in the network. One of the main advantages of this Public Blockchain configuration is the reduced need for special central database servers and system manager, thereby leading to cost reduction. These have, generally, a token association for designing to reward participants in the network. The examples for this category are Bitcoin, Litecoin, Ethereum, Monero, and Dash, among others.

Private Blockchains

The second category is Private Blockchains, also known as Permissioned Blockchains. Total privileges of reading and writing rights in the source code of blockchain are limited only to the owners/proprietors; and hence, sometimes also called as Closed Blockchain. These Blockchains normally reside within the organisations. A Private Blockchain has restrictions on access and on who can participate in transaction and validation operations. It is a platform in which only the owner of the blockchain has the right to make changes in rules or other terms and conditions. External consumers cannot run a full node, start mining, make transactions or audit the blockchain in a Blockchain explorer. Private Blockchain is private property of an individual or an organization. Private Blockchain networks are deployed for voting, digital identity, asset ownership, and supply chain management (SCM) etc. The transactions per second (TPS) rate is higher in the case of Private Blockchains; however, these are highly scalable. The general activities included in Private Blockchain are access, visibility, storage, and execution. The best example for this sort of blockchain is Bankchain. Another example is MONAX.

Federated Blockchains

Another main category of Blockchains is Federated or Consortium Blockchains. This type inherits a mixture of characteristics of both Public and Private Blockchains. Hence, these may be considered as semi-decentralized. The Consortium Blockchain provides efficiency and security of public blockchains while still allowing for some degree of central control, monitoring and safeguarding. Like Public Blockchain, these are distributed systems and like Private Blockchain, Permissioned Blockchains. Only permitted members with prior approval or voting can become the part of network to carry out the transactions. This kind of Blockchain is between the companies and among the organizations for their day-to-day to financial business operations. Quorum, Hyperledger and Corda blockchains are some of best examples falling under Federated/Consortium Blockchain category.

BLOCKCHAIN COMPONENTS

Blockchain Technology phenomena are having immense applications in various different sectors. Because of the many advantages of blockchain and allied technologies, many startup companies are also mushrooming under the banner of blockchain solutions. Many existing companies are also collaborating for interoperable technological development. For example, Hyperledger is an open-source community focused on developing a suite of stable frameworks, tools and libraries for enterprise-grade blockchain deployments. In this project, Intel, IBM, CISCO, CLS, IC3, Accenture, London Stock Exchange and many more companies are members for the development of Blockchain Technology applications. Many IT/ITeS giants and global financial technology companies have already experienced the first-mover advantages in Blockchain global business. However, new startups are also sharing blockchain commercial profits.

The goal of blockchain technology is to create a decentralized environment where no third party is in control of the transactions and data (Yli-Huumo et al., 2016). Blockchain technology facilitates systems to develop a democratic, open, and scalable digital economy (Wang et al., 2016). As disruptive innovation of the Internet era, it combines several computer technologies, including distributed data storage, point-to-point transmission, consensus mechanisms, and encryption algorithms (Zhang, 2016). The

Blockchain concept involves diverse technologies including distributed digital ledgers, mining process, cryptocurrencies, Proof of Work/Stake (PoW/PoS), smart contracts, security and so on.

The next section elaborates in detail different Blockchain technology components including Distributed Digital Ledgers, Mining Process, Proof-of-Work/&Stake, Smart Contracts, Data Integrity and Security.

Distributed Digital Ledgers

Now days, this term is becoming the buzzword in financial industry. In a digital system, the digital ledger consists of records of digital transactions, maintained at multiple points within a network. Therefore, the online open distributed digital ledgers consist of different nodes in the form of users or computers or systems in the connected blockchain system. These users undertake the transactions at any time. The transactional data records are saved in the form of blocks, and added or inter-linked to the existing blocks in the blockchain. These digital ledgers are saved as separate files or else in a plain form in a database. These blocks are a kind of online data structure keeping all transactions in a distributed network. The chains are a sequence of blocks in a specific order with user, amount, place, date and time with the help of consensus algorithms. All these blocks are recognized by hash technique (e.g. SHA256 Cryptographic Hash Algorithm) on the header of the block. Thus, the Distributed Digital Ledgers are at the heart of the entire Blockchain technology at the back-end level.

Mining Process

The Blockchain business has exponentially grown since 2017. With the development of blockchain technology, Bitcoin mining has become highly popular (Qin et al., 2018). One of the most vital components in blockchain technologies is the mining process. The process is similar to the mining process of ores. In order to create new cryptocurrencies and transactions, this process plays an important role in Blockchain technologies. In mining, blocks are created in about 10 minutes each, after which the solvers of the computation challenges are rewarded currency (Lindman et al., 2017). Mining involves using specialized computer hardware to find a particular mathematical hash function, with the reward for success being payment in new bitcoins/cryptocurrencies (Easley et al., 2019). Miners are actors, who play a crucial role both in creating new cryptocurrencies and in verifying transactions on the blockchain. In Proof-of-Work-based blockchain networks, the block miners participate in a crypto-puzzle solving competition to win the reward of publishing i.e., mining new blocks (Liu et al., 2018). In Blockchain pool mining, Pay-Per-Last-N-Shares is one of the most commonly used reward mechanisms in practice, in which the mining pools will distribute the reward among the miners whose reported shares fall in the last N shares, according to the proportion of the number of shares of the miner in the last N shares (Qin et al., 2018).

Proof-of-Work and Proof of Stake

The Proof-of-Work and Proof-of-Stake are two technical terms people come across in Blockchain technology. There is a misconception about these terms that they are similar. The Proof-of-Work is abbreviated as PoW and Proof-of-Stake as PoS. Both of these are consensus mechanisms that allow distinguishing a valid from an invalid blockchain. This implies that this algorithm resolves the issue of trust between the participants of the network. Some studies state that Cynthia Dwork and Moni Naorin first mentioned the Proof-of-Work concept in 1993 in a journal article. However, some say that Markus Jakobsson and

Ari Juels coined the term "Proof of Work" in 1999. In Bitcoin, hashing is used for 'Proof of Work', a mechanism that links consensus with computing power, making duplication of participants influential to consensus outcomes (Aste et al., 2017).

As regards the Proof of Stake, it is a type of consensus algorithm. Some studies say that Proof of Stake is a substitute process for transaction verification on a blockchain. The role of Proof-of-Stake is to achieve distributed consensus in the blockchain network. In Proof-of-Stake based cryptocurrencies, the creator of the next block is chosen via various combinations of random selection and wealth or age, i.e. the stake. Proof-of-Stake means a form of proof of ownership of the currency. Coin age consumed by a transaction can be considered a form of Proof-of-Stake. We expect Proof-of-Stake designs to become a potentially more competitive form of peer-to-peer crypto-currency than Proof-of-Work designs due to the elimination of dependency on energy consumption (King & Nadal, 2012). The Proof-of-Stake consensus protocol is an interestingly attractive one, which provides the block-inclusion decision-making power to those entities that have stakes in the system irrespective of blockchain's length or history of the public ledger (Tosh et al., 2017).

Smart Contracts

The emerging concept under the umbrella of blockchain technology is Smart Contracts. As automation is becoming the prime part of any kind of business, the contracts between two business parties are also becoming automatic, without any physical presence. The smart contracts are about the business rules implied by the agreement to do the transactions, where parties involved could be individuals or organizations. There is no third-party involvement in the process. These rules and regulations are developed and embedded in the blockchain technology and are encoded with the help of different programming languages.

Smart contracts are computer programs that can be correctly executed by a network of mutually distrusting nodes, without the need of an external trusted authority (Atzei et al. 2017). The transactional agreements between businesses parties by the signatures are verifiable automatically with the help of predefined rules. The validation process of cryptocurrencies between individuals is done using digital signatures and ring signatures. Emerging smart contract systems over decentralized cryptocurrencies allow mutually distrustful parties to transact safely without trusted third parties (Kosba et al., 2016). Thus, this process reduces the cost of travelling, demands lesser material cost, requires lesser manual process, is timesaving, and can be done in real time.

Data Integrity

Data is an invaluable resource. It guides all business decisions in most of the computer-aided human activities. Threats to data integrity are thus of paramount relevance, as tampering with data may maliciously affect crucial business decisions (Gaetani et al., 2017). Data is a vital component in the entire financial transaction process as well. When the cryptocurrencies transactions from different participants are occurring between/among them, irrespective of the currency type, the exact amount of cryptocurrency conversion takes place automatically. The best part is that there are different interoperability techniques, that will help transactions with smoothening operations without failure. In most cases, the data is not at all centrally kept in one place. All the blocks of records of distributed ledgers are stored in the distributed environments with the help of miners witness as proof of transactions. As per the authors' knowledge, central servers, the cloud storages and advanced storage paradigms like data lakes concepts may not be required, as there is no requirement of central repository, except big data storage organizations.

In blockchain technologies, data integrity refers to the assurance of data accuracy and consistency in transaction over the entire life cycle. It is also responsible for the design and usage of any blockchain system and the maintenance of data; that stores, processes, or retrieves data. When we create a transaction in a connected network and is added as a new record of the block to the chain, this block information cannot be modified or changed due to the blockchain technology's immutable nature. Each record, once stored at UCX using the trusted storage feature, will generate a unique hash for the file's content. Put simply, the blockchain integration will ensure transparency, auditability and security of the information processed in the government systems. Due to its strong data integrity guarantees, blockchain can be employed to ensure log integrity, but its current performance limitations hinder actual exploitations (Aniello et al., 2017). Thus, data integrity in Blockchain technologies is about the data corrections, accuracy, backups and availability.

Data Security

Security and Privacy are among the most vital aspects of any business information system. Even though the terms are different, in a broader way their objective is ensuring the privacy for the miner, giving authentication for sender and receiver, securing the transactions in the process end and minimizing the noise errors. The most attractive advantage of blockchain is that the public ledger cannot be modified or deleted after all nodes have approved the data. This is why blockchain is well known for its data integrity and security characteristics (Yli-Huumo et al., 2016). The degree of trust between users determines the technological configuration of a distributed ledger. The online ledger is shared in the network but at the same time, participants get the privacy of their own transactions. Identity of the online financial transactions are not linked to a transaction due to privacy concern, however, all the transactions are authenticated, while identity kept confidential. Besides, for the security of transactions, many cryptography tools and techniques are used at the node level to process these transactions smoothly. Cryptography techniques are the backbone for the blockchain technology. This term 'cryptography' is derived from two Latin words: crypto which means secret, and graph that means writing. That the entire cryptocurrencies transactions happen through secret writing between two parties. The RSA (Rivest–Shamir–Adleman) algorithm is a well-known cryptographic technique for data transmissions among security mechanisms of data communications. In effect, all the cryptocurrencies use private and public keys at the time of online transactions. The encryption key is public and distinct from the decryption key, which is kept secret (private). Based on the same technique, the blockchain technologies security mechanisms are developed for peer-peer secured transactions.

BLOCKCHAIN CASE STUDIES

Laroiya et al. (2020) contemplate that the blockchain technology has the potential to not only 'revolutionize' various industries, but also to 'transform' our lives. The authors quote an IBM survey based on more than three thousand executives from across the world. The survey reported that around 80 per cent of the respondents were either already employing some blockchain technology in their businesses, or were planning to do the same. The authors reported that the technology is being deployed even by the governments, for more transparency in services like transferring payments to public, for removing undesired red-tapes, etc. Wang and Filippi (2020) foresee blockchain as a huge contributor towards achieving a vision of a global self-sovereign identity system. While a sacrosanct definition is yet to emerge, self-sovereign identity can be generally defined as a system wherein individuals have the say in deciding what aspect of their personal identity information can be disclosed in different contexts (Wang & Filippi, 2020).

The focus of this section is to collate case studies from different industries across the globe. For better exposition, this section is divided into four sub-sections, each section focussing on the application of blockchain in different sectors. To exhibit that the phenomenon is global and sweeps across the national boundaries, an effort is made to present cases from varying geographies. Developed as well as emerging economies are endeavoured to be captured.

Banking and Insurance Sectors

In the words of Arnold (2017): barely a day goes by without a fresh announcement about how banks are seeking to use blockchain technology to transform sizeable chunks of their business...Blockchain is the hottest buzzword in the sector...

The financial sector is the first among all the sectors to have witnessed an important application of blockchain technology – in the form of 'crypto-finance' (Casey et al., 2018). Ever since, the magnum as well as the further potential of transformation has been significant. A review of articles, based on financial technology, has discovered 'blockchain' to be one of the most researched aspects of FinTech (Sangwan et al., 2020). Besides, Madakam & Kollu (2020) observe that in blockchain, there is a great a potential to build a radically better financial system. Highlighting the potential and the magnitude of adoption, Mappo (2019) provided a list of more than 200 banks and other financial institutions, which either already used or were soon to use this technology. As of today, more than a year ahead of the report, the count is trusted to have increased substantially. Many authors have highlighted many potential ways in which blockchain can positively change the banking and insurance sectors (e.g. Campbell, 2017; Bramblet, 2018; Harris & Wonglimpiyarat, 2019; Mappo, 2019; Laroiya et al., 2020):

- Payment settlements including cross-border payments can become easier and faster
- Security can be enhanced and therefore it can lead to fraud reduction
- Administrative costs can be minimized by going paperless, and hence low transaction costs
- Transparency among the parties involved in insurance contracts can improve
- Access to information can become faster and more accurate
- Higher efficiency can even translate into lower insurance premiums
- Turnaround time for different processes can reduce
- Owing to other benefits, customer satisfaction can rise.

Substantial savings have been exhibited by use cases on personal auto insurance firms in the US market (Bramblet, 2018). According to a survey of bankers, analysts and consultants conducted by The Financial Times (Arnold, 2017), the five areas expected to undergo the maximum changes are: i) Clearing and settlement, ii) payments, iii) trade finance, iv) identity (customers and other parties), and v) syndicated loans.

The revolution has also touched the central banks of the nations. Priyaranjan et al. (2020) provide details about the projects undertaken by the central banks of different countries on the application of distributed ledger technology. Gil-Pulgar (2019) reported that according to IBM, it is expected that to ensure their continued hold on monetary matters, the central banks might come up with cryptocurrency (Central Bank Digital Currency or CBDC) in the coming five years. The losing of monopoly could also persuade these erstwhile monopolists to look into any lacunae in their existing system and amend. The pace of the dynamism can be grasped by the fact that in stark contrast to this finding. The same study a year ago had reported that the central banks would not launch cryptocurrency in the near future (Esteves, 2018). According to IBM Blockchain, with the CBDC, some lacunae of the existing payment systems can be fixed. The CBDC might bring with it the following advantages (Esteves, 2018):

- Credit risk can be done away with, reducing the volatility of the currency
- By enabling the central banks to issue tokens, liquidity risk can be taken care of
- The operating cost and the complexity of the payment system can be minimised
- The speed and efficiency of the payment system can be enhanced
- Owing to decentralization, real-time settlement of CBDC can be conceived of.

Even the insurance sector has not remained aloof of the development. Bramblet (2018) reported that with an expected compound annual growth rate (CAGR) of 84.9 per cent, the market for blockchain in the insurance sector might grow to $1.39 billion by the year 2023 (it stood at $64.5 million in 2018). A Technology Vision 2019 survey conducted by Accenture reported that more than 80 per cent of the respondents who were insurance executives either already employed or planned to employ the blockchain technology. Another survey by the World Economic Forum and Accenture together reported that 65 of the respondents (insurance executives) believed that the distributed ledger technology was a necessity to adopt to ensure competitiveness. Acknowledging the growing significance of blockchain, Abdeen et al. (2019) proposed a blockchain-based framework for Takaful, the counterpart of insurance contracts in Islamic banking.

The authors Abdeen et al. (2019) state blockchain as: *currently the only viable solution to offer security, transparency, integrity of resources and ensure trustworthiness among customer*. In addition, the application of blockchain in various other financial aspects have been reported or explored. Chang et al. (2020) talk about the possible role of blockchain in trade financing (usage of Letter of Credit). Naheem (2019) discuss the role blockchain technology can play in regulations relating to anti-money laundering. While it is evident that the application of blockchain in the financial services industry is humungous, and many examples can be cited to validate the argument, two case studies – one from an emerging economy (India) and another from a developed economy (Germany) - are presented here to bring home the case in point.

Case: State Bank of India (SBI)

State Bank of India is the largest public commercial bank of India in terms of deposits, assets and profits (State Bank of India, 2020). SBI also holds the honour of hatting the highest number of branches and employees among the commercial banks. It has a long history, and its roots can be traced back to the year 1806. The bank boasts of donning an international presence. The bank has been one of the firsts among Indian banks to embrace the opportunities offered by blockchain.

In February 2017, SBI announced its plan to employ blockchain for prevention of fraud (Mehta, 2017). BankChain was conceived for implementing this proposal (and many others that followed). BankChain describes itself as "a community of banks for exploring, building and implementing block-chain solutions" (BankChain, 2020). At present, it has 37 members, which hail from across the border as well. It has a partnership with stalwarts like Microsoft, IBM, and Intel. As of May 12, 2020, it lists as many as 24 projects, it is involved in. BankChain was proposed to bring many players on-board, to ensure compatibility and ease sharing among themselves. Not only documents, but also even resources can be shared to bring symbiosis. Figure 2 presents a timeline of the progression of announcements and implementation of blockchain at SBI.

Figure 2. Timeline and SBI's blockchain journey

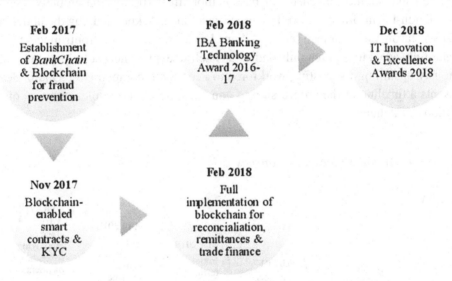

In November 2017, the Bank announced its plan to launch blockchain-enabled smart contracts and Know Your Customer (KYC). The bank also revealed its upcoming innovation centre to explore the applicability of the latest technologies in its operations (ET Bureau, 2017). In February 2018, the bank further revealed its plan to fully implement blockchain for management of reconciliation, remittances, and trade financing during the financial year 2019-20 (Bose, 2018). These initiatives have won the bank various accolades. The bank bagged awards in Indian Bank Association (IBA) Banking Technology Award 2016-17 (SBI in the news, 2018) held in February 2018. SBI was the runner up in Best Use of Digital and Channels Technology for its deliveries that provided convenience to customers. The bank has endeavoured to apply the latest technologies in various services, thereby improving efficiency. Chatbots is one such example that utilizes blockchain. Further, in December 2018, the bank bagged the Best BFSI (Banking, Financial Services and Insurance) in terms of Implementations of Cognitive Technologies Award for AI, blockchain, and digital category (IT Innovation & Excellence Awards 2018). Computer Society of India organized the award. In addition, the bank also won the awards for other technologies. It won the Best Technology Bank of the Year award for its continuous success in launching technology-based customer services. The bank has successfully launched AI, ML and RPA based processes. Further, it was chosen a winner for the most innovative project using Information Technology (IT) for its project 'Automated Real-Time Customer Emotion Feedback (ARTCEF). The bank employed AI, ML and Cognitive to capture customer emotions (and thus, feedback) using a camera. This case hails from an economy (India) where the adoption and maturity level of blockchain was measured to be low in 2016 (Yadav et al., 2018). With huge potential still untapped, the blockchain implementation so far can be just a tip of the iceberg, and continuous progress shall change the face of the banking sector in the times to come.

Case: Allianz SE (Societas Europaea)

The Allianz Company, founded in 1890 in Berlin (Germany), is the market leader in the insurance sector of Germany (Allianz, 2020). As a group, the company has presence in more than 70 nations and employs circa 147,000 human resources. Its customer base is more than 100 million globally. The company is into both life and non-life insurance, as well as into re-insurance. Acknowledging the undeniable technological alteration staring the insurance sector, Allianz has been among the frontrunners to welcome the change and gainfully adapt to it. It not only dedicates itself to explore new solutions, but it also believes in simultaneously upskilling its existing workforce to keep them competitive (Allianz Search, 2020). Figure 3 presents a timeline of the progression of announcements and implementation of blockchain-related operations by Allianz.

Figure 3. Timeline of Allianz's blockchain journey

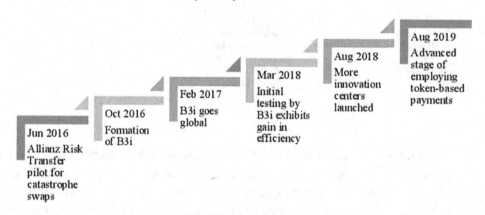

Towards the outcome of Allianz's Disruptive Technologies division and Nephila, one of the early steps of the journey began when Allianz Risk Transfer pilot was successfully run in June 2016. Eventually, Allianz employed blockchain-based smart contracts for managing contracts relating to catastrophe bonds and swaps (Bramblet, 2018). Allianz has been a founding member of the Blockchain Insurance Industry Initiative (B3i), a consortium with a focus on insurance. The consortium was established in October 2016 with an objective of aiding implementation of blockchain in the insurance sector. It also enjoyed the backing of stalwarts like American International Group (AIG) and American Insurance Association (AIA). In February 2017, B3i attracted members from across the globe, giving it an international stature. One of the aims of the consortium was to improve data sharing among the members. It was believed that the application would enhance customer satisfaction by offering improved services.

The consortium also went ahead to develop a prototype smart contract management system. Further, more members joined in October 2017; and the consortium converted into a start-up in 2018 (Bramblet, 2018; Allianz Search, 2020). In March 2018, B3i, the blockchain start-up, exhibited gains in efficiency of up to 30 per cent in the initial testing of its first product. The start-up aimed to commercialize the blockchain-based solutions in the field of insurance and reinsurance.

In August 2018, Allianz Partners established three innovation centres to further explore and employ disruptive technologies including blockchain. With one centre already functioning since 2014, the total went up to four. Pirus (2019) reported in August 2019 that Allianz Global Corporate & Specialty SE was in the process of developing a token-based electronic payment system. The firm visualizes a blockchain-based system for insurance-related payments of different categories.

With the progress observed so far at frequent intervals, the embracing of blockchain still seems a work-in-progress, and many new surprises hopefully await to see the light of the day. Thus, the banking and insurance sectors moved towards employing more of the blockchain technology. The next section will discuss another set of two domain specific blockchain applications in real estate and smart cities.

Real Estate and Smart Cities

The blockchain applications are immense and uncountable as we already discussed in the above sections. Yet another set of sectors that embraced the blockchain technology include real estate and smart cities. Grover et al. (2019) report that the application of blockchain technology in the real estate sector has reached the confirmation stage of the innovation-decision process. The confirmation stage implies that the real estate sector has put the blockchain technology in use, and the results are better than the ones obtained from the previously applicable systems. Wouda and Opdenakker (2019) proposed a blockchain-based application that could improve the efficiency and the speed of transacting in any commercial real estate. Further, according to Laroiya et al. (2020), the real estate sector is expected to gain from the ability of blockchain to maintain data related to ownership records, which cannot be tampered with. Karamitsos et al. (2018) recognize benefits such as more efficient database management, easier to build trust among the parties involved, doing away with the requirements of intermediaries, and more effective invoice management. Moreover, it has applications in Smart Cities/Smart Urban spaces. According to Xie et al. (2019), *blockchain as an emerging technology has many good features, such as trust-free, transparency, pseudonymity, democracy, automation, decentralization, and security. These features of blockchain are helpful to improve smart city services and promote the development of smart cities.*

Focusing on smart cities, Feroz (2020) stated that blockchain could take care of the issues like security, transparency, innovation, and others, which are the heartbeat of a smart city. Adding to it, Shilpi and Ahad (2020) believe that blockchain could be the answer to a safe exchange of information across various components of a smart city system. It is also perceived as the go-to technology for efficient usage of resources, and for keeping frauds in check (Rotuna et al., 2019). Hakak et al. (2020) propose a conceptual framework on the application of blockchain technology for developing a secure smart city. One can use the blockchain applications in Smart Homes, Smart Buildings, and Land registration purposes. Congruent to the pattern of its predecessor, two cases, one based on a developed economy (United States) and another based on an emerging economy (UAE) are presented in this section.

Case: Sotheby's International Realty (SIR)

SIR is a real estate platform that aims to connect the sellers of real estate to their prospective buyers. Established in 1976, the firm now positions itself as a luxury brand and words like 'finest', 'most prestigious', 'exceptional', 'extraordinary', 'distinctive', 'world-class', 'most cherished', and 'connoisseur' stud its web portal (Sotheby's International Realty, 2006-2020). As the name explicitly suggests, the firm is a global player, with its headquarters in the United States of America. As of March 2020, the firm had presence in 70 countries and territories across the globe. More than 23,000 independent sales associates were affiliated with the SIR, and the company had a turnover of $114 billion in the year 2019 (Couch, 2020).

The firm has won various accolades over the years, for example, *Best in Category for Real Estate Franchisee Satisfaction Award* (by Franchise Business Review) continuously for seven years. The brand defines itself as "dedicated to innovation", and this is why blockchain had to happen to the firm. SIR holds the honour of introducing Bitcoin, a blockchain-based cryptocurrency to the world of real estate transactions (Chowdhury, 2019). September 2017 witnessed the first of its kind transaction, when a house was sold for Bitcoin by Kuper SIR, Texas.

SIR holds another 'first'. It was the first luxury real estate firm to collaborate with a tokenization platform. In December 2019, UK SIR collaborated with Smartlands (tokenization platform) to explore the application of blockchain in the real estate sector. The collaboration targeted exploring the employment of Security Token Offering (STO) for the ownership of real estates (Lane, 2019). STO is a crypto token, which is issued to an investor as a proof of her/his investment in the underlying asset. What makes it different from the issuance of other documents as proof (viz., print or digital certificate) is the fact that the record of investment is maintained on a blockchain (Pauw, 2019). Further, the worth is enhanced as law recognizes the STOs. With the marriage of blockchain and real estate, many more applications are expected to be seen in times to come.

Case: Dubai as Smart City

Located in western Asia, Dubai is a city in the United Arab Emirates (UAE). It is one of the most affluent emirates of the UAE, and often called 'a city of skyscrapers' (Davidson, 2020). The author identifies two factors contributing to the magnificent growth witnessed by the city: efficient administrative system, and the welcoming approach for businesses. The city has successfully positioned itself as a global city, and it globally reckoned for business and tourism (Bishr, 2018).

Launched in 2014, Dubai's Smart City strategy targets to make it "the world's smartest city by 2021" (Dubai, 2020). The city is currently pursuing one of the most comprehensive integration programmes involving Information and Communication Technology (ICT), with more than 545 initiatives in progress or under planning. These initiatives are expected to contribute substantially towards the Gross Domestic Products (GDP) of the city. Some of these are:

- Endeavouring to transfer essential government services to the online mode
- Moving towards a smart transportation system of Buses, Metro, Taxi using smart cards
- Providing access to high-speed Wi-Fi throughout the city for free
- Pursuing to achieve a data-driven economy by deploying massive technologies in city axes

As already implied earlier, the city warmly embraces new technologies for building a mark on the world's map. From 1999 to 2015, Dubai has witnessed launch of several strategies (Bishr, 2018). The latest on the list is blockchain strategy launched in October 2016. Figure 4 summarizes the relevant projects. The objective of Dubai's blockchain strategy is to become the first Blockchain-powered city.

Figure 4. Dubai's ICT initiatives - 1999 onwards [Adapted from Bishr (2018)]

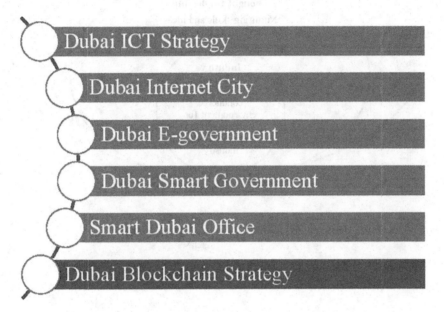

Different players commit the government of Dubai to provide a conducive environment for employment of blockchain across the city and across industries. The print media (The Economic Times) has already called Dubai as 'the world capital of blockchain development' (Mediawire, 2020). As stated by the Director General of the Smart Dubai Office, there are three pillars of the Blockchain strategy, as depicted in Figure 5 (Bishr, 2018).

As of February 2020, the city had already put in use 24 use cases of blockchain across as many as eight industries. Refer to Figure 6, adapted from Mediawire (2020). Further, the city had launched the Dubai Blockchain Platform and the Dubai Blockchain Policy (Mediawire, 2020). The Dubai Blockchain Platform engages IBM as a partner, and aids the Dubai government units in developing use cases. The Dubai Blockchain Policy is a manual covering all the learnings of Dubai in implementation of blockchain, and aims to act as a guide for others across the globe. The most interesting part, the Policy is accessible for free by the world.

All these initiatives have led to the growth rate of blockchain market in Dubai being higher than the world average (Mediawire, 2020). With the ecstatic vision of making Dubai 'the happiest city on earth' (Smart Dubai, 2020), the authors (and probably the world) very hopefully await how the progress of the city unfolds. It might act as 'path-paver' and lead the world to a new unseen sphere. Currently all upcoming smart cities projects across the globe including PlanIT Valley in Portugal, Masdar in UAE, Padova in Italy, and Smart City Kochi in India in brainstorming of this technology implementation as part of civic service facilities.

Figure 5. Dubai's Blockchain strategy

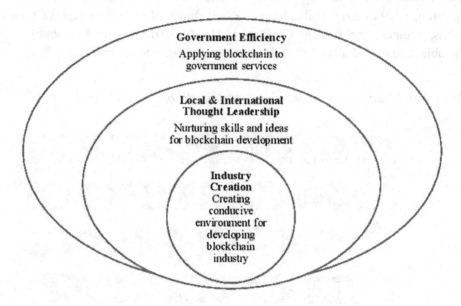

Figure 6. Dubai blockchain strategy implementation across sectors

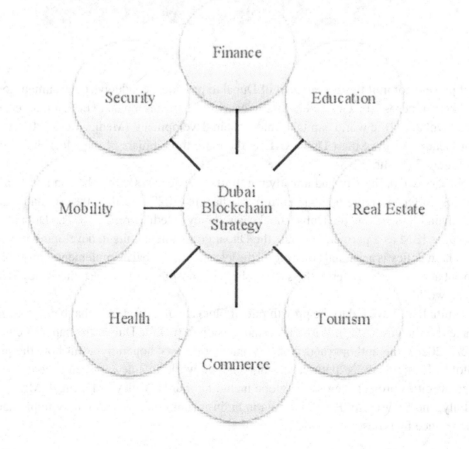

Manufacturing and Supply Chain Firms

As Shah (2018) reminds us: blockchain is a technology that is attractive to manufacturers looking to solve a problem... But it's expected that ... with the wider availability of cheap, ubiquitous computing—blockchain applications will become relevant to even the most stodgy manufacturers.

While the financial sector appears as the frontrunner when one thinks of blockchain applications, the technology has successfully exhibited its applicability in various other sectors. This sub-section focuses on the manufacturing and the supply chain sectors.

Researchers have identified multiple areas through which blockchain is redefining the manufacturing sector and supply chain, viz. data protection, communication, trust among unseen players, process improvement, management of intellectual property rights, and keeping an eye on the maintenance of certain tangible assets (Shah, 2018; Kurpjuweit et al., 2019; Kasten, 2020). Similarly, for the automotive sector, Dorri et al. (2017) proposed that the blockchain technology could address issues such as data privacy, and vehicle security. Further, in the words of Fraga-Lamas and Fernández-Caramés (2019), *One of the latest technologies that can benefit the automotive industry is blockchain, which can enhance its data security, privacy, anonymity, traceability, accountability, integrity, robustness, transparency, trustworthiness, and authentication, as well as provide long-term sustainability and higher operational efficiency to the whole industry.* In this section, the stories of two firms, which are adopting Blockchain technologies, one originating from an emerging economy (China) and the other from a developed economy (Japan) are included as the cases. Besides, there are many global and local manufacturing, automobile, and supply chain companies set to employ blockchain technologies for their day-to-day business operations.

Case: Toyota Motor Corporation (Toyota)

Toyota Motor Corporation is the market leader in the automotive sector of Japan, besides holding a sturdy position at the global level. Headquartered in Japan, the firm has roots dated 1933. The firm fathers close to 600 subsidiaries across geography. The firm is into the manufacturing of automobiles, commercial vehicles, industrial vehicles, and spare parts (Duignan, 2020). Nurturing innovation can be stated as a part of culture of the firm. With an aim to boost research, Toyota Research Institute was established in 2015 in the United States. Further, recently, the firm explicated its commitment to providing continued services in the novel CASE areas, including connected cars, autonomous /automated driving, Shared and Electric (Toyota, 2020). The initial small steps of the firm evident to public in the world of blockchain, can be traced back to December 2016, when the firm, in partnership with blockchain-active firms like Digital Garage Inc., invited proposals for Toyota Next Open Innovation program. The aim was to employ innovative technologies and solutions for business problems. The Toyota Research Institute, in collaboration with Massachute Institute of Technology (MIT) Media Lab and other industry partners, announced exploring blockchain technology for developing mobility ecosystem (Toyota Canada Newsroom, 2017). In May 2017, the plan was announced with a belief of accelerating the progress of autonomous driving technique. In April 2019, The Toyota Motor Corporation and Toyota Financial Services Corporation together set up Toyota Blockchain Lab, a virtual organization for exploring the applications of blockchain in business ideas. In May 2019, the firm collaborated with The University of Tokyo and Trende Inc. to begin the testing of blockchain-based electricity trading system. The firms had a vision

Figure 7. Timeline of Toyota's blockchain journey

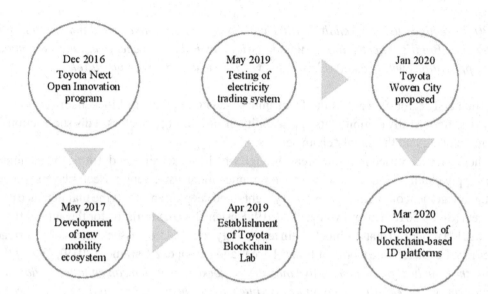

of developing next-generation electricity systems that could enable individuals and businesses to trade electricity among themselves.

The firm proposed its plan, in January 2020, to build Toyota Woven City in Japan. With a vision to improve the lifestyle in future, it is expected to be a 'living laboratory' for researchers, providing them with real-life environment for developing technologies (Toyota Woven City, 2020). The Toyota Blockchain Lab in March 2020 announced its plan to pool in partner companies and thus, expand collaborations more than ever (Toyota, 2020). The Lab also worked on global collaboration among Toyota Group companies for symbiotic use of resources. Furthermore, the firm revealed development of a blockchain-based ID (Identifier) platform for individuals as well as vehicles, built in collaboration with Securitize (Bourne, 2020). The platforms can be employed multifariously i.e. personal ID platform can be harnessed by employers to maintain employee-related benefits; vehicle ID platform can be harnessed to maintain records related to vehicle registration, maintenance, and others. Figure 7 summarizes the blockchain journey of Toyota. With many proposals already in pipeline, the best might yet to come from the visionary portfolio of Toyota.

Case: Alibaba.com

Alibaba Group is a conglomerate, with Alibaba.com being one of its businesses operating in the area of e-commerce. Headquartered in China, the Group was founded in 1999 (Alibaba Group, 2020). As of the end of 2019, the Group employed more than 116,000 employees. The Group is into multiple businesses, viz., commerce, cloud computing, innovation, digital media and entertainment. It might appear young by age, but it is mighty by deeds and has already proved its mettle in several fields. Alibaba.com is a leading platform for global wholesale and trade. In 2018, the company held the honour of being China's largest integrated international online wholesale marketplace by revenue (Alibaba Group, 2020). The customer base of the company spreads across more than 190 countries. Besides, the company provides supply chain services to its members.

The employment of blockchain by Alibaba should not come as a surprise since even the foundations of the Group was based on leveraging technologies. The founders believed that innovation and technology could be capitalized on, to provide a level playing field to a smaller business competing with bigger counterparts. The company endeavours to act as a platform for merchants and other business players to help them grow their market reach using new technologies. In 2017, Alibaba organized annual Computing Conference, with blockchain as one of the themes. One of its businesses already offers Blockchain as a Service (BaaS). In October 2018, the Group expanded the customer base for its offering BaaS to cover Asia, Europe and the United States. The Group also owns an initiative called 'Charities on the Chain', which is blockchain-based charity recordkeeping that provides transparency and traceability of donations (Ledger Insights, 2020).

Alibaba had collaborated with Australia Post and PwC in March 2017, with an aim to explore the possible role of blockchain in fighting the problem of food fraud. A year later, in April 2018, Alibaba while shipping products (food items/health supplements) from Australia and New Zealand to China (Barbaschow, 2018) undertook a pilot test of applying blockchain for supply chain. The vice president of the Group had announced in March 2019 that the Group was considering the usage of blockchain for cross-border supply chain (Yakubowski, 2019). In March 2020, the group announced its plan to employ blockchain for its supply chain, with an objective of enhancing the transparency of the chain (Kastelein, 2020). It can enable the customers to track the source of origin and current position of goods in the supply chain. The customers can access the details about logistics for any product by scanning a Quick Response (QR) code (Peng, 2020). Peng (2020) also further reported that Alibaba foresaw the following benefits of engaging in the blockchain-based supply chain:

- It can ease the tracking of goods
- It can avoid the problem of mismatch between goods and logistics information
- It can assist in clearly defining the responsibility of the concerned party in the supply chain

In addition, as Sharma (2019) reported, the blockchain technology can also help in verifying the authenticity of the goods, by making the entries of the ledger tamper-proof. All these benefits are expected to enhance consumer confidence (Barbaschow, 2018). With another application of blockchain aimed at enhancing the consumer experience and many giants including Alibaba already in the fray, the supply chain is poised to witness changes in the rules of the game.

Energy and Telecom

The other set of industries enjoying the disruption with the advent of blockchain technology are the network-operating sectors, especially energy and telecom. Andoni et al. (2019) report on the evident rise in the number of blockchain-based start-ups and projects in the energy sector. Based on their review, the authors conclude that the blockchain might be the answer to some of the problems thriving in this sector. Teufel et al. (forthcoming) argue that blockchain technologies can be employed for the trading of energy, storage of information, and achieving greater transparency in transactions. The authors coin the term 'blockchain energy' to refer to blockchain technologies employable in the energy domain. Acknowledging that the applications also involve challenges, the authors especially mention the need to address the challenge of cybersecurity. Further, anticipating that the future of the energy sector would involve a decentralization of energy generators, Worner et al. (2019) foresee blockchain to play a pertinent role in the process.

On similar lines as the energy sector, decentralization is seen in the future of the telecom sector as well. Kabbinale et al. (2020) believe that with the onset of decentralization, blockchain technology would be the platform to record the economic aspects of the transactions in a transparent manner. Cryptocurrencies and smart contracts would also come to the rescue. Praveen et al. (forthcoming) propose that with the stepping up of 5G technology in the telecom, blockchain would provide the required enhanced privacy and security to the parties involved. Khalaf et al. (2020) propose a new algorithm of blockchain technology, that they perceive would be relevant for the new generation of telecom. Adding a different angle, Lee (2018) proposed the usage of blockchain for ID as a Service (BIDaaS), which could be employed for identity management of mobile users. Wang et al. (2019) summarize possible blockchain networks' application in telecom.

Similar to the previous sections, the cases that follow are based on companies originating from an emerging (South Africa) and a developed (Finland) economy.

Case: Sun Exchange (SE)

Sun Exchange is the world's first peer-to-peer solar leasing platform (Sun Exchange, 2019). The installation partners of the company provide installation and maintenance services to owners of solar cells, who lease out their solar cells to business houses. This service puts in the hands of people in general, a source to earn money by merely owning solar cells and offering them on lease. With roots emanating from South Africa, the company was started in 2014, and the central idea that drove the founder was concerned about climate change. The founder's realization about the speed, ease and efficiency of sending cryptocurrency for international remittance was what fits the piece of blockchain into this jigsaw puzzle. The payments to owners of solar cells are made either in local currency, or in cryptocurrency. As of March 2018, the company had members spread across 70 countries. As of 2019, the number rose to 155, a growth of 121 per cent in a year.

Sun Exchange was awarded the *Best Bitcoin/Blockchain in Africa Award* two years in a row – 2016 and 2017. In June 2017, SE won the Smart Dubai Office Global Blockchain Challenge competing against 20 blockchain-based players from across the globe. In March 2018, the company launched SUNEX Network token sale for public, a platform to 'monetize sunshine' and earn cryptocurrency by leasing solar cells. It is proposed to act as an insurance fund for solar projects. Year 2019 brought many more awards and recognition, one of them being the Disruptor Daily's *Blockchain in Energy Use Case Awards*. The company operates a blockchain-based framework that maintains records of owners of the solar cells and their earnings. Being tamper-proof, these records act as the basis for regulators to compute toll charges and apply through smart contracts. Records of both the consumers and the sellers are recorded on blockchain platform, and this eases the requirement of administering these records.

While this minimizes the administrative expenses, blockchain is also expected to contribute in reducing carbon emission (Sun Exchange, 2019; Ellsmoor, 2019a). The company reports of having saved 1,280 tonnes of CO_2 as of 2019. By resorting to solar energy, SE also contributes in saving the non-renewable sources from getting consumed. In addition, the projects also aid the consumers in saving their expenses on energy. The company has reported savings to the tune of 30 per cent by schools and other organizations. Talking about the applications of blockchain in the energy sector in general, Ellsmoor (2019b) states that many of the new entrants are employing blockchain technology for maintaining smart grid. By sharing data with consumers in real-time, the system enables them to choose their source of purchase of energy. This, in turn, enhances the efficiency of allocation and pricing, by making the market competitive. With the company so young and still in the stage of exploring and expanding, the benefits from application of blockchain in the energy sector are expected to boom in the times to come.

Case: Nokia

Nokia is a Finnish company founded in 1865, with operations in telecommunication, information technology, and consumer electronics (Nokia, 2020b). The tagline of the company, "We create the technology to connect the world", reveals the technology-centric nature of Nokia. The company boasts of …adapting to the needs of an ever-changing world for over 150 years, and of being acknowledged for …leadership in shaping the future of technology (Nokia, 2020a). The company offers products and services from end consumers to service providers to industries and sectors. The company is into providing network equipment, software, services, and licensing opportunities at a global platform. As of 2019, Nokia employed more than 98,000 employees across five continents. In 2019, the company was reported to be the top ranked telecom service provider as per market share (Nokia, 2019).

In December 2016, Nokia initiated and established Open Ecosystem Network, a hub to act as a platform for open collaboration and innovation. It attracted participation from various industries, and in its first year of operation, launched 100 projects on recent innovations like blockchain (Cangl, 2017). In April 2018, Nokia announced of entering into partnership with a blockchain start-up with an aim to make mobile connections available to remote rural population (Coleman, 2018). In May 2018, Nokia also announced of collaboration with a blockchain data platform Streamr (and a software company OSIsoft) to aid Nokia customers to control their own data, and to enter into transactions with IoT devices (Floyd, 2018). The participants can transact real-time data for cryptocurrency employing smart contracts. Nokia offers Sensing as a Service (SaaS) to its clients, who are operators. The service enables the operators to remotely monitor their network assets. While improving the operational efficiency of the service providers, this digitization also provides them a new source of revenue, the blockchain-based smart contracts for which are created automatically (Nokia, 2020c). In April 2019, Nokia's SaaS was employed by an Israeli telecom company Cellcom Israel. The companies together also employed blockchain-based IoT data shop to enhance transparency of data and provide better innovation opportunities (Kfar-Saba, 2019). In August 2019, IBM, in collaboration with Nokia and other players, launched a blockchain network *Trust Your Supplier* (Crouse, 2019). The network aims to provide digital identities to suppliers, and thus improve supplier management. According to David Post, managing director of IBM Blockchain Ventures, the presence of Nokia and Vodafone as founding members of the platform would help in exploring the ways the network would benefit the telecom sector. More innovations, more collaborations, and the resulting ecosystems are sure to discover more ideas and bring for telecom, newer blockchain-based faces.

CONCLUSION

The Blockchain Technologies phenomenon is highly attractive. Its advantages and applications are numerous and so this technology is of interest to nearly all business corporations. This disruptive financial technology is nothing but capability to conduct transactions anytime from anywhere with any device by anyone for smoothening financial operation in the network. Therefore, all organisations in finance, insurance, mobility, manufacturing, supply chain, judicial, governance, education, healthcare, energy, real estate, tourism, hotel and service sectors are attempting to adopt this technology for operational efficiency. From barter systems to coins minting, currency notes, credit/debit cards and even the online transactions and financial apps, none are comparable to this innovative disruptive technology.

This book chapter explores the systematic literature, concepts, and components. Moreover, detailed different case studies are discussed in the book chapter. Still a lot of research is going on for the development related to new tools, techniques, mining process, new cryptocurrencies, securing the transactions for even better financial operations. We are hearing a lot about cryptocurrencies, these days, which are essential in our daily transactions. Different digital currencies like Bitcoin, Blackcoin, Litecoin, Ripple, Monero, Tither, LibrexCoin, and Zcash are becoming popular but there are also concerns. The reason is that there is no clear official permission from the governments to adopt these cryptocurrencies for business activities. However, hoping that in the coming years, the world all over will definitely embrace this disruptive technology for business as well as personal financial needs.

ACKNOWLEDGMENT

The infrastructure, including library, databases, computational devices, and technological support, provided by FORE School of Management, New Delhi is gratefully appreciated.

REFERENCES

Abdeen, M., Jan, S., Khan, S., & Ali, T. (2019). Employing Takaful Islamic Banking through state of the art blockchain: A case study. *International Journal of Advanced Computer Science and Applications*, *10*(2), 648–654. doi:10.14569/IJACSA.2019.0101283

Alibaba Group. (2020). *Home*. Retrieved from https://www.alibabagroup.com/en/global/home

Allianz. (2020). *At a glance*. Retrieved from https://www.allianz.com/en/about-us/who-we-are/at-a-glance.html

Andoni, M., Robu, V., Flynn, D., Abram, S., Geach, D., Jenkins, D., McCallum, P., & Peacock, A. (2019). Blockchain. *Renewable & Sustainable Energy Reviews*, *100*(February), 143–174. doi:10.1016/j.rser.2018.10.014

Aniello, L., Baldoni, R., Gaetani, E., Lombardi, F., Margheri, A., & Sassone, V. (2017, September). A prototype evaluation of a tamper-resistant high performance blockchain-based transaction log for a distributed database. In *2017 13th European Dependable Computing Conference (EDCC)* (pp. 151-154). IEEE.

Arnold, M. (2017). *Five ways banks are using blockchain*. Retrieved from https://www.ft.com/content/615b3bd8-97a9-11e7-a652-cde3f882dd7b

Aste, T., Tasca, P., & Di Matteo, T. (2017). Blockchain technologies: The foreseeable impact on society and industry. *Computer, 50*(9), 18-28.

Atzei, N., Bartoletti, M., & Cimoli, T. (2017, April). A survey of attacks on ethereum smart contracts (sok). In *International conference on principles of security and trust* (pp. 164-186). Springer.

BankChain. (2020). *Home*. Retrieved from https://www.bankchaintech.com/index.php

Barbaschow, A. (2018). *Alibaba pilots blockchain supply chain initiative down under*. Retrieved from https://www.zdnet.com/article/alibaba-pilots-blockchain-supply-chain-initiative-down-under/

Bayer, D., & Haber, S., & Stornetta, W. S. (1992, March). Improving the Efficiency and Reliability of Digital Time-Stamping. *Sequences.*, *2*, 329–334.

Bishr, A. B. (2018). Dubai: A city powered by Blockchain. *Innovations/Blockchain for Global Development II, 12*(3/4), 4-8.

Blidholm, G., & Johnson, M. (2018). *The adoption of distributed ledger technology in trade and export finance operations of Swedish banks*. Academic Press.

Bose, S. (2018). *SBI to deploy blockchain in three functions in FY19*. Retrieved from https://www.financialexpress.com/industry/sbi-to-deploy-blockchain-in-three-functions-in-fy19/1058852/

Bourne, J. (2020). *Toyota and Securitize develop blockchain-based ID platform*. Retrieved from https://blockchaintechnology-news.com/2020/03/toyota-and-securitize-develop-blockchain-based-id-platform/

Bramblet, J. (2018). *Ultimate guide to blockchain in insurance*. Retrieved from https://insuranceblog.accenture.com/ultimate-guide-to-blockchain-in-insurance

Brito, J., & Castillo, A. (2013). Bitcoin: A primer for policymakers. Mercatus Center at George Mason University.

Bureau, E. T. (2017). *SBI to use blockchain for smart contracts and KYC by next month*. Retrieved from https://economictimes.indiatimes.com/industry/banking/finance/banking/sbi-to-use-blockchain-for-smart-contracts-and-kyc-by-next-month/articleshow/61715860.cms?from=mdr

Campbell, R. (2017). *Which major banks have adopted or are adopting the blockchain?* Retrieved from https://blockchain.works-hub.com/learn/Which-Major-Banks-Have-Adopted-or-Are-Adopting-the-Blockchain

Cangl, G. (2017). *Year one: Open Ecosystem Network has a lot to celebrate*. Retrieved from https://www.nokia.com/blog/year-one-open-ecosystem-network-lot-celebrate/

Casey, M., Crane, J., Gensler, G., Johnson, S., & Narula, N. (2018). *The impact of blockchain technology on finance: A catalyst for change (Geneva Reports on the World Economy 21)*. International Center for Monetary and Banking Studies.

Casey, M. J. (2015, Apr. 15). Moneybeat/BitBeat: Blockchains without coins stir tensions in Bitcoin Community. *The Wall Street Journal*.

Chang, S. E., Luo, H. L., & Chen, Y. C. (2020). Blockchain. *Sustainability*, *12*(1), 1–16. doi:10.3390u12010188

Chowdhury, N. (2019). Inside Blockchain, Bitcoin, and Cryptocurrencies. CRC Press.

Coeckelbergh, M., & Reijers, W. (2016). Cryptocurrencies as narrative technologies. *ACM SIGCAS Computers and Society*, *45*(3), 172–178. doi:10.1145/2874239.2874264

Coleman, L. (2018). *Why Nokia is partnering with a crypto startup to build an IoT network*. Retrieved from https://www.ccn.com/nokia-community-hosted-networks-to-bring-revenue-opportunities-to-remote-areas/

Couch, M. (2020). *Sotheby's International Realty opens first office in Ukraine*. Retrieved from https://www.sothebysrealty.com/extraordinary-living-blog/sothebys-international-realty-opens-first-office-in-ukraine

Crosby, M. N., Pattanayak, P., Verma, S., & Kalyanaraman, V. (2016). Blockchain technology: Beyond bitcoin. *Applied Innovation Review*, *2*, 6–19.

Crouse, M. (2019). *IBM's blockchain network gives digital identities to suppliers*. Retrieved from https://www.fiercetelecom.com/telecom/ibm-s-blockchain-network-gives-digital-identities-to-suppliers

Dash, & Behera, P. C. (2017). Blockchain. *International Journal of Information Science and Computing*, *4*(1), 27–39. doi:10.5958/2454-9533.2017.00004.7

Davidson, C. (2020). *Dubai-United Arab Emirates*. Retrieved from https://www.britannica.com/place/Dubai-United-Arab-Emirates

Dorri, A., Steger, M., Kanhere, S. S., & Jurdak, R. (2017). BlockChain: A distributed solution to automotive security and privacy. *IEEE Communications Magazine*, *55*(12), 119–125. doi:10.1109/MCOM.2017.1700879

Dubai. (2020). *How advanced ICT drives Dubai's Smart City*. Retrieved from https://www.visitdubai.com/en/business-in-dubai/why-dubai/news-and-insights/becoming-the-worlds-smartest-city

Duignan, B. (2020). *Toyota Motor Corporation*. Retrieved from https://www.britannica.com/topic/Toyota-Motor-Corporation.

Easley, D., O'Hara, M., & Basu, S. (2019). From mining. *Journal of Financial Economics*, *134*(1), 91–109. doi:10.1016/j.jfineco.2019.03.004

Ellsmoor, J. (2019a). *Meet 5 companies spearheading blockchain for renewable energy*. Retrieved from https://www.forbes.com/sites/jamesellsmoor/2019/04/27/meet-5-companies-spearheading-blockchain-for-renewable-energy/#52efffb5f2ae

Ellsmoor, J. (2019b). *Blockchain is the next big thing for renewable energy*. Retrieved from https://www.forbes.com/sites/jamesellsmoor/2019/04/27/blockchain-is-the-next-big-thing-for-renewable-energy/#164c089d48c1

Esteves, R. (2018). *IBM survey: No major central bank will implement CBDCs in the near-term*. Retrieved from https://www.newsbtc.com/2018/10/27/ibm-survey-no-major-central-bank-will-implement-cbdcs-in-the-near-term/

Extance, A. (2015). The future of cryptocurrencies: Bitcoin and beyond. *NATNews*, *526*(7571), 21. PMID:26432223

Felin, T., & Lakhani, K. (2018). What problems will you solve with blockchain? *MIT Sloan Management Review*, *60*(1), 32–38.

Feroz, N. (2020). A systematic review of blockchain-based services for security upgradation of a smart city. *EAI Endorsed Transactions on Smart Cities*. . doi:10.4108/eai.13-7-2018.163840

Floyd, D. (2018). *Nokia is letting consumers monetize their data with blockchain.* Retrieved from https://www.coindesk.com/streamr-announces-partnership-with-nokia-osisoft

Fraga-Lamas, P., & Fernández-Caramés, T. M. (2019). A review on blockchain technologies for an advanced and cyber-resilient automotive industry. *IEEE Access: Practical Innovations, Open Solutions*, *7*(January), 17578–17598. doi:10.1109/ACCESS.2019.2895302

Gaetani, E., Aniello, L., Baldoni, R., Lombardi, F., Margheri, A., & Sassone, V. (2017). *Blockchain-based database to ensure data integrity in cloud computing environments.* Academic Press.

Gatteschi, V., Lamberti, F., Demartini, C., Pranteda, C., & Santamaría, V. (2018). Blockchain. *Future Internet*, *10*(2), 20. doi:10.3390/fi10020020

Gil-Pulgar, J. (2019). *IBM: Central banks will launch digital currencies within 5 years.* Retrieved from https://bitcoinist.com/ibm-central-bank-issued-cryptocurrency-five-years/

Grigoriadou, V. (2019). Blockchain. *Homo Virtualis*, *2*(1), 50–56. doi:10.12681/homvir.20194

Grover, P., Kar, A. K., & Janssen, M. (2019). Diffusion of blockchain technology - Insights from academic literature and social media analytics. *Journal of Enterprise Information Management*, *32*(5), 735–757. doi:10.1108/JEIM-06-2018-0132

Haber, S., & Stornetta, W. S. (1991, January). How to time-stamp a digital document. *Journal of Cryptology*, *3*(2), 99–111. doi:10.1007/BF00196791

Hakak, S., Khan, W. Z., Gilkar, G. A., Imran, M., & Guizani, N. (2020). Securing smart citiessmart cities. *IEEE Network*, *34*(1), 8–14. doi:10.1109/MNET.001.1900178

Harris, W. L., & Wonglimpiyarat, J. (2019). Blockchain. *Foresight*, *21*(6), 625–639. doi:10.1108/FS-12-2018-0113

Hütten, M. (2017). *Soft Spots of Hard Code: The Emergence, Proliferation, and Pitfalls of the Blockchain Technology* (Doctoral dissertation). Goethe University of Frankfurt.

Insights, L. (2020). *Alibaba's cross-border e-commerce platform uses blockchain for traceability.* Retrieved from https://www.ledgerinsights.com/alibaba-blockchain-cross-border-e-commerce-kaolo-traceability/

IT Innovation & Excellence Awards 2018. (2018). *Overview.* Retrieved from https://www.csimumbai.org/it2025-18/award.html

Janssen, M., Weerakkody, V., Ismagilova, E., Sivarajah, U., & Irani, Z. (2020). A framework for analysing blockchain technology adoption: Integrating institutional, market and technical factors. *International Journal of Information Management*, *50*, 302–309. doi:10.1016/j.ijinfomgt.2019.08.012

Kabbinale, A. R., Dimogerontakis, E., Selimi, M., Ali, A., Navarro, L., Sathiaseelan, A., & Crowcroft, J. (2020). Blockchain. *Concurrency and Computation*, *32*(12), e5349. doi:10.1002/cpe.5349

Karamitsos, I., Papadaki, M., & Al Barghuthi, N. B. (2018). Design of the blockchain smart contract: A use case for real estate. *Journal of Information Security*, *9*(03), 177–190. Security doi:10.4236/jis.2018.93013

Kastelein, R. (2020). *Alibaba Group implementing blockchain technology for the world's largest eCommerce site*. Retrieved from https://www.the-blockchain.com/2020/03/23/alibaba-group-implementing-blockchain-technology-for-the-worlds-largest-ecommerce-site/

Kasten, J. E. (2020). Engineering and manufacturing on the blockchain: A systematic review. *IEEE Engineering Management Review*, *48*(1), 31–47. doi:10.1109/EMR.2020.2964224

Kfar-Saba. (2019). *Cellcom Israel to deploy Nokia's Sensing as a Service*. Retrieved from https://www.nokia.com/about-us/news/releases/2019/04/12/cellcom-israel-to-deploy-nokias-sensing-as-a-service/

Khalaf, O. I., Abdulsahib, G. M., Kasmaei, H. D., & Ogudo, K. A. (2020). A new algorithm on application of blockchain technology in live stream video transmissions and telecommunications. *International Journal of e-Collaboration*, *16*(1), 16–32. doi:10.4018/IJeC.2020010102

Khatal, S., Rane, J., Patel, D., Patel, P., & Busnel, Y. (2020, January). FileShare: A Blockchain and IPFS framework for Secure File Sharing and Data Provenance. *International Conference on Modelling, Simulation & Intelligent Computing (MoSICom 2020)*.

King, S., & Nadal, S. (2012). *Ppcoin: Peer-to-peer crypto-currency with proof-of-stake*. self-published paper.

Köhler, S., & Pizzol, M. (2019). Life Cycle Assessment of Bitcoin. *Environmental Science & Technology*, *53*(23), 13598–13606. doi:10.1021/acs.est.9b05687 PMID:31746188

Kosba, A., Miller, A., Shi, E., Wen, Z., & Papamanthou, C. (2016, May). Hawk: The blockchain model of cryptography and privacy-preserving smart contracts. In *2016 IEEE symposium on security and privacy (SP)* (pp. 839-858). IEEE.

Kurpjuweit, S., Schmidt, C. G., Klockner, M., & Wagner, S. M. (2019). BlockchainBlockchain. *Early View*, (Special Issue), jbl.12231. Advance online publication. doi:10.1111/jbl.12231

Lane, M. (2019). *The tokenisation revolution: Smartlands and Sotheby's partner up*. Retrieved from https://www.propertyinvestortoday.co.uk/breaking-news/2019/12/the-tokenisation-revolution-smartlands-and-sothebys-partner-in-joint-experiment?source=trending

Laroiya, C., Saxena, D., & Komalavalli, C. (2020). Applications of blockchain technology. In S. Krishnan, V. E. Balas, E. G. Julie, Y. H. Robinson, S. Balaji, & R. Kumar (Eds.), Handbook of Research on Blockchain Technology (pp. 213–243). Academic Press. doi:10.1016/B978-0-12-819816-2.00009-5

Lee, J.-H. (2018). BIDaaS: Blockchain. *IEEE Access: Practical Innovations, Open Solutions*, *6*, 2274–2278. doi:10.1109/ACCESS.2017.2782733

Lindman, J., Tuunainen, V. K., & Rossi, M. (2017). *Opportunities and risks of Blockchain Technologies–a research agenda*. Academic Press.

Liu, X., Wang, W., Niyato, D., Zhao, N., & Wang, P. (2018). Evolutionary game for mining. *IEEE Wireless Communications Letters*, 7(5), 760–763. doi:10.1109/LWC.2018.2820009

Lundström, S., & Öhman, S. (2019). *Generating Value through Blockchain Technology: The Case of Trade Finance*. Academic Press.

Madakam, S., & Kollu, S (2020). Blockchain Technologies Fundamentals–Perceptions, Principles, Procedures and Practices. *Journal of Social and Management Sciences, 345*.

Manrique, S. (2018). *Blockchain: A Proof of Trust*. Retrieved from: https://repository.tudelft.nl/islandora/object/uuid%3Ac1996e12-1462-4683-8716-72110c665d4c

Mappo. (2019). *Comprehensive List of Banks using Blockchain Technology*. Retrieved from https://medium.com/predict/comprehensive-list-of-banks-using-blockchain-technology-dc39ce5b6573

Martin, K. (2016, Sept. 27). CLS dips into blockchain to net new currencies. *Financial Times*.

Mediawire. (2020). *Dubai- the world capital of blockchain development*. Retrieved from https://economictimes.indiatimes.com/tech/ites/dubai-the-world-capital-of-blockchain-development/articleshow/74224682.cms

Mehta, S. (ET Bureau). (2017). *SBI takes lead in blockchain, to use it to prevent fraud*. Retrieved from https://economictimes.indiatimes.com/markets/stocks/news/sbi-takes-lead-in-blockchain-to-use-it-to-prevent-fraud/articleshow/57178212.cms

Mihigo, E. (2019). *Culture Within the 4th Industrial Revolution: How Botho can help Blockchain become a key driver of Sustainable Development in Botswana*. Academic Press.

Mushtaq, A., & Haq, I. U. (2019, February). Implications of Blockchain in Industry 4. O. In *2019 International Conference on Engineering and Emerging Technologies (ICEET)* (pp. 1-5). IEEE.

Naheem, M. A. (2019). Exploring the links between AML, digital currencies and blockchain technology. *Journal of Money Laundering Control*, 22(3), 515–526. doi:10.1108/JMLC-11-2015-0050

Nakamoto, S. (2008). *Bitcoin: A peer-to-peer electronic cash system*. https://bitcoin.org/bitcoin.pdf

Narayanan, A., Bonneau, J., Felten, E., Miller, A., & Goldfeder, S. (2016). Bitcoin and cryptocurrency technologies: a comprehensive introduction. Princeton University Press.

Nehaï, Z., & Guerard, G. (2017, May). Integration of the blockchain in a smart grid model. In *Proceedings of the 14th International Conference of Young Scientists on Energy Issues (CYSENI 2017), Kaunas, Lithuania* (pp. 25-26). Academic Press.

Nian, L. P., & Chuen, D. L. K. (2015). A light touch of regulation for virtual currencies. In *Handbook of Digital Currency* (pp. 309–326). Academic Press. doi:10.1016/B978-0-12-802117-0.00016-3

Nokia. (2019). *Nokia ranked as the top telecom software business by market share*. Retrieved from https://www.nokia.com/about-us/news/releases/2019/10/08/nokia-ranked-as-the-top-telecom-software-business-by-market-share/

Nokia. (2020a). *About us*. Retrieved from https://www.nokia.com/about-us/

Nokia. (2020b). *Nokia*. Retrieved from https://en.wikipedia.org/wiki/Nokia

Nokia. (2020c). *Search results*. Retrieved from https://www.nokia.com/search/global/en/blockchain

Pauw, C. (2019). *What is an STO, explained*. Retrieved from https://cointelegraph.com/explained/what-is-an-sto-explained

Peng, T. (2020). *Alibaba imports e-commerce platform adopts Blockchain Traceability System*. Retrieved from https://cointelegraph.com/news/alibaba-imports-e-commerce-platform-adopts-blockchain-traceability-system

Pirus, B. (2019). *Allianz in 'Advanced Stages' of accepting crypto for payment*. Retrieved from https://www.forbes.com/sites/benjaminpirus/2019/08/08/allianz-among-the-latest-entrants-into-token-based-payment-space-development/#53593b935c5e

Praveen, G., Chamola, V., Hassija, V., & Kumar, N. (2020). Blockchain. *Early*, *34*(6), 106–113. Advance online publication. doi:10.1109/MNET.001.2000005

Priyaranjan, N., Roy, M., & Dhal, S. (2020). Distributed ledger technology, blockchain and central banks. *RBI Bulletin*, (February), 41–53.

Qin, R., Yuan, Y., Wang, S., & Wang, F. Y. (2018, June). Economic issues in bitcoin mining and blockchain research. In *2018 IEEE Intelligent Vehicles Symposium (IV)* (pp. 268-273). IEEE. 10.1109/IVS.2018.8500377

Rotuna, C., Gheorghita, A., Zamfiroiu, A., & Anagrama, D. S. (2019). Smart City Ecosystem Using Blockchain *Informações Econômicas*, *23*(4), 41–50. doi:10.12948/issn14531305/23.4.2019.04

Salsman, R. M. (2013). The financial crisis was a failure of government, not free markets. *Forbes Magazine*, 19.

Sangwan, V., Harshita, H., Prakash, P., & Singh, S. (2020). Financial technology: A review of extant literature. *Studies in Economics and Finance*, *37*(1), 71–88. doi:10.1108/SEF-07-2019-0270

SBI in the News. (2018). *IBA Banking Technology Award 2016-17 held on 27/02/2018, Mumbai*. Retrieved from https://www.sbi.co.in/web/sbi-in-the-news

Scott, S. (1991). How to time-stamp a digital document. *Journal of Cryptology*.

Search, A. (2020). *Blockchain*. Retrieved from https://www.allianz.com/en/search.html#searchTerm=blockchain

Shah, A. (2018). The chain gang. *Mechanical Engineering (New York, N.Y.)*, *140*(5), 30–35. doi:10.1115/1.2018-MAY-1

Sharma, T. K. (2019). *Alibaba looks to implement blockchain for its complex supply chains*. Retrieved from https://www.blockchain-council.org/blockchain/alibaba-looks-to-implement-blockchain-for-its-complex-supply-chains/

Shi, X. (2019). *Do Core Developers Owe Fiduciary Duty to Users of Blockchain Platforms?* Available at SSRN 3526685.

Shilpi & Ahad, M. A. (2020). Blockchain technology and smart cities- A review. *EAI Endorsed Transactions on Smart Cities*. doi: . doi:10.4108/eai.13-7-2018.163846

Smart Dubai. (2020). *Our vision is to make Dubai the happiest city on earth*. Retrieved from https://www.smartdubai.ae/

Songara, A., & Chouhan, L. (2017, October). Blockchain: a decentralized technique for securing Internet of Things. *Conference on Emerging Trends in Engineering Innovations & Technology Management (ICET: EITM-2017)*.

Sotheby's International Realty. (2006-2020). *An extraordinary history*. Retrieved from https://www.sothebysrealty.com/eng/history

State Bank of India. (2020). *Investor relations*. Retrieved from https://www.sbi.co.in/web/investor-relations/investor-relations

Sun Exchange. (2019). *About Sun Exchange*. Retrieved from https://thesunexchange.com/about-us

Teufel, B., Sentic, A., & Barmet, M. (2020). Blockchain energy: Blockchain in future energy systems. *Journal of Electronic Science and Technology*. doi:10.1016/j.jnlest.2020.100011

Tosh, D. K., Shetty, S., Liang, X., Kamhoua, C., & Njilla, L. (2017, October). Consensus protocols for blockchain-based data provenance: Challenges and opportunities. In *2017 IEEE 8th Annual Ubiquitous Computing, Electronics and Mobile Communication Conference (UEMCON)* (pp. 469-474). IEEE.

Toyota. (2020). *Search*. Retrieved from https://search.newsroom.toyota.co.jp/en/all/search.x?q=blockchain&pagemax=20

Toyota Canada Newsroom. (2017). *Toyota Research Institute explores blockchain technology for development of new mobility ecosystem*. Retrieved from https://media.toyota.ca/releases/toyota-research-institute-explores-blockchain-technology-for-development-of-new-mobility-ecosystem

Toyota Woven City. (2020). *Welcome to woven city*. Retrieved from https://www.woven-city.global/

Wang, F., & Filippi, P. D. (2020). Self-sovereign identity in a globalized world: Credentials-based identity systems as a driver for economic inclusion. *Frontiers in Blockchain*, 2(January), 1–22. doi:10.3389/fbloc.2019.00028

Wang, H., Chen, K., & Xu, D. (2016). A maturity model for blockchain adoption. *Financial Innovation*, 2(1), 12.

Wang, W., Hoang, D. T., Hu, P., Xiong, Z., Niyato, D., Wang, P., Wen, Y., & Kim, D. I. (2019). A survey on consensus mechanisms and mining strategy management in blockchain networks. *IEEE Access : Practical Innovations, Open Solutions*, 7, 22328–22370. doi:10.1109/ACCESS.2019.2896108

Worner, A., Meeuw, A., Ableitner, L., Wortmann, F., Schopfer, S., & Tiefenbeck, V. (2019). Trading solar energy within the neighborhood: Field implementation of a blockchain-based electricity market. *Energy Informatics*, *2*(Supplement 1), 1–12. doi:10.118642162-019-0092-0

Wouda, H. P., & Opdenakker, R. (2019). Blockchain technology in commercial real estate transactions. *Journal of Property Investment & Finance*, *37*(6), 570–579. doi:10.1108/JPIF-06-2019-0085

Xie, J., Tang, H., Huang, T., Yu, F. R., Xie, R., Liu, J., & Liu, Y. (2019). A Survey of Blockchain Technology Applied to Smart Cities: Research Issues and Challenges. *IEEE Communications Surveys and Tutorials*, *21*(3), 2794–2830. doi:10.1109/COMST.2019.2899617

Yadav, S. S., Singh, S., & Harshita. (2018). FinTech: A new tint of glasses to see the age-old world of Finance. In *Emerging Perspectives in FinTech - The Experts' Voice* (pp. 4-7). Haryana: National Institute of Financial Management.

Yakubowski, M. (2019). *Alibaba exec: E-commerce giant considering blockchain use in complex supply chains.* Retrieved from https://cointelegraph.com/news/alibaba-exec-e-commerce-giant-considering-blockchain-use-in-complex-supply-chains

Yli-Huumo, J., Ko, D., Choi, S., Park, S., & Smolander, K. (2016). Where is current research on blockchain technology? A systematic review. *PLoS One*, *11*(10), e0163477.

Zhang, E. (2016). *Antshares Whitepaper1.0*. Academic Press.

ADDITIONAL READING

Durach, C. F., Blesik, T., von During, M. & Bick, M. (2020). Blockchain applications in supply chain transactions. Journal of Business Logistics, Early View, 1-18. . doi:10.1111/jbl.12238

Dutta, V. (ET Bureau) (2019). Infibeam Avenues & Primechain Technologies collaborate for cross border blockchain invoicing. Retrieved from https://cio.economictimes.indiatimes.com/news/corporate-news/infibeam-avenues-primechain-technologies-collaborate-for-cross-border-blockchain-invoicing/68948621 (accessed 11 May 2020).

ETCIO. (2017). State Bank of India partners with BankChain and Intel to deploy blockchain solutions. Retrieved from https://cio.economictimes.indiatimes.com/news/corporate-news/state-bank-of-india-partners-with-bankchain-and-intel-to-deploy-blockchain-solutions/61396719 (accessed 12 May 2020).

KEY TERMS AND DEFINITIONS

Bitcoin: It refers to a cryptocurrency introduced as 'peer-to-peer electronic cash system'. It permits transfer of electronic cash from one entity to the other, without involving any financial institution in between.

Blockchain Technology: It is a digital ledger database technology; wherein blocks of information are recorded, stacking one upon the other to form an interconnected chain. Each block carries a unique identity called hash, and the records are immutable.

Cryptocurrency: This refers to a digital currency, the units of which are created mostly without involvement of any government financial institution. The transaction records for cryptocurrencies are maintained using digital ledgers employing cryptography technique. Therefore, the name 'cryptocurrency'.

Data Integrity: This is the assurance of the data accuracy, and its consistency over its entire life cycle. It also includes ensuring the soundness of the system that collects, stores, processes, transfers, and retrieves data. Blockchain technology, being immutable, can ensure data integrity.

Data Security: Data security is keeping any digital database out of the reach of unauthorised entities and attacks. It involves ensuring the privacy for the miner, giving authentication for sender and receiver, securing the transactions in the process and minimizing the noise errors.

Digital Signatures: This is a digital authentication mechanism that is attached to any digital document to recognize the identity of the sender. Akin to a handwritten signature, it is employed as a means to authenticate that the content of a document are indeed being sent by the intended party.

Miner: Miner is an actor who participates in cryptocurrency transactions, and in turn, plays a crucial role both in creating new cryptocurrencies and in verifying transactions on the blockchain. It adds new blocks to the existing chain, and ensures that these additions are accurate.

Mining: This is the process of adding additional cryptocurrency transactions to the blockchain by the miners. It involves employment of powerful computers to solve complicated problems leading to creation of new cryptocurrency with the help of hash functions.

Proof-of-Work: Proof-of-Work is a consensus mechanism that allow distinguishing a valid from an invalid blockchain. In Bitcoin, hashing is used for 'Proof of Work'.

Smart Contracts: A smart contract is a digital code that enables the execution of a contract between two parties through blockchain, without involvement of any legal system. The transactions emanating out of the contract are also recorded on blockchain and are therefore immutable.

Chapter 11
Industry Use Cases on Blockchain Technology

Daniel Schönle

Furtwangen University of Applied Science, Germany

Kevin Wallis

Furtwangen University of Applied Science, Germany

Jan Stodt

(iD) https://orcid.org/0000-0001-9115-7668

Furtwangen University of Applied Science,

Germany

Christoph Reich

Furtwangen University, Germany

Dominik Welte

Offenburg University of Applied Science, Germany

Axel Sikora

Offenburg University of Applied Science, Germany

ABSTRACT

Digital transformation strengthens the interconnection of companies in order to develop optimized and better customized, cross-company business models. These models require secure, reliable, and traceable evidence and monitoring of contractually agreed information to gain trust between stakeholders. Blockchain technology using smart contracts allows the industry to establish trust and automate cross-company business processes without the risk of losing data control. A typical cross-company industry use case is equipment maintenance. Machine manufacturers and service providers offer maintenance for their machines and tools in order to achieve high availability at low costs. The aim of this chapter is to demonstrate how maintenance use cases are attempted by utilizing hyperledger fabric for building a chain of trust by hardened evidence logging of the maintenance process to achieve legal certainty. Contracts are digitized into smart contracts automating business that increase the security and mitigate the error-proneness of the business processes.

DOI: 10.4018/978-1-7998-6650-3.ch011

INTRODUCTION

Complex products and services require multi-level value chains and collaboration between companies, resulting and leading to complex business models with manifold cross-company relations. Building trust between all stakeholders and concerning all transactions is essential. A secure, reliable, immutable and traceable database supporting logging of actions, contracts and their fulfilment is necessarily required.

Blockchain Technology, also known as Distributed Ledger Technology (DLT), can be used to meet these requirements. Blockchains promise a reliable solution for decentralized accounting of involved stakeholders. It is well suited for safety-critical applications by using smart contracts for maintenance and monitoring with immutable logging. It provides the proof of authenticity for replacement parts through a documented supply-chain. All use cases in this chapter use private and permissioned blockchains. In contrast to popular public blockchain, there is no need for proof of work or proof of stake. All participants are required to authenticate themselves before they are allowed to join the network. Data-Blocks are added to the blockchain according to a consensus algorithm.

The transition from traditional methods to a distributed blockchain assists business and service processes by promising advantages such as a more efficient business, fail-safety, a quicker market launch, process efficiency, and cost reduction. The immutability of data provides security and enables the use of reliable automatic contract execution. However, benefits and disadvantages of the transition have to be balanced wisely. The blockchains smart contracts permit controlled data sharing between machine tools, operators and service providers. A digitization of contractual agreements between stakeholders occurs and cross-company processes begin to prosper. Thus, Blockchain technology creates new value-added opportunities in the context of digitization by threatening intermediary-focused business models. Companies can join forces and form consortia to represent their interests, building even cross-industry infrastructure platforms (Gratzke et al., 2017).

As of today, we are not aware of professional and large-scale usage of Blockchain technology in industrial production environments. However, other business sectors had an earlier start. Blockchain implementations in banking include the storage of information and its validation up to securities settlement (Mills et al., 2016). Blockchains can enable constant optimizations in the know-your-customer (KYC) processes (Moyano et al., 2017). Several projects have been found in supply chain management (SCM). The Everledger Project (www.everledger.io) uses IBM Hyperledger Fabric to secure the provenance of diamonds. A digital fingerprint of the diamond is created and stored in a blockchain to verify its provenance and ownership, and to store its characteristics so that all involved stakeholders, such as suppliers or intermediaries, can monitor transactions and each diamond's provenance.

This chapter is organized as follows: In the first section on "Industry Needs Trust", industry use cases and maintenance processes are inspected. Solutions using blockchain technology are presented. Trust, maintenance and blockchain in Industry 4.0 are therefore the subjects of the next section "Related Work", followed by a section on "Cross-Company Business Models Need Digital Contracts", in which smart contracts and smart contract templates are introduced and discussed. The implementation of maintenance processes using Hyperledger Fabric is described in "Tool and Machine Maintenance With Hyperledger Fabric". In the section "Discussion, Challenges, and Solutions", various challenges and solutions regarding blockchain and smart contracts are discussed. The final section summarizes achievements and provides an outlook on our future work.

INDUSTRY NEEDS TRUST

Trust surrounds us everywhere in everyday life (Rutter, 2001). Customers trust restaurants to follow the hygiene regulations and banks to handle their money responsibly. In business, companies work together with financial obligations up to hundreds of million dollars. Cooperation between companies without trust is impossible. Building trust between companies has become more difficult with frequently changing cooperation partners due to the fast-paced nature of todays' economy. Sako et al. (1998) defined four core aspects for successful cooperation; that all boil down to trust, viz.:

- Written contracts are a necessity in cooperation between companies, not only because of legal requirements, but also as a protection against fraudulent activities and a guarantee of expected behaviour. Existing natural-language contracts with a high level of ambiguities can be transformed into a digital form with clearly defined contract terms known as smart contracts. Refer to the section on "Smart Contracts (SC)".
- Uncertainties in cooperation between companies, created by ambiguous contracts, render decision-making more difficult. Existing natural-language contracts with a high level of ambiguities can be transformed into a digital form with clearly defined contract terms known as smart contracts. Refer to the section on "Smart Contracts (SC)".
- Bilateral and accurate exchange of information between companies is a core requirement for successful cooperation, otherwise errors with serious consequences will be made. In contrast to aspects that allow successful collaboration, there are aspects preventing dynamic collaboration (see Sako et al., 1998). Information exchange between companies can be automated and proven by recorded information in the blockchain or by initiating events within the blockchain to notify the blockchain participants. Refer to "BISS 4.0 Platform" for more information.
- In a traditional cooperation relationship, trust is created by demonstrating trustworthiness in a long-term trading relationship, preventing rapid change of cooperation partners. Trust in dynamic business relationships can be demonstrated by the proof of previous successful cooperation, which is maintained and protected by the blockchain. Refer to "Blockchain as Trust Anchor" for more details

Blockchain can help to support these requirements with reduced complexity, at lower cost, and with reduced effects of the negative aspects – as already stated in the above four bullet points.

Typical industrial use cases that might benefit from blockchain implementations can be found in areas such as the following:

- *Supply Chain Management:* The complexity of supply chains is steadily increasing. More and more goods are shipped across the globe, while the quality management during transportation is often still based on pen and paper. Data as a central component of supply chains needs to be transparent, available and reliable. When dealing with different suppliers, it is critical to trust in the quality of data of delivered products (Uca et al., 2017). Blockchain helps to share reliable data with authorized supply chain participants, to break down existing silos and to support new networks with transformative insight.
- *Product Traceability:* The more a customer knows about a certain product (e.g. what are the ingredients, when was it manufactured, who did the final quality control), the more trust he or she

has in the quality of the product. With product traceability it is possible for the customer to see who is to blame for problems. Consequently, claims for malfunctions can be handled more easily (Steinauer et al., 1997). Blockchain technology can help to create a product history about production time, location, quality and so forth. It can create transparency for all companies involved in the product processing chain.

- *Certification:* In order to obtain certifications e.g. ISO 9000 (ISO & IAF, 2020), the auditor needs to have trust in the company to follow the required guidelines specified in the certification. Trust has to exist the other way around as well: The company needs to be sure that the auditor is inspecting the company without any bias and in a completely independent manner (Kouakou et al., 2013). To prevent misuse of certificates, the blockchain can be used to verify certificates and to guarantee that certificates are authentic and were neither tampered nor forged. Once the information is stored in the blockchain, companies make their certificates transparent and help to build confidence.

This chapter is dedicated to maintenance use cases. Although industry is constantly shifting from manual work to autonomized manufacturing, the task of maintenance is still human-centred. Today, maintenance tasks are still logged via paper-based checklists, which is an unreliable process for data collection. Doubts about the correctness in the maintenance may be created by inadequate, incomplete or even manipulated maintenance reports. Trust in maintenance can be ensured by combining blockchains with digital evidence and mitigation of identity frauds. For example, to protect against tampered RFID markers, the markers can be physically embedded within parts as Physical Unclonable Functions (PUF) (Zimmermann et al., 2019) or placed on surfaces in an irremovable way. The scan of this physical evidence can prove the identity of spare parts or can indicate execution steps of the maintenance process.

Tools and Machine Maintenance

Availability, reliability and regulatory requirements have changed dramatically in recent times due to globalization and technological changes. They challenge asset management and maintenance professionals at various levels to make their activities more efficient. Changes in maintenance approaches and the use of technology will become even more essential to ensure more efficient and cost-effective processes (Campbell & Jardine, 2010).

As defined by DIN 31051 (DIN, 2012), maintenance consists of the tasks service, inspection, overhaul and improvement. Ran et al. (2019) investigated different maintenance methods and, as shown in Figure 1, defined three classes: i) *Reactive Maintenance*, where the system reacts to error events; in most cases, errors lead to unplanned production downtimes. ii) *Preventive Maintenance* achieves predictable production downtime by means of interval maintenance; here the maintenance planning is based on an expected failure behaviour, which hast to be predictable. iii) *Predictive Maintenance* measures the condition of the machine and its parts, achieving higher accuracy; it predicts the time when equipment is likely to fail or degrade and what maintenance activity has to be executed for prevention.

In this process, equipment productivity, maintenance frequency and maintenance costs need to be balanced. The process needs to be carried out according the regulations and the service provider needs to be able to prove this any time. The traditional paper-based maintenance process can be simplified through the use of blockchain, while simultaneously increasing the confidence in the maintenance process. Refer to "tool and machine maintenance with Hyperledger Fabric" for a detailed discussion of the benefits of using blockchain.

Figure 1. Maintenance plans: Reactive, Preventative, and Predictive

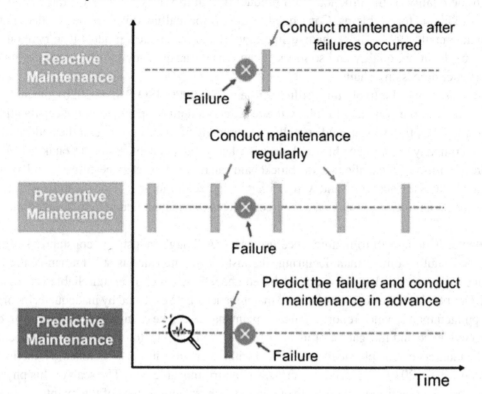

Tool Maintenance

In the area of mechanical manufacturing, tools are used as a precision device for cutting, punching or shaping metals and other materials (Canis, 2012). The manufacturer's specification is followed to maintain the high quality of work pieces. For example, the radius of punching tools, increased by wear-out over time, should not be larger than 0.1mm (Canadian Fabricating & Welding, 2018). Refer to Figure 2. A grinding process according to the specifications is necessary for maintenance to remove the abrasion and sharpen the edge again.

By following the maintenance recommendations, the condition of the tools and machines is ensured but also service and warranty contracts are fulfilled. In the section "cross-company business models need digital contracts", smart contracts are used to automate this process and providing a legal certainty by using blockchain technology.

Figure 2. Maintenance specification of a punching tool

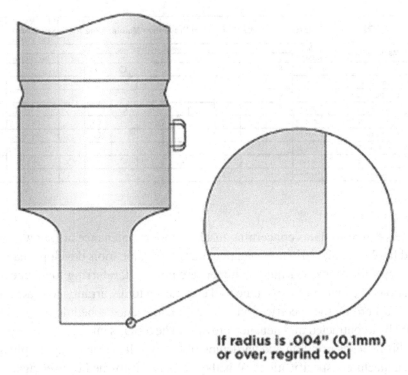

**If radius is .004" (0.1mm)
or over, regrind tool**

Machine Maintenance

Nowadays, many manufacturing machines are part of a complex system of collaborating machines (Zeng, 1997). With usage and age, the condition of the machine degrades. This holds especially true for all the mechanical parts. With ongoing degradation, productivity decreases and susceptibility to failures increases. Maintenance plans are developed according to the maintenance concept, with the goal to determine the optimum frequency to perform maintenance in equipment, in order to ensure its availability (Duarte et al., 2006; Jin et al., 2009). As the observance of the plan can get legal relevance, monitoring of maintenance tasks in the blockchain is a simple way to provide certainty. Table 1 shows a typical preventive maintenance plan for a punching machine (Balram, 2015).

Maintenance Partnerships

Maintenance can be performed by different parties, either by skilled in-house staff, by OEM staff or by a service provider being authorized by the OEM (Tenneson, 2017). Third-party maintenance is considered for different reasons, such as maintenance cost reduction, reduced management effort and delegation of employment risks (Bertolini et al., 2004). Subject of third-party maintenance can differ from single machines or machinery to general factory centred domains like infrastructure, fire prevention, cleaning or electricity (Gomez et al., 2009). Outsourcing of maintenance leads to a wide range of involved parties.

Table 1. Preventive maintenance plan for a punching machine.

VCIPL			Master List of Machines cum Preventive Maintenance Plan									QFM / MAINT / 04 Rev. Status: 01 Date : 15.04.2015			
Sr. No.	Machine Name	M/C Code	Preventive Maintenance Schedule												
			April	May	Jun	Jul	Aug	Sep	Oct	Nov	Dec	Jan	Feb	Mar
1	Belt Drop Hammer 1.5 Ton	FHM-01	O						O					
2	Belt Drop Hammer 2.5 Ton	FHM-02		O						O				
3	Power Press 300 Tons	FPP-01	O						O					
4	Induction Billet Heater	IBH-01	O						O					
5	Power Press 300 Tons	FPP-02		O						O				
6	Muffle Furnace	FMF-01		O						O				
7	Friction Press 300 Tons	SFP-01			O						O			
8	Power Press 100 Tons	SPP-01			O						O			
9	Power Press 100 Tons	SPP-02			O						O			

The stakeholders and procedures concerning machine tool maintenance are shown as an example in Figure 3, inspired by Wan et al. (2017). A manufacturer of machine tools develops maintenance schedules and tolerance specifications. Warranty contracts are provided, referring to a huge amount of such technical information. The owner of a machine tool contracts a tool warranty contract which binds him to observe the tool according the specifications. As the maintenance schedule triggers a maintenance, the tool is removed by a contracted maintenance provider. The tool is sent to a second service provider to get overhauled. This includes grinding and hardening of the tool. It is tested for compliance and recertified according manufacturers specifications. Whether sold as refurbished or used again, the certificate has to be verified.

Figure 3. Involvement of multiple stakeholders for maintenance

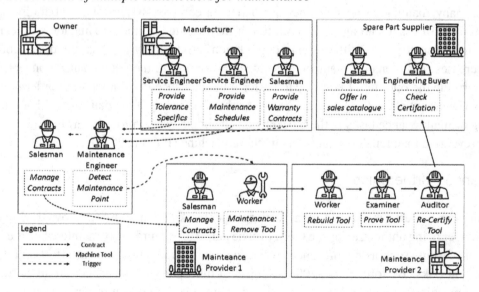

As seen in Castillo (2020), selling refurbished spare parts can be a lucrative business model, if the quality of the refurbishing process can be proven; this process can be refined by leveraging blockchain technology.

Figure 4 illustrates using blockchain technology within an example consortium of stakeholders, which are all involved in the maintenance process. A blockchain (service blockchain) can be used for the exchange of information amongst the maintenance partners. Private in-house information is kept secret in the "Shop Floor Blockchain". Details of these solutions can be found in the section "unwanted cross-company data transfer".

Figure 4. Involvement of multiple stakeholders for maintenance

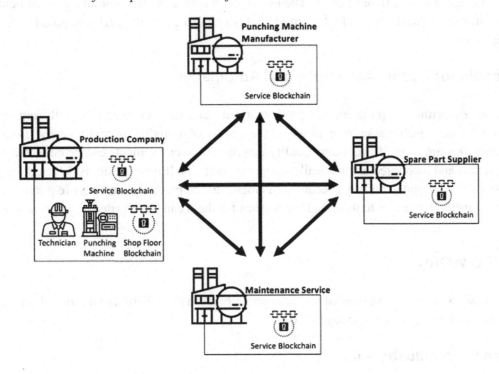

Blockchain technology can provide a maintenance audit trail, which is used to trace relevant events. Records of performed maintenance are kept in the blockchain and provide monitoring and verification for all stakeholders. This allows to investigate the cause of failure afterwards and serve as evidence for legal cases. Furthermore, it can be used as a reminder to keep track of upcoming maintenance. The "European Union Aviation Safety Agency" defined a maintenance audit trail for the aviation industry to define the compliant maintenance-state of aircraft (EASA, 2020).

Paper-Based Maintenance and Human Errors

Despite detailed maintenance plans and methods developed to prevent or at least mitigate the effects of human errors during the maintenance process (Abbassi et al., 2015), human errors still occur within its documentation frequently (Dhillon, 2013). The source of errors varies from lack of effective communication to operator fatigue and inadequate operator training (MacKenzie et al., 2007; Whittingham, 2004). These causes are summarized as human errors and are amplified with increasing numbers of stakeholders involved in the maintenance process. A major source of human error are paper-based records and their processing (Barchard et al., 2011). Prime examples of problems with paper-based documents are poor handwriting (falsified data due to incorrect interpretation), costly transport and storage of large quantities of documents, destruction or loss of documents or difficult to understand relationships between individual documents (Pandey, 2019).

Human errors can be reduced by replacing the paper-based documentation approach by a digitized approach (Watson et al., 2019) using automatic data collection (e.g. sensors, physical markers that cannot be copied (Jung et al., 2013; Wlodarczyk et al., 2017) and other automatically collectable data sources) in combination with blockchain. The use of smart contracts allows proofing of data-collection for correctness and plausibility. Refer to "smart contract challenges in industry and possible solutions" for more information.

Blockchain for Quality Assurance and Automation

Another process within the production of goods that can be carried out more efficiently and verifiably using blockchain is quality assurance, in which the quality of a product is continuously checked, and countermeasures are taken if necessary. Quality-determining measurements can be collected with the help of sensors and monitored automatically via smart contracts. If poor quality is detected, smart contracts can be used to automatically execute adjustments to the production process (e.g. adjustment of process parameters); changes to these and the reasons for them can be recorded in a traceable manner.

RELATED WORK

The related work section is partitioned into four parts: blockchain, reliability and traceability, contract agreements, and maintenance in Industry 4.0.

Blockchain in Industry 4.0

Integrating a blockchain into Industry 4.0 replaces existing error-prone procedures with software centred and documented processes (see Kshetri, 2017; Christidis et al., 2016). An architectural approach for integrating a blockchain into Industry 4.0 was introduced by Teslya et al. (2017). It proposes to use smart contracts to control resources in the production process. A blockchain security architecture, *IoTChain* (see Alphand et al., 2018), combines *ACE* as an authorization framework and *OSCAR* as an encryption framework for the application layer payload. Additional papers, which target blockchain in Industry 4.0, are focusing on preserving the privacy of data. Rahulamathavan et al. (2017) use decentralized attribute-based encryption and decryption for accessing sensor values. Another access control based on smart contracts is introduced by Zhang et al. (2018). They use different contract types such as: 1) accessing control contracts for specifying access control of multiple subject-object pairs, 2) judging contracts for evaluating misbehaviour of users during access control and 3) registering contracts for managing the other contracts. Despite the opportunities for blockchain and Industry 4.0, a profound understanding of the blockchain is essential, otherwise a serious financial loss can happen (Destefanis et al., 2018).

Reliability and Traceability in Industry 4.0

Following the digitization of all kinds of information, blockchain technology is currently being used to lay the foundation for the digitization of trust, monetary values and services using decentralized architectures. Beside Bitcoin and other financial services, most blockchain work is presently found in the area of supply chain management. For example, in the food industry, a strict environmental control has to be ensured (Caro et al., 2018; Tian, 2017), during transportation. This similarly applies to medical products (Bocek et al., 2017).

Contract Agreements in Industry 4.0

There are approaches to use blockchain technologies for smart contracts in Industry 4.0. Norta (2015) quite fundamentally describes ideas introducing blockchain to conventional business processes. A web API for Service Level Agreement (SLA) contracts was introduced by Nakashima et al. (2017). The work focuses on API specification for the orchestration of SLA contracts but disregards Industry 4.0 use cases where machines, sensors and suchlike are part of the SLA contract. Beside Industry 4.0 Pascale et al., 2017 discuss the use of smart contract SLAs for mobile communication providers.

Maintenance in Industry 4.0

Major maintenance research for Industry 4.0 was done in the area of predictive maintenance due to the rise of machine learning algorithms (Spendla et al., 2017; Yan et al., 2017). However, general research about the Industry 4.0 impact on traditional maintenance techniques was carried out by Beng (2018). It points out that the original Maintenance Management Model from Garg et al. (2006) needed to be updated. Industry 4.0, IoT and cyber-physical systems are new types of maintenance strategy categories. Kumar et al. (2017) describe the positive effects on technology, organization and operations of a maintenance model, which interacts with Industry 4.0.

CROSS-COMPANY BUSINESS MODELS NEED DIGITAL CONTRACTS

Typically, a contract is a legal document that defines an agreement between business partners and outlines the services provided, costs, resources and so on. Cross-company business models consist of several business services provided by several parties. To get a satisfactory service for the customer, the agreed quality of services between the business partners, have to be digitized, to enable automatic monitoring, compliance verification and initiation of actions in case contracts are violated.

Towards Digital Agreements

A business contract is a legal binding agreement between two or more persons or entities. As shown in Figure 5, there are different agreements at various management levels (Wallis et al., 2020) e.g.:

- Service Level Agreement: Specifying the quality of service at the IT operation level, which is measured and reported against criteria of technical infrastructures (e.g. bandwidth).

- Process Level Agreement: Specifying the quality of service at the process operation level, which is measured and reported against the context of business processes (e.g. production line processing time).
- Business Level Agreement: Specifying the quality of service at the business operation level, which is measured and reported against the context of business results (e.g. the number of produced work pieces).

Figure 5. Smart Contracts at different business levels

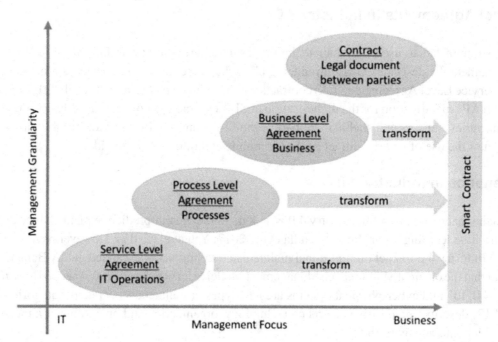

Usually, sophisticated reporting mechanisms are sufficient to document agreements retrospectively. However, to support the progressive digitization of business processes, do real-time reporting and launching appropriate actions, new approaches are needed to meet the near real-time requirements. Transforming these documents into a digital representation would allow the following:

- To model dependencies between the services at various agreement levels (see Figure 5).
- To document comprehensibly and unchangeably the specified quality of services of arbitrary complex systems.
- To monitor specified metrics and activities (workflows) and trigger actions by demand.

Smart Contracts (SC)

The goal of SC in blockchains is to enable non-repudiation and transparent traceability of previously paper-based contracts. They do not replace legal business contracts; they refine and specify parts to be automated. Implementations of SC range from simple processes to very complex processes, covering as many tasks as possible. An example for a simple process is the monitoring of conditions, such as sensor values. Comparison of simple conditions always leads to a clear result. An example for a complex process is the verification of a chained process step with various stakeholders involved. The comparison of complex conditions does not always lead to clear results and must be dealt with by further checks in order to obtain clear results. One limitation that has to be observed is the avoidance of non-deterministic functions and values. These are, among other things, the retrieval of the current time with an accuracy of seconds, the generation of random numbers or the query of sensor values (Alharby et al., 2017; Vukolić, 2017). To obtain these potential non-deterministic values, e.g. sensor data, they are retrieved outside the smart contract and are used as input parameters of smart contracts.

Smart Contract Templates (SCT)

To protect blockchain users against serious consequences such as losing assets, losing orders among competitors, while still providing ease of use, the SC templating schema is introduced. The SCT splits the required knowledge to create a smart contract into two domains - maintenance and blockchain - allowing each domain expert to concentrate on his domain without worrying about the inner workings of the other domain. The blockchain expert develops the smart contract basis, suitable for the specific domain. The maintenance domain expert identifies the essential properties of the paper-based maintenance service manuals. As seen in Figure 6, maintenance service manuals are analysed and essential properties, such as name, date, service intervals, service prices, behaviour on error and liability among others are identified. Essential properties are filled into the smart contract template by the maintenance expert and the smart contract is automatically generated and stored within the blockchain for execution.

Figure 6. Smart Agreement Contract Template workflow

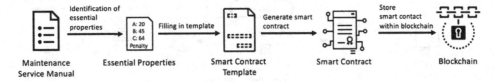

TOOL AND MACHINE MAINTENANCE WITH HYPERLEDGER FABRIC

Hyperledger Fabric (HLF or Fabric) is an open source permissioned blockchain developed by IBM (Hyperledger Foundation, 2020). Permissioned blockchains provide trust by restricting the user group while publishing all information to every participant. Therefore, the stakeholders have to know each other without trusting each other. An algorithm is used to achieve consensus about what is truth, whether a transaction is true according to the contracts and their referring data or not. The consensus algorithm raft will become byzantine fault tolerant in near future (IBM Corporation, 2020b). Smart Contracts are called Chaincode in Fabric and can be written in Go, node.js or Java (IBM Corporation, 2020a). Several client SDKs, which are used building applications to interact with Fabric, are provided in a number of different programming languages (Java, node.js, Python) (IBM Corporation, 2020c).

Maintenance Use Cases of an Industrial Robot

Epson introduced the T3-401S SCARA robot (ESR) as a versatile entry-level robot solution for production lines (Epson, 2019). An adoption of typical maintenance works for the ESR using blockchain is demonstrated in the following subsections. The use cases rely on the integration of BISS 4.0 which is described in detail later on. The stakeholders and procedures involved can be seen in Figure 7.

The stakeholders built a consortium to transform business transactions concerning service contracts. The owner uses the ESR for production, maintenance tasks are carried out by internal and external staff. For external maintenance, a cleaning service is contracted. Warranty contracts between the owner and the manufacturer (OEM) rely on compliant maintenance tasks. There are applications (Capture Interface and Registry Application) to perform transactions on the shared blockchain, represented in HLF as a channel. Every stakeholder keeps a copy of the ledger, the complete history of all transactions. Smart contracts are reading the channel for new transactions to succeed or fail, yielding a judgment of their contract fulfilment. The smart contracts concerning maintenance are based upon either (i) the maintenance plan, provided by the OEM and based on historical data or (ii) the Preventive Maintenance (PM), a system observing the condition of the ESR and reacting adaptive. The PM is based on previous sensor-collected machine data, which is interpreted and used for maintenance scheduling. The PM uses Machine Learning Technology to predict appropriate intervals and types of maintenance.

Figure 7. BISS 4.0 Platform Integration

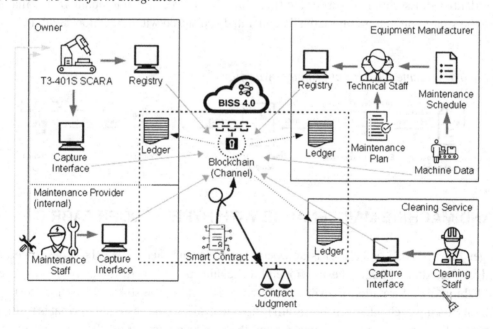

Planned Maintenance Use Case (PMUC)

In this use case a scheduled maintenance task is carried out without issues. The task is defined in the service manual, provided by the equipment manufacturer. The manual lists the maintenance tasks (MT), describing the task and peripheral information. Most relevant are inspection points, operation hours, maintenance procedures and the condition of the ESR (Epson, 2016). Two exemplary Tasks are: "Check whether unusual sound or vibration occurs" (MT1) on a daily basis; "Check looseness or backlash of bolts/screws. Tighten them if necessary" (MT2); either has to be done every 12 months or after 3000 hours of operation. Refer to Figure 8, that shows an excerpt from Epson T-Series robot safety and installation manual (Epson, 2016). The ESR must be powered on for MT1 and powered off for MT2. It is assumed that in-house staff can perform the maintenance, as no explicit expertise requirement is defined. The data documenting the maintenance has to be captured. The complete maintenance procedure includes the following:

1. Detection of an inspection point.
2. Maintenance staff checks the prerequisites and prepares the ESR for maintenance.
3. Maintenance procedures are carried out.
4. Additional step for data capture: Information on events and results of the maintenance are logged. This includes manual log data created by staff using the Capture Interface as well as automatic captured data by sensors of the machine and tools.
5. The emerged maintenance log is added to the blockchain for trusted persistence and traceability.

Failed Maintenance Use Case (FMUC)

This use case concerns a malfunction caused by insufficient cleaning and demonstrates how blockchain simplifies the proof of evidence in a legal case. An ESR is operating in a dust-laden environment, therefore frequent cleaning is required to ensure seamless operation. The cleaning task is performed by an external cleaning service. Predictive maintenance is used for scheduling. The dust burden is captured with a sensor measuring particle concentration.

Figure 8. Excerpt from Epson T-Series robot safety and installation manual

Inspection While the Power is OFF (Manipulator is not operating)

Inspection Point	Inspection Place	Daily	Monthly	Quarterly	Biannual	Annual
Check looseness or backlash of bolts/screws. Tighten them if necessary. (For the tightening torque, refer to *Tightening Hexagon Socket Head Cap Bolts*.)	End effector mounting bolts	√	√	√	√	√
	Manipulator mounting bolts	√	√	√	√	√
	Each joint	√	√	√	√	√
	Bolts/screws around shaft (T series)					√
	Bolts/screws securing motors, reduction gear units, etc.					√

While in-service, the predictive maintenance model of the ESR initiates a maintenance task which requires an overhaul of mechanical parts. The overhaul has to be performed earlier than specified in the manual causing costs and a delay in production. The financial impact of this incidence is subject to legal actions between the owner and the manufacturer (OEM). Both refuse compensation of costs. The blockchain is triggered to generate an audit trail. The audit trail reveals insufficient cleaning. The cleaning service did not perform all required cleaning tasks in time. This caused an increased wear due to the dust-laden air. The documented maintenance logs in the blockchain are used to identify the liability of the cleaning staff.

BISS 4.0 Platform

The BISS 4.0 Platform (Blockchain-Technologien im Schaltschrank or Blockchain in the Switch Cabinet) establishes a continuous trust of chain, digitizes SLA contracts and controls data exchange between companies on a policy basis (Hochschule Furtwangen, 2018). The application use cases "Reliable interactive maintenance plans" and "Reliable troubleshooting" are implemented and demonstrated in the BISS 4.0 platform.

Figure 9. BISS 4.0 Platform

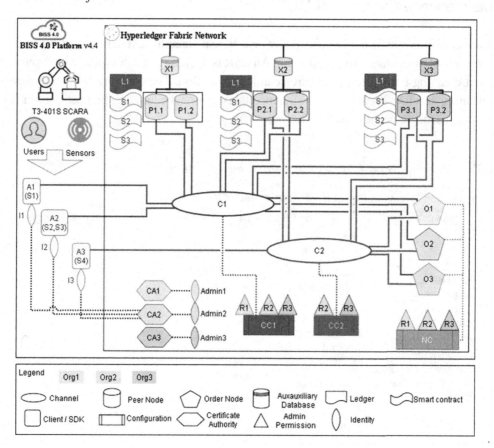

The architecture of BISS 4.0 fulfils the obvious requirements of the use cases MT1 and MT2 (as mentioned above), such as framing three organizations with different access levels, providing a trustful blockchain concept with separation of concerns and connecting machines like the ESR. Besides these, three goals were tracked concerning distributed computing: i) A consortium of stakeholders implementing equal rights for all participants; ii) A platform infrastructure which is fail-safe and redundant; and iii) A multi-tenant architecture. All used and developed components of BISS 4.0 are licensed as open source. Hyperledger Fabric (HLF) is used as the blockchain component.

Three organizations (see Figure 9), represented by three different colours, are collaborating using an HLF Channel (C1), that is red coloured. According to the use cases, these are a cleaning service as i) Org1/R1, the ESR-Owner; ii) as Org2/R2 and the ESR-OEM; and iii) as Org3/R3. Each organization is equipped with infrastructure on their own, as follows:

i) Two independent HLF Peer Nodes (P*.1, P*.2) connecting to C1 and both maintaining copies of the HLF Ledger (L1). The two peers per stakeholder are independent, residing on hardware in different locations providing fault safety. The smart contracts (S1-S3) are working on L1.

ii) An auxiliary database (X*), keeping information on token-information. For example, sensor data and evidence pictures are stored here; the blockchain stores the corresponding hashes. The database is implemented using CouchDB (Apache Software Foundation, 2020), replicating between the organizations.

iii) An HLF Certificate Authority, providing the ability to create certificates for identities.

iv) An HLF Orderer Node that participate in the consensus process to decide whether a transaction is valid. Valid transactions are sorted into blocks for distribution, building the blockchain. Each organization participate in the definition of the Network Configuration (NC) using their Admin Permissions. These Admin Permissions are also used to control the Configuration of Channel 1 (CC1) defining the Channel properties.

v) Client applications (A1, A2) that perform business transactions within the channels. A1 represents the Capture Interface Application, which is used to capture information concerning maintenance. On technical level, A1 puts data in C1. The ESR is connected by sensors, delivering data to A1 and A2. The cleaning service staff uses A1 to document their work, A1 is also used by the maintenance staff of the owner. A1 is using smart contract S1, concerning maintenance tasks. The Owner and the OEM have a rich full application (A2) to interact with each other, concerning maintenance tasks, warranty, part replacement, service contracts.

Identities in HLF are provided by the Membership Service Provider (MSP). The most often used MSP is the HLF Certificate Authority (Fabric-CA) (IBM Corporation, 2020d). It uses X.509 certificates in order to authenticate users and sign transactions. Typically, each organization has at least one Fabric-CA, which allows the administrator to enrol new users. In the configured BISS 4.0 (Figure 9), R1 (owner) has used CA2 to create users for A1 and A2. The Identity of the ESR and its sensors was certified and therefore documented in the blockchain.

Machine Integration into Blockchain

In order to be able to store and retrieve information from the blockchain network, the devices/machines need to be integrated into the network. Fabric provides different SDKs to solve this task. These SDKs offer interfaces for high level programming languages.

As industrial machines are closed systems which run on proprietary software, it is not possible to run custom code. Most of these machines run a programmable logic controller (PLC) which is feasible and extended with additional functionality. A common option is to integrate an OPC UA server. OPC UA is a machine to machine communication protocol which is designed for industrial automation (OPC Foundation, 2020). In recent years, this object-oriented protocol has become a de facto standard in the automation field. Machines of different vendors can be integrated by OPC UA using only one protocol. There are multiple, open source client OPC-UA-libraries available, which can be used in conjunction with the different Fabric SDKs (e.g. NodeOpcUa, 2020; FreeOpcUa, 2020).

Figure 10. Different ways to connect machines to Hyperledger Fabric

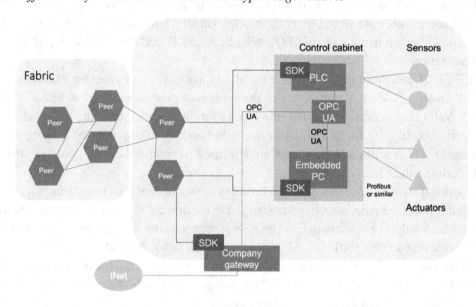

Depending on the specific machines and the networking capabilities of a company, there are different layers upon which it is feasible to implement the blockchain integration. Refer to Figure 10. The easiest way to connect a machine is by an embedded OPC UA server. The Fabric SDK runs on either a small embedded industrial PC next to or inside the machine or acts as a gateway to which all machines on the shop floor are connected to. The SDK runs directly on the machine if permission to install software is granted.

Maintenance Smart Contract and Templates

Transformation of the service manual into a maintenance smart contract involves experts of two domains: one entity familiar with maintenance and one entity familiar with blockchain and smart contract. The transformation consists out of two major steps: identification of essential properties of the maintenance tasks by the maintenance domain expert, and the creation of the maintenance smart contract by the blockchain domain expert.

Identification of Essential Maintenance Task Properties

The maintenance domain expert analyses the service manual for several properties e.g.:

- Type of maintenance task (manual, semi-automated, automated)
- Interval of maintenance task (daily, weekly, every X hours of operation, etc.)
- Condition to be met (e.g. torque, filling level, etc.)
- Required evidence (sensor value, scan of ID, picture of replaced part, etc.)

Results of the analysis regarding the two maintenance cases, MT1: *"check of unusual sound or vibration"* and MT2: *"check looseness of bolts and tighten if necessary"*, are shown in Table 2 below.

Table 2. Identified maintenance properties

Property	MT1	MT2
Type of maintenance task	Manual	Semi-automated
Interval of maintenance task	Daily	12 month or 3000 hours of operation
Condition to be met	No unusual sound or vibration	Bolt torque: 8.0 ± 0.4 N·M
Required evidence	Picture of sound meter result	Result of torque meter

Creation of Maintenance Smart Contract Template

Based on maintenance properties identified by the maintenance expert, the blockchain expert creates maintenance smart contracts and templates. Evaluation of the similarities between MT1 and MT2 reveals that both require some sort of evidence and feature some sort of comparison. These similarities are extracted into the template, to reduce code duplication and potential error sources. In addition, there are common smart contract functions that are included in maintenance smart contract templates:

- Saving content in the blockchain
- Retrieving content from the blockchain
- Triggering of events

The resulting smart contract template, created by the blockchain domain expert and based on the properties, is shown in Algorithm 1. Properties to be filled in by the maintenance expert are marked by a placeholder.

Figure 11. Algorithm 1: Maintenance Smart Contract Template

Algorithm 1 Maintenance Smart Contract Template

1: **for each** $\boxed{Interval}$ **do**
2:    Input: $\boxed{Value}$;
3:    inspection_result: Input;
4:    evidence: $\boxed{Evidence}$;
5:    **if** inspection_result == $\boxed{Condition\ value}$ **then**
6:      execute $\boxed{Action}$;
7:      store in blockchain $\boxed{Values}$;
8:      send $\boxed{Event}$;
9:    **else if** inspection_result $\leq \boxed{Condition\ value}$ **then**
10:      execute $\boxed{Action}$;
11:      store in blockchain $\boxed{Values}$;
12:      send $\boxed{Event}$;
13:    **else if** ... **then**
14:      ...
15:    **else**
16:      execute $\boxed{Action}$;
17:      store in blockchain $\boxed{Values}$;
18:      send $\boxed{Event}$;
19:    **end if**
20: **end for**

Resulting Maintenance Smart Contracts

After the maintenance domain expert has completed the maintenance smart contract template for both maintenance tasks, the maintenance smart contract is automatically generated. The two resulting smart contracts are shown in Algorithm 2 and Algorithm 3.

Figure 12. Algorithm 2: Smart Contract for Maintenance Task 1

Algorithm 2 Smart Contract for Maintenance Task 1

1: **for each** 24h **do**
2:    Input: "no unusual sound", hash(picture);
3:    inspection_result: "no unusual sound";
4:    evidence: hash(picture);
5:    **if** inspection_result == "no unusual sound" **then**
6:      store inspection_result and evidence in blockchain;
7:      send "Maintenance ok" event;
8:    **else**
9:      store inspection_result and evidence in blockchain;
10:      send "Maintenance failed" event;
11:    **end if**
12: **end for**

Figure 13. Algorithm 3: Smart Contract for Maintenance Task 2

Algorithm 3 Smart Contract for Maintenance Task 2

1: required_torque: 8.0 N·M
2: deviation: 0.4 N·M
3: **for each** 12 month or 3000 hours of operation **do**
4:     Input: 8.2 N·M
5:     measured_torque: 8.2 N·M;
6:     **if** (required_torque - deviation) $\leq$ measured_torque **then**
7:         store measured_torque in blockchain;
8:         send "Maintenance ok" event;
9:     **else if** (required_torque + deviation) $\geq$ measured_torque **then**
10:        store measured_torque in blockchain;
11:        send "Maintenance ok" event;
12:     **else**
13:        store measured_torque in blockchain;
14:        send "Maintenance failed" event;
15:     **end if**
16: **end for**

DISCUSSION, CHALLENGES, AND SOLUTIONS

Based on the aspects considered above, a practical example is discussed in detail in the following sub-sections. The problem is described, and a solution is presented. Furthermore, existing problems in the field of smart contracts are also discussed and solutions presented.

Figure 14. Diversification of Blockchains

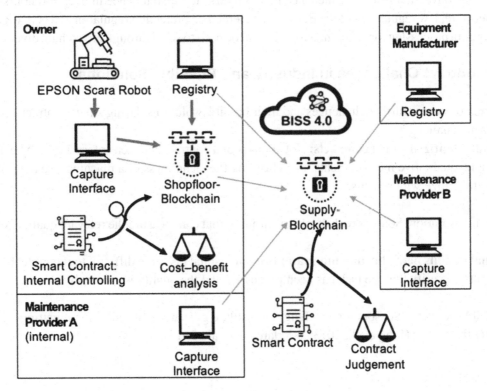

Unwanted Cross-Company Data Transfer

Data-transfer between enterprises may lead to data breaches. To ensure the separation of information, diversification of blockchains is introduced: A company-private blockchain (internal blockchain) containing detailed information, in addition to the all-purpose one (external blockchain).

The diversification reflects the data privacy borders of the stakeholders, with a self-centred perspective. Refer to Figure 11. Assuming the manufacturer using the machinery puts usage information of the machinery into the blockchain. Customers, OEMs and maintenance providers are connected to map business processes. Everyone on the blockchain can read changes of usage statistics. It is possible to read along and conclude about contracts, for example, processing of customer-orders. To solve this cross-company data access, data must be filtered before it is written to this blockchain (Service Blockchain). The complete data is stored in a private blockchain (Shop Floor Blockchain).

The Service Blockchain stores information generated and utilized by external service entities, such as maintenance records. The Shop Floor Blockchain provides data separation, storing private information generated and utilized by the manufacturing company, such as machine data and log files. This fragmentation grants data security and data privacy, while providing increased blockchain performance for all stakeholders. Machine data is stored exclusively in the Shop Floor Blockchain. Therefore, the service providers are not affected by the high amount of transactions imposed by storing machine data.

Another approach that prevents unwanted cross-company data transfer is the creation of an audit log and the use of qualitative descriptions (Stodt et al., 2020). If an auditable audit log of data transfer is to be created, P2P data transfers logged in blockchain can be used without direct insight into the data transfer. This way transferred data can be traced, but not the data content. However, if confidential data must be processed in a smart contract, the data is converted into a qualitative description. An example would be the conversion from "maintenance in 268 hours" to "maintenance in over 200 hours".

Furthermore, law regulations of the European general data protection regulation (EU GDPR), such as separating data processing for different purposes, can be used to solve through blockchain diversification.

Smart Contract Challenges in Industry and Possible Solutions

This section discusses further challenges and their possible solutions. Using smart contracts may cause the following challenges:

Partially digitized smart contracts: Not all parts of a contract between enterprises can be digitized. For example, qualitative measurements, like checking the cleanliness of a machine, are not possible or too costly to realize with sensors.

- Possible solution: Sensors with machine learning, that can measure the relevant qualitative values.

Manual actions being hard to integrate: Human manual tasks are difficult to integrate, because of the difficulty to verify that the task has been processed and the quality is acceptable.

- Possible solution: Sensors for checking the result, e.g. spare part replacement getting verified by an RFID marker (Jung et al., 2013; Wlodarczyk et al., 2017).

Identity management may be too costly: The identity of the blockchain participants is costly to be verified. For example, a sensor, delivering important information must be cryptographically identified and integrated into the blockchain.

- Possible solution: Usage of a gateway, which is responsible for the communication between sensor and blockchain. The gateway has to provide different features like a cryptographic module, multiple interfaces for sensors, etc.

Vulnerability of smart contracts: Smart contracts can themselves be poorly written and therefore pose a security risk in themselves (Atzei et al., 2017).

- Possible solution: Multiple test iterations, different test scenarios, and audit by experts.

False information becoming accidentally permanent: Parties could insert falsified data into the blockchain, which then becomes difficult to remove, because of the immutability characteristic.

- Possible solution: A validation system, which validates each value before it is stored inside the blockchain. Special caution is required because the validation system can be a single point of failure.

Possibility of smart contract code duplication: Smart contracts of a specific domain may feature code duplications, which reduces maintainability and increases the number of potential errors.

- Possible solution: Introduction of smart contract templates that contain common functions.

Complexity of smart contract updates: Smart contract updates that are required for updating flexible content (e.g. values of conditions) represent a high administrative burden.

- Possible solution: Replacement of flexible content by placeholders, storage of the flexible content in the blockchain, retrieval of the flexible content from the blockchain at the time of execution of the smart contract.

CONCLUSION AND FUTURE WORK

As the tool and machine maintenance process involves many alternating stakeholders, the impact of blockchain usage is enormous. Smart contracts are used to proof maintenance tasks, where every task-step is represented. Evidence of correct execution is stored in the blockchain. On successful execution, final actions of the contract, like payments, take place to complete the contract. The automation and ease of establishing trust reduces costs of contract processing. The precise monitoring of maintenance allows optimal operating of equipment enhancing productivity and reducing cost. The implementation of smart contracts is speeded up by modelling smart agreement contract templates. In addition, the reduced error-proneness of the process increases the security level.

For the proposed transformation of maintenance processes, Hyperledger Fabric has been used. By using the BISS 4.0 platform, an infrastructure had been developed including identity management. The integration of machines into blockchain was discussed and maintenance processes were digitized as smart contracts.

Despite the advantages of using blockchain technology, there are still some challenges such as the lack of complete contract digitization, scalability, secure incorporation of external information, data privacy protection, access management, etc. For some of these challenges, first solutions have been proposed in this chapter, although many of these are still under research. The outcome of this is to develop blockchain solutions regarding the maintenance topic, as most blockchain solutions focus solely on the traceability aspect within the supply chain topic.

In addition, there are other areas of the production industry that may benefit from the use of blockchain. One area is the dynamic machine payment, called "machine as a service" (EXOR, 2019). Two types of machine as a service are distinguished: payment per unit produced and selling of surplus production capacity. With the first type, a machine is sold to the customer at a low cost and an additional fee is charged per unit produced. With the second type, excess production capacity of a company can be sold to external companies, in order to utilize the machinery cost-efficient and generate additional income. Using "machine as a service", the blockchain obtains the role of a broker for supply and demand, payment service provider and documentation provider for securing evidence. In the area of environmental protection and resource conservation in production industry, the use of blockchain allows establishing a transparent binning process. Production output that does not correspond to first-class quality is re-labelled. A transparent binning process, logged and traceable by blockchain technology, creates trust in binned products.

ACKNOWLEDGMENT

This work has received funding from European Fonds for Regional Development (EFRE) and the Ministry of Science, Research and Art of Baden-Württemberg (MWK) in the framework of the project BISS 4.0 (biss40.in.hs-furtwangen.de).

REFERENCES

Abbassi, R., Khan, F., Garaniya, V., Chai, S., Chin, C., & Hossain, K. A. (2015). An integrated method for human error probability assessment during the maintenance of offshore facilities. *Process Safety and Environmental Protection*, *94*, 172–179. doi:10.1016/j.psep.2015.01.010

Alphand, O., Amoretti, M., Claeys, T., Dall'Asta, S., Duda, A., Ferrari, G., Rousseau, F., Tourancheau, B., Veltri, L., & Zanichelli, F. (2018). Iotchain: A blockchain security architecture for the internet of things. 2018 IEEE Wireless Communications and Networking Conference (WCNC), 1–6. doi:10.1109/WCNC.2018.8377385

Apache Software Foundation. (2020). Apache CouchDB. Retrieved May 30, 2020, from https://couchdb.apache.org

Atzei, N., Bartoletti, M., & Cimoli, T. (2017). A survey of attacks on ethereum smart contracts sok. Proceedings of the 6th International Conference on Principles of Security and Trust, 10204, 164–186. doi:10.1007/978-3-662-54455-6_8

Balram, J. (2015). Preventive Maintenance Plan. Scribd. Retrieved May 30, 2020, from https://www.scribd.com/doc/279104286/Preventive-Maintenance-Plan

Barchard, K. A., & Pace, L. A. (2011). Preventing human error: The impact of data entry methods on data accuracy and statistical results. *Computers in Human Behavior*, 27(5), 1834–1839. doi:10.1016/j.chb.2011.04.004

Beng, D. C. (2018). Industry 4.0 techniques as a maintenance strategy (a review paper). doi:10.13140/rg.2.2.18116.32644

Bertolini, M., Bevilacqua, M., Braglia, M., & Frosolini, M. (2004). An analytical method for maintenance outsourcing service selection. [Quality]. *International Journal of Quality & Reliability Management*, 21(7), 772–788. doi:10.1108/02656710410549118

Bocek, T., Rodrigues, B. B., Strasser, T., & Stiller, B. (2017). Blockchains everywhere - a use-case of blockchains in the pharma supply-chain. 2017 IFIP/IEEE Symposium on Integrated Network and Service Management (IM), 772–777. doi:10.23919/INM.2017.7987376

Campbell, J. D., & Jardine, A. K. (2010). *Maintenance excellence: optimizing equipment life-cycle decisions*. CRC Press.

Canadian Fabricating & Welding. (2018). Punching productively. Retrieved May 30, 2020, from https://www.canadianmetalworking.com/canadianfabricatingandwelding/article/fabricating/punching-productively

Canis, B. (2012). The tool and die industry: Contribution to US manufacturing and federal policy considerations. CRS Report for Congress, 1–17.

Caro, M. P., Ali, M. S., Vecchio, M., & Giaffreda, R. (2018). Blockchain-based traceability in agri-food supply chain management: A practical implementation. 2018 IoT Vertical and Topical Summit on Agriculture - Tuscany (IOT Tuscany), 1–4. doi:10.1109/IOTTUSCANY.2018.8373021

del Castillo, M. (2020). Honeywell Is Now Tracking $1 Billion In Boeing Parts On A Blockchain. Forbes. Retrieved June 29, 2020, from https://www.forbes.com/sites/michaeldelcastillo/2020/03/07/honeywell-is-now-tracking-1-billion-in-boeing-parts-on-a-blockchain/

Christidis, K., & Devetsikiotis, M. (2016). Blockchains and smart contracts for the internet of things. *IEEE Access: Practical Innovations, Open Solutions*, 4, 2292–2303. doi:10.1109/ACCESS.2016.2566339

Destefanis, G., Marchesi, M., Ortu, M., Tonelli, R., Bracciali, A., & Hierons, R. (2018, March). Smart contracts vulnerabilities: a call for blockchain software engineering? In *2018 International Workshop on Blockchain Oriented Software Engineering (IWBOSE)* (pp. 19-25). IEEE.

Dhillon, B. S. (2013). *Human reliability: With human factors*. Elsevier.

DIN. (2012). *DIN 31051: 2012 09–fundamentals of maintenance*. DIN.

Duarte, J. A. C., Craveiro, J. C. T. A., & Trigo, T. P. (2006). Optimization of the preventive maintenance plan of a series components system. *International Journal of Pressure Vessels and Piping, 83*(4), 244–248. doi:10.1016/j.ijpvp.2006.02.016

EASA. (2020). What does the term "detailed maintenance records" mean? Retrieved May 7, 2019, from https://www.easa.europa.eu/faq/19042

Epson. (2016). Robot system safety and installation (t3 / epson rc+ 7.0). Seiko Epson Corporation.

Epson. (2019). Epson SCARA t3-401s - epson. Retrieved May 9, 2019, from https://www.epson.de/en/products/robot/epson-scara-t3-401s-with-controller-built-in

EXOR. (2019). What is the Machines as a Service Business Model? Retrieved June 22, 2020, from https://www.exorint.com/en/blog/2019/04/26/what-is-the-machines-as-a-service-business-model

FreeOpcUa. (2020). OPC UA stack in python asyncio. Retrieved May 26, 2020, from https://github.com/FreeOpcUa/opcua-asyncio

Garg, A., & Deshmukh, S. (2006). Maintenance management: Literature review and directions. *Journal of Quality in Maintenance Engineering, 12*(3), 205–238. doi:10.1108/13552510610685075

Gomez, J., Crespo, A., Moreu, P., Parra, C., & Diaz, V. G. (2009). Outsourcing maintenance in services providers. Safety, reliability and risk analysis: Theory, methods and applications, 829–837.

Gratzke, P., Schatsky, D., & Piscini, E. (2017). Signals for Strategists: Banding together for Blockchain. Deloitte University Press. Retrieved from https://dupress.deloitte.com/dup-us-en/focus/tech-trends/2017/blockchain-trust-economy.html

Furtwangen, H. (2018). BISS:4.0. Retrieved May 30, 2020, from https://www.hs-furtwangen.de/forschung/forschungsprojekte/biss40/

Hyperledger Foundation. (2020). Hyperledger Open Source Blockchain Technologies. Hyperledger. Retrieved May 30, 2020, from https://www.hyperledger.org/

Corporation, I. B. M. (2020a). Fabric Chaincode. Retrieved May 26, 2020, from https://hyperledger-fabric.readthedocs.io/en/release-2.0/chaincode.html

Corporation, I. B. M. (2020b). Fabric Ordering Service. Retrieved May 26, 2020, from https://hyperledger-fabric.readthedocs.io/en/release-2.0/orderer/ordering service.html#raft

Corporation, I. B. M. (2020c). Fabric SDKs. Retrieved May 26, 2020, from https://hyperledger-fabric.readthedocs.io/en/release-2.0/fabric-sdks.html

Corporation, I. B. M. (2020d). Hyperledger Fabric CA. Retrieved May 26, 2020, from https://hyperledger-fabric-ca.readthedocs.io/en/release-1.4/

ISO & IAF. (2020). ISO 9001 Auditing Practices Group. Retrieved May 29, 2020, from https://committee.iso.org/home/tc176/iso-9001auditing-practices-group.html

Jin, Y.-L., Jiang, Z.-H., & Hou, W.-R. (2009). Integrating flexible-interval preventive maintenance planning with production scheduling. *International Journal of Computer Integrated Manufacturing*, 22(12), 1089–1101. doi:10.1080/09511920903207449

Jung, S. W., & Jung, S. (2013). Hrp: A hmac-based rfid mutual authentication protocol using puf. In *The international conference on information networking 2013 (ICOIN)*. IEEE.

Kouakou, D., Boiral, O., & Gendron, Y. (2013). ISO auditing and the construction of trusttrust. *Accounting, Auditing & Accountability Journal*, 26(8), 1279–1305. doi:10.1108/AAAJ-03-2013-1264

Kshetri, N. (2017). Can blockchain strengthen the internet of things? *IT Professional*, 19(4), 68–72. doi:10.1109/MITP.2017.3051335

Kumar, U., & Galar, D. (2017). *Maintenance in the era of industry 4.0: Issues and challenges. Quality, IT and business operations*. Springer Singapore.

MacKenzie, C., Holmstrom, D., & Kaszniak, M. (2007). Human factors analysis of the BP Texas City refinery explosion. *Proceedings of the Human Factors and Ergonomics Society Annual Meeting*, 51(20), 1444–1448. doi:10.1177/154193120705102015

Mills, D. C., Wang, K., Malone, B., Ravi, A., Marquardt, J., Badev, A. I., & Ellithorpe, M. (2016). *Distributed ledger technology in payments, clearing, and settlement*. Academic Press.

Moyano, J. P., & Ross, O. (2017). KYC optimization using distributed ledger technology. *Business & Information Systems Engineering*, 59(6), 411–423. doi:10.1007/s12599-017-0504-2

Nakashima, H., & Aoyama, M. (2017). An automation method of sla contract of web apis and its platform based on blockchain concept. 2017 IEEE International Conference on Cognitive Computing (ICCC), 32–39. doi:10.1109/IEEE.ICCC.2017.12

NodeOpcUa. (2020). OPC UA stack in node.js. Retrieved May 26, 2020, from https://github.com/node-opcua/node-opcua

Norta, A. (2015). Creation of smart-contracting collaborations for decentralized autonomous organizations. Perspectives in Business Informatics Research - 14th International Conference, BIR 2015, Tartu, Estonia, August 26-28, 2015, Proceedings, 3–17. 10.1007/978-3-319-21915-81

Pascale, E. D., McMenamy, J., Macaluso, I., & Doyle, L. (2017). Smart contract slas for dense small-cell-as-a-service. https://arxiv.org/abs/1703.04502

Rahulamathavan, Y., Phan, R. C. W., Rajarajan, M., Misra, S., & Kondoz, A. (2017). Privacy-preserving blockchain based iot ecosystem using attribute-based encryption. 2017 IEEE International Conference on Advanced Networks and Telecommunications Systems (ANTS), 1–6. doi:10.1109/ANTS.2017.8384164

Ran, Y., Zhou, X., Lin, P., Wen, Y., & Deng, R. (2019). A survey of predictive maintenance: Systems, purposes and approaches. arXiv preprint arXiv:1912.07383.

Rutter, J. (2001). From the sociology of trust towards a sociology of 'e-trust'. *International Journal of New Product Development & Innovation Management*, 2(4), 371–385.

Sako, M., & Helper, S. (1998). Determinants of trust. *Journal of Economic Behavior & Organization, 34*(3), 387–417. doi:10.1016/S0167-2681(97)00082-6

Spendla, L., Kebisek, M., Tanuska, P., & Hrcka, L. (2017). Concept of predictive maintenance of production systems in accordance with industry 4.0. 2017 IEEE 15th International Symposium on Applied Machine Intelligence and Informatics (SAMI), 405–410. doi:10.1109/SAMI.2017.7880343

Steinauer, D. D., Wakid, S. A., & Rasberry, S. (1997). Trust and traceability in electronic commerce. *StandardView, 5*(3), 118–124. doi:10.1145/266231.266239

Stodt, J., & Reich, C. (2020). Data confidentiality in p2p communication and smart contracts of blockchain in industry 4.0. Unpublished manuscript.

Tenneson, C. (2017). Competitive landscape: Partnering with third-party maintenance providers for data center and network maintenance cost optimization. Retrieved May 7, 2019, from https://www.gartner.com/en/documents/3756176

Teslya, N., & Ryabchikov, I. (2017). Blockchain-based platform architecture for industrial iot. 2017 21st Conference of Open Innovations Association (FRUCT), 321–329. doi:10.23919/FRUCT.2017.8250199

Tian, F. (2017). A supply chain traceability system for food safety based on haccp, blockchain internet of things. 2017 International Conference on Service Systems and Service Management, 1–6. doi:10.1109/ICSSSM.2017.7996119

Uca, N., Çemberci, M., Civelek, M., & Yılmaz, H. (2017). The effect of trust in supply chain on the firm performance through supply chain collaboration and collaborative advantage. *The Journal of American Science, 15*, 215–230.

Vukolić, M. (2017). Rethinking permissioned blockchains. *Proceedings of the ACM Workshop on Blockchain, Cryptocurrencies and Contracts*, 3–7.

Wallis, K., Stodt, J., Jastremskoj, E., & Reich, C. (2020). Agreements between enterprises digitized by smart contracts in the domain of industry 4.0. Unpublished manuscript.

Wan, S., Li, D., Gao, J., Roy, R., & Tong, Y. (2017). Process and knowledge management in a collaborative maintenance planning system for high value machine tools. *Computers in Industry, 84*, 14–24. doi:10.1016/j.compind.2016.11.002

Watson, K., & Smith, J. (2019). A digital approach to making a step change in reducing human error in procedures. SPE Offshore Europe Conference and Exhibition. doi:10.2118/195753-MS

Whittingham, R. (2004). The blame machine: Why human error causes accidents. Routledge. doi:10.4324/9780080472126

Wlodarczyk, K. L., Ardron, M., Waddie, A. J., Taghizadeh, M. R., Weston, N. J., & Hand, D. P. (2017). Tamper-proof markings for the identification and traceability of high-value metal goods. *Optics Express, 25*(13), 15216–15230. doi:10.1364/OE.25.015216 PubMed

Yan, J., Meng, Y., Lu, L., & Li, L. (2017). Industrial big data in an industry 4.0 environment: Challenges, schemes, and applications for predictive maintenance. *IEEE Access : Practical Innovations, Open Solutions, 5*, 23484–23491. doi:10.1109/ACCESS.2017.2765544

Zeng, S. W. (1997). Discussion on maintenance strategy, policy and corresponding maintenance systems in manufacturing. *Reliability Engineering & System Safety, 55*(2), 151–162. doi:10.1016/S0951-8320(96)00004-X

Zhang, Y., Kasahara, S., Shen, Y., Jiang, X., & Wan, J. (2018). Smart contract-based access control for the internet of things. IEEE Internet of Things Journal, 1–1. doi:10.1109/JIOT.2018.2847705

Zimmermann, L., Scholz, A., Tahoori, M. B., Aghassi-Hagmann, J., & Sikora, A. (2019). Design and evaluation of a printed analog-based differential physical unclonable function. IEEE Transactions on Very Large-Scale Integration (VLSI). *Systems, 27*(11), 2498–2510.

KEY TERMS AND DEFINITIONS

Chaincode: Smart Contracts are called Chaincode in Hyperledger Fabric. These are small computer programs that are executed in a distributed manner and represent a digitalised version of previously paper-based contracts. In Hyperledger Fabric, smart contracts can be programmed in Go, Java or Node. js and thus provide ease of use for the programmer. The process of executing the smart contracts is called a transaction.

Channel: A Hyperledger Fabric Channel provides private and confidential communication and represents a blockchain. Transactions are executed on a channel which are stored in the channel's ledger. Channels are used to hide certain information from specific Organizations.

ESR: This Epson T3-401S SCARA robot - a versatile entry-level robot solution for production lines.

Hyperledger Fabric: Hyperledger Fabric is a permissioned blockchain infrastructure, originally contributed by IBM and Digital Asset, providing a modular architecture with a delineation of roles between the nodes in the infrastructure, execution of Smart Contracts (called "chaincode" in Fabric) and configurable consensus and membership services.

Membership Service Provider: The Membership Service Provider (MSP) issues and maintains the identities of all nodes in the Hyperledger Fabric system. Issuing and maintaining the identities is handled via standard PKI methods based on digital signatures. Nodes take up to one of three roles: Client (executing the smart contract), Peers (maintaining a copy the blockchain and validation of the transaction), and Orderer (establishing the order of all transactions).

Orderer: This is a node type in Hyperledger Fabric. A group of Orderers form the ordering service, responsible for establishing the correct order of all transactions. In the process of ordering consensus (agreement) of the transactions is achieved. Hyperledger Fabric features three consensus implementations: Solo (for development purposes), Kafka (a crash fault tolerant consensus implementation), and Raft (a crash fault tolerant consensus algorithm).

Organization: Hyperledger Fabric uses Organizations to structure the stakeholders inside the network. Every user is part of an Organization which determines his access rights. Each Organization forms a trust domain, such that a node with the Organization trusts all node within the Organization but no node of another Organization. Each Organization issues the identities for its own members.

Peer: This is a node type in Hyperledger Fabric that provides access to the channels, executes smart contracts and keeps a copy of the Ledger. Peers validate the transactions to establish consensus. Peer communicate with each via is handled via Peer-to-peer communication.

SDK: This is short for Software Development Kit. In Hyperledger Fabric, various SDKs are available to provide easier interaction with the blockchain.

Shop Floor: The area where assembly or production is carried out, either by an automated system or by workers. This includes equipment, inventory, and storage areas.

Smart Contract: Template: Smart Contract Templates (SCT) reduce the required knowledge for defining a smart contract. A developer familiar with blockchain develops a smart contract that covers a wide range of possibilities and the SCT. The end user of the smart contract only needs to fill in parameters such as conditions and values. Resulting code represents a fully functional smart contract that can be used within the blockchain.

Chapter 12
Blockchain Technology in the Automotive Industry:
Use Cases and Statistical Evaluation

Atakan Gerger

https://orcid.org/0000-0002-3782-7613

Ege University, Turkey

ABSTRACT

Even though the automotive industry was among the key players of the industrial revolution in the last century, striking transformations experienced in other sectors did not have significant repercussions on this industry until a few years ago. However, general advancements in technology and Industry 4.0 have presented new opportunities for the reconfiguration of the business environment. Developments in cryptocurrencies such as bitcoin, in particular, have attracted the attention to what is known as blockchain technology. Several successful examples of blockchain applications in different industries have tempted the automotive industry to be rapidly involved with efforts in this direction. As a consequence, the application of the blockchain technology to highly diverse areas in the automotive industry was set in motion. The purpose of this chapter is to explore the application of blockchain technology in the automotive industry, to analyse its advantages and disadvantages, and to demonstrate its successful in general.

INTRODUCTION

The Blockchain (BC) technology has revolutionized several areas of society including manufacturing, commerce, banking, healthcare, automotive, and supply chain, to name but a few. The innovative approach of the BC which is based on trust and value is one of the primary attractive points of this revolution which offers new ways of doing business. Even though the automotive industry did not get acquainted with full digitalization until recently, it had and still has great potential for the future of personal mobility (Colonna, 2018). Today, along with the advancement of technology, the automotive industry has transformed from internal combustion engine vehicles to hybrid and electric automobiles. By virtue of the use of Industry 4.0 technologies such as Internet of Things (IoT), Automated Guided Vehicles

DOI: 10.4018/978-1-7998-6650-3.ch012

(AGV), Cloud Computing, Big Data Analytics (BDA), Robotics, Blockchain and Mobile Services and Technologies in the industry, the automotive industry began to become one of the most technologically advanced industries alongside the transformation of conventional vehicles to autonomous (self-driving) automobiles in line with its adaptation to the changing innovations. The fourth industrial revolution represents a new level of organization and control of the entire value creation chain across the life cycle of products. This cycle typically addresses the increasingly individualized customer demands, that range from the initial purchase order, to the development & production, to the delivery of a product to the end-user and, in the end, to the recycling process including the relevant services (Çetin Gerger, 2019; Kern & Wolff, 2019; Fraga-Lamas & Fernández-Caramés, 2019; Reinsel, Gantz, & Rydning, 2018).

As the automotive sector started to place the focus on autonomous vehicles, a very large amount of data is getting to be produced. To illustrate this point, the amount of data produced by an autonomous automobile is typically approximately 1 gigabyte every second. When this figure is benchmarked against data produced by all the autonomous vehicles used in a single metropolis alongside the growing number of autonomous automobiles with each passing day and against similar sources of data, a figure hugely enormous in size comes into view. Along with the generation of such an enormous amount of data, the need not only for safely storing data but also for statistically analysing and interpreting it comes to the forefront. As per the estimates of International Data Corp (IDCC), the amount of data generated across the globe, currently, is expected to reach around 175 zettabytes (ZB) by 2025 whilst it was 33 ZB in 2018. In view of the fact that 1 ZB is 1 trillion gigabytes, that is, 10^{21} (1,000,000,000,000,000,000,000) bytes, its manipulation requires new methods for analytics (Gerger, 2020; Gerger, 2019a; Gerger, 2019b; Pepper, 2012), and that is where Big Data techniques comes in.

As a result of the digitalization of the automotive sector together with Industry 4.0, cyber-attacks, unwanted losses, accidents, high costs, and operational inefficiencies are giving rise to inflated prices for parts and services and related security challenges. Such problems experienced in the sector are currently transferred to different and heterogeneous stakeholders positioned in the life cycle of vehicles production; the stakeholders being individual and corporate vehicle owners, service users, customers of logistics businesses or end-users. Industry 4.0 contributes to advancement in multiple domains which allow the positioning of sensors in large numbers. Some of them are as listed below (Fraga-Lamas & Fernández-Caramés, 2019):

- Implementation of big data techniques
- Improvements in connectivity and computational power
- Appearance of machine learning approaches
- Development of new computing paradigms (e.g. cloud, fog, mist and edge computing)
- Human-machine interfaces (HMI)
- Development of IoT and the use of robotics

The use of such sophisticated systems, equipped with autonomous networks, offer a variety of features and services. However, they bring about malicious attacks and additional risks which make cybersecurity even a more challenging issue. In scenarios in which the controlled systems are vehicles or vehicle-related systems, the public security becomes a matter of importance. Therefore, providing powerful cybersecurity services becomes a basic necessity (Blanco-Novoa, Fernández-Caramés, et al., 2018; Fraga-Lamas, Fernández-Caramés, et al., 2018; Fraga-Lamas, Fernández-Caramés, et al., 2017).

To this end, the automotive industry employs the Blockchain technology in order to optimize workings of all partners within the supply chain system.

The Blockchain technology refers to a large database or a distributed ledger system which is shared across a computer network. When a transaction is performed between two parties, it is added as the next block (within a Blockchain) after its verification using the consensus mechanism which is part of the Blockchain. The new verified block is then appended and linked to the previous last block. If a transaction is added to the BC, it becomes irreversible as response to alterations. Smart contracts are self-executing contracts that are also stored in BC. They contain all rules, terms & conditions, expiry dates and other related information that are necessary for the management of interaction between all relevant parties. Upon the fulfillment of terms & conditions of the smart contracts, the code is automatically executed. Smart contracts are stored within the Blockchain and these become operational upon the dispatch of a transaction to its address, and after it is verified and published across the general network (Mohanta, Panda, & Jena, 2018; Lee, Chua, Keoh, & Ohba, 2019).

By using the BC technology, smart vehicles of the future will provide advanced autonomous driving functionalities and will rely heavily on other vehicles, road infrastructure and a variety of cloud services. These data which are acquired through wireless interconnections will be used by any smart vehicle for enriching its own database which is composed of data collected via installed sensors such as cameras and radar systems for the purpose of further enhancing the security of autonomous driving functionalities. Moreover, they will facilitate the solution of problems such as driver's fatigue or distraction. Furthermore, data collected from vehicles which are equipped with limited smart technologies will be utilized far beyond just helping vehicle drivers during the trip (Stocker, Kaiser, & Fellmann, 2017; Stocker & Kaiser, 2016; Kaiser et al., 2018).

The purpose of this chapter is to explore the current applications of the BC technology in the automotive market and to shed light on its other likely areas of application. In discussing so, a holistic perspective is taken when the BC technology is examined.

AUTOMOTIVE INDUSTRY

The automotive industry is probably the largest in the industrialized countries and, therefore, in a constant development and change. An automobile or a vehicle requires the assembly of more than 20,000 parts which originate from thousands of suppliers across the world. In this sense, it has the most sophisticated supply chain of the world and is located in a highly competitive environment. The firms which operate in this industry aspire to improving the product quality and delivery, to cut down equipment and labor costs, wastefulness and fragility in the supply chain, and to develop engineering skills in the best manner. Low-quality components which enter the supply chain are likely to cause the vehicle manufacturers to have serious problems (Kern & Wolff, 2019; Hoyle, 2005). The main property of a product/service, which is required to satisfy customer needs or to be appropriate for the customer use, is the quality (Hoyle, 2000; Gerger, 2018; Gerger & Firuzan, 2020). Thus, the manufacturer alone does not have the full responsibility for all parts of any products used (Clarke, 2005); rather all parties across the supply chain share the collective responsibility. In today's world in the era of Industry 4.0 where everything is digitally connected to each other, all parties already have shared responsibility. Industry 4.0 represents a new level of organization of and control over the entire value creation chain during the life cycle of products. A vision of this fourth industrial revolution is to have the ability to auto control the machines and production systems based on data collected from connected devices. The most crucial characteristic of Industry 4.0 is the digitalization and automation. The digitalization in corporations alters business and operation models and develops and transforms supply chains and production methods for obtaining higher levels of reliability, agility and productivity. While the automotive industry was initially focused just on producing and selling automobiles, it has a more sophisticated ecosystem today. The stakeholders of this ecosystem are several, as presented in the list below (Fraga-Lamas & Fernández-Caramés, 2019; IBM Institute for Business Value, 2018; Lu et al., 2019; Kern & Wolff, 2019):

- Consumers, automobile owners and passengers
- Automobile entrepreneurs, technology firms
- Dealers/retailers
- OEMs/automobile makers
- Insurance companies
- Repair shops/garage services
- After-sale service departments
- Governments and public institutions
- Financial institutions
- Telecommunication and technology companies
- Scrap dealers/recycling agencies
- Academia
- Leasing and fleet companies
- Regulators and standards bodies
- Suppliers

Today, the automotive industry which aspires to create the best quality with the lowest cost in due time in parallel to the development of technology does not alone keep pace with this technological development, rather it is one of the sectors leading it. Researches indicate that the automotive industry occupies the position of leading practitioner in the area of smart factories. As the rationale for this keen interest in smart factories, several reasons, which range from developments in the productivity to significant cost savings, are proposed. It is possible to present the below categorization as the three primary reasons for the switch to smart factories:

- Firstly, along with the modernization and digitalization of operations, it enhances the productivity of factories in comparison to former conditions.
- Secondly, it makes it easier to identify quality problems which are impossible or difficult for human beings to notice. Moreover, it eliminates quality issues which are likely to arise from fatigue, absentmindedness or malicious intentions which are rooted in human nature.
- Thirdly, it offers cost savings by incorporating made-to-order or mass-customization capabilities.

Smart factories make use of digital technologies for the purpose of having crucial developments in areas such as productivity, quality, flexibility and services. Smart factories focus on three key technologies. These are as below:

- **Connectivity:** Using industrial IoT technologies for collecting data from existing equipment and new sensors.
- **Smart Automation**: Drones, advanced robots (cobots i.e. collaborative robots), machine learning, distributed control, and other smart devices and technologies.
- **Cloud-Based Data Management and Analytics:** Predictive Analytics, Artificial Intelligence (AI) practices.

The main property of a smart factory is the closed-loop, data-based optimization of end-to-end operations. Initially, developed analytics is used for decision support. However, the final goal is to have access to self-optimizing operations. Here, the factory constantly adapts to changes in the demand and supply and process deviations. It is observed that developments in the automotive industry took place in the last few years in particular. As per the results of the research by Capgemini (2019), while the ratio of interest of automotive firms in smart factories was 38% in 2017-2018, this figure reached 48% in 2019 (Winkler et al., 2020).

BLOCKCHAIN TECHNOLOGY

The BC is a technology which makes it possible to keep record of irreversible data of the distributed ledgers in a safe and encrypted format and, in no way, allows the retroactive alteration of transactions. The concept of Blockchain (BC) was, for the first time, introduced in 2008 in relation to Bitcoin by Satoshi Nakamoto. The BC offers a technological structure for challenging business problems. The Blockchain is defined as a decentralized distributed ledger which securely, verifiably and transparently stores all transactions executed across a peer-to-peer network. Data in this decentralized distributed ledger changes on the basis of the BC design. If the Blockchain is designed for the purpose of money transfers, as in the case of Bitcoin, then data about such transactions is stored in a block. If the Blockchain is designed for a supply chain, then all data that is supposed to be stored in the system across the supply chain are stored in many blocks. The block size is determined by the system. When a new block needs to be created, a structure called the Miner plays a key role in determining which blocks will be added to the system. These structures enable the processing of data which exist in blocks. In the BC technology, a new transaction to be added to the system is first created. This new operation (of creating a block) is posted across the network for verification and control, and, when the majority of nodes across the Blockchain approve this transaction in accordance with predetermined and previously authorized rules, this transaction is added to the chain as a new block. This transaction is recorded on several distributed nodes for ensuring the security. The feature, called Smart Contract and known as a critical property of the BC technology, provides the opportunity to perform safe transactions without the involvement of any third parties. These transactions come into being alongside a consistent verification process thanks to another network mechanism called Consensus. Upon the verification of the new record and its addition to the Blockchain, multiple copies are created in a decentralized manner in order to create the new Blockchain. Hence, by virtue of the BC technology, several problems in products/services such as traceability, compatibility, flexibility and the management of partners are eliminated (Emen, 2018; Güneşli, Yıldızbaşı & Eras, 2020; Kosba, Miller, Shi, et al., 2016; Saberi, Kouhizadeh, Sarkis & Shen, 2018; Liu, Kadıyala, & Cannistraci, 2018). On account of omitting the third party in conducting transactions, the security and productivity of transactions are enhanced and transaction costs are lowered (Dabbagh, Sookhak, & Safa, 2019).

The BC technology is being adopted by several industries at a fast rate. The scale indicating the adoption of this technology by each specific sector is displayed in Figure 1 (Pai et al., 2018).

Figure 1. Level of adoption of BC technology by each specific sector

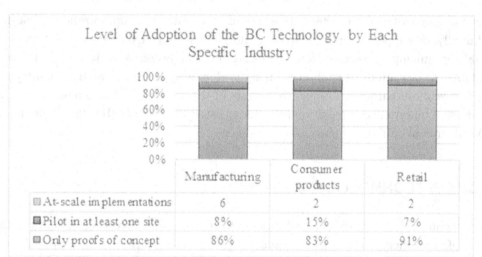

Upon the review of the ecosystem of the BC technology by country, it is discerned that the UK, the USA and France are taking the lead (Pai et al., 2018).

Figure 2. Use of the Blockchain technology as per the country ecosystems

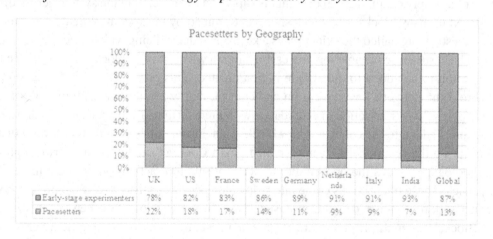

Principles of the BC technology are exhibited in Table 1 (Dobrovnik, Herold, Fürs, & Kummer, 2018; Iansiti & Lakhani, 2017).

Table 1. Principles of Blockchain technology

Distributed Database	Each party to the BC has access to the entire database and its history. No party controls data/information, and each party can directly verify the records of other parties to the transaction without intermediaries.
Peer-to-peer Transmission	The communication takes place directly between peers rather than through a central node. Each node stores and transfers data to other nodes.
Transparency with Pseudo Nymity	Each transaction and its associated value can be seen by each party who has access to the system. Each node or user has a unique alphanumeric address which identifies it and is composed of 30 plus characters. When transactions are performed between BC addresses, the users can prefer to remain anonymous or to authenticate their identities to other users.
Irreversibility of Records	When a transaction is entered in the database and accounts are updated, records cannot be altered as each transaction is tied to the preceding transactions. A variety of calculation algorithms and approaches are employed for ensuring that the record in the database becomes permanent, chronologically ordered and usable by all other users across the network.
Computational Logic	The digital structure of ledgers signifies that the BC transactions can be bound to a computational logic and, in essence, can be programmed. In other words, users can create algorithms and rules and automatically initiate the transactions between nodes (e.g. smart contracts).

According to a survey report, prepared by the World Economic Forum, approximately 10% of the Gross Domestic Product (GDP) at world scale will be stored in a Blockchain by 2027 (World Economic Forum, 2015). This estimate proves that the interest in the BC technology will grow even further and faster with each passing day.

Types of Blockchain

The BC technology can be grouped under three main categories as Public BC, Private/Permissioned BC and Consortium BC. They are as follows (Htet & Htet, 2019; Zheng, Shaoan Xie, et al., 2017):

- **Public Blockchain**: This is open to public and any interested party can participate in the network (e.g. for cryptocurrency transactions). All transactions which are performed across the general BC's are fully transparent. Each party can examine the transaction details. Moreover, the user can take part in the fulfillment of tasks such as approving transactions (mining) or performing simple user transactions.
- **Private/Permissioned Blockchain**: This is different from a public BC. Its features are presented below:
  - For joining the networks, participants are required to have an agreement.
  - Transactions are private and can be used solely by participants that are authorized by the ecosystem to join the network.
  - It is more centralized than public a public BC.

Private BC's are utilized by establishments or corporations that are interested in having cooperation with others and exchanging information or data but protecting the confidentiality of sensitive business data in a BC which is open to public. This BC type has a more centralized structure, and entities or members of the BC have authorizations.

- **Consortium Blockchain**: This variety of BC has all the advantages of a private BC and can be considered as its sub-category, rather than being a separate BC type. Nodes are separated across the network and act as a consensus system for new data or blocks which are processed across the network

Table 2. Types of Blockchain

Features	BC Types		
	Public	Private/Permissioned	Consortium
Agreement mechanism	No approval required	Approval Required	Approval required
Read permission	Open	Limited	Limited
Productivity	Low	High	High
Centrality	Distributed	Centralized	Distributed-Centralized
Data exchange	Impossible	Changeable	Changeable

Features of each Blockchain type differ from each other. Table 2 briefly summarizes the features (Baygin, Baygin, & Karakose, 2019).

Prominent Features of Blockchain Technology

Prominent features of the BC technology are listed below (Singh, BLOCKCHAIN TECHNOLOGY: A POTENTIAL GAME CHANGER FOR AUTOMOTIVE INDUSTRY, 2020):

- **Real-Time:** The analysis of recorded operations is fulfilled instantly, and disagreements are eliminated and the risk is lowered.
- **Reliable and Accessible:** As multiple participants share the same BC, a copy of the transaction is recorded in the computer of each user. By virtue of the fact that two passwords exist as public and private passwords, it is impossible to read or alter data.
- **Transparent**: Transactions are visible to all participants. Identical copies are stored in multiple computer systems. The control over stored data raises the level of trust.
- **Irreversible**: It is possible to make the transactions, which can promote the authenticity of records and simplify the back-office processes irreversible.
- **Immutable**: It is almost impossible to make alterations and commit fraud in a BC without being identified.
- **Digital**: Almost all documents or entities are expressed as codes and can be referenced with a ledger entry. In other words, the BC technology has a broad range of applications.

Blockchain Basics for Cybersecurity

As summarized in Figure 3, the Blockchain offers several security advantages which are essential to cyber-resistant applications (Fraga-Lamas & Fernández-Caramés, 2019).

Figure 3. Key features of the Blockchain in relation to cyber security

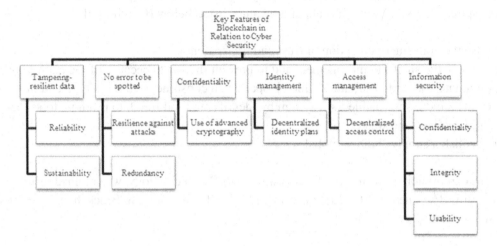

Information in a Blockchain is stored in an encrypted format which provides the system with security (Kalita, Boro, & Bhattacharyya, 2020). Each block is added to the compound value of the preceding blocks, and thus, it is cryptographically chained to the preceding blocks thereby assuring the integrity of the Blockchain. As long as an attacker does not take possession of the greater part of the network (which is highly unlikely), the Blockchain can prevent double-spending entries and inverse transactions. For admitting a newly proposed block, Blockchain systems rely on a consensus algorithm (Davi, Hatebur, Heisel, & Wirtz, 2019).

In light of security and confidentiality goals of an application of the BC technology, the below security measures are taken (Lu et al., 2019):

- **Confidentiality:** Third parties or those irrelevant to the transaction are not supposed to obtain information on objects which they do not own.
- **Authorization:** Third parties are not supposed to perform actions which are not relevant to their roles.
- **Accountability:** In the case where unwanted parties try to be part of a transaction or commit a malevolent behavior, the system is supposed to keep track of the erroneous behavior.

Merits and Demerits of Blockchain in Terms of Applications

The main advantage of the Blockchain over the available technologies is that it allows two or more parties to have transactions safely through the Internet without the intermediation of any third party. Exclusion of the third party does not only promote the security and productivity of operations but also lowers transaction costs (Çetin Gerger, 2013; Dabbagh, Sookhak & Safa, 2019). In the BC technology, the value is indicated by transaction records which are entered in a shared ledger, provide safe and auditable information, can be verified and include timestamp (English, Auer, & Domingue, 2016). Even if the BC technology is proactively used in several business and other sectors today, the areas of its application are increasingly broadened with each passing day. For instance, Wallmart works on the BC technology in cooperation with IBM for assuring food security and traceability. Together with the BC technology, Wallmart aspires to raise expectations about the values listed below (Galvin, 2017):

- To raise the consumer perception of trust and transparency.
- To improve the shelf life management and to prevent the waste because of the expired products.
- To eliminate counterfeit products which jeopardize a consumer or are likely to end in a disaster.
- To create a more sustainable food system by identifying food fraud, to promote food security and to avoid spoilage and waste.
- To establish a supply chain at global scale.

Upon the exploration of the reasons for investing in the BC technology, we obtained results as shown in Figure 4. It is discerned that the first three main factors for investing in Blockchain are cost savings, traceability and transparency (Pai et al., 2018).

Figure 4. Reasons for investing in Blockchain

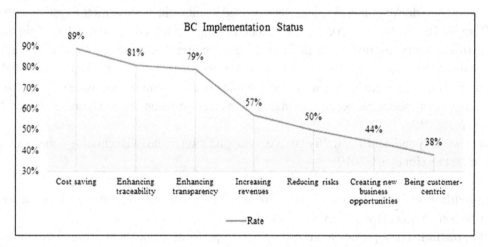

Blockchain applications vary across sectors. Advantages and disadvantages of the Blockchain can differ for sector to sector. Industries in which the Blockchain is employed, areas of application, and advantages and disadvantages are displayed in Table 3 (Baygin, Baygin, & Karakose, 2019).

Table 3. Advantages and disadvantages of the Blockchain technology across sectors

Industry	Area of Application	Advantages	Disadvantages
Governance	• Voting • Land transactions • Tax regulations • Education • Public services • Inheritance • Charity organizations • Labor rights • Authentication	• A transparent, reliable and verifiable system • Data security in the case of natural disasters • Protection of assets, reporting and accounting, accessibility, cost savings and effective collateral management	• Vulnerability of internet-based systems • Slow-down of the system due to newly-added blocks • Failure to maintain privacy under all circumstances • Selfish miners putting the system in trouble
Health	• Storing medical records • Health services	• Security of patient data • System with which the patient is actively involved rather than a system controlled by a centralized structure • Storage and analysis of health information as a whole	• Obligation to train the patient for enabling his/her involvement with the system • The possibility that the confidential data will be released due to technical failure although unauthorized access is not allowed.
Finance	• Mutual funds • Crypto exchanges • Stocks • Insurance • Credit records • Crowdfunding	• A fast, low-cost and simple system • Reliable system by virtue of controllable and non-tampering blocks • A recoverable system in the case of a failure	• Difficulty in implementing the entire BC structure due to the fact that banking systems which are used in daily life need a certain degree of centralization • Prolongation of the verification time for the system along with growing number of blocks and the subsequent slow-downs in the system
Technology	• Cloud storage • Data backup • IoT management • Cloud computing • Messaging applications	• Data consistency and rapid verification of operations • Enhancement of productivity and flexibility and low cost by virtue of eliminating third-party agents • The formation of fast moving systems with BC open-source code sharing	• Cost and capacity constraints • Manipulation of data • Cloud servers are susceptible to cyber-attacks during downtime • Data theft
Others	• Supply chain • Copyright protection • Food safety • Car-sharing • Internet advertisements • Forecasting systems • Energy management • Human rights • Customer recognition systems • Quality control • Logistics • Waste management	• Transforming the traditional structure for creating reliable, decentralized, scalable and unique structures • Ensuring integrity by creating a common database • Protection of author's copyright	• 51% of the BC is seized and the system is at great risk • Fork problem in the system • High cost of converting existing system infrastructure to BC structure • Uncertainty about regulations • Lack of clarity about smart contracts • Synchronization problem in non-interoperable systems

Merits and demerits of the BC technology vary but do also share similarities depending on the industry where the BC technology is used. That is why, addressing BC applications in a way to be specific to each industry will raise the likelihood of success.

Figure 5. Stages of adoption of Blockchain technology in the automotive industry

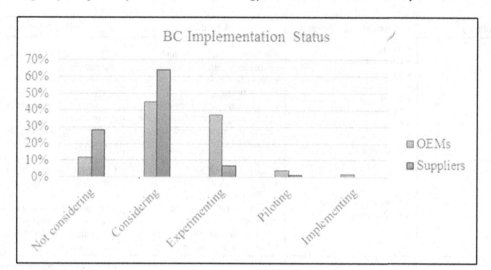

BLOCKCHAIN TECHNOLOGY IN AUTOMOTIVE INDUSTRY

As the Blockchain provides safer and traceable transactions, better access to information and transparency, it has the potential to promote the trust and cooperation between consumers and even vehicles. Advantages to be offered by the BC technology to the automotive ecosystem are to promote the cooperation between participants and to activate skills necessary for new business models of mobility. As well as activating a single source of data, the Blockchain can facilitate device-to-device transactions, smart contracts and real-time processing and locating. For automotive industry, the transparency of this supply chain signifies improvements and operational productivity in areas such as financial transactions between ecosystem participants, the verification of access to automobiles, customer experience and loyalty (IBM Institute for Business Value, 2018). However, data security is of high importance to the promotion of competitiveness and the protection of corporate secrets in the automotive industry. Without ensuring the data security, corporations acknowledge that systems should remain flexible enough to respond to the changing market conditions and customer needs even if they do not believe that new technologies will be extensively used. It is predicted that this topic will turn to be even more important in the future along with growing volume of data and computational advancements. Analyzing data with today's technology is remarkably effortless. For the purpose of eliminating the risks associated with the third parties, corporations store data in their own servers in countries which have the supportive regulatory framework. In such countries, corporations utilize firewalls and systems which have no internet access. Moreover, data are generally categorized in terms of sensitivity, and instructions specify the security category of data to be stored and where it should be stored. On the other hand, while certain data should be secured by corporations, some other data should be shared with partners in the supply chain. The data security should be ensured across the entire supply chain with more powerful interconnection systems. A disruption in its weakest entity poses a security threat to the entire network (Kern & Wolff, 2019).

In the automotive industry, the BC technology is successfully utilized in enterprise resource planning (ERP) software as well which is used in production planning phases (Winkler et al., 2020; Gerger & Firuzan, 2010).

Sector-specific research performed by IBM is particularly beneficial as it portrays to what extent OEMs and suppliers are prepared for the BC technology. Results of this research are demonstrated in Figure 5.

Use Cases of Blockchain Technology in Automotive Industry

Services to be fulfilled by using the BC technology in the automotive industry can be listed as follows (Fraga-Lamas & Fernández-Caramés, 2019; Zhao et al., 2018; Singh, 2020; Dorri, Steger, Kanhere & Jurdak, 2017; Rosado, Vasconcelos, & Correia, 2019):

- **Production Processes**: A production plant must effectively coordinate its suppliers in order to ensure the delivery of parts in due time and the optimization of stock levels. The BC technology is used for storing all data including WIP (work in progress) data for the assembly of each vehicle starting from the quality control records, which are created during the production process, to the final stage. Prior to introduction of Blockchain, an automobile manufacturer was obliged to wait for a few weeks or months before receiving the payment for a delivered vehicle from an importer/distributor/seller. The manufacturer was put through a slow flow of documentation owing to the multiple parties that controlled different steps in the supply chain. Through a Blockchain -based system, the process is shortened by ensuring the creation of transparency of information between multiple parties for the purpose of verifying banking documents and processing them faster.

- **Supply Chain**: Automotive supply chain is a sophisticated construct which is comprised of a variety of suppliers, distributors, dealers, regulatory agencies, insurance companies and so on. A Blockchain-based system can provide transparency between different parties. By using the BC technology in the supply chain, logistics services can be punctually developed, the number and costs of erroneous orders are lowered and inventory turnover is increased. As the Blockchain is highly secure, it is ideal for keeping records in between different parties. Relations between raw material suppliers, automotive suppliers, OEMs, dealers, repair shops, online after-sale retailers and other stakeholders include multiple parties in general and these parties are expected to reach a consensus over the agreement. Each party performs transactions in full security via the Blockchain instead of being directly involved in verifying and reconciling the transactions. For example, in case automobile parts were stolen, replaced and damaged in the delivery, it was assured that the manufacturer followed up these parts with full accuracy via the Blockchain concept. In the case of recalls, recall procedure is also facilitated as the Blockchain contains data on the history of the broken part. Whether the part had any modification or whether any manufacturing error occurred can be accurately checked.

- **Financial Transacions:** By virtue of the BC technology, all transactions which require the entry of manual data can lower operation costs and, among other things, facilitate revisions. The Blockchain will speed up these processes and keep them up-to-date during the lifecycle of an automobile. Finance providers for automobiles have in general no idea about drivers' real driving behaviors or repair and maintenance service history of the vehicle. A Blockchain-based system enables the exchange of information on driving models and repair and maintenance service history with a ledger which can be accessed by all parties. Data obtained about the wear and tear of a vehicle by means of the Blockchain automatically help the finance provider calculate the current value of the vehicle more accurately. Automatic financing contains a series of verification steps in which the Blockchain can be implemented for achieving better efficiency.

- **Secure Communication**: The BC technology has an applicability power in the case of both vehicle-to-vehicle and object-to-object secure communications. Today, autonomous vehicles establish communication with other vehicles, traffic lights and other unauthenticated devices. BC technology ensures that the communication is securely established only between relevant objects. Thus, unauthenticated persons are prevented from hacking these operations. A connected vehicle contains software-based navigation, vehicle-to-vehicle communication and several services which are likely to affect the security of vehicle and passenger. The Blockchain can be used for securely storing data which are sent and received by the systems. The enhanced encryption level prevents computer hackers from accessing or using these data. Along with the growth in the number of autonomous vehicles, millions of devices are in constant communication with each other. Therefore, it is essential that shared data be stored in safe databases requiring high-level authentication. Data which are shared in a ledger among automotive OEMs, part distributors, dealers, repair shops, insurance companies and other parties allow the part and equipment within the vehicle to recognize their own needs independently. For instance, a communication network of a car can offer recommendations to the driver about the repair needs of the car, and can communicate with remote users for updates or with suppliers in close proximity for spare parts. It can negotiate the price and arrange appointments for the service and subsequently process the payment for services.

- **Vehicle Safety and Data Security**: Having more communications with other vehicles or objects today make vehicles more sensitive to cyber-attacks which are likely to have fatal consequences. A Blockchain is an ideal place for storing data as data cannot be altered by virtue of strong cryptographic basis of the Blockchain technology which cannot be reverse-engineered. For instance, a common practice of an unethical car dealer is to sell a showroom vehicle and not to present information on this sale to the bank which provided the car dealer with loan for this vehicle. This practice enables the dealer to have the working capital necessary to pay for the wages of its employees and the supplies. If the bank finds about this undue process in time, it will immediately take action against the dealer. On the other hand, the bank can have no claim directly on the vehicle as the vehicle is sold legally, and at the same time, the financing extended to the dealer was already used. Alongside the transparency of data, the information asymmetry which makes this practice possible will not come into play. The BC technology instantaneously provides transparency, and provides more valuable service with the participation of more parties. It completely prevents such unethical operations.

- **Electric Vehicles:** As electric automobiles become more common, they will need a new machine-to-machine infrastructure which covers power suppliers, charging stations, automobile manufacturers, part suppliers and automobile owners. No firm can manage the sophisticated business of integrating its partners. No single entity is supposed to hold the ownership of the platform which is likely to create a monopoly. The security architecture proposed by the BC allows the data transfer between the vehicle and other IoT participants (e.g. smart house and user's smart devices). The other participants can be considered as the overlay nodes. For the protection of confidentiality, the vehicle owner can individually customize which data will be shared between these entities, and can upgrade the smart vehicle and its functionalities by introducing new services.

Table 4. Overcoming supply chain problems of automotive industry through BC technology

Problems encountered in conventional supply chains	How the BC technology can solve these problems?
Lack of traceability	Permission to control all transactions
Risks associated with multiple stakeholders	Irreversible - secure against undesired alterations
Lack of sensitivity	Real time
Mostly manual processing	Digitalized faster transactions
Legal compliance	Tampering-resilient data can be easily verified
Burden of reaching consensus	The single shared source of the truth

- **Insurance**: Insurance companies monitor the driving behaviors of their customers (braking, accelerating, lane changes and so on.) and evaluate these data. At the outset, when the vehicle owner selects such a flexible insurance model, the insurance company creates a pair of shared/private passcodes/keys for the vehicle through an account in the cloud. Thus, the insurance company knows the real identity of each account holder. The pair of keys is used by the vehicle for all transactions to be performed with the insurance company. Through the account, the vehicle stores all data in the cloud. These data are utilized by the insurance company for providing the user with flexible insurance services. As the insurance company knows about vehicle owner's identity by virtue of the information stored in the cloud, the company exchanges information with the relevant parties in the case of accidents or other cases where the need arises. As the data are stored by means of BC technology, malevolent actions are prevented. Vehicle owner can terminate his/her contract with the insurance company or can sell the vehicle any time he/she wishes. In such situations, the insurance company removes the account of the relevant vehicle from the cloud. Hence, the vehicle is prevented from having access to services and storing its data in the cloud any more.
- **Smart Charging Services**: As the number of electric vehicles constantly grows, the upward trend raises the demand for efficient and quick vehicle charging infrastructure. The desire of smart vehicle owners to connect the vehicle to the smart house, mobile devices etc. can require several sophisticated services. For instance, upon the acquisition of information on user's travel habits (e.g. through his/her calendars), the customization of pricing can be more individualized for each user. This information can be utilized for assuring that the vehicle is fully charged at the moment when the user needs it and also for selecting the most efficient and inexpensive charging cycle by avoiding the busiest charging periods.
- **Car-Sharing Services:** Today, the car-sharing services are rapidly growing. So as to provide such highly decentralized services, it is necessary for smart vehicles, car-pooling service providers and service users to be securely connected to each other. For securely changing the data such as the location of the vehicle, information for unlocking the doors of the vehicle and user's payment data, a secure communication channel is needed. By virtue of the decentralized structure of the Blockchain, only a registered and authorized user is permitted to find the location of the vehicle, to unlock its doors and to drive it. Information such as the user's real identity and travel route is securely stored.
- **Smart Contracts:** These are the computer programs which are written for the purpose of creating agreements between users of a Blockchain. By means of smart contracts, it is possible to ensure that provisions of a contract are automatically fulfilled and to make the violation of the contact

expensive or even prohibitive. The Blockchain creates a consensus which is based on minimum trust between network nodes for the purpose of creating smart contracts. For assuring the validity of the transaction, functions of the smart contract take effect and its terms are fulfilled.

Some other areas where the use of Blockchain will be more common for the collection and evaluation of data in the automotive industry in the future, are presented below (Kaiser et al., 2018):

- Emission data of vehicles
- Vehicle data (weight, number of passengers, manufacturing year, type, brand and so on)
- Environmental data (road condition, outside temperature, rainfall and so on)
- Traffic data (entities identified around the vehicle and including human beings and vehicles, the density rate of the streets and so on)
- Driver data (driver license, music channel, spiritual state, fatigue level, driving performance points, hearth rate and so on)
- Driving data (GPS location, inside temperature, start date, hour and destination)
- Other relevant data as a result of device connectivity

One of the areas where the BC technology is the most intensively used in the automotive industry is the supply chain. How the Blockchain solves the problems encountered in conventional supply chains is displayed in Table 4 (Pai et al., 2018).

Application of the BC technology is not limited only to the above areas. As in the case of other industries, areas of application of the Blockchain expand and get diversified in the automotive industry as well.

Strategy for Implementation of Blockchain Technology

Before deciding whether to apply the BC technology to operations, it is useful, first, to perform a well-structured situation analysis. To this end, analyzing the weaknesses and strengths of the firm is necessary for making a powerful start on Blockchain applications. Even though several techniques are utilized in this context, SWOT analysis which is one of the powerful tools of strategic management was preferred in this book chapter. The name SWOT is derived from the first letters of the words, Strengths, Weaknesses, Opportunities and Threats. This analysis is the comparison of opportunities and threats identified through the external analysis to the findings of the internal analysis, that is, organization's strengths and its weaknesses which are conducive to improvement (Hill & Westbrook, 1997; Özan, Polat, Gündüzalp, & Yaraş, 2015). In the application phase of the BC technology in the automotive industry, the evaluation of strengths and weaknesses is crucial. Strengths and weaknesses of the automotive industry are listed in Table 5 (Fraga-Lamas & Fernández-Caramés, 2019).

Table 5. SWOT analysis for enabling the expansion of BC to the automotive industry

POSITIVE	NEGATIVE
Strengths	**Weaknesses**
Internal ■ Operational productivity ■ Cyber resilience ■ No need for intermediaries that do not create value-added ■ Fast and simple transfers at low cost ■ Automated transactions through smart contracts, IoT enabler ■ Decline in human errors ■ Accountability, verified, timestamped and irreversible auditable data ■ No data loss, neither altered nor distorted ■ Security and modern encryption ■ Non-repudiation ■ Transparency ■ Global accessibility ■ Reliable platform of big data analysis ■ Decentralization ■ Traceability, asset provenance ■ Dynamic and fluid value exchange ■ Accountability, proof of ownership and rights	■ Nascent, in the early stage of development ■ Scalability issues ■ High power consumption ■ Low performance ■ Lack of interoperability ■ Confidentiality problems (in certain scenarios) ■ Criminal activities, malicious attacks ■ Dependent on inputs from external resources ■ Poor user experience, unfamiliarity of the customers ■ If users' credentials are lost (e.g. a wallet), no intermediary can be contacted ■ Being exposed to cryptocurrency volatility in cases of specific use ■ Limitation of the smart contract code programming model ■ Wallet and key management ■ Highly-qualified human resources (scarce and expensive) ■ Being too sophisticated (Mastering the BC concepts is difficult.) ■ Lack of trust in new technology suppliers ■ Core business scenarios or processes may not necessarily be well-suited to the application of BC ■ Poor corporate governance
Opportunities	**Threats**
External ■ Industrial competitive power (e.g. lower transaction costs, enhanced cyber security, full IoT automation) ■ Market diversification (e.g. supporting car-sharing) ■ Enabling new business models ■ Rebalancing of information symmetry between parties ■ Reducing fraud ■ Lowered systemic risks ■ Network effect ■ Large amount of heterogeneous data pushed into the BC by different actors for data analysis (big data applications) ■ Open-source code ■ Facilitation of the trans-boundary trade ■ Reducing the number of verification procedures ■ Digital twin enabler ■ Circular economy enabler	■ Perception of insecurity or unreliability ■ Technological vulnerabilities ■ Divergent block chains, ledger competition ■ Low-level adoption by important stakeholders ■ Institutional barriers to adoption ■ Medium term or long-term investment ■ Not adequate for external customers, lack of readiness for adoption

For the success of Blockchain applications in the automotive industry, it is important that, SWOT analysis is the first step.

Blockchain in Automotive Industry: Advantages and Disadvantages

Digital technologies which shape the future have presented a variety of connections and software to the automobiles and their manufacturers. In the context of IT data security, this situation has become a source of anxiety for all parties involved in the production and delivery value chain. However, the emergence of the BC technology has played a key role in relieving this anxiety.

Table 6. Challenges for the automotive industry in BC applications

Stakeholder	Challenges Likely To Be Faced
Car owners and lenders / buyers and sellers of pre-owned cars	• Lack of transparency about automobile's history • Unexpected vehicle maintenance and repair costs • Absence of trust in the outcome of maintenance and repair works • Lack of informed purchase options • Absence of car insurance options • Lack of trust in autonomous and IoT-connected vehicles • High-level transactional experience for consumers while reducing costs incurred by them
Fleet management companies / Car leasing or sharing (car-sharing, ride-sharing or ride-hailing) companies	• Lack of transparency about automobile's history • Unexpected vehicle maintenance and repair costs • Absence of trust in the outcome of maintenance and repair works • Lack of interoperability with business partners • High operational costs, low profit margins • High costs in car-sharing, ride-sharing and ride-hailing economy • Lack of trust in autonomous and IoT-connected vehicles
Car-sharing, ride-sharing or ride-hailing passengers	• Driving/riding cars more affordably • Better maintained cars • Lack of trust in autonomous and IoT-connected vehicles • Absence of a common platform for providing mobility • Lack of instant payments
Car entrepreneurs	• High vehicle leasing costs • Lower car-sharing, ride-sharing or ride-hailing partnership fees • Difficulties in setting up business, unfair competition • Lack of trust in autonomous and IoT-connected vehicles • Absence of information sharing
Car dealers and retailers	• Updated vehicle ownership records • Updated repair and maintenance records • Updated purchase records • Lack of trust in autonomous and IoT-connected vehicles • Absence of information sharing
OEM / Car manufacturers and suppliers	• High warranty claim costs • Forcing dealers to adhere to recommended maintenance and repair prices • Customer complaints because of automobile dealers' acts in violation of maintenance fees recommended by automobile manufacturers • Lack of control over the vehicle maintenance services performed by the authorized dealers • Low level of customer loyalty • Cyber-attacks and system failure risks in autonomous and IoT-connected vehicles • Control of logistics • Absence of information sharing
Insurance companies	• Inflexible and non-customized policy pricing • 5-10% of all claims across the world are fraudulent • Costly and inefficient claim management • Erroneous customer policy pricing • Lack of oversight over the quality and pricing for collision repair
Independent repair shops	• Underutilized capacity • Customer retention • Low profit margins • Lack of brand confidence
After-market (producers, distributors and retailers of spare parts, garages)	• Inefficient stock management • Counterfeit spare parts market • Lack of transparency in the warranty monitoring and enforcement • Low profit margins • Lack of brand confidence
Governments and public organizations	• Updated state records (e.g. vehicle maintenance records, ownership rights, vehicle taxes, traffic fine history) • Lack of trust in autonomous and IoT-connected vehicles • Adherence to the existing regulations especially in terms of driver liability or data protection • Enhanced interconnectivity along with open-source traffic data and infrastructure data offered through a data cloud, and eagerness to shift to digital radio and universal network coverage • Greater use of anonymization and pseudonymization in data collection, and processing comprehensive information and providing vehicle owners and drivers with information on which data are collected and by whom. • Real-time notifications about road conditions and traffic congestion • Reliable data for accident research and mitigating actions
Financial institutions	• Updated vehicle ownership records and automobile insurance, maintenance and lien records • Absence of a single reference point for all transactions
Telecommunication and tech companies, content and service providers	• Guaranteeing stable and secure vehicle-to-vehicle (V2V) and vehicle-to-infrastructure (V2I) communication to assure efficient and safe vehicle coordination and cooperation. • Lack of reliable connection between vehicles and between vehicles and infrastructure
Scrappage/recycle and environmental groups	• Control of greenhouse gas emissions • Full traceability of components • Long-term sustainability
Academia	• Guaranteeing vehicle safety, security, and autonomy • More efficient driving, development of the optimized Human-Machine Interfaces (HMI) • Tackling traffic management of highly and fully automated vehicles under mixed traffic conditions

The BC technology represents a breakthrough, which removes the need for a reliable third party for facilitating digital relationships, in recording and disseminating data. Even if there were several cases of the application of Blockchain in different sectors of the global economy, Blockchain applications intended for the automotive industry mostly remained at experimental and environmental level. That is the reason that the challenge for automotive industry is the conceptualization of a project which will spread the revolutionary benefits of this destructive technology to the entire automotive ecosystem (Car-nomic, 2020). To this end, the automotive industry should get acquainted with existing circumstances which will challenge it during the application of BC technology and seek solutions to these challenging circumstances. Fraga-Lamas and Fernández-Caramés (2017) have summarized certain potential inherent challenges in Blockchain applications to the said industry. These are listed in Table 6.

Even though there are said challenges, there are several advantages accompanying the BC technology in comparison to conventional methods. These are presented in Table 7 (Dorri, Steger, Kanhere, & Jurdak, 2017).

Table 7. BC Technology vs conventional methods - summary of advantages of BC

Areas of Application	Conventional Methods	Advantages Due To BC
Wireless Remote SW Update (WRSU)	• Central – not scalable • Partial participation – not addressing the entire value chain • Lack of confidentiality – A direct link between the vehicle and OEM can compromise driver's confidentiality (e.g. driver behaviors or locations). • Only the OEM can verify communications or history of updates	• Enabling decentralized data exchange and secure scalability • End-to-end: involving OEMs, vehicles, service centers, assembly lines and so on. • Protecting user's confidentiality (also for authentication) • Update history and authenticity of the software can be verified by all parties.
Insurance	• Existing systems are in general insecure, and this endangers the entire vehicle. • Users have no control on exchanged data. • In order to have access to the service, privacy-sensitive data should be constantly exchanged with the insurance company.	• Data exchange which is secure, decentralized and protects confidentiality • Users are able to control modified data. • Privacy-sensitive data are shared upon request instead of having data exchange constantly (e.g. accident occurred.).
Electric vehicles	• Centralized payment and accounting • User's locations and behaviors can be traced (e.g. using a specified charger on a certain day).	• Private and decentralized security, payments and accounting • User information such as the location data remains confidential.
Car-sharing services	• Centralized payment and accounting • Users can be traced through their identities. • Centralized authorization	• Private and decentralized security, payments and accounting • Users use modifiable credentials • Decentralized authorization

These advantages are not solely limited to the stated areas. Along with the expansion of the Blockchain literacy, areas of its application and advantages will be multiplied.

Best Practices

Blockchain technology offers powerful examples of its use that aims to transform several facets of the automotive industry. The Mobility Open Blockchain Initiative (MOBI) event in May 2018 is the most obvious manifestation of the increased pace of the Blockchain revolution in the automotive sector.

On this occasion, big car makers such as BWW, GM, Ford, Bosch and Renault Groupe and the leading Blockchain and technology enterprises such as IBM, Accenture, and ConsenSys came together. A further two-day colloquium which brought all MOBI members together was held in BMW Group IT Center in Munich in February 2019. The priority of the activity was designated as the promotion and development of common standards for enabling the implementation of Blockchain and distributed ledger technologies (DLT) in the mobility industry. Founders of MOBI aimed to use the BC technology with a view to shaping a mobility future which would be greener and safer and would raise the quality of life in cities. Moreover, the group works diligently on the areas of application of the Blockchain for making the mobility more secure, inexpensive and accessible.

MOBI performs researches on how the Blockchain can be used for meeting customer demands in the new digital mobility ecosystem. Some of the first projects of MOBI are focusing on secure mobility trade in the context of the following topics:

- mobility pricing and payments based on the usage
- identity, history and usage of the vehicle

MOBI partners aim only to develop clearly-defined universal standards and an open and independent platform which will enable the application of the BC technology across the sector. The leading manufacturers are currently pursuing a variety of Blockchain initiatives. Some of these are as briefly outlined below (IBM Institute for Business Value, 2018; Singh, 2020):

- **Ford**: This company launched a pilot study with a view to assuring the ethical procurement of cobalt, an element used in the production of lithium-ion car batteries. Thus, by means of BC technology, Ford are aspiring to ensure that child labor (child miner) is not employed in cobalt mining by following the supply chain of cobalt production and supply.
- **Volkswagen:** This car manufacturer is producing a BC-based tracking system for the purpose of preventing the odometer fraud which is commonly committed in the automotive industry. Hence, they aim to stop unfair car sellers from committing odometer fraud and to protect potential buyers.
- **Hyundai:** They announced a new partnership with IBM for the purpose of developing the BC technology and use of cloud-based AI. Here, IBM are focused on creating a finance ecosystem for the supply chain by means of open-source Hyper Ledger Fabric. The project aims to automate the manual processes, lower costs and delivery time, and hence enhance the customer experience.
- **Innogy SE (a member of RWE):** A short while ago, Innogy SE announced, via its enterprise Share & Charge, that it launched the installation of charge stations for electric automobiles to be operated through the BC technology across the country. This initiative aims to help electric automobile owners to charge their cars in charge stations set up by Share & Charge, which is the startup of Innogy Innovation Hub. This application is the first e-mobility community platform which relies on the BC technology.
- **Daimler AG:** Daimler AG have introduced a new Blockchain-based cryptocurrency, called MobiCoin, to the market. This currency is part of company's initiative which is designed to reward drivers for their environment-friendly driving habits. Drivers who achieve in obtaining MobiCoins will have the opportunity to use them for getting VIP tickets for activities such as Mercedes Cup Final or Fashion Week in Berlin.

STATISTICAL EVALUATION AND BIG DATA ANALYTICS

Big Data refers to data clusters which are characterized by big volume, high speed and diversity (Govindan, Cheng, Mishra, & Shukla, 2018). Prior to the fourth industrial revolution, in order to perform a statistical analysis about a population, a sample was required from the population based on the characteristics of the areas of interest. However, as accessing data is easy considering the necessary technologies being already available, it is possible to perform analysis directly on the population. With each passing day, these developments raise the importance of statistics even more in today's super intelligent society. For selecting the necessary data from among such large amount of data and analyzing them, the concept of Big Data came to the forefront. The concept of big data which appeared in 1997 for the first time (Cox and Ellsworth, 1997) was referred to in an article titled 'Application Controlled Demand Paging for Out-of-Core Visualization' which addressed the issue of insufficiency of storage devices (computer rams, external and internal hard disks and so on.) due to the large size of datasets (Cox & Ellsworth, 1997; Gerger, 2020). Big data is a new concept which defines any heterogeneous data that appear to be impossible to process through conventional database techniques (Gahi, Guennoun, & Mouftah, 2016). Big data is generated through several sources; some of the most renowned being sensors, smart devices (watches and bracelets), medical equipment, tablets, mobile phones, records of website use, social media, simulations, and so on (Schneider, 2012).

By virtue of the fact that data collection and capacity for data collection grow rapidly, creating networks gradually becomes more relevant to all domains and industries (Wu, Zhu, Wu, & Ding, 2014). It is the domain of big data analysis which supplements big data, and known also as the business intelligence and analytics. By analyzing critical business data, firms can better understand their businesses and markets, and take business decisions on time (Chen, Chiang, & Storey, 2012).

An OEM is able to perform statistical analyses through 'big data' technology for the purpose of optimizing the transportation network which includes transport time, truck loads and routes. Schaeffler, a first-level supplier, perceives the data analytics as a key opportunity for the future. By establishing a strategic partnership with IBM, the firm has already made efficiency enhancements in the production, by using the self-learning algorithms especially designed for big data analytics. In another example, cycle time of assembly stations is summed and analyzed to find out the probabilities of the process optimization such as the line balancing or raw material relocation (Kern & Wolff, 2019).

CONCLUSION

Along with the fast development of technology, in relation to the automotive industry, the traffic congestion also increases significantly, and this situation gives rise to a sharp rise in the amount of data generated by the connected devices. Statistical analysis of these data obtained from smart systems in a manner that is meaningful becomes a matter of considerable importance. In this scenario, the BC technology can help to do the following (Galvin, 2017):

- Saves time as it makes it possible to perform transactions instantly.
- Eliminates general expenses as it excludes intermediaries.
- Reduces risks as it prevents cybercrimes and fraud.
- Raises the trust as shared processes are recorded.

For enabling the digital transformation and the spread of the BC technology in the automotive industry, the relevant state authorities should pay attention to the following recommendations (**Kern & Wolff, 2019**):

- **Standardization**: Institutions which are involved with standardization efforts should be financed. Standardization institutions should be supported for the promotion of international cooperation, and free data conversion tools should be developed and be made available for use.
- **Data security**: The development of cooperation for the enhancement of data security and the adoption of laws intended for fighting international cybercrimes should be encouraged.
- **Qualifications of employees**: Continuing education efforts should be buttressed and the quality of schools and education in this area should be raised.

Even though the automotive industry is still at the initial stage of the Blockchain applications, it is observed that it makes rapid progress in several areas. Undoubtedly, with time, the digitalization of the automotive industry, along with this digitalization of other areas of application of the BC technology, will expand considerably. For this reason, it is important that all shareholders positioned in the automotive supply chain, particularly the big actors of the sector, invest in the BC technology and also train their employees for the required skills. Thus, in the industry with an already fiercely competitive atmosphere, firms will gain an advantage in terms of promoting the customer satisfaction.

REFERENCES

Allison, I. (2017). *Maersk and Ibm Want 10 Million Shipping Containers on the Global Supply Blockchain by Year-End.* International Business Times.

Baygin, N., Baygin, M., & Karakose, M. (2019). Blockchain Technology: Applications, Benefits and Challenges. *Conference: 2019 1st International Informatics and Software Engineering Conference (UBMYK).* 10.1109/UBMYK48245.2019.8965565

Blanco-Novoa, Ó., Fernández-Caramés, T. M., Fraga-Lamas, P., & Vilar-Montesinos, M. A. (2018). A Practical Evaluation of Commercial Industrial Augmented Reality Systems in an Industry 4.0 Shipyard. *IEEE Access: Practical Innovations, Open Solutions, 6,* 8201–8218. doi:10.1109/ACCESS.2018.2802699

Capgemini Research Institute. (2019). *Does blockchain hold the key to a new age of supply chain transparency and trust? How organizations have moved from blockchain hype to reality.* Capgemini Research Institute.

Carnomic. (2020). *Carnomic Blockchain-based Automotive Solution: White Paper Version 1.2.* Retrieved May 2, 2020, from https://www.carnomic.io/wp/Carnomic-White-Paper-en.pdf

Çetin Gerger, G. (2013). Legal Framework for the E-Taxation in Turkey. In Z. Mahmood (Ed.), *Developing E-Government Projects: Framworks and Methodologies* (pp. 165–180). IGI Global. doi:10.4018/978-1-4666-4245-4.ch008

Çetin Gerger, G. (2019). Tax Services and Tax Service Providers' Changing Role in the IoT and AmI Environment. In Guide to Ambient Intelligence in the IoT Environment (pp. 203-216). Cham, Switzerland: Springer Nature Switzerland. doi:10.1007/978-3-030-04173-1_9

Chen, H., Chiang, R. H., & Storey, V. C. (2012). Business intelligence and analytics: From big data to big impact. *Management Information Systems Quarterly*, *36*(4), 165–1188. doi:10.2307/41703503

Christidis, K., & Devetsikiotis, M. (2018). Blockchains and smart contracts for the internet of things. *IEEE Access: Practical Innovations, Open Solutions*, *2016*(4), 2292–2303.

Clarke, C. (2005). *Automotive production systems and standardization from Ford to the case of Mercedes-Benz*. Physica-Verlag. doi:10.1007/b138988

Colonna, S. (2018). *Blockchain opportunities in automotive market - spare parts case study*. Politecnico di Torino Corso di Laurea in Management Engineering.

Cox, M., & Ellsworth, D. (1997). Application-controlled demand paging for out-of-core visualization. In *Proceedings of the 8th Conference on Visualization'97* (pp. 235-244). Phoenix: IEEE.

Dabbagh, M., Sookhak, M., & Safa, N. S. (2019). The evolution of blockchain: A bibliometric study. *IEEE Access: Practical Innovations, Open Solutions*, *7*(8628982), 19212–19221. doi:10.1109/ACCESS.2019.2895646

Davi, L., Hatebur, D., Heisel, M., & Wirtz, R. (2019). Combining Safety and Security in Autonomous Cars Using Blockchain Technologies. *International Conference on Computer Safety, Reliability, and Security. SAFECOMP 2019*, *11699*, 223-234. doi:10.1007/978-3-030-26250-1_18

Dedeoğlu, D. (2019). *A'dan z'ye blockchain*. İnkılap Kitapevi.

Dobrovnik, M., Herold, D. M., Fürs, E., & Kummer, S. (2018). Blockchain for and in Logistics: What to Adopt and Where to Start. *Logistics*, *2*(18), 1–14. doi:10.3390/logistics2030018

Dorri, A., Steger, M., Kanhere, S. S., & Jurdak, R. (2017). BlockChain: A Distributed Solution to Automotive Security and Privacy. *IEEE Communications Magazine*, *55*(12), 1–7. doi:10.1109/MCOM.2017.1700879

Emen, E. (2018). Blokzincir (Blockchain) Teknolojisi. *Sanayi ve Teknoloji Bakanlığı Sanayi ve Verimlilik Genel Müdürlüğü Kalkınmada Anahtar Verimlilik Dergisi, 30*(353), 46-48. Retrieved from https://anahtar.sanayi.gov.tr/Files/Pdfs/anahta

English, M., Auer, S., & Domingue, J. (2016). Block Chain Technologies & The Semantic Web: A Framework for Symbiotic Development. In *Computer Science Conference for University of Bonn Students*, (pp. 47-61). Retrieved from http://cscubs.cs.uni-bonn.de/2016/

Fraga-Lamas, P., & Fernández-Caramés, T. M. (2019). A Review on Blockchain Technologies for an Advanced and Cyber-Resilient Automotive Industry. IEEE.

Fraga-Lamas, P., Fernández-Caramés, T. M., Blanco-Novoa, Ó., & Vilar-Montesinos, M. A. (2018). A Review on Industrial Augmented Reality Systems for the Industry 4.0 Shipyard. *IEEE Access: Practical Innovations, Open Solutions*, *6*, 3358–13375. doi:10.1109/ACCESS.2018.2808326

Fraga-Lamas, P., Fernández-Caramés, T. M., & Castedo, L. (2017). Towards the Internet of Smart Trains: A Review on Industrial IoT-Connected Railways. *Sensors (Basel), 17*(6), 1–44. doi:10.339017061457 PMID:28635672

Gahi, Y., Guennoun, M., & Mouftah, H. (2016). Big Data Analytics: Security and Privacy Challenges. In *Symposium on Computers and Communication (ISCC)* (pp. 1-6). Messina: IEEE. 10.1109/ISCC.2016.7543859

Galvin, D. (2017). *IBM and Walmart: Blockchain for Food Safety.* IBM Corporation.

Gerger, A. (2018). Use of Kobetsu Kaizen Method to Increase Efficiency in the Production Assembly: A Case Study. In Critical Debates in Social Science (pp. 54-70). FrontPage Publications Limited.

Gerger, A. (2019a). Endüstri 4.0 Üretim Sürecinde Süreç Değişkenliğinin Optimizasyonunda Heijunka Yöntemi. *Izmir Democracy University Social Sciences Journal, 2*(1), 1–17.

Gerger, A. (2019b). Toplum 5.0 ve Manisa. In *Manisa Ekonomisi ve Vizyonu* (pp. 239–261). Detay Yayıncılık.

Gerger, A. (2020). Success Factors And Best Practices in *Relation To The Use Of Newer Technologies at Connected Government Implementation. In Z. Mahmood (Ed.), Web 2.0 and Cloud Technologies for Implementing Connected Government* (pp. xx–xx). IGI Global.

Gerger, A., & Firuzan, A. R. (2010). Yalin alti sigma projelerinin başarisiz olma nedenleri. *Journal of Yaşar University, 20*(5), 3383–3393.

Gerger, A., & Firuzan, A. R. (2020). Taguchi based Case study in the automotive industry: Nonconformity decreasing with use of Six Sigma methodology. *Journal of Applied Statistics*, 1–17. doi:10.1080/02664763.2020.1837086

Govindan, K., Cheng, T. C., Mishra, N., & Shukla, N. (2018). Big data analytics and application for logistics and supply chain management. *Transportation Research Part E, Logistics and Transportation Review, 114*(May), 343–349. doi:10.1016/j.tre.2018.03.011

Güneşli, İ., Yıldızbaşı, A., & Eras, E. (2020). Otomotiv tedarik zincirinde blokzincir teknolojisi uygulamalarina ilişkin bir değerlendirme. *Journal of Industrial Engineering, 31*(1), 48–56.

Heutger, M., & Kueckelhaus, M. (2018). *Blockchain in Logistics.* DHL.

Hill, T., & Westbrook, R. (1997). SWOT Analysis: It's Time for a Product Recall. *Long Range Planning, 30*(1), 46–52. doi:10.1016/S0024-6301(96)00095-7

Hoyle, D. (2000). *Automotive quality systems handbook.* Elsevier Butterworth-Heinemann.

Hoyle, D. (2005). Quality systems handbook ISO/TS 16949:2002 (2nd ed.). Oxford: Elsevier Butterworth-Heinemann.

Htet, C. C., & Htet, M. (2019). A Secure Used Car Trading System based on Blockchain Technology. *2019 21th International Conference on Information Integration and Web-based Application and Services (iiWAS'2019).*

Huckle, S., Bhattacharya, R., White, M., & Beloff, N. (2016). Internet of things, blockchain and shared economy applications. *Procedia Computer Science, 98*, 461–466. doi:10.1016/j.procs.2016.09.074

Iansiti, M., & Lakhani, K. R. (2017, January-February). The truth about blockchain. *Harvard Business Review*. Retrieved from https://hbr.org/2017/01/the-truth-about-blockchain

IBM Institute for Business Value. (2018). *Daring to be first: How auto pioneers are taking the plunge into blockchain*. IBM Corporation.

Kaiser, C., Steger, M., Dorri, A., Festl, A., Stocker, A., Fellmann, M., & Kanhere, S. (2018). Towards a Privacy-Preserving Way of Vehicle Data Sharing – A Case for Blockchain Technology? *International Forum on Advanced Microsystems for Automotive Applications*, 111-122.

Kalita, K. P., Boro, D., & Bhattacharyya, D. K. (2020). Implementation of Minimally Shared Blockchains using Big Data Applications. *2020 Third ISEA Conference on Security and Privacy (ISEA-ISAP)*. 10.1109/ISEA-ISAP49340.2020.235000

Kern, J., & Wolff, P. (2019). The digital transformation of the automotive supply chain – an empirical analysis with evidence from Germany and China: Case study contribution to the OECD TIP Digital and Open Innovation project. *Sectoral Case Study*, 1-23.

Kosba, A., Miller, A., Shi, E., Wen, Z., & Papaman, C. (2016). Hawk: The Blockchain Model of Cryptography and Privacy-Preserving Smart Contracts. *2016 IEEE Symposium on Security and Privacy*, 839–858. 10.1109/SP.2016.55

Kshetri, N. (2017). Can Blockchain Strengthen the Internet of Things? *IT Professional, 19*(4), 68–72. doi:10.1109/MITP.2017.3051335

Lee, Z. E., Chua, R. L., Keoh, L. S., & Ohba, Y. (2019). Performance Evaluation of Big Data Processing at the Edge for IoT-Blockchain Applications. *2019 IEEE Global Communications Conference (GLOBECOM)*. 10.1109/GLOBECOM38437.2019.9013329

Liu, J., Kadiyala, A., & Cannistraci, P. (2018). *Enhancing Supply Chains with the Transparency and Security of Distributed Ledger Technology: Value Driven Supply Chain powered by Blockchain and IoT*. Deloitte Development LLC.

Lu, D., Moreno-Sanchez, P., Zeryihun, A., Bajpayi, S., Yin, S., Feldman, K., ... Kate, A. (2019). Reducing Automotive Counterfeiting using Blockchain: Benefits and Challenges. *IEEE International Conference on Decentralized Applications and Infrastructures (DAPPCON)*, 39-48. 10.1109/DAPPCON.2019.00015

Mathis, T. (2016). Blockchain: A Guide To Blockchain. *The Technology Behind Bitcoin and Other Cryptocurrencies., xx*, xx.

Mohanta, B. K., Panda, S. S., & Jena, D. (2018). An overview of smart contract and use cases in blockchain technology. *2018 9th International Conference on Computing, Communication and Networking Technologies (ICCCNT)*, 1-4.

Nakamato, S. (2008). *Bitcoin: A Peer-to-Peer Electronic Cash System*. Bitcoin.

Nooruddin, S. (2019). *All about Blockchain*. Vortex Institu of Ethical Hacking.

Özan, M. B., Polat, H., Gündüzalp, S., & Yaraş, Z. (2015). Eğitim Kurumlarında SWOT Analizi. *Turkish Journal of Educational Studies*, 2(1), 1–28.

Pai, S., Sevilla, M., Buvat, J., Schneider-Maul, R., Lise, O., Calvayrac, A., . . . Puttur, R. (2018). *Does blockchain hold the key to a new age in supply chain transparency and trust?* Capgemini.

Pepper, R. (2012, June 1). *Mobile Networks in a Zettabyte World Trends from Cisco's Visual Networking Index*. Retrieved from gsma.com: https://www.gsma.com/spectrum/wp-content/uploads/2012/06/Dr_Robert-_Pepper_Cisco_Public_Policy-Forum_Data_Demand.pdf

Reinsel, D., Gantz, J., & Rydning, J. (2018, November 1). *The Digitization of the World From Edge to Core*. Retrieved from Seagate: https://www.seagate.com/files/www-content/our-story/trends/files/idc-seagate-dataage-whitepaper.pdf

Rosado, T., Vasconcelos, A., & Correia, M. (2019). A Blockchain Use Case for Car Registration. In Essentials of Blockchain Technology (pp. 205-234). doi:10.1201/9780429674457-10

Saberi, S., Kouhizadeh, M., Sarkis, J., & Shen, L. (2018). Blockchain technology and its relationships to sustainable supply chain management. *International Journal of Production Research*, 57(7), 2117–2135. doi:10.1080/00207543.2018.1533261

Schneider, R. D. (2012). Hadoop for Dummies. Mississauga: John Wiley &.

Singh, K. (2020). Blockchain technology: A potential game changer for automotive industry. *International Journal of Advanced Research in Management and Social Sciences*, 9(3), 49–55.

Sözek, K. (2017). *Blockchain: Ultimate Step by Step Guide to Understanding Blockchain Technology, Bitcoin Creation, and the Future of Money*. CreateSpace Independent Publishing Platform.

Stocker, A., & Kaiser, C. (2016). Quantified car: potentials, business models and digital ecosystems. *E&i Elektrotechnik und Informationstechnik, 133*(7), 334–340.

Stocker, A., Kaiser, C., & Fellmann, M. (2017). Quantified Vehicles - Novel Services for Vehicle Life-cycle Data. *Journal of Business & Information. Systems Engineering, 59*(2), 1–6.

Timothy, L. (2017). *Blockchain for Transportation: Where the Future Starts*. Cleveland: TMWSystems, Inc.

Underwood, S. (2016). Blockchain beyond bitcoin. *Communications of the ACM, 59*(1), 5–17.

White, G. R. (2017). Future applications of blockchain in business and management: A delphi study. *Strategic Change, 2017*(26), 439–451. doi:10.1002/jsc.2144

Williams, S. P. (2019). *Blockchain: The Next Everything*. Scribner.

Winkler, M., Schneider-Maul, R., Puttur, R. K., Mehl, R., Buvat, J., & Nath, S. (2020). *How automotive organizations can maximize the smart factory potential*. Capgemini Research Institu.

World Economic Forum. (2015). *Deep shift Technology Tipping Points and Societal Impact. Survey Report*. WEF. Retrieved May 25, 2020, from http://www3.weforum.org/docs/WEF_GAC15_Technological_Tipping_Points_report_2015.pdf

Wu, X., Zhu, X., Wu, G.-Q., & Ding, W. (2014). Data mining with big data. *IEEE Transactions on Knowledge and Data Engineering*, *26*(1), 97–107. doi:10.1109/TKDE.2013.109

Zhao, D., Jia, G., Ren, H., Chen, C., Yu, R., Ge, P., & Liu, S. (2018). *Research on the Application of Block Chain in automobile industry. In IOP Conference Series: Materials Science and Engineering.* IOP Publishing., doi:10.1088/1757-899X/452/3/032076

Zheng, Z., Xie, S. S., Dai, H., Chen, X., & Wang, H. (2017). An Overview of Blockchain Technology: Architecture, Consensus, and Future Trends. *IEEE 6th International Congress on Big Data (Big Dats Congress'17.*

ADDITIONAL READING

Allison, I. (2017). *Maersk and Ibm Want 10 Million Shipping Containers on the Global Supply Blockchain by Year-End.* International Business Times.

Baygin, N., Baygin, M., & Karakose, M. (2019). Blockchain Technology: Applications, Benefits and Challenges. *Conference: 2019 1st International Informatics and Software Engineering Conference (UBMYK).* Ankara. 10.1109/UBMYK48245.2019.8965565

Blanco-Novoa, Ó., Fernández-Caramés, T. M., Fraga-Lamas, P., & Vilar-Montesinos, M. A. (2018). A Practical Evaluation of Commercial Industrial Augmented Reality Systems in an Industry 4.0 Shipyard. *IEEE Access: Practical Innovations, Open Solutions, 6,* 8201–8218. doi:10.1109/ACCESS.2018.2802699

Capgemini Research Institute. (2019). *Does blockchain hold the key to a new age of supply chain transparency and trust? How organizations have moved from blockchain hype to reality.* Capgemini Research Institute.

Carnomic. (2020). *Carnomic Blockchain-based Automotive Solution: White Paper Version 1.2.* Retrieved May 2, 2020, from https://www.carnomic.io/wp/Carnomic-White-Paper-en.pdf

Çetin Gerger, G. (2013). Legal Framework for the E-Taxation in Turkey. In Z. Mahmood (Ed.), *Developing E-Government Projects: Framworks and Methodologies* (pp. 165–180). IGI Global. doi:10.4018/978-1-4666-4245-4.ch008

Çetin Gerger, G. (2019). Tax Services and Tax Service Providers' Changing Role in the IoT and AmI Environment. In Guide to Ambient Intelligence in the IoT Environment (pp. 203-216). Cham, Switzerland: Springer Nature Switzerland. doi:10.1007/978-3-030-04173-1_9

Chen, H., Chiang, R. H., & Storey, V. C. (2012). Business intelligence and analytics: From big data to big impact. *Management Information Systems Quarterly*, *36*(4), 165–1188. doi:10.2307/41703503

Christidis, K., & Devetsikiotis, M. (2018). Blockchains and smart contracts for the internet of things. *IEEE Access: Practical Innovations, Open Solutions, 2016*(4), 2292–2303.

Clarke, C. (2005). *Automotive production systems and standardization from Ford to the case of Mercedes-Benz.* Physica-Verlag. doi:10.1007/b138988

Colonna, S. (2018). *Blockchain opportunities in automotive market - spare parts case study*. Politecnico Di Torino Corso di Laurea in Management Engineering.

Cox, M., & Ellsworth, D. (1997). Application-controlled demand paging for out-of-core visualization. *Proceedings of the 8th Conference on Visualization'97* (pp. 235-244). Phoenix: IEEE.

Dabbagh, M., Sookhak, M., & Safa, N. S. (2019). The evolution of blockchain: A bibliometric study. *IEEE Access: Practical Innovations, Open Solutions, 7*(8628982), 19212–19221. doi:10.1109/AC-CESS.2019.2895646

Davi, L., Hatebur, D., Heisel, M., & Wirtz, R. (2019). Combining Safety and Security in Autonomous Cars Using Blockchain Technologies. *International Conference on Computer Safety, Reliability, and Security. SAFECOMP 2019. 11699*, pp. 223-234. Springer, Cham. doi:10.1007/978-3-030-26250-1_18

Dobrovnik, M., Herold, D. M., Fürs, E., & Kummer, S. (2018). Blockchain for and in Logistics: What to Adopt and Where to Start. *Logistics, 2*(18), 1–14. doi:10.3390/logistics2030018

Dorri, A., Steger, M., Kanhere, S. S., & Jurdak, R. (2017). BlockChain: A Distributed Solution to Automotive Security and Privacy. *IEEE Communications Magazine, 55*(12), 1–7. doi:10.1109/MCOM.2017.1700879

Emen, E. (2018). Blokzincir (Blockchaın) Teknolojisi. *Sanayi ve Teknoloji Bakanlığı Sanayi ve Verim-lilik Genel Müdürlüğü Kalkınmada Anahtar Verimlilik Dergisi, 30*(353), 46-48. Retrieved from https://anahtar.sanayi.gov.tr/Files/Pdfs/anahta

English, M., Auer, S., & Domingue, J. (2016). Block Chain Technologies & The Semantic Web: A Framework for Symbiotic Development. *Computer Science Conference for University of Bonn Students*, (pp. 47-61). Bonn. Retrieved from http://cscubs.cs.uni-bonn.de/2016/

Fraga-Lamas, P., & Fernández-Caramés, T. M. (2019). A Review on Blockchain Technologies for an Advanced and Cyber-Resilient Automotive Industry. IEEE, 2169-3536.

Fraga-Lamas, P., Fernández-Caramés, T. M., Blanco-Novoa, Ó., & Vilar-Montesinos, M. A. (2018). A Review on Industrial Augmented Reality Systems for the Industry 4.0 Shipyard. *IEEE Access: Practical Innovations, Open Solutions, 6*, 3358–13375. doi:10.1109/ACCESS.2018.2808326

Fraga-Lamas, P., Fernández-Caramés, T. M., & Castedo, L. (2017). Towards the Internet of Smart Trains: A Review on Industrial IoT-Connected Railways. *Sensors (Basel), 17*(6), 1–44. doi:10.339017061457 PMID:28635672

Gahi, Y., Guennoun, M., & Mouftah, H. (2016). Big Data Analytics: Security and Privacy Challenges. *Symposium on Computers and Communication (ISCC)* (pp. 1-6). Messina: IEEE. 10.1109/ISCC.2016.7543859

Galvin, D. (2017). *IBM and Walmart: Blockchain for Food Safety*. 2017 IBM Corporation.

Gerger, A. (2018). Use of Kobetsu Kaizen Method to Increase Efficiency in the Production Assembly: A Case Study. In ritical Debates in Social Science (pp. 54-70). UK: FrontPage Publications Limited.

Gerger, A. (2019b). Toplum 5.0 ve Manisa. In *Manisa Ekonomisi ve Vizyonu* (pp. 239–261). Detay Yayıncılık.

Gerger, A. (2020). Success Factors And Best Practices. In *Relation To The Use Of Newer Technologies at Connected Government Implementation. In Z. Mahmood, Web 2.0 and Cloud Technologies for Implementing Connected Government* (pp. xx–xx). IGI Global.

Gerger, A., & Firuzan, A. R. (2010). YALIN ALTI SİGMA PROJELERİNİN BAŞARISIZ OLMA NEDENLERİ. *Journal of Yaşar University, 20*(5), 3383–3393.

Gerger, A., & Firuzan, A. R. (2020). Taguchi based Case study in the automotive industry: Nonconformity decreasing with use of Six Sigma methodology. *Journal of Applied Statistics*, ●●●, 1–17. doi:10.1080/02664763.2020.1837086

Govindan, K., Cheng, T. C., Mishra, N., & Shukla, N. (2018). Big data analytics and application for logistics and supply chain management. *Transportation Research Part E, Logistics and Transportation Review, 114*(May), 343–349. doi:10.1016/j.tre.2018.03.011

Heutger, M., & Kueckelhaus, M. (2018). *Blockchain in Logistics*. DHL.

Hill, T., & Westbrook, R. (1997). SWOT Analysis: It's Time for a Product Recall. *Long Range Planning, 30*(1), 46–52. doi:10.1016/S0024-6301(96)00095-7

Hoyle, D. (2000). *Automotive quality systems handbook*. Elsevier Butterworth-Heinemann.

Hoyle, D. (2005). Quality systems handbook ISO/TS 16949:2002 (2nd ed. ed.). Oxford: Elsevier Butterworth-Heinemann.

Htet, C. C., & Htet, M. (2019). A Secure Used Car Trading System based on Blockchain Technology. *In 2019 21th International Conference on Information Integration and Web-based Application and Services (iiWAS'2019)*. Munich.

Huckle, S., Bhattacharya, R., White, M., & Beloff, N. (2016). Internet of things, blockchain and shared economy applications. *Procedia Computer Science, 98*, 461–466. doi:10.1016/j.procs.2016.09.074

Iansiti, M., & Lakhani, K. R. (2017, January-February 1). The truth about blockchain. *Harvard Business Review*. Retrieved from https://hbr.org/2017/01/the-truth-about-blockchain

IBM Institute for Business Value. (2018). *Daring to be first: How auto pioneers are taking the plunge into blockchain*. IBM Corporation.

Kaiser, C., Steger, M., Dorri, A., Festl, A., Stocker, A., Fellmann, M., & Kanhere, S. (2018). Towards a Privacy-Preserving Way of Vehicle Data Sharing – A Case for Blockchain Technology? *In International Forum on Advanced Microsystems for Automotive Applications*, 111-122.

Kalita, K. P., Boro, D., & Bhattacharyya, D. K. (2020). Implementation of Minimally Shared Blockchains using Big Data Applications. *2020 Third ISEA Conference on Security and Privacy (ISEA-ISAP)*. Guwahati. 10.1109/ISEA-ISAP49340.2020.235000

Kern, J., & Wolff, P. (2019). The digital transformation of the automotive supply chain – an empirical analysis with evidence from Germany and China: Case study contribution to the OECD TIP Digital and Open Innovation project. *Sectoral Casw Study*, 1-23.

Kosba, A., Miller, A., Shi, E., Wen, Z., & Papaman, C. (2016). Hawk: The Blockchain Model of Cryptography and Privacy-Preserving Smart Contracts. *2016 IEEE Symposium on Security and Privacy*, (pp. 839–858). doi:10.1109/SP.2016.55

Kshetri, N. (2017). Can Blockchain Strengthen the Internet of Things? *IT Professional, 19*(4), 68–72. doi:10.1109/MITP.2017.3051335

Lee, Z. E., Chua, R. L., Keoh, L. S., & Ohba, Y. (2019). Performance Evaluation of Big Data Processing at the Edge for IoT-Blockchain Applications. *2019 IEEE Global Communications Conference (GLOBECOM)*. Waikoloa. 10.1109/GLOBECOM38437.2019.9013329

Liu, J., Kadıyala, A., & Cannistraci, P. (2018). *Enhancing Supply Chains with the Transparency and Security of Distributed Ledger Technology: Value Driven Supply Chain powered by Blockchain and IoT*. USA: Deloitte Development LLC.

Lu, D., Moreno-Sanchez, P., Zeryihun, A., Bajpayi, S., Yin, S., Feldman, K., ... Kate, A. (2019). Reducing Automotive Counterfeiting using Blockchain: Benefits and Challenges. *IEEE International Conference on Decentralized Applications and Infrastructures (DAPPCON)*, 39-48. 10.1109/DAPPCON.2019.00015

Mathis, T. (2016). Blockchain: A Guide To Blockchain. *The Technology Behind Bitcoin and Other Cryptocurrencies.*, *xx*, xx.

Mohanta, B. K., Panda, S. S., & Jena, D. (2018). An overview of smart contract and use cases in blockchain technology. *2018 9th International Conference on Computing, Communication and Networking Technologies (ICCCNT)*, (pp. 1-4).

Nakamato, S. (2008). *Bitcoin: A Peer-to-Peer Electronic Cash System*. Bitcoin.

Nooruddin, S. (2019). *All about Blockchain*. Vortex Institu of Ethical Hacking.

Özan, M. B., Polat, H., Gündüzalp, S., & Yaraş, Z. (2015). Eğitim Kurumlarında SWOT Analizi. *Turkish Journal of Educational Studies, 2*(1), 1–28.

Pai, S., Sevilla, M., Buvat, J., Schneider-Maul, R., Lise, O., Calvayrac, A., . . . Puttur, R. (2018). *Does blockchain hold the key to a new age in supply chain transparency and trust?* EU: Capgemini.

Pepper, R. (2012, June 1). *Mobile Networks in a Zettabyte World Trends from Cisco's Visual Networking Index*. Retrieved from gsma.com: https://www.gsma.com/spectrum/wp-content/uploads/2012/06/Dr_Robert-_Pepper_Cisco_Public_Policy-Forum_Data_Demand.pdf

Reinsel, D., Gantz, J., & Rydning, J. (2018, November 1). *The Digitization of the World From Edge to Core*. Retrieved from Seagate: https://www.seagate.com/files/www-content/our-story/trends/files/idc-seagate-dataage-whitepaper.pdf

Rosado, T., Vasconcelos, A., & Correia, M. (2019). A Blockchain Use Case for Car Registration. In Essentials of Blockchain Technology (pp. 205-234). doi:10.1201/9780429674457-10

Saberi, S., Kouhizadeh, M., Sarkis, J., & Shen, L. (2018). Blockchain technology and its relationships to sustainable supply chain management. *International Journal of Production Research, 57*(7), 2117–2135. doi:10.1080/00207543.2018.1533261

Schneider, R. D. (2012). Hadoop for Dummies ((Special Edition ed.). Mississauga: John Wiley &.

Sözek, K. (2017). *Blockchain: Ultimate Step by Step Guide to Understanding Blockchain Technology, Bitcoin Creation, and the Future of Money.* CreateSpace Independent Publishing Platform.

Stocker, A., & Kaiser, C. (2016). Quantified car: potentials, business models and digital ecosystems. *E&i Elektrotechnik und Informationstechnik, 133*(7), 334–340.

Stocker, A., Kaiser, C., & Fellmann, M. (2017). Quantified Vehicles - Novel Services for Vehicle Life-cycle Data. *Journal of Business & Information. Systems Engineering, 59*(2), 1–6.

Timothy, L. (2017). *Blockchain for Transportation: Where the Future Starts.* Cleveland: TMW Systems, Inc.

Underwood, S. (2016). Blockchain beyond bitcoin. *Communications of the ACM, 59*(1), 5–17.

White, G. R. (2017). Future applications of blockchain in business and management: A delphi study. *Strategic Change, 2017*(26), 439–451. doi:10.1002/jsc.2144

Williams, S. P. (2019). *Blockchain: The Next Everything.* Scribner.

Winkler, M., Schneider-Maul, R., Puttur, R. K., Mehl, R., Buvat, J., & Nath, S. (2020). *How automotive organizations can maximize the smart factory potential.* EU: Capgemini Research Institu.

World Economic Forum. (2015). *Deep shift Technology Tipping Points and Societal Impact. Survey Report.* WEF. Retrieved May 25, 2020, from http://www3.weforum.org/docs/WEF_GAC15_Techno-logical_Tipping_Points_report_2015.pdf

Wu, X., Zhu, X., Wu, G.-Q., & Ding, W. (2014). Data mining with big data. *IEEE Transactions on Knowledge and Data Engineering, 26*(1), 97–107. doi:10.1109/TKDE.2013.109

Zhao, D., Jia, G., Ren, H., Chen, C., Yu, R., Ge, P., & Liu, S. (2018). *Research on the Application of Block Chain in automobile industry. IOP Conference Series: Materials Science and Engineering.* IOP Publishing., doi:10.1088/1757-899X/452/3/032076

KEY TERMS AND DEFINITIONS

Automated Guided Vehicles (AGV): Automated Guided Vehicles are transport vehicles which automatically guide themselves without direct propulsion, as these are equipped with self-propulsion. These vehicles are autonomous vehicles which are employed for towing and/or carrying raw materials to. For example, warehouses.

Big Data: Big data refers to large amounts of heterogeneous data that cannot be easily processed using conventional database techniques. Big data characteristics include volume, variety, and velocity of data. This data is generated by many sources including smart sensors, smartwatches, wristbands, medical equipment/devices, tablets, mobile phones, web usage records, social media, and simulation.

Big Data Analytics: This refers to analysis of data clusters to gain business intelligence and determine logic and trends that exist in the data.

Blockchain (BC): This is an open, distributed ledger that can record transactions between two or more parties. more efficiently, securely, and permanently.

Cloud Computing: This refers to a distributed environment that houses networks, servers, storage spaces, software applications and virtualized hardware, which can be remotely accessed, utilized and released with minimum management effort, Environment acts as customizable common pool of data processing resources and used for providing on-demand network access.

Industry 4.0: Industry 4.0 emerged in Germany in 2011 to adopt digital technologies into development, production, and manufacturing. It involves automation, use of machine leaning and all forms of emerging technologies to achieve speed, efficiency and effectiveness of operations.

Internet of Thing (IoT): It refers to a network of inter-connected intelligent objects (computers, sensors, devices that have embedded processors, smart phones, etc.). These objects communicate with each other and transmit data between the connected smart devices.

Robotics: This refers to the use of machine learning, artificial intelligence and use of automation that employ these technologies; mainly to perform complex operations without much need of human intervention.

Statistics: Statistics is the science involved in the study of development of methods for collecting, analysing, interpreting and presenting data. Statistics is an interdisciplinary field, used in almost all scientific fields. Research questions in various scientific fields contribute to the development of new statistical methods and theories.

Chapter 13
Blockchain Reinventing the Healthcare Industry:
Use Cases and Applications

Vijayaraghavan Varadharajan

Infosys Ltd, India

Divik Bansal

Infosys Ltd, India

Sanal J. Nair

Infosys Ltd, India

Rian Leevinson J

Infosys Ltd, India

ABSTRACT

The fragmented and disorganized nature of data in healthcare poses a variety of challenges to scientific research and medical applications. This mainly stems from the lack of traceability of transactions, complex disconnected networks, and lack of data interoperability. This complexity leads to difficulties in conducting research and clinical trials, and to the problem of counterfeit drugs in the market. This triggers lack of availability and accessibility of data for researchers and medical experts. Blockchain technology offers comprehensive solutions to these problems, and hence it has been of enormous interest in the healthcare sector. Blockchain technology with its innate transparency, traceability, data security, and distributed nature can help to overcome the data related problems in healthcare. This chapter provides an overview of the use of blockchain in the healthcare industry and explores various use-cases and applications. This chapter also discusses case-studies and various challenges faced while adapting blockchain in the healthcare industry.

DOI: 10.4018/978-1-7998-6650-3.ch013

INTRODUCTION

Blockchain technology is a decentralized and distributed data sharing platform without the need of a central authority. Transactions in blockchain are innately secure, tamperproof and trustworthy due to cryptographic algorithms and proof of work feature of consensus algorithms. In recent years, use of blockchain and digital ledger technologies have gained traction and entered different domains, largely due to the popularity of cryptocurrencies. After gaining popularity as a distributed ledger technology used for the implementation of the bitcoin cryptocurrency, blockchain has gained popularity in non-financial domains and hence is now considered as a general-purpose technology (Jovanovic et al, 2005).

The healthcare sector has excellent potential for the implementation of blockchain-enabled technologies and a variety of use-cases have been developed with the help of blockchain. Studies have shown a wide range of possibilities with the use of blockchain in healthcare. The main areas of application include Electronic Health Records (EHR), personal patient data, medical records storage systems, clinical trial support systems, data management for connected devices, administrative systems, and supply chain in the pharmaceutical industry.

The blockchain is predominantly used for improving complex, multiparty transactions, access control, data integrity and provenance which are some of the major challenges in the healthcare industry today. Blockchain enables the secure transfer of information amongst researchers, healthcare professionals and patients. It can be used to build integrated health management systems across different institutions, healthcare systems and clinics. It also enables efficient electronic health records and personal health record managements, which are an essential part of modern healthcare industry. Moreover, this also facilitates seamless data accessibility for biomedical and bioinformatics researchers, paving way for better scientific collaborations and research. Provenance is one of the key advantages of blockchain and it plays an impeccable part in the pharmaceutical supply chain, especially to prevent counterfeit drugs and adulterations in medicine.

These are extremely important application areas that could be revolutionized by blockchain. Moreover, the use of blockchain can also improve interoperability while preserving the confidentiality and security of data. It conforms to strict regulations in terms of the handling and storage of sensitive data and it contains inherent integrity.

The evolution of technology has brought fundamental changes in the design of healthcare systems. The drawbacks of conventional healthcare systems will be overcome by the next generation healthcare systems, that would be intelligent, better connected, collaborative, secure by design, and will focus on inclusive user experience. Artificial intelligence can munch on petabytes of data from distributed systems and generate meaningful insights about the libraries of chemical compounds, natural products, extracts, and active agents throughout the drug discovery. A wearable wristwatch or a personal health assistant on mobile devices could identify conditions of medical emergencies like heart failure, diabetes, asthma attacks, etc. and alert the physician. Similarly, Augmented Reality is helping to model the novel discoveries and make them accessible for academia. The convergence of digital technologies such as Machine learning, IoT, Blockchain, and Augmented Reality will bring an unprecedented level of collaboration, trigger innovation in medical research, and facilitate newer concepts like precision medicine, population health, and help to create decision support systems for physicians. Blockchain enables trust, data integrity, data security, verifiability and better control over sensitive information moving between many devices, organizations, platforms and algorithms.

With humans being accustomed to a more sedentary lifestyle and a rapid increase in the aging population, there has been a considerable increase in the cost of healthcare and a growing risk of chronic diseases. Perhaps a more meaningful and long-term benefit lies in precision genome medicine. Currently, genome sequencing is finding its use in cancer research, characterizing genetic disease, and in predicting an individual's probable response to treatment. Advancement in the genome research together with technologies such as machine learning and blockchain would help to create a global genome knowledge repository or decision support database (Mattick et al., 2014). The global decision support systems could drastically improve the diagnosis and therapy for chronic diseases, personalized drug prescription, and pre-empting an epidemic based on the larger population data.

Healthcare and Life sciences organizations around the world, currently, appear to be struggling because of aging populations, rising healthcare costs, a growing number of patients with complex health conditions. Healthcare providers are a team of multidisciplinary experts and healthcare professionals to deliver healthcare services. Predominantly the interaction with the healthcare professionals have been dominated by the doctors or physicians. With a more patient-centric approach where several interdisciplinary professionals are involved in the care plan, it becomes extremely important to maintain a patient health record centrally. This record must be secure and most importantly provides an accurate track of the patient's health records since the very beginning.

One of the main issues with the health record is that we may lose the records of a health condition which existed years before. Several healthcare start-ups and industry veterans have taken up this challenge and using blockchain for building the new generation of smart solutions. Although extensive theoretical research has been conducted on the use cases involving blockchain in healthcare, there are many challenges and hurdles in implementing such solutions in the healthcare sector.

Lack of flexibility in existing systems, resistance to change, initial investment costs, lack of awareness about blockchain technology are some major hurdles in real life implementations. Moreover, most of the current research focuses on frameworks, algorithms, application designs, architectures or models. They do not showcase prototypes or deployable solutions which could convince healthcare professionals to adopt blockchain based solutions.

In this chapter, we explore how blockchain technology can be used in the healthcare industry and discuss various use cases and applications. The chapter begins with a brief introduction about the global healthcare and life sciences industry and blockchain technology. In the next section, the industrial challenges and regulatory landscapes are reviewed. The subsequent section explores the relevance of blockchain technology in healthcare and blockchain related use-cases. The key industry initiatives and challenges in blockchain adaption are presented in the following sections.

INDUSTRY CHALLENGES

Some of the major challenges faced by industry is in the supply chain management. The amount of fraud and counterfeit items in the drug supply chain are extremely high. Studies estimate that almost $455 billion of world healthcare spending is lost due to fraud or corruption (Button & GEE, 2015). WHO states that damages from counterfeit medicine cost over billions of dollars every year and is a deeply concerning problem, especially in developing countries. In more than 50% of the cases, drugs purchased over the Internet from websites without physical address have been found to be counterfeit (WHO bulletin, 2010). Interpol says that up to 1 million people die every year due to counterfeit drugs

(Southwick, 2013). With all these counterfeit drugs, the amount of recalls is vast. During a drug recall, either counterfeit drugs, or non-counterfeit but tainted drugs, all those medicines need to be removed from the shelves of stores and from people's possession. The problem with this is that only some of the drugs do need to be recalled, not all of them. Because we would rather be safe than sorry, we remove all of them unnecessarily.

The second major problem in the industry is about data breaches. According to IBM, the average cost of a data breach in the healthcare industry is $6.5 million (IBM Security, 2019). Between 2009 and 2018, there were over 189 million healthcare records stolen in the US alone which is over 59% of the entire US population (HIPAA, 2019). Drug abuse is another major problem in the healthcare industry. According to (NIDA, 2018), the Opioid crisis is continuing to grow and 18 million people misused medication in 2017.

In the healthcare and life sciences industry, health records are not standardized, and the owners of records are the institutions where the information is gathered. This is a problem for patients because if they want to switch doctors or bring their records somewhere else for a different reason, there is no one place, they can go to collect these records. The result is that there is no single comprehensive record of a patient's health which makes diagnosing more difficult for doctors.

Another problem in the industry refers to concerns relating to medical researchers. The FDA estimates that almost 10% of clinical trials monitored feature mislabelled or mishandled data (FDA, 2013). Medical scientists have to collect their own patient data because they do not have consent to all patient's records or their records are not as accurate as they could be.

Cold chain logistics is yet another challenge in healthcare industry. Certain drugs need to stay refrigerated from production to consumption. This means that delivery trucks need to be refrigerated and the medicine must not rise above a specific critical temperature. If the drugs go above the prescribed temperature, they may not function correctly. Currently, there is no specific way to monitor the individual drug temperature levels. While the truck can be equipped with a temperature-controlled refrigeration unit, it is not necessarily providing constant feedback where the alert can be triggered when the critical temperature is surpassed.

Regulatory Landscape

The healthcare industry is one of the most regulated industry. However, data breaching issues are on rise as the technology improves. Because of these breaches as well as technology advances, there have been increased rules and regulations. Most of these regulations concern patient privacy. Regulatory policies like HIPAA (Health Insurance Portability and Accountability Act) in US, and GDPR (General Data Protection Regulation) in Europe, aim to protect individual's medical records and privacy. There are other US policies like the Medical Device Reporting (MDR) that mandate streamline reporting of medical device issues. Another policy that aims to streamline efficiency and make records reporting easier is HITECH whose goal is to motivate the adoption of Electronic Health Records (EHR). The policies like Integrating Healthcare Enterprises (IHE) create standards for easier and streamlined reporting. The Centres for Medicare and Medicaid have also been collecting and analysing records to uncover fraud. The Drug Supply Chain Security Act (DSCSA) mandates that by 2023, every product requires to be trackable, accessible, and unalterable by all parties along a product's chain of ownership (DSCSA, 2015). The goal is to combat counterfeit drugs and also to aid in drug recalls as it is easier to note exactly which drugs are tainted and need to be removed from the system.

RELEVANCE OF BLOCKCHAIN IN HEALTHCARE

Blockchain technology has the ability to influence business in the healthcare and life sciences field, this section explores relevance of blockchain in healthcare and some of its use cases.

Operational Efficiencies

Customers are seeing the improvement in operational efficiencies by utilizing blockchain technology. There are a variety of ways in which blockchain can improve the operational efficiencies of supply chains. Shared databases between various health insurers is one such example of the use of blockchain to improve operational efficiencies. It mainly helps improve the accuracy of demographic data present in the databases of healthcare providers. Shared Blockchain networks help to improve operational efficiencies, data accuracy and reduce costs.

Reduction in Expense Ratios

Once operational efficiencies are realized by first adopters, they will start to see their expense ratios getting reduced. Companies will be able to use blockchain technology to reorganize their expenses and save money. MELLODDY (Machine Learning Ledger Orchestration for Drug Discovery) is a consortium of companies working together to reduce this expense ratio (Galtier, 2020). The members of this consortium are using artificial intelligence and federated machine learning techniques to enable secured data sharing fortified by blockchain-based tamperproof audit records which make drug discovery more efficient, faster, and safer. They use secure, scalable and intelligent frameworks that can efficiently train and evaluate drug discovery related models. Moreover, by sharing their database without sharing their patented information, they are reducing their expense ratios dramatically.

Productivity Improvement

After successful implementation of operational efficiencies and reduced expense ratios, improving productivity is a key challenge for companies and organizations, although healthcare organizations are increasingly interested in advancing the use of electronic health records, as then the patients will be able to access their own data and this will increase productivity tremendously. However, every time that a patient pays visit to a new physician, their profile needs to be rebuilt through many questions and answers. The problem with this approach is that it is difficult for the patients to remember about all the doctors they have visited, treatments they have undergone and tests that they have taken. This could lead to loss of critical information and can be difficult for the doctor to diagnose and treat the patient as well. Something that the patient may not have considered relevant could be extremely relevant to the doctor and could affect the treatment prescribed.

This scenario is also encountered during clinical trials. During each clinical trial, medical researchers need to reconstruct the patient's medical history in order to have a more accurate study, but patient can forget about the past treatments. By having decentralized electronic health records, each doctor could add information to the patient's long record. This complete record can then be shared by the patient to whomever they want. Having a distributed electronic health record will greatly improve productivity.

Blockchain Potential in Healthcare

Healthcare is largely attributed to the Personal Healthcare services which involves the patient and healthcare providers. There have been significant achievements in healthcare practices involving prevention, diagnosis and treatment of diseases or illness. A good percentage of the world has much better access to healthcare services as compared to a few decades ago. Much has been achieved, much more still needs to be done in this field by leveraging technology in this digital age.

World Health Organization defines patient safety as the 'absence of preventable harm to a patient during the process of healthcare and reduction of risk of unnecessary harm associated with healthcare to acceptable minimum'. The industry has been under pressure to improve the patient safety, reduce the medical errors by employing secure and timely access to the information while controlling the costs associated with it.

Safety of Drug Supply Chain

Counterfeit medications have grown into a severe concern both in developed and the developing countries. Governing bodies in the United States of America, the European Union, Japan, India, South Korea, Turkey, China, and many others have introduced tough regulatory norms to guarantee the safety of the drug supply chain. This primarily includes strict regulations for barcoding and serialization. According to the recent WHO estimates, around 10.5% of the medical samples in the low or middle-income countries are found to be substandard or falsified (WHO, 2017).

One of the biggest challenges faced by the pharmaceutical companies and other stakeholders in the ecosystem relate to how to generate, verify, share and report the specific pieces of information for each shipment. Figure 1 shows the diverse stakeholders in the pharmaceutical supply chain. With many point-to-point interfaces required for issuing, verifying and reporting information, accuracy will continue to be a challenge with the current messaging architecture.

Figure 1. Stakeholders in a Pharmaceutical Supply Chain

A blockchain-based supply chain traceability solution has immense potential to tackle the issue of counterfeit drugs by tracking the movement of drugs throughout the lifecycle (Sylim, 2018). Several industries like manufacturing, retail, and mining, have applied blockchain or digital ledger technologies to build solutions to their supply-chain related challenges like provenance, proof of custody, inventory auditing and traceability. Blockchain's inherent design features of decentralization, encryption methods and immutable record-keeping, ensures that associated data can be distributed among stakeholders securely. In pharmaceutical industry similar methods can be utilised to prevent counterfeit medicines from entering the supply chain. Regardless, blockchain should not be considered as a replacement of the existing landscape in the supply chain. It is aimed at complementing the current IT system with the benefits of an immutable and shared ledger.

One of the benefits of blockchain is being able to securely track the provenance of any item though the network of stakeholders. This means that from the initial raw materials, all the way to the end consumer, the supply chain can be rigorously monitored. Every time a medicine changes hands, it would be recorded on an immutable ledger. By seeing the provenance of each drug, it is easy to verify if the drugs are counterfeit.

Another issue with the safety in Pharmaceutical supply chain are the drug recalls. Since each drug can be labelled individually, the process of drug recall is much simpler and easier. Not only can the affected drugs be taken off from the shelves, but the consumer can be automatically notified, not to take the drugs anymore.

Certain pharmaceutical products and medical devices must adhere to stringent storage and handling requirements along the supply chain during transportation (WHO Bulletib, 2010). The requirements include control of storage conditions like temperature, humidity, and air quality. Some of the main causes for drug recall include failed specifications, mislabelling, or drug contamination.

A blockchain solution can avoid drug recalls or support targeted recalls due to mislabelling, contamination and failed specifications (Bayanna, 2019). Blockchain-based traceability solutions will be secure, transparent, and able to establish provenance along the value chain of pharmaceutical products to trace back the material and information flow. All participants and authorities in the supply chain would be able to use this to ensure better compliance.

By using blockchain with connected IoT sensors, it is possible to have temperature sensors constantly monitoring temperatures of drugs and giving feedback in real-time. Technology will ensure that threshold temperature barriers are not crossed by alerting for corrective actions to maintain the ambient conditions. If the drug temperature rises above the critical temperature, the goods can automatically be shipped back and the drugs won't make it to retail outlets.

Blockchain technology has the characteristics of high security, decentralization, and tamper-proof. With intelligent devices being connected to a network and a wide verity of sensor data being generated and used to trigger automated processes, security of such a system is vital. The security can be ensured on the blockchain using cryptography and the data is encrypted by public-private keys during transmission. Moreover, only peers with valid credentials can perform transactions on the network. The terms of the contract written in smart contracts govern the validity of the transactions on the network. The contracts deployed after endorsement by the network stakeholders along with the consensus algorithms demonstrate the decentralized autonomy of these intelligent devices.

Specialty Drugs Provenance

Specialty Drugs are typically used to treat chronic, complex or rare medical conditions that can be progressive or fatal if left untreated. Such specialty drugs are very expensive and are generally not dispensed at most of the retail, and community pharmacies. This adds up additional costs like special handling, storage, transportation and in addition, they may need intensive monitoring and clinical oversight. Several stakeholders are involved in the end to end distribution of the medicine. Transaction details and sensor data is usually maintained in silos with the stakeholder and the data sharing is often inefficient. This adds to the complications over and above the operational costs.

Data or transaction issues cause complication, and this may lead to additional burden on the insurance. A blockchain-based end to end traceability of the specialty drugs along with automated monitoring of environmental parameters and use of smart contract to trigger alerts for preventive maintenance or initiate the drug refill would lead to a significant improvement in the logistics of speciality medicines. Autonomous actions would be possible for the refill, discard or replacement of the medicine. Patients are also enabled to access the provenance of the journey of the specialty medicine from the manufacturer including the environmental conditions, distributors and pharmacy details. Moreover, being able to identify the chain of custody of an expensive speciality medicine also allows safe return or redistribution of unused or donated medicines.

Interoperable Electronic Health Records

In the current scenario, a patient's Electronic Health Records (EHR) are managed and controlled by the healthcare providers. Getting a consolidated view of medical history, diagnosis and treatment becomes a challenge. For instance, if a patient consulted two different hospitals or providers for any medication for diagnostics services, the patient needs to go back to the individual providers and seek the medical records or the prescriptions. The current health services mostly revolve around the hospital or the provider. Additionally, there is no assurance of data privacy. The healthcare providers or institutions are often reluctant to share the health record data because of privacy concerns, and the fear that the shared data may be used to the competitive advantage of the others. This also leads to medication errors because of inaccurate or incomplete medical records between healthcare providers. An accurate health information exchange can benefit the patients by significantly reducing the healthcare costs, minimizing errors because of missing records and better coordination of care between different specialties with different healthcare providers.

Challenges exist with large scale health information exchanges because of: 1) privacy concerns related to the Personal Health Information (PHI), 2) the security risks associated with a single centralized database, 3) the errors in data exchange because of data mismatch in disjoint systems, and 4) a lack of control with the patients (Trehan, 2020). Enabling an efficient healthcare information exchange between the patient, healthcare providers and diagnostic centres would yield significant benefits for the patient, such as avoiding medication errors, duplicate testing and improving diagnosis.

An accurate medical history is very important part of healthcare and critically important during initial assessment for any health condition. Blockchain can store individual health records against a unique patient identifier. When a patient visits a new provider, the provider would share the diagnosis, medical reports or prescriptions electronically with the patients. The patients can receive the same on their own device like a mobile phone. The information may be shared by means of a QR code, email or electronic message (Kim J.W et al, 2019). The hash of the medical records is stored on the blockchain for future verification against any a possible attempt of tampering. The ownership of such patient-centric medical health record resides with the patient or their legal guardian and can be produced to a pharmacy or another provider with a time bound consent from the patient. The receiver of such medical records could easily verify the records against the hash stored on the blockchain to verify the authenticity. Such a verification would be required to verify a forgery, or a possible scenario of prescription abuse which is discussed later in the chapter.

For the information to be interoperable with other providers, the information on health records should be standardised. An international standard has already been created by Health Level Seven International (HL7). HL7 has created Fast Healthcare Interoperability Resources (FHIR), which is a standard describing the data formats and elements (known as "resources") and the Application Programming Interface (API) for exchanging electronic health records. Several standard specifications, relevant detailed documentation and examples can be found on the HL7 FHIR website (FHIR, 2019).

The patient could use the data on their electronic health records for various purposes such as receiving prescriptions from the pharmacy, filing insurance claims, visiting a new provider, providing consent to the clinical research organization to use his or her medical records for research purposes. The receiver of the information can verify the legitimacy of the records within seconds by verifying against the hash stored on the blockchain based distributed ledger.

The blockchain based Electronic Health Records system will also be able to integrate with legacy EHR systems to make the transition from old systems to new systems easier by preserving most of the user experience. By having an electronic health record, patient's information from all of their doctors can be captured and helps to build a complete view of the patient. By having this full record, the patient now has access to their own records and can share with whomever they would like.

Medical Records Data Breach

A medical data breach is a compromise of medical information, personal information, or medical billing information from health information systems. If compromised, medical records could be used to perform malevolent activities like personal identity theft, defamation, and sensationalization, etc. Apart from personal health details, patient records kept by healthcare organizations may also include a patient's financial data, like credit card numbers, telephone numbers and Aadhaar card number or social security numbers, etc. which can be misused for financial gains. In the biggest healthcare breach to date, over 78.8 million patient records were stolen in 2015 by unknown hackers (Mathews, 2015). The data breach gives access to the hackers to the database containing personal information such as names, social security numbers, addresses, email addresses, employment information, dates of births, etc. (Pierson, 2017).

In the last two years, almost 94% of healthcare organizations have witnessed a data breach (York & MacAlister, 2015). Despite the prevalence and cost, over half of the healthcare organizations still do not have the technologies or expertise needed to prevent or quickly detect a data breach. This lack of resources has created a need for pivotal shift in the industry. Figure 2 shows the noticeable data breach instances which have been reported publicly in multiple sources. Joseph Conn (2016), Steve Alder (2018), Kate Vinton (2015), Patrick Ouellette (2013), Davis (2019), Julie (2017), Singh (2019).

Figure 2. Some of the Biggest Data breaches in healthcare

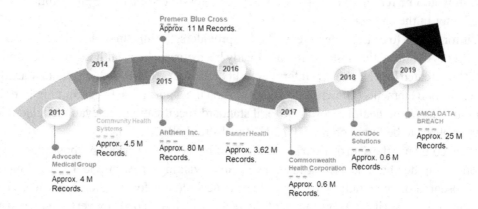

A blockchain based electronic health records would secure the patient's medical records on a blockchain based distributed application. The data is secured cryptographically and the transactions involving the medical records, are encrypted by public private key encryption. Hence ensuring high security, decentralised and tamper proof personal health records. The data is stored on a distributed network and access is provided only after the consent from the patient which is usually in the form of a time bound access which means the receiver may access the information only for a time period.

By storing everything in an encrypted blockchain, it is not necessarily stored on the individual's computer network. Hence, it is extremely secure and very difficult to breach. However, if a hospital's computer network gets hacked or if a major data breach occurs, the hospital and its data centre do not have to shut down. The data can be retrieved from other computers connected to the network. Ransomware is a notorious form of malware which encrypts data in the target system, thereby rendering the data inaccessible to the users. The hackers usually demand an exorbitant fee to grant access to the data again to the owners of the data. But in the case of a blockchain network, the hospital can access copies of the records through another computer that is attached to the blockchain. This distributed nature of data storage on a blockchain helps to address the issue of ransomware attacks.

Prescription Drugs Misuse and Abuse

Opioids, marijuana and some similar drugs have been considered for use in medical purposes; for example, as pain killers and stress relievers and are often used for cases where conventional medicines could not be prescribed, given the patient's health conditions.

The origin of the opioid crisis in the USA has its roots back in 1990s. It was declared as a public health emergency in the United States in October 2017 (Hargan, 2017). According to the sharable graphics on the CDC, approx. 184 people die of drug overdose everyday (Wilson, 2018). Moreover, over 450,000 people died from opioid overdose from 1999 to 2018. The main source of overdose is because of prescription misuse along with the illicit manufacturing or distribution of the synthetic opioids.

Blockchain based prescription drugs monitoring programs can act as viable solutions to prevent prescription drug abuse. With the help of blockchain technology, medical professionals will be able to examine the patient's prescription history and can even revoke prescriptions if they identify a potential misuse of drugs. Pharmacies could also verify the prescriptions against the hash stored on the blockchain network, thereby ensuring process efficiency and compliance.

Prescriptions and the number of allowed refills tracked on the blockchain based prescription management system ensuring increased process transparency and accountability in the supply chain. The chain of custody of a serialised drug could be established and help to verify the ownership and source of a prescribed medicine. Drugs tracked using the platform can be verified together with the physician and patient's details, thereby preventing the misuse of prescription drugs.

By using a blockchain system, an individual's prescription history can be stored on the blockchain. With this information, it is easy to see if the same person is going from doctor to doctor getting prescriptions and filling it at different pharmacies. Smart contracts on a blockchain based prescription management system can automatically flag users who could potentially be abusing drugs and the medical professional will be able to check and verify the misuse.

Along with tough prevention measures, it is also equally important to control the licencing, manufacturing and distribution of such synthetic drugs throughout the distribution process to the pharmacy and to the patient against a valid prescription. Tough measures in tracking legal prescriptions, using a blockchain based prescription drug monitoring program, will come with additional benefits in terms of interoperability and data privacy and accountability for the patients.

Clinical Trials

Vaccine or drug development is a lengthy and expensive process. It may take several years of research and trials to produce a licensed drug or a vaccine and it is often accompanied by high costs and failure rates (Fogel, 2018). Figure 3 illustrates the various phases in typical clinical trials.

Figure 3. Phases in Clinical trials

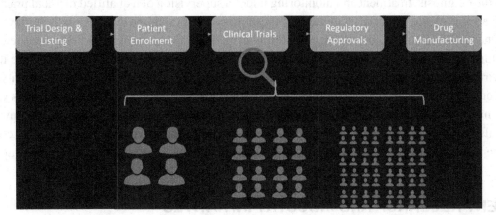

The increasing costs in a vaccine or drug development are a major constraint to the willingness of pharmaceutical companies to undertake clinical trials. The H1N1 influenza vaccine was one of the fastest vaccines developed, largely attributed to the similar work done on the influenza vaccine in the past. However, the vaccine was available to the masses only after the peak of the infection. Later the vaccine was incorporated in the commercially available influenza vaccine. In other cases, for example for SARS, Ebola and Zika, the vaccine was not available in the market on time. The epidemic ended on its due course causing suffering to the ones infected as well as causing financial losses to the drug manufacturers and other drug trials which were set aside for them (Lurie et all, 2020).

Study participants' recruitment, retention, and monitoring is a complex task and could account for up to 30% of the cost of the clinical trials (Sertkaya et al., 2016). Today, challenges exist in tracking clinical trial logistics, trial administration, and patient consent management. Many candidates do not opt into the studies because of trust issues and fearing that their privacy could be compromised. In some cases, the patient opts out of the trial simply because he cannot manage or lack of support to visit the trial site periodically to undergo the trial procedure.

Putting in perspective, in the gamut of challenges in the space of clinical trials, we visualize a digital technology backed ecosystem that can economize on the cost, while expediting the lifecycle with complete transparency and privacy. A decentralized blockchain-based solution to track and trace the movement of trial medicines throughout the supply chain, with real-time monitoring of the transport conditions using smart IoT devices and real-time monitoring of patient using connected medical devices would ensure that a patient could undergo most of the trial procedures from the comfort of their homes. Anonymized data collection and consent management process would allow the patient to share case records and diagnostic parameters, without compromising personally identifiable information and hence increase the rate of participation.

By having a patient's complete electronic health record on the blockchain, researchers can learn more than they would have before because of the availability of patient's health profile. Also, the data mishandling would be less problematic as there are better records. The patient is also allowed to give consent for different pieces of their health record so there is less concern about consent because the patient can clearly see who accessed their data and when they accessed it.

Traditionally, most clinical trials are run at sites, which are hospitals or clinics where the patient would undergo the diagnosis, treatment and monitoring under a supervision of a qualified medical practitioner. With the advent of site-less trials a number of these procedures could be done virtually at the patient's convenience at their home. A convergence of intelligent medical devices, artificial intelligence, tele-health and mobility together on a decentralized blockchain based platform enables the infrastructure required for the virtual site-less trials. The patient could enrol on a trial, undergo virtual consultation with the medical practitioner, get his medications and refills home delivered and record the trial results virtually and still maintaining the accountability at each step of the trial. It is not just a matter of convenience but will also enable to expand the reach of the clinical trials to remote patients who otherwise could not afford the travel required owing to a medical condition or unavailability of time or personal support.

CURRENT RESEARCH AND INDUSTRY INITIATIVES

There have been a variety of studies about the use of blockchain in healthcare, predominantly related to blockchain data management, electronic health records, drug discoverydrug discovery and clinical trials. Moreover, companies and research institutions are actively investigating the prospects of blockchain technology in healthcare. Most of these works are summarized by systematic reviews of research papers, articles and publications (Agbo 2019; Casino 2019). They provide a comprehensive overview about the current landscape and challenges faced while using blockchain in healthcare.

Yue et al. (2016) propose a Healthcare Data Gateway (HDG) based on the blockchain storage platform, which allows patients to process their own data without violating privacy. MedRec is a decentralized blockchain based record management system (Azaria et al., 2016). An attribute-based signature scheme with multiple authorities is proposed by Guo et al. (2018).

Guardtime is one of the pioneers in the field of blockchain and have been working on the world's first blockchain supported personal care record platform launched for the 30 million NHS patients in the UK (Guardtime, 2020). In a similar effort, Singapore government-owned deep technology development firm Innovate is working together with a Singapore based blockchain and healthcare analytics start-up, Medilot, and Singapore national university hospital and few others to build a blockchain powered electronic health record comprising of medical histories, treatment plans and more (Sregantan, 2018).

Government agencies, regulators around the world have been focusing on an important aspect of counterfeit drugs and medical devices which has been growing at an alarming rate. Moreover, there also exists an issue with identifying any critical issue leading to a drug recall and with target dissemination of recall information to the concerned distributors and pharmacies. A drug recall maybe because of different reasons like drug contamination, mislabelling or any failed specifications. Identifying such incidents early in the supply chain and preventing them is important. Regulators like in Europe took a centralized tracking and reporting solution to tackle this issue. At the same time several organizations are experimenting with the use of blockchain, as a solution to their pharma supply chain issues. Mediledger, backed by some of the leading pharmaceutical companies and technology solution providers, have been working on a project with the US FDA to tackle the issue of a serialized drug verification (AmerisourceBergen, 2020). The group in their reports, showcase how a blockchain-based solution can scale through and provide a solution to verify the serialized package or a lot of drugs in the supply chain without actually revealing the information to the public using the zero-knowledge proof solutions on blockchain. Some other organizations like Remedichain are working towards tracking expensive specialty medicines e.g. oral chemotherapy drugs and making it available to the needy (Boxler, 2019). Others like the Melloddy project involving the leading pharma companies is using blockchain to enforce data security and immutable audit trial in drug discovery and prevent leakage of proprietary information while enabling predictive performance (Galtier, 2020). The framework is an attempt to implement federated machine learning to improve collaboration and competitive data sharing among the pharmaceutical companies, i.e. the data never leaves their respective nodes. Only algorithms, predictive models, and non-sensitive metadata are exchanged on the network. Distributed ledger technology is being used here for orchestrating the computation and to establish traceability and authenticity of the information. Around 10 large pharmaceutical companies are involved in this project along with universities, research organizations, public bodies, non-profit organizations, and several technology vendors.

MedBlock also exhibits high information security, due to customized access control protocols and symmetric cryptography (FanKai et al, 2018). BlockHIE is a blockchain-based platform for healthcare information exchange. It uses a combination of two blockchains to handle different kinds of healthcare data. It also combines off-chain storage and on-chain verification to satisfy the requirements of both privacy and authentication. It also uses two fairness-based packing algorithms to improve the system (Shan et al, 2018).

Consortiums such as Coalesce Health Alliance are working on Healthcare data exchanges and provider data directories across the payer entities. Similarly, another consortium, Synaptic Health Alliance has been working in the US to handle the issue of provider data management which directly or indirectly impacts claims settlement, physician directories, physician referrals, credentialing and the information exchange. Others like IBM along with the leading insurance giants in the US have been working on claims adjudication, enabling health information exchange and provider directories.

Ancile (Dagher et al., 2018) is a framework that utilizes smart contracts in an Ethereum-based blockchain for heightened access control and employs advanced cryptographic techniques for further security. It is predominantly used by patients, medical service providers, and third parties. DPS is a Data Preservation System (DPS) for medical data using blockchain. It provides a reliable storage solution that provides data integrity and verifiability while preserving privacy of users. This allows the users to preserve their data ensuring verifiability of the originality and integrity of the data if needed. User privacy is enhanced using prudent data storage strategies and a variety of cryptographic algorithms.

FHIRChain is a blockchain-based architecture designed to handle shared clinical data. It follows the Fast Healthcare Interoperability Resources (FHIR) standard. FHIRChain can be used to build decentralized apps using digital health identities. This solution has been implemented and used to authenticate participants in collaborative decision making for remote cancer care (Zhang et al, 2018).

MedShare is a blockchain based system that provides data provenance, auditing and control for shared medical data in cloud repositories among big data entities. MedShare monitors entities that access data for malicious use from a data custodians' system (Xia et al., 2017). Data transitions, transactions and data sharing between entities and all other actions performed on the MedShare system, are recorded in a tamper-proof manner. The design employs smart contracts and an access control mechanism to effectively track the behaviour of the data across the system. If any malicious activity or violation of regulation is detected, access is immediately suspended. MedShare achieves data provenance and auditing while sharing medical data with entities such as research and medical institutions with minimal risk to data privacy.

Medium.io AG (Bocek et al., 2017) uses IoT devices that use blockchain technology to ensure data immutability and public accessibility of records. They also considerably reduce operational costs in traditional pharmaceutical supply-chains. The medical industry has many complex and strict environmental control process like temperature and humidity to ensure quality control and regulatory compliance over the transport of medical products. The sensor devices monitor the temperature of each parcel during the shipment to ensure adherence to regulations. This sensory data is transferred to the blockchain where a smart contract assesses against the product attributes.

HealthChain, a healthcare industry application, is formalized and developed on the foundation of blockchain using IBM Blockchain initiative (Ahram et al, 2017). The system is transferable to a wide range of industries like finance, government and manufacturing where both security and scalability must be attained. Information management is another excellent application of blockchain technology and one such system is MedBlock, it uses distributed ledger technology to enable efficient EMRs access and EMRs retrieval. It uses an improved consensus mechanism to achieve consensus of EMRs with considerably lesser energy consumption and network congestion.

Several pharma companies have been using technology to improve clinical trial support systems. The clinical trial systems involve a complicated sequence of data sharing between the sponsors, researchers, patients and regulators. Medrec is working on medical data management on the blockchain. It gives patient access to their transparent medical records. The data is secure and private, and it is only accessible by the patients who possess a private key. The data is mined by investigators and data providers are incentivized for contributing to the trials. Embleema is a consortium of medical researchers and patients that aims to provide better data to the researchers while paying participants. There is an app where a patient can upload their personal data such as medical, genomic, and lifestyle data. By having these records patient data does not need to be reconstructed for every clinical study they participate in. This saves money for the researchers as well as providing them better quality data.

Though the technology offers a good deal of promise, there is a fair bit of inertia to shift from the current mode of operations with a point to point interactions and limited information sharing. Several industry players are implementing solutions on blockchain and unlike the other technologies, regulators have come up to speed with the technology owing to its inherent principles of network integrity, security, privacy and inclusion which helps in larger adoption.

BLOCKCHAIN ADOPTION CHALLENGES

The industry is currently slow to adopt the widespread advances in blockchain technology. There are several main reasons because of which the adoption process is slow. The first reason is the lack of regulations. While there are certain incentives in place to adopt better technology, the differing regulations between various bodies makes it hard to adopt. Regulatory agencies like HIPAA and GDPR, want to ensure safety of patient records. However, the lack of international standards makes large scale solutions difficult.

Another reason is the network effect. This means that until widespread adoption is achieved, the solution is not effective. Blockchain gets stronger with every added organization; and adding those first ones are the most difficult. After a critical mass is reached, adoption will be much quicker and subsequent benefits will be more easily realizable. Moreover, there are no widely agreed upon standards in the blockchain industry. There are different blockchain networks out there, each offering has different benefits, but until there is a standard, it is hard for the industry to adopt. The various types of blockchain networks are not compatible so if one of your partners have one blockchain system, and another partner has a different system, it is hard to choose which one to adopt. Moreover, it is also important to account for evolving healthcare regulations, rules and standards.

Another reason for widespread adoption of blockchain technology being slow is that it is hard to forecast an accurate Return-On-Investment (ROI). This is predominantly due to the lack of large-scale real-life implementation in healthcare related use cases. Most pilot projects and prototypes are in early stages and have not been deployed to real life applications and hence their impact is not fully realized. While there have been reasons for slow adoption, companies and researchers continue to explore various ways for implementation of blockchain technology.

The fourth reason is the initial investment cost that is often the prime hurdle in evaluating blockchain use cases. While there may not be a direct return on investment immediately, the benefits of having a blockchain based system will be eventually realized. The return on investment should be clear for each party involved, not just the individual company because unless other stakeholders are convinced, implementation of the blockchain system will be a challenge. Hence, it is imperative that the stakeholders thoroughly understand the need for blockchain based systems, even if it involves a complete overhaul of existing legacy systems.

Mining in blockchain is expensive and uses a lot of computing power. While it is lucrative now with the high price of bitcoin, it is not the case in the healthcare industry. Mining should be done securely, while carefully accounting for resource intensity because it could end up costing the miners more money in computing resource consumption than the return that they receive. Some companies tend to incentivize miners by giving them access to anonymized data in return for their mining contributions (Azaria et al., 2016).

Another aspect to take into consideration when evaluating a blockchain system in the healthcare industry is government regulations. The healthcare and life sciences industries are highly regulated, and for a product or service to be successful in the space it should comply with all rules and regulations. For instance, all the new regulations within HIPAA or GDPR. If a company in the US does not comply with HIPAA or a company in Europe does not comply with GDPR regulations, then the company and its products are generally not allowed for commercial use. It is important not just to consider the current rules and regulations, but to consider the future scenarios as well.

CONCLUSION

A variety of problems and challenges, that are currently present in the healthcare industry, can be solved with the help of blockchain technology. As a trust mediator, it can enable novel healthcare solutions; and as an incentive machine, it can enable novel business models that may lead to new dynamics among various healthcare stakeholders like patients and providers. Similarly, blockchain based decentralized network and services may help to make medical data safe, secure, provide data integrity and data transparency among the stakeholders.

In this chapter, major use cases of blockchain such as medical data management and storage, use of blockchain in the pharmaceutical industry, drugs discovery, clinical trials etc. are explored. Examples of organizations and research institutions researching and developing blockchain-based applications for healthcare are also presented. However, despite the immense potential of blockchain technology and an enormous amount of interest around it, the technology still appears to be in a very early stage in terms of realization, implementation and application in the healthcare industry. Most blockchain based solutions are still in the research and experimenting stage.

Challenges such as integration with the existing systems, uncertainty in implementation and running costs, lack of flexibility and interoperability with legacy systems, technological and adoption barrier, regulatory compliance and scaling still need to be adequately addressed to achieve the widespread implementation of blockchain technology in the healthcare and other related sectors.

REFERENCES

Agbo, C. C., Mahmoud, Q. H., & Eklund, J. M. (2019). Blockchain Technology in Healthcare: A Systematic Review. *Health Care*, *7*, 56. PMID:30987333

Ahram, T., Sargolzaei, A., Sargolzaei, S., Daniels, J., & Amaba, B. (2017). Blockchain Technology Innovations. *Proceedings of the 2017 IEEE Technology & Engineering Management Conference (TEMSCON)*, 137–141. 10.1109/TEMSCON.2017.7998367

Alder. (2018). *2.65 Million Atrium Health Patients Impacted by Business Associate Data Breach.* https://www.hipaajournal.com/2-65-million-atrium-health-patients-impacted-by-business-associate-data-breach/

AmerisourceBergen. (2020). *MediLedger DSCSA Pilot Project.* Chesterbrook: Mediledger.

Azaria, A., Ekblaw, A., Vieira, T., & Lippman, A. (2016). Medrec: Using blockchain for medical data access and permission management. *Proc. of International Conference on Open and Big Data (OBD)*, 25–30.

BayannaK. (2019). Error! Hyperlink reference not valid.http://mdxblocks.com/wp-content/up-loads/2018/05/Product-traceability.pdf

Bocek, T., Rodrigues, B. B., Strasser, T., & Stiller, B. (2017). Blockchains everywhere—A use-case of blockchains in the pharma supply-chain. *Proceedings of the 2017 IFIP/IEEE Symposium on Integrated Network and Service Management (IM)*, 772–777. 10.23919/INM.2017.7987376

Boxler, D. (2019, April). Remedichain to Connect Patients with Costly Meds. *Drug Topics*, ●●●, 42–43.

Button, M., & Gee, J. (2015). *The Financial Cost of Healthcare Fraud*. https://www.researchgate.net/publication/299378586_The_Financial_Cost_of_Healthcare_Fraud

Casino, F., Dasaklis, T. K., & Patsakis, C. (2019). A systematic literature review of blockchain-based applications: Current status, classification and open issues. *Telematics and Informatics*, *36*, 55–81. doi:10.1016/j.tele.2018.11.006

Conn. (2016). *Banner Health cyberattack impacts 3.7 million people*. https://www.modernhealthcare.com/article/20160803/NEWS/160809954/banner-health-cyberattack-impacts-3-7-million-people

Dagher, G. G., Mohler, J., Milojkovic, M., & Marella, P. B. (2018). Ancile: Privacy-preserving framework for access control and interoperability of electronic health records using blockchain technology. *Sustainable Cities and Society*, *39*, 283–297.

Davis, J. (2019). *The 10 Biggest Healthcare Data Breaches of 2019, So Far*. https://healthitsecurity.com/news/the-10-biggest-healthcare-data-breaches-of-2019-so-far

Fan, K., Wang, S., Ren, Y., Li, H., & Yang, Y. (2018). MedBlock: Efficient and Secure Medical Data Sharing Via Blockchain. *Journal of Medical Systems*, *42*(8), 136. doi:10.100710916-018-0993-7 PMID:29931655

FDA. (2013). *Guidance for Industry: Oversight of Clinical Investigations — A Risk-Based Approach to Monitoring*. U.S. Department of Health and Human Services Food and Drug Administration.

FHIR. (2019, November 1). *HL7 FHIR Release 4*. Retrieved from https://www.hl7.org/: https://www.hl7.org/fhir/

Fogel, D. B. (2018). Factors associated with clinical trials that fail and opportunities for improving the likelihood of success: A review. *Contemp Clin Trials Commun.*

Galtier, M. (2020, February 17). *MELLODDY: a "Co-opetitive" Platform for Machine Learning across Companies Powered by Owkin Technology*. Retrieved from www.melloddy.eu: https://www.melloddy.eu/blog/melloddy-a-co-opetitive-platform-for-machine-learning-across-companies-powered-by-owkin-technology

Guardtime. (2020). *World's first blockchain-supported Personal Care Record Platform launched by Guardtime and partners to up to 30 million NHS patients in the UK*. Retrieved from guardtime: https://guardtime.com/blog/world-s-first-blockchain-supported-personal-care-record-platform-launched-by-guardtime-and-partners

Guo, R., Shi, H., Zhao, Q., & Zheng, D. (2018). Secure attribute-based signature scheme with multiple authorities for blockchain in electronic health records systems. *IEEE Access, 6,* 676–686.

Hargan, E. D. (2017, June 10). *U.S. Department of Health & Human Services.* Retrieved from https://www.hhs.gov/sites/default/files/opioid%20PHE%20Declaration-no-sig.pdf

HIPAA. (2019). Healthcare Data Breach Statistics. *HIPAA Journal.* https://www.hipaajournal.com/healthcare-data-breach-statistics/

Jovanovic, B., & Peter, L. R. (2005). *General Purpose Technologies. In Handbook of Economic Growth. Elsevier.* doi:10.3386/w11093

Kim, J. W., Lee, A. R., Kim, M. G., Kim, I. K., & Lee, E. J. (2019). Patient-centric medication history recording system using blockchain. *2019 IEEE International Conference on Bioinformatics and Biomedicine (BIBM)*, 1513-1517. 10.1109/BIBM47256.2019.8983032

Lurie, N. Saville, M., Hatchett, R., & Halton, J. (2020, March 20). *Developing Covid-19 Vaccines at Pandemic Speed.* NEJM.org.

Mathews, A. W. (2015). Anthem: Hacked Database Included 78.8 Million People. *The Wall Street Journal.*

Mattick, J. S., Dziadek, M. A., Terrill, B. N., Kaplan, W., Spigelman, A. D., Bowling, F. G., & Dinger, M. E. (2014). The impact of genomics on the future of medicine and health. *The Medical Journal of Australia, 201*(1), 17–20. doi:10.5694/mja13.10920 PMID:24999876

NIDA. (2018). *Opioid Overdose Crisis.* https://www.drugabuse.gov/drug-topics/opioids/opioid-overdose-crisis

Ouellette. (2013). *Advocate Medical Group endures massive data breach.* https://healthitsecurity.com/news/advocate-medical-group-endures-massive-data-breach

Pierson, B. (2017). *Anthem to pay record $115 million to settle U.S. lawsuits over data breach.* https://www.reuters.com/article/us-anthem-cyber-settlement/anthem-to-pay-record-115-million-to-settle-u-s-lawsuits-over-data-breach

Security, I. B. M. (2019). *Cost of a Data Breach Report 2020.* https://www.ibm.com/security/digital-assets/cost-data-breach-report/#/

Sertkaya, A., Wong, H. H., Jessup, A., & Beleche, T. (2016). Key cost drivers of pharmaceutical clinical trials. *Clinical Trials, 13*(2), 117–126. Advance online publication. doi:10.1177/1740774515625964 PMID:26908540

Shan, J., Jiannong, C., Hanqing W., Yanni, Y., Mingyu, M., & Jianfei, H. (2018). *BlocHIE: A Blockchain based platform for Healthcare Information Exchange.* . doi:10.1109/SMARTCOMP.2018.00073

Singh, H. (2019). *Top Cybersecurity Data Breaches of 2019.* https://www.appknox.com/blog/top-cybersecurity-data-breaches

Southwick, N. (2013). *Counterfeit Drugs Kill 1 Mn People Annually.* Interpol. https://www.insightcrime.org/news/brief/counterfeit-drugs-kill-1-million-annually-interpol/

Spitzer. (2017). *11 of the biggest healthcare cyberattacks of 2017*. https://www.beckershospitalreview. com/cybersecurity/11-of-the-biggest-healthcare-cyberattacks-of-2017.html

Sregantan, N. (2018, July 17). SGInnovate invests in Singapore meditech start-up MediLOT Technologies. *straitstimes*.

Sylim, P., Liu, F., Alvin, M., & Fontelo, P. (2018). Blockchain Technology for Detecting Falsified and Substandard Drugs in the Pharmaceuticals Distribution System (Preprint). *JMIR Research Protocols*, 7. Advance online publication. doi:10.2196/10163 PMID:30213780

Trehan, R., Bansal, D., & Nair, S. J. (2020). *Fostering Interoperable Healthcare Ecosystems Using Blockchain*. Retrieved from www.infosys.com/: https://www.infosys.com/blockchain/documents/fostering-interoperable-healthcare-ecosystems.pdf

Vinton. (2015). *Premera Blue Cross Breach May Have Exposed 11 Million Customers' Medical And Financial Data*. https://www.forbes.com/sites/katevinton/2015/03/17/11-million-customers-medical-and-financial-data-may-have-been-exposed-in-premera-blue-cross-breach/#1aa66d4675d9

WHO Bulletin - Technical Report Series. (2010). *WHO good distribution practices for pharmaceutical products*. WHO Technical Report Series, No. 957.

WHO. (2017). A study on the public health and socioeconomic impact of substandard and falsified medical products. WHO/EMP/RHT/2017.02.

WHO Bulletin (2010). Growing threat from counterfeit medicines. *Bulletin of the World Health Organization*, *88*(4), 241–320.

Wilson, N., Kariisa, M., Seth, P., Smith, H. I. V., & Davis, N. L. (2018). Drug and Opioid-Involved Overdose Deaths— United States, 2017–2018. *MMWR. Morbidity and Mortality Weekly Report*, *2020*(69), 290–297. PMID:32191688

Xia, Q., Sifah, E. B., Asamoah, K. O., Gao, J., Du, X., & Guizani, M. (2017). MeDShare: Trust-Less Medical Data Sharing Among Cloud Service Providers via Blockchain. *IEEE Access: Practical Innovations, Open Solutions*, *5*, 14757–14767. doi:10.1109/ACCESS.2017.2730843

York, T. W., & MacAlister, D. (2015). Hospital and Healthcare Security. Academic Press.

Yue, X., Wang, H., Jin, D., Li, M., & Jiang, W. (2016). Healthcare data gateways: Found healthcare intelligence on blockchain with novel privacy risk control. *Journal of Medical Systems*, *40*(10), 218.

Zhang, P., White, J., Schmidt, D. C., Lenz, G., & Rosenbloom, S. T. (2018). FHIRChain: Applying Blockchain to Securely and Scalably Share Clinical Data. *Computational and Structural Biotechnology Journal*, *16*, 267–278. doi:10.1016/j.csbj.2018.07.004 PMID:30108685

ADDITIONAL READING

DSCDA. (2015), Drug Supply Chain Security Act, https://www.fda.gov/drugs/drug-supply-chain-security-act-dscsa/title-ii-drug-quality-and-security-act, Accessed May 2020.

Hölbl, M., Kompara, M., Kamišali'c, M., & Zlatolas, L. N. (2018). A Systematic Review of the Use of Blockchain in Healthcare. *Symmetry*, *10*(10), 470. Advance online publication. doi:10.3390ym10100470

Ichikawa, D., Kashiyama, M., & Ueno, T. (2017). Tamper-Resistant Mobile Health Using Blockchain Technology. *JMIR mHealth and uHealth*, *5*(7), e111. doi:10.2196/mhealth.7938 PMID:28747296

Katuwal, G. J., Pandey, S., Hennessey, M., & Lamichhane, B. (2018), Applications of Blockchain in Healthcare: Current Landscape & Challenges, arXiv: 1812.02776

Li, H., Zhu, L., Shen, M., Gao, F., Tao, X., & Liu, S. (2018). Blockchain-Based Data Preservation System for Medical Data. *Journal of Medical Systems*, *42*(8), 141. doi:10.100710916-018-0997-3 PMID:29956058

KEY TERMS AND DEFINITIONS

CDS: CDS stands for clinical decision support systems that are health information technology systems designed to provide physicians and other health professionals with clinical decision support i.e. assistance with clinical decision-making task.

Distributed Ledger Technology (DLT): A distributed ledger is a consensus of replicated, shared, and synchronized digital data geographically spread across countries, organizations, or institutions. There is no central administrator or centralized data storage.

HL7: Health Level Seven or HL7 refers to a set of international standards for transfer of clinical and administrative data between software applications used by various healthcare providers.

NHS: The National Health Service (NHS) is the umbrella term for the publicly-funded healthcare systems of the United Kingdom comprising of NHS Scotland, NHS Whales and Health and Social Care in Northern Ireland.

NIDA: National Institute of Drug Abuse is the United States of America's federal agency supporting scientific research on drug use.

Opioids: These are substances that have effects similar those of morphine. Medically they are primarily used for pain relief, including anesthesia. Opioids include oxycodone, hydrocodone, morphine, etc.

Serialized Drug: Serialization of drugs is the process of assigning unique numbers to each unit of prescription product, which contains information about the product's origin, batch number and expiration date.

Smart Contract: A smart contract is a computer protocol intended to digitally facilitate, verify, or enforce the negotiation or performance of a contract. Smart contracts allow the performance of credible transactions without third parties. These transactions are trackable and irreversible.

WHO: The World Health Organization (WHO) is a specialized agency of the United Nations responsible for international public health. The WHO's broad mandate includes advocating for universal healthcare, monitoring public health risks, coordinating responses to health emergencies, and promoting human health and wellbeing.

Chapter 14
Blockchain Integration Into Supply Chain Operations:
An Analysis With Case Studies

Yigit Sever
Middle East Technical University, Turkey

Pelin Angin
Middle East Technical University, Turkey

ABSTRACT

Following the globalization initiated by containerization of logistics, supply chains might be due another revolution by the integration of the disruptive blockchain technology that addresses the current issues with the management of complex global supply chains. Blockchains are distributed digital ledgers that require no central authority to operate while offering a tamper-proof and transparent history of each transaction from the very beginning. Distributed nature of these ledgers ensure that every participant of the supply chain has access to trusted data. The industry has already begun experimenting with blockchain integration into their operations. For the majority of the organizations, however, these experiments stay in proof-of-concept stages or small pilot studies. In this chapter, the authors discuss the supply chain characteristics that make blockchain integration favorable, lay the groundwork for how blockchain can be used for supply chain operations and how it has been used so far.

INTRODUCTION

Supply chains are networks of independent organizations that create and deliver a product to a customer. These complex provenance networks often span multiple countries or even continents. Due to the sheer number of actors on a supply chain, organizations concern themselves only with their immediate links; the upstream actor they are buying from and the downstream actor they are selling to. Incidentally, no one organization has overall control of the whole network, but organizations have to manage their resources and capital to fulfill their niche on the supply chain.

DOI: 10.4018/978-1-7998-6650-3.ch014

Supply Chain Management is the collaboration and cooperation of resources, time, and capital of the organizations on the chain. There is a delicate balance between centralization that leads to efficient use of time and resources, and decentralization to deter opportunistic behavior and fraud (Azzi et al., 2019; Schmidt & Wagner, 2019). As mentioned above, supply chains are not centralized, so it is not feasible to think that organizations have adequate information about the provenance of their inputs below or they are liable to provide information to the parties above them. The lack of information causes wasted inventory space, uncertain delivery times and forces companies to plan with margins of errors that can lead to the bullwhip effect (Ivanov et al., 2018).

Blockchain technology became popular after it was used to power the cryptocurrency Bitcoin in 2008 (Nakamoto, 2008). Since then it has found many uses in other than the finance domain. The primary benefits of blockchain technology in the supply chain management context include: *transparency*, *traceability* and *decentralization*. Blockchain can be used as a tamper-proof, immutable ledger shared between all parties. Once adopted by the organizations on the supply chain, transactions between the participants can be committed to the blockchain with some consensus process verifying the legitimacy of the data. The transparency and traceability of the information go hand-in-hand with a permission system such that the owner of the data can allow access only to concerned parties. All parties along the chain including the customers at the end can verify the provenance of the product they get and confirm that it is not counterfeit, sourced with unethical or questionable labor practices or contaminated in some way.

The industry has been conducting pilot studies for blockchain integration to the supply chain including food (IBM, 2017) and logistics (Moise & Chopping, 2018) industries. The literature has also suggested extensible frameworks (El Maouchi & Ersoy, 2018) and targeted applications such as a counterfeit-proof electronics supply chain (Xu et al., 2019). Internet of Things (IoT) is another field that can highly benefit from the *digitization* and *interoperability* that blockchain technology provides. IoT encompasses devices that have network access, collect data and act autonomously. With the developments in big data and machine learning fields, there is apparent value in collecting data to optimize operations and make informed decisions.

This chapter presents supply chain basics and identifies potential issues with the current supply chain management solutions. Then, the usefulness of blockchain for supply chain management is presented. The drawback of blockchain integration is examined alongside common criticisms against the technology and a discussion about when blockchain is not the viable solution. Finally, use cases from real life and literature is given in detail and open questions, as well as future research directions, are reviewed. Preliminary information regarding supply chains and current problems with it are presented for the rest of the section.

Supply Chain

A supply chain is the collection of organizations that ultimately deliver value to an end customer. A typical view of a supply chain, also depicted in Figure 1, starts with the natural resources that suppliers provide for manufacturers, which are then built into components and finally into products for the consumer market, with distributors handling the flow throughout the network.

In order to deliver the final product, intermediate organizations interact with their suppliers, customers and logistics handlers, creating a material, component, information and capital flow in this network. It is important for the network to allow bidirectional flow to get feedback and handle refunds from the customers at each level and ultimately from the end user.

The modern supply chain operates at a global level. The globalization was initiated after shipping costs became negligible in terms of distance, causing production to be done on the cheapest lot with the cheapest labor instead of near resources or transport hubs (Levinson, 2008). Since procurement is done on a global scale, competition occurs on the global stage as well.

In the article, *The Box: How the Shipping Container Made the World Smaller and the World Economy Bigger* (Levinson, 2008), the author argues that the widespread adoption of the shipping container inadvertently caused the shipping costs to be negligible and kickstarted the modern global supply chains. This should not be mistaken with the *invention* of the shipping containers. Previous attempts to adopt containerization failed because the implementation was tried on just parts of the supply chain. For instance, the ship owners only implemented up to what made sense for their equipment. As a result, the next organization, down the line, had to deal with the non-standard logistics decisions of their supplier. Packing already packaged goods to yet another package and unpacking them at destination to sort through them caused the businesses to avoid containers. Yet, the benefits of the containers became apparent as the network effect led the whole supply network to support shipping containers; from the design of the ships to the docks and the packaging of the products. In short, the true potential of containerization was only realized when the "old ways" of the logistics side of the business were abandoned.

Figure 1. An overview of an end-to-end supply chain.

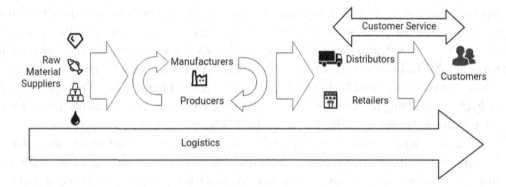

Does blockchain have the potential to disrupt the supply chain business, similar to what shipping containers did previously? Blockchain brings cryptocurrency connotations alongside, which is led by the success story that is Bitcoin, but also malicious actors or frauds such as Onecoin (Department of Justice, 2019). The story of how a company achieved a 289 percent increase in their share price only for it to crash back down in the same day, just by adding *Blockchain* to their name (Shapira & Leinz, 2017), which is indicative of the hype surrounding the technology. Another alternative to consider is this phase where businesses have not figured out how to utilize the potential of blockchain, similar to how businesses in the 1950's, who did not understand containerization, thought shipping containers were unnecessary or tried to keep the status quo for their own interests.

One of the most disruptive technologies the world has witnessed is the Internet (Babich & Hilary, 2020) which draws parallels from the dot-com bubble of the 1990s and the blockchain. This new and exciting technology might also go through the similar phases; hype, rapid adoption causing a bubble, then the crash and then stabilization. Following the dot-com bubble, the Internet is now the familiar way of doing business. Blockchain may go through similar phases and find a stable niche to fill once its benefits and drawbacks get properly figured out. Surveys conducted on adopters of blockchain from industry (e.g. Pawczuk et al., 2020) claim that the current phase of blockchain sentiment has already reached stabilization.

Problems with Supply Chains

Logistics under information asymmetry entail coordination, while keeping the international stage in mind where laws and ideologies differ across the borders during the journey of a product (Liu & Li, 2020). Any inefficiency during planning the operations results in non-optimal use of inventory and production facilities (Liotine & Ginocchio, 2020). This is directly tied to how operations of an organization are separated across the globe (Zhang, 2019). Furthermore, industry experts point to procurement and inventory costs as the main culprits to optimize using data driven long term planning (Kaçan, 2019). Supply chains with tiers of manufacturers, retailers and logistics entities are striving to create value for their organization. The paper-and-pen record keeping and the trail of hardcopy documents including invoices, certificates and bills of lading causes an environment where information is transient. Besides, the scarcity of information allows malicious actors to tamper with the documents through forgery or "double-spending" and robbery of container contents (Kshetri, 2018). The lack of comprehensive information has indirect consequences as well.

In competitive environments such as business negotiations, a negotiator tends to exploit the other party if there is an asymmetry between what two parties know of each other's resources (Boles et al., 2000). This phenomenon has been tested under laboratory conditions within supply chain negotiations as well (Inderfurth et al., 2013). In that study, the authors explain that if one party withholds information and acts upon it within their full capacity, the exploiting party receives benefit with the expense of the rest of the supply chain including higher retail prices for the end customer. In order to disclose information, the suggested method is using *screening contracts*. However, these contracts are set up manually, which hinders the efficiency of the supply chain, especially considering the tendency to operate under Just-in-Time (JiT) approach. Furthermore, the authors have found through experiments that communication and mutual trust increases the supply chain performance, yet this trust is fragile. The root cause of the issue still lies in the cumbersome nature of doing business with paper-based document trails, which makes information sharing harder than information withholding.

The lack of trust in an environment with asymmetric information access and limited information flow dictates entities' behavior. Babich & Hilary (2020) argue that retailers and suppliers on a supply chain would like to drive the price to their benefit by providing skewed information. For instance, suppliers forecast lower production to decrease the apparent supply, driving the price up. Retailers, on the other hand, present artificially inflated demands by forecasting higher sales to get the suppliers to increase their stock, driving the supply up and the prices down. Ultimately, both parties are exploiting the lack of widespread information.

The Bullwhip effect is a direct cause of competition under asymmetric access to information between parties. This effect dictates that when the variance of the presented demand to the manufacturers is higher than the variance of the production capacity of said manufacturer, they cannot make optimal decisions. The effect causes inventory mismanagement, reduced quality in customer service and inefficient distribution of production facilities (Schmidt & Wagner, 2019).

To summarize, the issues regarding supply chains have been identified as:

1. Difficulty of tracking and tracing
2. Not enough deterrence against unethical behavior, corruption
3. Arduous coordination efforts due to globalization and paper-based documents

BLOCKCHAIN TECHNOLOGY FOR SUPPLY CHAIN MANAGEMENT

This section starts by covering fundamental properties of blockchain technology. Then, a detailed presentation on blockchain aspects in relation to supply chain operations is given. Finally, how supply chain operations can benefit, from blockchain integration alongside Internet of Things technology, is discussed.

Blockchain

A blockchain is a series of cryptographically connected data blocks. Each block contains a timestamp, nonce value, reference to the previous block and the list of new transactions. The reference to the previous hash as well as the nonce value ensure that the blockchain is a continuous state and cannot be tampered with. A simplified structure of the blockchain is given in Figure 2.

For public blockchains such as Bitcoin, Proof-of-Work (PoW) provides *consensus* for the transactions and enables anyone to enter the system without time constraints or approval from a centralized authority. PoW is the process of finding a nonce value such that the list of transactions in the block combined with the nonce value yields a hash value within requirements. Since computing the hash value is computationally expensive, participants in the blockchain (called miners) have to expend CPU power and electricity to participate.

Bitcoin is the first successful realization of a cryptocurrency, a decentralized value system that is not backed up with a physical good. Previous "e-cash" systems failed because they relied on trusted central intermediaries. On the other hand, bitcoin is inherently tamper-proof because attackers are incentivized to contribute their resources to the value of the currency of the chain. If a malicious actor instead decides to spend resources to attack the currency, they would have to bolster more computation power than 51% of the participants to the network and even if they are successful, the currency loses value because of their efforts, rendering the gains worthless.

Blockchain implementations have been proposed according to different access classifications. *Bitcoin* is a fully public, open and permissionless network where participants can join the chain at any time. *Private blockchains* require authentication and authorization before participation in the form of network access or encryption. *Consortium blockchain* networks are extended private blockchains. They house validator nodes that govern which participant nodes can present consensus for transactions (Puthal et al., 2018). They are often built by organizations with a common goal but potentially competing interests, which is similar to how supply chains operate. Thus, consortium blockchain networks are often the starting point for pilot studies mentioned in this chapter.

Blockchain has a reputation for costly transactions in terms of time and electricity required. This is often discussed at the forefront among the disadvantages of blockchain implementations (Puthal et al., 2018). Since Bitcoin is a public ledger with no access requirements, the costly PoW has to be in place against 51% of attacks. The blockchain implementations for the supply chain operations have been drafted up to use permissioned or consortium structures, where the costly PoW is not required (Yiannas, 2018).

Figure 2. Simplified structure of a blockchain.

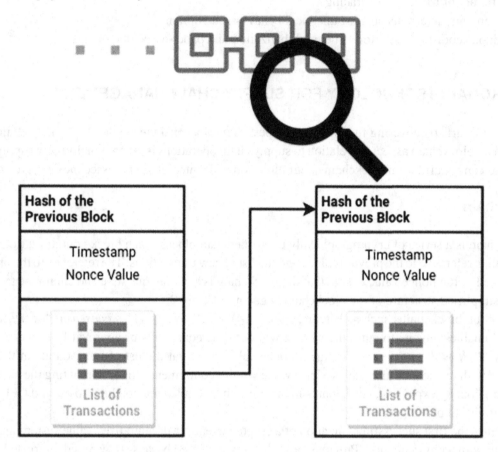

Smart contracts are used to extend the blockchain's capabilities further. They are programs that can be baked into the blockchain with their own addresses. They execute custom logic based on the blockchain state and transactions they receive (Christidis & Devetsikiotis, 2016). Since smart contracts are computer programs that run arbitrary scripts, they can be programmed to verify the quality standards of blockchain input using sensor data (Azzi et al., 2019).

Suitability of Blockchain for Supply Chain Management

In the literature, empirical studies on blockchain integration to the supply chain operations have been limited (Wamba & Queiroz, 2020). However, it is possible to derive the potential benefits of blockchain technology for supply chains from surveys done by research institutes, pilot studies by corporations, and framework proposals from the literature. In this section, the authors present certain suitable aspects of blockchain technology that could be or have been useful to manage supply chains.

In a survey conducted in 2018 regarding the potential uses of blockchain in operations of their companies, four out of five respondents said that their company will use blockchain primarily for the benefits towards traceability and transparency (Pai et al., 2018). These benefits include product tracking and provenance pinpointing.

Figure 3. Relation diagram of the suitable aspects of blockchain technology

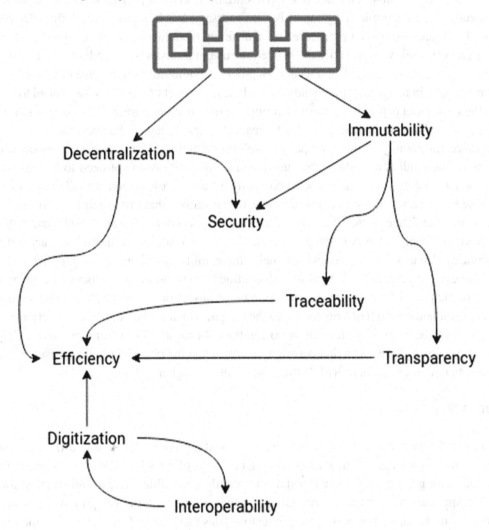

Through the blockchain integration to supply chain literature, it is common to come across notions such as "the problems that blockchain solves can be solved using other tools". As Babich & Hilary (2020) puts it; *Very few things are not technologically feasible without distributed ledger technology. However, some of these possibilities are not economically feasible, and for many, distributed ledger technology is more economical.* Kshetri (2018) addresses the same sentiment by saying that blockchain solves a *messaging problem* more than *a database problem.*

The following are the beneficial attributes the blockchain technology can offer to supply chain management. The relationship diagram of the aspects is provided in Figure 3.

Traceability

This refers to the ease of tracking the source of a product along the supply chain. Extending this idea to multiple levels, traceability is achieved when a product's journey through a supply network is available and can be accessed in a quick manner. Differentiation between perishable products such as food or pharmaceuticals or electronic components is not necessary. It is intuitive to think that electronics are put together from many components procured from different manufacturers but an ingredient for an item sitting on a grocery shelf was probably distributed for use in thousands of products at one point in the supply network (Yiannas, 2018). The traceability process should not only be possible, but be quick as well. In the blockchain integration pilot study by Walmart, a packet of mangoes was traced to the source farm with the traditional paper-based record keeping system in about a week (Yiannas, 2018). During a crisis related to food contamination, a week's traceability period may not be acceptable.

Furthermore, traceability allows a company to isolate contaminated batches should any occur or avoid unnecessary blame while the products that are traced to safe origins do not need to be wasted. Traceability is a valuable target to optimize when a company wants to present their ethical means of sourcing or sustainable business practices. In a holistic view, organizations that raise their traceability standards increase ethical compliance, reduce the cases of missing products during shipments and fraudulent products for the whole supply network (Chang et al., 2019). In electronics manufacturing, traceability helps with authenticity (Xu et al., 2019). Blockchain helps traceability as follows; every product or document is created alongside its digital twin. Real life transactions where products or documents change hands between the participants of the supply chain also create a transaction on the blockchain where the digital twin is exchanged and committed irreversibly to the ledger, which is shared between every entity in the network. The final recipient of the real life good can trace the digital token from creation to destination (Francisco & Swanson, 2018). The link between the token and the physical good is preserved using serial numbers, bar codes, sensors or RFID chips (Schmidt & Wagner, 2019).

Transparency

Transparency is the ease of access to the information about a product. It is subtly different from traceability since transparency deals with what the product consists of not where the product comes from. An edible product with good transparency translates to readily accessible allergen information for people with health complications or a trusted ingredient list that people with dietary preferences can rely on. Organizations with halal, kosher or organic product profiles can benefit from increasing their transparency – by way of gaining consumers' trust (Chang et al., 2019). Transparency is an open problem for supply chains because of too many stakeholders along the chains. For instance, in 2018, over 3.5 billion dollars were lost due to failure to disclose allergen information in food items (Maberry, 2018). Implementing blockchain technologies enables meeting transparency requirements by tracing the ingredients of a product through the chronologically sorted list of transactions.

Immutability

This is the finality of each transaction committed to the blockchain. Altering a previous transaction on the blockchain calls for altering subsequent transactions while the rest of the network is moving forwards with the correct shared state. Overall, immutability provides the basis of the traceability and transparency by securing the trust to the blockchain's state. Additional security measures that protect an organization's data storage integrity is alleviated with blockchain integration.

Efficiency

Integration of blockchain technologies brings the ability to integrate smart contracts to the supply networks. With smart contracts and the verification power of IoT devices, rote procurement processes can be offloaded to frictionless automation including ordering, payment and invoicing. Decentralization and traceability is relevant here for the elimination of the bullwhip effect. As mentioned before, JiT operations have been getting traction to optimize inventory and production facility utilization. Real time tracking through IoT sensors can lead to ahead-of-time operations with the ability to track even the minute details and small batches (Kshetri, 2018). Finally, dispute resolution between buyers and the sellers get benefit from the efficiency aspect with the immutable history of the transactions ready to audit for either party (Chang et al., 2019).

Digitization

As organizations reach interoperability milestones, transaction data such as bills of lading, certificates and product information as well as the product's journey can be available as raw data. Data aggregation is useful for decision making and optimization processes especially combined with big data applications and machine learning. IoT data, product journey, sensor readings such as temperature and humidity and even video data should be readily available for this purpose (Liu & Li, 2020). Digitization of transaction documents or elimination of paper trails is tied to the efficiency of transactions. For instance, logistics company Maersk has found that their shipments would wait unnecessarily in ports due to missing paperwork which would have been tied to the digital twin of the shipment with blockchain integration (Kshetri, 2018).

Decentralization

Decentralization for the present study is related to eliminating single points of failure within the supply chain. Integration of blockchain ensures accountability and trust across the supply network by ensuring that each participant has access to the shared and trusted state. The democratic consensus process confirms this further. The transparency aspect of blockchain integration stems from decentralization as well; the ledger is distributed to all parties. Current supply chain transactions establish validation by assigning the arbitration of trust to a third party verifier, driving up the cost of a transaction (Zhang, 2019). After widespread blockchain adoption, these verifiers will be shifted towards the entry points of the supply chain to assure correct human or sensor input to the blockchain. The rest of the transactions along the supply chain are between blockchain participants, and verification of those transactions are handled through the consensus mechanisms (Babich & Hilary, 2020).

Security

Security follows from both immutability and decentralization. Immutability protects the record keeping system from loss of integrity while decentralization provides protection from attacks against accessibility (Min, 2019). Traditional database management systems need to have protection against these threats while ledgers run on blockchain technology are intrinsically secure. Additionally, through the choice of appropriate consensus algorithms and validator nodes, the blockchain can be secured in the presence of untrusted nodes (Toyoda et al., 2017). It should be noted that untrusted does not necessarily equate to malicious. Competing participants with potentially diverging interests (Babich & Hilary, 2020) also calls for security measures. Finally, blockchain integration is used for secure document exchange and storage with cryptographic security and is used for "identity validation for assets and individuals" (Kshetri, 2018).

Interoperability

As mentioned before, current supply chain information exchange is majorly done manually, with pen-and-paper methods, but organizations keep their records on traditional database management systems. These systems are tailored to the organizations and are effectively walled gardens in terms of data access from third parties. Interoperability in this context refers to systems readily accepting each other's communications and data. Standardized blockchain transactions or API requirements are part of interoperability as well. Interoperability is not necessarily a direct benefit of blockchain integration but an important milestone when gradual adoption of blockchain integration of organizations happens. Blockchain integration after reaching the interoperability milestones allows for the digitization of the supply chain and the opportunity to use Internet of things (IoT) devices and sensors for enhancing the quality requirements tracking. The temperature, pressure or other variables of the products shipment can be tracked in real time and through smart contracts, committed to the blockchain automatically. GPS trackers and the chronological ordering of blocks allows for real time tracking and pinpointing of goods during transit (Kshetri, 2018).

Use of Smart Contracts and IoT

In the context of blockchain technology, tokenization is the process of creating a digital twin for a physical or intangible asset, by constructing a representation for it, to be input to the blockchain (Schmidt & Wagner, 2019); (Cameron-Huff, 2017). The resulting token is a record of proof for the whole or parts of the digitized asset. The owner of a block therefore owns the whole physical good (i.e. an amount of gold bars), parts of the physical good (i.e. some share in a real estate) or, if the asset is intangible, record of emission allowance or top-level domain names.

Inputting data to the blockchain involves tokenizing the physical goods or digital assets. Once tokenized, blockchain handles the security, mainly integrity, of the ownership of the assets in a cryptographically verifiable way with clear timestamps (Christidis & Devetsikiotis, 2016), even against the presence of malicious nodes, even in permissioned networks (Azzi et al., 2019).

With the leeway offered by the tokenization and secure transmission of data with blockchain, literature has suggested ways to harness the previously mentioned smart contracts for increasing efficiency in supply chain operations. Figure 4 illustrates a shipment of cargo using IoT sensors and blockchain integration.

Liu & Li (2020) have proposed a blockchain framework with a multi-chain structure where the sensitive account data is separated from transaction data and the data generated by IoT devices. This framework addresses the separate access frequencies and data requirements of three types of data while offering the ability to define access restrictions for each of them. El Maouchi & Ersoy (2018) suggested and empirically analyzed a generic supply chain traceability framework powered by blockchain. Their framework is proposed for a public blockchain structure and assumes secure input from the environment.

Figure 4. Real time product tracking using blockchain and IoT sensors.

Reyna et al. (2018) conducted a literature survey on blockchain and IoT integration. The authors suggest that blockchain integration can help IoT communications by providing data reliability. Furthermore, blockchain can provide unique identifiers for each device on the network and a trusted authentication scheme. They have identified three communication architectures for use in blockchain integration. The first one is *IoT-IoT* where IoT devices communicate directly with each other for low latency applications while blockchain only provides the addressing and authentication framework. The second architecture is *IoT-Blockchain,* where IoT devices have to use blockchain as a database to query and act autonomously. The transactions are immutably committed to the blockchain for this architecture. The third architecture is the *Hybrid approach* in which the previous two architectures are combined, where appropriate, to create a full operation definition. The authors claim that the hybrid approach is the best way to integrate IoT to blockchain applications since it leverages the real-time capabilities of IoT with the aforementioned benefits of the blockchain.

Bumblauskas et al. (2020) conducted a pilot study alongside a company regarding egg tracking in the United States. The company used temperature and humidity sensors to collect data about the transit of the eggs from the farm to the customers. During the proof-of-concept study, consumers could scan a QR code in the grocery stores with their smartphones to access the provenance of the carton of eggs they are holding. Behnke & Janssen (2020) have documented *boundary conditions* for a dairy supply chain to meet traceability requirements. Authors have conducted interviews with the organizations on dairy supply chains during 4 case studies. They found that the standardization of data and the selection of governance structure are the main driving factors of blockchain integration.

On the other hand, (Marsal-Llacuna, 2018) claims that a system with blockchain integration that relies on IoT data requires massive computing power and will not be feasible. However, the author only considered public blockchain structures where the limiting factor is the expensive PoW consensus algorithm.

ADOPTING BLOCKCHAIN TECHNOLOGY FOR SUPPLY CHAIN MANAGEMENT

While all of the suitable aspects of blockchain require an ensemble of organizations with a common goal and diverging interests to participate in the blockchain and provide consensus for the transactions, the interoperability aspect requires a much stronger action. While the blockchain is inherently decentralized, the standards for transactions, characteristics of the blockchain and the technical details like the choice of consensus method or the existence of validator nodes has to be agreed upon. Adoption of blockchain technology can propagate in two directions: top down integration is possible when a large retail corporation requires its suppliers to join the blockchain, or bottom up approach when suppliers at the start of the supply chain start participating in the blockchain and showcase the benefits to the distribution companies (Kshetri, 2018).

This section is dedicated to the details of the blockchain integration process, mainly the parameters of the blockchain and the initial data input issues.

Blockchain Modes of Operation

Blockchain networks operate under two basic access principles; permissioned and permissionless. According to Wüst & Gervais (2018), permissionless or decentralized mode of operation is the use case that could leverage the true potential of blockchain technology. Furthermore, if all of the parties of a network are fully trusted, then a private permissioned blockchain implementation is redundant and a traditional database system should be used instead. A supply chain is not a network where all parties are trusted due to the competition, they are in.

Environment to Blockchain Input

The integrity assurance of blockchain is at its weakest at the time of initial human or sensor input to the blockchain (Schmidt & Wagner, 2019). The threat actors here are rouge/malicious humans and malfunctioning or tampered sensors (Wüst & Gervais, 2018). Babich & Hilary (2020) call the potentially insecure input to the immutable blockchain transition the *state zero problem*.

The transactions on the blockchain are agreed upon by both the buyer and the seller during consensus. Babich & Hilary (2020) say that this is only a partial solution. However, Rodney & Zuckerman (2019) claim that use of IoT sensors fully solve the issue. This finding is supported by Queiroz et al. (2019) as well, who identified IoT devices to be especially useful for ensuring that the initial input from the environment to blockchain is legitimate. These sensors may include temperature and weight sensors, barcodes and RFID tags. For perishable materials such as pharmaceuticals and food items, gel-like trackers that do not disrupt the items can be used. Literature has also suggested successful PoW techniques that identify fraudulent food items without opening their containers (Ha, Leng et al., 2020). Value of these proposals are apparent when considering the statement by a wine authenticator "The value of fraudulent fine wine in circulation may be as much as $1 billion" (Adam Lechmere, 2016). The diversity of these methods underlines the interoperability requirements of blockchain implementations as well as the redundancy that could be established by using multiple sensors and sensing technologies.

Consensus

Another avenue for reaching consensus over the requirements and quality standards for assets in a transaction is relying on external *oracles*. Simply put, oracles are 3rd party entities that actors on the blockchain rely to verify the authenticity of transactions. The use of oracles inadvertently skews the decentralized nature of the blockchain platform by implementing trust on a central authority. The company ChainLink (Ellis et al., 2017) have suggested a decentralized oracle structure to solve this issue.

Depending on the access requirements of the blockchain network, a suitable consensus algorithm should be utilized. Permissionless or public networks use expensive PoW to reach consensus in an environment with no trust. Since blockchains for supply networks fall into the consortium blockchains category, expensive PoW is not preferred. Algorithms like Practical Byzantine Fault Tolerance that work under permissioned settings and provide resistance to $\frac{1}{3}$ of the network acting malicious are suitable.

CASE STUDIES

The blockchain emerged as a linked series of transactions, thought as the driving power of a new currency. For the purposes of supply chains, the core idea of keeping an unchangeable chronology of all transactions within the system has carried over. Blockchain can be hard to untangle from its Bitcoin roots and the hype that still surrounds it. However, the seemingly simple idea of all transactions being agreed on and final can be built upon. In the end, thinking about blockchain as a shared data storage, that all writers and readers can trust. is the basis of all implementations.

Blockchain technology has caught the interest of organizations, especially the food industry and retail. The most commonly cited reasons for this interest are the outbreaks stemming from contaminated food.

Between April and May 2018, Capgemini Research Institute asked 731 organizations on various supply chains about the blockchain adoption progress in their organization. 447 organizations responded with an even split into manufacturing, retail and consumer products. Among the answers; only 3% are using blockchain in their daily operations, 10% are doing a pilot study with blockchain, while 87% use it as a proof of concept. The survey has also found that the most popular benefit of blockchain in supply chain operations for organizations is traceability and transparency. A more tangible benefit is the management of supplier contracts. (Pai et al., 2018).

Recently, Deloitte Insights have conducted a survey of 1,488 senior executives and practitioners from 14 countries, between February 6 to March 3, 2020, on the organizational stance on blockchain (Pawczuk et al., 2020). Since the research institute has been conducting similar surveys for the past 3 years, they have gathered some data for the adoption progress of blockchain over the years. For instance, the percentage of respondents that replied that blockchain is a top 5 priority for their organization climbed up from 43% to 53%. The authors of the survey report this finding as indicative that "blockchain is now an integral way of doing business". Among the answers that saw a rise in positive answers e.g. "My organization or project will lose a competitive advantage if we don't adopt blockchain technology and Our executive team believes there is a compelling business case for the use of blockchain technology within my organization or project" are further indications of this adoption. However, positive answers to "Blockchain is overhyped" has also risen.

Blockchain technology requires decentralization of work. A blockchain implementation planned to be used only within an organization is a waste of potential and resources. This type of closed implementations of blockchain as data storage should be left to traditional data storage solutions like databases (Wüst & Gervais, 2018). Furthermore, decentralization is possible only with proper onboarding procedures and adoption incentives so that different parties, even competitors, participate to the blockchain and be a part of the democratic consensus process.

In order to ease the inventory management, Walmart required its top 100 suppliers to adopt RFID tags by January 2005. This is an example of top-down propagation of adoption, discussed under the Adoption of Blockchain in Supply Chains section. A major retail-forced adoption of an innovation to smooth off the transition phase is the uphill phase of the network effect. Similarly, an organization with enough incentive can hasten the adoption of blockchain. On the other hand, according to the founder of the blockchain for automotive industry initiative MOBI, Chris Ballinger, *the network effects will be very strong* in the industries that use blockchain technology and *if you're not in at the very start, it may be too late* (Shiraz Ahmed, 2018).

Traceability is an integral requirement for supply chains that deal with food. It is well justified by retailers, manufacturers and consumers. Retailers would like to pinpoint the provenance of items in case of contamination or similar issues that would lead to a recall process for the product. Manufacturers would like to avoid misplaced blame when their product is not the cause of an outbreak so that they do not have to issue recalls or lose reputation tied to their brand in the face of the public. Finally, customers would like to purchase food items that are held up to standards (Tan et al., 2018). Pai et al. (2018) have reported that "a typical beverage recall would have cost 8 million dollars in 2017 and 456 food recalls in the United States is estimated to cost 3.5 billion dollars". For the majority of the recalls, the culprit is undeclared allergen information (Maberry, 2018). In other words, the food industry lost upwards of 3.5 billion dollars due to lack of transparency and traceability. It is no wonder that the initial surge of blockchain adoption in supply chains targeted the food industry.

Traceability has another value proposition for organizations that would like to gain the trust of the customers through concern for environmental causes and sustainability. An estimated €966 billion opportunity exists for brands that make their sustainability credentials clear (Unilever NV, 2017). Survey done on five countries and 20 thousand participants found that customers are conscious of the environmental impacts of their products and given choice, would prefer brands that are sourced and produced sustainably. This is especially true for customers in developing countries. For organizations that are integrating sustainability into their operations, blockchain is part of the solution for conveying this stance to customers. The tuna fish tracking pilot study done by Provenance gives further insight on how the initial sourcing process of the materials can be input to the blockchain and propagated up the supply chain all the way to the customers.

During the rest of this section, the authors present the real-life use cases of blockchain integration to supply chains in accordance to accounts by the organizations that conducted the studies.

Tuna Tracking by Provenance

Provenance is a London based blockchain startup. They have been conducting pilot studies for different supply chains with reports and documentations of their experiences. During these studies, the company worked with organizations and people from fashion, textile, cosmetics and coffee industries to name a few. The most extensive report, which is covered in this chapter, is given for the yellowfin and skipjack tuna fish tracking in Indonesia.

In a 6 month long pilot study in 2016, Provenance built a blockchain for the end-to-end traceability for tuna fish in Indonesia (Provenance, 2016). Traceability of tuna sourcing is especially important for the region due to unethical sourcing practices with the extreme examples reaching to the point of slavery. Provenance identified that the fishermen have access to mobile phones and set up their system to work with simple SMS messages as input. They used smart tagging to tokenize the fish in the form of NFC-enabled smart stickers.

The aim of the pilot study was to aid the industry of the region with the proof of compliance to standards. Fishermen are certified for their compliance to sustainable catching as well as protecting them against unethical labor practices. Another aim was to prevent "double-spending" of certificates. A holistic view for the study regarding the company is "exploring how these new technologies could form the basis for an open system for traceability powering consumer-facing transparency for food and other physical goods".

The pilot study has successfully demonstrated the possibility of integrating blockchain to an end-to-end supply chain, starting from the source all the way to the consumer. The data that flows through the supply chain and committed to the blockchain has been successfully ensured to be interoperable.

Food Tracking by Walmart

Improving supply chains that deal with food items has been the focus of recent research. Food items are especially susceptible to fraud and tampering due to the large amounts they get shipped in (McKenzie, 2018). While fraud and tampering, such as dilution or faking, is detrimental to consumer health, disastrous consequences stem from outbreaks that use contaminated foodstuff as disease vectors. One particular case of E. coli outbreak during 2006 is of interest since the offending batch of spinach that hospitalized 102 people and caused the death of 3 has found to have originated from a single lot (Centers for Disease Control and Prevention, 2006). There is an apparent value in the ability to identify the procurement of food items.

When the president for food safety of Walmart realized the difficulties surrounding the tracing and tracking food origins, they conducted a simple experiment (Yiannas, 2018). They purchased a packet of sliced mangoes and asked their team during a meeting to track down the farm that harvested the product that they are holding in their hand. The supply chain involving the mangoes used pen and paper methods for keeping a ledger of mangoes. This paper trail is not scalable and the information available in one party is not directly available in another. Furthermore, as discussed earlier on in this chapter, due to sheer complexity of supply chains, organizations are aware of only the neighboring portions of the supply chain. Eventually, it took 6 days, 18 hours and 26 minutes for the team to track down the farm that harvested the mangoes. Leaving non-essential goals such as informing customers about the ethical harvesting processes aside, that is potentially a week for an organization to gather data during a potential outbreak from contaminated food.

After the successful pilot study, Walmart invited other food retail companies and together they formed a coalition of ten Foundation Partners composed of both suppliers and retailers, which include Walmart, Kroger, Wegmans, Tyson, Driscolls, Nestle, Unilever, Danone, McCormick, and Dole. As the consortium, the pilot study continued and "as of May 2018, Walmart has already tracked nearly two dozen SKUs involving 2.6 million food packages across 166,000 traceability events on the blockchain in production environments".

A decentralized system fails if it is not interoperable. The current consensus going forward from those who applied blockchain on the field are implementing open systems with simple onboarding processes and robust data input. Blockchain should be decentralized but the implementation should not be monopolized. No single food retailer can mandate better food traceability, food manufacturers in one country cannot do it alone, nor can any single country's regulatory agencies. Better food traceability requires collaboration, and it must be people led and technology enabled.

When consumers visit a grocery store, they want to know whether the ingredients in their product have been sourced ethically. While it is not a constantly present concern, news of disregarded labor practices or sourcing through slave labor would upset consumers as well. Furthermore, customers prefer sustainable methods that are not harmful to the environment. Some consumers have strict dietary requirements such as vegetarians and vegans. Requirements of others go beyond the ingredients list and reach to the sourcing process; for instance, halal food requirements are concerned with the slaughtering process of the animals. Finally, allergen information should be covered under transparency.

High Value Items Tracking by Everledger

Everledger is a blockchain platform, founded for meeting the traceability and provenance demands of high-value items such as diamonds, wines, and luxury goods. The case of luxury goods draws a contrary case from the previous case studies since foodstuffs are relatively low-value items that require atomistic risk evaluation where the journey of a product from the farm to the plate of a customer can be planned in steps. High-value items that Everledger deal with require holistic solutions due to the increased threat to the high-value items (Kshetri, 2018). For instance, to overcome the state zero problems, Everledger's operations include "scan and verify every diamond manually before its data is stored on the blockchain", which the company has done for over 2 million diamonds, as reported in a 2019 study (Schmidt & Wagner, 2019).

Everledger has identified that customers have been raising ethical concerns regarding the provenance of the diamonds (George, 2020b). Their initiative to use blockchain technology was motivated by the immutability it provides (Price, 2015) which is the basis for transparency. The authentication process of high-value diamonds are tied to certifications and regulations; hence Everledger assigned Chow Tai Fook Jewellery Group to certify traceability, truthfulness, thoughtfulness and transparency; and independent diamond grading authority, Gemological Institute of America (GIA), to certify the physical attributes of each diamond as verifiers (George, 2020a). Similar to how Walmart presented its product's traceability and transparency credentials, end customers can use their smartphones to access this information (George, 2020a).

CONCLUSION

Blockchain technology, with implementation details set aside, is a shared state with strong guarantees that the said state can be traced back to the very beginning, and is the same for every participant. Starting from this modest definition, it is possible to build some truly disruptive systems that can change how business, supply chains, energy grids, or communication systems operate.

Following the examples and case studies presented in this chapter, the next obstacle for blockchain integration to supply chains is the adoption phase. The network effect dictates that the adoption will be slow while the incentive to join the blockchain is low due to the lack of participants to the network. Presented surveys, that were conducted on industry professionals, indicate that the rapid adoption process might be getting closer.

The truly beneficial aspects of blockchain, namely digitization and efficiency which bring the ability to collect, learn from, and act upon data autonomously require interoperability. If the adoption phase of the blockchain leaves the industry with segmented networks that do not integrate with each other than each chain's value will get lower.

This chapter gave an overview of the aspects of blockchain that is beneficial for actors on the supply chain and presented some real-life use cases that gave valuable insight into the theoretical benefits of blockchain in real markets.

It should be noted that the future work of blockchain integration to the supply chain is vast. For instance, coordination of consortium blockchains, meeting the data processing requirements borne out of IoT devices, and securing the blockchain input against malicious actors or sensors are open questions.

REFERENCES

Ahmed, S. (2018, May 2). Automakers, suppliers team up to develop blockchain technology. *Automotive News*. https://www.autonews.com/article/20180502/MOBILITY/180509974/automakers-suppliers-team-up-to-develop-blockchain-technology

Azzi, R., Chamoun, R. K., & Sokhn, M. (2019). The power of a blockchain-based supply chain. *Computers & Industrial Engineering, 135*, 582–592. doi:10.1016/j.cie.2019.06.042

Babich, V., & Hilary, G. (2020). Distributed Ledgers and Operations: What Operations Management Researchers Should Know About Blockchain Technology. *Manufacturing & Service Operations Management, 22*(2), 223–240. doi:10.1287/msom.2018.0752

Behnke, K., & Janssen, M. F. W. H. A. (2020). Boundary conditions for traceability in food supply chains using blockchain technology. *International Journal of Information Management, 52*, 101969. doi:10.1016/j.ijinfomgt.2019.05.025

Boles, T. L., Croson, R. T. A., & Murnighan, J. K. (2000). Deception and Retribution in Repeated Ultimatum Bargaining. *Organizational Behavior and Human Decision Processes, 83*(2), 235–259. doi:10.1006/obhd.2000.2908 PMID:11056070

Bumblauskas, D., Mann, A., Dugan, B., & Rittmer, J. (2020). A blockchain use case in food distribution: Do you know where your food has been? *International Journal of Information Management, 52*, 102008. doi:10.1016/j.ijinfomgt.2019.09.004

Cameron-Huff, A. (2017, March 30). *How Tokenization Is Putting Real-World Assets on Blockchains: How Tokenization Is Putting Real-World Assets on Blockchains | Nasdaq*. https://www.nasdaq.com/articles/how-tokenization-putting-real-world-assets-blockchains-2017-03-30

Centers for Disease Control and Prevention. (2006, October 6). *Multistate Outbreak of E. coli O157:H7 Infections Linked to Fresh Spinach (FINAL UPDATE)*. https://www.cdc.gov/ecoli/2006/spinach-10-2006.html

Chang, Y., Iakovou, E., & Shi, W. (2019). *Blockchain in Global Supply Chains and Cross Border Trade: A Critical Synthesis of the State-of-the-Art, Challenges and Opportunities*. https://arxiv.org/abs/1901.02715

Christidis, K., & Devetsikiotis, M. (2016). Blockchains and Smart Contracts for the Internet of Things. *IEEE Access: Practical Innovations, Open Solutions, 4*, 2292–2303. doi:10.1109/ACCESS.2016.2566339

Department of Justice. (2019, March 8). *Manhattan U.S. Attorney Announces Charges Against Leaders Of "OneCoin," A Multibillion-Dollar Pyramid Scheme Involving The Sale Of A Fraudulent Cryptocurrency*. https://www.justice.gov/usao-sdny/pr/manhattan-us-attorney-announces-charges-against-leaders-onecoin-multibillion-dollar

El Maouchi, M., & Ersoy, O. (2018). *TRADE: A Transparent, Decentralized Traceability System for the Supply Chain*. doi:10.18420/BLOCKCHAIN2018_01

Ellis, S., Juels, A., & Nazarov, S. (2017). *ChainLink A Decentralized Oracle Network*. ChainLink. https://link.smartcontract.com/whitepaper

Francisco, K., & Swanson, D. (2018). The Supply Chain Has No Clothes: Technology Adoption of Blockchain for Supply Chain Transparency. *Logistics, 2*(1), 2. doi:10.3390/logistics2010002

George, C. (2020a). *Unraveling hidden value in diamond sourcing*. Everledger. https://www.everledger.io/concept-paper/unraveling-hidden-value-in-diamond-sourcing/

George, C. (2020b, May 1). *Diamond Provenance at every link of the value chain*. Everledger. https://www.everledger.io/diamond-provenance-at-every-link-of-the-value-chain/

Ha, U., Leng, J., Khaddaj, A., & Adib, F. (2020). Food and liquid sensing in practical environments using RFIDs. *17th USENIX Symposium on Networked Systems Design and Implementation (NSDI 20)*, 1083–1100. https://www.usenix.org/conference/nsdi20/presentation/ha

IBM. (2017, August 22). IBM Announces Major Blockchain Collaboration with Dole, Driscoll's, Golden State Foods, Kroger, McCormick and Company, McLane Company, Nestlé, Tyson Foods, Unilever and Walmart to Address Food Safety Worldwide. *PR Newswire*. https://www.prnewswire.com/news-releases/ibm-announces-major-blockchain-collaboration-with-dole-driscolls-golden-state-foods-kroger-mccormick-and-company-mclane-company-nestle-tyson-foods-unilever-and-walmart-to-address-food-safety-worldwide-300507604.html

Inderfurth, K., Sadrieh, A., & Voigt, G. (2013). The Impact of Information Sharing on Supply Chain Performance under Asymmetric Information. *Production and Operations Management, 22*(2), 410–425. doi:10.1111/j.1937-5956.2012.01372.x

Ivanov, D., Tsipoulanidis, A., & Schönberger, J. (2018). Global Supply Chain and Operations Management: A Decision-Oriented Introduction to the Creation of Value (2nd ed.). Springer.

Kaçan, M. (2019, October 17). *5 main drivers of supply chain costs*. ICRON. https://icrontech.com/blog_item/5-main-drivers-of-supply-chain-costs/

Kshetri, N. (2018). 1 Blockchain's roles in meeting key supply chain management objectives. *International Journal of Information Management*, *39*, 80–89. doi:10.1016/j.ijinfomgt.2017.12.005

Lechmere, A. (2016, December 5). Wine Vault Offers Security in a Digital Age. *Wine-Searcher*. https://www.wine-searcher.com/m/2016/12/wine-vault-offers-security-in-a-digital-age

Levinson, M. (2008). *The Box: How the Shipping Container Made the World Smaller and the World Economy Bigger*. Princeton University Press.

Liotine, M., & Ginocchio, D. (2020). The supply blockchain: Integrating blockchain technology within supply chain operations. In *Technology in Supply Chain Management and Logistics* (pp. 57–89). Elsevier. doi:10.1016/B978-0-12-815956-9.00004-1

Liu, Z., & Li, Z. (2020). A blockchain-based framework of cross-border e-commerce supply chain. *International Journal of Information Management*, *52*, 102059. doi:10.1016/j.ijinfomgt.2019.102059

Maberry, T. (2018, February 6). A Look Back at 2017 Food Recalls. *Food Safety Magazine*. https://www.foodsafetymagazine.com/enewsletter/a-look-back-at-2017-food-recalls/

Marsal-Llacuna, M.-L. (2018). Future living framework: Is blockchain the next enabling network? *Technological Forecasting and Social Change*, *128*, 226–234. doi:10.1016/j.techfore.2017.12.005

McKenzie, J. (2018, February 4). Wal-Mart and IBM want to harness blockchain to improve food safety. *The Counter*. https://thecounter.org/blockchain-food-traceability-walmart-ibm/

Min, H. (2019). Blockchain technology for enhancing supply chain resilience. *Business Horizons*, *62*(1), 35–45. doi:10.1016/j.bushor.2018.08.012

Moise, I., & Chopping, D. (2018, January 16). Maersk and IBM Partner on Blockchain for Global Trade. *The Wall Street Journal*. https://www.wsj.com/articles/maersk-and-ibm-partner-on-blockchain-for-global-trade-1516111543

Nakamoto, S. (2008). *Bitcoin: A peer-to-peer electronic cash system*. Academic Press.

Pai, S., Sevilla, M., Buvat, J., Schneider-Maul, R., Lise, O., Calvayrac, A., Karanam, T., & Puttur, R. (2018). *Does Blockchain hold the key to a new age in Supply Chain transparency and trust?* Capgemini Research Institute. https://www.capgemini.com/research/does-blockchain-hold-the-key-to-a-new-age-in-supply-chain-transparency-and-trust/

Pawczuk, L., Holdowsky, J., Massey, R., & Hansen, B. (2020). *Deloitte's 2020 Global Blockchain Survey*. Deloitte Insights. https://www2.deloitte.com/content/dam/insights/us/articles/6608_2020-global-blockchain-survey/DI_CIR%202020%20global%20blockchain%20survey.pdf

Price, R. (2015, August 28). This London startup could make diamond theft a thing of the past—And that's just the start. *Business Insider*. https://www.businessinsider.com/everledger-ledger-diamonds-blockchain-tech-theft-fraud-2015-8

Provenance. (2016). *From shore to plate: Tracking tuna on the blockchain*. Provenance. https://www.provenance.org/tracking-tuna-on-the-blockchain

Puthal, D., Malik, N., Mohanty, S. P., Kougianos, E., & Das, G. (2018). Everything You Wanted to Know About the Blockchain: Its Promise, Components, Processes, and Problems. *IEEE Consumer Electronics Magazine*, *7*(4), 6–14. doi:10.1109/MCE.2018.2816299

Queiroz, M. M., Telles, R., & Bonilla, S. H. (2019). Blockchain and supply chain management integration: A systematic review of the literature. *Supply Chain Management*, *25*(2), 241–254. doi:10.1108/SCM-03-2018-0143

Reyna, A., Martín, C., Chen, J., Soler, E., & Díaz, M. (2018). On blockchain and its integration with IoT. Challenges and opportunities. *Future Generation Computer Systems*, *88*, 173–190. doi:10.1016/j.future.2018.05.046

Rodney, J. D., & Zuckerman, N. (2019, February 11). How blockchain can strengthen the military supply chain. *Vanguard Magazine*. https://vanguardcanada.com/2019/02/11/how-blockchain-can-strengthen-the-military-supply-chain/

Schmidt, C. G., & Wagner, S. M. (2019). Blockchain and supply chain relations: A transaction cost theory perspective. *Journal of Purchasing and Supply Management*, *25*(4), 100552. doi:10.1016/j.pursup.2019.100552

Shapira, A., & Leinz, K. (2017, December 21). *Long Island Iced Tea Soars After Changing Its Name to Long Blockchain*. Bloomberg.Com. https://www.bloomberg.com/news/articles/2017-12-21/crypto-craze-sees-long-island-iced-tea-rename-as-long-blockchain

Tan, B., Yan, J., Chen, S., & Liu, X. (2018). The impact of blockchain on food supply chain: The case of Walmart. *International Conference on Smart Blockchain*, 167–177. 10.1007/978-3-030-05764-0_18

Toyoda, K., Takis Mathiopoulos, P., Sasase, I., & Ohtsuki, T. (2017). A Novel Blockchain-Based Product Ownership Management System (POMS) for Anti-Counterfeits in the Post Supply Chain. *IEEE Access, 5*, 17465–17477. doi:10.1109/ACCESS.2017.2720760

Unilever, N. V. (2017, May 1). *Report shows a third of consumers prefer sustainable brands*. Unilever Global Company Website. https://www.unilever.com/news/press-releases/2017/report-shows-a-third-of-consumers-prefer-sustainable-brands.html

Wamba, S. F., & Queiroz, M. M. (2020). Blockchain in the operations and supply chain management: Benefits, challenges and future research opportunities. *International Journal of Information Management*, *52*, 102064. doi:10.1016/j.ijinfomgt.2019.102064

Wüst, K., & Gervais, A. (2018). Do you Need a Blockchain? *2018 Crypto Valley Conference on Blockchain Technology (CVCBT)*, 45–54. 10.1109/CVCBT.2018.00011

Xu, X., Rahman, F., Shakya, B., Vassilev, A., Forte, D., & Tehranipoor, M. (2019). Electronics Supply Chain Integrity Enabled by Blockchain. *ACM Transactions on Design Automation of Electronic Systems, 24*(3), 31:1–31:25. doi:10.1145/3315571

Yiannas, F. (2018). A New Era of Food Transparency Powered by Blockchain. *Innovations: Technology, Governance, Globalization*, *12*(1–2), 46–56. doi:10.1162/inov_a_00266

Zhang, J. (2019). Deploying Blockchain Technology in the Supply Chain. In Blockchain and Distributed Ledger Technology (DLT). IntechOpen. doi:10.5772/intechopen.86530

ADDITIONAL READING

Di Vaio, A., & Varriale, L. (2020). Blockchain technology in supply chain management for sustainable performance: Evidence from the airport industry. *International Journal of Information Management*, *52*, 102014. doi:10.1016/j.ijinfomgt.2019.09.010

Frizzo-Barker, J., Chow-White, P. A., Adams, P. R., Mentanko, J., Ha, D., & Green, S. (2020). Blockchain as a disruptive technology for business: A systematic review. *International Journal of Information Management*, *51*, 102029. doi:10.1016/j.ijinfomgt.2019.10.014

Kamble, S. S., Gunasekaran, A., & Sharma, R. (2020). Modeling the blockchain enabled traceability in agriculture supply chain. *International Journal of Information Management*, *52*, 101967. doi:10.1016/j.ijinfomgt.2019.05.023

Liotine, M., & Ginocchio, D. (2020). The supply blockchain: Integrating blockchain technology within supply chain operations. In *Technology in Supply Chain Management and Logistics* (pp. 57–89). Elsevier., doi:10.1016/B978-0-12-815956-9.00004-1

Lu, Q., & Xu, X. (2017). Adaptable Blockchain-Based Systems: A Case Study for Product Traceability. *IEEE Software*, *34*(6), 21–27. doi:10.1109/MS.2017.4121227

Pawczuk, L., Holdowsky, J., Massey, R., & Hansen, B. (2020). Deloitte's 2020 Global Blockchain Survey. Deloitte Insights. https://www2.deloitte.com/content/dam/insights/us/articles/6608_2020-global-blockchain-survey/DI_CIR%202020%20global%20blockchain%20survey.pdf

Provenance. (2016). From shore to plate: Tracking tuna on the blockchain. Provenance. https://www.provenance.org/tracking-tuna-on-the-blockchain

Tian, F. (2016). An agri-food supply chain traceability system for China based on RFID blockchain technology. 2016 13th International Conference on Service Systems and Service Management (ICSSSM), 1–6. 10.1109/ICSSSM.2016.7538424

Tönnissen, S., & Teuteberg, F. (2020). Analysing the impact of blockchain-technology for operations and supply chain management: An explanatory model drawn from multiple case studies. *International Journal of Information Management*, *52*, 101953. doi:10.1016/j.ijinfomgt.2019.05.009

Wamba, S. F., & Queiroz, M. M. (2020). Blockchain in the operations and supply chain management: Benefits, challenges and future research opportunities. *International Journal of Information Management*, *52*, 102064. doi:10.1016/j.ijinfomgt.2019.102064

Wong, L.-W., Leong, L.-Y., Hew, J.-J., Tan, G. W.-H., & Ooi, K.-B. (2020). Time to seize the digital evolution: Adoption of blockchain in operations and supply chain management among Malaysian SMEs. *International Journal of Information Management*, *52*, 101997. doi:10.1016/j.ijinfomgt.2019.08.005

Yiannas, F. (2018). A New Era of Food Transparency Powered by Blockchain. *Innovations: Technology, Governance, Globalization, 12*(1–2), 46–56. doi:10.1162/inov_a_00266

KEY TERMS AND DEFINITIONS

Blockchain: Blockchain refers to a decentralized history of transactions shared between various participant. The blocks of a blockchain are connected chronologically where each block is linked to the previous block. Changing an arbitrary transaction requires altering every block, while the rest of the network is following the longest chain.

Internet of Things (IoT): This refers to inter-connection of processing devices (computers, mobile phones, sensors, smart watches, and other smart devices) via the Internet to communicate, share and process data. Applications include Internet of Vehicles, Industrial IoT, smart cities, etc.

Interoperability: Interoperability is the degree of communication between two or more systems. When interoperability between systems is high, then they can communicate, share data, and use each other's functionalities. When the interoperability is low between systems then additional effort is required to translate one system's data types and communication protocols to the other, if possible.

Proof-of-Work (PoW): This is a computationally intensive task used in public open blockchain networks. It requires the participants to increment a nonce value to calculate a hash using the list of waiting transactions. The resulting hash value should be lower than a set limit. This busywork is in place mainly to select the transactions to commit to blockchain while protecting the network from malicious actors, as adversaries cannot bolster enough computational power to divert the blockchain.

Smart Contracts: Smart contracts are computer programs that can be assigned an address on a blockchain. Their code can execute and address transactions to other parties on the blockchain according to the state of the blockchain or according to the transactions they receive based on certain pre-defined terms. Smart contracts are useful to introduce automation to the blockchain.

State Zero Problem: Any input to the blockchain is irreversible so the tokenization process is delicate. If any mistakes occur or a malicious actor alters the information, the blockchain moves forwards with the erroneous information. If the tokenization process is secure, then the immutability characteristic of blockchain technology guarantees that the blockchain handles the rest of the security requirements.

Supply Chain: Supply chains refer to how a product's raw materials are sourced, constructed, assembled, distributed, and sold to a customer. These consist of multiple organizations that often span across countries.

Tokenization: This is the process of creating a representation of a physical item or asset to be used in the blockchain. This token is exchanged during transactions that match the journey of the asset, from sender to the receiver.

Compilation of References

Abbas, Q. E., & Sung-Bong, J. (2019). A Survey of Blockchain and Its Applications. *2019 International Conference on Artificial Intelligence in Information and Communication (ICAIIC)*, 1–3. 10.1109/ICAIIC.2019.8669067

Abbassi, R., Khan, F., Garaniya, V., Chai, S., Chin, C., & Hossain, K. A. (2015). An integrated method for human error probability assessment during the maintenance of offshore facilities. *Process Safety and Environmental Protection, 94*, 172–179. doi:10.1016/j.psep.2015.01.010

Abdeen, M., Jan, S., Khan, S., & Ali, T. (2019). Employing Takaful Islamic Banking through state of the art blockchain: A case study. *International Journal of Advanced Computer Science and Applications, 10*(2), 648–654. doi:10.14569/IJACSA.2019.0101283

Active Business Systems. (2020). *Blockchain and the ERP*. Available at: https://www.activebs.com/en/news/2018/blockchain-and-erp

Agbo, C. C., Mahmoud, Q. H., & Eklund, J. M. (2019). Blockchain Technology in Healthcare: A Systematic Review. *Health Care, 7*, 56. PMID:30987333

Aggarwal, S., Chaudhary, R., Aujla, G. S., Kumar, N., Choo, K.-K. R., & Zomaya, A. Y. (2019). Blockchain. *Journal of Network and Computer Applications, 144*, 13–48. doi:10.1016/j.jnca.2019.06.018

Ahmed, S. (2018, May 2). Automakers, suppliers team up to develop blockchain technology. *Automotive News*. https://www.autonews.com/article/20180502/MOBILITY/180509974/automakers-suppliers-team-up-to-develop-blockchain-technology

Ahram, T., Sargolzaei, A., Sargolzaei, S., Daniels, J., & Amaba, B. (2017), Blockchain technology innovations. *2017 IEEE Technology Engineering Management Conference (TEMSCON)*, 137–141. 10.1109/TEMSCON.2017.7998367

Ainsworth, R., & Shact, A. (2016). Blockchain (Distributed Ledger Technology) Solves VAT Fraud. SSRN. doi:10.2139srn.2853428

AinsworthR.AlwohaibiM.CheethamM.TirandC. (2018), A Vatcoin Solution To MTIC Fraud: Past Efforts, Present Technology, and the EU's 2017 Proposal. Boston University School of Law, Law & Economics Series Paper No. 18-08. SSRN: https://ssrn.com/abstract=3151394

Alammary, A., Alhazmi, S., Almasri, M., & Gillani, S. (2019). Blockchain-Based Applications in Education: A Systematic Review. *App. Sci., 9*(12), 2400. doi:10.3390/app9122400

Albishi, S., Soh, B., Ullah, A., & Algarni, F. (2017). Challenges and Solutions for Applications and Technologies in the Internet of Things. *Procedia Computer Science, 124*, 608–614. doi:10.1016/j.procs.2017.12.196

Alder. (2018). *2.65 Million Atrium Health Patients Impacted by Business Associate Data Breach*. https://www.hipaa-journal.com/2-65-million-atrium-health-patients-impacted-by-business-associate-data-breach/

Alexander, C. A., & Wang, L. (2019), Cybersecurity, Information Assurance, and Big Data Based on Blockchain. 2019 SoutheastCon, 1–7. doi:10.1109/SoutheastCon42311.2019.9020582

Alibaba Group. (2020). *Home*. Retrieved from https://www.alibabagroup.com/en/global/home

Ali, M. S., Vecchio, M., Pincheira, M., Dolui, K., Antonelli, F., & Rehmani, M. H. (2019). Applications of Blockchains in the Internet of Things. *IEEE Communications Surveys and Tutorials, 21*(2), 1676–1717. doi:10.1109/COMST.2018.2886932

Alkhalsi, Z. (2018). *IMF Chief: Cryptocurrency Regulation Is 'Inevitable'*. https://money.cnn.com/2018/02/11/investing/lagarde- bitcoin-regulation/index.html

Allianz. (2020). *At a glance*. Retrieved from https://www.allianz.com/en/about-us/who-we-are/at-a-glance.html

Allison, I. (2017). *Maersk and Ibm Want 10 Million Shipping Containers on the Global Supply Blockchain by Year-End*. International Business Times.

Alphand, O., Amoretti, M., Claeys, T., Dall'Asta, S., Duda, A., Ferrari, G., Rousseau, F., Tourancheau, B., Veltri, L., & Zanichelli, F. (2018). Iotchain: A blockchain security architecture for the internet of things. 2018 IEEE Wireless Communications and Networking Conference (WCNC), 1–6. doi:10.1109/WCNC.2018.8377385

Alvarado, J., & Halgamuge, M. N. (2019). New Era in the Supply Chain Management With Blockchain: A Survey. In Industry 4.0 and Hyper-Customized Smart Manufacturing Supply Chains (pp. 1–37). IGI Global.

AmerisourceBergen. (2020). *MediLedger DSCSA Pilot Project*. Chesterbrook: Mediledger.

Andoni, M., Robu, V., Flynn, D., Abram, S., Geach, D., Jenkins, D., McCallum, P., & Peacock, A. (2019). Blockchain. *Renewable & Sustainable Energy Reviews, 100*(February), 143–174. doi:10.1016/j.rser.2018.10.014

Andriole, S. J. (2020). Blockchain cybersecurity. *IT Professional, 22*(1), 13–16. doi:10.1109/MITP.2019.2949165

Aniello, L., Baldoni, R., Gaetani, E., Lombardi, F., Margheri, A., & Sassone, V. (2017, September). A prototype evaluation of a tamper-resistant high performance blockchain-based transaction log for a distributed database. In *2017 13th European Dependable Computing Conference (EDCC)* (pp. 151-154). IEEE.

Apache Software Foundation. (2020). Apache CouchDB. Retrieved May 30, 2020, from https://couchdb.apache.org

Arnold, M. (2017). *Five ways banks are using blockchain*. Retrieved from https://www.ft.com/content/615b3bd8-97a9-11e7-a652-cde3f882dd7b

Arslan, S. S., Jurdak, R., Jelitto, J., & Krishnamachari, B. (2019). Advancements in Distributed Ledger Technology for Internet of Things. *Internet of Things, 9*, 100114. doi:10.1016/j.iot.2019.100114

Asatiani, A., & Penttinen, A. (2016). Turning Robotic Process Automation into Commercial Success – Case OpusCapita. *Journal of Information Technology Teaching Cases, 6*(2), 67–74. doi:10.1057/jittc.2016.5

Asquith, R. (2016). *How Blockchain could shape tax automation?* https://www.avalara.com/vatlive/en/vat-news/how-Blockchain-could-shape-tax-automation.html

Aste, T., Tasca, P., & Di Matteo, T. (2017). Blockchain technologies: The foreseeable impact on society and industry. *Computer, 50*(9), 18-28.

Atack, J., & Neal, L. (2009). *The origins and development of financial markets and institutions: From the seventeenth century to the present*. Cambridge University Press. doi:10.1017/CBO9780511757419

Atzei, N., Bartoletti, M., & Cimoli, T. (2017). A survey of attacks on ethereum smart contracts sok. Proceedings of the 6th International Conference on Principles of Security and Trust, 10204, 164–186. doi:10.1007/978-3-662-54455-6_8

Atzei, N., Bartoletti, M., & Cimoli, T. (2017, April). A survey of attacks on ethereum smart contracts (sok). In *International conference on principles of security and trust* (pp. 164-186). Springer.

Azaria, A., Ekblaw, A., Vieira, T., & Lippman, A. (2016). Medrec: Using blockchain for medical data access and permission management. *Proc. of International Conference on Open and Big Data (OBD)*, 25–30.

Azzi, R., Chamoun, R. K., & Sokhn, M. (2019). The power of a blockchain-based supply chain. *Computers & Industrial Engineering*, *135*, 582–592. doi:10.1016/j.cie.2019.06.042

Babich, V., & Hilary, G. (2020). Distributed Ledgers and Operations: What Operations Management Researchers Should Know About Blockchain Technology. *Manufacturing & Service Operations Management*, *22*(2), 223–240. doi:10.1287/msom.2018.0752

Bakon, K. A., Elias, N. F., & Abusamhadana, G. A. O. (2020). Culture and Digital Divide Influence on Government Success of Developing Countries: A Literature Review. *Journal of Theoretical and Applied Information Technology*, *98*(9).

Bal, A. (2015). *Bitcoin Transactions: Recent Tax Developments and Regulatory Responses*. https://www.ibfd.org/sites/ibfd.org/files/content/pdf/dfi_2015_05_int_2.pdf

Balram, J. (2015). Preventive Maintenance Plan. Scribd. Retrieved May 30, 2020, from https://www.scribd.com/doc/279104286/Preventive-Maintenance-Plan

BankChain. (2020). *Home*. Retrieved from https://www.bankchaintech.com/index.php

Baravalle, A., Lopez, M. S., & Lee, S. W. (2016). Mining the Dark Web: Drugs and Fake Ids. *2016 IEEE 16th International Conference on Data Mining Workshops (ICDMW)*, 350–356. 10.1109/ICDMW.2016.0056

Barbaschow, A. (2018). *Alibaba pilots blockchain supply chain initiative down under*. Retrieved from https://www.zdnet.com/article/alibaba-pilots-blockchain-supply-chain-initiative-down-under/

Barchard, K. A., & Pace, L. A. (2011). Preventing human error: The impact of data entry methods on data accuracy and statistical results. *Computers in Human Behavior*, *27*(5), 1834–1839. doi:10.1016/j.chb.2011.04.004

Barnaghi, P., Wang, W., Henson, C., & Taylor, K. (2012). Semantics for the Internet of Things: Early progress and back to the future. *International Journal on Semantic Web and Information Systems*, *8*(1), 1–21. doi:10.4018/jswis.2012010101

Barratt, M. J., Ferris, J. A., & Winstock, A. R. (2016). Safer scoring? Cryptomarkets, social supply and drug market violence. *The International Journal on Drug Policy*, *35*, 24–31. doi:10.1016/j.drugpo.2016.04.019 PMID:27241015

Bartolomé, A., Castañeda, L., Torlà, C. B., & Adell, J. (2017), Blockchain in Education: Introduction and Critical Review of the state of the art. *EDUTEC, Revista Electrónica de Tecnología Educativa*.

BayannaK. (2019). Error! Hyperlink reference not valid.http://mdxblocks.com/wp-content/uploads/2018/05/Product-traceability.pdf

Bayer, D., & Haber, S., & Stornetta, W. S. (1992, March). Improving the Efficiency and Reliability of Digital Time-Stamping. *Sequences.*, *2*, 329–334.

Baygin, N., Baygin, M., & Karakose, M. (2019). Blockchain Technology: Applications, Benefits and Challenges. *Conference: 2019 1st International Informatics and Software Engineering Conference (UBMYK)*. 10.1109/UBMYK48245.2019.8965565

Begley, R. (2017). *Information and Records Management and Blockchain Technology: Understanding its Potential* (Masters Dissertation). Northumbria University, New Castle.

Behnke, K., & Janssen, M. F. W. H. A. (2020). Boundary conditions for traceability in food supply chains using blockchain technology. *International Journal of Information Management, 52*, 101969. doi:10.1016/j.ijinfomgt.2019.05.025

Bélanger, F., & Carter, L. (2008). Trust and Risk in E-Government Adoption. *The Journal of Strategic Information Systems, 17*(2), 165–176. doi:10.1016/j.jsis.2007.12.002

Beng, D. C. (2018). Industry 4.0 techniques as a maintenance strategy (a review paper). doi:10.13140/rg.2.2.18116.32644

Benhamouda, F., Halevi, S., & Halevi, T. (2018). Supporting Private Data on Hyperledger Fabric with Secure Multiparty Computation. In *2018 IEEE International Conference on Cloud Engineering (IC2E)*. Orlando, FL: IEEE. 10.1109/IC2E.2018.00069

Bertolini, M., Bevilacqua, M., Braglia, M., & Frosolini, M. (2004). An analytical method for maintenance outsourcing service selection. [Quality]. *International Journal of Quality & Reliability Management, 21*(7), 772–788. doi:10.1108/02656710410549118

Bhasin, H. (2019, April). *3 Main Types of Blockchain: Classification of Blockchain.* Available at: https://www.marketing91.com/types-of-blockchain/

Bhasin, H. (2019, April). *3 Main Types of Blockchain: Classification of Blockchain.* Available at: https://www.marketing91.com/types-of-Blockchain/

Bhatia, S., Douglas, E. K., & Most, M. (2020). *Blockchain and records management: disruptive force or new approach?* Retrieved 17 May 2020, from https://www.emerald.com/insight/0956-5698.htm

Bishr, A. B. (2018). Dubai: A city powered by Blockchain. *Innovations/Blockchain for Global Development II, 12*(3/4), 4-8.

Bitcoin. (2020). *Bitcoin developer.* Retrieved from Learn Bitcoin and start building Bitcoin-based applications: https://developer.bitcoin.org/

BitPremier. (2019). *Cryptocurrency Exchange Reviews.* https://www. bitpremier.com/best-exchanges

Blanco-Novoa, Ó., Fernández-Caramés, T. M., Fraga-Lamas, P., & Vilar-Montesinos, M. A. (2018). A Practical Evaluation of Commercial Industrial Augmented Reality Systems in an Industry 4.0 Shipyard. *IEEE Access: Practical Innovations, Open Solutions, 6*, 8201–8218. doi:10.1109/ACCESS.2018.2802699

Blidholm, G., & Johnson, M. (2018). *The adoption of distributed ledger technology in trade and export finance operations of Swedish banks.* Academic Press.

Bocek, T., Rodrigues, B. B., Strasser, T., & Stiller, B. (2017). Blockchains everywhere - a use-case of blockchains in the pharma supply-chain. 2017 IFIP/IEEE Symposium on Integrated Network and Service Management (IM), 772–777. doi:10.23919/INM.2017.7987376

Bocek, T., Rodrigues, B. B., Strasser, T., & Stiller, B. (2017). Blockchains everywhere—A use-case of blockchains in the pharma supply-chain. *Proceedings of the 2017 IFIP/IEEE Symposium on Integrated Network and Service Management (IM)*, 772–777. 10.23919/INM.2017.7987376

Boles, T. L., Croson, R. T. A., & Murnighan, J. K. (2000). Deception and Retribution in Repeated Ultimatum Bargaining. *Organizational Behavior and Human Decision Processes, 83*(2), 235–259. doi:10.1006/obhd.2000.2908 PMID:11056070

Bose, S. (2018). *SBI to deploy blockchain in three functions in FY19.* Retrieved from https://www.financialexpress.com/industry/sbi-to-deploy-blockchain-in-three-functions-in-fy19/1058852/

Bourne, J. (2020). *Toyota and Securitize develop blockchain-based ID platform*. Retrieved from https://blockchaintech-nology-news.com/2020/03/toyota-and-securitize-develop-blockchain-based-id-platform/

Boxler, D. (2019, April). Remedichain to Connect Patients with Costly Meds. *Drug Topics*, ●●●, 42–43.

Bralić, V., Kuleš, M., & Stančić, H. (2017). A Model for Long-Term Preservation of Digital Signature Validity: Trust-Chain. In *Future2017: Integrating ICT in Society, 2017*. Retrieved 30 March, 2020, https://www.researchgate.net/publication/321171227_A_Model_for_Long

Bramblet, J. (2018). *Ultimate guide to blockchain in insurance*. Retrieved from https://insuranceblog.accenture.com/ultimate-guide-to-blockchain-in-insurance

Brennan, C., & Lunn, W. (2016), The trust disrupter, https://www.finextra.com/finextra-downloads/newsdocs/docu-ment-1063851711.pdf, Accessed August 2016

Brito, J., & Castillo, A. (2013). Bitcoin: A primer for policymakers. Mercatus Center at George Mason University.

Bumblauskas, D., Mann, A., Dugan, B., & Rittmer, J. (2020). A blockchain use case in food distribution: Do you know where your food has been? *International Journal of Information Management*, *52*, 102008. doi:10.1016/j.ijinfomgt.2019.09.004

Bureau, E. T. (2017). *SBI to use blockchain for smart contracts and KYC by next month*. Retrieved from https://eco-nomictimes.indiatimes.com/industry/banking/finance/banking/sbi-to-use-blockchain-for-smart-contracts-and-kyc-by-next-month/articleshow/61715860.cms?from=mdr

Burke, F. G. (1992). Chaos through communications: archivists, records managers, and the communications phenomenon. In The Archival Imagination: Essays in Honour of Hugh A. Taylor (pp. 154-77). Academic Press.

Button, M., & Gee, J. (2015). *The Financial Cost of Healthcare Fraud*. https://www.researchgate.net/publication/299378586_The_Financial_Cost_of_Healthcare_Fraud

Byon/Alacrity. (2020, May). *Blockchain in Education: three Promising Reforms*. Available at: https://alacritys.net/2020/05/27/blockchain-in-education-three-promising-reforms/

Cai, C., Duan, H., & Wang, C. (2018). Tutorial: Building Secure and Trustworthy Blockchain Applications, 2018 IEEE Cybersecurity Development. SecDev. doi:10.1109/SecDev.2018.00023

Cameron-Huff, A. (2017, March 30). *How Tokenization Is Putting Real-World Assets on Blockchains: How Tokenization Is Putting Real-World Assets on Blockchains | Nasdaq*. https://www.nasdaq.com/articles/how-tokenization-putting-real-world-assets-blockchains-2017-03-30

Campbell, R. (2017). *Which major banks have adopted or are adopting the blockchain?* Retrieved from https://blockchain.works-hub.com/learn/Which-Major-Banks-Have-Adopted-or-Are-Adopting-the-Blockchain

Campbell, J. D., & Jardine, A. K. (2010). *Maintenance excellence: optimizing equipment life-cycle decisions*. CRC Press.

Canadian Fabricating & Welding. (2018). Punching productively. Retrieved May 30, 2020, from https://www.canadian-metalworking.com/canadianfabricatingandwelding/article/fabricating/punching-productively

Cangl, G. (2017). *Year one: Open Ecosystem Network has a lot to celebrate*. Retrieved from https://www.nokia.com/blog/year-one-open-ecosystem-network-lot-celebrate/

Canis, B. (2012). The tool and die industry: Contribution to US manufacturing and federal policy considerations. CRS Report for Congress, 1–17.

Capgemini Research Institute. (2019). *Does blockchain hold the key to a new age of supply chain transparency and trust? How organizations have moved from blockchain hype to reality.* Capgemini Research Institute.

Caprio, G. (2013). Securities settlement systems. In Handbook of Key Global Financial Markets, Institutions, and Infrastructure (pp. 547–563). Academic Press.

Çarkacıoğlu, A. (2016). *Kripto-Para Bitcoin.* Sermaye Piyasası Kurulu Araştırma Dairesi.

Carnomic. (2020). *Carnomic Blockchain-based Automotive Solution: White Paper Version 1.2.* Retrieved May 2, 2020, from https://www.carnomic.io/wp/Carnomic-White-Paper-en.pdf

Caro, M. P., Ali, M. S., Vecchio, M., & Giaffreda, R. (2018). Blockchain-based traceability in agri-food supply chain management: A practical implementation. 2018 IoT Vertical and Topical Summit on Agriculture - Tuscany (IOT Tuscany), 1–4. doi:10.1109/IOTTUSCANY.2018.8373021

Carstens, A. (2018). *Money in the Digital Age: What Role for Central Banks?* Lecture at House of Finance, Goethe Univ. https://www.bis.org/ speeches/sp180206.pdf

Casey, M. J. (2015, Apr. 15). Moneybeat/BitBeat: Blockchains without coins stir tensions in Bitcoin Community. *The Wall Street Journal.*

Casey, M., Crane, J., Gensler, G., Johnson, S., & Narula, N. (2018). *The impact of blockchain technology on finance: A catalyst for change (Geneva Reports on the World Economy 21).* International Center for Monetary and Banking Studies.

Casino, F., Dasaklis, T. K., & Patsakis, C. (2019). A systematic literature review of blockchain-based applications: Current status, classification and open issues. *Telematics and Informatics, 36,* 55–81. doi:10.1016/j.tele.2018.11.006

Centers for Disease Control and Prevention. (2006, October 6). *Multistate Outbreak of E. coli O157:H7 Infections Linked to Fresh Spinach (FINAL UPDATE).* https://www.cdc.gov/ecoli/2006/spinach-10-2006.html

Çetin Gerger, G. (2019). Tax Services and Tax Service Providers' Changing Role in the IoT and AmI Environment. In Guide to Ambient Intelligence in the IoT Environment (pp. 203-216). Cham, Switzerland: Springer Nature Switzerland. doi:10.1007/978-3-030-04173-1_9

Çetin Gerger, G. (2013). Legal Framework for the E-Taxation in Turkey. In Z. Mahmood (Ed.), *Developing E-Government Projects: Framworks and Methodologies* (pp. 165–180). IGI Global. doi:10.4018/978-1-4666-4245-4.ch008

Çetin Gerger, G., & Bozdoğanoğlu, B. (2017). *Evaluation of the problems regarding taxation of electronic commerce in the context of informal economy and tax evasion.* Issues in Public Sector Economics, Peter Lang.

Chadha, S., & Kumar, U. (2017). Ransomware: Let's fight back! *2017 International Conference on Computing, Communication and Automation (ICCCA),* 925–930. 10.1109/CCAA.2017.8229926

Chandrasekaran, N., Somanah, R., Rughoo, D., Dreepaul, R. K., Cunden, T. S. M., & Demkah, M. (2019). Digital Transformation from Leveraging Blockchain Technology, Artificial Intelligence, Machine Learning and Deep Learning. In S. Satapathy, V. Bhateja, R. Somanah, X. S. Yang, & R. Senkerik (Eds.), *Information Systems Design and Intelligent Applications. Advances in Intelligent Systems and Computing* (Vol. 863). Springer. doi:10.1007/978-981-13-3338-5_25

Chang, Y., Iakovou, E., & Shi, W. (2019). *Blockchain in Global Supply Chains and Cross Border Trade: A Critical Synthesis of the State-of-the-Art, Challenges and Opportunities.* https://arxiv.org/abs/1901.02715

Chang, S. E., Luo, H. L., & Chen, Y. C. (2020). Blockchain. *Sustainability, 12*(1), 1–16. doi:10.3390u12010188

Chaterera, F. (2013). *Records surveys and the management of public records in Zimbabwe* (Masters Dissertation). University of South Africa, Pretoria.

Chaterera, F., Masuku, M., Bhebhe, S., Ngoepe, M. S., & Katuu, S. (2018). *Enterprise digital records management in Zimbabwe*. Retrieved 16 April, 2020, from https://interparestrust.org/assets/public/dissemination/AF03ZimbabweLit-ReviewJuly2018.pdf

Chaterera, F. (2012). Towards harnessing e-government adoption in Zimbabwe. 2012. *Mousaion: South African Journal of Information Studies, 30*(2), 78–93.

Chaterera-Zambuko, F. (2019). *The integrity and authenticity of records: is Blockchain the silver bullet?* Paper presented at the 3rd Records Management Conference on Records management and sustainable development, Mombasa, Kenya.

Chen, P.-W., Jiang, B.-S., & Wang, C.-H. (2017). Blockchain-based payment collection supervision system using pervasive Bitcoin digital wallet. *2017 IEEE 13th International Conference on Wireless and Mobile Computing, Networking and Communications (WiMob)*, 139–146. 10.1109/WiMOB.2017.8115844

Cheng, S., Zeng, B., & Huang, Y. Z. (2017). Corrigendum: Research on Application Model of Blockchain Technology in Distributed Electricity Market. *IOP Conference Series. Earth and Environmental Science, 93*, 012065. doi:10.1088/1755-1315/93/1/012065

Chen, H., Chiang, R. H., & Storey, V. C. (2012). Business intelligence and analytics: From big data to big impact. *Management Information Systems Quarterly, 36*(4), 165–1188. doi:10.2307/41703503

Chen, S., Xu, H., Liu, D., Hu, B., & Wang, H. (2014). A Vision of IoT: Applications, Challenges, and Opportunities with China Perspective. *IEEE Internet of Things Journal, 1*(4).

Chen, Y. (2012), Challenges and Opportunities of Internet of Things, In *17th Asia and South Pacific Design Automation Conference* (pp. 383-388) IEEE. 10.1109/ASPDAC.2012.6164978

Chikomba, A. (2018). *Management of digital records in selected financial services parastatals in Zimbabwe* (Masters Dissertation). University of South Africa, Pretoria.

Chowdhury, N. (2019). Inside Blockchain, Bitcoin, and Cryptocurrencies. CRC Press.

Christidis, K., & Devetsikiotis, M. (2016). Blockchains and smart contracts for the internet of things. *IEEE Access : Practical Innovations, Open Solutions, 4*, 2292–2303. doi:10.1109/ACCESS.2016.2566339

Christidis, K., & Devetsikiotis, M. (2016). Blockchains and Smart Contracts for the Internet of Things. *IEEE Access: Practical Innovations, Open Solutions, 4*, 2292–2303. doi:10.1109/ACCESS.2016.2566339

Christidis, K., & Devetsikiotis, M. (2018). Blockchains and smart contracts for the internet of things. *IEEE Access: Practical Innovations, Open Solutions, 2016*(4), 2292–2303.

Christin, N. (2014). Commentary on Barratt *et al.* (2014): Steps towards characterizing online anonymous drug marketplace customers [Commentary]. *Addiction (Abingdon, England), 109*(5), 784–785. doi:10.1111/add.12519 PMID:24720826

CitiusTech. (2018, May). *Blockchain for Healthcare*. Available at: https://www.ehidc.org/sites/default/fi:les/resources/files/blockchain-for-healthcare-341.pdf

CitiusTech. (2018, May). *Blockchain for Healthcare*. Available at: https://www.ehidc.org/sites/default/fi:les/resources/files/Blockchain-for-healthcare-341.pdf

Clark, D. (2016). *10 Ways Blockchain could be used in education*. Available at: https://oeb.global/oeb-insights/10-ways-blockchain-could-be-used-in-education

Clarke, C. (2005). *Automotive production systems and standardization from Ford to the case of Mercedes-Benz*. Physica-Verlag. doi:10.1007/b138988

Coeckelbergh, M., & Reijers, W. (2016). Cryptocurrencies as narrative technologies. *ACM SIGCAS Computers and Society*, *45*(3), 172–178. doi:10.1145/2874239.2874264

Coin Telegraph. (2015). *How Estonia Brought Blockchain Closer to Citizens: GovTech Case Studies*. https://cointelegraph.com/news/how-estonia-brought-Blockchaincloser-to-citizens-govtech-case-studies

CoinMarketCap. (2019). *All Cryptocurrencies*. https://coinmarketcap.com/all/views/all

Coleman, L. (2018). *Why Nokia is partnering with a crypto startup to build an IoT network*. Retrieved from https://www.ccn.com/nokia-community-hosted-networks-to-bring-revenue-opportunities-to-remote-areas/

Collis, J., & Hussey, R. (2014). *Business Research* (4th ed.). Macmillan. doi:10.1007/978-1-137-03748-0

Colonna, S. (2018). *Blockchain opportunities in automotive market - spare parts case study*. Politecnico di Torino Corso di Laurea in Management Engineering.

Columbus, L. (2019). *How Blockchain Can Improve Manufacturing in 2019*. Available at: https://www.forbes.com/sites/louiscolumbus/2018/10/28/how-blockchain-can-improve-manufacturing-in-2019

Committee on Capital Markets Regulation. (2019). *Blockchain and Securities Clearing and Settlement*. https://www.capmktsreg.org/wp-content/uploads/2019/04/CCMR_statement_ Blockchain_Securities_Settlement-Final.pdf

Composer. (2020, June 23). *Typical Hyperledger Composer Solution Architecture*. Retrieved from Hyperledger Composer: https://hyperledger.github.io/composer/v0.19/introduction/solution-architecture

Concise Software. (2020). *10 Use Cases of Blockchain in Banking*. Available at: https://concisesoftware.com/10-use-cases-of-blockchain-in-banking

Conn. (2016). *Banner Health cyberattack impacts 3.7 million people*. https://www.modernhealthcare.com/article/20160803/NEWS/160809954/banner-health-cyberattack-impacts-3-7-million-people

ConsenSys. (2016). *5 Incredible Blockchain IoT Applications*. Available at: https://blockgeeks.com/5-incredible-blockchain-iot-applications/

Consensys. (2020). *Blockchain Use Cases-Blockchain in Supply Chain Management*. Retrieved from https://consensys.net/blockchain-use-cases/supply-chain-management/

Consensys. (2020). *Smart Dubai: Blockchain Case Study for Government in the UAE*. Available at: https://consensys.net/Blockchain-use-cases/government-and-the-public-sector/smart-dubai/

Consensys. (2020a). *Real World Blockchain Case Studies*. Available at: https://consensys.net/Blockchain-use-cases/case-studies/

Cooper, M. C., Lambert, D. M., & Pagh, J. D. (1997). Supply Chain Management: More Than a New Name for Logistics. *International Journal of Logistics Management*, *8*(1), 1–14. doi:10.1108/09574099710805556

Corporation, I. B. M. (2020a). Fabric Chaincode. Retrieved May 26, 2020, from https://hyperledger-fabric.readthedocs.io/en/release-2.0/chaincode.html

Corporation, I. B. M. (2020b). Fabric Ordering Service. Retrieved May 26, 2020, from https://hyperledger-fabric.readthedocs.io/en/release-2.0/orderer/ordering service.html#raft

Corporation, I. B. M. (2020c). Fabric SDKs. Retrieved May 26, 2020, from https://hyperledger-fabric.readthedocs.io/en/release-2.0/fabric-sdks.html

Corporation, I. B. M. (2020d). Hyperledger Fabric CA. Retrieved May 26, 2020, from https://hyperledger-fabric-ca.readthedocs.io/en/release-1.4/

Couch, M. (2020). *Sotheby's International Realty opens first office in Ukraine*. Retrieved from https://www.sothebysrealty.com/extraordinary-living-blog/sothebys-international-realty-opens-first-office-in-ukraine

Cox, M., & Ellsworth, D. (1997). Application-controlled demand paging for out-of-core visualization. In *Proceedings of the 8th Conference on Visualization'97* (pp. 235-244). Phoenix: IEEE.

Crosby, M. N., Pattanayak, P., Verma, S., & Kalyanaraman, V. (2016). Blockchain technology: Beyond bitcoin. *Applied Innovation Review*, 2, 6–19.

Crouse, M. (2019). *IBM's blockchain network gives digital identities to suppliers*. Retrieved from https://www.fierce-telecom.com/telecom/ibm-s-blockchain-network-gives-digital-identities-to-suppliers

Crypto Digest. (2020). *EOS Platform: What you should know*. Available at: https://cryptodigestnews.com/eos-platform-what-you-should-know-58da830d2aa8

Dabbagh, M., Sookhak, M., & Safa, N. S. (2019). The evolution of blockchain: A bibliometric study. *IEEE Access: Practical Innovations, Open Solutions*, 7(8628982), 19212–19221. doi:10.1109/ACCESS.2019.2895646

Dagher, G. G., Mohler, J., Milojkovic, M., & Marella, P. B. (2018). Ancile: Privacy-preserving framework for access control and interoperability of electronic health records using blockchain technology. *Sustainable Cities and Society*, 39, 283–297.

Dai, F., Shi, Y., Meng, N., Wei, L., & Ye, Z. (2017), From Bitcoin to cybersecurity: A comparative study of blockchain application and security issues. *2017 4th International Conference on Systems and Informatics (ICSAI)*, 975–979. 10.1109/ICSAI.2017.8248427

Daley, S. (2020, March). *25 Blockchain Applications & Real World Use Cases Disrupting the Status Quo*. Available at: https://builtin.com/Blockchain/Blockchain-applications

Dash, & Behera, P. C. (2017). Blockchain. *International Journal of Information Science and Computing*, 4(1), 27–39. doi:10.5958/2454-9533.2017.00004.7

Davidson, C. (2020). *Dubai-United Arab Emirates*. Retrieved from https://www.britannica.com/place/Dubai-United-Arab-Emirates

Davi, L., Hatebur, D., Heisel, M., & Wirtz, R. (2019). Combining Safety and Security in Autonomous Cars Using Blockchain Technologies. *International Conference on Computer Safety, Reliability, and Security. SAFECOMP 2019*, *11699*, 223-234. doi:10.1007/978-3-030-26250-1_18

Davis, F. D. (1989). *Perceived usefulness, perceived ease of use, and user acceptance of information technology*. Retrieved 12 May, 2020, from http://www.jstor.org/stable/249008

Davis, J. (2019). *The 10 Biggest Healthcare Data Breaches of 2019, So Far*. https://healthitsecurity.com/news/the-10-biggest-healthcare-data-breaches-of-2019-so-far

Davor, D., & Domagoj, S. (2018). Blockchain Applications in Supply Chain. *SMART Supply Network*, 21-46.

De, N. (2018). *Germany Won't Tax you for Buying Coffee with Bitcoin*. https://www.coindesk.com/germany-considers-crypto-legal-equivalent-to-fiat-for-tax-purposes/

Dedeoğlu, D. (2019). *A'dan z'ye blockchain*. İnkılap Kitapevi.

del Castillo, M. (2020). Honeywell Is Now Tracking $1 Billion In Boeing Parts On A Blockchain. Forbes. Retrieved June 29, 2020, from https://www.forbes.com/sites/michaeldelcastillo/2020/03/07/honeywell-is-now-tracking-1-billion-in-boeing-parts-on-a-blockchain/

Deloitte. (2017). *Blockchain Technology and Its Potential in Taxes.* https://www2.deloitte.com/content/dam/Deloitte/pl/Documents/Reports/pl_Blockchain-technology-and-its-potential-in-taxes-2017-EN.PDF

Department of Justice. (2019, March 8). *Manhattan U.S. Attorney Announces Charges Against Leaders Of "OneCoin," A Multibillion-Dollar Pyramid Scheme Involving The Sale Of A Fraudulent Cryptocurrency.* https://www.justice.gov/usao-sdny/pr/manhattan-us-attorney-announces-charges-against-leaders-onecoin-multibillion-dollar

Destefanis, G., Marchesi, M., Ortu, M., Tonelli, R., Bracciali, A., & Hierons, R. (2018, March). Smart contracts vulnerabilities: a call for blockchain software engineering? In *2018 International Workshop on Blockchain Oriented Software Engineering (IWBOSE)* (pp. 19-25). IEEE.

Dhillon, B. S. (2013). *Human reliability: With human factors.* Elsevier.

Di Grigorio, M. (2017). *Blockchain: a new tool to cut costs.* Retrieved 30 March, 2020 https://www.pwc.com/m1/en/media-centre/articles/Blockchain-new-tool-to-cut-costs.html

Dickinson, K. (2015). *Financial market operations management.* Wiley.

Dignum, V. (2017). Responsible Artificial Intelligence: Designing AI for Human Values. *ITU Journal: ICT Discoveries, 1.*

Dikshit, P., & Singh, K. (2017). Efficient weighted threshold ECDSA for securing bitcoin wallet. *2017 ISEA Asia Security and Privacy (ISEASP)*, 1–9. doi:10.1109/ISEASP.2017.7976994

DIN. (2012). *DIN 31051: 2012 09–fundamentals of maintenance.* DIN.

Dobrovnik, M., Herold, D. M., Fürs, E., & Kummer, S. (2018). Blockchain for and in Logistics: What to Adopt and Where to Start. *Logistics, 2*(18), 1–14. doi:10.3390/logistics2030018

Dohertya, N. F., Anastakisa, L., & Fulfordb, H. (2011). Reinforcing the corporate security of information resources: A critical review of the role of the acceptable use policy. *International Journal of Information Management, 31*, 201–209.

Doku, R., Rawat, D. B., Garuba, M., & Njilla, L. (2019). LightChain: On the Lightweight Blockchain for the Internet-of-Things. *2019 IEEE International Conference on Smart Computing (SMARTCOMP)*, 444–448, 10.1109/SMARTCOMP.2019.00085

Dorri, A., Steger, M., Kanhere, S. S., & Jurdak, R. (2017). BlockChain: A distributed solution to automotive security and privacy. *IEEE Communications Magazine, 55*(12), 119–125. doi:10.1109/MCOM.2017.1700879

DTCC. (2016). *Embracing Disruption.* https://www.dtcc.com/~/media/Files/PDFs/DTCC-Embracing-Disruption.pdf

Duarte, J. A. C., Craveiro, J. C. T. A., & Trigo, T. P. (2006). Optimization of the preventive maintenance plan of a series components system. *International Journal of Pressure Vessels and Piping, 83*(4), 244–248. doi:10.1016/j.ijpvp.2006.02.016

Dubai. (2020). *How advanced ICT drives Dubai's Smart City.* Retrieved from https://www.visitdubai.com/en/business-in-dubai/why-dubai/news-and-insights/becoming-the-worlds-smartest-city

Dube, C., & Gumbo, V. (2017). Technology Acceptance Model for Zimbabwe: The case of the retail industry in Zimbabwe. *Applied Economics and Finance, 4*(3), 56–76. doi:10.11114/aef.v4i3.2208

Dubovitskaya, A., Novotny, P., Xu, Z., & Wang, F. (2019). *Applications of Blockchain Technology for Data-Sharing in Oncology: Results from a Systematic Literature Review. Oncology and Informatics - Review.* doi:10.1159/000504325

Duignan, B. (2020). *Toyota Motor Corporation*. Retrieved from https://www.britannica.com/topic/Toyota-Motor-Corporation.

Duranti, L., & Rogers, C. (2019). *Trusting in records and data online*. Retrieved 12 May, 2020, from https://www.researchgate.net/publication/337398175_Trusting_Records_and_Data_in_the_Cloud_The_Creation_Management_and_Preservation_of_Trustworthy_Digital_Content

Duranti, L. (2001). The impact of digital technology on archival science. *Archival Science*, *1*(1), 39–55. doi:10.1007/BF02435638

Duranti, L. (2009). From digital diplomatics to digital records forensics. *Archivaria: Journal of the Association of Canadian Archivists*, *68*, 39–66.

EASA. (2020). What does the term "detailed maintenance records" mean? Retrieved May 7, 2019, from https://www.easa.europa.eu/faq/19042

Easley, D., O'Hara, M., & Basu, S. (2019). From mining. *Journal of Financial Economics*, *134*(1), 91–109. doi:10.1016/j.jfineco.2019.03.004

EC. (2019). *Urgency for an EU blacklist of third countries in line with the Anti-Money Laundering Directive*. https://www.europarl.europa.eu/doceo/document/TA-8-2019-0216_EN.html

Economic Point. (2020). *What is the Ethereum Platform*. Available at: https://economicpoint.com/ethereum

Efanov, D., & Roschin, P. (2018). The All-Pervasiveness of the Blockchain Technology. *Procedia Computer Science*, *123*, 116–12. doi:10.1016/j.procs.2018.01.019

El Maouchi, M., & Ersoy, O. (2018). *TRADE: A Transparent, Decentralized Traceability System for the Supply Chain*. doi:10.18420/BLOCKCHAIN2018_01

Ellis, S., Juels, A., & Nazarov, S. (2017). *ChainLink A Decentralized Oracle Network*. ChainLink. https://link.smartcontract.com/whitepaper

Ellsmoor, J. (2019a). *Meet 5 companies spearheading blockchain for renewable energy*. Retrieved from https://www.forbes.com/sites/jamesellsmoor/2019/04/27/meet-5-companies-spearheading-blockchain-for-renewable-energy/#52efffb5f2ae

Ellsmoor, J. (2019b). *Blockchain is the next big thing for renewable energy*. Retrieved from https://www.forbes.com/sites/jamesellsmoor/2019/04/27/blockchain-is-the-next-big-thing-for-renewable-energy/#164c089d48c1

Emen, E. (2018). Blokzincir (Blockchaın) Teknolojisi. *Sanayi ve Teknoloji Bakanlığı Sanayi ve Verimlilik Genel Müdürlüğü Kalkınmada Anahtar Verimlilik Dergisi*, *30*(353), 46-48. Retrieved from https://anahtar.sanayi.gov.tr/Files/Pdfs/anahta

English, M., Auer, S., & Domingue, J. (2016). Block Chain Technologies & The Semantic Web: A Framework for Symbiotic Development. In *Computer Science Conference for University of Bonn Students*, (pp. 47-61). Retrieved from http://cscubs.cs.uni-bonn.de/2016/

Epson. (2016). Robot system safety and installation (t3 / epson rc+ 7.0). Seiko Epson Corporation.

Epson. (2019). Epson SCARA t3-401s - epson. Retrieved May 9, 2019, from https://www.epson.de/en/products/robot/epson-scara-t3-401s-with-controller-built-in

Esteban Koberg, A. L. (2018). A systematic review of sustainable supply chain management in global supply chains. *Journal of Cleaner Production*, 1084–1098.

Esteves, R. (2018). *IBM survey: No major central bank will implement CBDCs in the near-term.* Retrieved from https://www.newsbtc.com/2018/10/27/ibm-survey-no-major-central-bank-will-implement-cbdcs-in-the-near-term/

Ethereum. (2020, June 23). *Ethereum is a global, open-source platform for decentralized applications.* Retrieved from ethereum.org: https://ethereum.org/

Euroclear and Oliver Wyman. (2016). *Blockchain in Capital Markets: The Prize and the Journey.* Brussels: Euroclear, Oliver Wyman. https://www.euroclear.com/en/campaigns/Blockchain-in-capital-markets.html

European Central Bank. (2007). *The securities custody industry.* https://www.ecb.europa.eu/pub/pdf/scpops/ecbocp68.pdf

European Central Bank. (2015). *TARGET2-Securities successfully launched today.* https://www.ecb.europa.eu/press/pr/date/2015/html/pr150622_2.en.html

European Central Bank. (2016). *Distributed ledger technologies in securities post-trading.* https://www.ecb.europa.eu/pub/pdf/scpops/ecbop172.en.pdf

European Securities and Market Authority. (2016). *The distributed ledger technology applied to securities markets.* https://www.esma.europa.eu/press-news/esma-news/esma-assesses-usefulness-distributed-ledger-technologies

Europol. (2020). *Economic Crime.* https://www.europol.europa.eu/crime-areas-and-trends/crime-areas/economic-crime/mtic-missing-trader-intra-community-fraud

Eva, M. (2015). Custody chains and asset values: Why crypto-securities are worth contemplating. *The Cambridge Law Journal, 73*(3), 505–533.

Evans, N. (2003). *Business innovation and disruptive technology harnessing the power of breakthrough technology for competitive advantage.* Upper Saddle River, NJ: Financial Times Prentice Hall.

Everett, S., Calitz, A. P., & Greyling, J. (2017). The case for a 'sovereign' distributed securities depository for securities settlement. *Journal of Securities Operations & Custody, 9*(3), 269-292. https://www.henrystewartpublications.com/jsoc/v9

EXOR. (2019). What is the Machines as a Service Business Model? Retrieved June 22, 2020, from https://www.exorint.com/en/blog/2019/04/26/what-is-the-machines-as-a-service-business-model

Extance, A. (2015). The future of cryptocurrencies: Bitcoin and beyond. *NATNews, 526*(7571), 21. PMID:26432223

Faccia, N., & Mosteanu, R. (2019). Tax Evasion_Information System and Blockchain. Journal of Information Systems & Operations Management, 13(1), 65-74.

Fan, K., Wang, S., Ren, Y., Li, H., & Yang, Y. (2018). MedBlock: Efficient and Secure Medical Data Sharing Via Blockchain. *Journal of Medical Systems, 42*(8), 136. doi:10.100710916-018-0993-7 PMID:29931655

Fanusie, Y. J., & Robinson, T. (2018). *Bitcoin Laundering: An Analysis of Illicit Flows into Digital Currency Services.* https://www.fdd.org/analysis/2018/01/10/bitcoin-laundering-an-analysis-of-illicit-flows-into-digital-currency-services/

FDA. (2013). *Guidance for Industry: Oversight of Clinical Investigations — A Risk-Based Approach to Monitoring.* U.S. Department of Health and Human Services Food and Drug Administration.

Feki, M. A., Kawsar, F., Boussard, M., & Trappeniers, L. (2013). The Internet of Things: The Next Technological Revolution. *Computer, 46*(2), 24–25. doi:10.1109/MC.2013.63

Felin, T., & Lakhani, K. (2018). What problems will you solve with blockchain? *MIT Sloan Management Review, 60*(1), 32–38.

Fenwick, M., & Vermeulen, E. P. M. (2019). Decentralisation is Coming: The Future of Blockchain. *The JBBA*, *2*(2), 2019. doi:10.31585/jbba-2-2-(8)2019

Feroz, N. (2020). A systematic review of blockchain-based services for security upgradation of a smart city. *EAI Endorsed Transactions on Smart Cities*. . doi:10.4108/eai.13-7-2018.163840

Ferrer, E. C. (2019), The Blockchain: A New Framework for Robotic Swarm Systems. *Proceedings of the Future Technologies Conference (FTC) 2018*.

FHIR. (2019, November 1). *HL7 FHIR Release 4*. Retrieved from https://www.hl7.org/: https://www.hl7.org/fhir/

Financial Stability Board. (2009). *Addressing SIFIs*. https://www.fsb.org/what-we-do/policy-development/systematically-important-financial-institutions-sifis/

Floreani, J., & Polato, M. (2014). *The economics of the global stock exchange industry*. Palgrave Macmillan. doi:10.1057/9781137321831

Floyd, D. (2018). *Nokia is letting consumers monetize their data with blockchain*. Retrieved from https://www.coindesk.com/streamr-announces-partnership-with-nokia-osisoft

Fogel, D. B. (2018). Factors associated with clinical trials that fail and opportunities for improving the likelihood of success: A review. *Contemp Clin Trials Commun*.

Fraga-Lamas, P., & Fernández-Caramés, T. M. (2019). A Review on Blockchain Technologies for an Advanced and Cyber-Resilient Automotive Industry. IEEE.

Fraga-Lamas, P., & Fernandez-Carames, T. M. (2019). A Review on Blockchain. *IEEE Access: Practical Innovations, Open Solutions*, *7*, 17578–17598. doi:10.1109/ACCESS.2019.2895302

Fraga-Lamas, P., Fernández-Caramés, T. M., Blanco-Novoa, Ó., & Vilar-Montesinos, M. A. (2018). A Review on Industrial Augmented Reality Systems for the Industry 4.0 Shipyard. *IEEE Access: Practical Innovations, Open Solutions*, *6*, 3358–13375. doi:10.1109/ACCESS.2018.2808326

Fraga-Lamas, P., Fernández-Caramés, T. M., & Castedo, L. (2017). Towards the Internet of Smart Trains: A Review on Industrial IoT-Connected Railways. *Sensors (Basel)*, *17*(6), 1–44. doi:10.339017061457 PMID:28635672

Francisco, K., & Swanson, D. (2018). The Supply Chain Has No Clothes: Technology Adoption of Blockchain for Supply Chain Transparency. *Logistics*, *2*(1), 2. doi:10.3390/logistics2010002

Fraser, J. G., & Bouridane, A. (2017). Have the security flaws surrounding BITCOIN effected the currency's value? *2017 Seventh International Conference on Emerging Security Technologies (EST)*, 50–55. 10.1109/EST.2017.8090398

FreeOpcUa. (2020). OPC UA stack in python asyncio. Retrieved May 26, 2020, from https://github.com/FreeOpcUa/opcua-asyncio

Furtwangen, H. (2018). BISS:4.0. Retrieved May 30, 2020, from https://www.hs-furtwangen.de/forschung/forschungsprojekte/biss40/

Gaetani, E., Aniello, L., Baldoni, R., Lombardi, F., Margheri, A., & Sassone, V. (2017). *Blockchain-based database to ensure data integrity in cloud computing environments*. Academic Press.

Gahi, Y., Guennoun, M., & Mouftah, H. (2016). Big Data Analytics: Security and Privacy Challenges. In *Symposium on Computers and Communication (ISCC)* (pp. 1-6). Messina: IEEE. 10.1109/ISCC.2016.7543859

Galtier, M. (2020, February 17). *MELLODDY: a "Co-opetitive" Platform for Machine Learning across Companies Powered by Owkin Technology*. Retrieved from www.melloddy.eu: https://www.melloddy.eu/blog/melloddy-a-co-opetitive-platform-for-machine-learning-across-companies-powered-by-owkin-technology

Galvin, D. (2017). *IBM and Walmart: Blockchain for Food Safety*. IBM Corporation.

Gao, Z., Xu, L., Chen, L., Zhao, X., Lu, Y., & Shi, W. (2018). CoC: A Unified Distributed Ledger Based Supply Chain Management System. *Journal of Computer Science and Technology*, 237–248.

Garg, A., & Deshmukh, S. (2006). Maintenance management: Literature review and directions. *Journal of Quality in Maintenance Engineering*, *12*(3), 205–238. doi:10.1108/13552510610685075

Garson, B. (2018, June). *Blockchain Beyond the Hype*. Available at: https://www.mckinsey.com/business-functions/mckinsey-digital/our-insights/blockchain-beyond-the-hype-what-is-the-strategic-business-value?cid=other-eml-nsl-mip-mck-oth-1807&hlkid=5424a29008e445239371a81cc83b3dbb&hctky=10291646&hdpid=bb9f89f0-458b-4b4e-a1ee-ad99e602294e

Garson, B. (2018, June). *Blockchain Beyond the Hype*. Available at: https://www.mckinsey.com/business-functions/mckinsey-digital/our-insights/Blockchain-beyond-the-hype-what-is-the-strategic-business-value?cid=other-eml-nsl-mip-mck-oth-1807&hlkid=5424a29008e445239371a81cc83b3dbb&hctky=10291646&hdpid=bb9f89f0-458b-4b4e-a1ee-ad99e602294e

Gartner. (2020). *Gartner hype cycle for emerging technologies identifies three key trends that organizations must track to gain competitive advantage*. https://www.gartner.com/newsroom/id/3412017

Gatteschi, V., Lamberti, F., Demartini, C., Pranteda, C., & Santamaría, V. (2018). Blockchain. *Future Internet*, *10*(2), 20. doi:10.3390/fi10020020

Gauteng Province. (2020). *Online Admissions*. https://www.gdeadmissions.gov.za/Home/VideoTutorial

Gauteng Provincial Government. (2020). *Digital Platform*. https://www.gov.za/

Gennaro, R., Goldfeder, S., & Narayanan, A. (2016). Threshold-Optimal DSA/ECDSA Signatures and an Application to Bitcoin Wallet Security. In M. Manulis, A.-R. Sadeghi, & S. Schneider (Eds.), Applied Cryptography and Network Security (pp. 156–174). Springer International Publishing. doi:10.1007/978-3-319-39555-5_9

George, C. (2020a). *Unraveling hidden value in diamond sourcing*. Everledger. https://www.everledger.io/concept-paper/unraveling-hidden-value-in-diamond-sourcing/

George, C. (2020b, May 1). *Diamond Provenance at every link of the value chain*. Everledger. https://www.everledger.io/diamond-provenance-at-every-link-of-the-value-chain/

Gerçek, A., & Bakar Türegün, F. (2018). Şirketlerde Vergi Riski Algısı Ve Vergi Riski Yönetimi Üzerine Bir Araştırma. *Muhasebe ve Vergi Uygulamaları Dergisi*, *11*(3), 307–332. doi:10.29067/muvu.368807

Gerger, A. (2018). Use of Kobetsu Kaizen Method to Increase Efficiency in the Production Assembly: A Case Study. In Critical Debates in Social Science (pp. 54-70). FrontPage Publications Limited.

Gerger, A. (2020). Technologies for Connected Government Implementation: Success Factors and Best Practices. In Z. Mahmood (Ed.), Web 2.0 and Cloud Technologies for Implementing Connected Government. IGI Global.

Gerger, A. (2019a). Endüstri 4.0 Üretim Sürecinde Süreç Değişkenliğinin Optimizasyonunda Heijunka Yöntemi. *Izmir Democracy University Social Sciences Journal*, *2*(1), 1–17.

Gerger, A. (2019b). Toplum 5.0 ve Manisa. In *Manisa Ekonomisi ve Vizyonu* (pp. 239–261). Detay Yayıncılık.

Gerger, A. (2020). Success Factors And Best Practices in *Relation To The Use Of Newer Technologies at Connected Government Implementation. In Z. Mahmood (Ed.), Web 2.0 and Cloud Technologies for Implementing Connected Government* (pp. xx–xx). IGI Global.

Gerger, A., & Firuzan, A. (2020). Taguchi based Case study in the automotive industry: Nonconformity decreasing with use of Six Sigma methodology. *Journal of Applied Statistics*, 1–17. Advance online publication. doi:10.1080/0266476 3.2020.1837086

Gerger, A., & Firuzan, A. R. (2010). Yalin alti sigma projelerinin başarisiz olma nedenleri. *Journal of Yaşar University*, *20*(5), 3383–3393.

Gibson, C., & Kirk, T. (2016). *Blockchain 101 for asset managers*. https://www.klgates.com/files/Publication/921292ec-0e76-4b4b-adf4-036b15c175fe/Presentation/PublicationAttachment/6489032d-7722-4dcc-a10c-09e7e9b4350e/Block-chain_101_for_Asset_Managers.pdf

Gil-Pulgar, J. (2019). *IBM: Central banks will launch digital currencies within 5 years*. Retrieved from https://bitcoinist.com/ibm-central-bank-issued-cryptocurrency-five-years/

Gomez, J., Crespo, A., Moreu, P., Parra, C., & Diaz, V. G. (2009). Outsourcing maintenance in services providers. Safety, reliability and risk analysis: Theory, methods and applications, 829–837.

Gorham, M., & Singh, N. (2009). *Electronic exchanges: The global transformation from pits to bits*. Elsevier.

Gorog, C., & Boult, T. E. (2018). Solving Global Cybersecurity Problems by Connecting Trust Using Blockchain. *2018 IEEE International Conference on Internet of Things (IThings) and IEEE Green Computing and Communications (GreenCom) and IEEE Cyber, Physical and Social Computing (CPSCom) and IEEE Smart Data (SmartData)*, 1425–1432. 10.1109/Cybermatics_2018.2018.00243

Gourisetti, S. N. G., Mylrea, M., & Patangia, H. (2019). Evaluation and Demonstration of Blockchain. *IEEE Transactions on Engineering Management*, 1–15. doi:10.1109/TEM.2019.2928280

Govindan, K., Cheng, T. C., Mishra, N., & Shukla, N. (2018). Big data analytics and application for logistics and supply chain management. *Transportation Research Part E, Logistics and Transportation Review*, *114*(May), 343–349. doi:10.1016/j.tre.2018.03.011

Goyal, S. (2018, Nov). *The History of Blockchain Technology: Must Know Timeline*. Available at: https://101blockchains.com/history-of-blockchain-timeline/

Gräther, W., Schütte, J., Kolvenbach, S., Torres, C. F., Ruland, R., & Wendland, F. (2018). Blockchain for Education: Lifelong Learning Passport, In W. Prinz & P. Hoschka (Eds.), *Proceedings of the 1st ERCIM Blockchain Workshop 2018, Reports of the European Society for Socially Embedded Technologies*. Academic Press.

Gratzke, P., Schatsky, D., & Piscini, E. (2017). Signals for Strategists: Banding together for Blockchain. Deloitte University Press. Retrieved from https://dupress.deloitte.com/dup-us-en/focus/tech-trends/2017/blockchain-trust-economy.html

Gravetter, F. J., & Wallnau, L. B. (2009). *Statistics for the Behavioral Sciences* (8th ed.). Wadsworth.

Grech, A., & Camilleri, A. F. (2017). *Blockchain in Education, JRC Science for Policy Report*. European Commission. doi:10.2760/60649

Greener, S. (2008). *Business research methods*. http://web.ftvs.cuni.cz/hendl/metodologie/introduction-to-research-methods.pdf

Grigoriadou, V. (2019). Blockchain. *Homo Virtualis*, *2*(1), 50–56. doi:10.12681/homvir.20194

Grinberg, R. (2011). Bitcoin: An Innovative Alternative Digital Currency. *Hastings Science & Technology Law Journal, 4*, 164. https://papers.ssrn.com/sol3/papers.cfm?abstract_id=1817857

Grover, P., Kar, A. K., & Janssen, M. (2019). Diffusion of blockchain technology - Insights from academic literature and social media analytics. *Journal of Enterprise Information Management, 32*(5), 735–757. doi:10.1108/JEIM-06-2018-0132

Guardtime. (2020). *World's first blockchain-supported Personal Care Record Platform launched by Guardtime and partners to up to 30 million NHS patients in the UK.* Retrieved from guardtime: https://guardtime.com/blog/world-s-first-blockchain-supported-personal-care-record-platform-launched-by-guardtime-and-partners

Güneşli, İ., Yıldızbaşı, A., & Eras, E. (2020). Otomotiv tedarik zincirinde blokzincir teknolojisi uygulamalarına ilişkin bir değerlendirme. *Journal of Industrial Engineering, 31*(1), 48–56.

Guo, R., Shi, H., Zhao, Q., & Zheng, D. (2018). Secure attribute-based signature scheme with multiple authorities for blockchain in electronic health records systems. *IEEE Access, 6*, 676–686.

Güven, V., & Şahinöz, E. (2018). Blokzincir - Kripto Paralar - Bitcoin. Satoshi Dünyayı Değiştiriyor. Kronik Kitap.

Ha, U., Leng, J., Khaddaj, A., & Adib, F. (2020). Food and liquid sensing in practical environments using RFIDs. *17th USENIX Symposium on Networked Systems Design and Implementation (NSDI 20),* 1083–1100. https://www.usenix.org/conference/nsdi20/presentation/ha

Haber, S., & Stornetta, W. S. (1991, January). How to time-stamp a digital document. *Journal of Cryptology, 3*(2), 99–111. doi:10.1007/BF00196791

Hakak, S., Khan, W. Z., Gilkar, G. A., Imran, M., & Guizani, N. (2020). Securing smart citiessmart cities. *IEEE Network, 34*(1), 8–14. doi:10.1109/MNET.001.1900178

Hameed, S., Khan, F. I., & Hameed, B. (2018). Understanding Security Requirements and Challenges in Internet of Things (IoT): A Review. Journal of Computer Networks and Communications.

Hance, M. (2020). *What is Blockchain and How Can it be Used in Education?* Available at: https://mdreducation.com/2018/08/20/blockchain-education/

Hargan, E. D. (2017, June 10). *U.S. Department of Health & Human Services.* Retrieved from https://www.hhs.gov/sites/default/files/opioid%20PHE%20Declaration-no-sig.pdf

Harris, L. (2004). Trading and Exchanges: Market Microstructure for Practitioners. Oxford: Oxford UK

Harris, W. L., & Wonglimpiyarat, J. (2019). Blockchain. *Foresight, 21*(6), 625–639. doi:10.1108/FS-12-2018-0113

Hassebo, A., Obaidat, M. A., & Ali, M. (2018). *Commercial 4G LTE Cellular Networks for Supporting Emerging IoT Applications in Internet of Things.* Mechatronics and their Applications International Conference, as a part of the Advances in Science and Engineering Technology Multi-Conference (ASET), Dubai, UAE.

He, D., Habermeier, K., Leckow, R., Haksar, V., Almeida, Y., Kashima, M., Kyriakos-Saad, N., Oura, H., Saadi Sedik, T., Stetsenko, N., & Verdugo Yepes, C. (2016). Virtual Currencies and Beyond: Initial Con-siderations. *IMF Staff Discussion Notes, 16*(3), 1. Advance online publication. doi:10.5089/9781498363273.006

He, S., Wu, Q., Luo, X., Liang, Z., Li, D., Feng, H., Zheng, H., & Li, Y. (2018). A Social-Network-Based Cryptocurrency-Cryptocurrency. *IEEE Access: Practical Innovations, Open Solutions, 6*, 7654–7663. doi:10.1109/ACCESS.2018.2799385

Heutger, M., & Kueckelhaus, M. (2018). *Blockchain in Logistics.* DHL.

Hill, T., & Westbrook, R. (1997). SWOT Analysis: It's Time for a Product Recall. *Long Range Planning*, *30*(1), 46–52. doi:10.1016/S0024-6301(96)00095-7

Hinton, P. R., McMurray, I., & Brownlow, C. (2004). *SPSS Explained*. Routledge. doi:10.4324/9780203642597

HIPAA. (2019). Healthcare Data Breach Statistics. *HIPAA Journal*. https://www.hipaajournal.com/healthcare-data-breach-statistics/

HMRC. (2019). *Crypto Assets: Tax for Individuals*. https://www.gov.uk/government/publications/tax-on-cryptoassets/cryptoassets-for-individuals

Hofmann, P., Samp, C., & Urbach, N. (2019). (2019), Robotic Process Automation. *Electronic Markets*. Advance online publication. doi:10.100712525-019-00365-8

Holotescu, C. (2018). *Understanding Blockchain technology and how to get involved*. Paper presented at the 14th International Scientific Conference eLearning and Software for Education, Bucharest, Romania.

Houben, R., & Snyers, A. (2018). *Cryptocurrencies and Blockchain*. https://www.europarl.europa.eu/cmsdata/150761/TAX3%20Study%20on%20cryptocurrencies%20and%20Blockchain.pdf

Hoyle, D. (2005). Quality systems handbook ISO/TS 16949:2002 (2nd ed.). Oxford: Elsevier Butterworth-Heinemann.

Hoyle, D. (2000). *Automotive quality systems handbook*. Elsevier Butterworth-Heinemann.

Htet, C. C., & Htet, M. (2019). A Secure Used Car Trading System based on Blockchain Technology. *2019 21th International Conference on Information Integration and Web-based Application and Services (iiWAS'2019)*.

Huckle, S., Bhattacharya, R., White, M., & Beloff, N. (2016). Internet of things, blockchain and shared economy applications. *Procedia Computer Science*, *98*, 461–466. doi:10.1016/j.procs.2016.09.074

Hütten, M. (2017). *Soft Spots of Hard Code: The Emergence, Proliferation, and Pitfalls of the Blockchain Technology* (Doctoral dissertation). Goethe University of Frankfurt.

Huynh, T. T., Nguyen, T. D., & Tan, H. (2019). A Survey on Security and Privacy Issues of Blockchain Technology. *2019 International Conference on System Science and Engineering (ICSSE)*, 362–367. 10.1109/ICSSE.2019.8823094

Hyperledger Fabric. (2020). *Hyperledger Fabric*. Available at: https://hyperledger-fabric.readthedocs.io/en/release-2.0/whatis.html

Hyperledger Foundation. (2020). Hyperledger Open Source Blockchain Technologies. Hyperledger. Retrieved May 30, 2020, from https://www.hyperledger.org/

Hyperledger. (2020a, June 23). *Hyperledger Fabric*. Retrieved from Hyperledger: https://www.hyperledger.org/use/fabric

Hyperledger. (2020b, June 23). *Private data*. Retrieved from Hyperledger Fabric: https://hyperledger-fabric.readthedocs.io/en/release-2.0/private-data/private-data.html

Iansiti, M., & Lakhani, K. R. (2017, January-February). The truth about blockchain. *Harvard Business Review*. Retrieved from https://hbr.org/2017/01/the-truth-about-blockchain

IBINEX. (2019). *Global Cryptocurrency Market Report*. https://www.financemagnates.com/wp-content/uploads/2018/10/Global-Cryptocurrency-Market-Report.pdf

IBM Institute for Business Value. (2018). *Daring to be first: How auto pioneers are taking the plunge into blockchain*. IBM Corporation.

IBM. (2017, August 22). IBM Announces Major Blockchain Collaboration with Dole, Driscoll's, Golden State Foods, Kroger, McCormick and Company, McLane Company, Nestlé, Tyson Foods, Unilever and Walmart to Address Food Safety Worldwide. *PR Newswire*. https://www.prnewswire.com/news-releases/ibm-announces-major-blockchain-collaboration-with-dole-driscolls-golden-state-foods-kroger-mccormick-and-company-mclane-company-nestle-tyson-foods-unilever-and-walmart-to-address-food-safety-worldwide-300507604.html

IEEE Spectrum. (2020, April). *Spanish Researchers Use Blockchain and AI to Flatten the Curve*. Available at: https://spectrum.ieee.org/news-from-around-ieee/the-institute/ieee-member-news/researchers-spain-Blockchain-ai-app-flatten-the-curve

IMF Monetary and Capital Markets, Legal and Strategy and Policy Review Departments. (2016). *Virtual Currencies and Beyond: Initial Considerations Prepared by an IMF Staff Team1*. https://www.imf.org/external/pubs/ft/sdn/2016/sdn1603.pdf

Inderfurth, K., Sadrieh, A., & Voigt, G. (2013). The Impact of Information Sharing on Supply Chain Performance under Asymmetric Information. *Production and Operations Management, 22*(2), 410–425. doi:10.1111/j.1937-5956.2012.01372.x

Infura. (2020). *Partnering with Horizon Games to Power a New Dimension of Gaming*. Available at: https://infura.io/customers/skyweaver

Insights, L. (2020). *Alibaba's cross-border e-commerce platform uses blockchain for traceability*. Retrieved from https://www.ledgerinsights.com/alibaba-blockchain-cross-border-e-commerce-kaolo-traceability/

International Organization for Standardization. (2016). *ISO 15489-1:2016 Information and Documentation–Records Management–Part1: Concepts and Principles*. ISO.

Iron Mountain. (2020). *What is Blockchain and why should records management professionals care?* Retrieved 6 May, 2020, from https://www.ironmountain.com/resources/general-articles

IRS. (2014). *Virtual Currency Guidance: Virtual Currency Is Treated as Property for U.S. Federal Tax Purposes; General Rules for Property Transactions Apply*. IRS. https://www.irs.gov/uac/newsroom/irs-virtual-currency-guidance

I-Scope. (2020). *Blockchain and the Internet of Things: the IoT blockchain opportunity and challenge*. Available at: https://www.i-scoop.eu/internet-of-things-guide/blockchain-iot/

I-Scope. (2020). *Blockchain and the Internet of Things: the IoT Blockchain opportunity and challenge*. Available at: https://www.i-scoop.eu/internet-of-things-guide/Blockchain-iot/

ISO & IAF. (2020). ISO 9001 Auditing Practices Group. Retrieved May 29, 2020, from https://committee.iso.org/home/tc176/iso-9001auditing-practices-group.html

ISO. (2016). *Information technology*. Patent No. ISO/IEC 10118–1:2016.

IT Innovation & Excellence Awards 2018. (2018). *Overview*. Retrieved from https://www.csimumbai.org/it2025-18/award.html

ITU. (2018). *Measuring the Information Society Report Volume 2*. Retrieved 30 March, 2020, from https://www.itu.int/en/ITU-D/Statistics/Documents/publications/misr2018/MISR-2018-Vol-2-E.pdf

Ivanov, D., Tsipoulanidis, A., & Schönberger, J. (2018). Global Supply Chain and Operations Management: A Decision-Oriented Introduction to the Creation of Value (2nd ed.). Springer.

Janssen, M., Weerakkody, V., Ismagilova, E., Sivarajah, U., & Irani, Z. (2020). A framework for analysing blockchain technology adoption: Integrating institutional, market and technical factors. *International Journal of Information Management*, *50*, 302–309. doi:10.1016/j.ijinfomgt.2019.08.012

Jin, Y.-L., Jiang, Z.-H., & Hou, W.-R. (2009). Integrating flexible-interval preventive maintenance planning with production scheduling. *International Journal of Computer Integrated Manufacturing*, *22*(12), 1089–1101. doi:10.1080/09511920903207449

John, C. (2019). *Blockchain for contract and records management*. Retrieved 26 March, 2020, fromhttps://medium.com/vdcconsortium/Blockchain

Johnston, S., & Lewis, A. (2017). New Frontiers: Tax Agencies Explore Blockchain. *Tax Notes International, 86*(9), 16-19. https://www.taxnotes.com/tax-notes-international/tax-system-administration/new-frontiers-tax-agencies-explore-Blockchain/2017/04/03/18884661

Jones, A. (2018). *Blockchain brings proof of authenticity to records management*. Retrieved 20 March, 2020, https://www.alfresco.com/blogs/digital-transformation/Blockchain

Jones, D., Cranston, M., Behrens, S., & Jamieson, K. (2005). *What makes ICT implementation successful: A case study of online assignment submission*. Retrieved 29 March, 2020, from https://djon.es/blog/wp-content/uploads/2008/12/oasissubmit_v3.pdf

Jovanovic, B., & Peter, L. R. (2005). *General Purpose Technologies. In Handbook of Economic Growth. Elsevier*. doi:10.3386/w11093

Jung, S. W., & Jung, S. (2013). Hrp: A hmac-based rfid mutual authentication protocol using puf. In *The international conference on information networking 2013 (ICOIN)*. IEEE.

Kabbinale, A. R., Dimogerontakis, E., Selimi, M., Ali, A., Navarro, L., Sathiaseelan, A., & Crowcroft, J. (2020). Blockchain. *Concurrency and Computation*, *32*(12), e5349. doi:10.1002/cpe.5349

Kaçan, M. (2019, October 17). *5 main drivers of supply chain costs*. ICRON. https://icrontech.com/blog_item/5-main-drivers-of-supply-chain-costs/

Kaiser, C., Steger, M., Dorri, A., Festl, A., Stocker, A., Fellmann, M., & Kanhere, S. (2018). Towards a Privacy-Preserving Way of Vehicle Data Sharing – A Case for Blockchain Technology? *International Forum on Advanced Microsystems for Automotive Applications*, 111-122.

Kalita, K. P., Boro, D., & Bhattacharyya, D. K. (2020). Implementation of Minimally Shared Blockchains using Big Data Applications. *2020 Third ISEA Conference on Security and Privacy (ISEA-ISAP)*. 10.1109/ISEA-ISAP49340.2020.235000

Kalusopa, T., & Ngulube, P. (2012). Developing an e-records readiness framework for labour organisations in Botswana. *Information Development*, *28*(3), 199–215. doi:10.1177/0266666912446209

Kaplanov, N. M. (2012). Nerdy Money: Bitcoin, the private digital currency, and the case against its regulation. *Temple Law Review*. https://papers.ssrn.com/sol3/papers.cfm?abstract_id=2115203

Karamitsos, I., Papadaki, M., & Al Barghuthi, N. B. (2018). Design of the blockchain smart contract: A use case for real estate. *Journal of Information Security*, *9*(03), 177–190. Security doi:10.4236/jis.2018.93013

Karp, N. (2015). *Blockchain Technology: The Ultimate disruption in the Financial System*. https://www.bbvaresearch.com/wp-content/uploads/2015/07/150710_US_EW_Blockchain Technology.pdf

Kashyap, P. (2018, Feb). *What are Different Types of Blockchain and its Components?* Available at: http://www.be-ingcrypto.com/what-are-different-types-of-Blockchain-and-its-components/

Kastelein, R. (2020). *Alibaba Group implementing blockchain technology for the world's largest eCommerce site.* Retrieved from https://www.the-blockchain.com/2020/03/23/alibaba-group-implementing-blockchain-technology-for-the-worlds-largest-ecommerce-site/

Kasten, J. E. (2020). Engineering and manufacturing on the blockchain: A systematic review. *IEEE Engineering Management Review, 48*(1), 31–47. doi:10.1109/EMR.2020.2964224

Kaushal, P. K., Bagga, A., & Sobti, R. (2017). Evolution of bitcoin and security risk in bitcoin wallets. *2017 International Conference on Computer, Communications and Electronics (Comptelix)*, 172–177. 10.1109/COMPTELIX.2017.8003959

Keakopa, S. (2007). Policies and Procedures for the Management of Electronic Records in Botswana, Namibia and South Africa. *ESARBICA Journal, 26*(1), 54–64. doi:10.4314/esarjo.v26i1.31015

Keatinge, T., Carlisle, D., & Keen, F. (n.d.). *Virtual currencies and terrorist financing: assessing the risks and evaluating responses.* Study commissioned by the Directorate General for Internal Policies, Policy Department for Citizens. https://www.titanium-project.eu

Kemoni, H., Ngulube, P., & Stilwell, C. (2007). Public records and archives as tools for good governance: Reflections within the recordkeeping scholarly and practitioner communities. *ESARBICA Journal: Journal of the Eastern and Southern Africa Regional Branch of the International Council on Archives, 26*(1), 3–18. doi:10.4314/esarjo.v26i1.31012

Kenton, W. (2020, June 24). *Hyperledger Fabric.* Retrieved from Investopedia: https://www.investopedia.com/terms/h/hyperledger-fabric.asp

Kern, J., & Wolff, P. (2019). The digital transformation of the automotive supply chain – an empirical analysis with evidence from Germany and China: Case study contribution to the OECD TIP Digital and Open Innovation project. *Sectoral Case Study*, 1-23.

Kfar-Saba. (2019). *Cellcom Israel to deploy Nokia's Sensing as a Service.* Retrieved from https://www.nokia.com/about-us/news/releases/2019/04/12/cellcom-israel-to-deploy-nokias-sensing-as-a-service/

Khalaf, O. I., Abdulsahib, G. M., Kasmaei, H. D., & Ogudo, K. A. (2020). A new algorithm on application of blockchain technology in live stream video transmissions and telecommunications. *International Journal of e-Collaboration, 16*(1), 16–32. doi:10.4018/IJeC.2020010102

Khatal, S., Rane, J., Patel, D., Patel, P., & Busnel, Y. (2020, January). FileShare: A Blockchain and IPFS framework for Secure File Sharing and Data Provenance. *International Conference on Modelling, Simulation & Intelligent Computing (MoSICom 2020).*

Khatoon, A. (2020). Blockchain-Based Smart Contract System for Healthcare Management. *Electronics (Basel), 9*(94), 1–23. doi:10.3390/electronics9010094

Khodjaeva, M., Obaidat, M. A., & Salane, D. (2019). Mitigating Threats and Vulnerabilities of RFID in IoT through Outsourcing Computations Using Public Key Cryptography. In *Security, Privacy and Trust in the IoT Environment.* Springer-Cham.

Kim, J. W., Lee, A. R., Kim, M. G., Kim, I. K., & Lee, E. J. (2019). Patient-centric medication history recording system using blockchain. *2019 IEEE International Conference on Bioinformatics and Biomedicine (BIBM)*, 1513-1517. 10.1109/BIBM47256.2019.8983032

King, S., & Nadal, S. (2012). *Ppcoin: Peer-to-peer crypto-currency with proof-of-stake.* self-published paper.

Kızıl, E. (2019). Türkiye'de Kripto Paranın Vergilendirilmesi ve Muhasebeleştirilmesi. *Mali Çözüm, 29*(155), 179–196.

Köhler, S., & Pizzol, M. (2019). Life Cycle Assessment of Bitcoin. *Environmental Science & Technology, 53*(23), 13598–13606. doi:10.1021/acs.est.9b05687 PMID:31746188

Ko, K., Lee, C., Jeong, T., & Hong, J. W.-K. (2018). Design of RPC-based Blockchain Monitoring Agent. In *2018 International Conference on Information and Communication Technology Convergence (ICTC)*. Jeju, South Korea: IEEE. 10.1109/ICTC.2018.8539456

Komgo. (2020). *Streamlining Trade Finance*. Available at: https://komgo.io/

Konakçı, A. E. (2018). *Prag Metro Sistemi Artık 10 Bitcoin ATM'sine Sahip!* https://koinbulteni.com/prag-metro-sistemi-artik-10-bitcoin-atmsine-sahip-19118

Korman, Z. (2017). *On Blockchain, Intermediaries and Hype*. https://www.zkorman.com/writing/blockchain/

Kosba, A., Miller, A., Shi, E., Wen, Z., & Papamanthou, C. (2016, May). Hawk: The blockchain model of cryptography and privacy-preserving smart contracts. In *2016 IEEE symposium on security and privacy (SP)* (pp. 839-858). IEEE.

Kosba, A., Miller, A., Shi, E., Wen, Z., & Papaman, C. (2016). Hawk: The Blockchain Model of Cryptography and Privacy-Preserving Smart Contracts. *2016 IEEE Symposium on Security and Privacy*, 839–858. 10.1109/SP.2016.55

Kouakou, D., Boiral, O., & Gendron, Y. (2013). ISO auditing and the construction of trusttrust. *Accounting, Auditing & Accountability Journal, 26*(8), 1279–1305. doi:10.1108/AAAJ-03-2013-1264

KPMG. (2018). *The Changing Landscape of Disruptive Technologies*. https://home.kpmg/by/en/home/insights/2018/06/the-changing-landscape-of-disruptive-technologies.html

Kshetri, N. (2017). Blockchain privacy. *Telecommunications Policy, 41*(10), 1027–1038. doi:10.1016/j.telpol.2017.09.003

Kshetri, N. (2017). Can Blockchain Strengthen the Internet of Things? *IT Professional, 19*(4), 68–72. doi:10.1109/MITP.2017.3051335

Kshetri, N. (2017). Can blockchain strengthen the internet of things? *IT Professional, 19*(4), 68–72. doi:10.1109/MITP.2017.3051335

Kshetri, N. (2018). Blockchain's roles in meeting key supply chain management objectives. *International Journal of Information Management, 39*, 80–89. doi:10.1016/j.ijinfomgt.2017.12.005

Kshetri, N., & Voas, J. (2017). Do Crypto-Currencies Fuel Ransomware? *IT Professional, 19*(5), 11–15. doi:10.1109/MITP.2017.3680961

Kumar, U., & Galar, D. (2017). *Maintenance in the era of industry 4.0: Issues and challenges. Quality, IT and business operations*. Springer Singapore.

Kurpjuweit, S., Schmidt, C. G., Klockner, M., & Wagner, S. M. (2019). BlockchainBlockchain. *Early View*, (Special Issue), jbl.12231. Advance online publication. doi:10.1111/jbl.12231

Lacity, L. P., & Willcocks, M. C. (2016). A New Approach to Automating Service. *MIT Sloan Management Review, 58*(1).

Lane, M. (2019). *The tokenisation revolution: Smartlands and Sotheby's partner up*. Retrieved from https://www.propertyinvestortoday.co.uk/breaking-news/2019/12/the-tokenisation-revolution-smartlands-and-sothebys-partner-in-joint-experiment?source=trending

Laroiya, C., Saxena, D., & Komalavalli, C. (2020). Applications of blockchain technology. In S. Krishnan, V. E. Balas, E. G. Julie, Y. H. Robinson, S. Balaji, & R. Kumar (Eds.), Handbook of Research on Blockchain Technology (pp. 213–243). Academic Press. doi:10.1016/B978-0-12-819816-2.00009-5

Lechmere, A. (2016, December 5). Wine Vault Offers Security in a Digital Age. *Wine-Searcher.* https://www.wine-searcher.com/m/2016/12/wine-vault-offers-security-in-a-digital-age

Lee, J.-H. (2018). BIDaaS: Blockchain. *IEEE Access: Practical Innovations, Open Solutions, 6,* 2274–2278. doi:10.1109/ACCESS.2017.2782733

Lee, Z. E., Chua, R. L., Keoh, L. S., & Ohba, Y. (2019). Performance Evaluation of Big Data Processing at the Edge for IoT-Blockchain Applications. *2019 IEEE Global Communications Conference (GLOBECOM).* 10.1109/GLOBECOM38437.2019.9013329

Lemieux, V. L. (2017). *A typology of Blockchain recordkeeping solutions and some reflections on their implications for the future of archival preservation.* Retrieved 26 April, 2020, from https://www.researchgate.net/publication/322511343

Lemieux, V. L., Hofman, J. D., Batista, D., & Joo, A. (2019). *Blockchain technology and recordkeeping.* Retrieved 26 March, 2020, from http://armaedfoundation.org/wp-content/uploads/2019/06/AIEF-Research-Paper-Blockchain-Technology-Recordkeeping.pdf

Lemieux, V. L. (2016). Trusting records: Is Blockchain technology the answer? *Records Management Journal, 26*(2), 110–139. doi:10.1108/RMJ-12-2015-0042

Lemieux, V. L. (2019). Blockchain and Public Record Keeping: Of Temples, Prisons, and the (Re) Configuration of Power. *Frontiers in Blockchain, 2*(5), 1–14. doi:10.3389/fbloc.2019.00005

Levinson, M. (2008). *The Box: How the Shipping Container Made the World Smaller and the World Economy Bigger.* Princeton University Press.

Lewis, A. (2015). *A Gentle Introduction to Blockchain Technology.* Retrieved 17 July, 2020, from https://bitsonblocks.net/2015/09/09/gentle-introduction-Blockchain-technology/

Lindman, J., Tuunainen, V. K., & Rossi, M. (2017). *Opportunities and risks of Blockchain Technologies–a research agenda.* Academic Press.

Liotine, M., & Ginocchio, D. (2020). The supply blockchain: Integrating blockchain technology within supply chain operations. In *Technology in Supply Chain Management and Logistics* (pp. 57–89). Elsevier. doi:10.1016/B978-0-12-815956-9.00004-1

Litecoin. (2020, June 23). *The Cryptocurrency For Payments: Based on Blockchain Technology.* Retrieved from https://litecoin.org/

Liu, J., Kadıyala, A., & Cannistraci, P. (2018). *Enhancing Supply Chains with the Transparency and Security of Distributed Ledger Technology: Value Driven Supply Chain powered by Blockchain and IoT.* Deloitte Development LLC.

Liu, Y., Chen, X., Zhang, L., Tang, C., & Kang, H. (2017). An Intelligent Strategy to Gain Profit for Bitcoin Mining Pools. *2017 10th International Symposium on Computational Intelligence and Design (ISCID), 2,* 427–430. 10.1109/ISCID.2017.184

Liu, Y., Liu, X., Zhang, L., Tang, C., & Kang, H. (2017). An efficient strategy to eliminate malleability of bitcoin transaction. *2017 4th International Conference on Systems and Informatics (ICSAI),* 960–964. 10.1109/ICSAI.2017.8248424

Liu, X., Wang, W., Niyato, D., Zhao, N., & Wang, P. (2018). Evolutionary game for mining. *IEEE Wireless Communications Letters*, *7*(5), 760–763. doi:10.1109/LWC.2018.2820009

Liu, Z., & Li, Z. (2020). A blockchain-based framework of cross-border e-commerce supply chain. *International Journal of Information Management*, *52*, 102059. doi:10.1016/j.ijinfomgt.2019.102059

Li, W., Sforzin, A., Fedorov, S., & Karame, G. (2017). Towards Scalable and Private Industrial Blockchains. In *BCC '17: Proceedings of the ACM Workshop on Blockchain, Cryptocurrencies and Contracts* (pp. 9-14). ACM. 10.1145/3055518.3055531

Li, Z., Bahramirad, S., Paaso, A., Yan, M., & Shahidehpour, M. (2019). Blockchain. *The Electricity Journal*, *32*(4), 58–72. doi:10.1016/j.tej.2019.03.008 PMID:32524086

Loader, D. (2002). *Clearing, settlement, and custody*. Butterworth-Heinemann.

Lohachab, A., Lohachab, A., & Jangra, A. (2020). Comprehensive Survey of Prominent Cryptographic Aspects for Securing Communication in Post-Quantum IoT networks. *Internet of Things*, *9*, 100174. doi:10.1016/j.iot.2020.100174

Lu, D., Moreno-Sanchez, P., Zeryihun, A., Bajpayi, S., Yin, S., Feldman, K., ... Kate, A. (2019). Reducing Automotive Counterfeiting using Blockchain: Benefits and Challenges. *IEEE International Conference on Decentralized Applications and Infrastructures (DAPPCON)*, 39-48. 10.1109/DAPPCON.2019.00015

Luka, M. (2012). The Impacts of ICTs on Banks: A Case study of the Nigerian Banking Industry. *International Journal of Advanced Computer Science and Applications*, *3*(9), 145–149.

Lundström, S., & Öhman, S. (2019). *Generating Value through Blockchain Technology: The Case of Trade Finance*. Academic Press.

Lurie, N. Saville, M., Hatchett, R., & Halton, J. (2020, March 20). *Developing Covid-19 Vaccines at Pandemic Speed*. NEJM.org.

Maaghul, R. (2019, Oct). *Blockchain in Education: The Future of Records Management*. Available at: https://blogs.odem.io/blockchains-bright-future-in-the-education-industry

Maberry, T. (2018, February 6). A Look Back at 2017 Food Recalls. *Food Safety Magazine*. https://www.foodsafetymagazine.com/enewsletter/a-look-back-at-2017-food-recalls/

MacKenzie, C., Holmstrom, D., & Kaszniak, M. (2007). Human factors analysis of the BP Texas City refinery explosion. *Proceedings of the Human Factors and Ergonomics Society Annual Meeting*, *51*(20), 1444–1448. doi:10.1177/154193120705102015

Madakam, S., & Kollu, S (2020). Blockchain Technologies Fundamentals–Perceptions, Principles, Procedures and Practices. *Journal of Social and Management Sciences, 345*.

Madakam, S., Holmukhe, R. M., & Jaiswal, D. K. (2019). The Future Digital Work Force: Robotic Process Automation (RPA). *Journal of Information Systems and Technology Management*, *16*, 1–17. doi:10.4301/S1807-1775201916001

Makridakis, S., Polemitis, A., Giaglis, G., & Louca, S. (2018). *Blockchain: The Next Breakthrough in the Rapid Progress of AI*. Artificial Intelligence-Emerging Trends and Applications. doi:10.5772/intechopen.75668

Malhotra, M. (2020, March). *A comprehensive list of blockchain platforms to look for in 2020*. Available at: https://www.valuecoders.com/blog/technology-and-apps/a-comprehensive-list-of-Blockchain-platforms-to-look-for-in-2019/

Manrique, S. (2018). *Blockchain: A Proof of Trust*. Retrieved from: https://repository.tudelft.nl/islandora/object/uuid%3Ac1996e12-1462-4683-8716-72110c665d4c

Mappo. (2019). *Comprehensive List of Banks using Blockchain Technology*. Retrieved from https://medium.com/predict/comprehensive-list-of-banks-using-blockchain-technology-dc39ce5b6573

MarketWatch. (2020, June). *Blockchain Technology Market Share, Growth to record over US $25 billion by 2025 – Press Release*. Available at: https://www.marketwatch.com/press-release/Blockchain-technology-market-share-growth-to-record-over-us-25-billion-by-2025-2020-06-09

Marr, B. (2018). *Artificial Intelligence and Blockchain: 3 Major Benefits of Combining These Two Mega-Trends*. https://www.forbes.com/sites/bernardmarr/2018/03/02/artificial-intelligenceand-blockchain-3-major-benefits-of-combining-these-two-mega-trends/

Marsal-Llacuna, M.-L. (2018). Future living framework: Is blockchain the next enabling network? *Technological Forecasting and Social Change*, *128*, 226–234. doi:10.1016/j.techfore.2017.12.005

Martin, K. (2016, Sept. 27). CLS dips into blockchain to net new currencies. *Financial Times*.

Martin, S. (2017). *Blockchain use cases for food traceability and control. Swedish county councils and regions: Kairos Future*. Retrieved from Kairos Future: https://tinyurl.com/y7hh6nup

Martucci, B. (2018). *What Is Cryptocurrency: How it Works, History & Bitcoin Alternatives*. https://www.moneycrashers.com/cryptocurrency-history-bitcoin-alternatives/

Marutha, N. S. (2019). *Using Blockchain technology to interconnect the entire healthcare universe for patients' records sharing*. Paper presented at the School of Arts Triennial Conference, Pretoria, South Africa.

Mathews, A. W. (2015). Anthem: Hacked Database Included 78.8 Million People. *The Wall Street Journal*.

Mathis, T. (2016). Blockchain: A Guide To Blockchain. *The Technology Behind Bitcoin and Other Cryptocurrencies.*, *xx*, xx.

Matonis, J. W. (1995). *Digital Cash and Monetary Freedom*. Economic Notes No. 63. http://libertarian.co.uk/lapubs/econn/econn063.pdf

Mattick, J. S., Dziadek, M. A., Terrill, B. N., Kaplan, W., Spigelman, A. D., Bowling, F. G., & Dinger, M. E. (2014). The impact of genomics on the future of medicine and health. *The Medical Journal of Australia*, *201*(1), 17–20. doi:10.5694/mja13.10920 PMID:24999876

Maurer, F. K., Neudecker, T., & Florian, M. (2017). Anonymous CoinJoin Transactions with Arbitrary Values. *2017 IEEE Trustcom/BigDataSE/ICESS*, 522–529. doi:10.1109/Trustcom/BigDataSE/ICESS.2017.280

McKemmish, S. (2013). *Record keeping and archiving in the cloud: is there a silver lining?* Retrieved 1 July, 2020, from https://infoz.ffzg.hr/INFuture/2013/papers/1-02%20McKemmish,%20Recordkeeping%20and%20Archiving%20in%20the%20Cloud.pdf

McKenzie, J. (2018, February 4). Wal-Mart and IBM want to harness blockchain to improve food safety. *The Counter*. https://thecounter.org/blockchain-food-traceability-walmart-ibm/

Mediawire. (2020). *Dubai- the world capital of blockchain development*. Retrieved from https://economictimes.indiatimes.com/tech/ites/dubai-the-world-capital-of-blockchain-development/articleshow/74224682.cms

Mehta, S. (ET Bureau). (2017). *SBI takes lead in blockchain, to use it to prevent fraud*. Retrieved from https://economictimes.indiatimes.com/markets/stocks/news/sbi-takes-lead-in-blockchain-to-use-it-to-prevent-fraud/articleshow/57178212.cms

Mehta, I. S., Chakraborty, A., Choudhury, T., & Sharma, M. (2017). Efficient approach towards bitcoin security algorithm. *2017 International Conference on Infocom Technologies and Unmanned Systems (Trends and Future Directions) (ICTUS)*, 807–810. 10.1109/ICTUS.2017.8286117

Meiklejohn, S., Pomarole, M., Jordan, G., Levchenko, K., McCoy, D., Voelker, G. M., & Savage, S. (2013). A fistful of bitcoins: Characterizing payments among men with no names. *Proceedings of the 2013 Conference on Internet Measurement Conference*, 127–140. 10.1145/2504730.2504747

Meyvaert, E. (2020, June 22). *Siemens Mindsphere and SettleMint's distributed middleware: the perfect match!* Retrieved from Medium: https://updates.settlemint.io/siemens-mindsphere-and-settlemints-distributed-middleware-the-perfect-match-b1ce77335c09

Mihigo, E. (2019). *Culture Within the 4th Industrial Revolution: How Botho can help Blockchain become a key driver of Sustainable Development in Botswana*. Academic Press.

Mills, D. C., Wang, K., Malone, B., Ravi, A., Marquardt, J., Badev, A. I., & Ellithorpe, M. (2016). *Distributed ledger technology in payments, clearing, and settlement*. Academic Press.

Min, H. (2019). Blockchain technology for enhancing supply chain resilience. *Business Horizons*, *62*(1), 35–45. doi:10.1016/j.bushor.2018.08.012

Mire, S. (2018, Nov). *Blockchain For Manufacturing: 10 Possible Use Cases*. Available at: https://www.disruptordaily.com/blockchain-use-cases-manufacturing

Mirzayi, S., & Mehrzad, M. (2017). Bitcoin, an SWOT analysis. *2017 7th International Conference on Computer and Knowledge Engineering (ICCKE)*, 205–210. 10.1109/ICCKE.2017.8167876

Mnjama, N., & Wamukoya, J. (2007). Egovernment and Records Management: An Assessment Tool for E-records Readiness in Government. *The Electronic Library*, *25*(3), 274–284. doi:10.1108/02640470710754797

Moatlhodi, T., & Kalusopa, T. (2016). An Assessment of E-Records Readiness at the Ministry of Labour and Home Affairs, Gaborone, Botswana. Mousaion. *South African Journal of Information Studies*, *34*(3), 1–22.

Modi, R. (2018). *Solidity Programming Essentials*. Packt Publishing.

Mohanta, B. K., Panda, S. S., & Jena, D. (2018). An overview of smart contract and use cases in blockchain technology. *2018 9th International Conference on Computing, Communication and Networking Technologies (ICCCNT)*, 1-4.

Mohanta, B. K., Jena, D., Panda, S. S., & Sobhanayak, S. (2019). Blockchain privacy. *Internet of Things*, *8*, 100107. doi:10.1016/j.iot.2019.100107

Moise, I., & Chopping, D. (2018, January 16). Maersk and IBM Partner on Blockchain for Global Trade. *The Wall Street Journal*. https://www.wsj.com/articles/maersk-and-ibm-partner-on-blockchain-for-global-trade-1516111543

Mokhaoli, V. (2020). *Parents Plead with Lesufi to Bring Back Manual School Registrations, Eyewitness News*. https://ewn.co.za/2020/01/15/parents-plead-with-lesufi-to-bring-back-manual-school-registrations

Moloi, J., & Mutula, S. (2007). E-records management records management. *Information Development*, *23*(4), 290–306. doi:10.1177/0266666907084765

Moore, M. (Ed.). (2016). *Cybersecurity Breaches and Issues Surrounding Online Threat Protection*. IGI Global.

Morgan Stanley. (2016). *Global insight: Blockchain in banking: Disruptive threat or tool?* https://www.the-blockchain.com/docs/Morgan-Stanley-blockchain-report.pdf

Mori, T. (2016). Financial Technology: Blockchain and Securities Settlement. Deoitte and Touceh Tomatsu.

Morley, M. (2020, Feb). *Top 5 Use Cases of Blockchain in the Supply Chain in 2020*. Available at: https://blogs.opentext.com/blockchain-in-the-supply-chain/

Mosweu, O. (2014). *Factors affecting the adoption and use of Document Workflow Management System (DWMS) by Action Officers and Records Officers at the Ministry of Trade and Industry in Botswana* (MA Dissertation). University of Botswana, Gaborone.

Mosweu, O. (2016). Critical success factors in electronic document and records management. *ESARBICA Journal, 35*, 1–13.

Mosweu, O., Bwalya, J., & Mutshewa, A. (2017). A probe into the factors for adoption and usage of electronic document and records management records management. *Information Development, 33*(1), 97–110. doi:10.1177/0266666916640593

Mosweu, T. L., & Kenosi, L. (2018). Implementation of the Court Records Management System in the delivery of justice at the Gaborone Magisterial District, Botswana. *Records Management Journal, 28*(3), 234–251. doi:10.1108/RMJ-11-2017-0033

Mosweu, T., Luthuli, L., & Mosweu, O. (2019). Implications of cloud - computing services in Africa: Achilles heels of the digital era? *South African Journal of Information Management, 21*(1), 1–12. doi:10.4102ajim.v21i1.1069

Motsaathebe, L., & Mnjama, N. (2007). The management of High Court records in Botswana. *Records Management Journal, 19*(3), 173–189. doi:10.1108/09565690910999175

Mougayar, W. (2016). *The Business Blockchain: Promise, Practice, and Application of the Next Internet Technology*. John Wiley & Sons. http://ebookcentral.proquest.com

Moyano, J. P., & Ross, O. (2017). KYC optimization using distributed ledger technology. *Business & Information Systems Engineering, 59*(6), 411–423. doi:10.1007/s12599-017-0504-2

MultiChain. (2020). *MultiChain for Developers*. Available at: https://www.multichain.com/developers/

Mushtaq, A., & Haq, I. U. (2019, February). Implications of Blockchain in Industry 4. O. In *2019 International Conference on Engineering and Emerging Technologies (ICEET)* (pp. 1-5). IEEE.

Mylrea, M., & Gourisetti, S. N. G. (2017). Blockchain for smart grid resilience: Exchanging distributed energy at speed, scale and security. Resilience Week. doi:10.1109/RWEEK.2017.8088642

Naheem, M. A. (2019). Exploring the links between AML, digital currencies and blockchain technology. *Journal of Money Laundering Control, 22*(3), 515–526. doi:10.1108/JMLC-11-2015-0050

Nakamato, S. (2008). *Bitcoin: A Peer-to-Peer Electronic Cash System*. Bitcoin.

Nakamoto, S. (2008). *Bitcoin: A peer-to-peer electronic cash system*. Academic Press.

Nakamoto, S. (2008). *Bitcoin: A peer-to-peer electronic cash system*. https://bitcoin.org/bitcoin.pdf

Nakamoto, S. (2008). *Bitcoin: A Peer-to-Peer Electronic Cash System*. https://bitcoin.org/bitcoin.pdf

Nakamoto, S. (2008). *Bitcoin: A Peer-To-Peer Electronic Cash System*. https://bitcoin.org/bitcoin.pdf

Nakamoto, S. (2008). *Bitcoin: A peer-to-peer electronic cash system*. Retrieved 20 July, 2020, from https://bitcoin.org/bitcoin.pdf

Nakamoto, S. (2008). *Bitcoin: A Peer-to-Peer Electronic Cash System*. www.bitcoin.org

Nakamoto, S. (2019). Bitcoin: A Peer-to-Peer Electronic Cash System. *Manubot.* https://git.dhimmel.com/bitcoin-whitepaper/

Nakashima, H., & Aoyama, M. (2017). An automation method of sla contract of web apis and its platform based on blockchain concept. 2017 IEEE International Conference on Cognitive Computing (ICCC), 32–39. doi:10.1109/IEEE.ICCC.2017.12

Narayanan, A., Bonneau, J., Felten, E., Miller, A., & Goldfeder, S. (2016). Bitcoin and cryptocurrency technologies: a comprehensive introduction. Princeton University Press.

Narayanan, A., Bonneau, J., Felten, E., Miller, A., & Goldfeder, S. (2016). Bitcoin and Cryptocurrency Technologies: A Comprehensive Introduction. Princeton University Press.

Narbayeva, S., Bakibayev, T., Abeshev, K., Makarova, I., Shubenkova, K., & Pashkevich, A. (2020). Blockchain Technology. *Transportation Research Procedia, 44,* 168–175. doi:10.1016/j.trpro.2020.02.024

Natarajan, H., Krause, S., & Gradstein, H. (2017). *Distributed Ledger Technology (DLT) and Blockchain.* FinTech note, no. 1. http://documents.worldbank.org/curated/en/177911513714062215/pdf/122140-WP-PUBLIC-Distributed-Ledger-Technology-and-Blockchain-Fintech-Notes.pdf

National Archives and Records Administration (NARA). (2019). *Blockchain white paper.* Retrieved 2 May, 2020, from: http://www.archives.gov>policy

Natoli, C., & Gramoli, V. (2016). *The blockchain anomaly.* https://arxiv.org/pdf/1605.05438v1.pdf

Nehaï, Z., & Guerard, G. (2017, May). Integration of the blockchain in a smart grid model. In *Proceedings of the 14th International Conference of Young Scientists on Energy Issues (CYSENI 2017), Kaunas, Lithuania* (pp. 25-26). Academic Press.

Nengomasha, C. T., & Chikomba, A. (2018). Status of EDRMS implementation in the public sector in Zimbabwe and Namibia. *Records Management Journal, 28*(3), 252–264. doi:10.1108/RMJ-08-2017-0023

Ngoepe, M. (2009). Organising public records to achieve service delivery: The role of the National Archives and Records Service of South Africa's Functional Subject File Plan in Government Departments. *ESARBICA Journal: Journal of the Eastern and Southern Africa Regional Branch of the International Council on Archives, 28*(1), 41–56. doi:10.4314/esarjo.v28i1.44397

Ngulube, P. (2011). Cost analysis and the effective management of records throughout their life cycle. *Journal of the South African Society of Archivists, 44,* 3–18.

Ngulube, P., & Tafor, V. F. (2006). An overview of the management of public records and archives in the member countries of the East and Southern Africa Regional Branch of the International Council on Archives (ESARBICA). *Journal of the Society of Archivists, 27,* 69–86.

Nian, L. P., & Chuen, D. L. K. (2015). A light touch of regulation for virtual currencies. In *Handbook of Digital Currency* (pp. 309–326). Academic Press. doi:10.1016/B978-0-12-802117-0.00016-3

NIDA. (2018). *Opioid Overdose Crisis.* https://www.drugabuse.gov/drug-topics/opioids/opioid-overdose-crisis

Nkala, G., Ngulube, P., & Mangena, S. (2012). E-Records readiness at the National Archives of Zimbabwe. *Mousaion, 30*(2), 108–116.

NodeOpcUa. (2020). OPC UA stack in node.js. Retrieved May 26, 2020, from https://github.com/node-opcua/node-opcua

Nokia. (2019). *Nokia ranked as the top telecom software business by market share.* Retrieved from https://www.nokia.com/about-us/news/releases/2019/10/08/nokia-ranked-as-the-top-telecom-software-business-by-market-share/

Nokia. (2020a). *About us.* Retrieved from https://www.nokia.com/about-us/

Nokia. (2020b). *Nokia.* Retrieved from https://en.wikipedia.org/wiki/Nokia

Nokia. (2020c). *Search results.* Retrieved from https://www.nokia.com/search/global/en/blockchain

Nooruddin, S. (2019). *All about Blockchain.* Vieh Group.

Norta, A. (2015). Creation of smart-contracting collaborations for decentralized autonomous organizations. Perspectives in Business Informatics Research - 14th International Conference, BIR 2015, Tartu, Estonia, August 26-28, 2015, Proceedings, 3–17. 10.1007/978-3-319-21915-81

Norton Life Lock. (2020). *2019 data breaches: 4 billion records breached so far.* Retrieved 2 May, 2020, from:https://us.norton.com/internetsecurity-emerging-threats-2019-data-breaches.html

Notheisen, B., Hawlitschek, F., & Weinhardt, C. (2017). *Breaking Down the Blockchain Hype - Towards a Blockchain Market Engineering Approach.* Retrieved 18 May 2020, https://www.researchgate.net/publication/317828531

O'Connor, D. (2004). *The Basics of Economics.* Greenwood.

Obaidat, M. A., Khodjaeva, M., Obeidat, S., Salane, D., & Holst, J. (2019). Security Architecture Framework for Internet of Things. IEEE 10th Annual Ubiquitous Computing, Electronics & Mobile Communication Conference (UEMCON), 154-157. doi:10.1109/UEMCON47517.2019.8993096

Obaidat, M. A., Obeidat, S., Holst, J., Al Hayajneh, A., & Brown, J. (2020, May). A Comprehensive and Systematic Survey on the Internet of Things: Security and Privacy Challenges, Security Frameworks, Enabling Technologies, Threats, Vulnerabilities and Countermeasures, in Computers Journal. *MDPI, 9,* 44.

Oksiiuk, O., & Dmyrieva, I. (2020). Security and privacy issues of blockchain technology. *2020 IEEE 15th International Conference on Advanced Trends in Radioelectronics, Telecommunications and Computer Engineering (TCSET),* 1–5. 10.1109/TCSET49122.2020.235489

OpenChain. (2020). *Overview of OpenChain.* Available at: https://docs.openchain.org/en/latest/general/overview.html

OpenZeppelin. (2020). *The standard for secure Blockchain applications.* Available at: https://openzeppelin.com/

Ouellette. (2013). *Advocate Medical Group endures massive data breach.* https://healthitsecurity.com/news/advocate-medical-group-endures-massive-data-breach

Özan, M. B., Polat, H., Gündüzalp, S., & Yaraş, Z. (2015). Eğitim Kurumlarında SWOT Analizi. *Turkish Journal of Educational Studies, 2*(1), 1–28.

Pai, S., Sevilla, M., Buvat, J., Schneider-Maul, R., Lise, O., Calvayrac, A., . . . Puttur, R. (2018). *Does blockchain hold the key to a new age in supply chain transparency and trust?* Capgemini.

Pai, S., Sevilla, M., Buvat, J., Schneider-Maul, R., Lise, O., Calvayrac, A., Karanam, T., & Puttur, R. (2018). *Does Blockchain hold the key to a new age in Supply Chain transparency and trust?* Capgemini Research Institute. https://www.capgemini.com/research/does-blockchain-hold-the-key-to-a-new-age-in-supply-chain-transparency-and-trust/

Pascale, E. D., McMenamy, J., Macaluso, I., & Doyle, L. (2017). Smart contract slas for dense small-cell-as-a-service. https://arxiv.org/abs/1703.04502

Pauw, C. (2019). *What is an STO, explained.* Retrieved from https://cointelegraph.com/explained/what-is-an-sto-explained

Pawczuk, L., Holdowsky, J., Massey, R., & Hansen, B. (2020). *Deloitte's 2020 Global Blockchain Survey.* Deloitte Insights. https://www2.deloitte.com/content/dam/insights/us/articles/6608_2020-global-blockchain-survey/DI_CIR%20 2020%20global%20blockchain%20survey.pdf

Peng, T. (2020). *Alibaba imports e-commerce platform adopts Blockchain Traceability System.* Retrieved from https:// cointelegraph.com/news/alibaba-imports-e-commerce-platform-adopts-blockchain-traceability-system

Pepper, R. (2012, June 1). *Mobile Networks in a Zettabyte World Trends from Cisco's Visual Networking Index.* Retrieved from gsma.com: https://www.gsma.com/spectrum/wp-content/uploads/2012/06/Dr_Robert-_Pepper_Cisco_Public_Policy-Forum_Data_Demand.pdf

Perboli, G., Musso, S., & Rosano, M. (2018). Blockchain in Logistics and Supply Chain: A Lean Approach for Designing Real-World Use Cases. *IEEE Access: Practical Innovations, Open Solutions, 6,* 62018–62028. doi:10.1109/ ACCESS.2018.2875782

Pierson, B. (2017). *Anthem to pay record $115 million to settle U.S. lawsuits over data breach.* https://www.reuters.com/ article/us-anthem-cyber-settlement/anthem-to-pay-record-115-million-to-settle-u-s-lawsuits-over-data-breach

Pilkington, M. (2015). *Blockchain Technology: Principles and Applications.* http://ssrn.com/abstract=2662660

Pirus, B. (2019). *Allianz in 'Advanced Stages' of accepting crypto for payment.* Retrieved from https://www. forbes.com/sites/benjaminpirus/2019/08/08/allianz-among-the-latest-entrants-into-token-based-payment-space-development/#53593b935c5e

Poelstra, A. (2014). *Distributed consensus from proof of stake is impossible.* https://download.wpsoftware.net/bitcoin/ old-pos.pdf

Pólvora, A., Nascimento, S., Lourenço, J. S., & Scapolo, F. (2020). Blockchain. *Technological Forecasting and Social Change, 157,* 120091. doi:10.1016/j.techfore.2020.120091

Prasad, D. (2016). *A Study of ICT Use for Service Delivery in the Public Sector of Palau, Samoa, Kiribati and the Solomon Islands.* Retrieved 19 May 2020, from https://www.researchgate.net/publication/314281757

Praveen, G., Chamola, V., Hassija, V., & Kumar, N. (2020). Blockchain. *Early, 34*(6), 106–113. Advance online publication. doi:10.1109/MNET.001.2000005

Prewett, K., Dorsey, R. W., & Kumar, G. (2019). A Primer on Taxation of Investment in Cryptocurrencies. *Journal of Taxation of Investments, 36*(4), 3. Retrieved April 2020, from http://search.ebscohost.com/login.aspx?direct=true&db =edb&AN=138241160&site=eds-live

Price, R. (2015, August 28). This London startup could make diamond theft a thing of the past—And that's just the start. *Business Insider.* https://www.businessinsider.com/everledger-ledger-diamonds-blockchain-tech-theft-fraud-2015-8

Priyaranjan, N., Roy, M., & Dhal, S. (2020). Distributed ledger technology, blockchain and central banks. *RBI Bulletin,* (February), 41–53.

Project Khokha: An Enterprise Ethereum Banking and Finance Case Study. (2020). Available at: https://pages.consensys.net/consensys-banking-and-finance-project-khokha-v2?utm_campaign=Enterprise%20Ethereum%20&utm_source=Website&utm_medium=Direct&utm_term=EntEth&utm_content=CaseStudyKhokha

Provenance. (2016). *From shore to plate: Tracking tuna on the blockchain.* Provenance. https://www.provenance.org/ tracking-tuna-on-the-blockchain

Puthal, D., Malik, N., Mohanty, S. P., Kougianos, E., & Das, G. (2018). Everything You Wanted to Know About the Blockchain: Its Promise, Components, Processes, and Problems. *IEEE Consumer Electronics Magazine, 7*(4), 6–14. doi:10.1109/MCE.2018.2816299

Qiang, Y., Fang, Y., & Gonzalez, J. J. (2012). Managing security risks during new technology adoption. *Computers & Security, 31*, 859–869.

Qin, R., Yuan, Y., Wang, S., & Wang, F. Y. (2018, June). Economic issues in bitcoin mining and blockchain research. In *2018 IEEE Intelligent Vehicles Symposium (IV)* (pp. 268-273). IEEE. 10.1109/IVS.2018.8500377

Quamara, S., & Singh, A. K. (2016). Bitcoins and secure financial transaction processing, recent advances. *2016 2nd International Conference on Applied and Theoretical Computing and Communication Technology (ICATccT)*, 216–219. 10.1109/ICATCCT.2016.7911995

Queiroz, M. M., Telles, R., & Bonilla, S. H. (2019). Blockchain and supply chain management integration: A systematic review of the literature. *Supply Chain Management, 25*(2), 241–254. doi:10.1108/SCM-03-2018-0143

Quorum. (2020, June 23). *The proven blockchain solution for business*. Retrieved from Evolve with Quorum: https://www.goquorum.com/

R3. (2020). *Corda Enterprise: A Next-Gen Blockchain Platform*. Available at: https://www.r3.com/corda-platform/

Radif, M., Fan, I. S., & McLaughlin, P. (2016). *Employment Technology Acceptance Model (TAM) to adopt Learning Management System (LMS) in Iraqi Universities*. Paper presented at the 10th annual International Technology, Education and Development Conference, Valencia, Spain. Retrieved 2 May, 2020, from: https://www.researchgate.net/publication/298953343_EMPLOYMENT_TECHNOLOGY_ACCEPTANCE_MODEL_TAM

Rahulamathavan, Y., Phan, R. C. W., Rajarajan, M., Misra, S., & Kondoz, A. (2017). Privacy-preserving blockchain based iot ecosystem using attribute-based encryption. 2017 IEEE International Conference on Advanced Networks and Telecommunications Systems (ANTS), 1–6. doi:10.1109/ANTS.2017.8384164

Rakemane, D., & Serema, B. C. (2018). Electronic records management practices at the Companies and Intellectual Property Authority in Gaborone, Botswana. *Journal of the South African Society of Archivists, 51*, 148–169.

Ram, A. J. (2018). Taxation of the bitcoin: Initial insights through a correspondence analysis. *Meditari Accountancy Research, 26*(2), 214-240. http://www.emeraldinsight.com/doi/10.1108/MEDAR-10-2017-0229

Ran, Y., Zhou, X., Lin, P., Wen, Y., & Deng, R. (2019). A survey of predictive maintenance: Systems, purposes and approaches. arXiv preprint arXiv:1912.07383.

Reader, S. (2018). *Self-learning: why it's essential for you in the 21st Century*. Retrieved 6 May, 2020, from: https://medium.com/wondr-blog/self-learning-why-its-essential-for-us-in-the-21st-century-9e9729abc4b8

Reid, F., & Harrigan, M. (2013). An Analysis of Anonymity in the Bitcoin System. In Y. Altshuler, Y. Elovici, A. B. Cremers, N. Aharony, & A. Pentland (Eds.), Security and Privacy in Social Networks (pp. 197–223). Springer. doi:10.1007/978-1-4614-4139-7_10

Reinsel, D., Gantz, J., & Rydning, J. (2018, November 1). *The Digitization of the World From Edge to Core*. Retrieved from Seagate: https://www.seagate.com/files/www-content/our-story/trends/files/idc-seagate-dataage-whitepaper.pdf

Rejeb, A., Keogh, J. G., & Treiblmaier, H. (2019). Leveraging the Internet of Things and Blockchain Technology in Supply Chain Management. *Future Internet, 11*(7), 161. doi:10.3390/fi11070161

Reyna, A., Martín, C., Chen, J., Soler, E., & Díaz, M. (2018). On Blockchain and its Integration with IoT. Challenges and Opportunities. *Future Generation Computer Systems, 88*, 173–190. doi:10.1016/j.future.2018.05.046

Ripple. (2020). *University Blockchain Research Initiative.* Available at: https://ubri.ripple.com/faq/

Robinson, J. (2018, Aug). *The Future of Blockchain in Transportation.* Available at: https://www.fleetio.com/blog/future-of-blockchain-in-transportation

Robinson, J. (2018, Aug). *The Future of Blockchain in Transportation.* Available at: https://www.fleetio.com/blog/future-of-Blockchain-in-transportation

Rodney, J. D., & Zuckerman, N. (2019, February 11). How blockchain can strengthen the military supply chain. *Vanguard Magazine.* https://vanguardcanada.com/2019/02/11/how-blockchain-can-strengthen-the-military-supply-chain/

Rogers, E. M. (2003). *Diffusion of innovations* (5th ed.). Free Press.

Rosado, T., Vasconcelos, A., & Correia, M. (2019). A Blockchain Use Case for Car Registration. In Essentials of Blockchain Technology (pp. 205-234). doi:10.1201/9780429674457-10

Rosic, A. (1916). *What is Blockchain Technology? A Step-by-Step Guide For Beginners.* Available at: https://blockgeeks.com/guides/what-is-blockchain-technology/

Rosic, A. (1916). *What is Blockchain Technology? A Step-by-Step Guide For Beginners.* Available at: https://blockgeeks.com/guides/what-is-Blockchain-technology/

Rotuna, C., Gheorghita, A., Zamfiroiu, A., & Anagrama, D. S. (2019). Smart City Ecosystem Using Blockchain *Informações Econômicas, 23*(4), 41–50. doi:10.12948/issn14531305/23.4.2019.04

Rutter, J. (2001). From the sociology of trust towards a sociology of 'e-trust'. *International Journal of New Product Development & Innovation Management, 2*(4), 371–385.

Saberi, S., Kouhizadeh, M., Sarkis, J., & Shen, L. (2018). Blockchain technology and its relationships to sustainable supply chain management. *International Journal of Production Research, 57*(7), 2117–2135. doi:10.1080/00207543.2018.1533261

Sadhya, V., & Sadhya, H. (2018), Barriers to Adoption of Blockchain Technology. *Twenty-fourth Americas Conference on Information Systems*, New Orleans.

Sako, M., & Helper, S. (1998). Determinants of trust. *Journal of Economic Behavior & Organization, 34*(3), 387–417. doi:10.1016/S0167-2681(97)00082-6

Salah, K., Rehman, M. H., Nizamuddin, N., & Al-Fuqaha, A. (2019). Blockchain for AI: Review and Open Research Challenges. *IEEE Access: Practical Innovations, Open Solutions, 7*, 10127–10149. doi:10.1109/ACCESS.2018.2890507

Salsman, R. M. (2013). The financial crisis was a failure of government, not free markets. *Forbes Magazine, 19.*

Sangwan, V., Harshita, H., Prakash, P., & Singh, S. (2020). Financial technology: A review of extant literature. *Studies in Economics and Finance, 37*(1), 71–88. doi:10.1108/SEF-07-2019-0270

Saunders, M., Lewis, P., & Thornhill, A. (2012). *Research methods for business students.* Pearson Education Limited.

SBI in the News. (2018). *IBA Banking Technology Award 2016-17 held on 27/02/2018, Mumbai.* Retrieved from https://www.sbi.co.in/web/sbi-in-the-news

Schipor, F. G.-L. (2019). Risks and Opportunities in the Cryptocurrency Market. *Ovidius University Annals, Series Economic Sciences, 19*(2), 879–883. http://search.ebscohost.com/login.aspx?direct=true&db=obo&AN=142315464&site=eds-live

Schmidt, C. G., & Wagner, S. M. (2019). Blockchain and supply chain relations: A transaction cost theory perspective. *Journal of Purchasing and Supply Management, 25*(4), 100552. doi:10.1016/j.pursup.2019.100552

Schneider, R. D. (2012). Hadoop for Dummies. Mississauga: John Wiley &.

Scott, S. (1991). How to time-stamp a digital document. *Journal of Cryptology*.

Search, A. (2020). *Blockchain*. Retrieved from https://www.allianz.com/en/search.html#searchTerm=blockchain

Security, I. B. M. (2019). *Cost of a Data Breach Report 2020*. https://www.ibm.com/security/digital-assets/cost-data-breach-report/#/

Senthilkumar, D. (2020). Cross-Industry Use of Blockchain Technology and Opportunities for the Future: Blockchain Technology and Aritificial Intelligence. In Cross-Industry Use of Blockchain Technology and Opportunities for the Future: Blockchain Technology and Aritificial Intelligence. IGI Global.

Sertkaya, A., Wong, H. H., Jessup, A., & Beleche, T. (2016). Key cost drivers of pharmaceutical clinical trials. *Clinical Trials, 13*(2), 117–126. Advance online publication. doi:10.1177/1740774515625964 PMID:26908540

Shah, A. (2018). The chain gang. *Mechanical Engineering (New York, N.Y.), 140*(5), 30–35. doi:10.1115/1.2018-MAY-1

Shahaab, A., Hewage, R. M. C., & Khan, I. (2020). Managing Gender Change Information on Immutable Blockchain in Context of GDPR. The JBBA, 3(1).

Shan, J., Jiannong, C., Hanqing W., Yanni, Y., Mingyu, M., & Jianfei, H. (2018). *BlocHIE: A Blockchain based platform for Healthcare Information Exchange.* . doi:10.1109/SMARTCOMP.2018.00073

Shanmugam, B., Azam, S., Yeo, K. C., Jose, J., & Kannoorpatti, K. (2017). A critical review of Bitcoins usage by cybercriminals. *2017 International Conference on Computer Communication and Informatics (ICCCI)*, 1–7. 10.1109/ICCCI.2017.8117693

Shapira, A., & Leinz, K. (2017, December 21). *Long Island Iced Tea Soars After Changing Its Name to Long Blockchain*. Bloomberg.Com. https://www.bloomberg.com/news/articles/2017-12-21/crypto-craze-sees-long-island-iced-tea-rename-as-long-blockchain

Sharma, M. (2019), Blockchain for Cybersecurity: Working Mechanism, Application areas and Security Challenges. *2019 2nd International Conference on Intelligent Computing, Instrumentation and Control Technologies (ICICICT), 1*, 1182–1187. 10.1109/ICICICT46008.2019.8993204

Sharma, T. K. (2019). *Alibaba looks to implement blockchain for its complex supply chains*. Retrieved from https://www.blockchain-council.org/blockchain/alibaba-looks-to-implement-blockchain-for-its-complex-supply-chains/

Sharples, M., & Domingue, J. (2016). The Blockchain and Kudos: A Distributed System for Educational Record, Reputation and Reward. In K. Verbert, M. Sharples, & T. Klobučar (Eds.), Lecture Notes in Computer Science: Vol. 9891. *Adaptive and Adaptable Learning. EC-TEL 2016.* Springer. doi:10.1007/978-3-319-45153-4_48

Shehhi, A. A., Oudah, M., & Aung, Z. (2014). Investigating factors behind choosing a cryptocurrency. *2014 IEEE International Conference on Industrial Engineering and Engineering Management*, 1443–1447. 10.1109/IEEM.2014.7058877

Shi, X. (2019). *Do Core Developers Owe Fiduciary Duty to Users of Blockchain Platforms?* Available at SSRN 3526685.

Shilpi & Ahad, M. A. (2020). Blockchain technology and smart cities- A review. *EAI Endorsed Transactions on Smart Cities.* doi: . doi:10.4108/eai.13-7-2018.163846

Shonhe, L., & Grand, B. (2019). Implementation of electronic records electronic records. *Records Management Journal, 30*(1), 43–62. doi:10.1108/RMJ-03-2019-0013

Shrestha, B., Halgamuge, M. N., & Treiblmaier, H. (2020). Using Blockchain for Online Multimedia Management: Characteristics of Existing Platforms. In Blockchain and Distributed Ledger Technology Use Cases (pp. 289–303). Springer.

Shumsky, P. (2019, Sep). *Blockchain Use Cases For Banks In 2020.* Available at: https://www.finextra.com/blogposting/17857/blockchain-use-cases-for-banks-in-2020

Siemens. (2019). *Trusted Traceability - Blockchain and the Internet of Things.* uremberg, Germany: Siemens AG 2019. Retrieved from https://assets.new.siemens.com/siemens/assets/api/uuid:de496ba4-0081-48f5-965b-4963879b2d43/version:1557493248/vrfb-b10033-00-7600sbblockchainfb-144.pdf

Sigauke, D. T., & Nengomasha, C. (2012), *Challenges and prospects facing the digitization of historical records for their preservation within the national archives of Zimbabwe.* Paper presented at the 2nd International Conference on African Digital libraries and Archives (ICADLA-2), University of Witwatersrand, Johannesburg, South Africa. Retrieved 16 April, 2020, from https://core.ac.uk/download/pdf/39670341.pdf

Sigauke, D. T., Nengomasha, C., & Chabikwa, S. (2016). Management of email as electronic records in state universities in Zimbabwe: Findings and implications for the National Archives of Zimbabwe. *ESARBICA Journal, 35,* 14–29.

Silcock, R. (2001). What is e-Government? *Parliamentary Affairs, 54*(1), 88–101. doi:10.1093/pa/54.1.88

Singh, H. (2019). *Top Cybersecurity Data Breaches of 2019.* https://www.appknox.com/blog/top-cybersecurity-data-breaches

Singh, N. (2020, May). *Permissioned vs. Permissionless Blockchain: A Comparison Guide.* Available at: https://101blockchains.com/permissioned-vs-permissionless-blockchains/

Singh, N. (2020, May). *Permissioned vs. Permissionless Blockchain: A Comparison Guide.* Available at: https://101Blockchains.com/permissioned-vs-permissionless-Blockchains/

Singh, K. (2020). Blockchain technology: A potential game changer for automotive industry. *International Journal of Advanced Research in Management and Social Sciences, 9*(3), 49–55.

Smart Dubai. (2020). *Our vision is to make Dubai the happiest city on earth.* Retrieved from https://www.smartdubai.ae/

Songara, A., & Chouhan, L. (2017, October). Blockchain: a decentralized technique for securing Internet of Things. *Conference on Emerging Trends in Engineering Innovations & Technology Management (ICET: EITM-2017).*

Sotheby's International Realty. (2006-2020). *An extraordinary history.* Retrieved from https://www.sothebysrealty.com/eng/history

Southwick, N. (2013). *Counterfeit Drugs Kill 1 Mn People Annually.* Interpol. https://www.insightcrime.org/news/brief/counterfeit-drugs-kill-1-million-annually-interpol/

Sözek, K. (2017). *Blockchain: Ultimate Step by Step Guide to Understanding Blockchain Technology, Bitcoin Creation, and the Future of Money.* CreateSpace Independent Publishing Platform.

Spendla, L., Kebisek, M., Tanuska, P., & Hrcka, L. (2017). Concept of predictive maintenance of production systems in accordance with industry 4.0. 2017 IEEE 15th International Symposium on Applied Machine Intelligence and Informatics (SAMI), 405–410. doi:10.1109/SAMI.2017.7880343

Spitzer. (2017). *11 of the biggest healthcare cyberattacks of 2017.* https://www.beckershospitalreview.com/cybersecurity/11-of-the-biggest-healthcare-cyberattacks-of-2017.html

Sregantan, N. (2018, July 17). SGInnovate invests in Singapore meditech start-up MediLOT Technologies. *straitstimes.*

State Bank of India. (2020). *Investor relations.* Retrieved from https://www.sbi.co.in/web/investor-relations/investor-relations

Steinauer, D. D., Wakid, S. A., & Rasberry, S. (1997). Trust and traceability in electronic commerce. *StandardView, 5*(3), 118–124. doi:10.1145/266231.266239

Stocker, A., & Kaiser, C. (2016). Quantified car: potentials, business models and digital ecosystems. *E&i Elektrotechnik und Informationstechnik, 133*(7), 334–340.

Stocker, A., Kaiser, C., & Fellmann, M. (2017). Quantified Vehicles - Novel Services for Vehicle Lifecycle Data. *Journal of Business & Information. Systems Engineering, 59*(2), 1–6.

Stodt, J., & Reich, C. (2020). Data confidentiality in p2p communication and smart contracts of blockchain in industry 4.0. Unpublished manuscript.

Strobel, V., Ferrer, E. C., & Dorigo, M. (2018). Managing Byzantine Robots via Blockchain Technology in a Swarm Robotics Collective Decision-Making Scenario. *Proc. 17th Int. Conf. Auto. Agents MultiAgent Syst. International Foundation for Autonomous Agents and Multiagent Systems: Stockholm, Sweden*, 541–549.

Sun Exchange. (2019). *About Sun Exchange.* Retrieved from https://thesunexchange.com/about-us

Swan, M. (2015), Financial Services. In Blockchain: Blueprint for a new economy. O'Reilly

Swanson, T. (2015). *Consensus-as-a-service: A brief report on the emergence of permissioned, distributed ledger systems.* https://www.weusecoins.com/assets/pdf/library/Consensus-as-a-service%20-%20a%20brief%20report%20on%20the%20emergence%20of%20permissioned %20distributed%20ledger.pdf

Syed, R., Suriadi, S., Adams, M., Bandara, W., Leemans, S. J. J., Ouyanga, C., Hofstede, A. H. M., de Weerd, I., Wynn, M. T., & Reijers, H. A. (2020). Robotic Process Automation: Contemporary Themes and Challenges. *Computers in Industry, 115*, 103162. doi:10.1016/j.compind.2019.103162

Sylim, P., Liu, F., Alvin, M., & Fontelo, P. (2018). Blockchain Technology for Detecting Falsified and Substandard Drugs in the Pharmaceuticals Distribution System (Preprint). *JMIR Research Protocols, 7.* Advance online publication. doi:10.2196/10163 PMID:30213780

Tama, B. A., Kweka, B. J., Park, Y., & Rhee, K.-H. (2017). A critical review of blockchain and its current applications. *2017 International Conference on Electrical Engineering and Computer Science (ICECOS)*, 109–113. 10.1109/ICECOS.2017.8167115

Tan, B., Yan, J., Chen, S., & Liu, X. (2018). The impact of blockchain on food supply chain: The case of Walmart. *International Conference on Smart Blockchain*, 167–177. 10.1007/978-3-030-05764-0_18

Tan, Y. H., & Thoen, W. (2001). Toward a Generic Model of Trust for Electronic Commerce. *International Journal of Electronic Commerce, 5*(2), 61–67.

Tasca, P., & Tessone, C. J. (2019). *A Taxonomy of Blockchain Technologies: Principles of Identification and Classification, Ledger.* LedgerJournal.org.

Tenneson, C. (2017). Competitive landscape: Partnering with third-party maintenance providers for data center and network maintenance cost optimization. Retrieved May 7, 2019, from https://www.gartner.com/en/documents/3756176

Tepper School of Business. (2020). *Tepper Blockchain Initiative*. Available at: https://www.cmu.edu/tepper/faculty-and-research/initiatives/Blockchain-initiative/

Terazono, E. (2017). *Bitcoin Gets Official Blessing in Japan*. https://www.ft.com/content/b8360e86-aceb-11e7-aab9-abaa44b1e130

Teslya, N., & Ryabchikov, I. (2017). Blockchain-based platform architecture for industrial iot. 2017 21st Conference of Open Innovations Association (FRUCT), 321–329. doi:10.23919/FRUCT.2017.8250199

Teufel, B., Sentic, A., & Barmet, M. (2020). Blockchain energy: Blockchain in future energy systems. *Journal of Electronic Science and Technology*. doi:10.1016/j.jnlest.2020.100011

The Citizen. (2020). *Frustration and Anger over Dept's Online Registration System, The Citizen*. https://citizen.co.za/news/south-africa/education/2228424/frustration-and-anger-over--depts-online-registration-system/

The Economist. (2014). *Cryptocurrencies – the great hiccup*. https://www.economist.com/news/finance-and-economics/21596971-bitcoin-growing-too-fast-its-technology-keep-up-great-hiccup

Thummavet, P. (2020, June 22). *Demystifying Hyperledger Fabric: Fabric Architecture*. Retrieved from Medium: https://tinyurl.com/y9yn33k5

Tian, F. (2017). A supply chain traceability system for food safety based on haccp, blockchain internet of things. 2017 International Conference on Service Systems and Service Management, 1–6. doi:10.1109/ICSSSM.2017.7996119

Timothy, L. (2017). *Blockchain for Transportation: Where the Future Starts*. Cleveland: TMWSystems, Inc.

Tornatzky, L. G., & Fleischer, M. (1990). *The processes of technological innovation*. Academic Press.

Tosh, D. K., Shetty, S., Liang, X., Kamhoua, C., & Njilla, L. (2017, October). Consensus protocols for blockchain-based data provenance: Challenges and opportunities. In *2017 IEEE 8th Annual Ubiquitous Computing, Electronics and Mobile Communication Conference (UEMCON)* (pp. 469-474). IEEE.

Totolo, A. (2007), *Information Technology Adoption by Principals in Botswana Secondary Schools*. Retrieved 30 April, 2020, from https://www.researchgate.net/publication/242407711_Information_Technology_Adoption_by_Principals_in_Botswana_Secondary_Schools

Toyoda, K., Ohtsuki, T., & Mathiopoulos, P. T. (2017). Identification of High Yielding Investment Programs in Bitcoin via Transactions Pattern Analysis. *GLOBECOM 2017 - 2017 IEEE Global Communications Conference*, 1–6. 10.1109/GLOCOM.2017.8254420

Toyoda, K., Takis Mathiopoulos, P., Sasase, I., & Ohtsuki, T. (2017). A Novel Blockchain-Based Product Ownership Management System (POMS) for Anti-Counterfeits in the Post Supply Chain. *IEEE Access*, 5, 17465–17477. doi:10.1109/ACCESS.2017.2720760

Toyota Canada Newsroom. (2017). *Toyota Research Institute explores blockchain technology for development of new mobility ecosystem*. Retrieved from https://media.toyota.ca/releases/toyota-research-institute-explores-blockchain-technology-for-development-of-new-mobility-ecosystem

Toyota Woven City. (2020). *Welcome to woven city*. Retrieved from https://www.woven-city.global/

Toyota. (2020). *Search*. Retrieved from https://search.newsroom.toyota.co.jp/en/all/search.x?q=blockchain&pagemax=20

Trehan, R., Bansal, D., & Nair, S. J. (2020). *Fostering Interoperable Healthcare Ecosystems Using Blockchain*. Retrieved from www.infosys.com/: https://www.infosys.com/blockchain/documents/fostering-interoperable-healthcare-ecosystems.pdf

Tschorsch, F., & Scheuermann, B. (2016). Bitcoin. *IEEE Communications Surveys and Tutorials, 18*(3), 2084–2123. doi:10.1109/COMST.2016.2535718

Turkanović, M., Hölbl, M., Košič, K., Hericko, M., & Kamisalic, A. (2018). EduCTX: A Blockchain-Based Higher Education Credit Platform. *IEEE Access: Practical Innovations, Open Solutions, 6*, 5112–5127. doi:10.1109/AC-CESS.2018.2789929

Turnbaugh, R. C. (1997). Information Technology, Records, and State Archives. *The American Archivist, 60*(2), 184–200. doi:10.17723/aarc.60.2.e6247tm502671537

Uca, N., Çemberci, M., Civelek, M., & Yılmaz, H. (2017). The effect of trust in supply chain on the firm performance through supply chain collaboration and collaborative advantage. *The Journal of American Science, 15*, 215–230.

Uçma Uysal, T., & Aldemír, C. (2018). Dijital Kamu Mali Yönetim Sistemi ve Blok Zinciri Teknolojisi. *Muhasebe ve Vergi Uygulamaları Dergisi, 11*(3), 505–522. doi:10.29067/muvu.415066

Uğurlu, M. (2018). *Kripto Paraların Gelişimi ve Vergisel Konular.* https://coin-turk.com/kripto-paralarin-gelisimi-ve-vergisel-konular

Underwood, S. (2016). Blockchain beyond bitcoin. *Communications of the ACM, 59*(1), 5–17.

UNESCO. (2003). *Internet in education.* Retrieved 3 May, 2020, from https://iite.unesco.org/pics/publications/en/files/3214612.pdf

Unilever, N. V. (2017, May 1). *Report shows a third of consumers prefer sustainable brands.* Unilever Global Company Website. https://www.unilever.com/news/press-releases/2017/report-shows-a-third-of-consumers-prefer-sustainable-brands.html

Upadhyaya, R., & Jain, A. (2016). Cyber ethics and cybercrime: A deep dwelved study into legality, ransomware, underground web and bitcoin wallet. *2016 International Conference on Computing, Communication and Automation (ICCCA),* 143–148. 10.1109/CCAA.2016.7813706

Uskenbayeva, R., Kalpeyeva, Z., Satybaldiyeva, R., Moldagulova, A., & Kassymova, A. (2019), Applying of RPA in Administrative Processes of Public Administration. In *2019 IEEE 21st Conference on Business Informatics (CBI)* (Vol. 2, pp. 9-12). IEEE.

Uti, T. (2018). *Bangkok's Revenue Department Will Use Blockchain Technology to Prevent Tax Evasion.* https://Blockchainreporter.net/bangkoks-revenue-department-will-use-Blockchain-technology- to-prevent-tax-evasion/

van der Aalst, W. M. P., Bichler, M., & Heinzl, A. (2018). Robotic Process Automation. *Business & Information Systems Engineering, 60*(4), 269–272. doi:10.100712599-018-0542-4

Van Der Horst, L., Choo, K.-K. R., & Le-Khac, N.-A. (2017). Process Memory Investigation of the Bitcoin. *IEEE Access: Practical Innovations, Open Solutions, 5*, 22385–22398. doi:10.1109/ACCESS.2017.2759766

Vance, T. R., & Vance, A. (2019). Cybersecurity in the Blockchain Era: A Survey on Examining Critical Infrastructure Protection with Blockchain-Based Technology. *2019 IEEE International Scientific-Practical Conference Problems of Infocommunications, Science and Technology (PIC S&T),* 107–112. 10.1109/PICST47496.2019.9061242

Venkatesh, V., Morris, M. G., Davis, G. B., & Davis, F. D. (2003). *User Acceptance of Information Technology: Toward a Unified View.* Retrieved 16 April 2020, from https://www.researchgate.net/publication/220259897

Vinton. (2015). *Premera Blue Cross Breach May Have Exposed 11 Million Customers' Medical And Financial Data.* https://www.forbes.com/sites/katevinton/2015/03/17/11-million-customers-medical-and-financial-data-may-have-been-exposed-in-premera-blue-cross-breach/#1aa66d4675d9

Vukolić, M. (2017). Rethinking permissioned blockchains. *Proceedings of the ACM Workshop on Blockchain, Cryptocurrencies and Contracts, 3*–7.

Wall, E., & Malm, G. (2016). *Using blockchain technology and smart contracts to create a distributed securities depository.* http://lup.lub.lu.se/student-papers/record/8885750

Wallis, K., Stodt, J., Jastremskoj, E., & Reich, C. (2020). Agreements between enterprises digitized by smart contracts in the domain of industry 4.0. Unpublished manuscript.

Wamba, S. F., & Queiroz, M. M. (2020). Blockchain in the operations and supply chain management: Benefits, challenges and future research opportunities. *International Journal of Information Management, 52,* 102064. doi:10.1016/j.ijinfomgt.2019.102064

Wamboye, E., Tochkov, K., & Sergi, B. S. (2015). Technology adoption and growth in sub-Saharan African countries. *Comparative Economic Studies, 57*(1), 136–167. doi:10.1057/ces.2014.38

Wang, F., & Filippi, P. D. (2020). Self-sovereign identity in a globalized world: Credentials-based identity systems as a driver for economic inclusion. *Frontiers in Blockchain, 2*(January), 1–22. doi:10.3389/fbloc.2019.00028

Wang, H., Chen, K., & Xu, D. (2016). A maturity model for blockchain adoption. *Financial Innovation, 2*(1), 12.

Wang, Q., Li, X., & Yu, Y. (2018). Anonymity. *IEEE Access: Practical Innovations, Open Solutions, 6,* 12336–12341. doi:10.1109/ACCESS.2017.2787563

Wang, W., Hoang, D. T., Hu, P., Xiong, Z., Niyato, D., Wang, P., Wen, Y., & Kim, D. I. (2019). A survey on consensus mechanisms and mining strategy management in blockchain networks. *IEEE Access : Practical Innovations, Open Solutions, 7,* 22328–22370. doi:10.1109/ACCESS.2019.2896108

Wang, Y., & Gao, J. (2018). A Regulation Scheme Based on the Ciphertext-Policy Hierarchical Attribute-Based Encryption in Bitcoin. *IEEE Access: Practical Innovations, Open Solutions, 6,* 16267–16278. doi:10.1109/ACCESS.2018.2814620

Wan, S., Li, D., Gao, J., Roy, R., & Tong, Y. (2017). Process and knowledge management in a collaborative maintenance planning system for high value machine tools. *Computers in Industry, 84,* 14–24. doi:10.1016/j.compind.2016.11.002

Watson, K., & Smith, J. (2019). A digital approach to making a step change in reducing human error in procedures. SPE Offshore Europe Conference and Exhibition. doi:10.2118/195753-MS

Westerkamp, M., Victor, F., & Küpper, A. (2018). Blockchain-Based Supply Chain Traceability: Token Recipes Model Manufacturing Processes. In *IEEE/ACM Int'l Conference on Cyber, Physical and Social Computing (CPSCom).* Halifax, NS, Canada: IEEE Xplore. 10.1109/Cybermatics_2018.2018.00267

White, A. K. (2018). *Blockchain Discover the Technology Behind Smart Contracts, Wallets, Mining and Cryptocurrency.* CreateSpace Independent Publishing Platform.

White, G. R. (2017). Future applications of blockchain in business and management: A delphi study. *Strategic Change, 2017*(26), 439–451. doi:10.1002/jsc.2144

Whittingham, R. (2004). The blame machine: Why human error causes accidents. Routledge. doi:10.4324/9780080472126

WHO Bulletin - Technical Report Series. (2010). *WHO good distribution practices for pharmaceutical products.* WHO Technical Report Series, No. 957.

WHO Bulletin (2010). Growing threat from counterfeit medicines. *Bulletin of the World Health Organization*, *88*(4), 241–320.

WHO. (2017). A study on the public health and socioeconomic impact of substandard and falsified medical products. WHO/EMP/RHT/2017.02.

Williams, S. P. (2019). *Blockchain: The Next Everything*. Scribner.

Wilson, N., Kariisa, M., Seth, P., Smith, H. I. V., & Davis, N. L. (2018). Drug and Opioid-Involved Overdose Deaths— United States, 2017–2018. *MMWR. Morbidity and Mortality Weekly Report*, *2020*(69), 290–297. PMID:32191688

Winkler, M., Schneider-Maul, R., Puttur, R. K., Mehl, R., Buvat, J., & Nath, S. (2020). *How automotive organizations can maximize the smart factory potential.* Capgemini Research Institu.

Winnesota. (2020). *How Blockchain is Revolutionising the World of Transportation and Logistics.* Available at: https://www.winnesota.com/blockchain

Witscad. (2020). *Blockchain Characteristics.* Available at: https://witscad.com/course/blockchain-fundamentals/chapter/blockchain-characteristics

Witscad. (2020). *Blockchain Characteristics.* Available at: https://witscad.com/course/Blockchain-fundamentals/chapter/Blockchain-characteristics

Wlodarczyk, K. L., Ardron, M., Waddie, A. J., Taghizadeh, M. R., Weston, N. J., & Hand, D. P. (2017). Tamper-proof markings for the identification and traceability of high-value metal goods. *Optics Express*, *25*(13), 15216–15230. doi:10.1364/OE.25.015216 PubMed

World Bank Group. (2017). *FinTech Note No: 1, Distributed Ledger Technology (DLT) and Blockchain.* Author.

World Economic Forum. (2015). *Deep shift Technology Tipping Points and Societal Impact. Survey Report.* WEF. Retrieved May 25, 2020, from http://www3.weforum.org/docs/WEF_GAC15_Technological_Tipping_Points_report_2015.pdf

World Economic Forum. (2015). *The Future of Financial Services.* http://www3.weforum.org/docs/WEF_The_future__of_financial_services.pdf

World Federation of Exchanges. (2016). *Financial market infrastructures and distributed ledger technology.* https://www.world-exchanges.org/home/index.php/files/18/Studies%20-%20Reports/349/WFE%20IOSCO%20AMCC%20DLT%20report.pdf

Worner, A., Meeuw, A., Ableitner, L., Wortmann, F., Schopfer, S., & Tiefenbeck, V. (2019). Trading solar energy within the neighborhood: Field implementation of a blockchain-based electricity market. *Energy Informatics*, *2*(Supplement 1), 1–12. doi:10.118642162-019-0092-0

Wouda, H. P., & Opdenakker, R. (2019). Blockchain technology in commercial real estate transactions. *Journal of Property Investment & Finance*, *37*(6), 570–579. doi:10.1108/JPIF-06-2019-0085

Wüst, K., & Gervais, A. (2018). Do you Need a Blockchain? *2018 Crypto Valley Conference on Blockchain Technology (CVCBT)*, 45–54. 10.1109/CVCBT.2018.00011

Wu, X., Zhu, X., Wu, G.-Q., & Ding, W. (2014). Data mining with big data. *IEEE Transactions on Knowledge and Data Engineering*, *26*(1), 97–107. doi:10.1109/TKDE.2013.109

Xia, Q., Sifah, E. B., Asamoah, K. O., Gao, J., Du, X., & Guizani, M. (2017). MeDShare: Trust-Less Medical Data Sharing Among Cloud Service Providers via Blockchain. *IEEE Access: Practical Innovations, Open Solutions*, *5*, 14757–14767. doi:10.1109/ACCESS.2017.2730843

Xie, J., Tang, H., Huang, T., Yu, F. R., Xie, R., Liu, J., & Liu, Y. (2019). A Survey of Blockchain Technology Applied to Smart Cities: Research Issues and Challenges. *IEEE Communications Surveys and Tutorials, 21*(3), 2794–2830. doi:10.1109/COMST.2019.2899617

Xing, B., & Marwala, T. (2018). *The Synergy of Blockchain and Artificial Intelligence.* https://arxiv.org/ftp/arxiv/papers/1802/1802.04451.pdf

Xu, X., Rahman, F., Shakya, B., Vassilev, A., Forte, D., & Tehranipoor, M. (2019). Electronics Supply Chain Integrity Enabled by Blockchain. *ACM Transactions on Design Automation of Electronic Systems, 24*(3), 31:1–31:25. doi:10.1145/3315571

Yadav, S. S., Singh, S., & Harshita. (2018). FinTech: A new tint of glasses to see the age-old world of Finance. In *Emerging Perspectives in FinTech - The Experts' Voice* (pp. 4-7). Haryana: National Institute of Financial Management.

Yakubowski, M. (2019). *Alibaba exec: E-commerce giant considering blockchain use in complex supply chains.* Retrieved from https://cointelegraph.com/news/alibaba-exec-e-commerce-giant-considering-blockchain-use-in-complex-supply-chains

Yan, J., Meng, Y., Lu, L., & Li, L. (2017). Industrial big data in an industry 4.0 environment: Challenges, schemes, and applications for predictive maintenance. *IEEE Access : Practical Innovations, Open Solutions, 5*, 23484–23491. doi:10.1109/ACCESS.2017.2765544

Yassein, M. B., Shatnawi, F., Rawashdeh, S., & Mardin, W. (2019). Blockchain Technology: Characteristics, Security and Privacy; Issues and Solutions. *2019 IEEE/ACS 16th International Conference on Computer Systems and Applications (AICCSA),* 1–8, 10.1109/AICCSA47632.2019.9035216

Yeasmin, S., & Baig, A. (2019). Unblocking the Potential of Blockchain. *2019 International Conference on Electrical and Computing Technologies and Applications (ICECTA),* 1–5. 10.1109/ICECTA48151.2019.8959713

Yeoh, P. (2017). Regulatory issues in Blockchain technology. *Journal of Financial Regulation and Compliance, 25*(2), 196–208. doi:10.1108/JFRC-08-2016-0068

Yiannas, F. (2018). A New Era of Food Transparency Powered by Blockchain. *Innovations: Technology, Governance, Globalization, 12*(1-2), 46–56. doi:10.1162/inov_a_00266

Yilmaz, K. (2013). European Journal of Education. *European Journal of Education, 48*, 311–325. doi:10.1111/ejed.12014

Yin, W., Wen, Q., Li, W., Zhang, H., & Jin, Z. (2018). An Anti-Quantum Transaction Authentication Approach in Blockchain. *IEEE Access: Practical Innovations, Open Solutions, 6*, 5393–5401. doi:10.1109/ACCESS.2017.2788411

Yli-Huumo, J., Ko, D., Choi, S., Park, S., & Smolander, K. (2016). Where is current research on blockchain technology? A systematic review. *PLoS One, 11*(10), e0163477.

Yoo, S. (2017). Blockchain based financial case analysis and its implications. *Asia Pacific Journal of Innovation and Entrepreneurship., 11*(3), 312–321. doi:10.1108/APJIE-12-2017-036

York, T. W., & MacAlister, D. (2015). Hospital and Healthcare Security. Academic Press.

Yue, X., Wang, H., Jin, D., Li, M., & Jiang, W. (2016). Healthcare data gateways: Found healthcare intelligence on blockchain with novel privacy risk control. *Journal of Medical Systems, 40*(10), 218.

Zaky, D. (2020, March). *What is Blockchain Technology and How Does It Work?* Available at: https://fxdailyreport.com/Blockchain-technology/

Zeng, S. W. (1997). Discussion on maintenance strategy, policy and corresponding maintenance systems in manufacturing. *Reliability Engineering & System Safety*, 55(2), 151–162. doi:10.1016/S0951-8320(96)00004-X

Zhang, J. (2019). Deploying Blockchain Technology in the Supply Chain. In Blockchain and Distributed Ledger Technology (DLT). IntechOpen. doi:10.5772/intechopen.86530

Zhang, Y., Kasahara, S., Shen, Y., Jiang, X., & Wan, J. (2018). Smart contract-based access control for the internet of things. IEEE Internet of Things Journal, 1–1. doi:10.1109/JIOT.2018.2847705

Zhang, E. (2016). *Antshares Whitepaper1.0*. Academic Press.

Zhang, P., White, J., Schmidt, D. C., Lenz, G., & Rosenbloom, S. T. (2018). FHIRChain: Applying Blockchain to Securely and Scalably Share Clinical Data. *Computational and Structural Biotechnology Journal*, *16*, 267–278. doi:10.1016/j.csbj.2018.07.004 PMID:30108685

Zhang, Y., & Li, J. (2016, June 30). An Automatic Identification Authentic Work Anti-counterfeiting Algorithm Based on DWT-DCT. *International Journal of Security and Its Applications*, *10*(6), 135–144. doi:10.14257/ijsia.2016.10.6.14

Zhao, D., Jia, G., Ren, H., Chen, C., Yu, R., Ge, P., & Liu, S. (2018). *Research on the Application of Block Chain in automobile industry. In IOP Conference Series: Materials Science and Engineering.* IOP Publishing., doi:10.1088/1757-899X/452/3/032076

Zhao, J. L., Fan, S., & Yan, J. (2016). Overview of Business Innovations and Research Opportunities in Blockchain and Introduction to the Special Issue. *Financial Innovation*, *2*(1), 28. doi:10.118640854-016-0049-2

Zheng, Z., Xie, S. S., Dai, H., Chen, X., & Wang, H. (2017). An Overview of Blockchain Technology: Architecture, Consensus, and Future Trends. *IEEE 6th International Congress on Big Data (Big Dats Congress'17*.

Zheng, Z., Xie, S., Dai, H., Chen, X., & Wang, H. (2017). An Overview of Blockchain Technology: Architecture, Consensus, and Future Trends. In *2017 IEEE International Congress on Big Data (BigData Congress).* Honolulu, HI: IEEE. 10.1109/BigDataCongress.2017.85

Zhiliang, D., Yongjun, R., Yepeng, L., Xiang, Y., Zixuan, S., & Hye-Jin, K. (2019). *Blockchain-Based Trusted Electronic Records Preservation in Cloud Storage.* Retrieved 16 July 2020, from https://vntechindia.com/wp-content/uploads/2020/04/004.pdf

Zikratov, I. A., Lebedev, I. S., Gurtov, A. V., & Kuzmich, E. V. (2014). Securing Swarm Intellect Robots with a Police Office Model. *2014 IEEE 8th International Conference on Application of Information and Communication Technologies (AICT),* 1-5. 10.1109/ICAICT.2014.7035906

Zimmermann, L., Scholz, A., Tahoori, M. B., Aghassi-Hagmann, J., & Sikora, A. (2019). Design and evaluation of a printed analog-based differential physical unclonable function. IEEE Transactions on Very Large-Scale Integration (VLSI). *Systems*, 27(11), 2498–2510.

Zohar, A. (2015). *Bitcoin. Communications of the ACM*. doi:10.1145/2701411

Zuckerman, M. J. (2018). S. *Korea to Tax Crypto Exchanges 24.2 Percent, in Line with Existing Tax Policy*. https://cointelegraph.com/news/s-korea-to-tax-crypto-exchanges-242-percent-in-line-with-existing-tax-policy

About the Contributors

Zaigham Mahmood is a published author/editor of thirty-two books on subjects including Electronic Government, Cloud Computing, Data Science, Big Data, Fog Computing, Internet of Things, Internet of Vehicles, Industrial IoT, Smart Cities, Ambient Intelligence, Project Management, and Software Engineering, including: Cloud Computing: Concepts, Technology & Architecture which is also published in Korean and Chinese languages. Additionally, he is developing two new books to appear later in the year. He has also published more than 150 articles and book chapters and organized numerous conference tracks and workshops. Professor Mahmood is Editor-in-Chief of Journal of E-Government Studies and Best Practices, Editor-in-Chief of the IGI book series on E-Government and Digital Divide, Technology Consultant at Debesis Education UK and Professor at the Shijiazhuang Tiedao University in Hebei, China. He further holds positions as Foreign Professor at NUST and IIU in Islamabad Pakistan. He has also served as a Reader (Associated Professor) at the University of Derby UK, and Professor Extraordinaire at the North West University South Africa. Professor Mahmood is a certified cloud computing instructor and a regular speaker at international conferences devoted to Distributed Computing and E-Government. Professor Mahmood's book publications can be viewed at: https://www.amazon.co.uk/Zaigham-Mahmood/e/B00B29OIK6.

* * *

Kamalani Aiyar received her Master's degree in Information Technology from Charles Sturt University (CSU) in Melbourne, in 2020. She completed her BIT (Bachelor in Information Technology) from the University of Colombo, Sri Lanka in 2006. She has experience in teaching IT subjects for more than 10 years in Sri Lanka. Her current research interests include blockchain technology, emerging technologies, and data security.

Pelin Angin is Assistant Professor of Computer Engineering at Middle East Technical University. She completed her B.S. in Computer Engineering at Bilkent University in 2007 and her Ph.D. in Computer Science at Purdue University, USA in 2013. Between 2014-2016, she worked as a Visiting Assistant Professor and Postdoctoral Researcher at Purdue University. Her research interests lie in the fields of cloud computing and IoT security, distributed systems, 5G networks and blockchain. She is among the founding members of the Systems Security Research Laboratory and an affiliate of the Wireless Systems, Networks and Cybersecurity Laboratory at METU. She serves on the editorial boards of multiple journals on IoT and mobile computing. Her work in security has been published at high impact journals including IEEE Transactions on Dependable and Secure Computing, Computers & Security and IEEE Access among others.

Divik Bansal is a Principal Consultant, Blockchain Service, at Infosys limited in India and handles global engagements in Healthcare, Life Sciences, Energy and Utilities in Blockchain. He also offers executive level advise and thought leadership focusing on how blockchain can be applied to specific business units and how to it can leveraged by public or private sector organizations. He also has expertise to undertake assessment of corporate strategy to evaluate blockchain potential applicability and business impact.

John Breslin is a Personal Professor (Personal Chair) in Electronic Engineering at the College of Science and Engineering at the National University of Ireland Galway, where he is Director of the TechInnovate / AgInnovate programmes. John has taught electronic engineering, computer science, innovation and entrepreneurship topics during the past two decades. Associated with three SFI Research Centres, he is a Co-Principal Investigator at Confirm (Smart Manufacturing) and Insight (Data Analytics), and a Funded Investigator at VistaMilk (AgTech). He has written 200+ peer-reviewed academic publications (h-index of 41, 7100 citations, best paper awards from IoT, DL4KGS, SEMANTiCS, ICEGOV, ESWC, PELS), and co-authored the books "Old Ireland in Colour", "The Social Semantic Web" and "Social Semantic Web Mining". He co-created the SIOC framework (Wikipedia article), implemented in hundreds of applications (by Yahoo, Boeing, Vodafone, etc.) on at least 65,000 websites with 35 million data instances.

Joseph Brown received the B.S. degree in computer science and information security from John Jay College of Criminal Justice. Currently he is a researcher at the Center for Cybercrime Studies at John Jay College of Criminal Justice. His research interest includes authentication techniques, online privacy, IoT security & privacy and digital forensics. Outside of academics, he works as a project manager in a multimedia consumer software business which he also operates, and provides cybersecurity consulting and solutions at Mandala Labs.

Andre Calitz is a Professor in the Department of Computing Sciences at Nelson Mandela University in Port Elizabeth, South Africa. He has two doctorates, a PhD in Computer Science and a Doctorate in Business Administration (DBA). He is a rated NRF researcher and has published extensively in international journals and conferences. He received the 2016 and 2018 NMU Research Excellence Award. He has been an IT consultant on projects for businesses such as Volkswagen, Mercedes Benz, Firestone and Nelson Mandela Bay Municipality. He is a Fellow of the Institute of IT Professionals of South Africa.

Güneş Çetin Gerger is an Assoc. Prof. Dr. at the Faculty of Applied Sciences. She has a BA degree in public finance at İzmir Dokuz Eylül University. She has an MA and Ph.D. degree in Public Finance at Manisa Celal Bayar University. Her research mostly focuses on taxpayer's rights, tax compliance behaviour, tax literacy, taxation of e-commerce, digitalization in tax administrations. She completed a scientific research project in TÜBİTAK as a researcher entitled "Improving Taxpayer's Right in Turkey, Starting from Various Countries Successful Applications". She is working on a scientific research project in TÜBİTAK as a researcher entitled "Measurement and Improvement of Tax Literacy in Turkey, and Analysis of The Impact on Tax Compliance". She has lectured for ten years about Public Finance,

Turkish Tax System, Taxation Theory and Policy, Public Budget, Tax Law, Tax Audit, Expenditure Tax Analysis in Manisa Celal Bayar University.

Forget Chaterera-Zambuko holds a Doctor of Literature and Philosophy in Information Sciences. She holds a Master in Information Science, Masters in Museum Studies, Bachelor Honours Degree in Archaeology and a Postgraduate Diploma in Tertiary Education. She is currently a Postdoctoral Fellow in the History Department at Sorbonne University Abu Dhabi and a Research Fellow in the Department of Information Science at the University of South Africa (UNISA). She is a rated researcher in the Y category by the National Research Foundation of South Africa. Forget Chaterera-Zambuko serves in the International Council on Archives' (ICA) New Professional Programme (2019 – 2020 cohort). She was Zimbabwe's lead researcher for the InterPARES Project Africa Team Phase four. Her research interests include access and use of documentary heritage, displaced archives, archival diplomatics, Blockchain and other emerging technologies.

Steve Everett is a Senior manager at the Canadian Derivative Clearing Corporation in Toronto, Canada. He obtained his master's degree from Nelson Mandela University in South Africa in 2017. In his present role, he introduces new technology and products across markets and leverages the existing capabilities within the TMX Group. He has gained extensive experience in Blockchain technologies relating to the securities settlement industry.

Atakan Gerger is a graduate of Automotive Technology studied at the Ege University; his second degree was received from Business Administration from Anadolu University in Turkey. He has a master's degree in Total Quality Management and a Ph.D. degree in Statistics obtained in 2017 from Dokuz Eylül University in Turkey. He is currently working in the Aerospace Industry as a Continuous Improvement and Lean Production Manager. He is also a Lean Six Sigma, Industry 4.0, continuous improvement, quality systems, manufacturing management and statistical methods professional, with aerospace and automotive industry background. Atakan Gerger has authored or co-authored over 15 articles including 4 book chapters and one book. Atakan research areas include Statistics, Quality Management, Manufacturing Management, Aerospace Engineering, Big Data, Machine Learning, Connected Government, Industry 4.0, Society 5.0, Web 2.0 and Continuous Improvement.

Jean Greyling is a Professor in the Department of Computing Sciences at Nelson Mandela University in Port Elizabeth, South Africa. He holds a PhD in Computer Science and specialises in teaching programming related subjects in the department. He has a passion for engaging with schools to make scholars/learners aware of the career opportunities in computing. This has resulted in a project using mobile apps and tangible tokens, to introduce scholars/learners to programming without the use of computers. This project has received various local, national and global accolades, including an acknowledgement by UNESCO for the impact it has on education to disadvantaged communities.

Malka N. Halgamuge is a Researcher in the Department of Electrical and Electronic Engineering of the University of Melbourne, and she has also obtained her Ph.D. from the same department in 2007. She is passionate about research and teaching university students (Data Science, Business Intelligence using Big Data, Internet of Things (IoT), Sensor Network, Blockchain, Bioelectromagnetics, and Hyperthermia). She has published more than 90 peer-reviewed technical articles attracting over 1400 Google Scholar

Citations with h-index = 21, and her Research Gate RG Score is 38.27. She is currently supervising a PhD student at the University of Melbourne, and 4 PhD students completed their theses in 2013, 2015 and 2018 with her as the principal supervisor. She successfully sought 7 short-term research fellowships at premier Universities in the World. She excels in major commercial work related to the investigation of electromagnetic radiation hazards safety assessment and the provision of extensive technical reports. This work allows her to help organizations and individuals to promote precautionary approaches to the use of technology, and access to contribute in Media.

Harshita is Assistant Professor of Finance at Institute of Management Technology Ghaziabad, Delhi NCR. She is certificate holder of CFA Institute's Investment Foundations programme and is awardee of Junior Research Fellowship from The University Grants Commission. Her Alma Maters are IIT Delhi (PhD, Finance), Shri Ram College of Commerce (Masters in Commerce) and Daulat Ram College (Bachelors in Commerce, Honors). She has published journal articles with publishers of international repute and presented papers at prestigious institutes and societies. One of her publications has earned the Emerald Literati Award for Outstanding Paper. During the doctoral study, she received financial assistance from the Research Promotional Fund at IIT Delhi for paper presentation at an international conference. She was awarded CBSE Merit Scholarship for her outstanding performance in the XII Board examination and has secured first position at the district level in the CBSE X Board examination.

Rian Leevinson is a Senior Associate Analyst at Infosys Limited India with over 2.7 years of experience, working in the field of data science, machine learning, NLP, statistics, computer vision and predictive analytics. He also researches about emerging technologies and integration of technology with society. His research areas include applications of Industrial IoT, emerging technologies for smart cities, intelligent traffic management systems in smart cities, chatbot testing and quantum machine learning. He has experience in building data driven solutions to industrial problems. He is skilled in Python, R, Rshiny, Azure ML Studio, Azure data services and Azure AutoML. He is experienced in domains and sectors such as finance, e-commerce, transportation and logistics. His areas of interest include data science, advanced machine learning, quantum computing, intelligent autonomous systems and astronomy.

Somayya Madakam is an Assistant Professor in IT at FORE School of Management, New Delhi after completing the UGC-Junior Research Fellowship. He has worked for the Tata Institute of Social Sciences (TISS), Mumbai as a Systems Analyst-cum-Programmer. Due to interest in research and academia, in 2012, he joined the National Institute of Industrial Engineering (NITIE), Mumbai for a Fellow Program in Management where he completed his thesis on "Internet of Things (IoT) Technologies in Smart Cities: An Exploratory Study in India". He has presented his academic research work in both inter/national conferences including at Bangkok (Thailand), Dubai (UAE), Alicante (Spain), Fairfax (USA), and Porto (Portugal). He also published more than 20 articles in journals or as book chapters and posters. He is an evangelist on "The New Language of Publications".

Neha Mason was born in Dehradun, India. She received the B.Com. [Hons] degree from Delhi University in 2010 and the M.I.T degree from the University of Charles Sturt University (CSU), Melbourne in 2018. Her professional degree includes a semi-qualified Chartered Accountant from the Institute of Chartered Accountants of India. Her research interest includes cryptocurrencies and the Legal and Ethical Implications of these.

Olefhile Mosweu is currently a Postdoctoral Research Fellow at the University of Johannesburg, South Africa. He holds a Doctoral degree in Information Science from the University of South Africa, BA (English and History), Post Graduate Diploma in Education and Masters in Archives and Records Management from the University of Botswana, Masters in Business Administration from Amity University, India, and a Diploma in Human Resources Management from Botswana Open University. He has worked in the public sector of Botswana as an archives and records management professional. He has authored several articles in reputable journals. He regularly reviews book chapters and journal articles in the eastern and Southern Africa region. He is also an editorial member of the Journal of the South African Society of Archivists. His research interests are in archival education, digital records management, research methodology, knowledge management and the impact of Industry 4.0 technologies on records management. He has been a Research Assistant and member of Team Africa in the Int. Research on Permanent Authentic Records in Electronic Systems project (InterPARES Trust) (2013 – 2018).

Sanal Nair is a Senior Consultant at Blockchain Service line at Infosys limited in India. Sanal is responsible for business solution development for Healthcare and Lifesciences engagements in blockchain practice. He has 13+ years of IT and Consulting experience. He works closely with clients and development teams enabling use case enrichment through design thinking workshops, development of blockchain implementations and enterprise application integration.

Muath Obaidat is an Assistant Professor of Computer Science and Information Security at John Jay College of Criminal Justice of the City University of New York and a member of the Center for Cybercrime Studies. He received his Ph.D. in Electrical Engineering from The Department of Electrical Engineering at the Graduate Center of the City University of New York. He has Master of Science in computer engineering from New Jersey Institute of Technology (NJIT) and computer science degree from Monmouth University. He has numerous scientific article publications in journals and respected conference proceedings. His research interests lie in the area of digital forensics, ubiquitous Internet of Things (IoT) security and privacy. His recent research crosscuts the areas wireless network protocols, cloud computing and security. He serves on multiple conferences and workshop program and organizing committees. In addition, he is a peer reviewer for many International high impact journals.

Christoph Reich is professor, since 2002, at the faculty of computer science at the university of applied science in Furtwangen (HFU) and teaches network technologies, IT protocols, IT security, Cloud Computing, and Machine Learning. He is CIO of the HFU Information and Media Centre, and scientific director of the IT data centre, Online-Services, Learning-Services, and library department. He is head of the Institute of Data Science, Cloud Computing and IT-Security (IDACUS; idacus.hs- furtwangen. de). Several founded research projects (FP7 EU, BMBF, MWK) have been accomplished successfully.

Daniel Schönle is member of the Institute for Data Science, Cloud Computing and IT-security. He is a member of the faculty of computer science at the University of Applied Science in Furtwangen (HFU). His research topics include blockchain technology, machine learning, digital twins, chatbots and self- adapting learning environments. In 2019, he received his M.Sc. degree in computer science from the University of Applied Science in Furtwangen (HFU) with focus on machine learning. He worked in the aerospace industry and information technology industry after his diploma in computer science in 2005 majoring artificial intelligence and IT security.

Yigit Sever is a research assistant at Middle East Technical University, Department of Computer Engineering. He is pursuing his PhD degree in the same department with Dr. Pelin Angin as his advisor. He has completed his undergraduate degree in computer engineering at TED University in 2016 and his Master's degree in computer engineering at Hacettepe University in 2019. His research interests include blockchain and cyber security.

Nhlanhla Andrew Sibanyoni holds a PhD in information Systems from University of South Africa. The title of the thesis is "Towards Assessing Persuasive Mobile Technology for South Africa Learners Studying Mathematics". He also has a Master's in Business Information System from Tshwane University of Technology. He is currently a Systems Operational Manager at one of the leading international companies. He has over 20 years of ICT industry experience with specialisation in SAP Portal, Business Object and holds several specialist certifications in ICT including Business Information Warehouse and ITIL IT Service Management. He has full life project implementation experience at various industries such as ICT, Travel, Insurance, Government, pharmaceutical, Mining and Food and Beveridge and motor manufacturing.

Axel Sikora is professor, since 2011, at the Offenburg University of Applied Science, where he lectures about Embedded Systems and Communication. He is also the head of the Institute of Reliable Embedded Systems and Communication Electronics (ivESK). Before coming to Offenburg, he taught at the Duale Hochschule Baden-Württemberg Lörrach for twelve years and worked in the telecommunications and semiconductor industry. His focus of research has always been on embedded connectivity, especially wireless connectivity of low powered devices. Over the course of his career, he authored and co-authored multiple books and papers. Additionally, he is on the program committees of several international conferences.

Jan Stodt is a member of the Institute for Data Science, Cloud Computing and IT-security and a member of the faculty of computer science at the University of Applied Science in Furtwangen (HFU). He received his B. Sc. degree in computer science from the University of Applied Science in Furtwangen (HFU) in 2017 and his M. Sc. degree in computer science for the University of Applied Science in Furtwangen (HFU) in 2019.

Subhasis Thakur received the PhD degree from Griffith University, Australia, in 2013. He has worked as a research fellow with the University of Liverpool, the University of L'Aquila and the National University of Ireland. He is leading several blockchain projects at Insight Centre for Data Analytics. His research interests include multi-agent systems, game theory, and cloud computing.

Vijayaraghavan Varadharajan is a Principal Research Scientist at Infosys Limited in India, researching in the field of Quantum Computing, XAI, FoW, Security analytics, Cloud security, Security assessment, Authentication and Privacy protection. He has over 19 years of experience as a researcher in industry and academia. He also focuses on Emerging technology & Business opportunity identification, Incubation and Venture assessment for Investments. Dr. Vijay has six granted US patents and has filed many US and Indian patents in key technology areas. He has published 50+ research publications in International journals & conferences and served as a Technical Reviewer, Program Committee member and Chair for many conferences around the globe.

Kevin Wallis received his B.Sc. in 2014 and M.Sc. in 2016 in Computer Science and Software Engineering from the University of Applied Sciences Vorarlberg. He is currently pursuing a cooperative PhD between the University of Freiburg and the University of Applied Sciences Furtwangen on thetopic of Cyber Security in Industry 4.0 environments. Furthermore, his research topics involve blockchain security and implementation as well as the development of distributed data validation systems to increase data quality during data profiling. One of the goals is to minimize the success probability of attacks on data validation systems and thus increase the overall security of industrial systems.

Dominik Welte is a member of the Institute of Reliable Embedded Systems and Communication Electronics (ivESK) at Offenburg University of Applied Science. This is also where he received his B. Sc. (2016) and M. Sc. (2018) degrees in Computer Science.

Kosala Yapa Bandara is a principal investigator, researcher, architect, and developer at the Insight Centre for Data Analytics at NUI Galway, Ireland. Kosala received the PhD from Dublin City University, Ireland in 2012. He has worked as a software engineer and senior software engineer in multinational software companies in Ireland. Kosala has played leading roles as a lecturer, senior lecturer, undergraduate project manager, PhD supervisor, PhD examiner, head of academic departments, and member of academic boards including the university council. He has worked as a postdoctoral researcher at Dublin City University and University College Cork prior to joining with NUI Galway. His research interests include blockchain, multi-agent systems, cloud computing, service-oriented architecture, and the semantic web.

Index

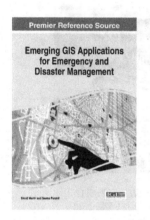

www.igi-global.com

Publisher of Peer-Reviewed, Timely, and Innovative Academic Research Since 1988

IGI Global's Transformative Open Access (OA) Model:
How to Turn Your University Library's Database Acquisitions Into a Source of OA Funding

Well in advance of Plan S, IGI Global unveiled their OA Fee Waiver (Read & Publish) Initiative. Under this initiative, librarians who invest in IGI Global's InfoSci-Books and/or InfoSci-Journals databases will be able to subsidize their patrons' OA article processing charges (APCs) when their work is submitted and accepted (after the peer review process) into an IGI Global journal.

How Does it Work?

Step 1: **Library Invests in the InfoSci-Databases:** A library perpetually purchases or subscribes to the InfoSci-Books, InfoSci-Journals, or discipline/subject databases.

Step 2: **IGI Global Matches the Library Investment with OA Subsidies Fund:** IGI Global provides a fund to go towards subsidizing the OA APCs for the library's patrons.

Step 3: **Patron of the Library is Accepted into IGI Global Journal (After Peer Review):** When a patron's paper is accepted into an IGI Global journal, they option to have their paper published under a traditional publishing model or as OA.

Step 4: **IGI Global Will Deduct APC Cost from OA Subsidies Fund:** If the author decides to publish under OA, the OA APC fee will be deducted from the OA subsidies fund.

Step 5: **Author's Work Becomes Freely Available:** The patron's work will be freely available under CC BY copyright license, enabling them to share it freely with the academic community.

Note: This fund will be offered on an annual basis and will renew as the subscription is renewed for each year thereafter. IGI Global will manage the fund and award the APC waivers unless the librarian has a preference as to how the funds should be managed.

Hear From the Experts on This Initiative:

"I'm very happy to have been able to make one of my recent research contributions *freely available* along with having access to the *valuable resources* found within IGI Global's InfoSci-Journals database."

– Prof. Stuart Palmer,
Deakin University, Australia

"Receiving the support from IGI Global's OA Fee Waiver Initiative *encourages me to continue my research work without any hesitation*."

– Prof. Wenlong Liu, College of Economics and Management at Nanjing University of Aeronautics & Astronautics, China

For More Information, Scan the QR Code or Contact:
IGI Global's Digital Resources Team at eresources@igi-global.com.

Printed in the United States
by Baker & Taylor Publisher Services